RitualSong

CHOIR EDITION

G-4500C

RitualSong

A HYMNAL AND SERVICE BOOK FOR ROMAN CATHOLICS
CHOIR EDITION

GIA PUBLICATIONS, INC.
CHICAGO

Cover design by Adam Kochlin reminds us that grace is
achieved through the waters of Baptism and we are saved by
the cross of redemption. This was witnessed by "The
Twelve," rejected by Judas, and commemorated in the
Eucharist.

The liturgical texts are reproduced by authority of the
Committee on the Liturgy of the National Conference of
Catholic Bishops.

Book design is based upon *Worship—Third Edition* by
Michael Tapia.

Published with ecclesiastical approval, Archdiocese of
Chicago, January 24, 1996.

ISBN 0-941050-86-6

1 2 3 4 5 6 7 8 9 10 11 12 13 14 15 16 17 18 19 20

PREFACE

If seriousness can be measured by the resources and amount of time expended on an effort, this publisher could be regarded as having produced its first serious hymnal in 1975. That book, *Worship II,* was the product of extensive preparation by a committee of competent editors. But that was just the beginning.

GIA has always firmly believed in a bound hymnal as the ideal printed resource for the worshiping community. In a time when the Church is marked by a diversity of approaches to worship, it has become increasingly clear that no single hymnal/service book can satisfy all. *RitualSong* is the seventh hymnal for parish worship published by GIA in these twenty-one years. Two of those have been replaced by revisions, which are among the five choices currently available to Roman Catholic parishes from this publisher.

Worship II was eventually replaced in 1986 by *Worship—Third Edition,* GIA's premier classical hymnal. And *Gather,* a collection of contemporary "folk-style" music published in 1988 as a companion book to *Worship,* was replaced in 1995 by *Gather—Second Edition. Worship* and *Gather* used together offer parishes the most extensive repertoire available today in a published program. A spinoff of these hymnals, *Gather Comprehensive,* is the entire *Gather—Second Edition* with a significant amount of organ-based music added.

Since the first publication of *Worship* and *Gather,* GIA has heard some parish musicians and liturgists speak of using the combination of these two books as perhaps the ideal, but nonetheless one that was not suitable for their particular parish circumstances. These pastoral practitioners have ultimately influenced GIA's decision to combine the substance of *Worship* and *Gather* into one book, *RitualSong.*

The editors of *RitualSong* set out to create a truly comprehensive hymnal, reflective of the growing trend in the Church today toward an eclectic approach to selecting music for liturgy.

While *RitualSong* may be thought of as the best of *Worship* and *Gather* somewhat equally combined into one book, it is actually much more. *RitualSong* is a fairly even mix of those two earlier hymnals in terms of style, quality, and much of the content, but it actually contains many things never before included in a single hymnal or combination program.

RitualSong contains more psalms and canticles than any other published hymnal, including up to five different settings of some of the psalms that are used most frequently. It has more service music than any other hymnal GIA has ever published, and it offers a collection of 500 hymns and songs—many appearing for the first time in a GIA hymnal.

In the psalter section, many psalms list recommended verses for use with a particular refrain. One must be careful to distinguish between the use of "Vs" and "St" in these designations. "Verses" refers to biblical verses, and "stanzas" refers to groupings, generally of four lines. In Psalm 16 (#34), for example, we find eleven biblical verses and a doxology, grouped into seven stanzas. The pew edition shows this format most clearly because the psalm verses are printed poetically rather than interlined with music.

Special recognition for this project is given to Jeffry Mickus (project coordinator), Marc Southard (typesetting, music engraving, and book layout), Alec Harris (technical coordinator), Clarence Reiels and Edwina Schaufler (proofreaders), Victoria Krystansky (copyright permissions and editorial services), and last but far from least, one who is clearly the world's most experienced and competent hymnal indexer, Robert H. Oldershaw.

Michael A. Cymbala
Project Director
Robert J. Batastini
Senior Editor
David Anderson
Marty Haugen
Jean McLaughlin
Editors
Edward J. Harris
Publisher

Contents

Hymns

Appendix

Indexes

The Liturgy of the Hours

When darkness gives way before the sun's light and a new day begins, people of all religions have had their rites of morning: words and songs and gestures with which to pray. It has been the same at the end of the day's light, and again in the last moments before sleep.

Christians, following the example of their Jewish ancestors, continued to pray at morning and evening and night. These moments are the hinges of daily life. As they came round each day they have been occasions to repeat what every child has learned by heart: words to praise God for a new morning, to thank the Father for Christ who is our light as evening comes, to invoke God's strong protection through the hours of night.

The daily prayers of Christians were fashioned at first from very simple things: the sign of the cross, the Lord's Prayer, a few verses and songs and short psalms, intercessions. And for most Christians morning and night remain times for such simple prayers always said by heart.

The pages of this present section offer a form of daily prayer that grew from this same tradition. When Christians have gathered in the early morning, at day's end, just before retiring, the simple prayers for the individual have grown more elaborate. The daily assemblies of Christians gave shape to what became known as the divine office or "liturgy of the hours." In recent times, these prayers have been restored to some of their original simplicity and are again being prayed in parish churches and Christian households.

In using and in adapting the forms of morning, evening and night prayer given below, two things are especially important. First, these are not to be prayers which could be prayed any time. Rather, they are prayers (in word, song, gesture, silence) which are prompted by the morning itself, by the evening, by the night. Their content and pace should reflect what is unique to each of these moments. Second, these prayers are not meant to be followed in and read from books. The assembly's parts are to be gradually learned by heart. Simplicity, repetition, care for times of silence, the use of refrains: all make it possible for these prayers to belong fully to those who assemble.

Appointed antiphons, readings, intercessions and prayers for each day can be found in **Worship—Liturgy of the Hours—Leader's Edition** *(GIA) or* **Christian Prayer***.*

INVITATORY

All make the sign of the cross on their lips.

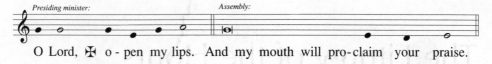

O Lord, ✠ o-pen my lips. And my mouth will pro-claim your praise.

2 PSALM 95

The psalm may begin with an appropriate antiphon.

A. ADVENT

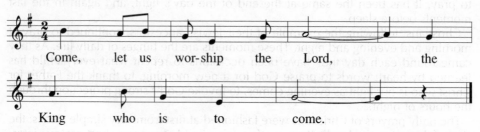

Come, let us wor-ship the Lord, the King who is to come.

B. CHRISTMAS

Christ is born for us; come, let us a - dore him.

C. LENT

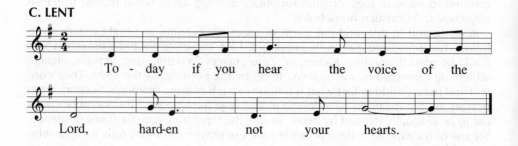

To - day if you hear the voice of the Lord, hard-en not your hearts.

D. EASTER

The Lord is ris - en, al - le - lu - ia.

E. GENERAL

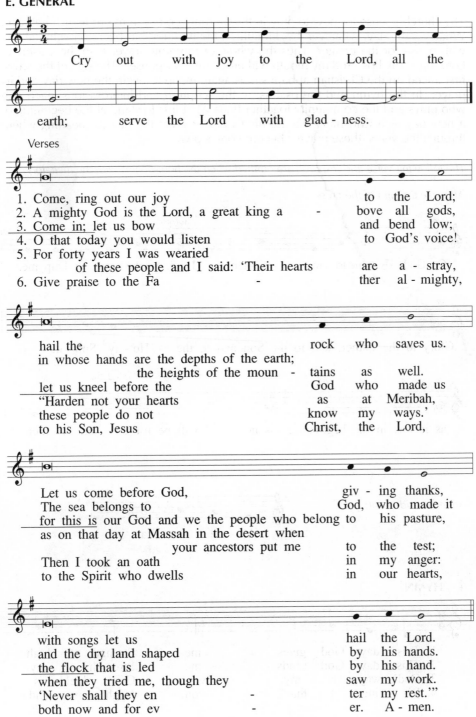

Cry out with joy to the Lord, all the earth; serve the Lord with glad - ness.

Verses

1. Come, ring out our joy   to the Lord;
2. A mighty God is the Lord, a great king a - bove all gods,
3. Come in; let us bow   and bend low;
4. O that today you would listen   to God's voice!
5. For forty years I was wearied
     of these people and I said: 'Their hearts   are a - stray,
6. Give praise to the Fa - ther al - mighty,

hail the   rock who saves us.
in whose hands are the depths of the earth;
     the heights of the moun - tains as well.
let us kneel before the   God who made us
"Harden not your hearts   as at Meribah,
these people do not   know my ways.'
to his Son, Jesus   Christ, the Lord,

Let us come before God,   giv - ing thanks,
The sea belongs to   God, who made it
for this is our God and we the people who belong to his pasture,
as on that day at Massah in the desert when
     your ancestors put me   to the test;
Then I took an oath   in my anger:
to the Spirit who dwells   in our hearts,

with songs let us   hail the Lord.
and the dry land shaped   by his hands.
the flock that is led   by his hand.
when they tried me, though they   saw my work.
'Never shall they en - ter my rest.'"
both now and for ev - er. A - men.

Text: Antiphons, © 1974, ICEL; Psalm 95, © 1963, 1993, The Grail, GIA Publications, Inc., agent
Music: Howard Hughes, SM, © 1974, ICEL

3 MORNING PRAYER/LAUDS

The church's sense for how to pray in the morning comes from our Jewish heritage. Whatever the day, whatever the difficulties, the tradition has been to begin the day with praise for the creator. Thus the whole of morning prayer is in the verse: "O Lord, open my lips. And my mouth will proclaim your praise." The sign of the cross, first traced on the Christian at baptism, is again made to begin the new day and its prayer. In the hymn and the psalms, in the scripture and intercessions, each one who prays and the community together finds what it is to stand at the beginning of a new day as a Christian. The morning's prayer gives the day its meaning when, through the years, these prayers become one's own.

The following verse and response are omitted when the hour begins with the invitatory.

All make the sign of the cross.

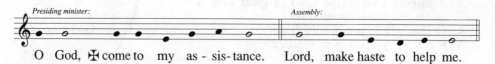

Presiding minister: O God, ✠ come to my as-sis-tance. *Assembly:* Lord, make haste to help me.

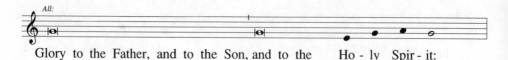

All: Glory to the Father, and to the Son, and to the Ho - ly Spir - it:

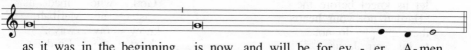

as it was in the beginning, is now, and will be for ev - er. A-men.

Added outside Lent:

Al - le - lu - ia.

4 HYMN

1. This day God gives me Strength of high
2. This day God sends me Strength as my
3. God's way is my way, God's shield is
4. Ris - ing I thank you, Might - y and

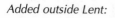

heav - en,	Sun and moon shin - ing,	Flame in my
guar - dian,	Might to up - hold me,	Wis - dom as
'round me,	God's host de - fends me,	Sav - ing from
strong One,	King of cre - a - tion,	Giv - er of

hearth,	Flash - ing of light - ning,	Wind in its
guide.	Your eyes are watch - ful,	Your ears are
ill.	An - gels of heav - en,	Drive from me
rest,	Firm - ly con - fess - ing	God in three

swift - ness,	Depths of the o - cean,	Firm - ness of earth.
lis - t'ning,	Your lips are speak - ing,	Friend at my side.
al - ways	All that would harm me,	Stand by me still.
Per - sons,	One - ness of God - head,	Trin - i - ty blest.

Text: Ascribed to St. Patrick; James Quinn, S.J., b.1919, © 1969. Used by permission of Selah Publishing Co., Inc., Kingston, N.Y.
Tune: BUNESSAN, 5 5 5 4 D; Gaelic; acc. by Marty Haugen, b.1950, © 1987, GIA Publications, Inc.

PSALMODY   5

The singing of one or more psalms is a central part of Morning Prayer. Psalm 63/Ant. II (no. 89) is one of the premier morning psalms. Psalm 51/Ant. V (no. 82) is commonly substituted for Psalm 63 on Wednesday and Friday, as well as during Lent. Other appropriate psalms for morning are Psalms 5, 8, 33, 42, 66, 72, 80, 85, 93, 95, 98, 100, 118, 148, 149 and 150.

READING

RESPONSE TO THE WORD OF GOD   6

A. ADVENT

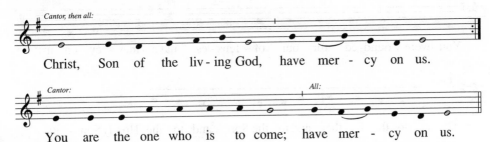

Cantor, then all:

Christ, Son of the liv - ing God, have mer - cy on us.

Cantor: All:

You are the one who is to come; have mer - cy on us.

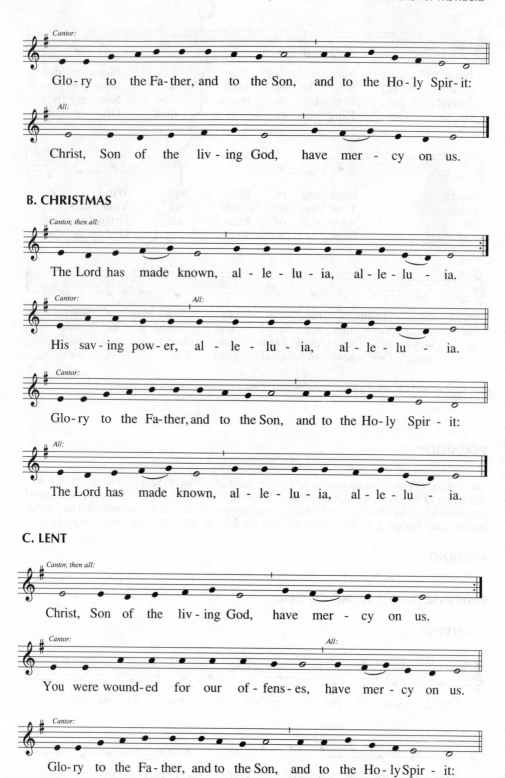

Cantor:

Glo-ry to the Fa-ther, and to the Son, and to the Ho-ly Spir-it:

All:

Christ, Son of the liv-ing God, have mer - cy on us.

B. CHRISTMAS

Cantor, then all:

The Lord has made known, al - le - lu - ia, al - le - lu - ia.

Cantor: *All:*

His sav-ing pow-er, al - le - lu - ia, al - le - lu - ia.

Cantor:

Glo-ry to the Fa-ther, and to the Son, and to the Ho-ly Spir - it:

All:

The Lord has made known, al - le - lu - ia, al - le - lu - ia.

C. LENT

Cantor, then all:

Christ, Son of the liv - ing God, have mer - cy on us.

Cantor: *All:*

You were wound-ed for our of - fens - es, have mer - cy on us.

Cantor:

Glo-ry to the Fa-ther, and to the Son, and to the Ho-ly Spir - it:

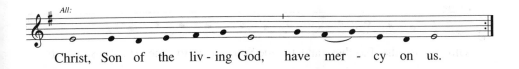

All:

Christ, Son of the liv-ing God, have mer - cy on us.

D. EASTER

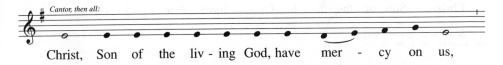

Cantor, then all:

Christ, Son of the liv-ing God, have mer - cy on us,

al - le - lu - ia, al - le - lu - ia.

Cantor: *All:*

You have ris - en from the dead, al - le - lu - ia, al - le - lu - ia.

Cantor:

Glo - ry to the Fa - ther, and to the Son, and to the Ho - ly Spir - it:

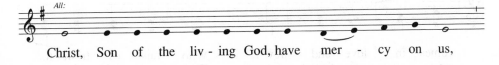

All:

Christ, Son of the liv-ing God, have mer - cy on us,

al - le - lu - ia, al - le - lu - ia.

E. GENERAL

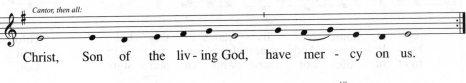

Cantor, then all:

Christ, Son of the liv-ing God, have mer - cy on us.

Cantor: *All:*

You are seat-ed at the right hand of the Fa-ther, have mer - cy on us.

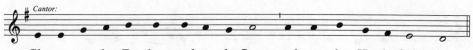

Glo-ry to the Fa-ther, and to the Son, and to the Ho-ly Spir-it:

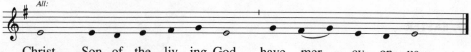

Christ, Son of the liv-ing God, have mer-cy on us.

Text: *Liturgy of the Hours,* © 1974, ICEL
Tune: Robert Le Blanc, © 1986, GIA Publications, Inc.

7 GOSPEL CANTICLE

All make the sign of the cross.

1. Now ✠ bless the God of Is - ra - el, Who
2. Re - mem - ber - ing the cov - e - nant, God
3. In ten - der mer - cy, God will send The

comes in love and pow'r, Who rais - es from the
res - cues us from fear, That we might serve in
day - spring from on high, Our ris - ing sun, the

roy - al house De - liv - 'rance in this hour. Through
ho - li - ness And peace from year to year; And
light of life For those who sit and sigh. God

ho - ly proph - ets   God has sworn   To
you, my child, shall   go be - fore   To
comes to guide our   way to peace,   That

free   us   from   a - larm,   To save us from the
preach, to proph - e - sy,   That all may know the
death shall reign no more.   Sing prais - es to the

heav - y   hand   Of   all   who wish   us   harm.
ten - der   love,   The   grace   of   God most   high.
Ho - ly   One!   O   wor - ship   and   a - dore!

Text: *Benedictus*, Luke 1:68-79; Ruth Duck, b.1947, © 1992, GIA Publications, Inc.
Tune: FOREST GREEN, CMD; English; harm. by Ralph Vaughan Williams, 1872-1958, © Oxford University Press

INTERCESSIONS   8

In place of the following, a more familiar form may be used.

Cantor:

1. In you, O Lord, is the source of   life.
2. Send forth your light and your   truth.
3. Fill us each morning with your constant   love.
4. Let us see your mighty   acts.
5. Lord our God, may your blessing be up   -   on us.

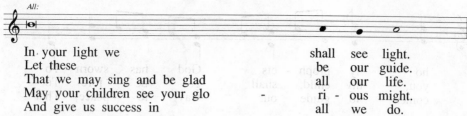

All:

In your light we	shall	see	light.
Let these	be	our	guide.
That we may sing and be glad	all	our	life.
May your children see your glo -	ri -	ous	might.
And give us success in	all	we	do.

Praise God in Song, © 1979, GIA Publications, Inc.

9 LORD'S PRAYER

Our Fa - ther, who art in heav - en, hal - lowed be thy name;

thy king - dom come; thy will be done on earth as it

is in heav - en. Give us this day our dai - ly bread;

and for - give us our tres - pass - es as we for - give

those who tres - pass a - gainst us; and lead us not

in - to temp - ta - tion, but de - liv - er us from e - vil.

All:

For the king - dom, the pow'r, and the

glo - ry are yours, now and for ev - er.

Music: Traditional chant, adapt. by Robert Snow, 1964; acc. by Robert J. Batastini, © 1975, 1993, GIA Publications, Inc.

The concluding prayer follows.

DISMISSAL

Priest or deacon: The Lord be with you. *Assembly:* And also with you.

Priest or deacon: May almight - y God bless you, the Fa - ther, and the Son, and the Holy Spir - it.

All: A - men! A - men!

Music: David Clark Isele, © 1979 GIA Publications, Inc.

Priest or deacon: Go in peace. *Assembly:* Thanks be to God.

Dismissal, if the leader is not a priest or deacon:

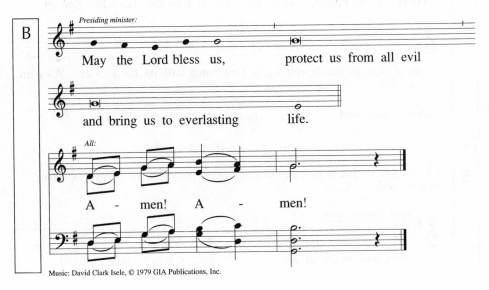

Presiding minister: May the Lord bless us, protect us from all evil and bring us to everlasting life.

All: A - men! A - men!

Music: David Clark Isele, © 1979 GIA Publications, Inc.

11 EVENING PRAYER/VESPERS

The church gathers in the evening to give thanks for the day that is ending. In the earliest tradition, this began with the lighting of the lamps as darkness fell and the hymn of praise of Christ who is "radiant Light. . .of God the Father's deathless face." The evening psalms and the Magnificat bring the day just past to focus for the Christian: "God has cast down the mighty from their thrones, and has lifted up the lowly"; "God has remembered the promise of mercy, the promise made to our ancestors." Prayers of intercession are almost always part of the church's liturgy, but those which conclude evening prayer are especially important. As day ends, the church again and again lifts up to God the needs and sorrows and failures of all the world. Such intercession is the daily task and joy of the baptized.

Appointed antiphons, readings, intercessions, prayers for each day and seasonal settings of the evening thanksgiving can be found in **Worship—Liturgy of the Hours—Leader's Edition** *(GIA) or* **Christian Prayer.**

All make the sign of the cross.

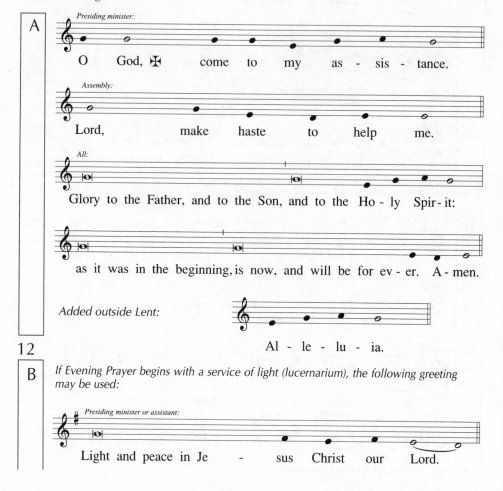

A

Presiding minister:

O God, ✠ come to my as - sis - tance.

Assembly:

Lord, make haste to help me.

All:

Glory to the Father, and to the Son, and to the Ho - ly Spir - it:

as it was in the beginning, is now, and will be for ev - er. A - men.

Added outside Lent:

Al - le - lu - ia.

12

B

If Evening Prayer begins with a service of light (lucernarium), the following greeting may be used:

Presiding minister or assistant:

Light and peace in Je - sus Christ our Lord.

Assembly:

Thanks be to God.

HYMN 13

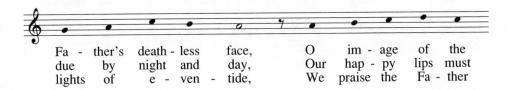

1. O ra - diant Light, O Sun di - vine Of God the
2. O Son of God, the source of life, Praise is your
3. Lord Je - sus Christ, as day - light fades, As shine the

Fa - ther's death - less face, O im - age of the
due by night and day, Our hap - py lips must
lights of e - ven - tide, We praise the Fa - ther

Light sub - lime That fills the heav'n - ly dwell - ing place.
raise the strain Of your es - teemed and splen - did name.
with the Son, The Spir - it blest, and with them one.

Text: *Phos Hilaron* Greek, c.200; tr. by William G. Storey, ©
Music: JESU DULCIS MEMORIA, LM; Mode I; acc. by Richard Proulx, © 1975, GIA Publications, Inc.

Optional

If the lucernarium is celebrated, the evening thanksgiving may be sung: 14

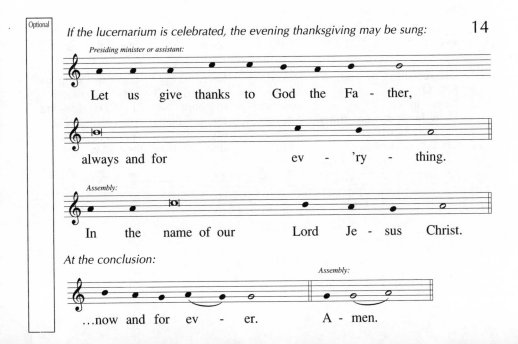

Presiding minister or assistant:

Let us give thanks to God the Fa - ther,

always and for ev - 'ry - thing.

Assembly:

In the name of our Lord Je - sus Christ.

At the conclusion:

Assembly:

...now and for ev - er. A - men.

PSALMODY

The singing of one or more psalms is a central part of Evening Prayer. Psalm 141, given below, is one of the premier evening psalms (see also no. 188 and 189). It is customary to use incense as it is sung. Other appropriate psalms for evening are Psalms 19, 23, 27, 84, 91, 104, 117, 118, 121, 122, 130 and 145.

15 PSALM 141/INCENSE PSALM

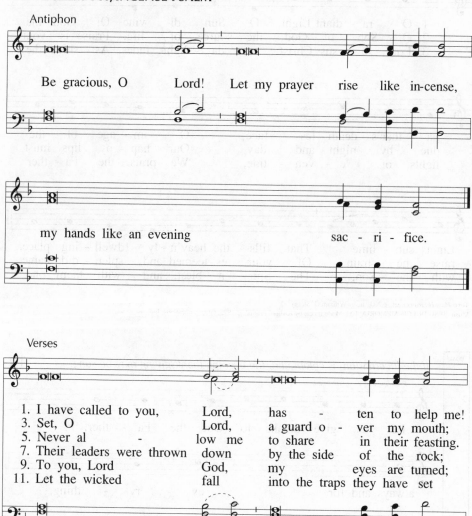

Antiphon

Be gracious, O Lord! Let my prayer rise like in-cense,

my hands like an evening sac - ri - fice.

Verses

1. I have called to you,   Lord,   has   -   ten   to   help me!
3. Set, O   Lord,   a guard o - ver   my mouth;
5. Never al -   low me   to share   in   their feasting.
7. Their leaders were thrown   down   by the side of   the rock;
9. To you, Lord   God,   my   eyes are turned;
11. Let the wicked   fall   into the traps they have set

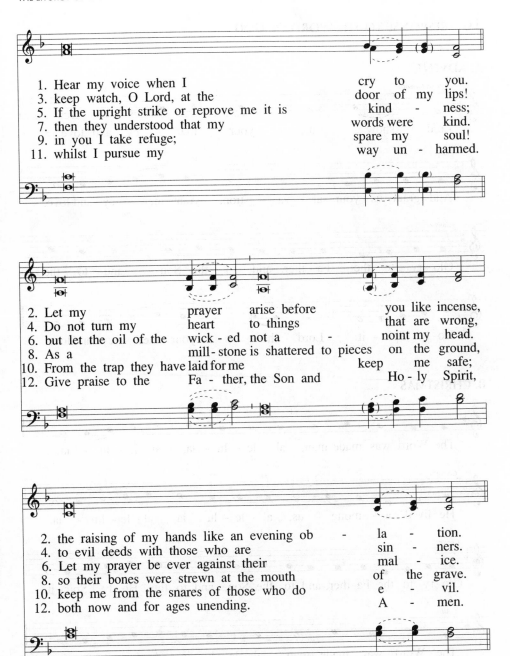

1. Hear my voice when I cry to you.
3. keep watch, O Lord, at the door of my lips!
5. If the upright strike or reprove me it is kind - ness;
7. then they understood that my words were kind.
9. in you I take refuge; spare my soul!
11. whilst I pursue my way un - harmed.

2. Let my prayer arise before you like incense,
4. Do not turn my heart to things that are wrong,
6. but let the oil of the wick - ed not a - noint my head.
8. As a mill- stone is shattered to pieces on the ground,
10. From the trap they have laid for me keep me safe;
12. Give praise to the Fa - ther, the Son and Ho - ly Spirit,

2. the raising of my hands like an evening ob - la - tion.
4. to evil deeds with those who are sin - ners.
6. Let my prayer be ever against their mal - ice.
8. so their bones were strewn at the mouth of the grave.
10. keep me from the snares of those who do e - vil.
12. both now and for ages unending. A - men.

Text: Psalm 141; © 1963, 1993, The Grail, GIA Publications, Inc.
Music: KONTAKION; Russian Orthodox Liturgy, adapt. by Richard Proulx, © 1985, GIA Publications, Inc.

READING

16   RESPONSE TO THE WORD OF GOD

A. ADVENT

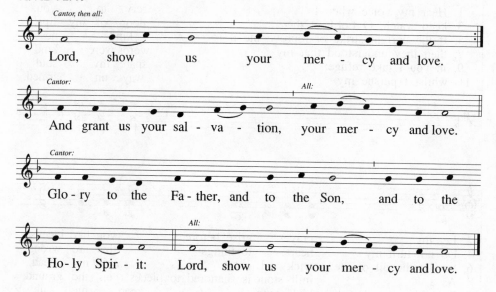

Cantor, then all:

Lord, show us your mer - cy and love.

Cantor: *All:*

And grant us your sal - va - tion, your mer - cy and love.

Cantor:

Glo - ry to the Fa - ther, and to the Son, and to the

All:

Ho - ly Spir - it: Lord, show us your mer - cy and love.

B. CHRISTMAS

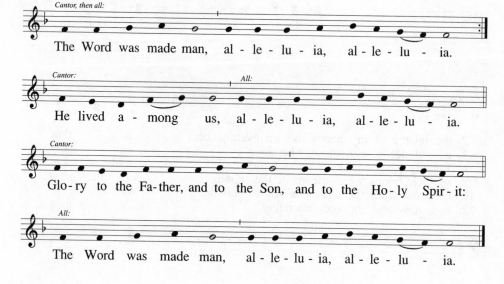

Cantor, then all:

The Word was made man, al - le - lu - ia, al - le - lu - ia.

Cantor: *All:*

He lived a - mong us, al - le - lu - ia, al - le - lu - ia.

Cantor:

Glo - ry to the Fa - ther, and to the Son, and to the Ho - ly Spir - it:

All:

The Word was made man, al - le - lu - ia, al - le - lu - ia.

C. LENT

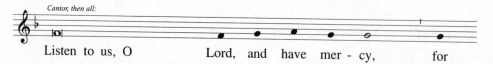

Cantor, then all:

Listen to us, O Lord, and have mer - cy, for

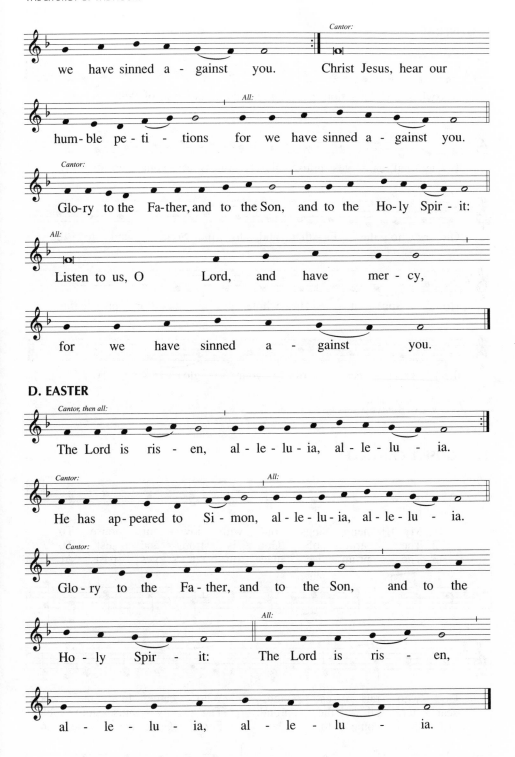

we have sinned a - gainst you.   *Cantor:* Christ Jesus, hear our

All: hum- ble pe - ti - tions for we have sinned a - gainst you.

Cantor: Glo-ry to the Fa-ther, and to the Son, and to the Ho-ly Spir - it:

All: Listen to us, O Lord, and have mer - cy,

for we have sinned a - gainst you.

D. EASTER

Cantor, then all: The Lord is ris - en, al - le - lu - ia, al - le - lu - ia.

Cantor: He has ap- peared to Si - mon, *All:* al - le - lu - ia, al - le - lu - ia.

Cantor: Glo - ry to the Fa - ther, and to the Son, and to the

All: Ho - ly Spir - it: The Lord is ris - en,

al - le - lu - ia, al - le - lu - ia.

E. GENERAL

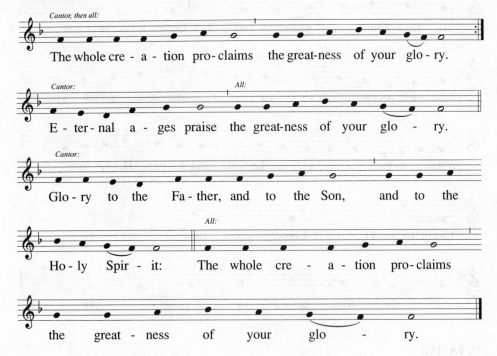

Cantor, then all:

The whole cre - a - tion pro - claims the great-ness of your glo - ry.

Cantor: ... *All:*

E - ter - nal a - ges praise the great-ness of your glo - ry.

Cantor:

Glo - ry to the Fa - ther, and to the Son, and to the

All:

Ho - ly Spir - it: The whole cre - a - tion pro - claims

the great - ness of your glo - ry.

Text: *Liturgy of the Hours,* © 1974, ICEL
Music: Robert Le Blanc, © 1986, GIA Publications, Inc.

17 GOSPEL CANTICLE

1. My ✠ heart sings out with joy - ful praise To
2. The arm of God is strong and just To
3. The prom - ise made in a - ges past At

God who rais - es me, Who came to me when
scat - ter all the proud. The ty - rants tum - ble
last has come to be, For God has come in

I was low And changed my des - ti - ny. The
from their thrones And van - ish like a cloud. The
pow'r to save, To set all peo - ple free. Re -

Ho - ly One, the Liv - ing God, Is
hun - gry all are sat - is - fied; The
mem - b'ring those who wait to see Sal -

al - ways full of grace To those who seek their
rich are sent a - way. The poor of earth who
va - tion's dawn - ing day, Our Sav - ior comes to

Mak - er's will In ev - 'ry time and place.
suf - fer long Will wel - come God's new day.
all who weep To wipe their tears a - way.

Text: *Magnificat*, Luke 1:46-55; Ruth Duck, b.1947, © 1992, GIA Publications, Inc.
Tune: KINGSFOLD, CMD; English traditional; harm. by Ralph Vaughan Williams, 1872-1958, © Oxford University Press

18   INTERCESSIONS

The response will be indicated by the leader.

LORD'S PRAYER

Our Fa-ther, who art in heav-en, hal-lowed be thy name;

thy king-dom come; thy will be done on earth as it

is in heav-en. Give us this day our dai-ly bread;

and for-give us our tres-pass-es as we for-give

those who tres-pass a-gainst us; and lead us not

in-to temp-ta-tion, but de-liv-er us from e - vil.

All:

For the king-dom, the pow'r, and the

glo-ry are yours, now and for ev - er.

Music: Traditional chant, adapt. by Robert Snow, 1964; acc. by Robert J. Batastini, © 1975, 1993, GIA Publications, Inc.

The concluding prayer follows.

DISMISSAL

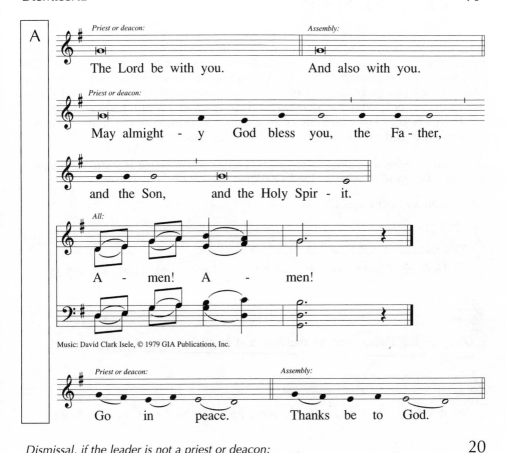

Music: David Clark Isele, © 1979 GIA Publications, Inc.

Dismissal, if the leader is not a priest or deacon:

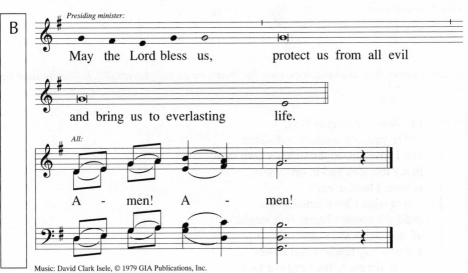

Music: David Clark Isele, © 1979 GIA Publications, Inc.

All may conclude the celebration by exchanging a sign of peace.

21 NIGHT PRAYER/COMPLINE

The church's prayers at night are direct and simple. The Christian remembers with sorrow the day's evil and failure, and places this before the mercy of God. Before surrendering to sleep, there is prayer for God's protection through the night and an expression of acceptance: "Now, Lord, you may dismiss your servant." The night prayer concludes by binding together the sleep of this night with the final falling asleep in the Lord: "May the all-powerful Lord grant us a restful night and a peaceful death." Night's last words are often a gentle invocation of our mother, "When this exile is ended, show us your womb's blessed fruit, Jesus."

Appointed antiphons, readings, intercessions and prayers for each day can be found in **Worship—Liturgy of the Hours—Leader's Edition** *(GIA) or* **Christian Prayer***.*

All make the sign of the cross.

Presiding minister:
O God, ✠ come to my as-sis-tance.

Assembly:
Lord, make haste to help me.

All:
Glory to the Father, and to the Son, and to the Ho-ly Spir-it:

as it was in the beginning, is now, and will be for ev-er. A-men.

Added outside Lent:
Al-le-lu-ia.

A brief examination of conscience may be made. At its conclusion, the following may be said:

> **Optional**
>
> I confess to almighty God,
> and to you, my brothers and sisters,
> that I have sinned through my own fault
> in my thoughts and in my words,
> in what I have done,
> and in what I have failed to do;
> and I ask blessed Mary, ever virgin,
> all the angels and saints,
> and you, my brothers and sisters,
> to pray for me to the Lord our God.

HYMN 22

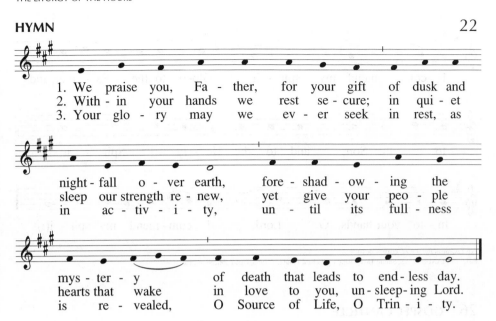

1. We praise you, Fa - ther, for your gift of dusk and
2. With - in your hands we rest se - cure; in qui - et
3. Your glo - ry may we ev - er seek in rest, as

night - fall o - ver earth, fore - shad - ow - ing the
sleep our strength re - new, yet give your peo - ple
in ac - tiv - i - ty, un - til its full - ness

mys - ter - y of death that leads to end - less day.
hearts that wake in love to you, un - sleep - ing Lord.
is re - vealed, O Source of Life, O Trin - i - ty.

Text: Benedictine Nuns of St. Mary's Abbey, West Malling, Kent, © 1967
Music: TE LUCIS ANTE TERMINUM, LM; adapt. by Howard Hughes, SM, © 1982, GIA Publications, Inc.

PSALMODY 23

The proper psalms for Night Prayer are: Sunday, Psalm 91/Ant. III (no. 122); Monday, Psalm 86/Ant. II (no. 115); Tuesday, Psalm 143:1-11 (no. 190); Wednesday, Psalm 31:1-6/Ant. III (no. 63) and Psalm 130/Ant. III (no. 175); Thursday, Psalm 16/Ant. I (no. 34); Friday, Psalm 88 (no. 116); and Saturday, Psalm 4/Ant. I (no. 29) and Psalm 134 (no. 181).

READING 24

RESPONSORY 25

Cantor:
In - to your hands, O Lord, I com - mend my spir - it.

All:
In - to your hands, O Lord, I com - mend my spir - it.

Cantor:
You have re - deemed us, Lord God of truth.

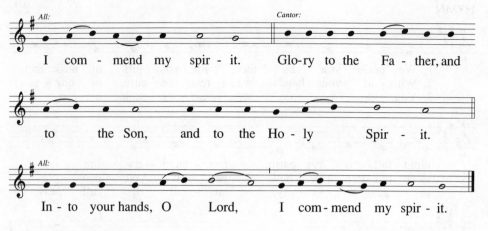

All: I com-mend my spir-it. **Cantor:** Glo-ry to the Fa-ther, and to the Son, and to the Ho-ly Spir-it. **All:** In-to your hands, O Lord, I com-mend my spir-it.

Text: *Liturgy of the Hours,* © 1974, ICEL
Music: IN MANUS TUAS; Sarum Tone, adapt. by Richard Proulx, © 1986, GIA Publications, Inc.

26 GOSPEL CANTICLE

Antiphon

Pro-tect us, Lord, as we stay a-wake; watch o-ver us as we sleep, that a-wake we may keep watch with Christ, and, a-sleep, rest in his peace.

Verse 1

1. Lord, ✠ now you let your ser-vant go in peace: your word has been ful-filled. **D.C.**

Verse 2

2. My own eyes have seen the sal-va-tion which you have prepared in the sight of ev-'ry peo-ple. **D.C.**

Verse 3

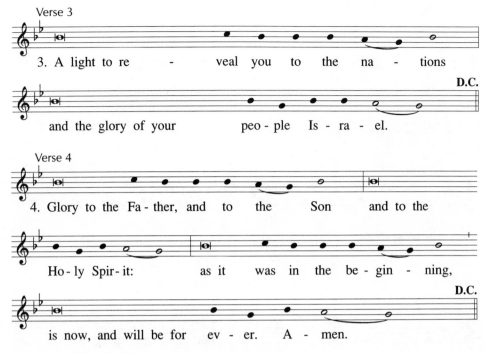

3. A light to re - veal you to the na - tions
and the glory of your peo - ple Is - ra - el.

D.C.

Verse 4

4. Glory to the Fa - ther, and to the Son and to the
Ho - ly Spir - it: as it was in the be - gin - ning,
is now, and will be for ev - er. A - men.

D.C.

Text: *Liturgy of the Hours,* © 1974, ICEL
Music: NUNC DIMITTIS; Sarum tone, adapt. by Richard Proulx, © 1986, GIA Publications, Inc.

PRAYER

27

CONCLUSION

Presiding minister:

May the all-powerful Lord grant us a restful night and a peaceful death.

All:

A - men! A - men!

Music: David Clark Isele, © 1979, GIA Publications, Inc.

The Marian antiphon, "Salve Regina," no. 894, or during Easter season, "Regina Caeli," no. 584, may follow.

28 Psalm 1: Happy Are They

Antiphon

Hap-py are they who hope, who hope in the Lord.

Text: *Lectionary for Mass,* © 1969, 1981, ICEL
Music: Robert J. Thompson, © 1975, GIA Publications, Inc.

Psalm Tone

Repeat for 6-line stanza

Music: Robert Kennedy Knox, © 1979

Gelineau Tone

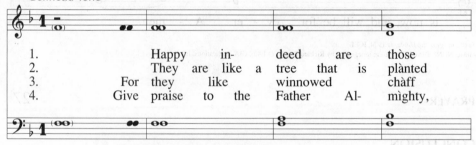

1. Happy in- deed are thòse
2. They are like a tree that is plànted
3. For they like winnowed chàff
4. Give praise to the Father Al- mìghty,

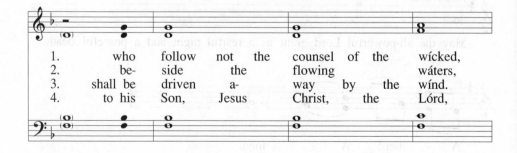

1. who follow not the counsel of the wícked,
2. be- side the flowing wáters,
3. shall be driven a- way by the wínd.
4. to his Son, Jesus Christ, the Lórd,

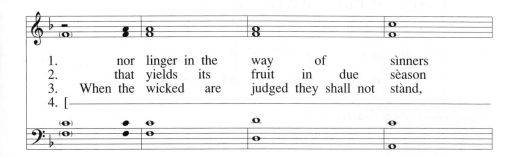

1. nor linger in the way of sìnners
2. that yields its fruit in due sèason
3. When the wicked are judged they shall not stànd,
4. [

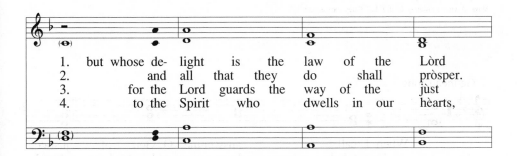

1. nor sit in the company of scórners,
2. and whose leaves shall never fáde;
3. nor find room among those who are júst;
4.]

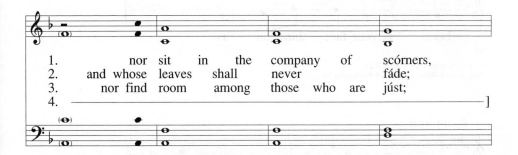

1. but whose de- light is the law of the Lòrd
2. and all that they do shall pròsper.
3. for the Lord guards the way of the jùst
4. to the Spirit who dwells in our hèarts,

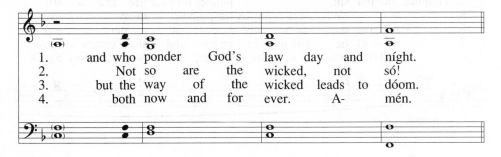

1. and who ponder God's law day and níght.
2. Not so are the wicked, not só!
3. but the way of the wicked leads to dóom.
4. both now and for ever. A- mén.

Text: Psalm 1; The Grail
Music: Joseph Gelineau, SJ
© 1963, 1993, The Grail, GIA Publications, Inc., agent

29 Psalm 4: Have Mercy, Lord

Antiphon I

Have mer-cy, Lord, and hear my prayer.

Text: *Liturgy of the Hours,* © 1974, ICEL
Music: Eugene Englert, © 1986, GIA Publications, Inc.

Antiphon II (Vs. 2.4.7.8.9)

Lord, let your face shine on us.

Text: *Lectionary for Mass,* © 1969, ICEL
Music: Robert LeBlanc, © 1986, GIA Publications, Inc.

Psalm Tone

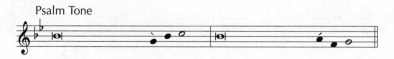

Music: A. Gregory Murray, OSB, © L. J. Carey and Co., Ltd.

Gelineau Tone

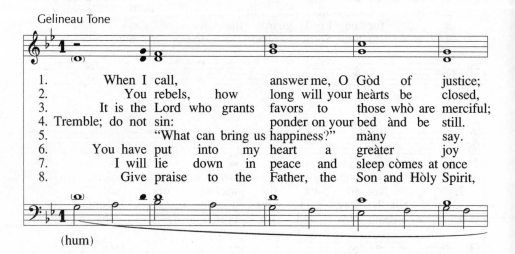

1. When I call, answer me, O Gòd of justice;
2. You rebels, how long will your heàrts be closed,
3. It is the Lord who grants favors to those whò are merciful;
4. Tremble; do not sin: ponder on your bed ànd be still.
5. "What can bring us happiness?" màny say.
6. You have put into my heart a greàter joy
7. I will lie down in peace and sleep còmes at once
8. Give praise to the Father, the Son and Hòly Spirit,

(hum)

1. from anguish you re-leased me, have mercý and hear me!
2. will you love what is futile and seek whát is false?
3. the Lord hears me when-evér I call.
4. Make justice your sacrifice and trust ín the Lord.
5. Lift up the light of your face on ús, O Lord.
6. than they have from a-bundance of corn ánd new wine.
7. for you alone, Lord, make me dwéll in safety.
8. both now and for ages un-endíng. A- men.

(hum)

Text: Psalm 4; The Grail
Music: Joseph Gelineau, SJ
© 1963, 1993, The Grail, GIA Publications, Inc., agent

30 Psalm 4: Let Your Face Shine upon Us

Refrain

Lord, let your face shine up - on us, shine up -
on us, shine up - on us.

Verses 1, 2

1. Lis - ten to my song, Hear me when I call, Oh
2. You have called my name, set your seal up - on my

Lord, my God, be gra - cious,
heart, you hear me

hear my prayer.
when I call.

Verse 3

3. Fill me with your joy, grant to me your peace - ful rest, to dwell in safe - ty with my Lord.

Text: Psalm 4:2, 4, 9; Marty Haugen
Music: Marty Haugen
© 1980, GIA Publications, Inc.

31 Psalm 8: How Great Is Your Name

Antiphon I

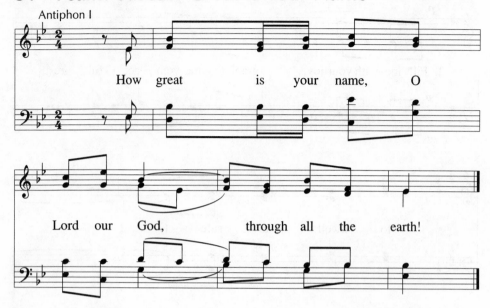

How great is your name, O
Lord our God, through all the earth!

Text: Psalm 8:2; The Grail
Music: A. Gregory Murray, OSB
© 1963, The Grail, GIA Publications, Inc., agent

Antiphon II (St. 3-5)

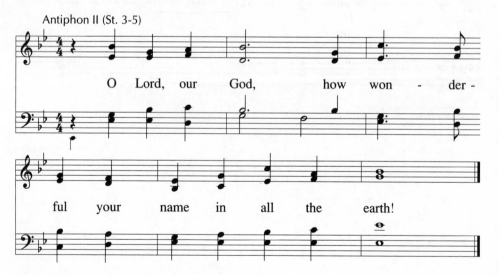

O Lord, our God, how won - der -
ful your name in all the earth!

Text: *Lectionary for Mass,* © 1969, 1981, ICEL
Music: J. Robert Carroll, © 1975, GIA Publications, Inc.

Psalm Tone

Music: Chant tone 5; acc. by Robert J. Batastini, © 1975, GIA Publications, Inc.

Gelineau Tone

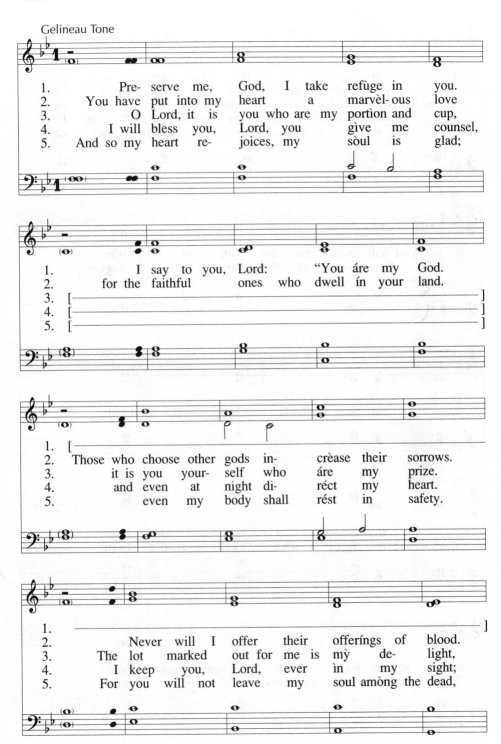

1.   Pre- serve me,   God,   I   take   refùge in   you.
2. You have put into my heart   a   marvèl- ous love
3.   O Lord, it is you who are my portìon and cup,
4.   I will bless you, Lord, you   gìve me counsel,
5. And so my heart re- joices, my   sòul is glad;

1.   I say to you, Lord: "You áre my God.
2. for the faithful   ones who dwell ín your land.
3. [   ]
4. [   ]
5. [   ]

1. [
2. Those who choose other gods in-   crèase their sorrows.
3.   it is you your- self who áre my prize.
4.   and even   at   night di- réct my heart.
5.   even   my body shall rést in safety.

1.   ]
2.   Never will I offer their offeríngs of blood.
3. The lot marked out for me is mỳ de- light,
4. I keep you, Lord, ever ìn my sight;
5. For you will not leave my soul amòng the dead,

1. My happiness lies in yóu a- lone."
2. Never will I take their name upón my lips.
3. welcome in- deed the heritage that fálls to me!
4. since you are at my right hand, I sháll stand firm.
5. nor let your be- loved knów de- cay.

6. You will show me the pàth of life,
7. Give praise to the Fathèr Al- mighty,

6. [   ]
7. to his Son, Jesus Chríst, the Lord,

6. the fullness of joy ín your presence,
7. to the Spirit who dwells ìn our hearts,

6. at your right hand happinéss for ever.
7. both now and for evér. A- men.

Text: Psalm 16; The Grail
Music: Joseph Gelineau, SJ
© 1963, 1993, The Grail, GIA Publications, Inc., agent

Psalm 16: Keep Me Safe, O God   35

Refrain

mf *a tempo*

Keep me safe, O God: you are my hope;

you are my hope,   O God.

1.
rit.

2. *To verses*
Last time

Verses*

mf

1. I	say	to	God,	"you	are	my
2. I	find	in	God	al -	ways	my
3. I	bless	my	God:	God	who	has
4. I	keep	my	God	al -	ways	be -
5. And	so	my	heart	al -	ways	is
6. For	you	will	not	ev -	er	a -
7. The	path	of	life	you	have	re -

on	-	ly	God,	I	have	no
cup		of	joy;	and	God	will
coun	-	seled	me.	At	night	my
fore		my	eyes;	with	God	be -
glad		in	God;	my	bod -	y
ban	-	don	me,	or	let	your
vealed		to	me,	and	in	your

* Verses may be selected according to liturgical need.

good	ex -	cept	in	you."
keep	my	life	se -	cure.
heart	gives	coun -	sel	too.
side	me	I'm	se -	cure.
too	shall	dwell	se -	cure.
ser -	vant	lose	the	path.
pres -	ence	is	my	joy.

Text: Psalm 16; John Foley, SJ, © 1993, GIA Publications, Inc.; refrain trans., © 1969, ICEL
Music: John Foley, SJ, © 1993, GIA Publications, Inc.

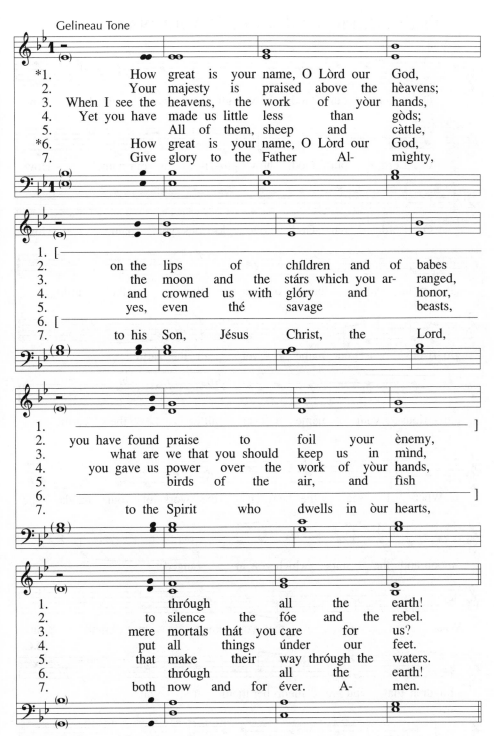

Gelineau Tone

*1. How great is your name, O Lòrd our God,
2. Your majesty is praised above the hèavens;
3. When I see the heavens, the work of yòur hands,
4. Yet you have made us little less than gòds;
5. All of them, sheep and càttle,
*6. How great is your name, O Lòrd our God,
7. Give glory to the Father Al- mìghty,

1. [
2. on the lips of chíldren and of babes
3. the moon and the stárs which you ar- ranged,
4. and crowned us with glóry and honor,
5. yes, even thé savage beasts,
6. [
7. to his Son, Jésus Christ, the Lord,

1.   ]
2. you have found praise to foil your ènemy,
3. what are we that you should keep us in mìnd,
4. you gave us power over the work of yòur hands,
5. birds of the air, and fìsh
6.   ]
7. to the Spirit who dwells in òur hearts,

1. thróugh all the earth!
2. to silence the fóe and the rebel.
3. mere mortals thát you care for us?
4. put all things únder our feet.
5. that make their way thróugh the waters.
6. thróugh all the earth!
7. both now and for éver. A- men.

*Omitted when Antiphon I is used.

Text: Psalm 8; The Grail
Music: Joseph Gelineau, SJ
© 1963, 1993, The Grail, GIA Publications, Inc., agent

32   Psalm 8: How Glorious Is Your Name

Refrain

Soprano:

O Lord,   our God,   how glo-rious your   name!   How

Alto & Melody:

O Lord,   our God,   how glo-ri-ous is your name!   How

Tenor: unis.

Bass:

O Lord,   our God,   how glo-rious your   name!   How

glo - rious   your   name o - ver   all   the   earth!

glo-ri-ous   is your name o - ver   all the earth!

glo - rious   your   name o - ver   all   the   earth!

Verse 1

1. When   I   see   the heav-ens,   the work of your   hands,   the

moon and the   stars   which you ar - ranged,

What   are   we   that you keep   us   in   mind?   Your

D.C.

chil-dren that   you re - mem-ber them   at   all?

Verse 2

2. Yet   you have made   us   lit-tle   less   than gods,   with

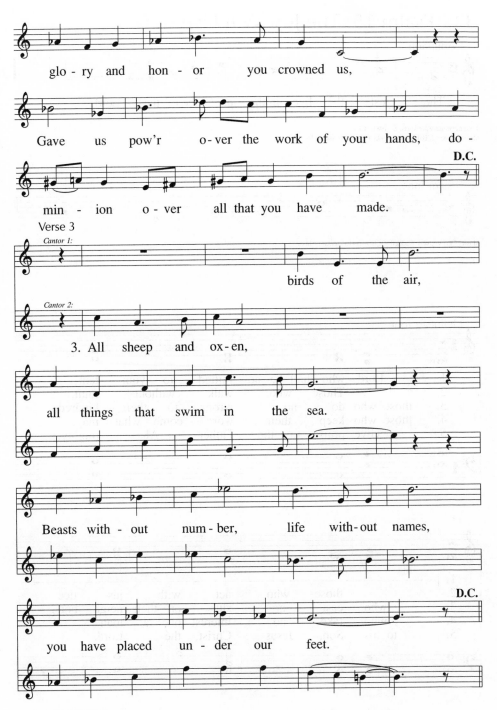

Text: Psalm 8:4-5, 6-7, 8-9; Rory Cooney
Music: Rory Cooney
© 1990, GIA Publications, Inc.

33 Psalm 15: The Just Will Live

Antiphon

The just will live in the pres-ence of the Lord.

Text: *Lectionary for Mass,* © 1981, ICEL
Music: Robert J. Batastini, © 1995, GIA Publications, Inc.

Psalm Tone

Omit for stanza 1

Music: Chrysogonus Waddell, OCSO, © Gethsemani Abbey

Gelineau Tone

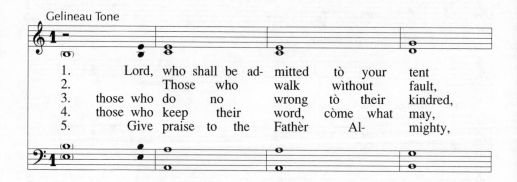

1.		Lord, who shall be ad-	mitted	tò your	tent
2.		Those who	walk	wìthout	fault,
3.	those who do	no	wrong	tò their	kindred,
4.	those who keep	their	word,	còme what	may,
5.	Give praise to	the	Fathèr	Al-	mighty,

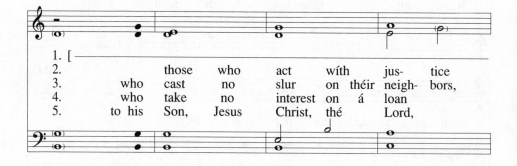

1. [					
2.		those who	act	wíth	jus- tice
3.	who cast	no	slur	on théir	neigh- bors,
4.	who take	no	interest	on á	loan
5.	to his	Son, Jesus	Christ,	thé	Lord,

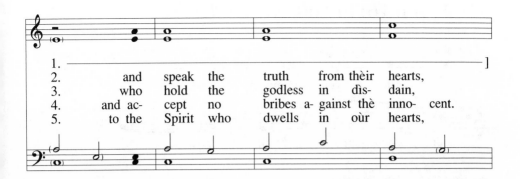

1.
2. and speak the truth from thèir hearts,
3. who hold the godless in dìs- dain,
4. and ac- cept no bribes a- gainst thè inno- cent.
5. to the Spirit who dwells in oùr hearts,

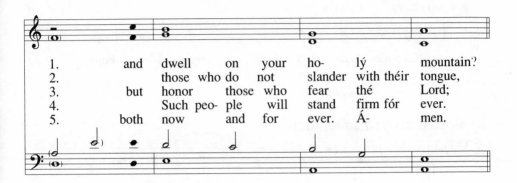

1. and dwell on your ho- lý mountain?
2. those who do not slander with théir tongue,
3. but honor those who fear thé Lord;
4. Such peo- ple will stand firm fór ever.
5. both now and for ever. Á- men.

Text: Psalm 15; The Grail
Music: Joseph Gelineau, SJ
© 1963, 1993, The Grail, GIA Publications, Inc., agent

34 Psalm 16: In You, My God

Antiphon I

In you, my God, my bod-y will rest in hope.

Antiphon II (Vs. 5.8.9-10.11)

Keep me safe, O God; you are my hope.

Antiphon III (Vs. 1-2.5.7-8.9-10.11)

Lord, you will show us the path of life.

Antiphon IV (Vs. 1-2.5.7-8.9-10.11)

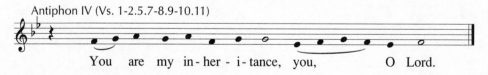

You are my in-her-i-tance, you, O Lord.

Psalm Tone

Omit for 3-line stanza   Repeat for 5-line stanza

Psalm 16: You Will Show Me the Path of Life   36

Refrain I

You will show me the path of life, you, my hope and my shel-ter;

To verses

In your pres-ence is end-less joy, at your side is my home for - ev - er.

Refrain II

To verses

Keep me safe, O God, I take ref - uge in you.

Refrain III

To verses

You are my in - her - i - tance, O Lord.

Verses

unis.   *div.*

1. Faith-ful God, I look to you, you a - lone my life and
2. From of old you are my her - i - tage, you my wis - dom and my
3. So my heart shall sing for joy, in your arms I rest se -

for - tune, nev - er shall I look to oth - er gods,
safe - ty, through the night you speak with - in my heart,
cure - ly, you will not a - ban - don me to death,

poco. rit.   *To refrain*

you shall be my one hope.
si - lent - ly you teach me.
you shall not de - sert me.

Text: Psalm 16:1-2, 6-8, 9-10; Marty Haugen, © 1988, GIA Publications, Inc.; refrain III trans., © 1969, ICEL
Music: Marty Haugen; refrain II and III adapt. by Diana Kodner © 1988, 1994, GIA Publications, Inc.

37 Psalm 17: Lord, When Your Glory Appears

Refrain

Lord, when your glo-ry ap-pears, my joy, my joy will be full,

1. my joy, my joy will be full.

2. joy will be full.

Verses

1. Hear, O Lord, a just suit, at-
2. My steps are fast in your path, my
3. Keep me in your gen-tle care.

tend to my out-cry. Hear the pray'r of my
feet have fal-tered not. I call and you an-swer
Hide me un-der your wings. In jus-tice shall I see your

D.C.

lips; lips with-out de-ceit.
me; in-cline your ear to me.
face, on wak-ing shall I be con-tent.

Text: Psalm 17:1, 5-6, 8-9, 15; Roy James Stewart, © 1993, GIA Publications, Inc.; refrain trans. © 1969, ICEL
Music: Roy James Stewart, © 1993, GIA Publications, Inc.

Psalm 18: I Love You, Lord, My Strength   38

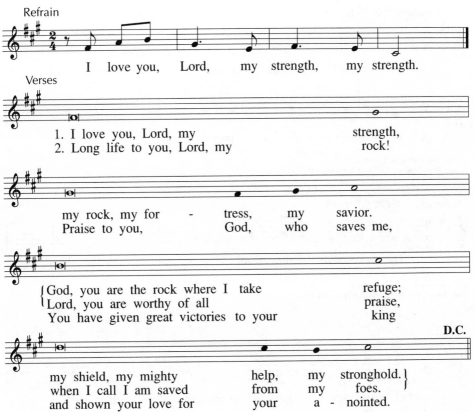

Refrain

I love you, Lord, my strength, my strength.

Verses

1. I love you, Lord, my strength,
2. Long life to you, Lord, my rock!

   my rock, my for - tress, my savior.
   Praise to you, God, who saves me,

   {God, you are the rock where I take refuge;
   {Lord, you are worthy of all praise,
   You have given great victories to your king

   D.C.

   my shield, my mighty help, my stronghold.
   when I call I am saved from my foes.
   and shown your love for your a - nointed.

Text: Psalm 18:2-3, 3-4, 47, 51; © 1963, 1993, The Grail, GIA Publications, Inc., agent; refrain trans. © 1969, ICEL
Music: Michel Guimont, © 1994, GIA Publications, Inc.

39 Psalm 19: Lord, You Have the Words

Antiphon I (St. 5-8)

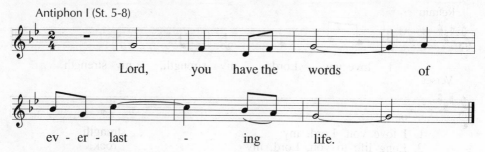

Lord, you have the words of ev - er - last - ing life.

Text: *Lectionary for Mass,* © 1969, ICEL
Music: Richard Proulx, © 1975, GIA Publications, Inc.

Antiphon II (St. 5.7.9.10)

The pre-cepts of the Lord give joy to the heart.

Text: *Lectionary for Mass,* © 1969, ICEL
Music: Randolph Currie, © 1986, GIA Publications, Inc.

Antiphon III (St. 1-2)

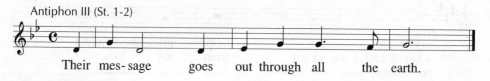

Their mes-sage goes out through all the earth.

Text: *Lectionary for Mass,* © 1969, ICEL
Music: James J. Chepponis, © 1986, GIA Publications, Inc.

Antiphon IV (St. 5.6.7.11)

Your words, Lord, are spir - it and life.

Text: *Lectionary for Mass,* © 1969, ICEL
Music: Chrysogonus Waddell, OCSO, © 1986, GIA Publications, Inc.

Psalm Tone

Repeat for stanzas 2-4

Music: A. Gregory Murray, OSB, © L. J. Carey and Co., Ltd.

Gelineau Tone

1. The heavens pro- claim the glory of God,
2. No speech, no word, no vòice is heard
3. There God has placed a tent fòr the sun;
4. At the end of the sky is the rising òf the sun;

(hum)

1. and the firmament shows forth the work óf God's hands.
2. [   ]
3. [   ]
4. [   ]

(hum)

1. Day unto day takes ùp the sto- ry
2. yet their span ex- tends through áll the earth,
3. it comes forth like a bridegroom coming fróm his tent,
4. to the furthest end of the sky ís its course.

(hum)

1. and night unto night makes knówn the message.
2. their words to the utmost bounds óf the world.
3. re- joices like a champion to rún its course.
4. There is nothing con- cealed from its búrning heat.

(hum)

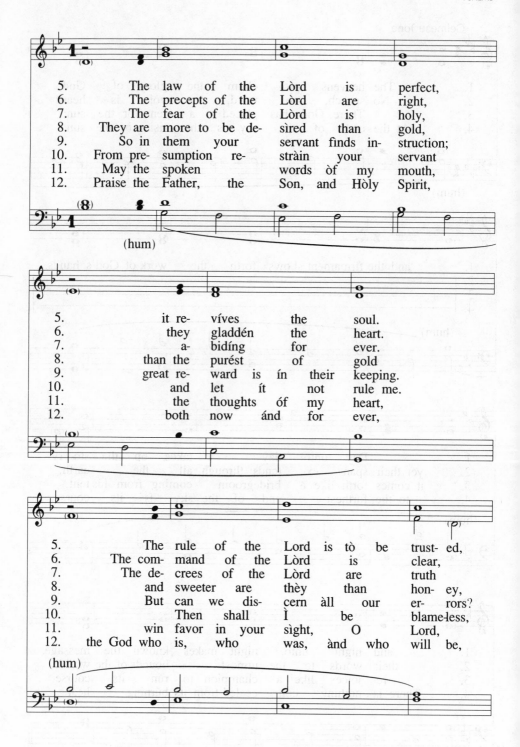

5. The law of the Lòrd is perfect,
6. The precepts of the Lòrd are right,
7. The fear of the Lòrd is holy,
8. They are more to be de- sìred than gold,
9. So in them your servant finds in- struction;
10. From pre- sumption re- stràin your servant
11. May the spoken words òf my mouth,
12. Praise the Father, the Son, and Hòly Spirit,

(hum)

5. it re- víves the soul.
6. they gladdén the heart.
7. a- bidíng for ever.
8. than the purést of gold
9. great re- ward is ín their keeping.
10. and let ít not rule me.
11. the thoughts óf my heart,
12. both now ánd for ever,

5. The rule of the Lord is tò be trust- ed,
6. The com- mand of the Lòrd is clear,
7. The de- crees of the Lòrd are truth
8. and sweeter are thèy than hon- ey,
9. But can we dis- cern àll our er- rors?
10. Then shall Ì be blame-less,
11. win favor in your sìght, O Lord,
12. the God who is, who was, ànd who will be,

(hum)

5.		it gives	wisdom	tó	the	simple.
6.		it gives	light	tó	the	eyes.
7.		and	all	óf	them	just.
8.		than	honey	fróm	the	comb.
9.		From	hidden	fáults	ac-	quit us.
10.			clean	fróm	grave	sin.
11.		my	rescuér,	my		rock!
12.			world	without		end.

(hum)

Text: Psalm 19; The Grail
Music: Joseph Gelineau, SJ
© 1963, 1993, The Grail, GIA Publications, Inc., agent

40 Psalm 19: Lord, You Have the Words

Refrain

Final ending

Lord, you have the words of ev-er-last-ing life.

Verse 1

1. The law of the Lord is per-fect, re-fresh-ing the soul; the Lord's rule is to be trust-ed, the sim-ple find wis-dom.

Verse 2

2. The fear of the Lord is ho-ly, a-bid-ing for ev-er; the de-crees of the Lord are true, all of them just.

Verse 3

3. The pre-cepts of the Lord are right, they glad-den the heart, the com-mand of the Lord is clear, giv-ing light to the eye.

Verse 4

4. They are worth more than gold, than the fin-est gold, sweet-er than hon-ey, than hon-ey from the comb.

Text: Psalm 19:8, 9, 10, 11; David Haas, © 1983, GIA Publications, Inc.; refrain trans., © 1969 ICEL
Music: David Haas, © 1983, GIA Publications, Inc.

Psalm 22: I Will Praise You, Lord   41

Refrain

I will praise you, Lord, in the as-sem - bly of your peo - ple.

Verses

1. My vows I will pay before those who fear God.
2. All the earth shall remember and return to the Lord,
3. My soul shall live for God and my children too shall serve.

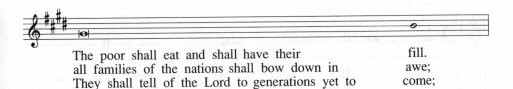

The poor shall eat and shall have their fill.
all families of the nations shall bow down in awe;
They shall tell of the Lord to generations yet to come;

Those who seek the Lord shall praise the Lord.
They shall bow down in awe, all the mighty of the earth,
declare to those unborn, the faithful - ness of God.

D.C.

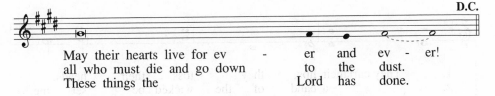

May their hearts live for ev - er and ev - er!
all who must die and go down to the dust.
These things the Lord has done.

Text: Psalm 22:26-27, 28, 30, 31-32; © 1963, 1993, The Grail, GIA Publications, Inc., agent; refrain trans. © 1969, ICEL
Music: Michel Guimont, © 1994, GIA Publications, Inc.

42   Psalm 22: My God, My God

Antiphon

My God,   my   God,   why have you for - sak-en me?

Text: Psalm 22:1; © 1963, The Grail, GIA Publications, Inc., agent
Music: Frank Schoen, © 1975, GIA Publications, Inc.

Psalm Tone

Music: Chant tone 8-g; acc. by Richard Proulx, © 1985, GIA Publications, Inc.

Gelineau Tone

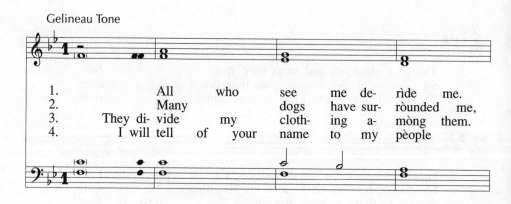

1.   All   who   see   me de-   rìde   me.
2.   Many   dogs   have sur-   ròunded   me,
3. They di- vide   my   cloth- ing a-   mòng   them.
4.   I will tell   of   your   name   to   my   pèople

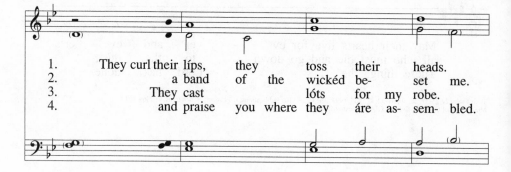

1. They curl their líps,   they   toss   their   heads.
2.   a band   of   the   wickéd be-   set   me.
3.   They cast   lóts   for   my   robe.
4.   and praise   you where they   áre   as- sem- bled.

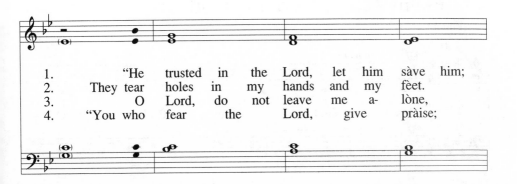

1.   "He   trusted   in   the   Lord,   let   him   sàve   him;
2. They tear   holes   in   my   hands   and   my   fèet.
3.   O   Lord,   do   not   leave   me   a-   lòne,
4. "You who   fear   the   Lord,   give   pràise;

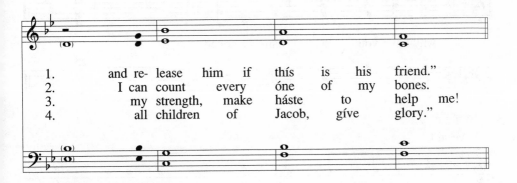

1.   and re- lease   him   if   thís   is   his   friend."
2.   I can count   every   óne   of   my   bones.
3.   my strength,   make   háste   to   help   me!
4.   all children   of   Jacob,   gíve   glory."

Text: Psalm 22:8-9, 17-18, 19-20, 23-24; The Grail
Music: Joseph Gelineau, SJ

43 Psalm 22: My God, My God

Refrain

♩=76

mf *a tempo*

My God, my God, O

Last time rit.

why have you a - ban - doned me?

Verse 1

1. All who see me laugh at me, they

mock me and they shake their heads: "He re-lied on the

poco rit. **D.C.**

Lord, let the Lord be his ref - uge."

Verse 2

2. As dogs a - round me, they cir-cle me a - bout.

poco rit. **D.C.**

Wound-ed me and pierced me, I can num-ber all my bones.

Verses 3, 4

3. My cloth - ing they di - vid - ed, for my
4. I will praise you to my peo - ple, and pro -

gar - ments cast - ing lots, O Lord, do not de -
claim you in their midst, O fear the Lord, my

poco rit. **D.C.**

sert me, but hast - en to my aid.
peo - ple, give glo - ry to God's name.

Text: Psalm 22:8-9, 17-18; 19-20; 23-24; Marty Haugen, © 1983, GIA Publications, Inc.; refrain trans. © 1969, ICEL
Music: Marty Haugen, © 1983, GIA Publications, Inc.

44 Psalm 23: The Lord Is My Shepherd

Refrain

Descant:
The Lord is my shep - herd, I shall not want. The

Melody:
The Lord is my shep - herd, I shall not want. The

rit.
Lord's my shep - herd, I shall not want.

rit.
Lord is my shep - herd, I shall not want.

Verses

Melody:
1. The pas - tures are fresh where you give me rest;
2. Though I am brought down to the val - ley deep,
3. A feast you have held in the sight of foes;
4. To - day and for all of my days to come

Harmony:
1. The pas - tures are fresh where you give me rest; Calm
2. Though I am brought down to the val - ley deep, No
3. A feast you have held in the sight of foes; Oil
4. To - day and for all of my days to come Good -

Calm wa - ters lift up my soul. You
No e - vil great will I fear; The
Oil has a - noint - ed my head; My
Good - ness and love fol - low me, And

wa - ters lift up my soul. You
e - vil great will I fear; The
has a - noint - ed my head; My
ness and love fol - low me, And

lead me on paths that are right - eous and good; Your
strength of your rod and the pow'r of your staff Will
cup o - ver - flows with your mer - cy and love: With
now I will dwell in the house of the Lord As

lead me on paths that are right-eous and good; Your
strength of your rod and the pow'r of your staff Will
cup o - ver - flows with your mer - cy and love: With
now I will dwell in the house of the Lord As

rit.   **D.C.**

name is hal-lowed by all.
give me com - fort and cheer.
bless - ings great am I fed.
long as life there shall be.

name is hal - lowed by all.
give me com - fort and cheer.
bless - ings great am I fed.
long as life there shall be.

Text: Psalm 23; Randall Sensmeier
Music: Randall Sensmeier
© 1994, GIA Publications, Inc.

45 Psalm 23: My Shepherd Is the Lord

Antiphon I

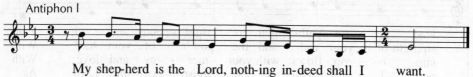

My shep-herd is the Lord, noth-ing in-deed shall I want.

Text: Psalm 23; The Grail
Music: Joseph Gelineau, SJ
© 1963, The Grail, GIA Publications, Inc., agent

Antiphon II

The Lord is my shep - herd, noth-ing shall I

want: he leads me by safe paths, noth-ing shall I fear.

Text: Psalm 23; The Grail
Music: A. Gregory Murray, OSB
© 1963, The Grail, GIA Publications, Inc., agent

Antiphon III

Descant:

The Lord is my shep - herd;

Melody:

The Lord is my shep-herd; there is

noth - ing I shall want.

noth - ing I shall want.

Text: *Lectionary for Mass*, © 1969, ICEL
Music: Richard Proulx, © 1975, GIA Publications, Inc.

Antiphon IV

I shall live in the house of the Lord all the days of my life.

Text: *Lectionary for Mass,* © 1969, ICEL
Music: Robert J. Batastini, © 1975, GIA Publications, Inc.

Psalm Tone

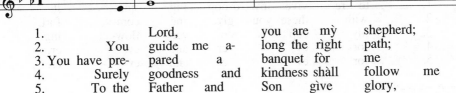

Omit for 4-line stanza

Music: Richard Proulx, © 1975, GIA Publications, Inc.

Gelineau Tone

1. Lord, you are mỳ shepherd;
2. You guide me a- long the rìght path;
3. You have pre- pared a banquet fòr me
4. Surely goodness and kindness shàll follow me
5. To the Father and Son gìve glory,

1. there is nothing Í shall want.
2. You are true tó your name.
3. in the sight óf my foes.
4. all the days óf my life.
5. give glory tó the Spirit.

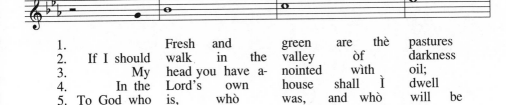

1. Fresh and green are thè pastures
2. If I should walk in the valley òf darkness
3. My head you have a- nointed wìth oil;
4. In the Lord's own house shall Ì dwell
5. To God who is, whò was, and whò will be

1. where you give me ré- pose.
2. no evil would Í fear.
3. [
4. [
5. [

1. Near restful waters yòu lead me,
2. You are there with your crook and yòur staff;
3.]
4.]
5.]

1. to re- vive my droop- íng spir- it.
2. with these you give mé com- fort.
3. my cup is o- vér- flow- ing.
4. for ev- er ánd ev- er.
5. for ev- er ánd ev- er.

Text: Psalm 23; The Grail
Music: Joseph Gelineau, SJ
© 1963, 1993, The Grail, GIA Publications, Inc., agent

Psalm 23: Nada Me Falta   46

Refrain

El Se - ñor es mi pas - tor, na-da me fal - ta. El Se -
ñor es mi pas - tor, na-da me fal - ta - rá.

Verse 1

1. El Se - ñor es mi pas - tor, na - da me fal - ta: En
ver-des pra - de - ras me_ha - ce re - cos - tar; Me con - du - ce ha-cia
fuen - tes tran-qui- las y re - pa - ra mis fuer-zas.

D.C.

Verse 2

2. Me guía por el sen-de-ro jus - to en gra-cia de su nom-bre.
Aun - que ca - mi - ne por ca - ña - das os - cu - ras, na - da te -
mo por-que tú vas con - mi - go: tu va - ra y tu ca -
ya - do me so - sie - gan.

D.C.

Verse 3

3. Pre - pa - ras u - na me - sa an - te mí, en - fren - te de

mis en - e - mi - gos; me un - ges la ca - be - za con per -

D.C.

fu - me, y mi co - pa re - bo - sa.

Verse 4

4. Tu bon - dad y tu en - gen - cia me a - com - pa - ñan.

To - dos los dí - as de mi vi - da, y ha - bi - ta - ré en la

D.C.

ca - sa del Se - ñor por siem - pre.

Text: Psalm 23, *Leccionario Edicion Hispanoamericana*; Donna Peña
Music: Donna Peña; acc. by Diana Kodner
© 1988, 1993, GIA Publications, Inc.

Psalm 24: We Long to See Your Face 47

Refrain I

O God, this is the peo-ple that longs to see your face. O God, this is the peo-ple that longs to see your face.

Refrain II

O-pen wide your gates; Let the King of Glo-ry in! O-pen wide your gates; Let the King of Glo-ry in!

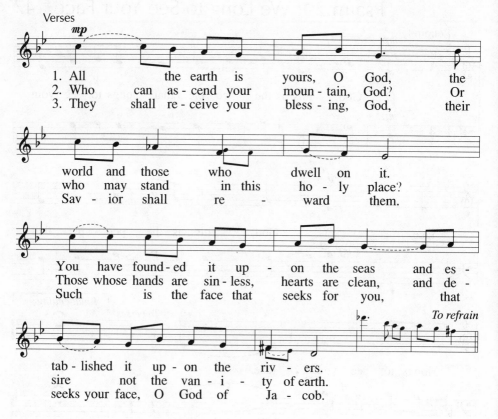

Verses

mp

1. All the earth is yours, O God, the
2. Who can as-cend your moun-tain, God? Or
3. They shall re-ceive your bless-ing, God, their

world and those who dwell on it.
who may stand in this ho - ly place?
Sav - ior shall re - ward them.

You have found-ed it up - on the seas and es -
Those whose hands are sin - less, hearts are clean, and de -
Such is the face that seeks for you, that

To refrain

tab - lished it up - on the riv - ers.
sire not the van - i - ty of earth.
seeks your face, O God of Ja - cob.

Text: Psalm 24; Kevin Keil, © 1993, GIA Publications, Inc.; refrain I trans. © 1969, ICEL
Music: Kevin Keil, © 1993 GIA Publications, Inc.

48 Psalm 24: Let the Lord Enter

Antiphon

Let the Lord en-ter; he is king of glo-ry.

Text: *Lectionary for Mass*, © 1969, ICEL
Music: Richard Proulx, © 1975, GIA Publications, Inc.

Psalm Tone

Music: Howard Hughes, SM, © 1986, GIA Publications, Inc.

Gelineau Tone

1. The Lord's is the earth and its fullness,
2. Who shall climb the mountain of the Lord?
3. They shall re- ceive blessings from the Lord

1. the world and all its peoples.
2. Who shall stand in God's holy place?
3. and re- ward from the God who saves them.

1. It is God who set it on the seas;
2. Those with clean hands and pure heart,
3. These are the ones who seek,

1. who made it firm on the waters.
2. who de- sire not worthless things.
3. seek the face of the God of [ ] Ja- cob.

Text: Psalm 24:1-2, 3-4, 5-6; The Grail
Music: Joseph Gelineau, SJ
© 1963, 1993, GIA Publications, Inc., agent

49 Psalm 24: Who Is This King

Refrain

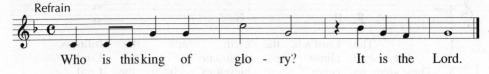

Who is this king of glo - ry? It is the Lord.

Verses

1. O gates, lift high your heads;   grow higher, an - cient doors.
2. Who is the king of glory?   The Lord, the mighty, the valiant,
3. O gates, lift high your heads;   grow higher, an - cient doors.
4. Who is the king of glory?   The Lord of heaven - ly armies.

D.C.

Let the king of glo - ry enter!
the Lord, the valiant in war.
Let the king of glo - ry enter!
This is the king of glory.

Text: Psalm 24:7, 8, 9, 10; © 1963, 1993, The Grail, GIA Publications, Inc., agent; refrain trans. © 1969, ICEL
Music: Michel Guimont, © 1995, GIA Publications, Inc.

50 Psalm 25: To You, O Lord

Antiphon

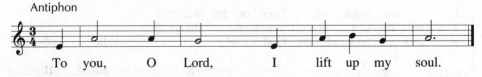

To you, O Lord, I lift up my soul.

Text: Psalm 25:1; © 1963, The Grail, GIA Publications, Inc., agent
Music: Robert J. Thompson, © 1975, GIA Publications, Inc.

Psalm Tone

Repeat for 5-line stanza

Music: Chrysogonus Waddell, OCSO, © Gethsemani Abbey

Gelineau Tone

1.   Lord,   make   me   knòw   your   ways.
2.   The Lord   is   gòod   and   upright,
3.   God's ways   are   steadfastness ànd   truth

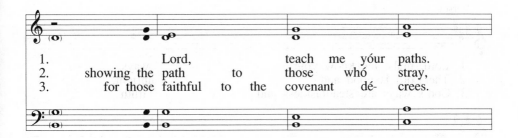

1.   Lord,   teach   me   yóur   paths.
2.   showing the path   to   those   whó   stray,
3.   for those faithful   to   the   covenant dé-   crees.

1.   Make me walk   in   your   truth,   ànd   teach   me,
2.   guiding the humble in   thè   right   path,
3.   The Lord's friendship is   for   thè   God-fearing;

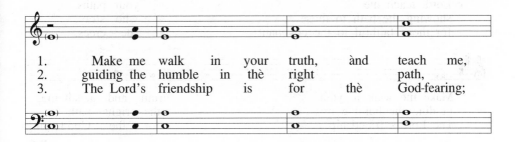

1.   { for   you   are   God   mý   savior. }
       { In   you   I   hope all the dáy long. }
2.   and   teaching   the   way   to   thé   poor.
3.   and the   covenant   is   ré-   vealed to them.

Text: Psalm 25:4-5, 8-9, 10, 14; The Grail
Music: Joseph Gelineau, SJ
© 1963, 1993, The Grail, GIA Publications, Inc., agent

51 Psalm 25: To You, O Lord

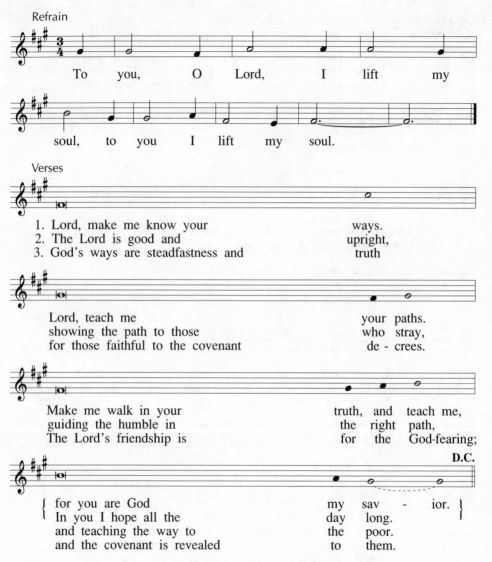

Refrain

To you, O Lord, I lift my soul, to you I lift my soul.

Verses

1. Lord, make me know your ways.
2. The Lord is good and upright,
3. God's ways are steadfastness and truth

Lord, teach me your paths.
showing the path to those who stray,
for those faithful to the covenant de - crees.

Make me walk in your truth, and teach me,
guiding the humble in the right path,
The Lord's friendship is for the God-fearing;

D.C.

{ for you are God my sav - ior. }
{ In you I hope all the day long. }
and teaching the way to the poor.
and the covenant is revealed to them.

Text: Psalm 25:4-5, 8-9, 10, 14; © 1963, 1993, The Grail, GIA Publications, Inc., agent; refrain trans. © 1969, ICEL
Music: Michel Guimont, © 1995, GIA Publications, Inc.

Psalm 25: Levanto Mi Alma   52

Refrain

Oh Dios mí-o,   le-van-to mi al - ma,   le-van-to a

ti Se - ñor,   mi sal - va - ción.

Verse 1

1. Só-lo en ti   con-fi-o,   es-ta-ré sin ver-güen-za.

Y no tri-un-fa-ran   mis e-ne-mi-gos. No hay du - das.   D.C.

Verse 2

2. Mues-tra-me tus   ca-mi-nos. En-se-ña-me tus   sen-das.

Guí-a-me Se-ñor   en tu ver-dad   y a mi sal-va-ción.   D.C.

Verse 3

3. To-do el día   es-pe-ro en ti,   es-pe-ro por tu

bon-dad.   No re-cuer-des Se-ñor los pe-ca-dos de mi ju-ven-

tud,   si-no,   da-me tu a - mor.   D.C.

Verse 4

4. Mis o-jos es-tan   en Yah-veh.   Mi-ra-me y ten

com - pa - sión, por - que_es - toy so - lo y es -

toy des - di - cha - do.

D.C.

Text: Psalm 25; Donna Peña
Music: Donna Peña; acc. by Diana Kodner
© 1988, 1993, GIA Publications, Inc.

53 Psalm 25: To You, O Lord

Refrain I *mf*

To you, O Lord, I lift my

soul, to you, I lift my soul.

Last time / To verses

Last time

Refrain II

Your ways, O Lord, are

love and truth, to those who

keep your cov - e - nant.

Verse 1
1. Lord, make me know your ways,
teach me your paths and keep me in the way of your

poco rit.   **D.C.**
truth, for you are God, my Sav - ior.

Verse 2 *mp*
2. For the Lord is good and right - eous, reveal - ing the way to those who wan - der,

rit.   **D.C.**
gen - tly lead - ing the poor and the hum - ble.

Verse 3 *f*
3. To the ones who seek the Lord, who look to God's
mf
word, who live God's love, God will al - ways be

mp   *poco rit.*   **D.C.**
near, and will show them mer - cy.

Text: Psalm 25:4-5, 8-9, 12-14; Marty Haugen, © 1982, GIA Publications, Inc.; refrain trans. © 1969, ICEL
Music: Marty Haugen, © 1982, GIA Publications, Inc.

54 Psalm 25: Remember Your Mercies

Refrain I

Re-mem-ber your mer - cies, O Lord.

Refrain II

Teach me your ways, O Lord.

Verses *piu mosso*

1. Your ways, O Lord, make known to me, teach me your
2. Re - mem - ber your com - pas-sion, Lord, and your kind - ness of
3. ⸢ Good and just is the Lord, the sin - ners know the

paths. Guide me, teach me, for
old. Re - mem-ber this, and not my sins, in your
way. God guides the meek to jus - tice, and

To refrain

you are my Sav - ior.
good - ness, O Lord.
teach - es the hum - ble.

Text: Psalm 25:4-5, 6-7, 8-9; David Haas, © 1985, GIA Publications, Inc.; refrain trans. © 1969, ICEL
Music: David Haas, © 1985, GIA Publications, Inc.

Psalm 27: I Believe That I Shall See 55

Antiphon I (St. 1.2.3)

I be-lieve that I shall see the good things of the

Lord in the land of the liv - ing.

Antiphon II (St. 1.3.4.5 or 1.2.5)

The Lord is my light and my sal - va - tion.

Psalm Tone

Repeat for 6-line stanza

Gelineau Tone

1. The Lord is my light ànd my help;
2. {There is one thing I ask òf the Lord,
    to live in the house òf the Lord,
3. O Lord, hear my voice whèn I call;
4. {It is your face, O Lord, thàt I seek;
    Dis- miss not your servànt in anger;
5. I am sure I shall see thè Lord's goodness

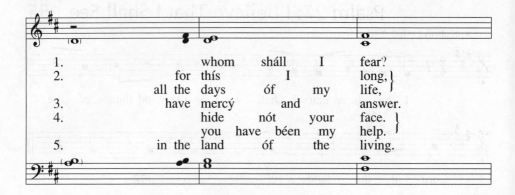

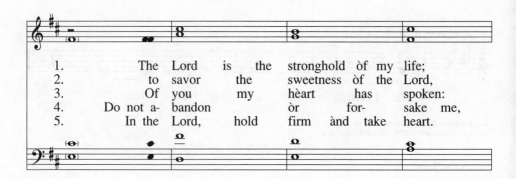

Text: Psalm 27:1, 4, 7-8, 8-9, 13-14; The Grail
Music: Joseph Gelineau, SJ
© 1963, 1993, The Grail, GIA Publications, Inc., agent

Psalm 27: In the Land of the Living   56

Refrain *mf*

I be-lieve I shall see the good things of the Lord in the

To verses | Final ending

land of the liv - ing.

Verses *mp*

1. The Lord is my light, the Lord is my help, of
2. ⁊ When I cry out, O Lord, hear my voice! Have
3. There is on - ly one thing I ask of the Lord: to

whom should I be a - fraid? The Lord is the strong-hold
mer - cy on me and an - swer. My heart has told me,
live in God's house for - ev - er, to sa - vor the sweet-ness

D.C.

of my life, be-fore whom should I shrink?
"seek his face!" It is your face, Lord, I seek.
of the Lord, to be - hold his tem - ple.

57   Psalm 27: The Lord Is My Light

Refrain

The Lord is my light and my sal - va - tion, of whom should I be a - fraid, of whom should I be a - fraid?

whom should I be a-fraid,

Verse 1 *mf*

1. The Lord is my light and my help; whom should I fear? The Lord is the strong - hold of my life; be-fore whom should I shrink?

poco rit. **D.C.**

Verse 2 *mf*

2. There is one thing I ask of the Lord; for this I long: to live in the house of the Lord all the days of my life.

poco rit. **D.C.**

Verse 3

3. I be - lieve I shall see the good - ness of the Lord in the land of the liv - ing; hope in God, and take heart. Hope in the Lord!

Text: Psalm 27:1-2, 4, 13-14; David Haas
Music: David Haas
© 1983, GIA Publications, Inc.

58 Psalm 29: The Lord Will Bless His People

Antiphon

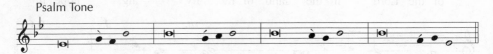

The   Lord will   bless his   peo - ple with   peace.

Text: *Lectionary for Mass*, © 1981, ICEL
Music: Robert J. Batastini, © 1995, GIA Publications, Inc.

Psalm Tone

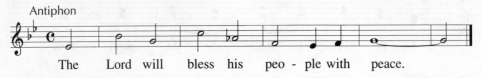

Music: Laurence Bevenot, OSB, © 1969, Ampleforth Abbey Trustees

Gelineau Tone

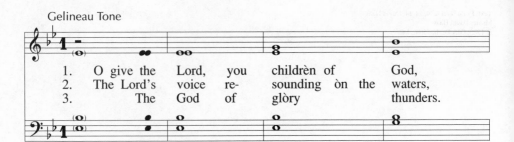

1.   O give the   Lord,   you   childrèn of   God,
2.   The Lord's   voice re-   sounding òn the   waters,
3.   The   God   of   glòry   thunders.

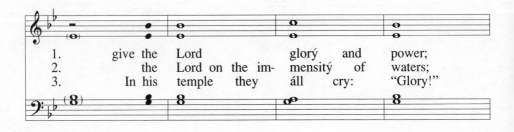

1.   give the   Lord   glorý   and   power;
2.   the   Lord on the im-   mensitý   of   waters;
3.   In his   temple   they   áll   cry: "Glory!"

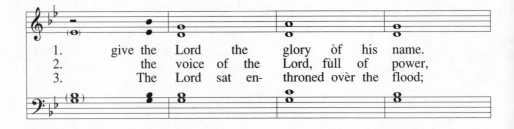

1.   give the   Lord   the   glory òf   his   name.
2.   the   voice of the   Lord, fùll   of   power,
3.   The   Lord   sat en-   throned ovèr the   flood;

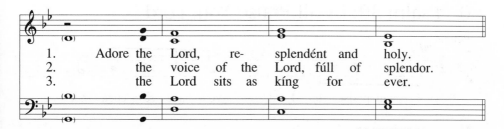

1. Adore the Lord, re- splendént and holy.
2. the voice of the Lord, fúll of splendor.
3. the Lord sits as kíng for ever.

Text: Psalm 29:1-2, 3-4, 3, 9-10; The Grail
Music: Joseph Gelineau, SJ
© 1963, 1993, The Grail, GIA Publications, Inc., agent

Psalm 30: I Will Praise You, Lord 59

Refrain

I will praise you, Lord, for you have res-cued me.

Verses

1. I will praise you, Lord, you have rescued me
2. Sing psalms to the Lord, you faithful ones,
3. The Lord listened and had pity.

and have not let my enemies rejoice o - ver me.
give thanks to his ho - ly name.
The Lord came to my help.

O Lord, you have raised my soul from the dead,
God's anger lasts a moment; God's favor all through life.
For me you have changed my mourning in - to dancing,

D.C.

restored me to life from those who sink into the grave.
At night there are tears, but joy comes with dawn.
O Lord my God, I will thank you for ev - er.

Text: Psalm 30:2, 4, 5-6, 11-13; © 1963, 1993, The Grail, GIA Publications, Inc., agent; refrain trans. © 1969, ICEL
Music: Michel Guimont, © 1995, GIA Publications, Inc.

60   Psalm 30: I Will Praise You, Lord

Refrain *mf*

I will praise you, Lord, you have res-cued me,

I will praise you, Lord, for your mer-cy. I will praise you, Lord,

you have res-cued me: I will praise you, Lord.

Last time

Verse 1 *mp*

1. I will praise you, Lord, you have res-cued me and have

not let my en-e-mies re-joice o-ver me. O

f   *dim.*

Lord, you have raised my soul from the dead, re-

D.C.

stored me to life from those who sink in-to the grave.

Verse 2 *mp*

2. Sing psalms to the Lord, all you faith-ful,

give thanks to his ho-ly name. God's

an - ger lasts but a mo - ment; God's fa - vor through life. At

night there are tears but joy comes with dawn.

Verse 3

3. The Lord lis - tened and had pit - y.

The Lord came to my help. For

me you have changed my mourn - ing in - to danc - ing; O

Lord my God, I will thank you for ev - er.

Text: Psalm 30:2, 4, 5-6, 11-13; © 1963, 1993, The Grail, GIA Publications, Inc., agent; refrain, Paul Inwood, © 1985
Music: Paul Inwood, © 1985
Published by OCP Publications

61 Psalm 31: I Put My Life in Your Hands / Pongo Mi Vida

Refrain

mp

Ab - ba, Ab - ba, I put my life in your
Ab - ba, Ab - ba, pon - go mi vi - da en tus

Descant:

Ab - ba, Ab - ba, I put my
Ab - ba, Ab - ba, pon - go mi

Melody:

hands. Ab - ba, Ab - ba, I put my
ma - nos. Ab - ba, Ab - ba, pon - go mi

1.- 2. 3.

life in your hands.
vi - da en tus ma - nos.

life in your hands.
vi - da en tus ma - nos.

Verse 1

1. In you, O Lord I take ref - uge; let me
1. En ti bus - co pro - tec - ción. No me de -

nev - er be put to shame. In your
frau - des nun - ca ja - más. Pon - me a

jus - tice res - cue me, in your
sal - vo pues tú e - res jus - to. En tus

D.C.

hands   I   com - mend   my   spir - it.
ma - nos en - co - mien - do mi es - pí - ri - tu.

Verse 2

2. For   all   my foes   re - proach me;   all my
2. En   ti   pon - go to - da mi   fe   hab - la -

friends   are   now   put   to   flight.   I   am for -
ré   de   tu   bon - dad,   por fa -

got - ten,   like   the   dead,   like a
vor es - tá siem - pre con - mi - go.   Tú

D.C.

dish   that   now   is   bro - ken.
ha - ces la luz del ca - os.

Verse 3   *f*

3. I   place   my trust   in   you;   in your
3. Tú   e - res mi es - pe - ran - za;   Só - lo

f

ff

hands   is   my   des - ti - ny.   Let   your
tú   mi   sal - va - ción.   Con   tu

ff

face shine up - on your ser - vant, in your
mi - se - ri - cor - dia, ven. Es -

hands I will place my life.
cu - cha mi o - ra - ción.

Text: Psalm 31; David Haas; Spanish trans. by Jeffrey Judge
Music: David Haas

62 Psalm 31: Father, I Put My Life in Your Hands

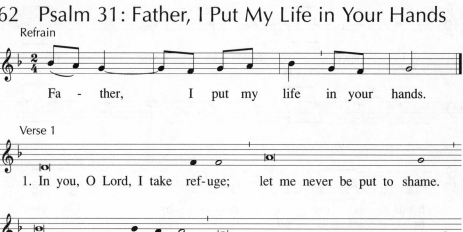

Refrain

Fa - ther, I put my life in your hands.

Verse 1

1. In you, O Lord, I take ref-uge;   let me never be put to shame.

In your justice res-cue me.   Into your hands I commend my spir - it;

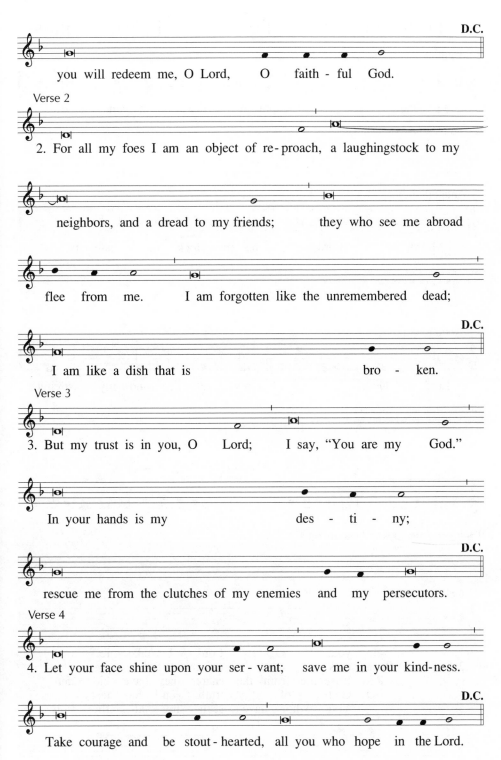

D.C.

you will redeem me, O Lord, O faith - ful God.

Verse 2

2. For all my foes I am an object of re-proach, a laughingstock to my

neighbors, and a dread to my friends; they who see me abroad

flee from me. I am forgotten like the unremembered dead;

D.C.

I am like a dish that is bro - ken.

Verse 3

3. But my trust is in you, O Lord; I say, "You are my God."

In your hands is my des - ti - ny;

D.C.

rescue me from the clutches of my enemies and my persecutors.

Verse 4

4. Let your face shine upon your ser - vant; save me in your kind-ness.

D.C.

Take courage and be stout - hearted, all you who hope in the Lord.

Text: Psalm 31:2, 6, 12-13, 15-16, 17-25; *New American Bible,* © 1970, Confraternity of Christian Doctrine; refrain trans. © 1969, ICEL
Music: Howard Hughes, SM, © 1980, GIA Publications, Inc.

63　Psalm 31: Father, I Put My Life in Your Hands

Antiphon I (Vs. 2.6.12-13.15-16.17.25)

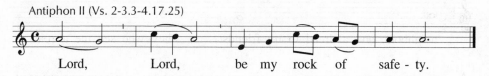

Fa - ther,　　I put my life in your hands.

Text: *Lectionary for Mass,* © 1969, 1981, ICEL
Music: S. DeLaSalle McKeon, CSJ, © 1975, GIA Publications, Inc.

Antiphon II (Vs. 2-3.3-4.17.25)

Lord,　　Lord,　　be my rock of safe - ty.

Text: *Lectionary for Mass,* © 1969, 1981, ICEL
Music: Marie Kremer, © 1986, GIA Publications, Inc.

Antiphon III

Lord　God,　　be my ref - uge and my strength.

Text: *Liturgy of the Hours,* © 1974, ICEL
Music: Randolph Currie, © 1986, GIA Publications, Inc.

Psalm Tone

Omit for 3-line stanza

Music: A. Gregory Murray, OSB, © L. J. Carey and Co., Ltd.

Gelineau Tone

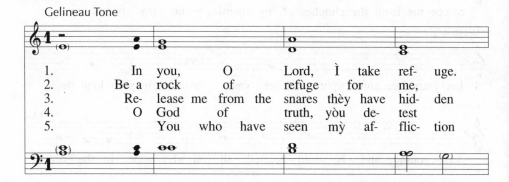

1.　　In you,　O　Lord, Ì take ref - uge.
2.　Be a rock　of　refùge for me,
3.　Re- lease me from the snares thèy have hid- den
4.　O God　of　truth, yòu de- test
5.　You who have seen mỳ af- flic - tion

1. Let me never be pút to shame.
2. a mighty stronghóld to save me,
3. for you are my réfuge, Lord.
4. those who worship false and émpty gods.
5. and taken heed of my sóul's dis- tress,

1. In your justice, sèt me free,
2. for you are my ròck, my stronghold.
3. Into your hands I com- mènd my spirit.
4. As for me, I trust ìn the Lord;
5. have not handed me over tò the enemy,

1. hear me and speedily réscue me.
2. For your name's sake, lead mé and guide me.
3. It is you who will re- déem me, Lord.
4. let me be glad and re- joice ín your love.
5. but set my féet at large.

6. Have mercy on mè, O Lord,
7. For my life is spènt with sorrow
8. In the face of àll my foes
9. Those who see me ìn the street
10. I have heard the slander òf the crowd,
11. But as for me, I trùst in you, Lord;
12. Let your face shine òn your servant.
13. Let them be silenced ìn the grave,

6.		for	I am	ín	dis-	tress.
7.	and my	yéars		with		sighs.
8.			I am	á	re-	proach,
9.		run	far a-	wáy	from	me.
10.			fear is	áll	a-	round me,
11.	I say:	"You		áre	my	God.
12.			Save me	ín	your	love.
13.		let	lying	líps	be	mute,

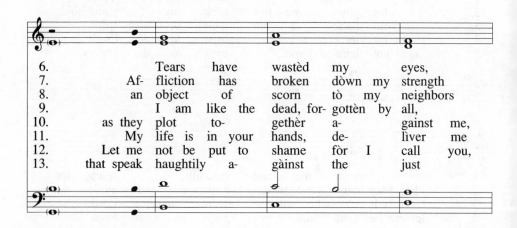

6.		Tears	have	wastèd	my	eyes,
7.	Af-	fliction	has	broken	dòwn my	strength
8.	an	object	of	scorn	tò my	neighbors
9.		I am	like the	dead, for-	gottèn by	all,
10.	as they	plot	to-	gethèr	a-	gainst me,
11.	My	life is	in your	hands,	de-	lìver me
12.	Let me	not be	put to	shame	fòr I	call you,
13.	that speak	haughtily	a-	gàinst	the	just

6.		my	throat	ánd	my	heart.
7.	and my	bones		wáste	a-	way.
8.	and of	fear		tó	my	friends.
9.		like a	thing	thrówn	a-	way.
10.	as they	plan	to	táke	my	life.
11.	from the	hands	of	thóse	who	hate me.
12.	let the	wickéd		be		shamed!
13.	with	pride		ánd	con-	tempt."

14. How great is the gòodness, Lord,
15. You hide them in the shelter òf your presence
16. Blessed be the Lord whò has shown me
17. "I am far re- moved fròm your sight"
18. Love the Lord, àll you saints.
19. Be strong, let your hèart take courage,

14. that you keep for thóse who fear you,
15. from hú- man plots;
16. such a stéad- fast love
17. I said in mý a- larm.
18. The Lord guárds the faithful
19. all who hope ín the Lord.

14. that you show to thòse who trust you
15. you keep them safe with-ìn your tent
16. [ ]
17. Yet you heard the voice òf my plea
18. but in turn will re- pay tò the full
19. Praise the Father, the Son, and Hòly Spirit,

14. in the síght of all.
15. from dis- pút- ing tongues.
16. in a fortí- fied city.
17. when I críed for help.
18. those who áct with pride.
19. for ev- ér and ever.

Text: Psalm 31; The Grail
Music: Joseph Gelineau, SJ
© 1963, 1993, The Grail, GIA Publications, Inc., agent

64   Psalm 32: I Turn to You, Lord

Slowly

I turn to you, Lord, in times of

trou-ble and you fill me with the joy of sal - va -

1.
tion.   I

2.
Last time
tion.   *To verses*
(2. But)

Verse 1

1. Hap - py   the one whose sin   is for - giv - en, whose

sin   is re - mit - ted   by the   Lord.

Hap-py   the one   whom the Lord im - putes   no guilt, whose

spir - it has no guile.

(SATB)
I

Verse 2

now I ac - knowl-edge all my sin, my

guilt I hide not from the Lord.

I will con-fess my sin to the Lord, my God, Lord for -

give the guilt of my sin.

D.S.
(SATB)
I

Verse 3

3. Re - joice, re - joice in the Lord our God, ex -

ult, you who are just. O come, come ring out your

joy all you up - right of heart.

D.S.
(SATB)
I

Text: Psalm 32:1-2, 5, 11; Roy James Stewart, © 1993, GIA Publications, Inc., refrain trans. © 1969, ICEL
Music: Roy James Stewart, © 1993, GIA Publications, Inc.

65 Psalm 32: Lord, Forgive the Wrong

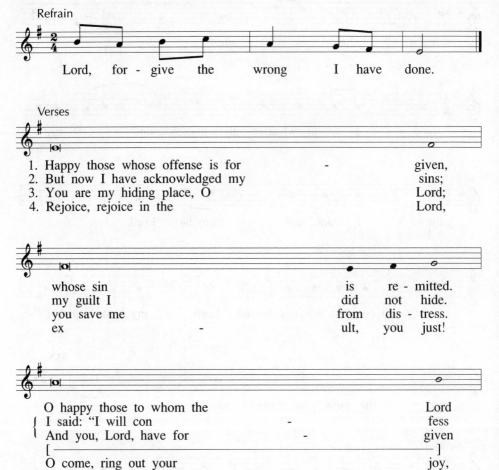

Refrain

Lord, for - give the wrong I have done.

Verses

1. Happy those whose offense is for - given,
2. But now I have acknowledged my sins;
3. You are my hiding place, O Lord;
4. Rejoice, rejoice in the Lord,

whose sin   is   re - mitted.
my guilt I   did not hide.
you save me   from dis - tress.
ex -   ult, you just!

O happy those to whom the   Lord
I said: "I will con -   fess
And you, Lord, have for -   given
[———————————————————————————————————]
O come, ring out your   joy,

D.C.

im -   putes no   guilt, }
in whose spirit   is   no   guile. }
my offense   to   the Lord." }
the guilt   of   my   sin. }
(You surround me with cries of   de - liverance.)
all you up -   right of   heart.

Text: Psalm 32:1-2, 5, 7, 11; © 1963, 1993, The Grail, GIA Publications, Inc., agent; refrain trans. © 1969, ICEL
Music: Michel Guimont, © 1995, GIA Publications, Inc.

Psalm 33: Let Your Mercy Be on Us   66

Refrain III

Hap-py are the peo - ple the Lord has cho - sen,

unis.   *div.*

Last time 𝄐   *To verses*

cho - sen to be his own.

Verse 1

1. Your words, O God, are truth in - deed, and all your works are ev - er faith - ful; you love jus - tice and right, your com -

To refrain

pas - sion fills all cre - a - tion.

Verse 2

2. See how the eye of God is watch - ing, ev - er guard-ing all who wait in hope, to de - liv - er them from death and sus -

To refrain

tain them in time of fam - ine.

Verse 3

3. Ex - ult, you just, in the Lord, for praise is the song of the right - eous! How hap - py the peo - ple of God, the ones whom God has cho - sen!

poco rit. *To refrain*

Verse 4

4. Our soul is wait - ing for God, for God is our help and our shield. May your kind - ness, O God, be up - on us who place our hope in you.

poco rit. *To refrain*

Text: Psalm 33:1, 4-5, 12, 18-19, 20, 22; Marty Haugen; refrain I trans. © 1969, ICEL; refrains II, III, and verses © 1987, 1994 GIA Publications, Inc.
Music: Marty Haugen; refrain III adapt. by Diana Kodner, © 1987, 1994, GIA Publications, Inc.

67 Psalm 33: Happy the People

Antiphon I (St. 2.4.6.7 or 1.6.7)

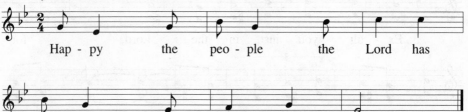

Hap - py   the   peo - ple   the   Lord   has
cho - sen   to   be   his   own.

Text: *Lectionary for Mass,* © 1969, 1981, ICEL
Music: Columba Kelly, OSB, © 1975, GIA Publications, Inc.

Antiphon II (St. 2.3.5.7)

The   earth   is   full   of   the
good - ness   the   good - ness   of the   Lord.

Text: *Lectionary for Mass,* © 1969, 1981, ICEL
Music: J. Robert Carroll, © 1975, GIA Publications, Inc.

Psalm Tone

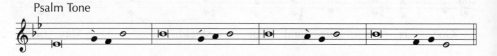

Music: Lawrence Bevenot, OSB, © 1969, Ampleforth Abbey Trustees

Gelineau Tone

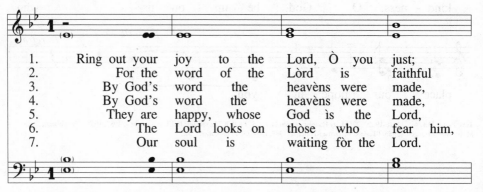

1. Ring out your joy to the Lord, Ò you just;
2. For the word of the Lòrd is faithful
3. By God's word the heavèns were made,
4. By God's word the heavèns were made,
5. They are happy, whose God ìs the Lord,
6. The Lord looks on thòse who fear him,
7. Our soul is waiting fòr the Lord.

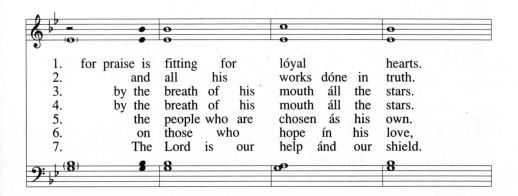

1. for praise is fitting for lóyal hearts.
2. and all his works dóne in truth.
3. by the breath of his mouth áll the stars.
4. by the breath of his mouth áll the stars.
5. the people who are chosen ás his own.
6. on those who hope ín his love,
7. The Lord is our help ánd our shield.

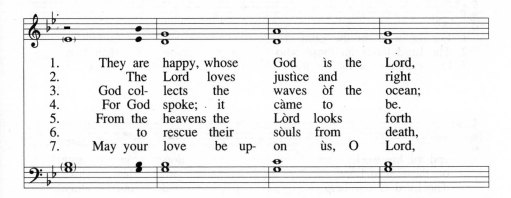

1. They are happy, whose God is the Lord,
2. The Lord loves justìce and right
3. God col- lects the waves òf the ocean;
4. For God spoke; it càme to be.
5. From the heavens the Lòrd looks forth
6. to rescue their sòuls from death,
7. May your love be up- on ùs, O Lord,

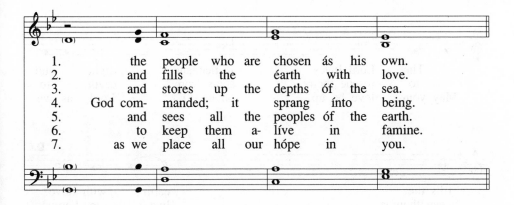

1. the people who are chosen ás his own.
2. and fills the éarth with love.
3. and stores up the depths óf the sea.
4. God com- manded; it sprang ínto being.
5. and sees all the peoples óf the earth.
6. to keep them a- líve in famine.
7. as we place all our hópe in you.

Text: Psalm 33:1 & 12, 4-5, 6-7, 6 & 9, 12-13, 18-19, 20 & 22; The Grail
Music: Joseph Gelineau, SJ
© 1963, 1993, The Grail, GIA Publications, Inc., agent

68   Psalm 33: Lord, Let Your Mercy

Refrain

Lord, let your mer - cy be on us, as we

place our trust in you.

Verses

1. For the word of the Lord is   faithful
2. The Lord looks on those who   fear him,
3. Our soul is waiting for the   Lord.

and all his works   done in truth.
on those who hope   in his love,
The Lord is our help   and our shield.

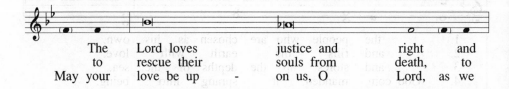

The   Lord loves   justice and   right and
to   rescue their   souls from   death, to
May your   love be up -   on us, O   Lord, as we

D.C.

fills the   earth with love.
keep them a -   live in famine.
place all our   hope in you.

Text: Psalm 33:4-5, 18-19, 20, 22; © 1963, 1993, The Grail, GIA Publications, Inc., agent; refrain trans. © 1969, ICEL
Music: Michel Guimont, © 1995, GIA Publications, Inc.

Psalm 34: The Cry of the Poor   69

Text: Psalm 34:2-3, 6-7, 18-19, 23; John Foley, SJ
Music: John Foley, SJ
© 1978, 1990, John B. Foley, SJ, and New Dawn Music

70 Psalm 34: Taste and See

Refrain

Taste and see the good-ness of the Lord, the good - ness of the Lord.

To verses   *Last time*

Verse 1

1. I will bless the Lord at all times, God's praise ev-er in my mouth. Glo-ry in the Lord for ev - er, and the low-ly will hear and be glad.

poco rit.   **D.C.**

Verse 2

2. Glo - ry in the Lord with me, let us to -
geth - er ex - tol God's name.
I sought the Lord, who an - swered me and de -
liv - ered me from all my fears.

poco rit.   **D.C.**

Verse 3

3. Look to God that you might be ra - diant with
joy, and your fac - es free from all shame.
The Lord hears the suf - fer - ing
souls, and saves them from all dis - tress.

poco rit.   **D.C.**

Text: Psalm 34:2-3, 4-5, 6-7; Marty Haugen, © 1980, GIA Publications, Inc.; refrain trans. © 1969, ICEL
Music: Marty Haugen, © 1980, GIA Publications, Inc.

71 Psalm 34: Taste and See

Refrain I (St. 1.2.3.4 or 1.5.6.7 or 1.8.9.10.11)

Taste and see the good - ness of the Lord.

Refrain II (Vs. 2-3.17-18.19.23)

The Lord hears the cry of the poor.

Verses

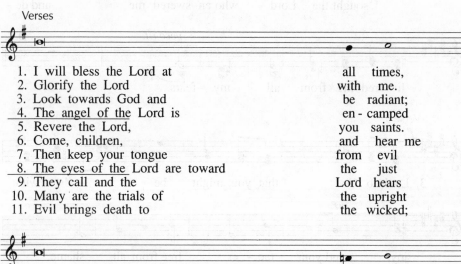

1. I will bless the Lord at   all times,
2. Glorify the Lord   with me.
3. Look towards God and   be radiant;
4. The angel of the Lord is   en - camped
5. Revere the Lord,   you saints.
6. Come, children,   and hear me
7. Then keep your tongue   from evil
8. The eyes of the Lord are toward   the just
9. They call and the   Lord hears
10. Many are the trials of   the upright
11. Evil brings death to   the wicked;

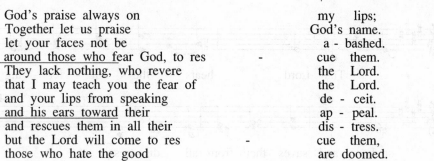

God's praise always on   my lips;
Together let us praise   God's name.
let your faces not be   a - bashed.
around those who fear God, to res -   cue them.
They lack nothing, who revere   the Lord.
that I may teach you the fear of   the Lord.
and your lips from speaking   de - ceit.
and his ears toward their   ap - peal.
and rescues them in all their   dis - tress.
but the Lord will come to res -   cue them,
those who hate the good   are doomed.

in the Lord my soul shall make — its boast.
I sought the Lord and — was heard;
When the poor cry out the — Lord hears them
Taste and see that the Lord — is good.
Strong lions suffer want and — go hungry
Who are those who long — for life
Turn aside from evil and — do good;
The face of the Lord rebuffs — the wicked
The Lord is close to the bro - ken- hearted;
keeping guard over all — their bones,
The Lord ransoms the souls of — the faithful.

D.C.

The humble shall hear — and be glad.
from all my ter - rors set free.
and rescues them from all — their dis - tress.
They are happy who seek ref - uge in God.
but those who seek the Lord — lack no bless - ing.
and many days, to enjoy — their pros - per - ity?
seek and strive — af - ter peace.
to destroy their remembrance — from the earth.
those whose spirit is crushed — God will save.
not one of their bones — shall be bro - ken.
None who trust in God shall — be con - demned.

Text: Psalm 34; © 1963, 1993, The Grail, GIA Publications, Inc., agent; refrain trans. © 1969, ICEL
Music: Michel Guimont, © 1995, GIA Publications, Inc.

72 Psalm 34: Taste and See

Refrain

Taste and see, taste and see that the Lord is good, the Lord is good. 4. The

Verses

1. I will bless the Lord at all times, his
2. Glo - ri - fy the Lord with me, to -
3. Look up - on the Lord and be ra - diant;
4. an - gel of the Lord is with his peo - ple to
5. Saints of the Lord, re - vere him;
6. Chil - dren of the Lord come and hear, and
7. Keep e - vil words from your tongue, your

praise al - ways on my lips. The
geth - er let us praise his name. I
hide not your face from the Lord. He
res - cue those who trust in him.
those who fear him lack noth - ing.
learn the fear of the Lord.
lips from speak - ing de - ceit.

Lord shall be the glo - ry of my soul; the
sought the Lord: he an - swered me; he
heard the cry of the poor; he
Taste and see the good - ness of the Lord; seek
Li - ons suf - fer want and go hun-gry, but
Who is he who longs for life, whose
Turn a - side from e - vil and do good; ʔ

D.C.

hum - ble shall hear and be glad.
set me free from all my fear.
res - cued them from all their woes.
ref - uge in him and be glad.
those who seek him lack no bless - ing.
on - ly love is for his wealth?
seek and strive af - ter peace.

Text: Psalm 34; Stephen Dean
Music: Stephen Dean
© 1981, Stephen Dean, published by OCP Publications

73 Psalm 34: Taste and See

Antiphon I (St. 1.2.3.4 or 1.5.6.7 or 1.8.9.10.11)

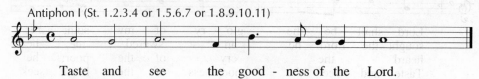

Taste and see the good-ness of the Lord.

Text: *Lectionary for Mass,* © 1969, 1981, ICEL
Music: Richard Proulx, © 1975, GIA Publications, Inc.

Antiphon II (St. 1-4)

The an-gel of the Lord will res-cue those who fear him.

Text: *Lectionary for Mass,* © 1969, 1981, ICEL
Music: Howard Hughes, SM, © 1975, GIA Publications, Inc.

Psalm Tone

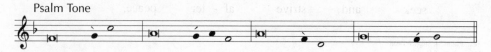

Music: Richard Proulx, © 1986, GIA Publications, Inc.

Gelineau Tone

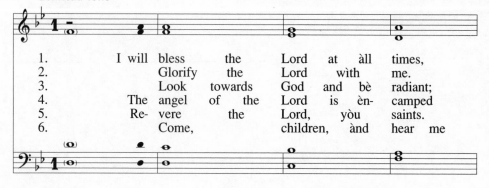

1.	I will bless	the	Lord	at	àll	times,
2.		Glorify	the	Lord	with	me.
3.		Look	towards	God	and	bè	radiant;
4.	The	angel	of the	Lord	is	èn-	camped
5.	Re-	vere	the	Lord,	yòu	saints.
6.		Come,		children,	ànd	hear me

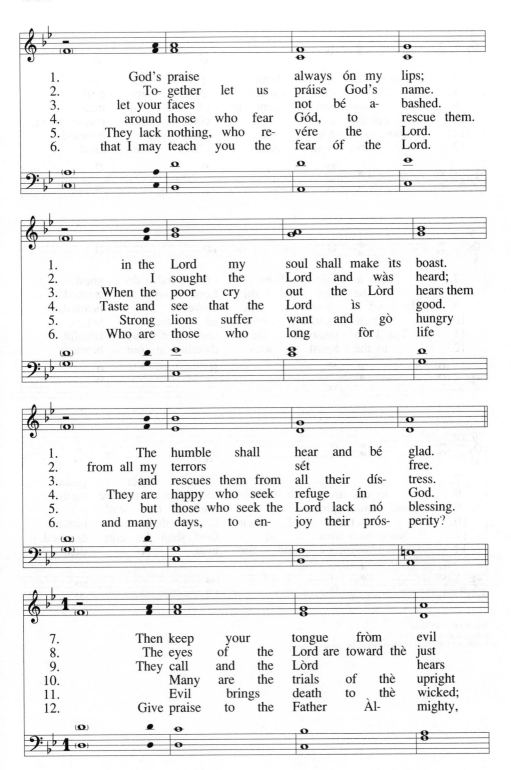

1. God's praise   always ón my   lips;
2. To-gether let us   práise God's   name.
3. let your faces   not bé a-   bashed.
4. around those who fear   Gód, to   rescue them.
5. They lack nothing, who re-   vére the   Lord.
6. that I may teach you the   fear óf the   Lord.

1. in the Lord my   soul shall make ìts   boast.
2. I sought the   Lord and wàs   heard;
3. When the poor cry   out the Lòrd   hears them
4. Taste and see that the   Lord ìs   good.
5. Strong lions suffer   want and gò   hungry
6. Who are those who   long fòr   life

1. The humble shall   hear and bé   glad.
2. from all my terrors   sét   free.
3. and rescues them from   all their dís-   tress.
4. They are happy who seek   refuge ín   God.
5. but those who seek the Lord lack nó   blessing.
6. and many days, to en-   joy their prós-   perity?

7. Then keep your   tongue fròm   evil
8. The eyes of the   Lord are toward thè   just
9. They call and the   Lòrd   hears
10. Many are the   trials of thè   upright
11. Evil brings   death to thè   wicked;
12. Give praise to the   Father Àl-   mighty,

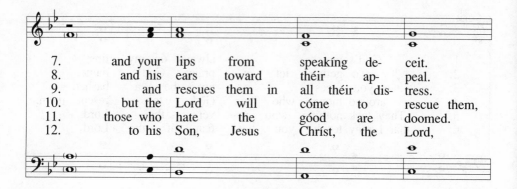

7.	and your	lips	from	speakíng de-	ceit.
8.	and his	ears	toward	théir ap-	peal.
9.	and	rescues	them in	all théir dis-	tress.
10.	but the	Lord	will	cóme to	rescue them,
11.	those who	hate	the	góod are	doomed.
12.	to his	Son,	Jesus	Chríst, the	Lord,

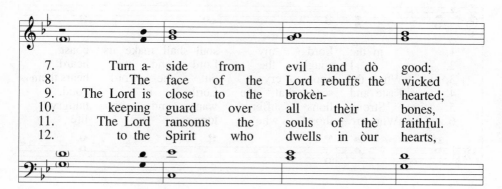

7.	Turn a-	side	from	evil and dò	good;
8.	The	face	of the	Lord rebuffs thè	wicked
9.	The Lord is	close	to the	brokèn-	hearted;
10.	keeping	guard	over	all théir	bones,
11.	The Lord	ransoms	the	souls of thè	faithful.
12.	to the	Spirit	who	dwells in òur	hearts,

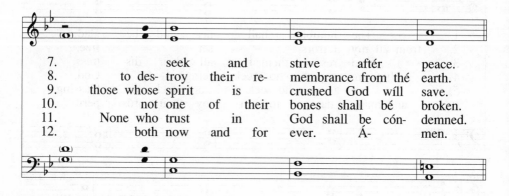

7.		seek	and	strive aftér	peace.
8.	to des-	troy	their re-	membrance from thé	earth.
9.	those whose	spirit	is	crushed God wíll	save.
10.	not	one	of their	bones shall bé	broken.
11.	None who	trust	in	God shall be cón-	demned.
12.	both	now	and for	ever. Á-	men.

Text: Psalm 34; The Grail
Music: Joseph Gelineau, SJ
© 1963, 1993, The Grail, GIA Publications, Inc., agent

Psalm 40: Here I Am　74

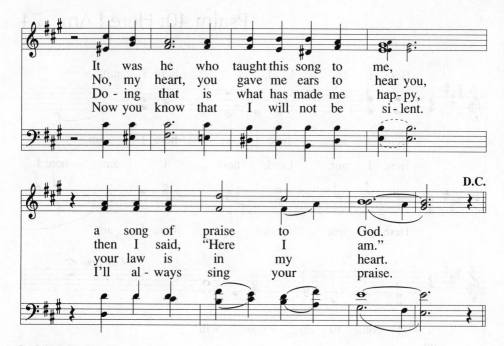

It was he who taught this song to me,
No, my heart, you gave me ears to hear you,
Do - ing that is what has made me hap- py,
Now you know that I will not be si - lent.

D.C.

a song of praise to God.
then I said, "Here I am."
your law is in my heart.
I'll al - ways sing your praise.

Text: Psalm 40; Rory Cooney
Music: Rory Cooney
© 1971, 1991, North American Liturgy Resources

75 Psalm 40: Here Am I

Antiphon I (Vs. 2.4.7-8.8-9.10 or st. 4.5.6.7)

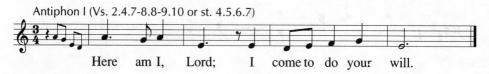

Here am I, Lord; I come to do your will.

Text: *Lectionary for Mass,* © 1969, 1981, ICEL
Music: Richard Proulx, © 1986, GIA Publications, Inc.

Antiphon II (St. 1.2.3.8)

Lord, come to my aid!

Text: *Lectionary for Mass,* © 1969, 1981, ICEL
Music: Robert J. Batastini, © 1975, GIA Publications, Inc.

Psalm Tone

Omit for 3-line stanza

Music: A. Gregory Murray, OSB, © L. J. Carey and Co., Ltd.

Gelineau Tone

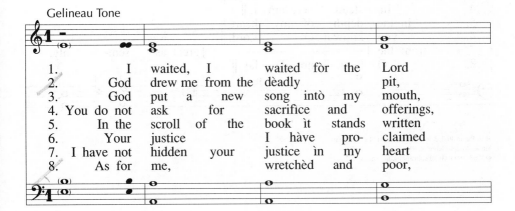

1.   I   waited, I   waited fòr the   Lord
2.   God   drew me from the   dèadly   pit,
3.   God   put   a   new   song intò   my   mouth,
4. You do not   ask   for   sacrifice   and   offerings,
5.   In the   scroll   of   the   book ìt   stands   written
6.   Your   justice   I   hàve   pro-   claimed
7. I have not   hidden   your   justice ìn   my   heart
8.   As for   me,   wretchèd   and   poor,

1.   who   stooped   dówn   to   me,
2.   from the   mír-   y   clay,
3.   praise   óf   our   God.
4.   but an   ó-   pen   ear.
5.   that   I   should   dó   your   will.
6.   in the   gréat   as-   sem-   bly.
7.   but de-   clared your   fáith-   ful   help.
8.   the   Lord   thínks   of   me.

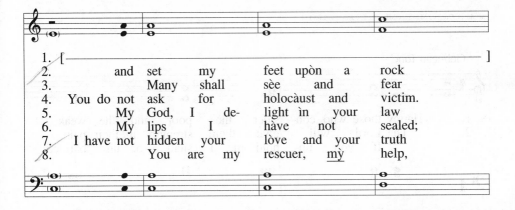

1. [——]
2.   and   set   my   feet upòn   a   rock
3.   Many   shall   sèe   and   fear
4. You do not   ask   for   holocàust and   victim.
5.   My   God, I   de-   light ìn   your   law
6.   My   lips   I   hàve   not   sealed;
7. I have not   hidden   your   lòve   and your   truth
8.   You   are   my   rescuer, <u>mỳ</u>   help,

1. and héard my cry.‖
2. and made my fóot- steps firm.‖
3. and shall trust ín the Lord.‖
4. In- stead, hére am I.‖
5. in the depth óf my heart.‖
6. you know ít, O Lord.‖
7. from the [——————————————] great ás- sem- bly.
8. O God, do nót de- lay.‖

Text: Psalm 40:2, 3, 4, 7-8, 8-9, 10, 11, 18; The Grail
Music: Joseph Gelineau, SJ
© 1963, 1993, GIA Publications, Inc., agent

76 Psalm 41: Lord, Heal My Soul

Antiphon

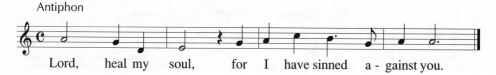

Lord, heal my soul, for I have sinned a - gainst you.

Text: *Lectionary for Mass*, © 1969, 1981, ICEL
Music: J. Robert Carroll, © 1975, GIA Publications, Inc.

Psalm Tone

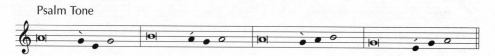

Music: A. Gregory Murray, OSB, © L. J. Carey and Co., Ltd.

Gelineau Tone

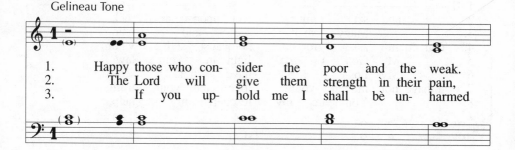

1. Happy those who con- sider the poor ànd the weak.
2. The Lord will give them strength ìn their pain,
3. If you up- hold me I shall bè un- harmed

1. The Lord will save them in the évil day,
2. will bring them back from sicknéss to health.
3. and set in your presence for éver- more.

1. will guard them, give them life, make them happy in the land
2. As for me, I said: "Lord, have mercỳ on me,
3. Blessed be the Lord, the Gòd of Israel

1. and will not give them up to the will óf their foes.
2. heal my soul for I have sínned a- gainst you."
3. from age to age. A- mén. A- men.

Text: Psalm 41: 2-3, 4-5, 13-14; The Grail
Music: Joseph Gelineau, SJ
© 1963, 1993, The Grail, GIA Publications, Inc., agent

77 Psalm 42-43: Like a Deer That Longs

Antiphon

Like a deer that longs for run-ning streams, my

soul longs for you, my God.

Text: *Lectionary for Mass,* © 1969, 1981, ICEL
Music: William A. Bauman, © 1975, GIA Publications, Inc.

Psalm Tone

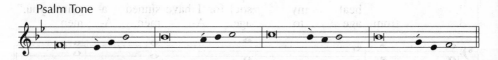

Music: Laurence Bevenot, OSB, © 1969, Ampleforth Abbey Trustees

Gelineau Tone

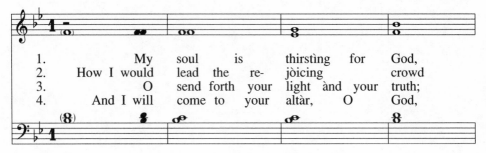

1.   My soul is   thirstìng for   God,
2. How I would lead the re- jòicing   crowd
3.   O send forth your light ànd your truth;
4. And I will come to your altàr,   O   God,

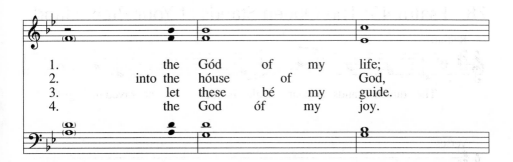

```
1.              the    Gód    of    my    life;
2.        into the    hóuse  of          God,
3.              let    these  bé    my    guide.
4.              the    God    óf    my    joy.
```

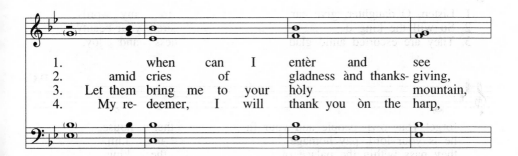

```
1.              when   can    I     entèr  and    see
2.        amid  cries  of            gladness ànd thanks- giving,
3.  Let them   bring  me     to    your  hòly          mountain,
4.  My re-  deemer,   I      will        thank you òn the harp,
```

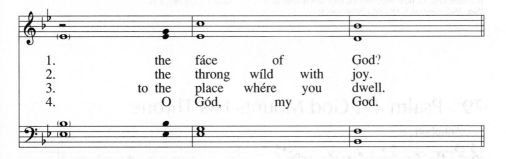

```
1.              the    fáce   of    God?
2.              the    throng wíld  with  joy.
3.        to the place  whére  you   dwell.
4.              O      Gód,   my    God.
```

Text: Psalm 42:3, 5; 43:3, 4; The Grail
Music: Joseph Gelineau, SJ
© 1963, 1993, The Grail, GIA Publications, Inc., agent

78 Psalm 45: The Queen Stands at Your Right Hand

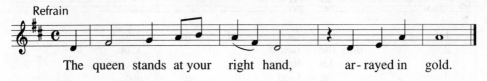

Refrain

The queen stands at your right hand, ar-rayed in gold.

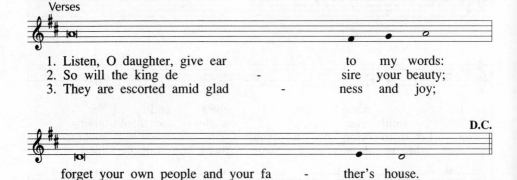

Verses

1. Listen, O daughter, give ear   to   my words:
2. So will the king de - sire   your beauty;
3. They are escorted amid glad - ness and joy;

D.C.

forget your own people and your fa - ther's house.
he is your lord, pay homage   to   him.
they pass within the palace of   the   king.

Text: Psalm 45:11, 12, 16; © 1963, 1993, The Grail, GIA Publications, Inc., agent; refrain trans. © 1969, ICEL
Music: Michel Guimont, © 1995, GIA Publications, Inc.

79 Psalm 47: God Mounts His Throne

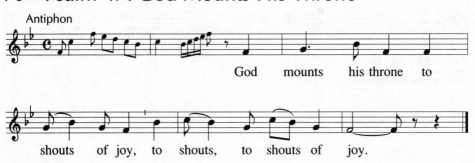

Antiphon

God mounts his throne to

shouts of joy, to shouts, to shouts of joy.

Text: Lectionary for Mass, © 1969, 1981, ICEL
Music: Richard Proulx, © 1975, GIA Publications, Inc.

Psalm Tone

Music: David Hurd, © 1973

Gelineau Tone

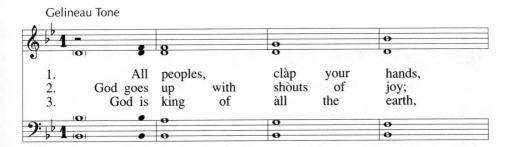

1. All peoples, clàp your hands,
2. God goes up with shòuts of joy;
3. God is king of àll the earth,

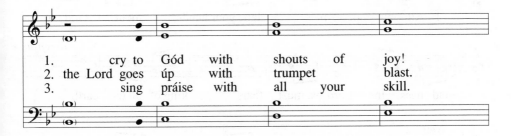

1. cry to Gód with shouts of joy!
2. the Lord goes úp with trumpet blast.
3. sing práise with all your skill.

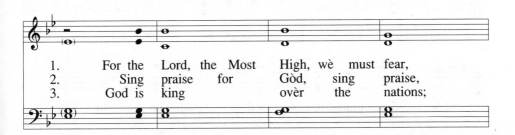

1. For the Lord, the Most High, wè must fear,
2. Sing praise for Gòd, sing praise,
3. God is king over the nations;

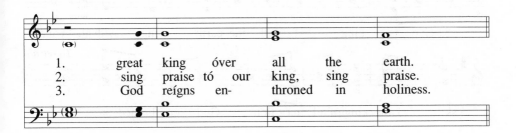

1. great king óver all the earth.
2. sing praise tó our king, sing praise.
3. God reígns en- throned in holiness.

Text: Psalm 47:2-3, 6-7, 8-9; The Grail
Music: Joseph Gelineau, SJ
© 1963, 1993, The Grail, GIA Publications, Inc., agent

80 Psalm 47: God Mounts His Throne

Ostinato Refrain*

1.
God mounts his throne to shouts of joy, O

2.

Final ending

sing your prais-es to the Lord!

Cantor: 1. All you
2. God goes
3. God is

Verses *(to be sung over ostinato)*

Verse 1

1. All you peo - ples, clap your hands, shout to God in

To refrain

glad - ness, the Lord we must fear, king of all the earth.

Verse 2

2. God goes up to shouts of joy, sound the trum - pet

To refrain

blast. Sing praise to our God, praise un - to our king!

Verse 3

3. God is king of all the earth, sing with all your

To refrain

skill to the king of all na - tions, God en - throned on high!

*May be sung in canon.

Text: Psalm 47:2-3, 6-7, 8-9; Marty Haugen, © 1983, GIA Publications, Inc.; refrain trans. © 1969, ICEL
Music: Marty Haugen, © 1983, GIA Publications, Inc.

Psalm 50: To the Upright   81

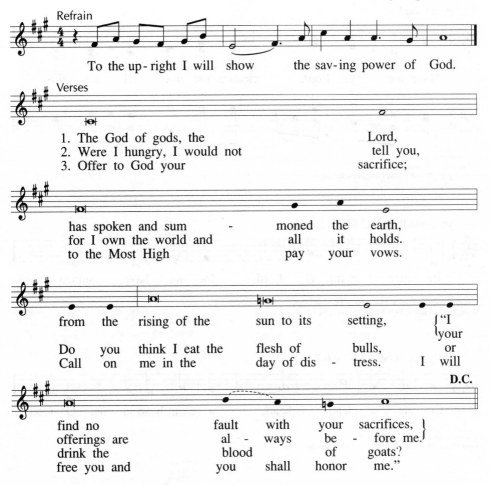

Refrain

To the up-right I will show the sav-ing power of God.

Verses

1. The God of gods, the Lord,
2. Were I hungry, I would not tell you,
3. Offer to God your sacrifice;

has spoken and sum - moned the earth,
for I own the world and all it holds.
to the Most High pay your vows.

from the rising of the sun to its setting, {"I
your
Do you think I eat the flesh of bulls, or
Call on me in the day of dis - tress. I will

D.C.

find no fault with your sacrifices, }
offerings are al - ways be - fore me.}
drink the blood of goats?
free you and you shall honor me."

Text: Psalm 50:1, 8, 12-13, 14-15; © 1963, 1993, The Grail, GIA Publications, Inc., agent; refrain trans. © 1969, ICEL
Music: Michel Guimont, © 1994, GIA Publications, Inc.

82 Psalm 51: Have Mercy, Lord

Antiphon I

Have mer - cy, Lord, cleanse me from all my sins.

Text: Psalm 51; The Grail
Music: Joseph Gelineau, SJ
© 1963, 1993, The Grail, GIA Publications, Inc., agent

Antiphon II (St. 1.2.6.7ab & 8cd)

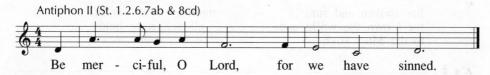

Be mer - ci-ful, O Lord, for we have sinned.

Text: *Lectionary for Mass*, © 1969, 1981, ICEL
Music: Patricia Craig, © 1975, GIA Publications, Inc.

Antiphon III (St. 1.6.7 or 6.7.9)

Cre - ate a clean heart, a clean heart in me, O God.

Text: *Lectionary for Mass*, © 1969, ICEL
Music: Frank Schoen, alt., © 1975, GIA Publications, Inc.

Antiphon IV (Vs. 3-4.12-13.17.19)

I will rise and go to my fa - ther.

Text: *Lectionary for Mass*, © 1969, 1981, ICEL
Music: James J. Chepponis, © 1986, GIA Publications, Inc.

Antiphon V

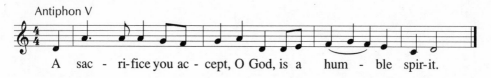

A sac - ri-fice you ac - cept, O God, is a hum - ble spir-it.

Text: *Praise God in Song*, 1979
Music: Michael Joncas, acc. by Robert J. Batastini
© 1979, 1995, GIA Publications, Inc.

Psalm Tone

Repeat for stanza 10

Music: Chrysogonus Waddell, OCSO, © Gethsemani Abbey

Gelineau Tone

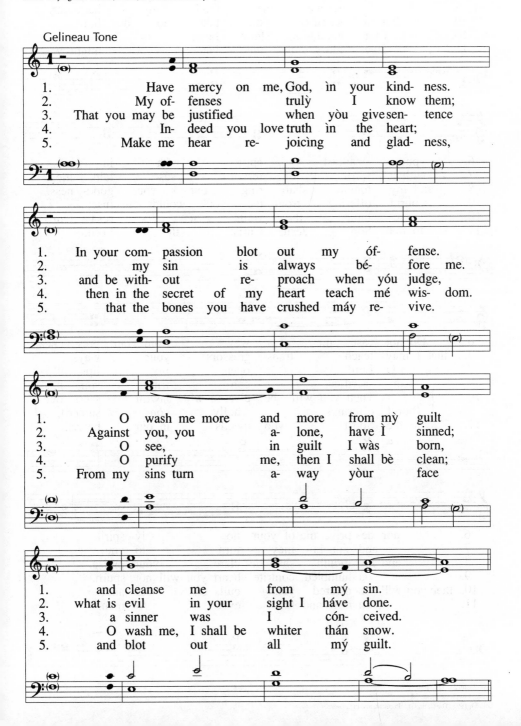

1. Have mercy on me, God, in your kind- ness.
2. My of- fenses truly I know them;
3. That you may be justified when you give sen- tence
4. In- deed you love truth in the heart;
5. Make me hear re- joicing and glad- ness,

1. In your com- passion blot out my óf- fense.
2. my sin is always bé- fore me.
3. and be with- out re- proach when yóu judge,
4. then in the secret of my heart teach mé wis- dom.
5. that the bones you have crushed máy re- vive.

1. O wash me more and more from mỳ guilt
2. Against you, you a- lone, have Ì sinned;
3. O see, in guilt I wàs born,
4. O purify me, then I shall bè clean;
5. From my sins turn a- way yòur face

1. and cleanse me from mý sin.
2. what is evil in your sight I háve done.
3. a sinner was I cón- ceived.
4. O wash me, I shall be whiter thán snow.
5. and blot out all mý guilt.

6. A pure heart cre- ate for mè, O God,
7. Give me a- gain the joy òf your help;
8. O rescue me, Gòd, my help- er,
9. For in sacrifice you take nò de- light,
10. In your goodness, show favòr to Zion;
11. Give glory to the Fathèr Al- might- y,

6. put a steadfast spirit with- in me.
7. with a spirit of fervor sús- tain me,
8. and my tongue shall ring out yóur good- ness.
9. burnt offering from me you would ré- fuse;
10. re- build the walls of Jé- rusa- lem.
11. to his Son, Jesus Christ, thé Lord,

6. Do not cast me a- way from yòur pres- ence,
7. that I may teach trans- gressors yòur ways
8. O Lord, open mỳ lips
9. my sacrifice, a con- trìte spir- it,
10. { Then you will be pleased with lawfùl sacri- fice, }
    { (burnt offerings wholly còn- sumed), }
11. to the Spirit who dwells in oùr hearts,

6. nor de- prive me of your ho- lý spirit.
7. and sinners may re- turn tó you.
8. and my mouth shall de- clare yóur praise.
9. a humbled, contrite heart you will nót spurn.
10. then you will be offered young bulls on yóur altar.
11. both now and for ever. Á- men.

Text: Psalm 51; The Grail
Music: Joseph Gelineau, SJ
© 1963, 1993, The Grail, GIA Publications, Inc., agent

Psalm 51: Be Merciful, O Lord 83

Refrain

mp

Lord, for we have sinned; be

Be mer-ci-ful, O Lord, we have sinned; be

mp

Be mer-ci-ful, O Lord, for we have sinned; be

Lord, for we have sinned. *Last time*

mer-ci-ful, O Lord, we have sinned. *Last time*

mer-ci-ful, O Lord, we have sinned.

Verse 1

1. Have mer-cy on me, God, in your kind-ness,

in your com-pas-sion, blot out my of-fense.

O wash me more and more from my guilt and my

D.C.

sor-row, and cleanse me from all of my sin.

Verse 2

2. My of-fens-es, tru-ly I know them, and my sins are

al - ways be - fore me; a- gainst you a - lone have I sinned, O

Lord, what is e - vil in your sight I have done. D.C.

Verse 3

3. Cre - ate in me a clean heart, O God, put your

stead - fast spir - it in my soul.

Cast me not a - way from your pres - ence, O Lord, and

take not your spir - it · from me. D.C.

Verse 4

4. Give back to me the joy of your sal - va - tion, let your

will - ing spir - it bear me up and

I shall teach your way to the ones who have wan - dered, and

bring them all home to your side. D.C.

Text: Psalm 51:3-4, 5-6, 12-13, 14-15; Marty Haugen, © 1983, GIA Publications, Inc.; refrain trans. © 1969, ICEL
Music: Marty Haugen, © 1983, GIA Publications, Inc.

Psalm 51: Create in Me   84

Refrain

Cre - ate in me,   cre - ate in me   a   clean heart, O   God.

Verses

1. A pure heart create for me,   O   God,
2. Give me again the joy of   your help;
3. For in sacrifice you take no   de - light,

put a steadfast spirit   with - in me.
with a spirit of fervor   sus - tain me,
burnt offering from me you would   re - fuse;

Do not cast me away from   your presence,
that I may teach transgressors   your ways
my sacrifice, a con   -   trite spirit,

D.C.

nor deprive me of your   ho - ly   spir - it.
and sinners may re   -   turn   to   you.
a humbled, contrite heart you   will   not   spurn.

Text: Psalm 51:12-13, 14-15, 18-19; © 1963, 1993, The Grail, GIA Publications, Inc., agent; refrain trans. © 1969, ICEL
Music: Michel Guimont, © 1995, GIA Publications, Inc.

85 Psalm 51: Create in Me

Refrains

I Cre-ate in me a clean heart, O God. God.
II I will a - rise and go to my God. God.

Verses

1. { Have mer - cy on me, O God. In the great-ness of your
2. { Stay close to me, O God. In your pres - ence keep me
3. Your sal - va - tion is joy to me. In your wis - dom show the

love, cleanse me from my sin. Wash me.
safe. Fill me with your spir - it. Re - new me.
way. Lead me back to you. Teach me.

Text: Psalm 51:3-4, 12-13, 14-15; David Haas
Music: David Haas
© 1987, GIA Publications, Inc.

Psalm 54: The Lord Upholds My Life 86

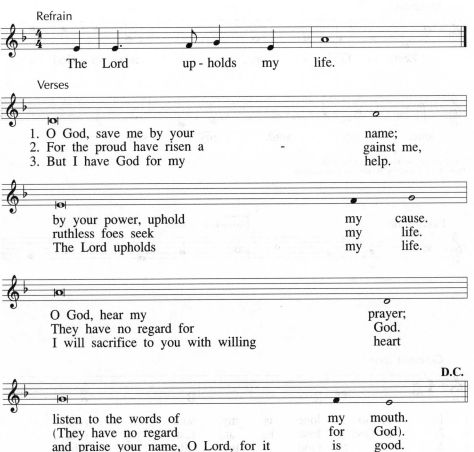

Refrain

The Lord up-holds my life.

Verses

1. O God, save me by your name;
2. For the proud have risen a - gainst me,
3. But I have God for my help.

by your power, uphold my cause.
ruthless foes seek my life.
The Lord upholds my life.

O God, hear my prayer;
They have no regard for God.
I will sacrifice to you with willing heart

D.C.

listen to the words of my mouth.
(They have no regard for God).
and praise your name, O Lord, for it is good.

Text: Psalm 54:3-4, 6-8, © 1963, 1986, The Grail, GIA Publications, Inc., agent; refrain trans. © 1969, ICEL
Music: Michel Guimont, © 1994, GIA Publications, Inc.

87 Psalm 62: Rest in God

Antiphon

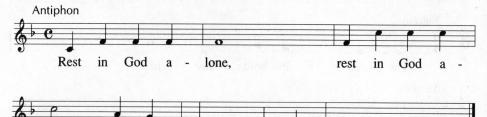

Rest in God a - lone, rest in God a - lone, my soul, my soul.

Text: *Lectionary for Mass,* © 1969, 1981, ICEL
Music: Robert J. Batastini, © 1975, GIA Publications, Inc.

Psalm Tone

Repeat for 5-line stanza

Music: Robert Knox Kennedy, © 1979

Gelineau Tone

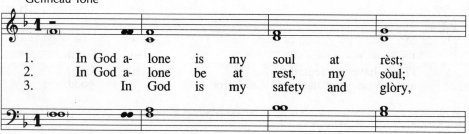

1. In God a-lone is my soul at rèst;
2. In God a-lone be at rest, my sòul;
3. In God is my safety and glòry,

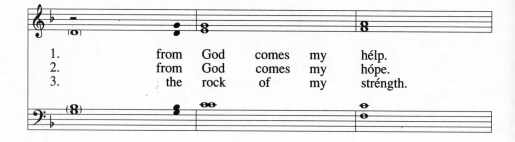

1. from God comes my hélp.
2. from God comes my hópe.
3. the rock of my stréngth.

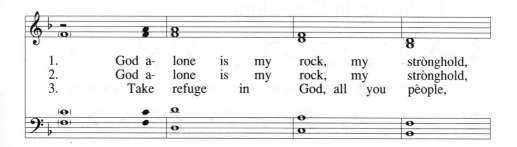

1. God a-lone is my rock, my stronghold,
2. God a-lone is my rock, my stronghold,
3. Take refuge in God, all you pèople,

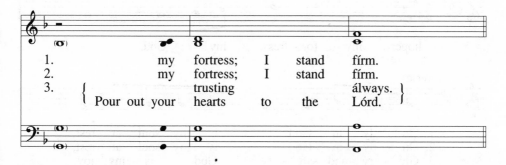

1. my fortress; I stand fírm.
2. my fortress; I stand fírm.
3. { trusting álways. }
   { Pour out your hearts to the Lórd. }

Text: Psalm 62:2-3, 6-7, 8-9; The Grail
Music: Joseph Gelineau, SJ
© 1963, 1993, The Grail, GIA Publications, Inc., agent

88　Psalm 62: In God Alone

Refrain

In God a-lone is my soul at rest, the God who is my help. The Lord is my rock, my strength and my hope; my for-tress, my God.

Verses

1. On - ly in God is my soul at rest, from my God comes my sal - va - tion. God is my rock, the sal - va - tion of my life. I shall not be shak - en, for the Lord is my strength!
2. On - ly in God is my soul at rest, from my God comes my hope. God is my rock, my sal - va - tion and my hope. I will rest in the Lord. I will not be a - fraid!
3. Glo - ry and safe - ty, God is my joy, God is my rock and my strength. God is my ref - uge, I trust with all my strength. Pour out your hearts, be - fore the Lord!

D.C.

Text: Psalm 62: 2-3, 6-7, 8-9; David Haas
Music: David Haas
© 1989, GIA Publications, Inc.

Psalm 63: My Soul Is Thirsting   89

Antiphon I

My soul is thirst-ing for you, O Lord, thirst-ing for you my God.

Text: *Lectionary for Mass*, © 1969, 1981, ICEL
Music: Richard Proulx, © 1975, GIA Publications, Inc.

Antiphon II

In the morn - ing I will sing, will sing glad songs of praise to you.

Text: *Praise God in Song*
Music: David Clark Isele
© 1979, GIA Publications, Inc.

Psalm Tone

Music : Richard Proulx, © 1986, GIA Publications, Inc.

Gelineau Tone

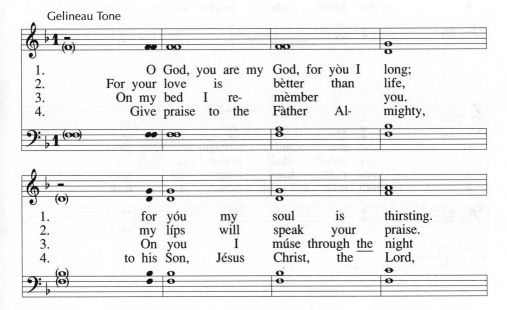

1. O God, you are my God, for yòu I long;
2. For your love is bètter than life,
3. On my bed I re- mèmber you.
4. Give praise to the Fàther Al- mighty,

1. for yóu my soul is thirsting.
2. my líps will speak your praise.
3. On you I múse through the night
4. to his Son, Jésus Christ, the Lord,

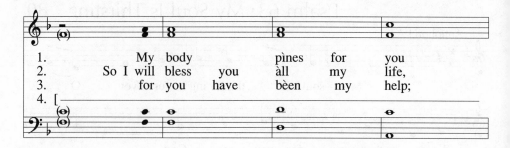

1. My body pìnes for you
2. So I will bless you àll my life,
3. for you have bèen my help;
4. [

1. like a dry, weary lánd without water.
2. in your name I will líft up my hands.
3. in the shadow of your wíngs I re- joice.
4.]

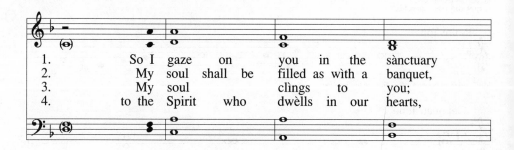

1. So I gaze on you in the sànctuary
2. My soul shall be filled as wìth a banquet,
3. My soul clìngs to you;
4. to the Spirit who dwèlls in our hearts,

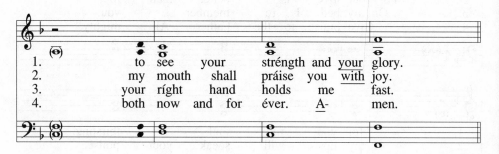

1. to see your stréngth and your glory.
2. my mouth shall práise you with joy.
3. your ríght hand holds me fast.
4. both now and for éver. A- men.

Text: Psalm 63:2-9; The Grail
Music: Joseph Gelineau, SJ
© 1963, The Grail, GIA Publications, Inc., agent

Psalm 63: My Soul Is Thirsting   90

With longing

Refrain

My soul is thirst-ing, my soul is thirst-ing,

To verses | *Last time*

my soul is thirst-ing for you, O Lord my God. God.

Verse 1

1. O God, you are my God whom I seek; O God, you are my

God whom I seek; for you my flesh pines, my soul

D.S.

thirsts like the earth, parched, life - less, with - out wa - ter.

Verse 2

2. Thus have I gazed toward you in your ho-ly place to see your

pow - er and your glo - ry. Your kind-ness is a great-er

D.S.

good than life it - self; my lips will glo - ri - fy you.

3. Thus will I bless you while I live; Lift-ing up my hands I will call up-on your name. As with a ban-quet shall my soul be sat-is-fied; with ex-ul-tant lips my mouth shall praise you.

Verse 4

4. For you have been my help, you have been my help; in the shad-ow of your wings I shout for joy. My soul clings fast to you; your right hand holds me firm; in the shad-ow of your wings I sing for joy.

Text: Psalm 63:2, 3-4, 5-6, 8-9; verses trans. © 1970, Confraternity of Christian Doctrine, Washington D.C.; refrain by Michael Joncas, © 1987, GIA Publications, Inc.
Music: Michael Joncas, © 1987, GIA Publications, Inc.

Psalm 63: My Soul Is Thirsting   91

Refrain

My soul is thirst-ing for you, O Lord, my God, O Lord, my God.

To verses | Last time

Verse 1

1. O Lord, you are my God whom I seek.

For you my soul pines.

Like the earth, parched and life-less

with-out wa-ter.

D.C.

Verse 2

2. I seek you in this ho-ly place,

to see your pow - er and glo - ry.

For your mer - cy is great - er than life, my

D.C.

lips glo - ri - fy you.

Verse 3

3. My God you are my help;

my soul clings fast to you.

In the shad - ow of your wings, I

D.C.

shout for joy.

Text: Psalm 63:2-4, 8-9; Roy James Stewart, © 1993, GIA Publications, Inc.; refrain trans. © 1969, ICEL
Tune: Roy James Stewart, © 1993, GIA Publications, Inc.

Psalm 65: The Seed That Falls on Good Ground   92

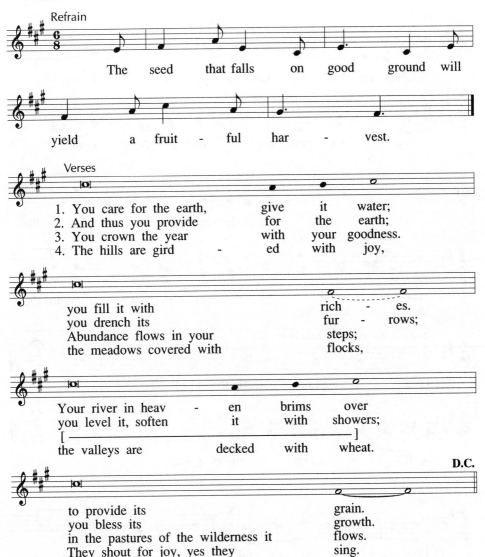

Refrain

The seed that falls on good ground will yield a fruit - ful har - vest.

Verses

1. You care for the earth, give it water;
2. And thus you provide for the earth;
3. You crown the year with your goodness.
4. The hills are gird - ed with joy,

you fill it with rich - es.
you drench its fur - rows;
Abundance flows in your steps;
the meadows covered with flocks,

Your river in heav - en brims over
you level it, soften it with showers;
[————————————————]
the valleys are decked with wheat.

D.C.

to provide its grain.
you bless its growth.
in the pastures of the wilderness it flows.
They shout for joy, yes they sing.

Text: Psalm 65:10-11, 12-13, 14; © 1963, 1993, The Grail, GIA Publications, Inc., agent; refrain trans. © 1969, ICEL
Music: Michel Guimont, © 1994, GIA Publications, Inc.

93 Psalm 66: Let All the Earth

Refrain

Melody:
Let all the earth cry out in joy to the Lord;

Tenor:
Alto:
Cry out in joy un - to the Lord

Let all the earth cry out in joy to the
Al - le - lu - ia,

Cry out in joy un - to the
Al - le - lu - ia,

1.-3. *To verses* | Last time rit.
Lord! Lord! to the Lord!
Lord! Lord! to the Lord!

Verses

1. Cry out in joy to the Lord, all peo-ples on
2. Lead - ing your peo - ple safe through fire and
3. Heark - en to me as I sing my love of the

earth, sing to the praise of God's name,
wa - ter, bring - ing their souls to life,
Lord, who an - swers the prayer of my heart.

pro - claim - ing   for   - ev - er,
we   sing   of   your   glo - ry,
God   leads   me   in   safe - ty,

D.C.

"tre - men - dous your   deeds   for   us."   Oh
your   love   is   e - ter - nal.   Oh
from   death   un - to   life.   Oh

Text: Psalm 66:1-3, 12, 16; Marty Haugen
Music: Marty Haugen
© 1982, GIA Publications, Inc.

94 Psalm 67: May God Bless Us in His Mercy

Refrain I

May God bless us in his mer - cy,

To verses

may God bless us in his mer - cy.

Refrain II

To verses

O God, O God, let all the na-tions praise you.

Verses

1. O God, be gracious and   bless us
2. Let the nations be glad and ex -   ult
3. Let the peoples praise you, O   God;

and let your face shed its light   up - on us.
for you rule the world   with justice.
let all the peo -   ples praise you.

So will your ways be known   up - on earth
With fairness you   rule the peoples,
May God still   give us blessing

To refrain

and all nations learn your sav -   ing help.
you guide the nations   on earth.
till the ends of the earth stand   in awe.

Text: Psalm 67:2-3, 5, 6, 6-8; © 1963, 1993, The Grail, GIA Publications, Inc., agent; refrain trans. © 1969, ICEL
Music: Michel Guimont, © 1994, GIA Publications, Inc.

Psalm 67: May God Bless Us in His Mercy 95

Antiphon I (St. 1.3.6ab & 5cd)

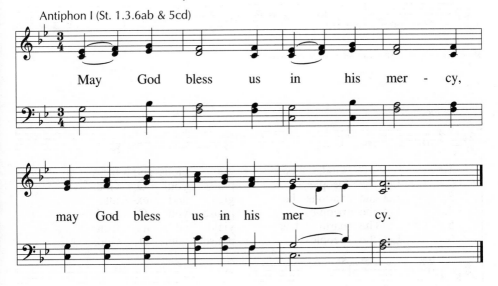

May God bless us in his mer - cy,

may God bless us in his mer - cy.

Text: *Lectionary for Mass,* © 1969, 1981, ICEL
Music: Robert J. Batastini, © 1975, GIA Publications, Inc.

Antiphon II (St. 1.3.6ab & 5cd)

O God, O God, let all the na-tions praise you!

Text: *Lectionary for Mass,* © 1969, 1981, ICEL
Music: Marie Kremer, © 1975, GIA Publications, Inc.

Antiphon III (St. 1.3.5)

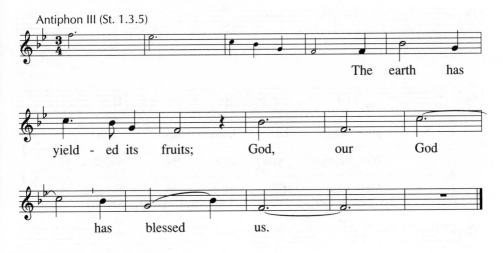

The earth has

yield - ed its fruits; God, our God

has blessed us.

Text: *Lectionary for Mass,* © 1969, 1981, ICEL
Music: Richard Proulx, © 1975, GIA Publications, Inc.

Psalm Tone   [Omit for 2-line stanza]

Gelineau Tone

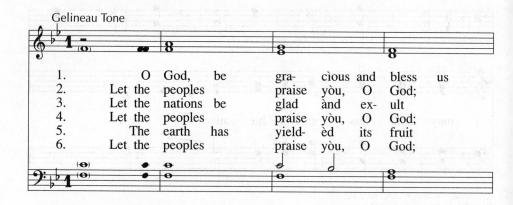

1.   O   God,   be   gra- cìous and   bless   us
2.   Let the peoples   praise yòu,   O   God;
3.   Let the nations be   glad   ànd   ex- ult
4.   Let the peoples   praise yòu,   O   God;
5.   The   earth   has   yield- èd   its   fruit
6.   Let the peoples   praise yòu,   O   God;

1.   and let your face shed its   líght   up- on   us.
2. [
3.   for you rule   the   wórld with justice.
4. [
5.   for God, our   Gód, has   blessed us.
6.   let all   the   péoples   praise you.

1.   So will your ways   be   known ùpon   earth
2.   ]
3.   With fairness you   rùle   the   peoples,
4.   ]
5.   May God   still   gìve   us   blessing
6.   To the Father, the   Son and Hòly Spirit,

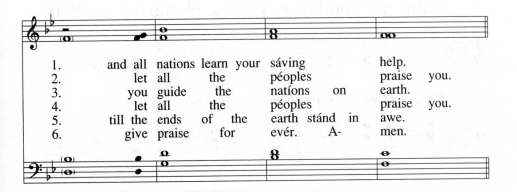

1. and all nations learn your sáving help.
2. let all the péoples praise you.
3. you guide the natíons on earth.
4. let all the péoples praise you.
5. till the ends of the earth stánd in awe.
6. give praise for evér. A- men.

Text: Psalm 67; The Grail
Music: Joseph Gelineau, SJ
© 1963, 1993, GIA Publications, Inc., agent

96 Psalm 68: You Have Made a Home for the Poor

Refrain

God, in your good-ness, you have made a home,

To verses

you have made a home for the poor.

Last time
rit.

home for the poor.

Text: *Lectionary for Mass,* © 1969, 1981, ICEL
Music: Rory Cooney, © 1991, GIA Publications, Inc.

Verses

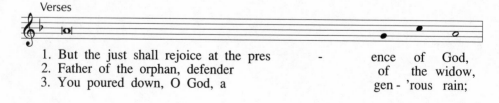

1. But the just shall rejoice at the pres - ence of God,
2. Father of the orphan, defender of the widow,
3. You poured down, O God, a gen - 'rous rain;

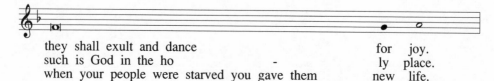

they shall exult and dance for joy.
such is God in the ho - ly place.
when your people were starved you gave them new life.

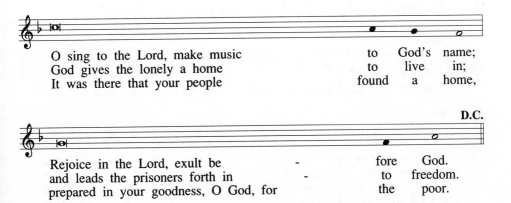

O sing to the Lord, make music   to   God's   name;
God gives the lonely a home   to   live   in;
It was there that your people   found   a   home,

D.C.

Rejoice in the Lord, exult be -   fore   God.
and leads the prisoners forth in -   to   freedom.
prepared in your goodness, O God, for   the   poor.

Text: Psalm 68:4-5, 6-7, 10-11; The Grail, © 1963, 1993, GIA Publications, Inc., agent
Music: Richard Proulx, © 1986, GIA Publications, Inc.

97 Psalm 69: Turn to the Lord in Your Need

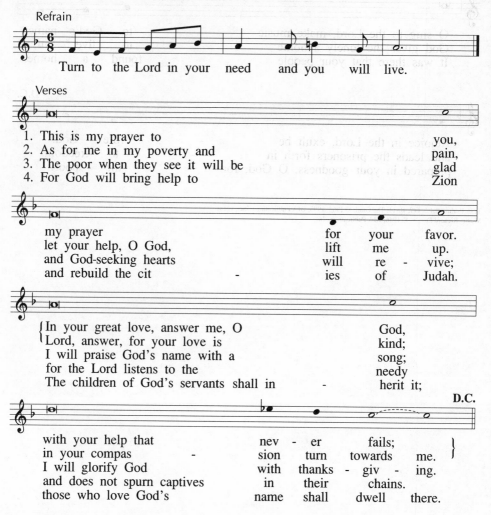

Refrain

Turn to the Lord in your need and you will live.

Verses

1. This is my prayer to you,
2. As for me in my poverty and pain,
3. The poor when they see it will be glad
4. For God will bring help to Zion

my prayer for your favor.
let your help, O God, lift me up.
and God-seeking hearts will re - vive;
and rebuild the cit - ies of Judah.

{ In your great love, answer me, O God,
{ Lord, answer, for your love is kind;
I will praise God's name with a song;
for the Lord listens to the needy
The children of God's servants shall in - herit it;

D.C.

with your help that nev - er fails;
in your compas - sion turn towards me.
I will glorify God with thanks - giv - ing.
and does not spurn captives in their chains.
those who love God's name shall dwell there.

Psalm 69: Lord, in Your Great Love   98

Antiphon

Lord,   in   your great   love,   an-swer me.

Text: *Lectionary for Mass,* © 1969, 1981, ICEL
Music: Alexander Peloquin, © 1975, GIA Publications, Inc.

Psalm Tone

Music: A. Gregory Murray, OSB, © L. J. Carey and Co., Ltd.

Gelineau Tone

1. It is for you that I sùffer   taunts,
2.   This is my prày er to   you,
3. The poor when they see it wìll be glad

1.   that shame   covérs my face,
2.   my prayer   fór your fa-   vor.
3.   and God-seeking   hearts wìll re-   vive;

1.   that I have become a stranger tò my family,
2. In your great love,   answer mè, O God,
3.   for the Lord   listens tò the needy

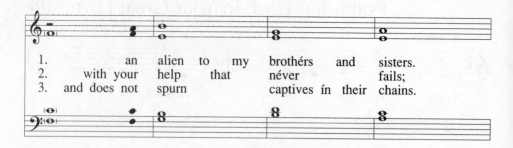

1.   an   alien   to   my   brothérs   and   sisters.
2.   with your   help   that   néver   fails;
3. and does not   spurn   captives ín their   chains.

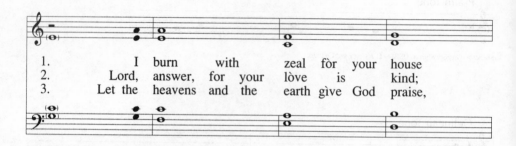

1.   I   burn   with   zeal   fòr   your   house
2.   Lord,   answer,   for   your   lòve   is   kind;
3.   Let the   heavens   and   the   earth gìve God   praise,

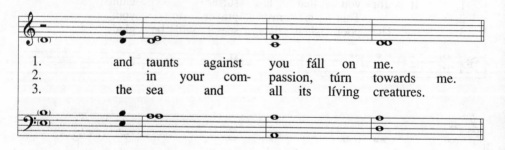

1.   and   taunts   against   you fáll   on   me.
2.   in   your   com-   passion, túrn   towards   me.
3.   the   sea   and   all   its   líving   creatures.

Text: Psalm 69:8-10, 14, 17, 33-35; The Grail
Music: Joseph Gelineau, SJ
© 1963, 1993, The Grail, GIA Publications, Inc., agent

Psalm 71: I Will Sing   99

Refrain

Gently flowing (♩ = 60)

I will sing of your sal - va-tion, I will sing, I will sing.

Optional Psalm Tone

Verse 1

p

1. In you, O Lord, I take rèf-uge; let me nev-er bé put to shame. In your jus - tice res-cue me, and de-liv-er me; in - cline your ear to mé and save me.

poco rit.

D.C.

Verse 2

mf

2. Be my rock of rèf-uge, a strong-hold to gíve me safe-ty, for you are my rock and my fòr-tress. O my

cresc. 3

ff *dim.* 3 ⌐3⌐ 3

D.C.

God, res-cue me from the hand óf the wick - ed.

Verse 3
3. For you are my hope, O Lòrd; my trust, O Gód, from my youth. On you I de - pend from bìrth; from my moth-er's wómb you are my strength.

D.C.

Verse 4
4. My mouth shall de - clare your jùs - tice, day by day, yóur sal - va - tion. O God, you have taught me from my yòuth, and till the pres - ent I pro - cláim your won - drous deeds.

D.C.

Text: Psalm 71:1-2, 3-4, 5-6, 15, 17; © 1963, 1993, The Grail, GIA Publications, Inc., agent; refrain trans. © 1969, ICEL
Music: Randolph Currie, © 1995, World Library Publications, Inc.; psalm tone: Richard Proulx, © 1986, GIA Publications, Inc.

Psalm 71: Since My Mother's Womb   100

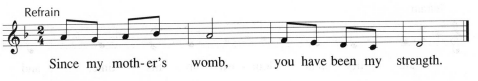

Refrain

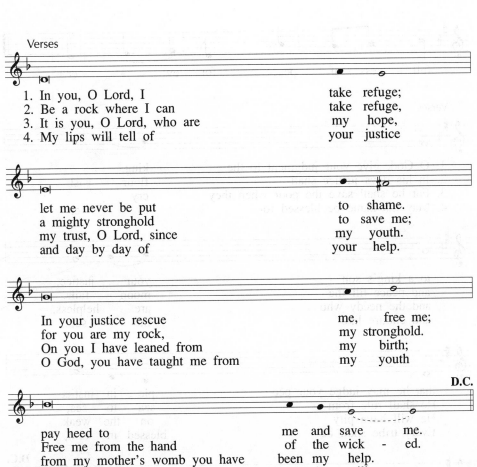

Since my moth-er's womb, you have been my strength.

Verses

1. In you, O Lord, I   take   refuge;
2. Be a rock where I can   take   refuge,
3. It is you, O Lord, who are   my   hope,
4. My lips will tell of   your   justice

let me never be put   to   shame.
a mighty stronghold   to   save me;
my trust, O Lord, since   my   youth.
and day by day of   your   help.

In your justice rescue   me,   free me;
for you are my rock,   my   stronghold.
On you I have leaned from   my   birth;
O God, you have taught me from   my   youth

D.C.

pay heed to   me and save   me.
Free me from the hand   of   the wick - ed.
from my mother's womb you have   been my   help.
and I proclaim your   won - der   still.

Text: Psalm 71:1-2, 3-4, 5-6, 15, 17; © 1963, 1993, The Grail, GIA Publications, Inc., agent; refrain trans. © 1969, ICEL
Music: Michel Guimont, © 1995, GIA Publications, Inc.

101 Psalm 72: Justice Shall Flourish

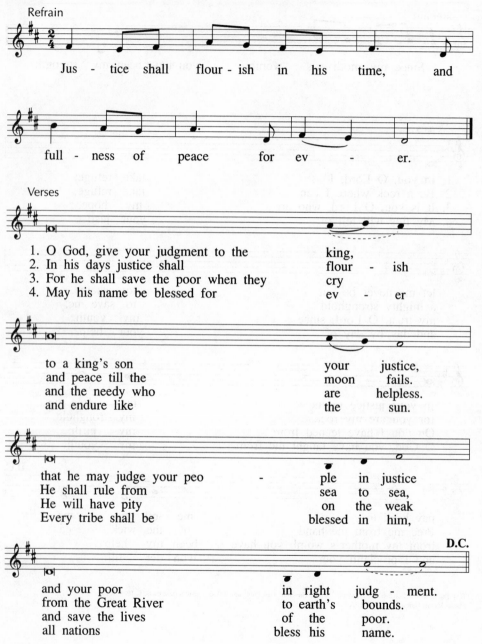

Refrain

Jus - tice shall flour - ish in his time, and

full - ness of peace for ev - er.

Verses

1. O God, give your judgment to the king,
2. In his days justice shall flour - ish
3. For he shall save the poor when they cry
4. May his name be blessed for ev - er

to a king's son your justice,
and peace till the moon fails.
and the needy who are helpless.
and endure like the sun.

that he may judge your peo - ple in justice
He shall rule from sea to sea,
He will have pity on the weak
Every tribe shall be blessed in him,

D.C.

and your poor in right judg - ment.
from the Great River to earth's bounds.
and save the lives of the poor.
all nations bless his name.

Text: Psalm 72:1-2, 7-8, 12-13, 17; © 1963, 1993, The Grail, GIA Publications, Inc., agent; refrain trans. © 1969, ICEL
Music: Michel Guimont, © 1995, GIA Publications, Inc.

Psalm 72: Every Nation on Earth   102

Verse 1

1. O God, with your judg-ment en - dow the king; with your jus - tice en - dow the king's son. With jus - tice he will gov - ern your peo - ple, your af - flict - ed ones with right judg - ment.

To refrain

Verse 2

2. Jus - tice shall flow'r in his days, last-ing peace 'til the moon be no more. May he rule from sea to sea, from the riv - er to the ends of the earth.

To refrain

Verse 3

3. The kings of Tar-shish and the Isles of-fer gifts, those from Se - ba and A - ra - bia bring trib - ute. All kings shall pay him their hom - age, all na - tions shall serve him.

To refrain

Verse 4

4. He res - cues the poor when they cry out, the af - flict - ed with no one to help. The low - ly and poor he shall pit - y, the lives of the poor he will save.

To refrain

Text: Psalm 72:1-2, 7-8, 10-11, 12-13; Michael Joncas
Music: Michael Joncas
© 1987, 1994, GIA Publications, Inc.

103　Psalm 72: Lord, Every Nation on Earth

Antiphon

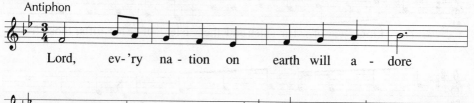

Lord, ev-'ry na-tion on earth will a-dore

you, ev-'ry na-tion on earth will a-dore you.

Text: *Lectionary for Mass,* © 1969, ICEL
Music: Marty Haugen, © 1995, GIA Publications, Inc.

Psalm Tone

Repeat for 6-line stanza

Music: Laurence Bevenot, OSB, © 1969, Ampleforth Abbey Trustees

Gelineau Tone

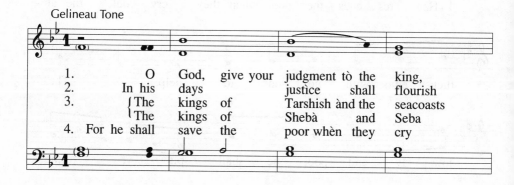

1. 　　　O God, give your judgment tò the king,
2. In his days 　　justìce shall flourish
3. {The kings of Tarshish ànd the seacoasts
   {The kings of Shebà and Seba
4. For he shall save the poor whèn they cry

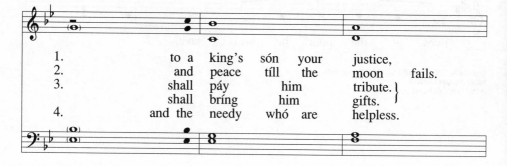

1. 　　to a king's són your justice,
2. 　　and peace tíll the moon fails.
3. 　　shall páy him tribute.}
　　　　shall bríng him gifts.}
4. 　　and the needy whó are helpless.

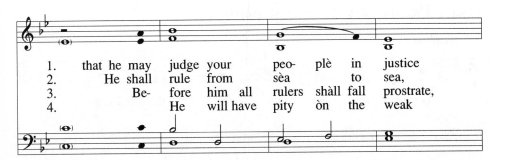

1. that he may judge your peo-plè in justice
2. He shall rule from sèa to sea,
3. Be- fore him all rulers shàll fall prostrate,
4. He will have pity òn the weak

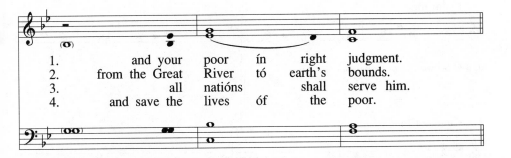

1. and your poor ín right judgment.
2. from the Great River tó earth's bounds.
3. all natións shall serve him.
4. and save the lives óf the poor.

Text: Psalm 72:1-2, 7-8, 10-11, 12-13; The Grail
Music: Joseph Gelineau, SJ
© 1963, 1993, The Grail, GIA Publications, Inc., agent

104 Psalm 78: Do Not Forget

Antiphon

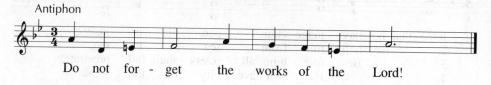

Do not for - get the works of the Lord!

Text: *Lectionary for Mass,* © 1969, 1981, ICEL
Music: Robert J. Batastini, © 1975, GIA Publications, Inc.

Psalm Tone

Music: Richard Proulx, © 1986, GIA Publications, Inc.

Gelineau Tone

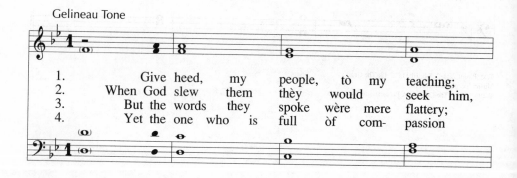

1. Give heed, my people, tò my teaching;
2. When God slew them thèy would seek him,
3. But the words they spoke wère mere flattery;
4. Yet the one who is full òf com- passion

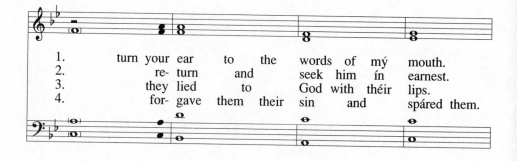

1. turn your ear to the words of mý mouth.
2. re- turn and seek him ín earnest.
3. they lied to God with théir lips.
4. for- gave them their sin and spáred them.

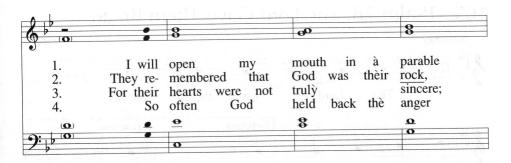

1. I will open my mouth in à parable
2. They re- membered that God was thèir rock,
3. For their hearts were not trulỳ sincere;
4. So often God held back thè anger

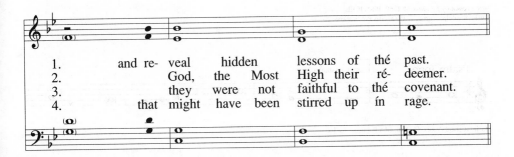

1. and re- veal hidden lessons of thé past.
2. God, the Most High their ré- deemer.
3. they were not faithful to thé covenant.
4. that might have been stirred up ín rage.

Text: Psalm 78:1-2, 34-35, 36-37, 38; The Grail
Music: Joseph Gelineau, SJ
© 1963, 1993, The Grail, GIA Publications, Inc., agent

105　Psalm 78: The Lord Gave Them Bread

Antiphon

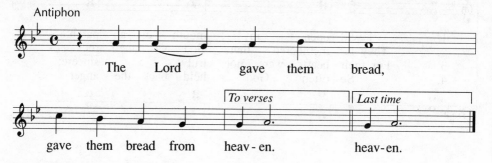

The Lord gave them bread,

gave them bread from heav-en.　heav-en.

To verses　*Last time*

Text: *Lectionary for Mass,* © 1969, 1981, ICEL
Music: Randolph Currie, © 1975, GIA Publications, Inc.

Psalm Tone　Omit for stanza 2

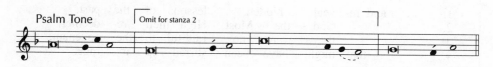

Music: Richard Proulx, © 1986, GIA Publications, Inc.

Gelineau Tone

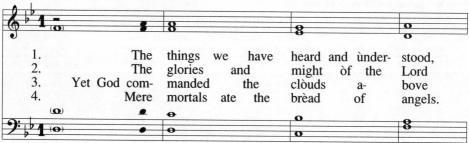

1.　　　　The things we have heard and ùnder- stood,
2.　　　　The glories and might òf the Lord
3. Yet God com- manded the clòuds a- bove
4.　　　Mere mortals ate the brèad of angels.

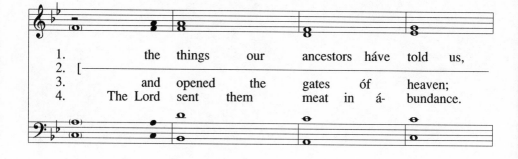

1.　　　the things our ancestors háve told us,
2. [
3.　　　and opened the gates óf heaven;
4. The Lord sent them meat in á- bundance.

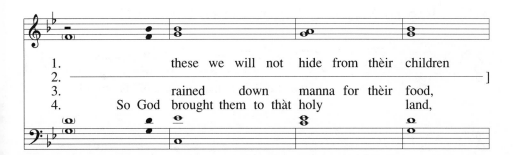

1.   these we will not hide from thèir children
2.
3.   rained   down   manna for thèir food,
4.   So God brought them to thàt holy   land,

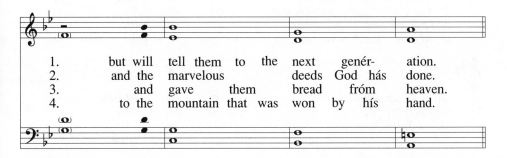

1.   but will tell them to the next genér-   ation.
2.   and the marvelous   deeds God hás   done.
3.   and   gave   them   bread fróm   heaven.
4.   to the mountain that was won by hís   hand.

Text: Psalm 78:3-4, 23-24, 25, 54; The Grail
Music: Joseph Gelineau, SJ
© 1963, 1993, The Grail, GIA Publications, Inc., agent

106 Psalm 80: The Vineyard of the Lord

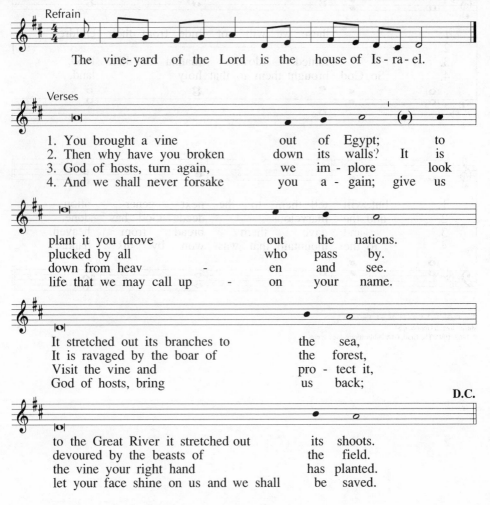

Refrain

The vine-yard of the Lord is the house of Is-ra-el.

Verses

1. You brought a vine out of Egypt; to
2. Then why have you broken down its walls? It is
3. God of hosts, turn again, we im - plore look
4. And we shall never forsake you a - gain; give us

plant it you drove out the nations.
plucked by all who pass by.
down from heav - en and see.
life that we may call up - on your name.

It stretched out its branches to the sea,
It is ravaged by the boar of the forest,
Visit the vine and pro - tect it,
God of hosts, bring us back;

D.C.

to the Great River it stretched out its shoots.
devoured by the beasts of the field.
the vine your right hand has planted.
let your face shine on us and we shall be saved.

Text: Psalm 80:9, 12-14, 15-16, 19-20; © 1963, 1993, The Grail, GIA Publications, Inc., agent; refrain trans. © 1969, ICEL
Music: Michel Guimont, © 1994, GIA Publications, Inc.

107 Psalm 80/85/Luke 1: Lord, Make Us Turn to You

Refrain

Lord, make us turn to you, show us your face, and

we shall be saved.

Verses
a tempo

Ps. 80
1. Shep - herd of Is - ra - el, heark - en from your
2. We are your cho - sen vine, on - ly by your
3. If you will dwell with us, we shall live a -

4. Lord, we are pres - ent here, show us your
Ps. 85
5. Lord, let sal - va - tion rain, show - er down your
6. See, Lord, we look to you, you a - lone can

7. You have done won - drous things, ho - ly is your
Lk. 1
8. You are my joy and song, I would have my
9. You fill all hun - gry hearts, send - ing the

throne and shine forth, O rouse your pow - er,
care do we live, reach out your hand, O
new in your love, O shine up - on us,
kind - ness and love, O speak your word of
jus - tice and peace, the earth shall bring forth
bring us to life, O walk be - fore us
name for all time, your mer - cy and your
life speak your praise, on me your love has
rich emp - ty forth, and hold - ing up in

poco rit. **D.C.**

and come to save us.
Lord, un - to your peo - ple.
great Lord of life.
peace un - to your peo - ple.
truth, the skies your love.
to light our path - ways.
love are with your peo - ple.
shown, your bless - ings giv - en.
love the meek and low - ly.

Text: Psalm 80:2-3, 15-16, 18-20; Psalm 85:9-14; Luke 1:46-55; Marty Haugen
Music: Marty Haugen
© 1982, GIA Publications, Inc.

108 Psalm 80: Lord, Make Us Turn to You

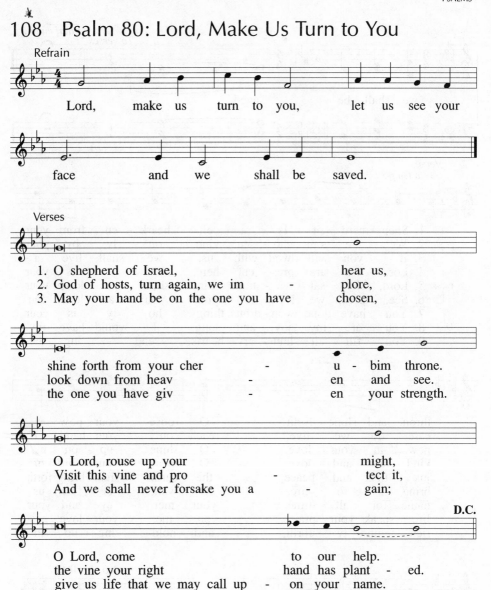

Refrain

Lord, make us turn to you, let us see your face and we shall be saved.

Verses

1. O shepherd of Israel, hear us,
2. God of hosts, turn again, we im - plore,
3. May your hand be on the one you have chosen,

shine forth from your cher - u - bim throne.
look down from heav - en and see.
the one you have giv - en your strength.

O Lord, rouse up your might,
Visit this vine and pro - tect it,
And we shall never forsake you a - gain;

O Lord, come to our help.
the vine your right hand has plant - ed.
give us life that we may call up - on your name.

Text: Psalm 80:2-3, 15-16, 18-19; © 1963, 1993, The Grail, GIA Publications, Inc., agent; refrain trans. © 1969, ICEL
Music: Michel Guimont, © 1995, GIA Publications, Inc.

Psalm 81: Sing with Joy to God   109

Antiphon

Sing with joy to God! Sing to God, our help!

Text: *Lectionary for Mass,* © 1969, 1981, ICEL
Music: Randolph Currie, © 1986, GIA Publications, Inc.

Psalm Tone

Music: Richard Proulx, © 1975, GIA Publications, Inc.

Gelineau Tone

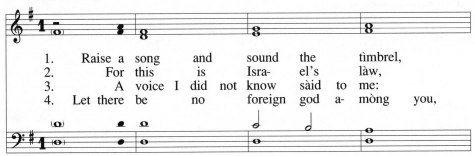

1. Raise a song and sound the tìmbrel,
2.   For this is Isra- el's làw,
3.   A voice I did not know sàid to me:
4. Let there be no foreign god a- mòng you,

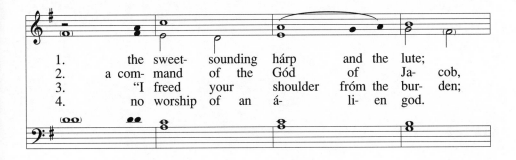

1.   the sweet- sounding hárp and the lute;
2.   a com- mand of the Gód of Ja- cob,
3.   "I freed your shoulder fróm the bur- den;
4.   no worship of an á- li- en god.

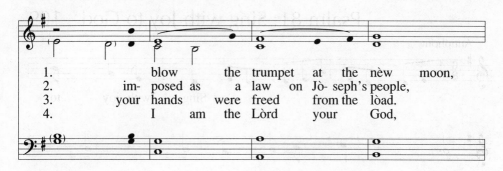

1. blow the trumpet at the nèw moon,
2. im- posed as a law on Jò- seph's people,
3. your hands were freed from the lòad.
4. I am the Lòrd your God,

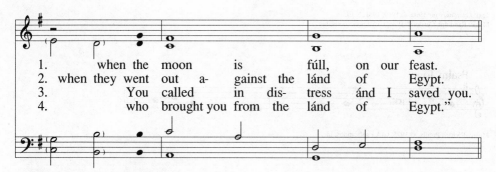

1. when the moon is fúll, on our feast.
2. when they went out a- gainst the lánd of Egypt.
3. You called in dis- tress ánd I saved you.
4. who brought you from the lánd of Egypt."

Text: Psalm 81:3-4, 5-6, 6-8, 10-11; The Grail
Music: Joseph Gelineau, SJ
© 1963, 1993, The Grail, GIA Publications, Inc., agent

Psalm 84: How Lovely Is Your Dwelling Place   110

Antiphon

How love-ly is your dwell-ing place, O Lord of hosts.

Text: Psalm 84:2, The Grail
Music: A. Gregory Murray, OSB
© 1963, The Grail, GIA Publications, Inc., agent

Psalm Tone

Repeat for 5-line stanza
Omit for 2-line stanza

Music: Chrysogonus Waddell, © Gethsemani Abbey

Gelineau Tone

1. How lovely is your dwèlling place,
2. My soul is longìng and yearn- ing,
3. The sparrow her- self finds a home
4. They are happy, who dwell in your house,
5. As they go through the Bìtter Val- ley
6. O Lord God of hosts, hèar my prayer,
7. One day with- in your courts
8. For the Lord God is a rampàrt, a shield.
9. Lord, Gòd of hosts,
10. Give praise to the Fathèr Al- might- y,

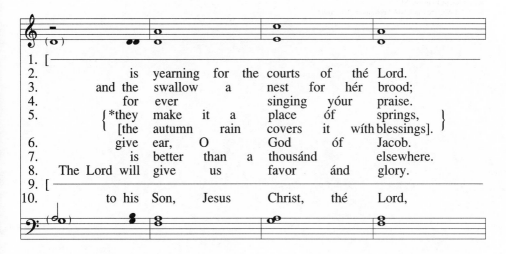

1. [
2. is yearning for the courts of thé Lord.
3. and the swallow a nest for hér brood;
4. for ever singing yóur praise.
5. { *they make it a place óf springs,
   [the autumn rain covers it with blessings]. }
6. give ear, O God óf Jacob.
7. is better than a thousánd elsewhere.
8. The Lord will give us favor ánd glory.
9. [
10. to his Son, Jesus Christ, thé Lord,

*Repeat the second musical phrase.

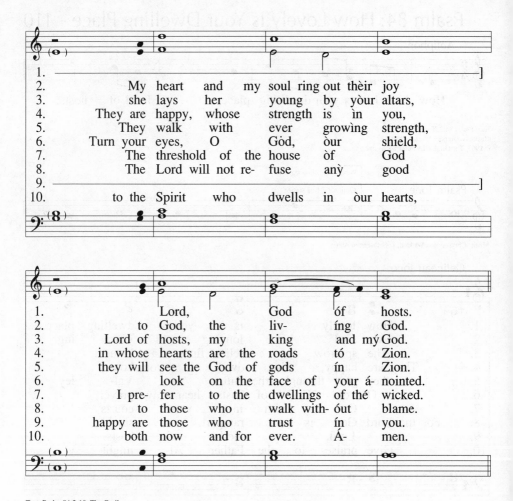

1.
2. My heart and my soul ring out thèir joy
3. she lays her young by yòur altars,
4. They are happy, whose strength is ìn you,
5. They walk with ever growìng strength,
6. Turn your eyes, O Gòd, òur shield,
7. The threshold of the house òf God
8. The Lord will not re- fuse anỳ good
9.
10. to the Spirit who dwells in òur hearts,

1. Lord, God óf hosts.
2. to God, the liv- íng God.
3. Lord of hosts, my king and mý God.
4. in whose hearts are the roads tó Zion.
5. they will see the God of gods ín Zion.
6. look on the face of your á- nointed.
7. I pre- fer to the dwellings of thé wicked.
8. to those who walk with- óut blame.
9. happy are those who trust ín you.
10. both now and for ever. Á- men.

Text: Psalm 84:2-10; The Grail
Music: Joseph Gelineau, SJ
© 1963, 1993, The Grail, GIA Publications, Inc., agent

Psalm 84: Happy Are They   111

Refrain
Optional canon

Hap-py are they who dwell in your house, O Lord, who dwell in your house, O Lord.

Verses

1. My soul yearns and pines for the courts of the Lord. My heart and my flesh cry to the living God.
2. The spar-row finds a home and the swal-low a nest; Your al-tars, O Lord, my King and my God.
3. Hap-py are they who a-bide in your house. You are their strength, your prais-es they will sing.

Text: Psalm 84:2, 3, 4, 5-6; Thomas J. Porter
Music: Thomas J. Porter

112 Psalm 85: Lord, Let Us See Your Kindness

Refrain

Lord,   let us see your   kind - ness;

Lord,   let us see your   kind - ness.   *Last time* ⌢

Verse 1

1. Let us hear   what our   God   pro - claims:

Peace   to the   peo - ple of   God,   sal - va - tion is

near   to the   ones   who   fear God.   **D.C.**

Verse 2

2. Kind - ness   and   truth,   jus - tice and peace;

truth   shall spring up   as the   wa - ter from   the earth,

jus - tice shall   rain from   the   heav - ens.

Verse 3

3. The   Lord   will   come   and you shall know his   love,

jus - tice shall   walk in   his   path - ways,   sal -

va - tion   the   gift   that   he   brings.

Text: Psalm 85:9-10, 11-12, 13-14; Marty Haugen, © 1983, GIA Publications, Inc.; refrain trans. © 1969, ICEL
Music: Marty Haugen, © 1983, GIA Publications, Inc.

113   Psalm 85: Lord, Let Us See Your Kindness

Antiphon I

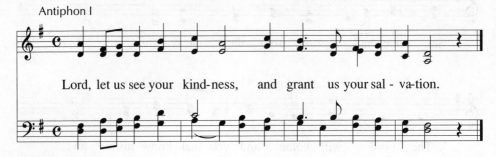

Lord, let us see your kind-ness,   and grant   us your sal - va-tion.

Text: *Lectionary for Mass,* © 1969, 1981, ICEL
Music: J. Robert Carroll, © 1975, GIA Publications, Inc.

Antiphon II

The   Lord   speaks   of   peace   to his   peo - ple.

Text: *Lectionary for Mass,* © 1969, 1981, ICEL
Music: Richard Proulx, © 1986, GIA Publications, Inc.

Psalm Tone

Music: Richard Proulx, © 1975, GIA Publications, Inc.

Gelineau Tone

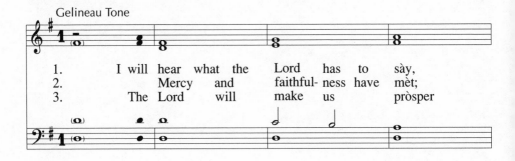

1.	I will	hear	what	the	Lord	has	to	sày,
2.		Mercy	and		faithful-	ness	have	mèt;
3.	The	Lord	will		make	us		pròsper

Text: Psalm 85:9-10, 11-12, 13-14; The Grail
Music: Joseph Gelineau, SJ
© 1963, 1993, The Grail, GIA Publications, Inc., agent

114 Psalm 85: Come, O Lord, and Set Us Free

Refrain I

Come, O Lord, and set us free.

Come, and set us free.

To verses | *Final ending*

Refrain II

Lord, let us see your kind - ness;
Lord, let us see your kind -

Lord, let us see your kind - ness;

Lord, grant us your sal - va - tion.

ness; Lord, grant us your sal - va -

Lord, grant us your sal - va - tion.

To verses

Final ending

tion.

Verses

1. Now I will hear what God pro - claims, the
2. Mer - cy and faith - ful - ness shall meet, in
3. Our God shall grant a - bun - dant gifts, the

Lord who speaks of peace. Near to us now, God's sav -
jus - tice and peace, em - brace. Truth shall blos - som from
earth shall yield its fruit. Jus - tice shall march be - fore

To refrain

ing love for those who be - lieve.
the earth as the heav - ens re - joice.
our God and guide us to peace.

Text: Psalm 85; refrains I and II, © 1969, ICEL; verses by Mike Balhoff, Gary Daigle, Darryl Ducote, © 1978, 1993, Damean Music.
Distributed by GIA Publications, Inc.
Music: Mike Balhoff, Gary Daigle, Darryl Ducote, © 1978, 1993, Damean Music. Distributed by GIA Publications, Inc.

115 Psalm 86: O Lord, Our God

Antiphon I

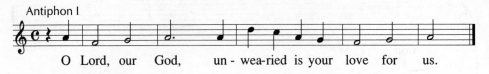

O Lord, our God, un - wea-ried is your love for us.

Text: *Liturgy of the Hours,* © 1974, ICEL
Music: John Schiavone, © 1986, GIA Publications, Inc.

Antiphon II

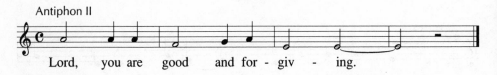

Lord, you are good and for - giv - ing.

Text: *Lectionary for Mass,* © 1969, 1981, ICEL
Music: Chrysogonus Waddell, OCSO, © 1986, GIA Publications, Inc.

Psalm Tone

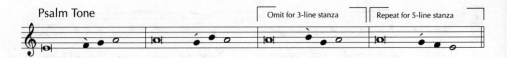

| Omit for 3-line stanza | Repeat for 5-line stanza |

Music: Laurence Bevenot, OSB, © 1969, Ampleforth Abbey Trustees

Gelineau Tone

1.	Turn your ear,	O	Lord, ànd give	an-	swer
2.	You are my God,	have	mercy òn me,	Lord,	
3.	O Lord,	you are	good ànd for-	giv-	ing,
4.	In the day	of dis-	tress Ì will	call	
5.	All the nations	shall	come tò a-	dore	you
6.	Show	me,	Lòrd, your	way	
7.	I will praise you, Lord my		God, with àll my	heart	
8.	The proud	have	risèn a-	gainst	me;
9.	But you,	God of	mercy ànd com-	pas-	sion,
10.	O give	your	strength tò your	ser-	vant
11.	Give praise	to the	Fathèr Al-	might-	y,

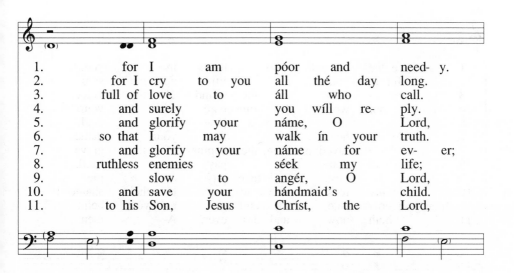

1. for I am póor and need- y.
2. for I cry to you all thé day long.
3. full of love to áll who call.
4. and surely you wíll re- ply.
5. and glorify your náme, O Lord,
6. so that I may walk ín your truth.
7. and glorify your náme for ev- er;
8. ruthless enemies séek my life;
9. slow to angér, O Lord,
10. and save your hándmaid's child.
11. to his Son, Jesus Christ, the Lord,

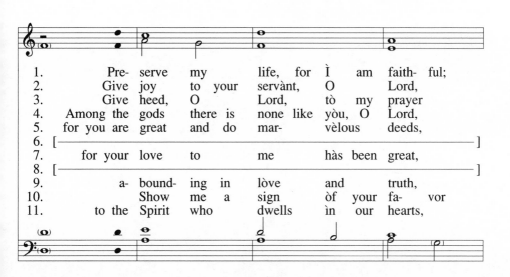

1. Pre- serve my life, for Ì am faith- ful;
2. Give joy to your servànt, O Lord,
3. Give heed, O Lord, tò my prayer
4. Among the gods there is none like yòu, O Lord,
5. for you are great and do mar- vèlous deeds,
6. [————————————————————————————————]
7. for your love to me hàs been great,
8. [————————————————————————————————]
9. a- bound- ing in lòve and truth,
10. Show me a sign òf your fa- vor
11. to the Spirit who dwells ìn our hearts,

1. save the servant who trústs in you.
2. for to you I lift úp my soul.
3. and at- tend to the sound óf my voice.
4. nor work to com- páre with yours.
5. you who a- lóne are God.
6. Guide my heart to féar your name.
7. you have saved me from the depths óf the grave.
8. to you they páy no heed.
9. turn and take pitý on me.
10. { that my foes may see tó their shame }
    { that you con- sole me and give mé your help. }
11. both now and for evér. A- men.

Text: Psalm 86; The Grail
Music: Joseph Gelineau, SJ
© 1963, 1993, The Grail, GIA Publications, Inc., agent

Psalm 88: Day and Night 116

Antiphon

Day and night I cry to you, my God.

Text: *Liturgy of the Hours,* © 1974, ICEL
Music: Suzanne Toolan, SM, © 1986, GIA Publications, Inc.

Psalm Tone

Music: Chrysogonus Waddell, OCSO, © Gethsemani Abbey

Gelineau Tone

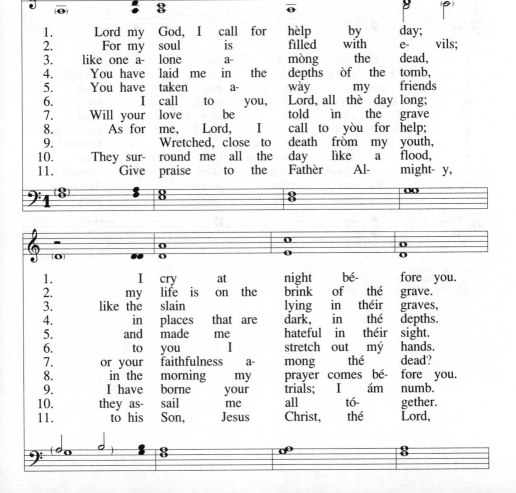

1. Lord my God, I call for help by day;
2. For my soul is filled with e- vils;
3. like one a- lone a- mòng the dead,
4. You have laid me in the depths òf the tomb,
5. You have taken a- wày my friends
6. I call to you, Lord, all thè day long;
7. Will your love be told ìn the grave
8. As for me, Lord, I call to yòu for help;
9. Wretched, close to death fròm my youth,
10. They sur- round me all the day lìke a flood,
11. Give praise to the Fathèr Al- might- y,

1. I cry at night bé- fore you.
2. my life is on the brink of thé grave.
3. like the slain lying in théir graves,
4. in places that are dark, in thé depths.
5. and made me hateful in théir sight.
6. to you I stretch out mý hands.
7. or your faithfulness a- mong thé dead?
8. in the morning my prayer comes bé- fore you.
9. I have borne your trials; I ám numb.
10. they as- sail me all tó- gether.
11. to his Son, Jesus Christ, thé Lord,

1. Let my prayer come into yòur presence.
2. I am reckoned as one in thè tomb;
3. like those you re- member nò more,
4. Your anger weighs down ùp- on me;
5. Im- prisoned, I cannot ès- cape;
6. Will you work your wonders for thè dead?
7. Will your wonders be known in thè dark
8. Lord, why do you rè- ject me?
9. Your fury has swept down ùp- on me;
10. Friend and neighbor you have taken à- way;
11. to the Spirit who dwells in òur hearts,

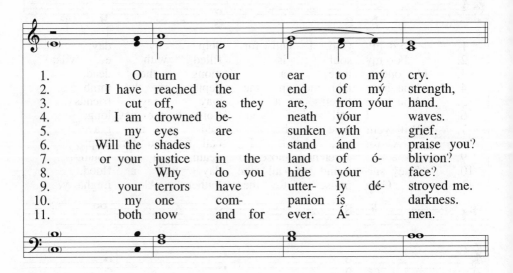

1. O turn your ear to mý cry.
2. I have reached the end of mý strength,
3. cut off, as they are, from yóur hand.
4. I am drowned be- neath yóur waves.
5. my eyes are sunken wíth grief.
6. Will the shades stand ánd praise you?
7. or your justice in the land of ó- blivion?
8. Why do you hide yóur face?
9. your terrors have utter- ly dé- stroyed me.
10. my one com- panion ís darkness.
11. both now and for ever. Á- men.

Text: Psalm 88; The Grail
Music: Joseph Gelineau, SJ
© 1963, The Grail, GIA Publications, Inc., agent

Psalm 89: For Ever I Will Sing 117

Refrain (St. 1.2.5 or 2.3.5 or 1.3.4)

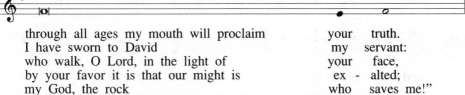

For ev - er I will sing the good-ness of the Lord.

Verses

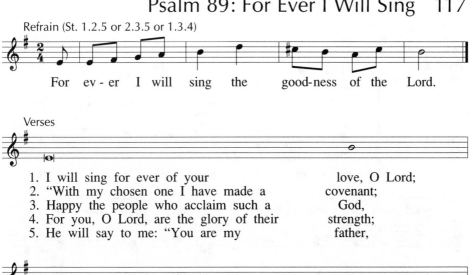

1. I will sing for ever of your   love, O Lord;
2. "With my chosen one I have made a   covenant;
3. Happy the people who acclaim such a   God,
4. For you, O Lord, are the glory of their   strength;
5. He will say to me: "You are my   father,

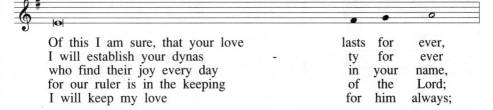

through all ages my mouth will proclaim   your   truth.
I have sworn to David   my   servant:
who walk, O Lord, in the light of   your   face,
by your favor it is that our might is   ex - alted;
my God, the rock   who   saves me!"

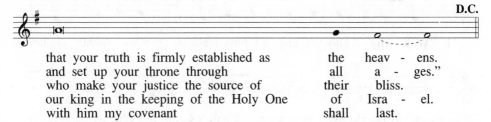

Of this I am sure, that your love   lasts   for   ever,
I will establish your dynas -   ty   for   ever
who find their joy every day   in   your   name,
for our ruler is in the keeping   of   the   Lord;
I will keep my love   for   him   always;

D.C.

that your truth is firmly established as   the   heav - ens.
and set up your throne through   all   a - ges."
who make your justice the source of   their   bliss.
our king in the keeping of the Holy One   of   Isra - el.
with him my covenant   shall   last.

Text: Psalm 89:2-3, 4-5, 16-17, 18-19, 27, 29; © 1963, 1993, The Grail, GIA Publications, Inc., agent; refrain trans. © 1969, ICEL
Music: Michel Guimont, © 1995, GIA Publications, Inc.

118 Psalm 89: For Ever I Will Sing

Verse 2

2. Hap - py   the peo - ple who ac - claim such a God,   who

walk,   O Lord, in the   light   of your face,   who   find   their joy ev - 'ry

slowing   *a tempo*   **D.C.**

day in your name, who make your jus - tice the   source   of   their bliss.

Verse 3

3. He   will   say   to   me: "You   are   my   fa - ther,   my

God,   the rock   who   saves me!"   I   will   keep   my   love   for   him

slowing   *a tempo*   **D.C.**

al - ways;   with   him   my   cov - e - nant   shall   last.

Alternate Verses
Verse 1

1. I   have found   Da - vid   my   ser - vant,   with my

ho - ly   oil   I   have a - noint - ed   him,   that   my

hand may ev-er be with him and my arm make him strong. *poco rit.* **D.C.**

Verse 2

2. My faith-ful-ness and love shall be with you, in my

2. My faith-ful-ness and love will be

Name your name will be ex - alt - ed. *poco rit.* **D.C.**

yours, and you will be ex - alt - ed.

Verse 3

3. He shall cry to me, "My rock of sal-

3. He shall cry to me, "My God, my rock of sal-

va - tion, my sal - va - tion." *poco rit.* **D.C.**

va - tion, my sal - va - tion."

Text: Psalm 89: 4-5, 16-17, 27-29; © 1963, 1993, The Grail, GIA Publications, Inc., agent, alt. verses 21-22, 25, 27; Marty Haugen, © 1988, 1994, GIA Publications, Inc.; refrain trans. © 1969, ICEL
Music: Marty Haugen, © 1988, 1994, GIA Publications, Inc.

Psalm 89: For Ever I Will Sing   119

Antiphon I (St. 1.2.5 or 2.3.5 or 1.3.4)

For ev - er I will sing the good - ness of the Lord.

Antiphon II (St. 1.2.5)

The Son of Da-vid will live for ev - er.

Psalm Tone

Gelineau Tone

1. I will sing for ever of your love, O Lord;
3. Happy the people who ac- claim such a God,
4. For you, O Lord, are the glory of their strength;

1. through all ages my mouth will pro- claim your truth.
3. who walk, O Lord, in the light of your face,
4. by your favor it is that our might is ex- alted;

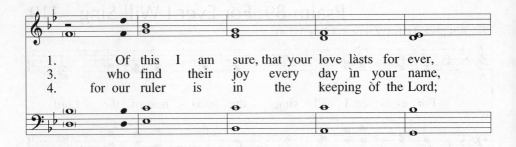

1. Of this I am sure, that your love làsts for ever,
3. who find their joy every day ìn your name,
4. for our ruler is in the keeping òf the Lord;

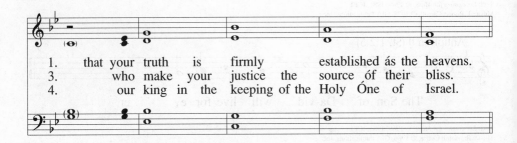

1. that your truth is firmly established ás the heavens.
3. who make your justice the source óf their bliss.
4. our king in the keeping of the Holy Óne of Israel.

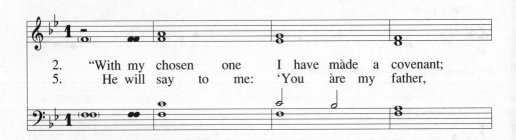

2. "With my chosen one I have màde a covenant;
5. He will say to me: 'You àre my father,

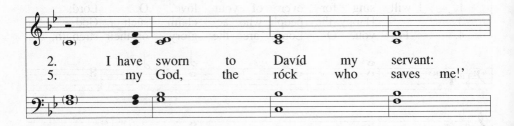

2. I have sworn to Davíd my servant:
5. my God, the róck who saves me!'

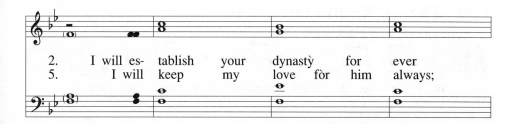

2. I will es- tablish your dynastỳ for ever
5. I will keep my love fòr him always;

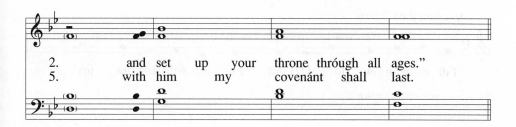

2. and set up your throne thróugh all ages."
5. with him my covenánt shall last.

Text: Psalm 89:2-3, 4-5, 16-17, 18-19, 27, 29; The Grail
Music: Joseph Gelineau, SJ
© 1963, 1993, The Grail, GIA Publications, Inc., agent

120   Psalm 90: In Every Age

Antiphon I (St. 2.3.7.8ab & 9cde)

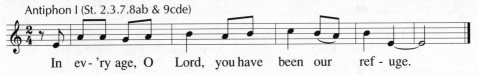

In ev-'ry age, O Lord, you have been our ref - uge.

Text: *Lectionary for Mass,* © 1969, 1981, ICEL
Music: Eugene Englert, © 1986, GIA Publications, Inc.

Antiphon II (St. 7.8.9)

Fill us with your love, O Lord, and we will sing for joy!

Text: *Lectionary for Mass,* © 1969, 1981, ICEL
Music: Robert J. Batastini, © 1975, 1995, GIA Publications, Inc.

Antiphon III (Vs. 2.3-4.12-13.14.16)

Lord, give suc - cess to the work of our hands.

Text: *Lectionary for Mass,* © 1969, 1981, ICEL
Music: Richard Proulx, © 1986, GIA Publications, Inc.

Psalm Tone

Repeat for 5-line stanza

Music: A. Gregory Murray, OSB, © L. J. Carey and Co., Ltd.

Gelineau Tone

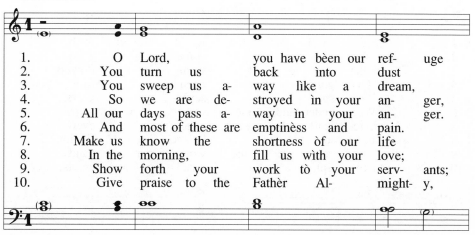

1.	O	Lord,	you have bèen our	ref-	uge
2.	You	turn us	back ìnto	dust	
3.	You	sweep us a-	way lìke a	dream,	
4.	So	we are de-	stroyed ìn your	an-	ger,
5.	All our	days pass a-	way ìn your	an-	ger.
6.	And	most of these are	emptinèss and	pain.	
7.	Make us	know the	shortness òf our	life	
8.	In the	morning,	fill us wìth your	love;	
9.	Show	forth your	work tò your	serv-	ants;
10.	Give	praise to the	Fathèr Al-	might-	y,

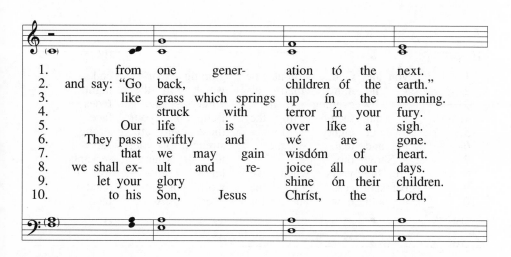

1.		from one gener-	ation tó the	next.	
2.	and say: "Go	back,	children óf the	earth."	
3.		like	grass which springs	up ín the	morning.
4.			struck with	terror ín your	fury.
5.		Our	life is	over líke a	sigh.
6.		They pass	swiftly and	wé are	gone.
7.		that	we may gain	wisdóm of	heart.
8.	we shall ex-	ult and re-	joice áll our	days.	
9.		let your	glory	shine ón their	children.
10.		to his	Son, Jesus	Chríst, the	Lord,

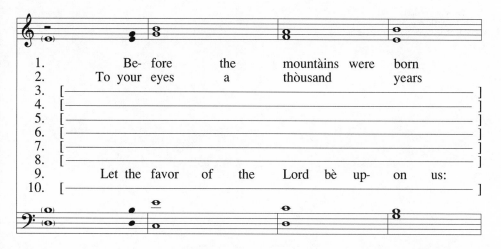

1.	Be-	fore the	mountàins were	born	
2.	To your	eyes a	thòusand	years	
3.	[				]
4.	[				]
5.	[				]
6.	[				]
7.	[				]
8.	[				]
9.	Let the	favor of	the Lord bè up-	on	us:
10.	[				]

1. or the earth or the wòrld brought forth,
2. are like yesterday, còme and gone,
3. In the morning it springs ùp and flowers;
4. Our guilt lies opèn be- fore you,
5. Our span is sevèn- ty years,
6. Who understands the power òf your anger
7. Lord, re- lent! Is your angèr for ever?
8. Give us joy to balance òur af- fliction
9. give suc- cess to the work òf our hands
10. to the Spirit who dwells ìn our hearts,

1. you are God, without be- ginníng or end.
2. no more than a watch ín the night.
3. by evening it withérs and fades.
4. our secrets in the light óf your face.
5. or eighty for those whó are strong.
6. and fears the strength óf your fury?
7. Show pity tó your servants.
8. for the years when we knéw mis- fortune.
9. (give suc- cess to the work óf our hands).
10. both now and for evér. A- men.

Text: Psalm 90; The Grail
Music: Joseph Gelineau, SJ
© 1963, 1993, GIA Publications, Inc., agent

Psalm 90: Fill Us with Your Love, O Lord 121

Refrain

Descant:
Fill us Lord, with your love, and

Melody:
Fill us with your love, O Lord, and

we will sing for joy!

we will sing for joy!

Verses 1, 2

1. Teach us to num-ber our days, that we may
2. Fill us at dawn with your kind-ness, that we may

gain wis-dom of heart. Re-turn, O Lord our
shout for joy and glad-ness. Make us glad for the days when you af-

D.C.

God, have pit-y on your ser-vants.
lict-ed us, for the years when we saw e-vil.

Verse 3

3. Let your work be seen by your ser-vants, and your glo-ry by their

D.C.

chil-dren. May your gra-cious care be ours. Pros-per the work of our hands.

Text: Psalm 90; Roy James Stewart, © 1993, GIA Publications, Inc.; refrain trans. © 1969 ICEL
Music: Roy James Stewart, © 1993, GIA Publications, Inc.

122 Psalm 91: My Refuge, My Stronghold

Antiphon I

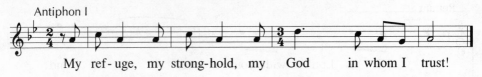

My ref-uge, my strong-hold, my God in whom I trust!

Text: The Grail
Music: A. Gregory Murray, OSB
© 1963, The Grail, GIA Publications, Inc., agent

Antiphon II

Call up-on the Lord and he will hear you.

Text: The Grail
Music: Joseph Gelineau, SJ
© 1963, The Grail, GIA Publications, Inc., agent

Antiphon III

Night holds no ter-rors for me sleep-ing un-der God's wings.

Text: *Liturgy of the Hours,* © 1974, ICEL
Music: Peter Hallock, acc. by Michael Connolly, © 1986, GIA Publications, Inc.

Psalm Tone

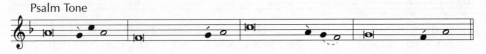

Music: Richard Proulx, © 1986, GIA Publications, Inc.

Gelineau Tone

1. Those who dwell in the shelter of thè Most High
2. It is God who will free you fròm the snare
3. You will not fear the terror òf the night
4. A thousand may fall àt your side,
5. Your eyes have onlỳ to look

1. and a- bide in the shade of the Ál- mighty
2. of the fowler who seeks to dé- stroy you;
3. nor the arrow that flies bý day,
4. ten thousand fall at yóur right,
5. to see how the wicked are ré- paid,

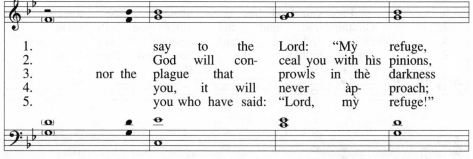

1. say to the Lord: "Mỳ refuge,
2. God will con- ceal you with hìs pinions,
3. nor the plague that prowls in thè darkness
4. you, it will never àp- proach;
5. you who have said: "Lord, mỳ refuge!"

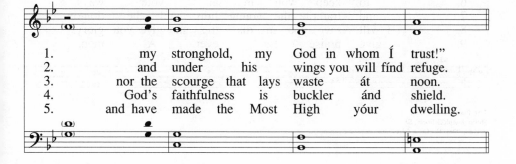

1. my stronghold, my God in whom Í trust!"
2. and under his wings you will fínd refuge.
3. nor the scourge that lays waste át noon.
4. God's faithfulness is buckler ánd shield.
5. and have made the Most High yóur dwelling.

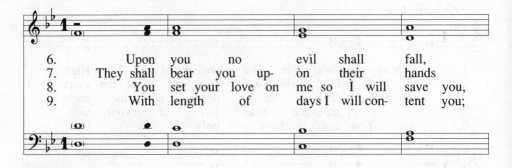

6. Upon you no evìl shall fall,
7. They shall bear you up- òn their hands
8. You set your love on me so Ì will save you,
9. With length of days I wìll con- tent you;

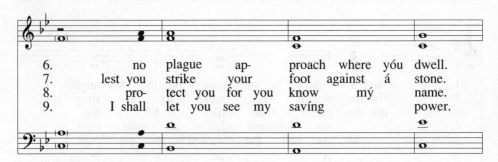

6. no plague ap- proach where yóu dwell.
7. lest you strike your foot against á stone.
8. pro- tect you for you know mý name.
9. I shall let you see my saving power.

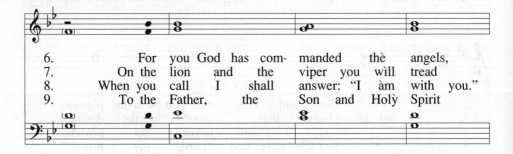

6. For you God has com- manded thè angels,
7. On the lion and the viper you wìll tread
8. When you call I shall answer: "I àm with you."
9. To the Father, the Son and Holỳ Spirit

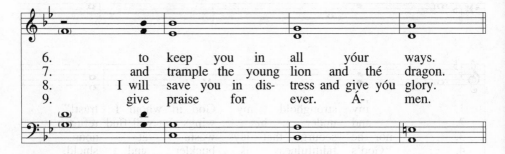

6. to keep you in all yóur ways.
7. and trample the young lion and thé dragon.
8. I will save you in dis- tress and give yóu glory.
9. give praise for ever. Á- men.

Text: Psalm 91; The Grail
Music: Joseph Gelineau, SJ
© 1963, 1993, The Grail, GIA Publications, Inc., agent

Psalm 91: Be with Me 123

Refrain

mf

Be with me, Lord, when I am in trou-ble, be

with me, Lord, I pray.

To verses

Last time

pray.

Verse 1

mf

1. You who dwell in the shel-ter of the Lord, Most High, who a-

bide in the shad-ow of our God, *f* say to the

Lord: "My ref-uge and for-tress, the God in whom I trust." D.C.

Verse 2

p div.

2. No e-vil shall be-fall you, no pain come near, for the

an-gels stand close by your side, *mp* guard-ing you

al - ways and bear - ing you gent - ly,

D.C.

watch - ing o - ver your life.

Verse 3   *mp*

3. Those who cling to the Lord live se - cure in God's

love, lift - ed high, those who trust in God's

div. **f**

name, call on the Lord who will

f

nev - er for - sake you. God will bring you sal -

D.C.

va - tion and joy.

Text: Psalm 91: 1-2, 10-11, 14-15; Marty Haugen
Music: Marty Haugen
© 1980, GIA Publications, Inc.

Psalm 92: Lord, It Is Good   124

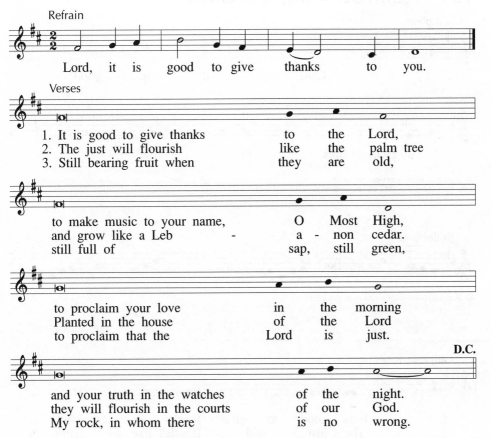

Refrain

Lord, it is good to give thanks to you.

Verses

1. It is good to give thanks to the Lord,
2. The just will flourish like the palm tree
3. Still bearing fruit when they are old,

to make music to your name, O Most High,
and grow like a Leb - a - non cedar.
still full of sap, still green,

to proclaim your love in the morning
Planted in the house of the Lord
to proclaim that the Lord is just.

D.C.

and your truth in the watches of the night.
they will flourish in the courts of our God.
My rock, in whom there is no wrong.

Text: Psalm 92:2-3, 13-14, 15-16; © 1963, 1993, The Grail, GIA Publications, Inc., agent; refrain trans. © 1969, ICEL
Music: Michel Guimont, © 1994, GIA Publications, Inc.

125   Psalm 92: Lord, It Is Good

Antiphon

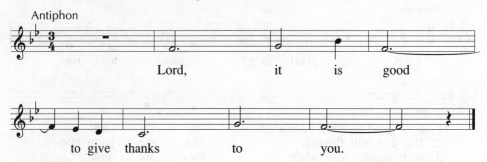

Lord,   it   is   good

to give thanks   to   you.

Text: *Lectionary for Mass,* © 1969, 1981, ICEL
Music: Richard Proulx, © 1975, GIA Publications, Inc.

Psalm Tone

Music: Richard Proulx, © 1986, GIA Publications, Inc.

Gelineau Tone

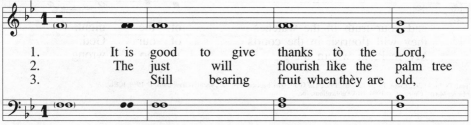

1.   It is   good   to   give   thanks tò   the   Lord,
2.   The   just   will   flourish lìke the   palm tree
3.   Still   bearing fruit when thèy are old,

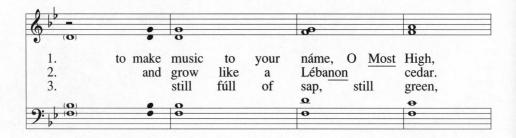

1.   to make music   to   your   náme, O <u>Most</u> High,
2.   and   grow   like   a   <u>Lébanon</u>   cedar.
3.   still   fúll   of   sap, still   green,

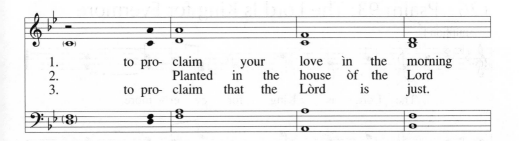

1. to pro- claim   your   love   in   the   morning
2.   Planted in   the   house òf   the Lord
3. to pro- claim   that   the   Lòrd is   just.

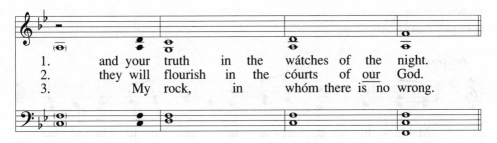

1. and your truth   in   the   wátches of   the night.
2. they will flourish in   the   córts   of   our   God.
3.   My   rock,   in   whóm there is no wrong.

Text: Psalm 92:2-3, 13-14, 15-16; The Grail
Music: Joseph Gelineau, SJ
© 1963, 1993, GIA Publications, Inc., agent

126 Psalm 93: The Lord Is King for Evermore

Antiphon I

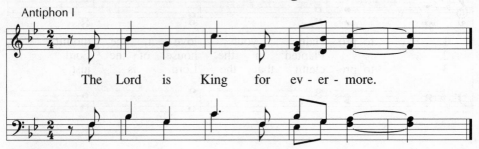

The Lord is King for ev-er-more.

Text: Psalm 93; The Grail
Music: A. Gregory Murray, OSB
© 1963, The Grail, GIA Publications, Inc., agent

Antiphon II

Al - le - lu - ia, al - le - lu - ia, al - le - lu - ia.

Music: A. Gregory Murray, OSB, © 1963, The Grail, GIA Publications, Inc, agent

Psalm Tone

Music: Psalm tone 8-g; acc. by Richard Proulx, © 1975, GIA Publications, Inc.

Gelineau Tone

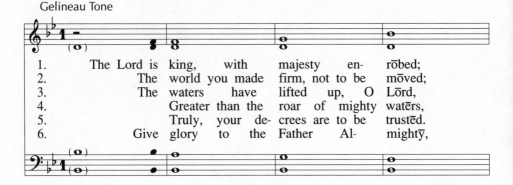

1. The Lord is king, with majesty en-rōbed;
2. The world you made firm, not to be mōved;
3. The waters have lifted up, O Lōrd,
4. Greater than the roar of mighty watērs,
5. Truly, your de-crees are to be trustēd.
6. Give glory to the Father Al-mightȳ,

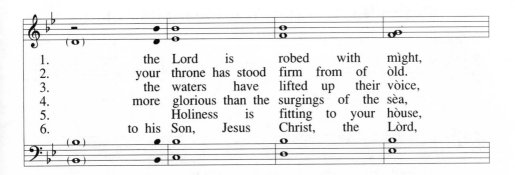

1.	the Lord is	robed with mìght,
2.	your throne has stood	firm from of òld.
3.	the waters have	lifted up their vòice,
4.	more glorious than the	surgings of the sèa,
5.	Holiness is	fitting to your hòuse,
6.	to his Son, Jesus	Christ, the Lòrd,

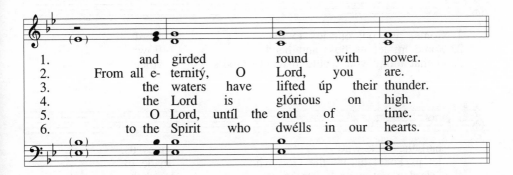

1.	and girded	round with power.
2.	From all e- ternitý, O	Lord, you are.
3.	the waters have	lifted úp their thunder.
4.	the Lord is	glórious on high.
5.	O Lord, untíl the	end of time.
6.	to the Spirit who	dwélls in our hearts.

Text: Psalm 93; The Grail
Music: Joseph Gelineau, SJ
© 1963, 1993, The Grail, GIA Publications, Inc., agent

127 Psalm 95: If Today You Hear His Voice

Refrain

If to - day you hear his voice,

hard - en not your hearts.

Verses

1. Come, ring out our joy to the   Lord;
2. Come in; let us bow and bend   low;
3. O that today you would listen to God's voice!

hail the rock who   saves us.
let us kneel before the God who made us
"Harden not your hearts as at Meribah,

Let us come before God, giv - ing thanks, with
for this   is our God { and we the
                 the
as on that day at Massah in the desert { when your
                when they

D.C.

songs let us   hail the Lord.
people who belong to his pasture, }
flock that is led by his hand. }
ancestors put me to the test; }
tried me, though they saw my work." }

Text: Psalm 95:1-2, 6-7, 8-9; © 1963, 1993, The Grail, GIA Publications, Inc., agent; refrain trans. © 1969, ICEL
Music: Michel Guimont, © 1995, GIA Publications, Inc.

Psalm 95: If Today You Hear His Voice   128

Refrain

If to - day you hear his voice, hard-en not your

hearts, hard - en not your hearts.

Last time *To verses*

Verse 1

1. Come, let us sing joy-ful-ly to the Lord; let us ac - claim the

rock of our sal - va - tion. Let us greet him with thanks-

giv - ing, sing joy - ful psalms to him.

D.C.

Verse 2

2. Come, let us bow down in wor-ship; let us kneel be -

fore the Lord who made us, for he is our

God and we the flock he guides.

Verse 3

3. O, that to - day you would hear his voice! Hard - en

not your hearts as in the days in the

des - ert where your fa - thers test - ed me.

Psalm 95: If Today You Hear God's Voice   129

Refrain

If to-day you hear God's voice,

hard-en not your hearts. If to-

day you hear God's voice, hard-en not your

hearts.

To verses | Final ending

Verse 1

1. Come, ring out our joy to the Lord,

hail the rock who saves us,

let us come now be - fore our God, with

songs let us hail the Lord.

Verse 2

2. Come, let us bow and bend low,

let us kneel be - fore God who made us,

for here is our God; we the peo -

ple, the flock that is led by God's hand.

Verse 3

3. O that to - day you would hear God's voice,

"Hard - en not your hearts, as

on that day in the des - ert, when your

par - ents put me to the test."

Text: Psalm 95:1-2, 6-7, 8-9; David Haas
Music: David Haas
© 1983, 1994, GIA Publications, Inc.

Psalm 96: Today Is Born Our Savior 130

Refrain ♩.= ca. 60

To - day is born our Sav-ior, Christ the Lord. To -

day is born our Sav - ior, Christ the Lord.

Verse 1

1. Sing to the Lord a new song; sing to the Lord, all you

D.C.

lands. Sing to the Lord; bless his name.

Verse 2

2. An-nounce his sal - va - tion, day af - ter day. Tell his glo-ry a -

D.C.

mong the na-tions; A - mong all peo-ples, his won - drous deeds.

Verse 3

3. Let the heav - ens be glad and the earth re -

joice; let the sea and what fills it re-sound;

let the plains be joy-ful and all that is in them!

Then shall all the trees of the for-est ex-ult. **D.C.**

Verse 4

4. They shall ex-ult be-fore the Lord, for he

comes; for he comes to rule the

earth. He shall rule the world with

jus-tice and the peo-ples with his con-stan-cy. **D.C.**

Music: Psalm 96; verses tr. © 1970, Confraternity of Christian Doctrine, Washington, D.C.; refrain tr. © 1969, ICEL
Music: Howard Hughes, SM, © 1976, GIA Publications, Inc.

Psalm 96: Great Is the Lord 131

Antiphon I

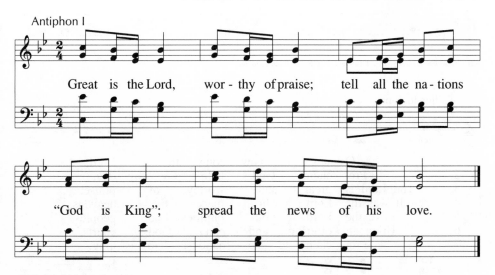

Great is the Lord, wor-thy of praise; tell all the na-tions

"God is King"; spread the news of his love.

Text: Psalm 96:3-4; The Grail
Music: Joseph Gelineau, SJ
© 1963, The Grail, GIA Publications, Inc., agent

Antiphon II

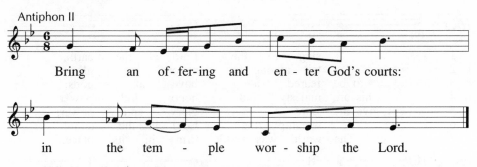

Bring an of-fer-ing and en-ter God's courts:

in the tem - ple wor - ship the Lord.

Text: Psalm 96:6; The Grail
Music: Clifford Howell, SJ
© 1963, 1993, The Grail, GIA Publications, Inc., agent

Antiphon III (St. 1.2.8.9)

To-day is born our Sav-ior, Christ the Lord.

Text: *Lectionary for Mass,* © 1969, 1981, ICEL
Music: Howard Hughes, SM, © 1975, GIA Publications, Inc.

Antiphon IV (Vs. 1.3.4-5.7-8.9-10)

Give the Lord glo-ry, glo-ry and hon - or.

Text: *Lectionary for Mass,* © 1969, 1981, ICEL
Music: Richard Proulx, © 1986, GIA Publications, Inc.

Psalm Tone

Music: Chant tone 5; acc. by Robert J. Batastini, © 1975, GIA Publications, Inc.

Gelineau Tone

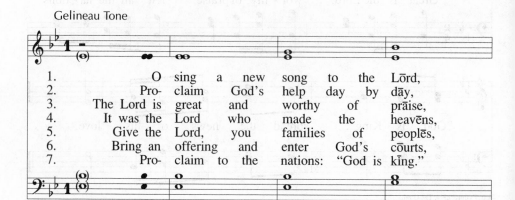

1.   O   sing   a   new   song   to   the   Lōrd,
2.   Pro-   claim   God's   help   day   by   dāy,
3. The Lord is   great   and   worthy   of   prāise,
4. It was the   Lord   who   made   the   heavēns,
5. Give the   Lord,   you   families   of   peoplēs,
6. Bring an   offering   and   enter   God's   cōurts,
7.   Pro-   claim   to   the   nations: "God is kīng."

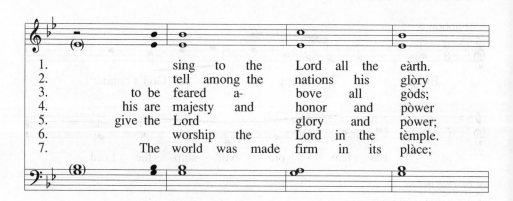

1.   sing   to   the   Lord   all   the   eàrth.
2.   tell   among the   nations   his   glòry
3.   to be   feared   a-   bove   all   gòds;
4.   his are   majesty   and   honor   and   pòwer
5.   give the   Lord   glory   and   pòwer;
6.   worship   the   Lord   in   the   tèmple.
7.   The   world   was   made   firm   in   its   plàce;

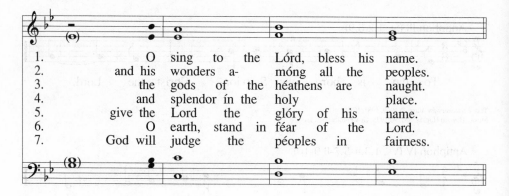

1.   O   sing   to   the   Lórd,   bless   his   name.
2.   and his   wonders a-   móng   all   the   peoples.
3.   the   gods   of   the   héathens   are   naught.
4.   and   splendor ín the   holy   place.
5.   give the   Lord   the   glóry   of   his   name.
6.   O   earth,   stand   in   féar   of   the   Lord.
7.   God will   judge   the   péoples   in   fairness.

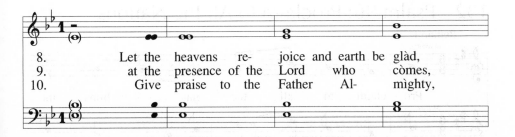

8. Let the heavens re- joice and earth be glàd,
9. at the presence of the Lord who còmes,
10. Give praise to the Father Al- mìghty,

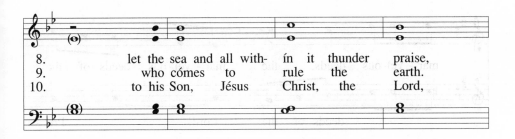

8. let the sea and all with- ín it thunder praise,
9. who cómes to rule the earth.
10. to his Son, Jésus Christ, the Lord,

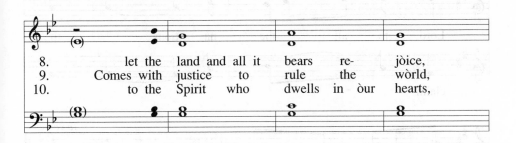

8. let the land and all it bears re- jòice,
9. Comes with justice to rule the wòrld,
10. to the Spirit who dwells in òur hearts,

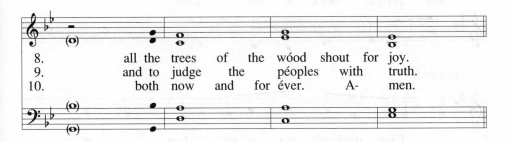

8. all the trees of the wóod shout for joy.
9. and to judge the péoples with truth.
10. both now and for éver. A- men.

Text: Psalm 96; The Grail
Music: Joseph Gelineau, SJ
© 1963, 1993, The Grail, GIA Publications, Inc., agent

132 Psalm 96: Proclaim to All the Nations

Refrain I

Descant:
Pro - claim   to   all   the   na - tions   the

Melody:
na - tions

mar - vel-ous deeds,   the   mar - vel- ous deeds of the

deeds of the   Lord!   Pro -

Lord, to all   the   na - tions   the

claim

To verses

mar - vel- ous deeds of the   Lord!

Refrain II

Descant:
Give the Lord glo - ry and hon - or.

Melody:
hon - or.

To verses

Give the Lord glo - ry and hon - or.

Verses 1, 3, 4

1. Sing to the Lord a new song.
3. Give to the Lord, you na - tions,
4. Wor - ship the Lord, and trem - ble, pro -

Sing to the Lord all you lands!
praise to the Lord of all! Sing
claim the one who reigns!

Sing to the Lord with all your heart,
glo - ry and praise and sing to the name,
Say to the na - tions: "The Lord is King;"

To refrain

and bless God's name!
a - bove all names!
who rules with jus - tice!

Verse 2

2. An - nounce sal - va - tion day by day, God's

glo - ry through - out the earth! A -

mong all the peo - ple in ev - 'ry land,

To refrain

God's won - drous deeds!

Text: Psalm 96:1-2, 3, 7-8, 9; David Haas, © 1989, GIA Publications, Inc.; refrains trans. © 1969, ICEL
Music: Marty Haugen; refrain I, David Haas; refrain II adapt. by Diana Kodner; © 1989, 1994, GIA Publications, Inc.

133 Psalm 97: The Lord Is King

Antiphon (St. 1.3.4 or 1.2.4)

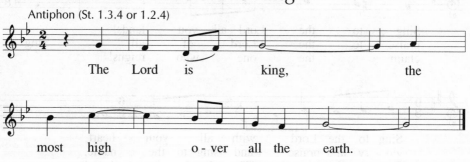

The Lord is king, the

most high o - ver all the earth.

Text: *Lectionary for Mass,* © 1969, 1981, ICEL
Music: Richard Proulx, © 1975, GIA Publications, Inc.

Psalm Tone

Music: Psalm tone 8-g; acc. by Richard Proulx, © 1975, GIA Publications, Inc.

Gelineau Tone

1. The Lord is king, let earth re- joice,
2. The mountains melt like wax
3. The skies pro- claim God's justice;
4. For you in- deed are the Lōrd

1.   let   all   the   cóastlands   be   glad.
2.   be-   fore   the   Lórd   of   all   the   earth.
3.   [
4.   [

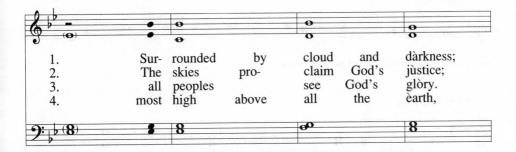

1.   Sur-   rounded   by   cloud   and   dàrkness;
2.   The   skies   pro-   claim   God's   jùstice;
3.   all   peoples   see   God's   glòry.
4.   most   high   above   all   the   èarth,

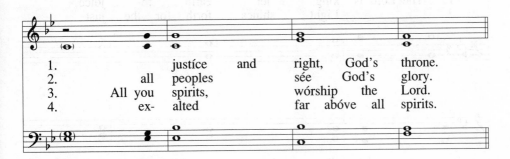

1.   justíce   and   right,   God's   throne.
2.   all   peoples   sée   God's   glory.
3.   All   you   spirits,   wórship   the   Lord.
4.   ex-   alted   far   abóve   all   spirits.

Text: Psalm 97:1-2, 5-6, 6-7, 9; The Grail
Music: Joseph Gelineau, SJ

134   Psalm 97: A Light Will Shine

Antiphon

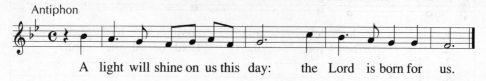

A light will shine on us this day: the Lord is born for us.

Psalm Tone

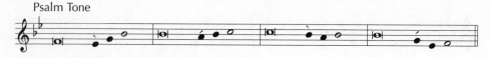

Gelineau Tone

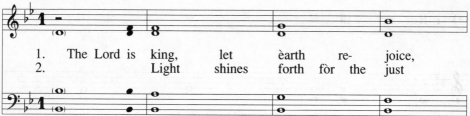

1.   The Lord is   king,   let   èarth   re-   joice,
2.   Light   shines   forth   fòr the   just

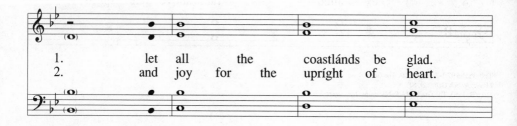

1.   let   all   the   coastlánds   be   glad.
2.   and   joy   for   the   upríght   of   heart.

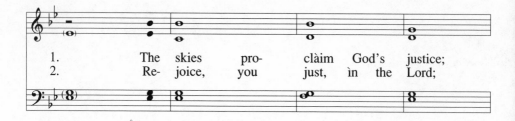

1.   The   skies   pro-   clàim   God's   justice;
2.   Re-   joice,   you   just,   ìn   the   Lord;

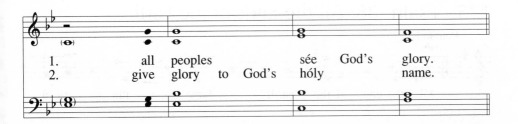

1.   all   peoples   sée   God's   glory.
2.   give   glory   to   God's   hóly   name.

Text: Psalm 97:1, 6, 11-12; The Grail
Music: Joseph Gelineau, SJ

135 Psalm 98: All the Ends of the Earth

Refrain III
unis.

The Lord comes to the earth to rule the earth with jus-tice. The Lord comes to the earth to rule the earth with jus-tice.

div.

To verses

Verse 1

1. Sing to the Lord a new song, for God has done won - drous deeds; whose right hand has won the vic - t'ry for us,

To refrain

God's ho - ly arm.

Verse 2

2. The Lord has made sal - va - tion known, and jus - tice re - vealed to all, re -

mem - ber - ing kind - ness and faith - ful - ness

To refrain

to Is - ra - el.

Verse 3

3. All of the ends of earth have seen sal -

va - tion by our God.

Joy - ful - ly sing out all you lands,

To refrain

break forth in song.

Verse 4

4. Sing to the Lord with harp and song, with

trum - pet and with horn.

Sing in your joy be - fore the king,

To refrain

the king, our Lord.

Text: Psalm 98:1, 2-3, 3-4, 5-6; David Haas, Marty Haugen
Music: David Haas, Marty Haugen; refrain II, III adapt. by Diana Kodner
© 1983, 1994, GIA Publications, Inc.

Psalm 98: All the Ends of the Earth 136

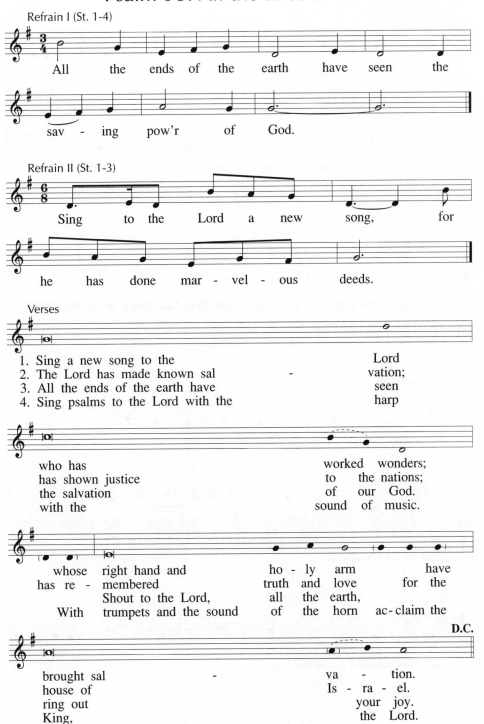

Refrain I (St. 1-4)

All the ends of the earth have seen the sav - ing pow'r of God.

Refrain II (St. 1-3)

Sing to the Lord a new song, for he has done mar - vel - ous deeds.

Verses

1. Sing a new song to the Lord
2. The Lord has made known sal - vation;
3. All the ends of the earth have seen
4. Sing psalms to the Lord with the harp

who has worked wonders;
has shown justice to the nations;
the salvation of our God.
with the sound of music.

whose right hand and ho - ly arm have
has re - membered truth and love for the
Shout to the Lord, all the earth,
With trumpets and the sound of the horn ac- claim the

D.C.

brought sal - va - tion.
house of Is - ra - el.
ring out your joy.
King, the Lord.

Text: Psalm 98:1, 2-3, 3-4, 5-6; © 1963, 1993, The Grail, GIA Publications, Inc., agent; refrains trans. © 1969, ICEL
Music: Michel Guimont, © 1995, GIA Publications, Inc.

137 Psalm 98: All the Ends of the Earth

Antiphon I (St. 1-4)

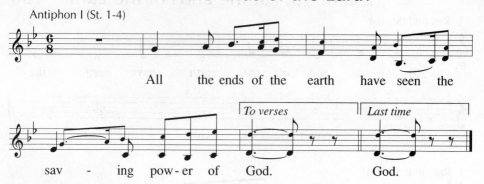

All the ends of the earth have seen the sav - ing pow-er of God. God.

Antiphon II (St. 1-3)

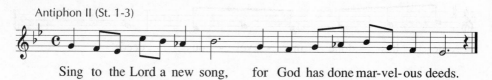

Sing to the Lord a new song, for God has done mar-vel-ous deeds.

Antiphon III (St. 1-3)

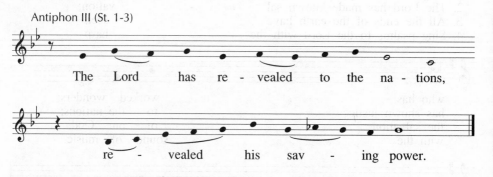

The Lord has re - vealed to the na - tions, re - vealed his sav - ing power.

Psalm Tone

Gelineau Tone

1. Sing a new song tò the Lord
2. The Lord has made knòwn sal- vation;
3. All the ends of the eàrth have seen
4. Sing psalms to the Lord wìth the harp

1. who hás worked wonders;
2. has shown justice tó the nations;
3. the sal- vation óf our God.
4. with the sóund of music.

1. whose right hand and hòly arm
2. has re- membered trùth and love
3. Shout to the Lord, àll the earth,
4. With trumpets and the sound òf the horn

1. have bróught sal- vation.
2. for the hóuse of Israel.
3. ring óut your joy.
4. acclaim the Kíng, the Lord.

Text: Psalm 98:1, 2-3, 3-4, 5-6; The Grail
Music: Joseph Gelineau, SJ
© 1963, 1993, The Grail, GIA Publications, Inc., agent

138 Psalm 100: We Are God's People

Ostinato Refrain

Sopranos:

We are God's peo - ple, the flock of the Lord.

Tenors:

Altos:

Last time

Verses 1, 3

1. Cry out with joy to the Lord, all you lands,
3. Go, now with - in the gates giv-ing thanks,

all you lands.   Serve the Lord now with
giv-ing thanks.   En - ter the courts sing-ing

To refrain

glad-ness,   come be - fore God sing-ing for joy!
praise,   give thanks and bless God's name!

Verse 2

2. Know that the Lord is God!   Know that the

Lord is God,   who made us, to God we be -

To refrain

long,   God's peo-ple, the sheep of the flock!

Verse 4

4. In - deed, how good is the Lord, whose mer-cy en -

To refrain

dures for ev-er, for the Lord, is faith-ful,

is faith-ful from age to age!

Text: Psalm 100:1-2, 3, 4, 5; David Haas
Music: David Haas

139 Psalm 100: Arise, Come to Your God

Antiphon I

A - rise,   come   to   your   God,

sing   him   your   songs   of   re - joic   -   ing.

Text: Joseph Gelineau
Music: Joseph Gelineau
© 1963, The Grail, GIA Publications, Inc., agent

Antiphon II

Al - le - lu - ia,   al - le - lu - ia,   al - le - lu - ia.

Music: A. Gregory Murray, OSB, © 1963, The Grail, GIA Publications, Inc., agent

Psalm Tone

Music: Chant tone 8-g; acc. by Richard Proulx, © 1975, GIA Publications, Inc.

Gelineau Tone

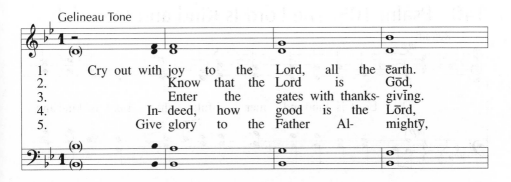

1. Cry out with joy to the Lord, all the earth.
2. Know that the Lord is God,
3. Enter the gates with thanks- giving.
4. In- deed, how good is the Lord,
5. Give glory to the Father Al- mighty,

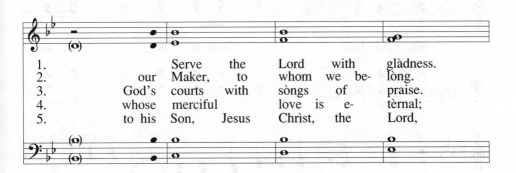

1. Serve the Lord with gladness.
2. our Maker, to whom we be- long.
3. God's courts with songs of praise.
4. whose merciful love is e- ternal;
5. to his Son, Jesus Christ, the Lord,

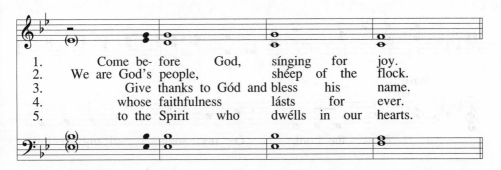

1. Come be- fore God, singing for joy.
2. We are God's people, sheep of the flock.
3. Give thanks to God and bless his name.
4. whose faithfulness lasts for ever.
5. to the Spirit who dwells in our hearts.

Text: Psalm 100; The Grail
Music: Joseph Gelineau, SJ
© 1963, 1993, The Grail, GIA Publications, Inc., agent

140   Psalm 103: The Lord Is Kind and Merciful

Refrain

The Lord is kind and mer - ci - ful; the Lord is kind and mer - ci - ful.

Slow to an - ger, rich in kind - ness, the Lord is kind and mer - ci - ful.

[1.-3. *To verses*] [4.]

Verse 1

1. Bless the Lord, O my soul; all my be - ing bless God's name. Bless the Lord, O my soul; for - get not all God's bless - ings.

D.C.

Verse 2

mp

2. The Lord is gra - cious and mer - ci - ful, slow to an - ger,

div. *p*

full of kind - ness. God is good to all cre - a - tion,

unis. D.C.

full of com - pas - sion.

Verse 3

mp

3. The good - ness of God is from age to age, bless - ing those who

div. *p*

choose to love. And jus - tice toward God's chil - dren; on

unis. D.C.

all who keep the cov - e - nant.

Text: Psalm 103; Jeanne Cotter
Music: Jeanne Cotter
© 1993, GIA Publications, Inc.

141   Psalm 103: The Lord Has Set His Throne

Antiphon I (St. 1.5.9)

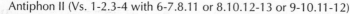

The Lord has set his throne in heav-en.

Text: *Lectionary for Mass,* © 1969, 1981, ICEL
Music: Marty Haugen, © 1986, GIA Publications, Inc.

Antiphon II (Vs. 1-2.3-4 with 6-7.8.11 or 8.10.12-13 or 9-10.11-12)

The Lord is kind and mer - ci - ful.

Text: *Lectionary for Mass,* © 1969, 1981, ICEL
Music: David Haas, © 1986, GIA Publications, Inc.

Antiphon III (St. 1-4)

The Lord's kind - ness is ev - er - last - ing to those who fear him.

Text: *Lectionary for Mass,* © 1969, 1981, ICEL
Music: Howard Hughes, SM, © 1975, GIA Publications, Inc.

Psalm Tone

Music: Richard Proulx, © 1975, GIA Publications, Inc.

Gelineau Tone

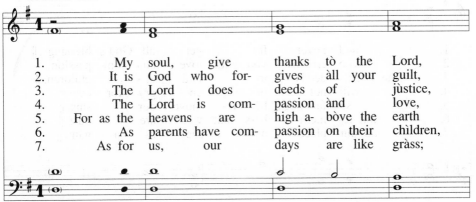

1.   My   soul,   give   thanks   tò   the   Lord,
2.   It is God   who for-   gives   àll   your   guilt,
3.   The   Lord   does   deeds   of   jùstice,
4.   The   Lord is   com-   passion ànd   love,
5.   For as the heavens   are   high a- bòve the earth
6.   As   parents have com- passion on their chìldren,
7.   As for   us,   our   days   are like   gràss;

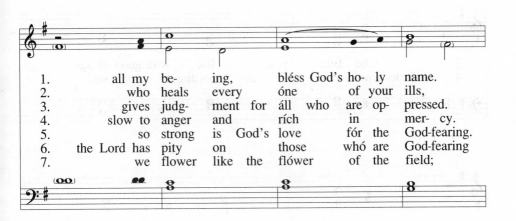

1.   all my be-   ing,   bléss God's ho- ly   name.
2.   who heals every   óne   of your ills,
3.   gives judg- ment for áll   who   are op- pressed.
4.   slow to anger   and   rích   in   mer- cy.
5.   so   strong is God's love   fór the God-fearing.
6.   the Lord has pity   on   those   whó are God-fearing
7.   we   flower like the flówer   of the   field;

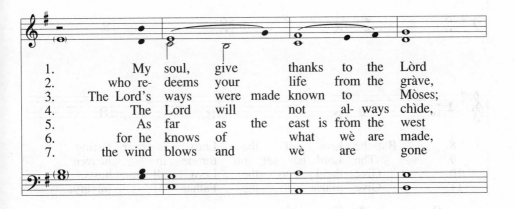

1.   My   soul,   give   thanks to   the   Lòrd
2.   who re- deems your   life   from the gràve,
3.   The Lord's ways were made known to   Mòses;
4.   The Lord will   not   al- ways chìde,
5.   As far   as   the   east is fròm the west
6.   for he knows of   what   wè are   made,
7.   the wind blows and   wè   are   gone

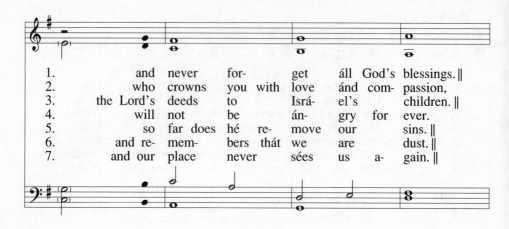

1.   and never for- get áll God's blessings. ‖
2.   who crowns you with love ánd com- passion,
3.   the Lord's deeds to Isrá- el's children. ‖
4.   will not be án- gry for ever.
5.   so far does hé re- move our sins. ‖
6.   and re- mem- bers thát we are dust. ‖
7.   and our place never sées us a- gain. ‖

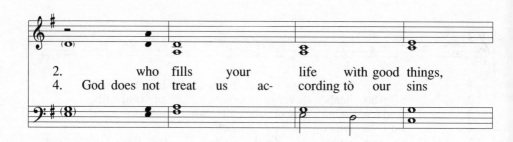

2.   who fills your life wìth good things,
4.   God does not treat us ac- cording tò our sins

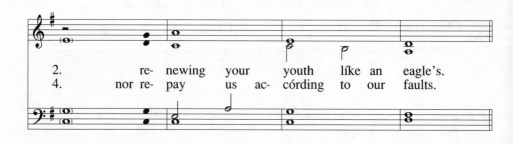

2.   re- newing your youth líke an eagle's.
4.   nor re- pay us ac- córding to our faults.

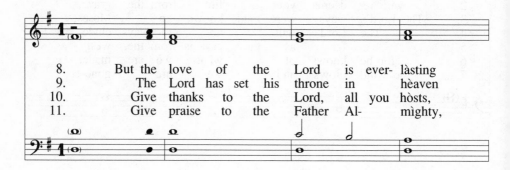

8.   But the love of the Lord is ever- làsting
9.   The Lord has set his throne in hèaven
10. Give thanks to the Lord, all you hòsts,
11. Give praise to the Father Al- mìghty,

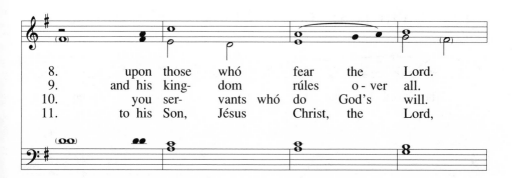

8. upon those whó fear the Lord.
9. and his king- dom rúles o - ver all.
10. you ser- vants whó do God's will.
11. to his Son, Jésus Christ, the Lord,

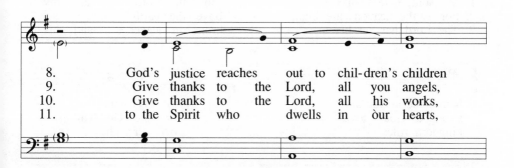

8. God's justice reaches out to chil-dren's children
9. Give thanks to the Lord, all you angels,
10. Give thanks to the Lord, all his works,
11. to the Spirit who dwells in òur hearts,

8. when they keep his cove- nant ìn truth,
9. mighty in power, ful- filling Gòd's word,
10. in ev- ery place where Gòd rules.
11. [————————————————————————————]

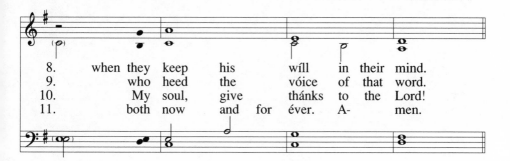

8. when they keep his wíll in their mind.
9. who heed the vóice of that word.
10. My soul, give thánks to the Lord!
11. both now and for éver. A- men.

Text: Psalm 103; The Grail
Music: Joseph Gelineau, SJ
© 1963, 1993, The Grail, GIA Publications, Inc., agent

142   Psalm 103: The Lord Has Set His Throne

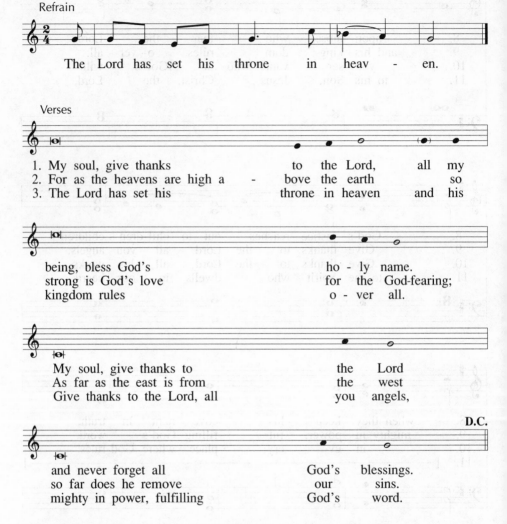

Refrain

The Lord has set his throne in heav - en.

Verses

1. My soul, give thanks   to   the Lord,   all   my
2. For as the heavens are high a   -   bove the earth   so
3. The Lord has set his   throne in heaven   and   his

being, bless God's   ho - ly name.
strong is God's love   for   the God-fearing;
kingdom rules   o - ver all.

My soul, give thanks to   the   Lord
As far as the east is from   the   west
Give thanks to the Lord, all   you   angels,

D.C.

and never forget all   God's   blessings.
so far does he remove   our   sins.
mighty in power, fulfilling   God's   word.

Text: Psalm 103:1-2, 11-12, 19-20; © 1963, 1993, The Grail, GIA Publications, Inc., agent; refrain trans. © 1969, ICEL
Music: Michel Guimont, © 1995, GIA Publications, Inc.

Psalm 103: The Lord Is Kind and Merciful   143

Refrain

The Lord is kind and mer-ci-ful, the

Lord is kind and mer-ci-ful.

Last time

Verse 1

mf

1. Bless the Lord, O my soul, and all my be-ing bless God's name;
bless the Lord, and for-get not God's ben-e-fits.

D.C.

Verse 2

mp

2. God par-dons all your in-iq-ui-ties, and com-forts your
sor-rows, re-deems your life from de-struc-tion and
crowns you with kind-ness.

D.C.

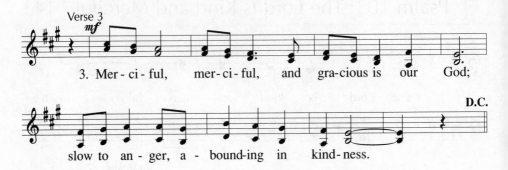

Verse 3

3. Mer - ci - ful, mer - ci - ful, and gra - cious is our God;

D.C.

slow to an - ger, a - bound-ing in kind - ness.

Text: Psalm 103:1-2, 3-4, 8; para. by Marty Haugen, © 1983, GIA Publications, Inc.; refrain trans. © 1969, ICEL
Music: Marty Haugen, © 1983, GIA Publications, Inc.

Psalm 104: Lord, Send Out Your Spirit   144

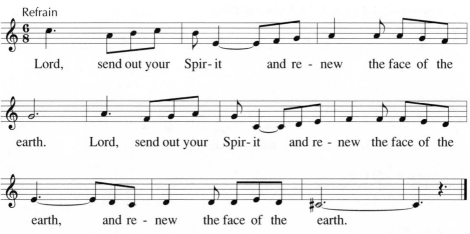

Lord, send out your Spir-it and re-new the face of the earth. Lord, send out your Spir-it and re-new the face of the earth, and re-new the face of the earth.

Text: *Lectionary for Mass,* © 1969, 1981, ICEL
Music: Alexander Peloquin, © 1971, GIA Publications, Inc.

Verses

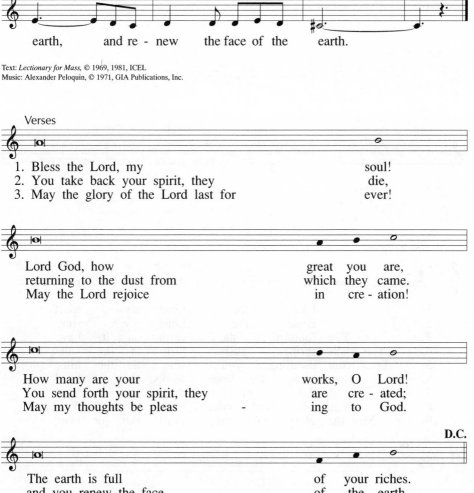

1. Bless the Lord, my   soul!
2. You take back your spirit, they   die,
3. May the glory of the Lord last for   ever!

Lord God, how   great you are,
returning to the dust from   which they came.
May the Lord rejoice   in   cre - ation!

How many are your   works, O Lord!
You send forth your spirit, they   are   cre - ated;
May my thoughts be pleas   -   ing   to God.

D.C.

The earth is full   of   your riches.
and you renew the face   of   the earth.
I find my joy   in   the Lord.

Text: Psalm 104:1, 24, 29-30, 31, 34; The Grail, © 1963, 1993, GIA Publications, Inc., agent
Music: David Anderson, © 1995, GIA Publications, Inc.

145   Psalm 104: Lord, Send Out Your Spirit

Antiphon (St. 1.3.4.5.6 or 1.6.7.8 or 2.8.9)

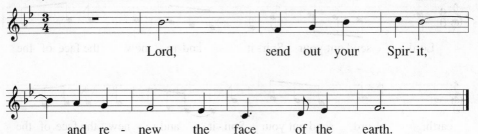

Lord, send out your Spir- it,

and re - new the face of the earth.

Text: *Lectionary for Mass,* © 1969, 1981, ICEL
Music: Richard Proulx, © 1975, GIA Publications, Inc.

Psalm Tone

Music: David Hurd, © 1986, GIA Publications, Inc.

Gelineau Tone

1.			Bless	the	Lòrd,	my	soul!
2.			Bless	the	Lòrd,	my	soul!
3.		You	founded	the	earth	òn	its	base,
4.	You make	springs	gush	forth	ìn	the	valleys;
5.	From your	dwelling	you	wa-	tèr	the	hills;
6.	How	many	are	your	wòrks,	O	Lord!
7.		All	of		these	lòok	to	you
8.		You	take	back	your	spirìt,	they	die,
9.	May the	glory	of	the	Lord	làst	for	ever!

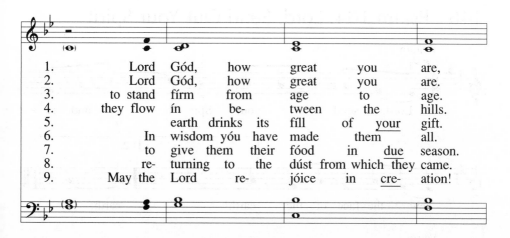

1.   Lord   Gód,   how   great   you   are,
2.   Lord   Gód,   how   great   you   are.
3.   to stand   fírm   from   age   to   age.
4.   they flow ín   be-   tween   the   hills.
5.   earth drinks its   fíll   of   your   gift.
6.   In   wisdom yóu have   made   them   all.
7.   to   give them their   fóod   in   due   season.
8.   re- turning to   the   dúst from which they came.
9.   May the Lord   re-   jóice   in   cre-   ation!

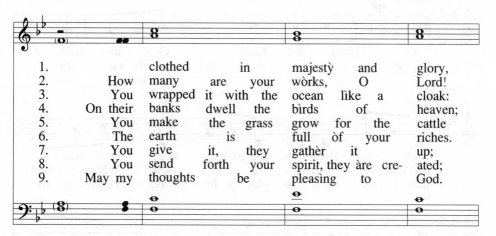

1.   clothed   in   majestỳ and   glory,
2.   How   many   are   your   wòrks,   O   Lord!
3.   You   wrapped it with the   ocean like a   cloak:
4.   On their banks   dwell the   bìrds   of   heaven;
5.   You   make   the   grass   grow for the   cattle
6.   The   earth   is   full   òf   your   riches.
7.   You   give   it,   they   gathèr   it   up;
8.   You   send   forth   your   spirit, they àre cre- ated;
9.   May my thoughts   be   pleasìng to   God.

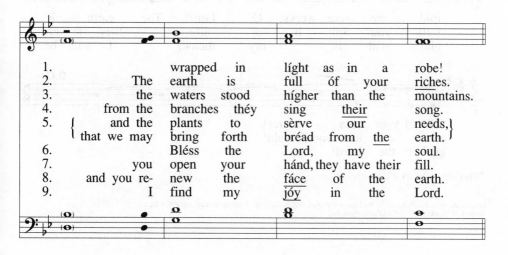

1.   wrapped   in   líght   as in   a   robe!
2.   The   earth   is   full   óf   your   riches.
3.   the   waters stood   hígher than the   mountains.
4.   from the branches théy   sing   their   song.
5.   { and the plants   to   sèrve   our   needs,}
     { that we may bring   forth   bréad from the   earth. }
6.   Bléss   the   Lord,   my   soul.
7.   you   open   your   hánd, they have their fill.
8.   and you re- new   the   fáce   of   the   earth.
9.   I   find   my   jóy   in the   Lord.

Text: Psalm 104:1-2, 1, 24, 5-6, 10, 12, 13-14, 24, 35, 27-28, 29-30, 31, 34; The Grail
Music: Joseph Gelineau, SJ
© 1963, 1993, The Grail, GIA Publications, Inc., agent

146　Psalm 104: Lord, Send Out Your Spirit

Refrain

f

Lord, send out your Spir-it, and re-new the face of the earth! earth!

Verses

mf

1. Bless the Lord, O my soul, O Lord, my God, you are great in-deed! How man-i-
2. If you take a-way their breath, they die and they re-turn to their dust. When you send
3. May his glo-ry last for all time; may the Lord be glad in his works. Pleas-ing to

fold are your works, O Lord! The earth is
forth your Spir-it of life, they are cre-
him will be my theme; I will be

f

D.C.

full of your crea-tures!
at-ed in your sight!
glad in the Lord!

May be sung as a canon.

Text: Psalm 104:1, 24, 29-30, 31, 34; Paul Lisicky, © 1985, GIA Publications, Inc.; refrain trans. © 1969, ICEL
Music: Paul Lisicky, © 1985, GIA Publications, Inc.

Psalm 107: Give Thanks to the Lord 147

Antiphon

Give thanks to the Lord, his love is ev-er-last-ing.

Text: *Lectionary for Mass*, © 1969, 1981, ICEL
Music: J. Robert Carroll, © 1975, GIA Publications, Inc.

Psalm Tone

Music: Richard Proulx, © 1975, GIA Publications, Inc.

Gelineau Tone

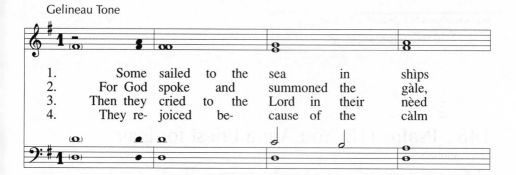

1. Some sailed to the sea in shìps
2. For God spoke and summoned the gàle,
3. Then they cried to the Lord in their nèed
4. They re-joiced be-cause of the càlm

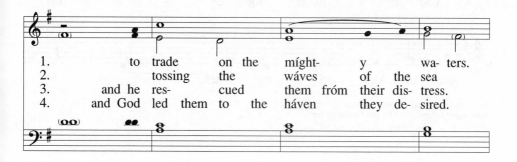

1. to trade on the míght-y wa-ters.
2. tossing the wáves of the sea
3. and he res-cued them fróm their dis-tress.
4. and God led them to the háven they de-sired.

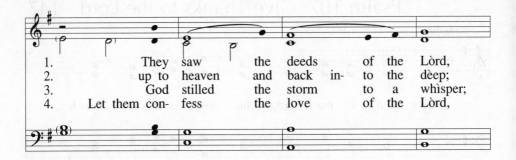

1. They saw   the deeds of the Lòrd,
2. up to heaven and back in- to the dèep;
3. God stilled the storm to a whìsper;
4. Let them con- fess the love of the Lòrd,

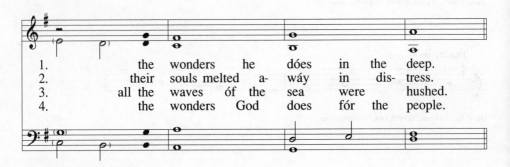

1. the wonders he dóes in the deep.
2. their souls melted a- wáy in dis- tress.
3. all the waves óf the sea were hushed.
4. the wonders God does fór the people.

Text: Psalm 107:23-24, 25-26, 28-29, 30-31; The Grail
Music: Joseph Gelineau, SJ
© 1963, 1993, The Grail, GIA Publications, Inc., agent

148   Psalm 110: You Are a Priest for Ever

Antiphon

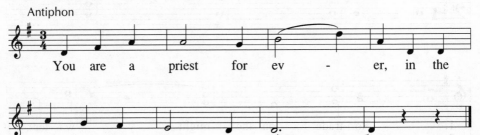

You are a priest for ev - er, in the

line of Mel - chi - ze - dek.

Text: *Lectionary for Mass,* © 1969, 1981, ICEL
Music: Robert J. Batastini, © 1975, GIA Publications, Inc.

Psalm Tone

Music: Richard Proulx, © 1975, GIA Publications, Inc.

Gelineau Tone

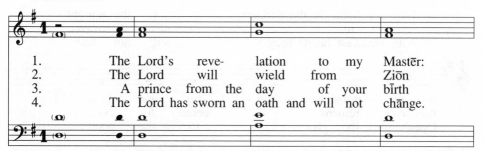

1. The Lord's reve- lation to my Mastēr:
2. The Lord will wield from Ziōn
3. A prince from the day of your bīrth
4. The Lord has sworn an oath and will not chānge.

1. "Sit on my ríght;
2. your scep- ter of pówer;
3. on the ho- ly móuntains;
4. "You are a priest for éver,

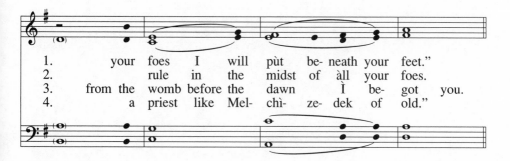

1. your foes I will pùt be- neath your feet."
2. rule in the midst of àll your foes.
3. from the womb before the dawn Ì be- got you.
4. a priest like Mel- chì- ze- dek of old."

Text: Psalm 110:1, 2, 3, 4; The Grail
Music: Joseph Gelineau, SJ
© 1963, 1993, The Grail, GIA Publications, Inc., agent

149   Psalm 112: A Light Rises in the Darkness

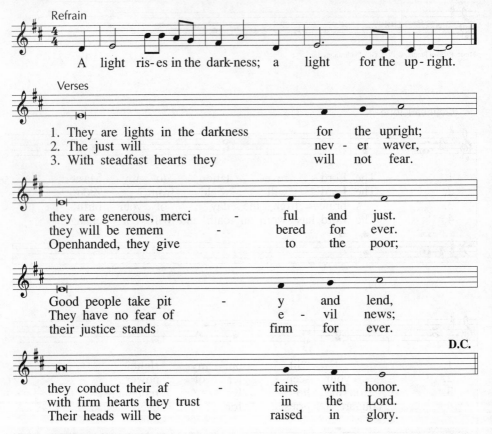

Refrain

A light ris-es in the dark-ness; a light for the up-right.

Verses

1. They are lights in the darkness   for   the upright;
2. The just will   nev - er   waver,
3. With steadfast hearts they   will   not   fear.

they are generous, merci -   ful   and   just.
they will be remem -   bered   for   ever.
Openhanded, they give   to   the   poor;

Good people take pit -   y   and   lend,
They have no fear of   e - vil   news;
their justice stands   firm   for   ever.

D.C.

they conduct their af -   fairs   with   honor.
with firm hearts they trust   in   the   Lord.
Their heads will be   raised   in   glory.

Text: Psalm 112:4-5, 6-7, 8-9; © 1963, 1993, The Grail, GIA Publications, Inc., agent; refrain trans. © 1969, ICEL
Music: Michel Guimont, © 1994, GIA Publications, Inc.

Psalm 113: Praise God's Name   150

Refrain

Al – le – lu – ia! Al – le – lu – ia!

Al – le – lu – ia! ia!

Verses 1, 2, 4

1. You ser-vants of the Lord, bless the Lord:
2. ⁷ High a-bove the na - tions the Lord is God;
4. ⁷ Glo - ry to the Fa - ther and glo - ry to the Son;

Bless-ed be the name for ev - er!
high a - bove the heav - ens God's glo - ry!
glo - ry to the Ho - ly Spir - it:

From east to west, praised be the name of the
Who is like God, en - throned on the stars a -
glo - ry and hon - or, wis - dom and pow - er for

D.C.

Lord our God!
bove earth and sky?
ev - er - more!

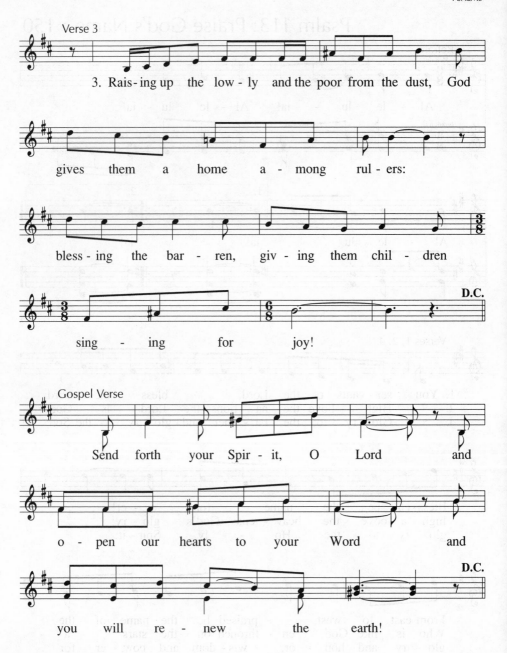

Verse 3

3. Rais-ing up the low - ly and the poor from the dust, God
gives them a home a - mong rul - ers:
bless - ing the bar - ren, giv - ing them chil - dren
sing - ing for joy!

D.C.

Gospel Verse

Send forth your Spir - it, O Lord and
o - pen our hearts to your Word and
you will re - new the earth!

D.C.

Text: Psalm 113; Michael Joncas
Music: Michael Joncas
© 1979, New Dawn Music

Psalm 113: Praise the Lord   151

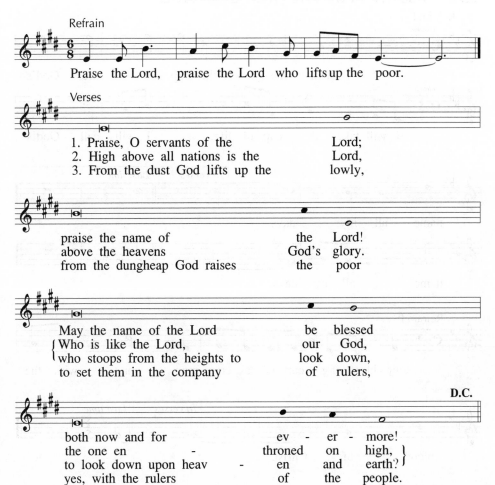

Refrain

Praise the Lord, praise the Lord who lifts up the poor.

Verses

1. Praise, O servants of the   Lord;
2. High above all nations is the   Lord,
3. From the dust God lifts up the   lowly,

praise the name of   the   Lord!
above the heavens   God's glory.
from the dungheap God raises   the   poor

May the name of the Lord   be   blessed
Who is like the Lord,   our   God,
who stoops from the heights to   look down,
to set them in the company   of   rulers,

D.C.

both now and for   ev - er - more!
the one en -   throned on   high,
to look down upon heav - en and earth?
yes, with the rulers   of   the   people.

Text: Psalm 113:1-2, 4-6, 7-8; © 1963, 1993, The Grail, GIA Publications, Inc., agent; refrain trans. © 1969, ICEL
Music: Michel Guimont, © 1994, GIA Publications, Inc.

152 Psalm 116: The Name of God

Refrain I

Descant:

I will take the cup of life, God's

Melody:

I will take the cup of life, I will call God's

name all my days. *To verses* / *Last time*

name all my days. *To verses* / *Last time*

Refrain II

Our bless-ing cup is a com-mun - ion with the

To verses / *Last time*

blood of Christ.

Refrain III

In the land of the liv - ing, I will walk with

To verses / *Last time*

God all my days.

Verse 1

1. How can I make a re - turn for the good-ness of God? This

sav-ing cup I will bless and sing, and call the name of God!

Verse 2

2. The dy-ing of those who keep faith is pre-cious to our God. I am your

ser-vant called from your hands, you have set me free!

Verse 3

3. To you I will of-fer my thanks and call up-on your name. You are my

prom-ise for all to see. I love your name, O God!

Text: Psalm 116; David Haas, © 1987, GIA Publications, Inc.; refrain II trans. © 1969, ICEL
Music: David Haas, © 1987, GIA Publications, Inc.

153 Psalm 116: I Will Take the Cup of Salvation

Antiphon I (Vs. 12-13.15-16.17-18)

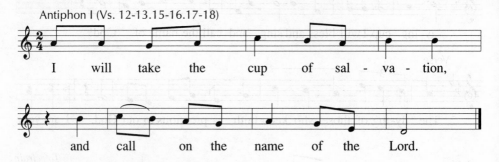

I will take the cup of sal - va - tion,

and call on the name of the Lord.

Text: *Lectionary for Mass,* © 1969, 1981, ICEL
Music: A. Gregory Murray, OSB, © 1975, GIA Publications, Inc.

Antiphon II (St. 6ab & 8cd.9.10 or vs. 1-2.3-4.5-6.8-9)

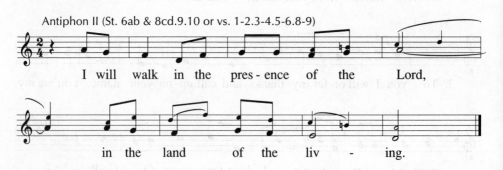

I will walk in the pres - ence of the Lord,

in the land of the liv - ing.

Text: *Lectionary for Mass,* © 1969, 1981, ICEL
Music: Richard Proulx, © 1975, GIA Publications, Inc.

Antiphon III (Vs. 12-13.15-16.17-18)

Our bless - ing - cup is a com -

mun - ion with the blood of Christ.

Text: *Lectionary for Mass,* © 1969, 1981, ICEL
Music: Alexander Peloquin, © 1975, GIA Publications, Inc.

Psalm Tone

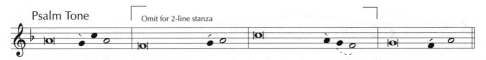

Omit for 2-line stanza

Music: Richard Proulx, © 1986, GIA Publications, Inc.

Gelineau Tone

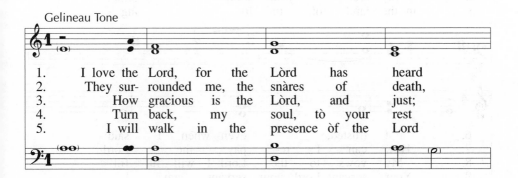

1. I love the Lord, for the Lòrd has heard
2. They sur- rounded me, the snàres of death,
3. How gracious is the Lòrd, and just;
4. Turn back, my soul, tò your rest
5. I will walk in the presence òf the Lord

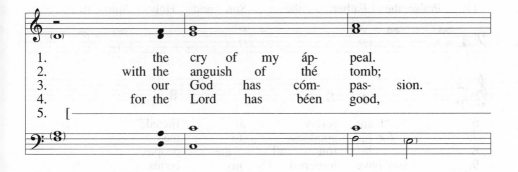

1. the cry of my áp- peal.
2. with the anguish of thé tomb;
3. our God has cóm- pas- sion.
4. for the Lord has béen good,
5. [

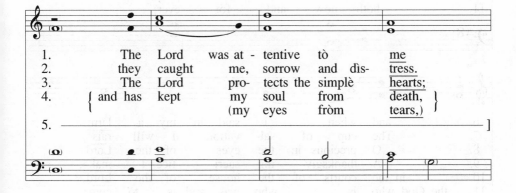

1. The Lord was at - tentive tò me
2. they caught me, sorrow and dìs- tress.
3. The Lord pro- tects the simplè hearts;
4. { and has kept my soul from death,
       (my eyes fròm tears,) }
5.]

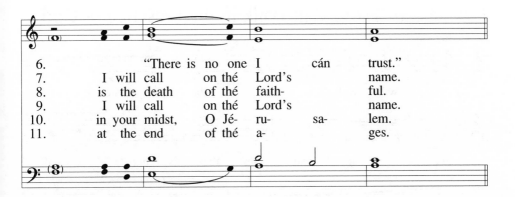

6. "There is no one I cán trust."
7. I will call on thé Lord's name.
8. is the death of thé faith- ful.
9. I will call on thé Lord's name.
10. in your midst, O Jé- ru- sa- lem.
11. at the end of thé a- ges.

Text: Psalm 116; The Grail
Music: Joseph Gelineau, SJ
© 1963, 1993, The Grail, GIA Publications, Inc., agent

154 Psalm 116: I Will Walk in the Presence of God

Refrain

I will walk in the pres - ence of God, in the land of the liv - ing; I will

Last time

walk in the pres - ence of God.

Verse 1

1. In my hour of de - spair, be - reft and be - trayed, I prayed, "Save me! Be my breath!" The death of a ser - vant cuts close to your

D.C.

heart, For God of the liv - ing you are.

Verse 2

2. Your ser - vant am I like my moth - er be - fore me. You re - store me, loos - ing my bonds.

My hands in thanks - giv - ing to God I will

raise. O join me in glo - ri - ous praise!

D.C.

Verse 3

3. My vows I will make, and may ev - 'ry - one

hear me! Draw near me, O ser - vants of God. I

stand here in the midst of them: Your house, your heart, Je -

D.C.

ru - sa - lem.

Text: Psalm 116 adapt. by Rory Cooney. © 1990, GIA Publications, Inc.; refrain trans. © 1969, ICEL
Music: Gary Daigle and Rory Cooney, © 1990, GIA Publications, Inc.

155   Psalm 116: Our Blessing-Cup

Refrain

Our bless-ing-cup is a com-mun-ion with the blood of the Lord.

To verses | *Final ending*

Verses

Descant:

Melody:

1. How can I make a re - turn to the
2. Pre - cious, in - deed, in the sight of the
3. Un - to your name I will of - fer my

Lord for all God has done for me?
Lord is the death of the faith - ful ones;
thanks for the debt that I owe to you.

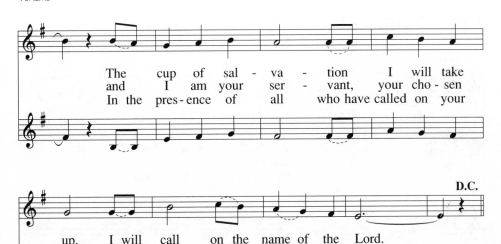

The cup of sal - va - tion I will take
and I am your ser - vant, your cho - sen
In the pres - ence of all who have called on your

up, I will call on the name of the Lord.
one, for you have set me free.
name, in the courts of the house of the Lord.

Text: Psalm 116:12-13, 15-16, 17-19; Marty Haugen
Music: Marty Haugen
© 1983, GIA Publications, Inc.

156 Psalm 117: Holy Is God, Holy and Strong

Refrain

Melody:

Ho - ly is God! Ho - ly and

Harmony:

Ho - ly is God!

strong! Ho - ly is God!

Ho - ly! Ho - ly! Ho - ly is God!

Ho-ly and strong! Ho - ly and liv - ing for ev-er!

Ho-ly and strong! Ho - ly and liv - ing for ev-er!

Verse 1

1. O praise the Lord, all you na - tions, ac -

claim God, all you peo - ples! Strong is God's

D.C.

love for us; the Lord is faith - ful for ev - er!

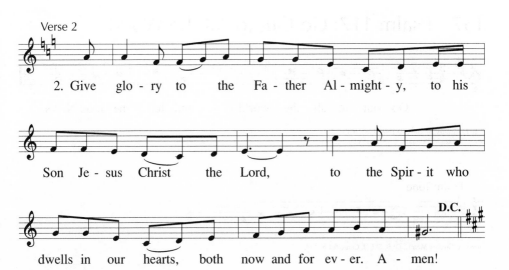

Verse 2

2. Give glo - ry to the Fa - ther Al - might - y, to his

Son Je - sus Christ the Lord, to the Spir - it who

dwells in our hearts, both now and for ev - er. A - men!

D.C.

Text: Psalm 117;© 1963, 1993, The Grail, GIA Publications, Inc., agent; refrain trans. © 1969, ICEL
Music: Michael Joncas, © 1979, GIA Publications, Inc.

157   Psalm 117: Go Out to All the World

Antiphon

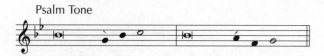

Go out to all the world, and tell the Good News.

Text: *Lectionary for Mass,* © 1969, 1981, ICEL
Music: Alexander Peloquin, © 1975, GIA Publications, Inc.

Psalm Tone

Music: A. Gregory Murray, OSB, © L. J. Carey & Co., Ltd.

Gelineau Tone

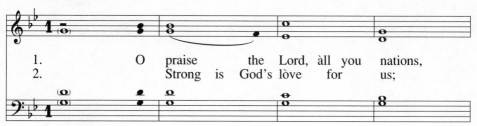

1. O praise the Lord, àll you nations,
2. Strong is God's lòve for us;

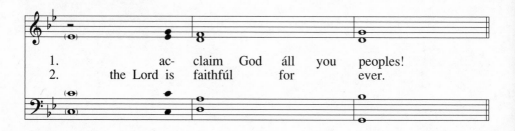

1. ac- claim God áll you peoples!
2. the Lord is faithfúl for ever.

Text: Psalm 117; The Grail
Music: Joseph Gelineau, SJ
© 1963, 1993, The Grail, GIA Publications, Inc., agent

Psalm 118: Let Us Rejoice   158

Refrain

This is the day the Lord has made, let us re-
Or: Al - le - lu - ia, al - le - lu - ia! Al - le -

joice and be glad; this is the day the Lord has
lu - ia! Al - le - lu - ia, al - le - lu -

made, let us re - joice and be glad!
ia! Al - le - lu - ia!

Verses 1, 2
Cantor: *Choir:*

1. Give thanks to the Lord, for God is good; God's
2. The hand of the Lord has struck with pow'r, God's

Verse 3

3. The stone which the build-ers re-ject-ed has be-come the cor-ner-stone, the Lord of love and mer-cy has brought won-der to our eyes!

mer-cy en-dures for ev — er; Let the house of
right hand is ex-alt — ed, I shall not die, but

Is-rael say: "God's mer-cy en — dures for ev — er."
live a-new, de-clar-ing the works of the Lord.

Text: Psalm 118:1-2, 16-17, 22-23; Marty Haugen, © 1983, GIA Publications, Inc.; refrain trans. © 1969, ICEL
Music: Marty Haugen, © 1983, GIA Publications, Inc.

Psalm 118: Give Thanks to the Lord   159

Antiphon

Give thanks to the Lord for he is good, his love is ev - er - last - ing.

Text: *Lectionary for Mass,* © 1969, 1981, ICEL
Music: Chrysogonus Waddell, OCSO, © 1986, GIA Publications, Inc.

Psalm Tone

Music: Richard Proulx, © 1986, GIA Publications, Inc.

Gelineau Tone

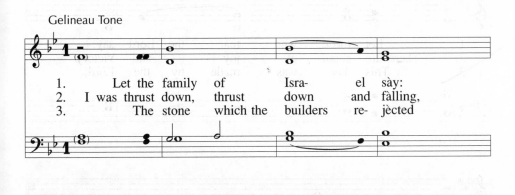

1.   Let the family   of   Isra-   el   sày:
2.   I was thrust down,   thrust   down   and   fàlling,
3.   The stone   which the   builders   re- jècted

1.   "God's love endures   for   éver."
2.   but the Lord was   my   hélper.
3.   has be- come   the   cornérstone.

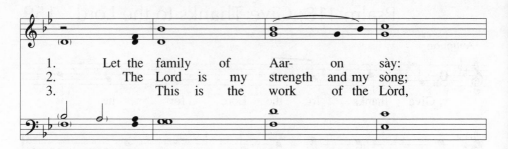

1. Let the family of Aar- on sày:
2. The Lord is my strength and my sòng;
3. This is the work of the Lòrd,

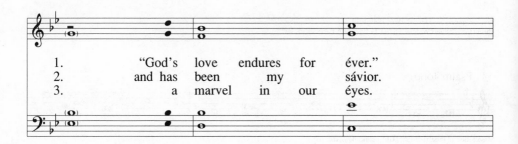

1. "God's love endures for éver."
2. and has been my sávior.
3. a marvel in our éyes.

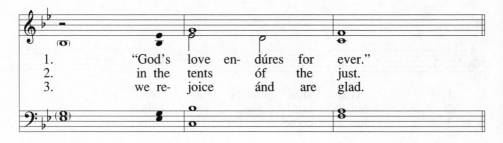

1. Let those who fear the Lord sày:
2. There are shouts of joy and vìctory
3. This day was made by the Lòrd;

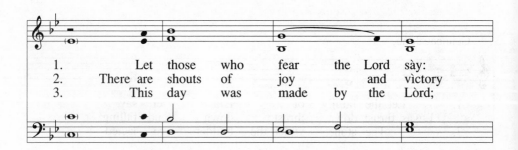

1. "God's love en- dúres for ever."
2. in the tents óf the just.
3. we re- joice ánd are glad.

Text: Psalm 118:2-4, 13-15, 22-24; The Grail
Music: Joseph Gelineau, SJ
© 1963, 1993, The Grail, GIA Publications, Inc., agent

Psalm 118: This Is the Day   160

Antiphon

Descant:

This is   the day   the

Melody: *1.

This is   the day   the

Lord   has   made;   re - joice,

2.

Lord   has   made;   let   us   re - joice,

re - joice,   re - joice and   be   glad.

let   us   re-joice,   let   us   re-joice and   be   glad.

*May be sung as a canon.

Text: *Lectionary for Mass*, © 1969, 1981, ICEL
Music: Richard Proulx, © 1975, GIA Publications, Inc.

Psalm Tone

Omit for 4-line stanza

Music: Richard Proulx, © 1975, GIA Publications, Inc.

Gelineau Tone

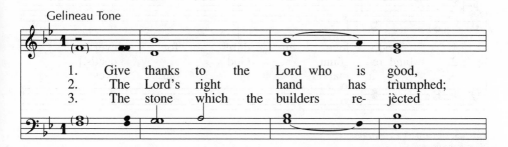

1. Give thanks to the Lord who is gòod,
2. The Lord's right hand has trìumphed;
3. The stone which the builders re- jècted

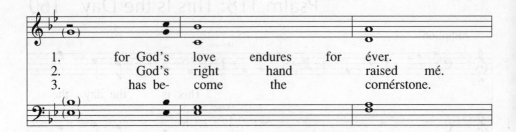

1. for God's love endures for éver.
2. God's right hand raised mé.
3. has be- come the cornérstone.

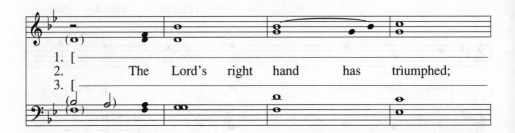

2. The Lord's right hand has trìumphed;

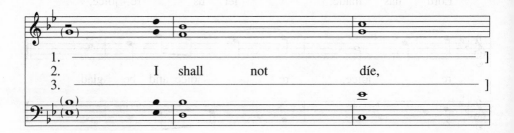

2. I shall not díe,

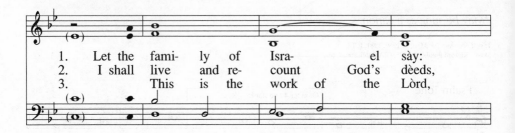

1. Let the fami- ly of Isra- el sày:
2. I shall live and re- count God's dèeds,
3. This is the work of the Lòrd,

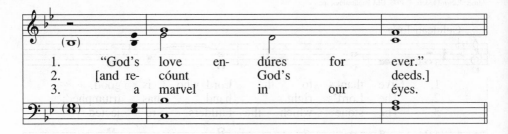

1. "God's love en- dúres for ever."
2. [and re- cóunt God's deeds.]
3. a marvel in our éyes.

Text: Psalm 118:1-2, 16-17, 22-23; The Grail
Music: Joseph Gelineau, SJ
© 1963, 1993, The Grail, GIA Publications, Inc., agent

Psalm 118: The Stone Rejected   161

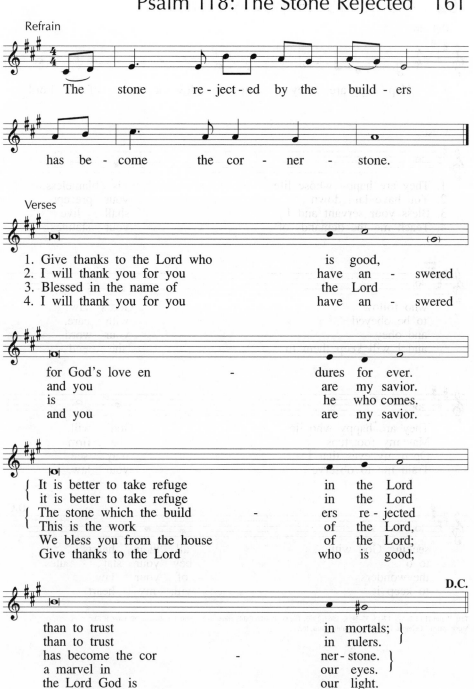

Refrain

The stone re - ject - ed by the build - ers
has be - come the cor - ner - stone.

Verses

1. Give thanks to the Lord who   is   good,
2. I will thank you for you   have   an - swered
3. Blessed in the name of   the   Lord
4. I will thank you for you   have   an - swered

for God's love en - dures   for   ever.
and you   are   my savior.
is   he   who comes.
and you   are   my savior.

It is better to take refuge   in   the   Lord
it is better to take refuge   in   the   Lord
The stone which the build - ers   re - jected
This is the work   of   the   Lord,
We bless you from the house   of   the   Lord;
Give thanks to the Lord   who   is   good;

D.C.

than to trust   in   mortals;
than to trust   in   rulers.
has become the cor - ner - stone.
a marvel in   our   eyes.
the Lord God is   our   light.
for God's love endures   for   ever.

Text: Psalm 118:1, 8-9, 21-23, 26, 21, 29; © 1963, 1993, The Grail, GIA Publications, Inc., agent; refrain trans. © 1969, ICEL
Music: Michel Guimont, © 1995, GIA Publications, Inc.

162 Psalm 119: Happy Are They

Refrain

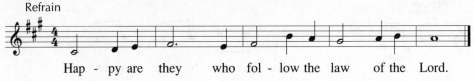

Hap - py are they who fol - low the law of the Lord.

Verses

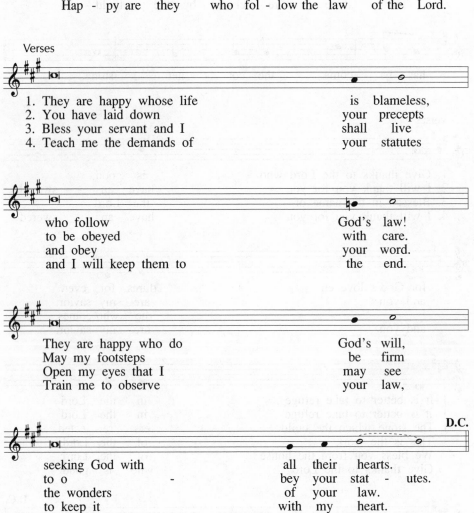

1. They are happy whose life   is blameless,
2. You have laid down   your precepts
3. Bless your servant and I   shall live
4. Teach me the demands of   your statutes

who follow   God's law!
to be obeyed   with care.
and obey   your word.
and I will keep them to   the end.

They are happy who do   God's will,
May my footsteps   be firm
Open my eyes that I   may see
Train me to observe   your law,

D.C.

seeking God with   all their hearts.
to o -   bey your stat - utes.
the wonders   of your law.
to keep it   with my heart.

Text: Psalm 119:1-2, 4-5, 17-18, 33-34; © 1963, 1993, The Grail, GIA Publications, Inc., agent; refrain trans. © 1969, ICEL
Music: Michel Guimont, © 1995, GIA Publications, Inc.

Psalm 119: Lord, I Love Your Commands   163

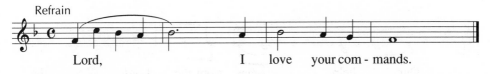

Text: *Lectionary for Mass,* © 1969, 1981, ICEL
Music: Robert J. Batastini, © 1986, GIA Publications, Inc.

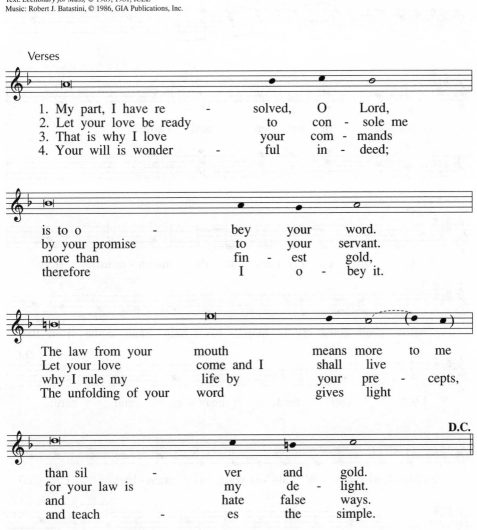

Text: Psalm 119:57, 72, 76-77, 127-128, 129-130; © 1963, 1993, The Grail, GIA Publications, Inc., agent
Music: Michel Guimont, © 1994, GIA Publications, Inc.

164 Psalm 121: Our Help Comes from the Lord

Refrain

Our help comes from the Lord, the mak - er of heav - en and earth.

Verse 1

1. I lift up my eyes to the moun - tains: from where shall come my help? My help shall come from the Lord who made heav - en and earth.

Verse 2

2. May God nev - er al - low you to stum - ble! Let God sleep not, your guard. Nei - ther sleep - ing nor slumb'r - ing, God, Is - ra - el's guard.

165 Psalm 122: I Rejoiced When I Heard

Antiphon

I re - joiced when I heard them say: let us

go to the house of the Lord.

Text: *Lectionary for Mass,* © 1969, 1981, ICEL
Music: Robert J. Batastini, © 1975, GIA Publications, Inc.

Psalm Tone

Music: Laurence Bevenot, OSB, © 1969, Ampleforth Abbey Trustees

Gelineau Tone

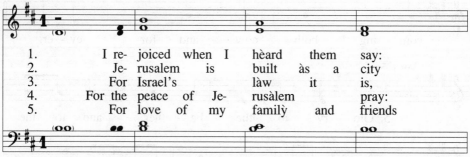

1. I re- joiced when I hèard them say:
2. Je- rusalem is built às a city
3. For Israel's làw it is,
4. For the peace of Je- rusàlem pray:
5. For love of my familỳ and friends

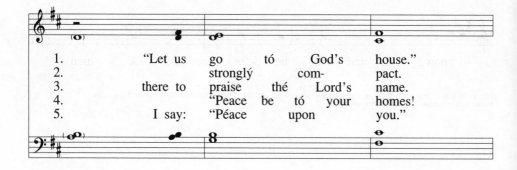

1. "Let us go tó God's house."
2. stronglý com- pact.
3. there to praise thé Lord's name.
4. "Peace be tó your homes!
5. I say: "Péace upon you."

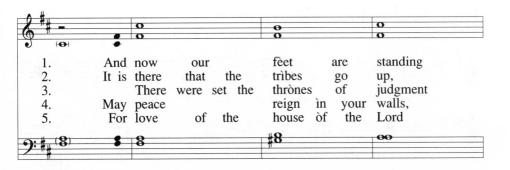

1. And now our feet are standing
2. It is there that the tribes go up,
3. There were set the thrones of judgment
4. May peace reign in your walls,
5. For love of the house òf the Lord

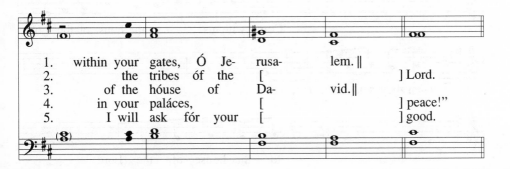

1. within your gates, Ó Je- rusa- lem. ‖
2. the tribes óf the [ ] Lord.
3. of the hóuse of Da- vid. ‖
4. in your paláces, [ ] peace!"
5. I will ask fór your [ ] good.

Text: Psalm 122; The Grail
Music: Joseph Gelineau, SJ
© 1963, 1993, The Grail, GIA Publications, Inc., agent

166 Psalm 122: I Was Glad

Refrain

f Cantor:
I was glad when they said to me,

f Assembly:
I was glad

"Come with us to the house of the Lord,

when they said to me,

to the house of the Lord!"

"Come with us to the house of the Lord!"

To verses | *Last time*

Verse 1

mf
1. I was glad when they said to me: "Come with us to the house of the

Lord." Now our feet are stand-ing firm with-

D.C.
in your gates, O Je - ru - sa - lem!

Verse 2

2. Je - ru - sa - lem— strong-ly built, walled a-round with u - ni - ty. It is there that the tribes of God are lift - ed high to the moun - tain of God! *D.C.*

Verse 3

3. Is - ra - el, this is your law: to praise the name of the Lord. Here are placed the judg - ment seats for the just, here the house of Da - vid! *D.C.*

Verse 4

4. For the love of my fam - 'ly and friends, "May the peace of God be with you!" For the love of the house of God I will pray, I will pray for your good! *D.C.*

Text: Psalm 122; David Haas
Music: David Haas
© 1994, GIA Publications, Inc.

167 Psalm 122: Let Us Go Rejoicing

Verse 3

3. For Is - ra - el's law is to praise God's name and there to give God thanks. There are set the judg - ment thrones for all of Da - vid's house.

D.C.

Verse 4

4. Pray for the peace of Je - ru - sa - lem! "May those who love you pros - per; May peace ev - er reign with - in your walls, and wealth with - in your build - ings!"

D.C.

Verse 5

5. For love of my fam - 'ly and love of my friends, I pray that peace be yours. For love of the house of the Lord our God I pray for your good.

D.C.

168 Psalm 123: Our Eyes Are Fixed on the Lord

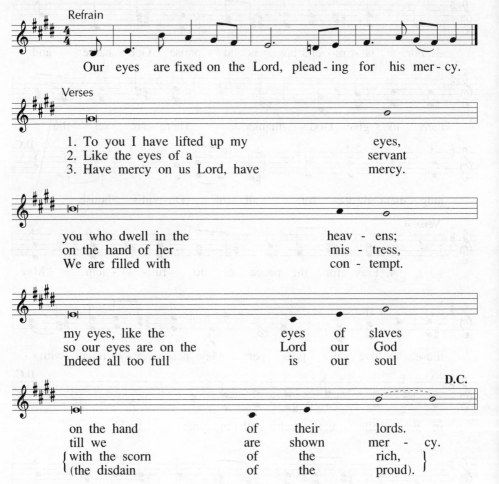

Refrain

Our eyes are fixed on the Lord, plead-ing for his mer-cy.

Verses

1. To you I have lifted up my eyes,
2. Like the eyes of a servant
3. Have mercy on us Lord, have mercy.

you who dwell in the heav - ens;
on the hand of her mis - tress,
We are filled with con - tempt.

my eyes, like the eyes of slaves
so our eyes are on the Lord our God
Indeed all too full is our soul

D.C.

on the hand of their lords.
till we are shown mer - cy.
{ with the scorn of the rich,
{ (the disdain of the proud). }

Text: Psalm 123:1-2, 3-4; © 1963, 1993, The Grail, GIA Publications, Inc., agent; refrain trans. © 1969, ICEL
Music: Michel Guimont, © 1994, GIA Publications, Inc.

Psalm 126: The Lord Has Done Great Things   169

Refrain

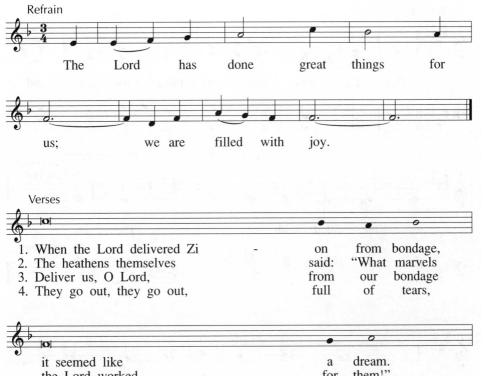

The Lord has done great things for us; we are filled with joy.

Verses

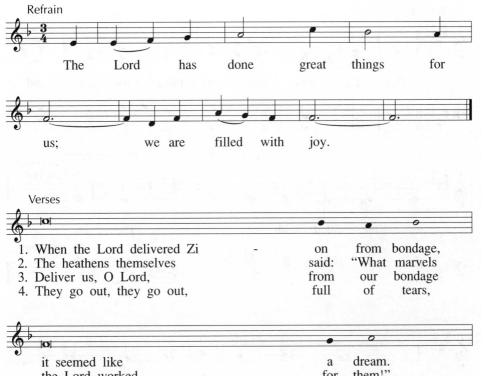

1. When the Lord delivered Zi - on   from bondage,
2. The heathens themselves   said: "What marvels
3. Deliver us, O Lord,   from   our   bondage
4. They go out, they go out,   full   of   tears,

it seemed like   a   dream.
the Lord worked   for   them!"
as streams in   dry   land.
carrying seed for   the   sowing;

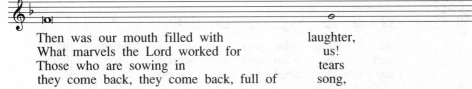

Then was our mouth filled with   laughter,
What marvels the Lord worked for   us!
Those who are sowing in   tears
they come back, they come back, full of   song,

D.C.

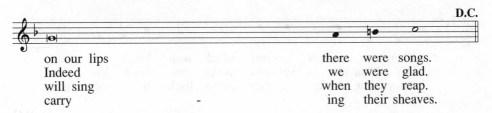

on our lips   there   were   songs.
Indeed   we   were   glad.
will sing   when   they   reap.
carry   -   ing   their sheaves.

Text: Psalm 126; © 1963, 1993, The Grail, GIA Publications, Inc., agent; refrain trans. © 1969, ICEL
Music: Michel Guimont, © 1995, GIA Publications, Inc.

170 Psalm 126: The Lord Has Done Great Things

Refrain

The Lord has done great things for us and

we are filled with joy. The joy.

Verses

1. When the Lord de - liv - ered Zi - on,
2. { The hea - then mar - velled at God,
3. They go out full of tears,

we were like peo - ple dream - ing.
and the won - ders he worked for them.
car - ry - ing seed for the sow - ing.

Then our mouth was filled with laugh - ter,
{ What mar - vel - ous works the Lord has done,
They come back, they come back full of song,

and our lips were filled with song.
and we are glad in - deed.
{ car - ry - ing their sheaves.

Text: Psalm 126:1-3, 6; Roy James Stewart, © 1993, GIA Publications, Inc.; refrain trans. © 1969, ICEL
Music: Roy James Stewart, © 1993, GIA Publications, Inc.

Psalm 126: The Lord Has Done Great Things   171

Antiphon

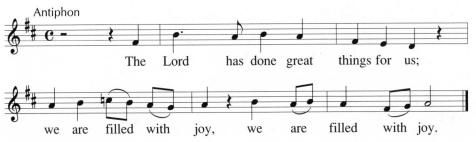

The Lord has done great things for us;
we are filled with joy, we are filled with joy.

Text: *Lectionary for Mass,* © 1969, 1981, ICEL
Music: Richard Proulx, © 1975, GIA Publications, Inc.

Psalm Tone

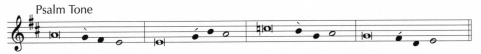

Music: Joseph B. Smith, © 1986, GIA Publications, Inc.

Gelineau Tone

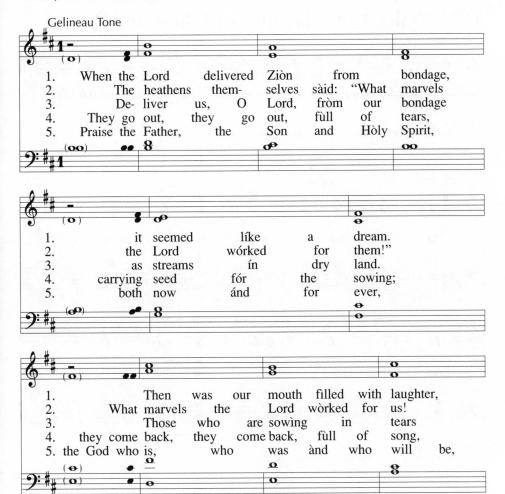

1. When the Lord   delivered Zìon   from   bondage,
2.   The heathens them-   selves sàid: "What   marvels
3.   De- liver   us,   O   Lord,   fròm   our   bondage
4.   They go out,   they   go   out,   fùll   of   tears,
5.   Praise the Father,   the   Son   and   Hòly   Spirit,

1.   it seemed   líke   a   dream.
2.   the Lord   wórked   for   them!"
3.   as streams   ín   dry   land.
4.   carrying seed   fór   the   sowing;
5.   both now   ánd   for   ever,

1.   Then   was   our   mouth   fílled   with   laughter,
2.   What marvels   the   Lord   wòrked   for   us!
3.   Those   who   are sowìng   in   tears
4.   they come back,   they   come back,   fùll   of   song,
5. the God who is,   who   was   ànd   who   will   be,

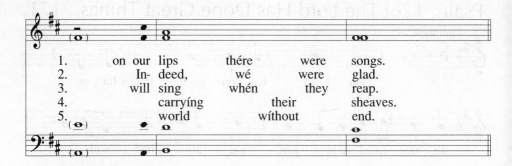

1. on our lips thére were songs.
2. In- deed, wé were glad.
3. will sing whén they reap.
4. carrying their sheaves.
5. world wíthout end.

Text: Psalm 126, The Grail
Music: Joseph Gelineau, SJ
© 1963, 1993, The Grail, GIA Publications. Inc., agent

172   Psalm 128: May the Lord Bless and Protect

Antiphon I

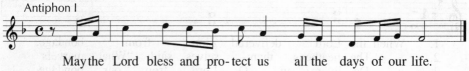

May the Lord bless and pro-tect us   all the days of our life.

Text: *Lectionary for Mass,* © 1969, 1981, ICEL
Music: A. Gregory Murray, OSB, © 1963, The Grail, GIA Publications, Inc., agent

Antiphon II

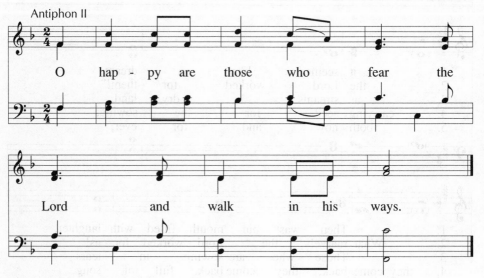

O hap - py are those who fear the

Lord and walk in his ways.

Text: *Lectionary for Mass,* © 1969, 1981, ICEL
Music: Joseph Gelineau, SJ, © 1963, The Grail, GIA Publications, Inc., agent

Psalm Tone

Music: Richard Proulx, © 1986, GIA Publications, Inc.

Gelineau Tone

1.   O blessed   are   you   who fèar the   Lord
2.   Your wife   like   a   frùitful   vine
3.   In- deed   thùs shall be   blessed
4. May you see   your   children's   children

1.   and wálk   in   God's   ways!
2.   in the héart   of   your   house;
3.   thóse who fear the   Lord.
4.   in a   hàppy   Je-   rusalem!

1.   By the labor of your   hands yòu shall   eat.
2.   your children like   shòots of the   olive,
3. May the Lord   blèss you from   Zion
4. [——————————————————————————]

1.   You will be happý   and   prosper.
2.   a- róund   your   table.
3.   all the dáys of   your   life!
4.   On Ísrael,   peace!

Text: Psalm 128; The Grail
Music: Joseph Gelineau, SJ
© 1963, 1993, The Grail, GIA Publications, Inc., agent

173 Psalm 128: Blest Are Those Who Love You

Refrain I

Blest are those who love you, hap-py those who fol-low you, blest are those who seek you, O God.

To verses

Last time

Refrain II

May the Lord bless us, May the Lord pro-tect us, all the days, all the days of our life.

To verses

Last time

Verse 1

1. Hap - py all those who fear the Lord, and walk in God's path - way; you will find what you

To refrain

long for: the rich - es of our God.

Verse 2

2. Your spouse shall be like a fruit - ful vine in the midst of your home, your chil - dren flour - ish like

To refrain

ol - ive plants re - joic - ing at your ta - ble.

Verse 3

3. May the bless - ings of God be yours all the days of your life, may the peace and the

To refrain

love of God live al - ways in your heart.

Text: Psalm 128:1-2, 3, 5; Marty Haugen
Music: Marty Haugen; refrain II adapt. by Diana Kodner
© 1987, 1993, GIA Publications, Inc.

174 Psalm 130: With the Lord There Is Mercy

Refrain

With the Lord there is mer - cy and the full - ness of re - demp - tion, call to him in your tri - als, he will an - swer when - ev - er you call. call.

To verses 1, 3, and last time

To verses 2, 4

Verses 1, 3

1. Out of the depths I cry to you, I cry to you, O Lord. Lord, o - pen your ears and hear my voice, at - tend to the sound of my plea.

3. Trust in the Lord, count on his word, wait for the Lord, my soul. I will wait for the Lord all the days of my life as sen - ti - nels wait for the dawn.

D.C.

Verses 2, 4

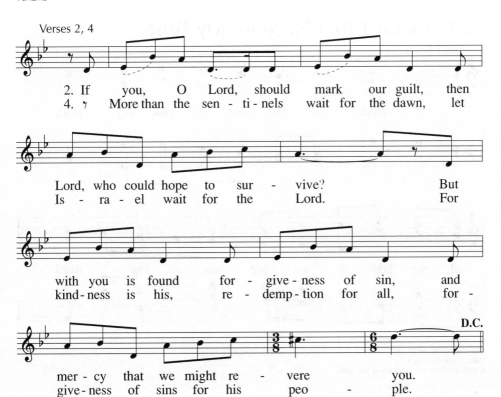

2. If you, O Lord, should mark our guilt, then
4. More than the sen - ti - nels wait for the dawn, let

Lord, who could hope to sur - vive? But
Is - ra - el wait for the Lord. For

with you is found for - give - ness of sin, and
kind - ness is his, re - demp - tion for all, for -

D.C.

mer - cy that we might re - vere you.
give - ness of sins for his peo - ple.

Text: Psalm 130; Michael Joncas
Music: Michael Joncas
© 1983, New Dawn Music

175 Psalm 130: I Place All My Trust

Antiphon I

I place all my trust in you, my God; all my hope is in your sav - ing word.

Text: Joseph Gelineau, SJ
Music: Joseph Gelineau, SJ
© 1963, The Grail, GIA Publications, Inc., agent

Antiphon II

If you, O Lord, should mark our sins, Lord, who would sur - vive?

Text: Psalm 130:3; The Grail
Music: Clifford W. Howell, SJ
© 1963, The Grail, GIA Publications, Inc., agent

Antiphon III

Out of the depths I cry to you, O Lord.

Text: *Liturgy of the Hours,* © 1974, ICEL
Music: Randolph Currie, © 1986, GIA Publications, Inc.

Antiphon IV

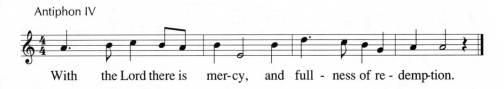

With the Lord there is mer-cy, and full - ness of re - demp-tion.

Text: *Lectionary for Mass,* © 1969, 1981, ICEL
Music: J. Robert Carroll, harm. by Richard Proulx, © 1975, GIA Publications, Inc.

Psalm Tone

Music: A. Gregory Murray, OSB, © L. J. Carey and Co., Ltd.

Gelineau Tone

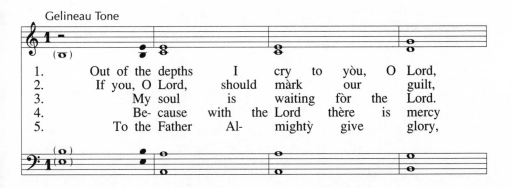

1. Out of the depths I cry to you, O Lord,
2. If you, O Lord, should màrk our guilt,
3. My soul is waiting fòr the Lord.
4. Be- cause with the Lord thère is mercy
5. To the Father Al- mightỳ give glory,

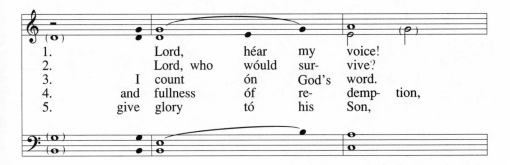

1. Lord, héar my voice!
2. Lord, who wóuld sur- vive'?
3. I count ón God's word.
4. and fullness óf re- demp- tion,
5. give glory tó his Son,

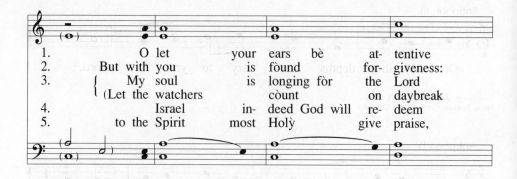

1. O let   your ears bè at- tentive
2. But with you is fòund for- giveness:
3. { My soul is longing fòr the Lord
    (Let the watchers còunt on daybreak
4. Israel in- deed God wìll re- deem
5. to the Spirit most Holỳ give praise,

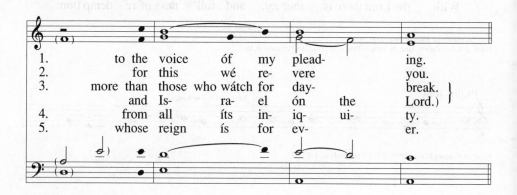

1. to the voice óf my plead- ing.
2. for this wé re- vere you.
3. more than those who wátch for day- break. }
    and Is- ra- el ón the Lord.) }
4. from all íts in- iq- ui- ty.
5. whose reign ís for ev- er.

Text: Psalm 130; The Grail
Music: Joseph Gelineau, SJ
© 1963, 1993, The Grail, GIA Publications, Inc., agent

Psalm 130: With the Lord There Is Mercy   176

3. Just as those who wait for the morn-ing light, e - ven

more I long for the Lord, my God, whose word to me shall

D.C.

ev - er be my com - fort.

Text: Psalm 130:1-2, 3-4, 5-6; Marty Haugen, © 1983, GIA Publications, Inc.; refrain trans. © 1969, ICEL
Music: Marty Haugen, © 1983, GIA Publications, Inc.

Psalm 130: If You, O God, Laid Bare Our Guilt   177

Refrain

If you, O God, laid bare our guilt,   O who could en-

dure it?   O who could en - dure it?

Verses

Melody: **f**

Harmony:

1. Out of the depths I cry to you.
2. If you, O God, lay bare our sin,
3. Wait - ing for you, our souls a - wait,
4. For with the Lord is stead - fast love:

mp   **f**   **mf**

Lord, hear my plea.   Let your ear be at - ten - tive
Lord, who can stand?   But with you is for - give - ness,
hop - ing in God.   Like the sen-t'nel for day - break,
pow'r to re - deem.   God will save us from sor - rows,

mp *rit.*   **D.C.**

to the sound   of my call.
so your name   is re - vered.
so our souls   wait for you.
bring us back   from our sin.

Text: Psalm 130; John Foley, SJ
Music: John Foley, SJ
© 1994, GIA Publications, Inc.

178 Psalm 131: My Soul Is Still

Refrain

In you, O Lord, I have found my peace, I have found my peace.

Verse 1

1. My heart is not proud, my eyes not a-bove you; You fill my soul. I am not filled with great things, nor with thoughts be - yond me.

D.C.

Verse 2

2. My soul is still, my soul stays qui - et, long-ing for you like a weaned child in its moth-er's arms; so is my soul a child with you.

D.C.

Text: Psalm 131; verses, David Haas, © 1985, GIA Publications, Inc.; refrain trans. © 1969, ICEL
Music: David Haas, © 1985, GIA Publications, Inc.

Psalm 131: In You, Lord   179

Antiphon

In you, Lord, in you, Lord,

in you, Lord, I have found my peace.

Text: *Lectionary for Mass,* © 1969, 1981, ICEL
Music: Robert J. Batastini, © 1975, GIA Publications, Inc.

Psalm Tone

Omit in stanza 3

Music: Richard Proulx, © 1986, GIA Publications, Inc.

Gelineau Tone

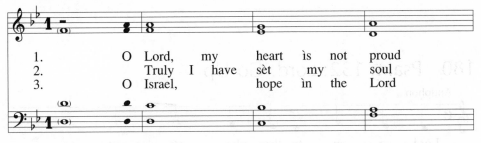

1. O Lord, my heart is not proud
2. Truly I have sèt my soul
3. O Israel, hope in the Lord

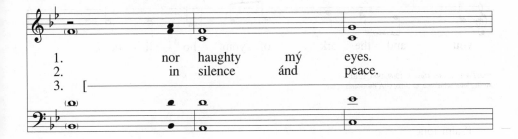

1. nor haughty mý eyes.
2. in silence ánd peace.
3. [

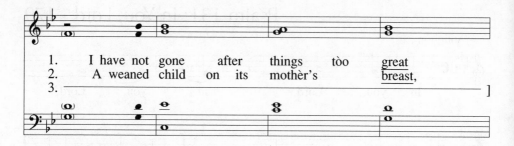

1. I have not gone after things tòo great
2. A weaned child on its mothèr's breast,
3. _____]

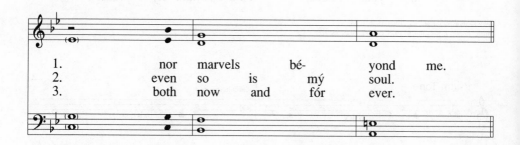

1. nor marvels bé- yond me.
2. even so is mý soul.
3. both now and fór ever.

Text: Psalm 131; The Grail
Music: Joseph Gelineau, SJ
© 1963, The Grail, GIA Publications, Inc., agent

180 Psalm 132: Lord, Go Up

Antiphon

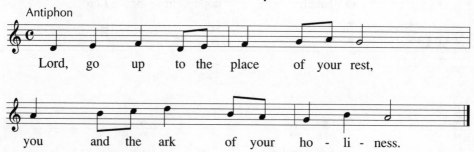

Lord, go up to the place of your rest,

you and the ark of your ho - li - ness.

Text: *Lectionary for Mass*, © 1969, 1981, ICEL
Music: John Schiavone, © 1986, GIA Publications, Inc.

Psalm Tone

Music: Richard Proulx, © 1986, GIA Publications, Inc.

Gelineau Tone

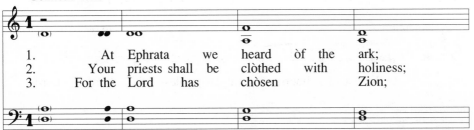

1. At Ephrata we heard òf the ark;
2. Your priests shall be clòthed with holiness;
3. For the Lord has chòsen Zion;

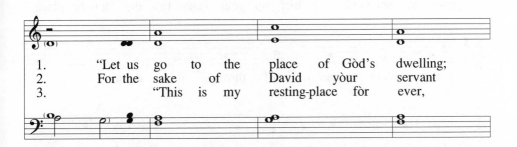

1. we found it in the plains óf Year- im.
2. your faithful shall ring out théir joy.
3. has de- sired it for á dwel- ling:

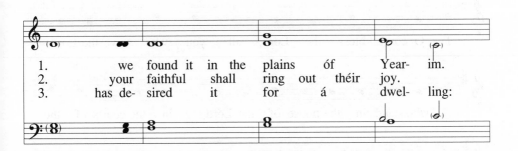

1. "Let us go to the place of Gòd's dwelling;
2. For the sake of David yòur servant
3. "This is my resting-place fòr ever,

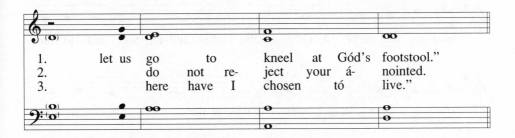

1. let us go to kneel at Gód's footstool."
2. do not re- ject your á- nointed.
3. here have I chosen tó live."

Text: Psalm 132:6-7, 9-10, 13-14; The Grail
Music: Joseph Gelineau, SJ
© 1963, 1993, The Grail, GIA Publications, Inc., agent

181 Psalm 134: In the Silent Hours of Night

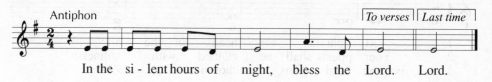

Antiphon · To verses · Last time

In the si - lent hours of night, bless the Lord. Lord.

Text: *Praise God in Song*
Music: Howard Hughes, SM
© 1979, GIA Publications, Inc.

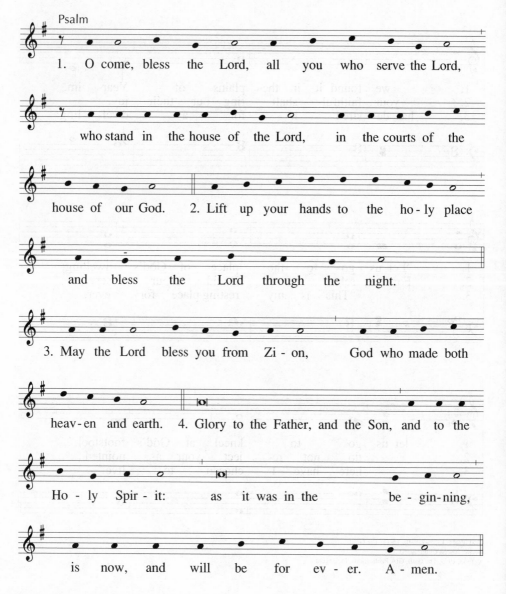

Psalm

1. O come, bless the Lord, all you who serve the Lord,

who stand in the house of the Lord, in the courts of the

house of our God. 2. Lift up your hands to the ho - ly place

and bless the Lord through the night.

3. May the Lord bless you from Zi - on, God who made both

heav-en and earth. 4. Glory to the Father, and the Son, and to the

Ho - ly Spir - it: as it was in the be - gin-ning,

is now, and will be for ev - er. A - men.

Text: Psalm 134; The Grail, © 1963, 1993, GIA Publications, Inc., agent
Music: Howard Hughes, SM, © 1979, GIA Publications, Inc.

Psalm 137: Let My Tongue Be Silent   182

Antiphon

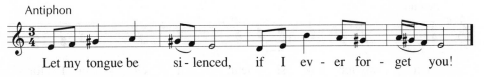

Let my tongue be si - lenced, if I ev - er for - get you!

Text: *Lectionary for Mass*, © 1969, 1981, ICEL
Music: Frank Schoen, © 1975, GIA Publications, Inc.

Psalm Tone

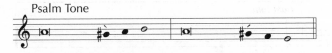

Music: A. Gregory Murray, OSB, alt., © L. J. Carey & Co., Ltd.

Gelineau Tone

1.   By the   rivers   of   Babylon
2.   For it was   there   that   they   asked   us,   our
3.   O   how   could   we   sing   the
4.   O   let   my   tongue

1. there we sat and   wept,   re-   mem-   bèr- ing   Zion;
2. captors,   for   songs, our op-   pres-   sòrs, for   joy.
3. song   of   the   Lord   on   a-   lì- en   soil?
4. cleave   to   my   mouth if I re-   mem-   bèr you   not,

1.   on the poplars   that   grew there we   hung úp our   harps.
2.   "Sing to us," they   said, "one   of   Zíon's   songs."
3. If I for- get   you, Je-   rusalem, let my   ríght   hand   wither!
4.   if I   prize   not Je-   rusalem a-   bove áll my   joys!

Text: Psalm 137:1-2, 3, 4-5, 6; The Grail
Music: Joseph Gelineau, SJ
© 1963, 1993, The Grail, GIA Publications, Inc., agent

183 Psalm 137: Let My Tongue Be Silent

Refrain

Let my tongue be si - lent, if ev - er I for -

To verses

get you!

Last time

get you!

Verse 1

1. By Ba-by-lon-ian riv-ers, we sat and wept, re-mem-b'ring Zi-on.

There on the pop-lars we re - tired our harps.

D.C.

Verse 2

2. For there our cap-tors de-mand-ed songs of joy:

"Sing to us one of the songs of Zi-on!"

D.C.

Verse 3

3. How can we sing the songs of the Lord while in a for - eign

land? How can we sing the

songs of the Lord while in a for-eign land?

poco rit. D.C.

Verse 4

4. If I should fail to re-mem-ber you, O

Zi - on, Let my tongue be si-lenced, let my

right hand be for - got-ten, If I do not con -

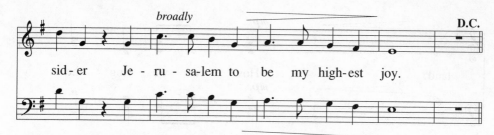

broadly D.C.

sid - er Je - ru - sa-lem to be my high-est joy.

Text: Psalm 137:1-6; Carl Johengen, © 1992, GIA Publications, Inc.; refrain trans. © 1969, ICEL
Music: Carl Johengen, © 1992, GIA Publications, Inc.

184 Psalm 138: In the Sight of the Angels

Antiphon I (St. 1.2.3.5)

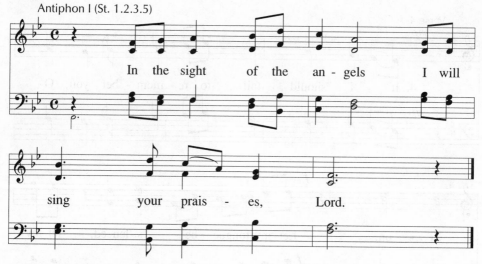

In the sight of the an - gels I will

sing your prais - es, Lord.

Text: *Lectionary for Mass,* © 1969, 1981, ICEL
Music: J. Robert Carroll, © 1975, GIA Publications, Inc.

Antiphon II (St. 1.2.4.5)

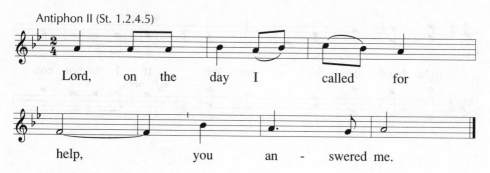

Lord, on the day I called for

help, you an - swered me.

Text: *Lectionary for Mass,* © 1969, 1981, ICEL
Music: Ralph C. Verdi, CPPs, © 1986, GIA Publications, Inc.

Antiphon III (St. 1.2.4ab & 5cd)

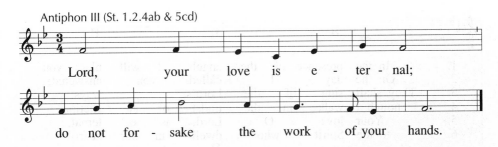

Lord, your love is e - ter - nal;
do not for - sake the work of your hands.

Text: *Lectionary for Mass,* © 1969, 1981, ICEL
Music: Richard Proulx, © 1975, GIA Publications, Inc.

Psalm Tone

Music: Laurence Bevenot, OSB, © 1969, Ampleforth Abbey Trustees

Gelineau Tone

1.   I thank you, Lord, with àll my heart,
2.   I thank you for your faithful- nèss and love
3. All the rulers on èarth shall thank you
4. The Lord is high yet looks òn the lowly
5.   You stretch out your hànd and save me,
6.   Give praise to the Fa- thèr Al- mighty,

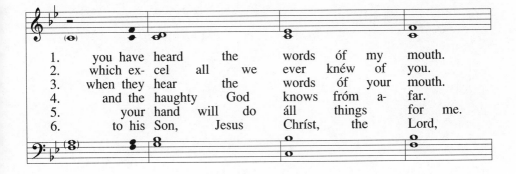

1. you have heard the words óf my mouth.
2. which ex- cel all we ever knéw of you.
3. when they hear the words óf your mouth.
4. and the haughty God knows fróm a- far.
5. your hand will do áll things for me.
6. to his Son, Jesus Chríst, the Lord,

1. In the presence of the angels Ì will bless you.
2. On the day I càlled, you answered;
3. They shall sing òf the Lord's ways:
4. Though I walk in the midst òf af- fliction
5. Your love, O Lord, ìs e- ternal,
6. to the Spirit who dwells ìn our hearts,

1. I will a- dore before your hóly temple.
2. you in- creased the strength óf my soul.
3. "How great is the glory óf the Lord!"
4. you give me life and frustráte my foes.
5. dis- card not the work óf your hands.
6. both now and for evér. A- men.

Text: Psalm 138; The Grail
Music: Joseph Gelineau, SJ
© 1963, 1993, The Grail, GIA Publications, Inc., agent

Psalm 138: In the Sight of the Angels   185

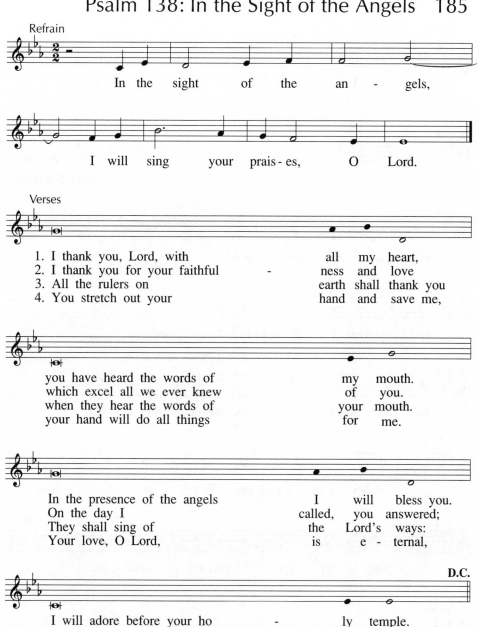

Refrain

In the sight of the an - gels,

I will sing your prais - es, O Lord.

Verses

1. I thank you, Lord, with   all   my   heart,
2. I thank you for your faithful   -   ness   and   love
3. All the rulers on   earth shall thank you
4. You stretch out your   hand and save me,

you have heard the words of   my   mouth.
which excel all we ever knew   of   you.
when they hear the words of   your   mouth.
your hand will do all things   for   me.

In the presence of the angels   I   will   bless you.
On the day I   called,   you   answered;
They shall sing of   the   Lord's   ways:
Your love, O Lord,   is   e - ternal,

D.C.

I will adore before your ho   -   ly   temple.
you increased the strength of   my   soul.
"How great is the glory of   the   Lord!"
discard not the work of   your   hands.

Text: Psalm 138:1-2, 2-3, 4-5, 7-8; © 1963, 1993, The Grail, GIA Publications, Inc., agent; refrain trans. © 1969, ICEL
Music: Michel Guimont, © 1995, GIA Publications, Inc.

186 Psalm 139: Guide Me, Lord

Refrain

Guide me, Lord, a - long the ev - er - last - ing way.

Verse 1

1. O Lord, you have probed me and you know me;
you know when I sit and when I stand; you
un - der - stand my thoughts from a - far.
My jour-neys and my rest you scru - ti - nize,
with all my ways you are fa - mil - iar.

D.C.

Verse 2

2. Ev - en be-fore a word is on my tongue, be - hold, O Lord,

you know the whole of it. Be - hind me and be -

fore, you hem me in and

rest your hand up - on me. Such

knowl-edge is too won-der-ful for me; too

D.C.

loft - y for me to at - tain.

Verse 3

3. Where can I go from your spir - it?

from your pres - ence where can I

flee? If I go up to the

heav-ens, you are there; if I sink to the

D.C.

neth - er world, you are pres - ent there.

Verse 4

4. If I take the

wings of the dawn, if I set - tle at the far - thest

lim - its of the sea, E - ven there

your hand shall guide me, and your

D.C.

right hand hold me fast.

Verse 5

3

5. If I say, "Sure - ly the

dark - ness shall hide me, and

night shall be my light"— For you,

darkness it-self is not dark,

D.C.

and night shines as the day.

Verse 6

6. Tru-ly you have

formed my in-most be - ing; you

knit me in my moth-er's womb. I

give you thanks that I am fear-ful-ly, won-der-f'ly

D.C.

made; won-der-ful are your works.

Verse 7

7. My soul al-so

you knew full well; nor was my frame

un - known   to   you   when   I   was   made

in   se - cret,   when   I   was   fash - ioned

in   the   depths   of   the   earth.

D.C.

Verse 8

8. Probe   me,   O

God, and know my   heart;   try   me,   and

know   my   thoughts;   See   if   my

way   is   crook - ed,   and

lead   me   in   the   way   of   old.

D.C.

Text: Psalm 139:1-15, 23-24; *New American Bible,* © 1970, Confraternity of Christian Doctrine
Music: Howard Hughes, SM, © 1979, GIA Publications, Inc.

Psalm 139: I Praise You   187

Refrain

I praise you, O Lord, for I am won-der-ful-ly made.

Verses

1. O Lord, you search me   and you know me,
2. For it was you who cre -   ated my being,
3. Already you   knew my soul,

you know my resting   and my rising,
knit me together in my   moth-er's womb.
my body held no se -   cret from you

you discern my purpose   from a - far.
I thank you for the wonder   of my being,
when I was being fash -   ioned in secret

D.C.

{ You mark when I walk   or lie down, }
all my ways lie o -   pen to you.
for the wonders of all   your cre - ation.
and molded in the depths   of the earth.

Text: Psalm 139:1-3, 13-14, 14-15; © 1963, 1993, The Grail, GIA Publications, Inc., agent; refrain trans. © 1969, ICEL
Music: Michel Guimont, © 1995, GIA Publications, Inc.

188 Psalm 141: Let My Prayer Rise Like Incense

Refrain

Let my prayer rise like in-cense be - fore you, O

Lord. Let my prayer rise like in-cense be - fore you, O

Lord, the lift-ing up of my hands like an eve-ning of - fer-

ing. Al - le - lu, al - le - lu - ia!

Verse 1

1. I have called to you, Lord; has-ten to

wick-ed not a-noint my head. Let my prayer be

ev - er a - gainst their mal - ice.

Verse 4

4. Their lead - ers were thrown down by the side of the

rock; then they un - der-stood that my

words were kind. As a mill-stone is

shat-tered to piec-es on the ground, so their bones were

strewn at the mouth of the grave.

Verse 5

5. To you, Lord God, my eyes are turned;

in you I take ref - uge; spare my soul!

From the trap they have laid for me keep me safe;

keep me from the snares of those who do e - vil.

Verse 6

6. Glo - ry to the Fa-ther, and to the Son,

and to the Ho - ly Spir - it:

as it was in the be - gin-ning, is now, and will be for

ev - er. A - men.

189 Psalm 141: Evening Offering

Refrain

Moderato ♩ = 140

mp

Let my prayer rise be - fore you like in - cense, O Lord,

mf

and my hands like an eve - ning of - f'ring.

Verses

mp

1. To you, O Lord, I call out for help. O
2. May my words, O Lord, speak on - ly your truth; my
3. Let your ho - ly ones con - front me in kind - ness; their
4. I look to you, O Lord, for my hope. For

hear my voice when I cry out to you. Let my
heart be filled with a long - ing for you. Keep my
words I hear as your wis - dom for me. But the
you, my God, are the strength of my soul. Keep me

prayer rise up be - fore you like in - cense, my
hands, O Lord, from all wick - ed deeds; let me
wick - ed ones shall nev - er mis - lead me; I will
safe from those who tempt me to sin, and

D.C.

hands lift - ed up at the end of the day.
not re - joice with those set a - gainst you.
pray for strength to con - quer their e - vil.
free my heart to rest in your peace.

Text: Psalm 141; Darryl Ducote
Music: Darryl Ducote; arr. by Gary Daigle
© 1985, 1993, Damean Music. Distributed by GIA. Publications, Inc.

Psalm 143: Do Not Hide Your Face   190

Antiphon

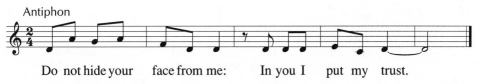

Do not hide your   face from me: In you I   put my   trust.

Text: *Liturgy of the Hours,* © 1974, ICEL
Music: Randolph Currie, © 1986, GIA Publications, Inc.

Psalm Tone*

*For this tone, use the following plan:
  2. Repeat C + D   6. Repeat C + D
  3. Repeat D for last line 7. Sing first 2 lines to A + D

Music: Chrysogonus Waddell, OCSO, © Gethsemani Abbey

Gelineau Tone

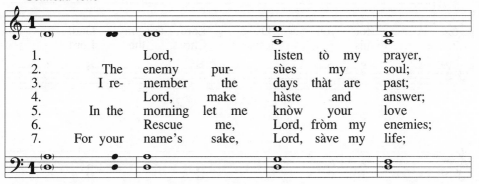

1.		Lord,	listen tò my	prayer,
2.	The	enemy pur-	sùes my	soul;
3.	I re-	member the	days thàt are	past;
4.		Lord, make	hàste and	answer;
5.	In the	morning let me	knòw your	love
6.		Rescue me,	Lord, fròm my	enemies;
7.	For your	name's sake,	Lord, sàve my	life;

1.		turn your	ear to my áp-	peal.
2.	has	crushed my	life to thé	ground;
3.	I	ponder	all yóur	works.
4.	for my	spirit	fails wíth-	in me.
5.	for I	put my	trust ín	you.
6.	I have	fled to	you fór	ref- uge.
7.	in your	justice save my	soul from dís-	tress.

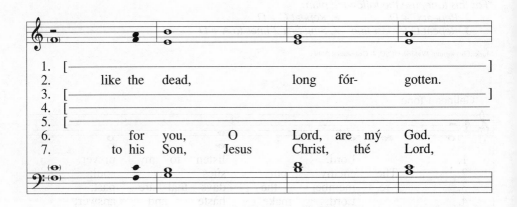

1. You are faithful, you are just; give answer.
2. has made me dwell in darkness
3. I muse on what your hand has wrought
4. Do not hide your face
5. Make me know the way I should walk;
6. Teach me to do your will
7. Give praise to the Father Almighty,

1. [—————————————————————————]
2. like the dead, long forgotten.
3. [—————————————————————————]
4. [
5. [
6. for you, O Lord, are my God.
7. to his Son, Jesus Christ, the Lord,

1. Do not call your servant to judgment
2. Therefore my spirit fails;
3. and to you I stretch out my hands.
4. —————————————————————————]
5. —————————————————————————]
6. Let your good spirit guide me
7. to the Spirit who dwells in our hearts,

1.		for	no	one	is	just	in	yóur	sight.
2.		my	heart	is		numb	wíth-	in	me.
3.	Like a	parched	land	my	soul	thirsts	fór	you.
4.	lest I be-	come	like		those	in	thé	grave.
5.	to	you	I		lift	up	mý	soul.
6.	in	ways	that	are	level		ánd	smooth.
7.	both	now	and	for	ever.	Á-		men.

Text: Psalm 143:1-11; The Grail
Music: Joseph Gelineau, SJ
© 1963, 1993, The Grail, GIA Publications, Inc., agent

191 Psalm 145: The Lord Is Near

Antiphon I (St. 1.2.5)

The Lord is near to all who call on him.

Text: *Lectionary for Mass,* © 1969, 1981, ICEL
Music: Robert J. Batastini, © 1995, GIA Publications, Inc.

Antiphon II (St. 3.4.5 or 2.4.5)

The hand of the Lord feeds us: he an-swers all our needs.

Text: *Lectionary for Mass,* © 1969, 1981, ICEL
Music: Columba Kelly, OSB, © 1975, GIA Publications, Inc.

Psalm Tone

Music: Douglas Mews, © 1981, ICEL

Gelineau Tone

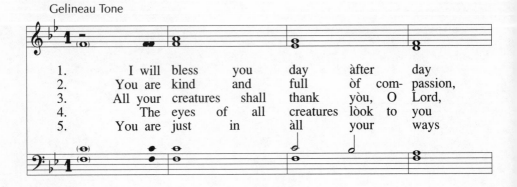

1.   I will bless you day àfter day
2.   You are kind and full òf com- passion,
3.   All your creatures shall thank yòu, O Lord,
4.   The eyes of all creatures lòok to you
5.   You are just in àll your ways

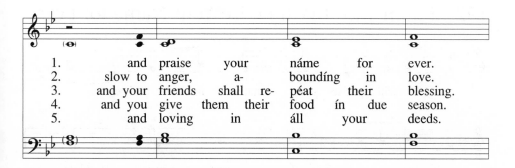

1. and praise your náme for ever.
2. slow to anger, a- bounding in love.
3. and your friends shall re- péat their blessing.
4. and you give them their food ín due season.
5. and loving in áll your deeds.

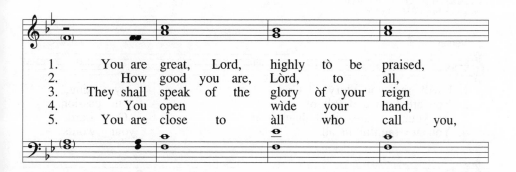

1. You are great, Lord, highly tò be praised,
2. How good you are, Lòrd, to all,
3. They shall speak of the glory òf your reign
4. You open wìde your hand,
5. You are close to àll who call you,

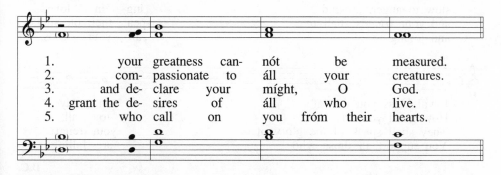

1. your greatness can- nót be measured.
2. com- passionate to áll your creatures.
3. and de- clare your míght, O God.
4. grant the de- sires of áll who live.
5. who call on you fróm their hearts.

Text: Psalm 145:2-3, 8-9, 10-11, 15-16, 17-18; The Grail
Music: Joseph Gelineau, SJ
© 1963, 1993, The Grail, GIA Publications, Inc., agent

192 Psalm 145: I Will Praise Your Name for Ever

Refrain

I will praise your name for ev -
er, my King and my God.

Text: *Lectionary for Mass,* © 1969, 1981, ICEL
Music: Leon Roberts, © 1987, GIA Publications, Inc.

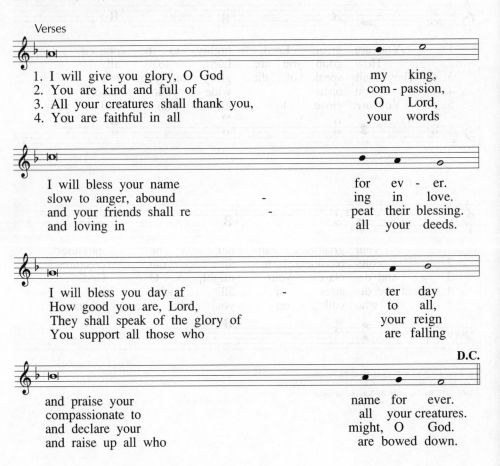

Verses

1. I will give you glory, O God — my king,
2. You are kind and full of — com - passion,
3. All your creatures shall thank you, O Lord,
4. You are faithful in all — your words

I will bless your name — for ev - er.
slow to anger, abound - ing in love.
and your friends shall re - peat their blessing.
and loving in — all your deeds.

I will bless you day af - ter day
How good you are, Lord, — to all,
They shall speak of the glory of — your reign
You support all those who — are falling

D.C.

and praise your — name for ever.
compassionate to — all your creatures.
and declare your — might, O God.
and raise up all who — are bowed down.

Text: Psalm 145:1-2, 8-9, 10-11, 13-14; © 1963, 1993, The Grail, GIA Publications, Inc., agent
Music: Paschal Jordan, OSB, © 1986, GIA Publications, Inc.

Psalm 145: I Will Praise Your Name   193

Refrain
Assembly:

I will praise your name, my King and my God. I will praise your name, my King and my God. I will praise your name, my King and my God.

To verses / *Last time*

King and my God. King and my God.

Verse 1

1. I will give you glo - ry, my God a - bove, and I will bless your name for ev - er. Ev - 'ry day

I will bless and praise your name for ev - er.

Verse 2

2. The Lord is full of grace and mer - cy,

who is kind and slow to an - ger. God is good in

ev - 'ry way, and full of com - pas - sion.

Verse 3

3. Let all your works give you thanks, O Lord, and

let all the faith - ful bless you. Let them speak of your

might, O Lord, the glo - ry of your king - dom.

Verse 4

4. The Lord is faith - ful in word and deed, and

al - ways near, his name is ho - ly. Lift - ing up all

those who fall, God rais - es up the low - ly.

Text: Psalm 145:1-2, 8-9, 10-11, 13b-14; David Haas
Music: David Haas
© 1983, GIA Publications, Inc.

Psalm 145: I Will Praise Your Name   194

Antiphon (St. 2.3.4 or 1.2.3.5)

I will praise your name for ev-er, my king and my God.

Text: *Lectionary for Mass,* © 1969, 1981, ICEL
Music: J. Robert Carroll, © 1975, GIA Publications, Inc.

Psalm Tone

Music: Douglas Mews, © 1981, ICEL

Gelineau Tone

1.	I will give you	glory,	O	Gòd	my	kìng,
2.	You are	kind	and	full	òf com-	passion,
3.	All your	creatures	shall	thank	yòu, O	Lord,
4.	To make	known	to	all your mìghty		deeds
5.	You are	faithful	in	àll	your	words

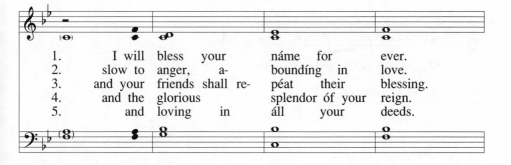

1.	I will bless your	náme for	ever.
2.	slow to anger, a-	boundíng in	love.
3.	and your friends shall re-	péat their	blessing.
4.	and the glorious	splendor óf your	reign.
5.	and loving in	áll your	deeds.

Psalm 145: I Will Praise Your Name   194

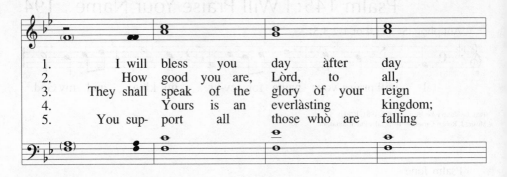

1.   I will bless you   day   àfter   day
2.   How good you are,   Lòrd,   to   all,
3.   They shall speak of the   glory òf your   reign
4.   Yours is an   everlàsting   kingdom;
5.   You sup- port all   those whò are   falling

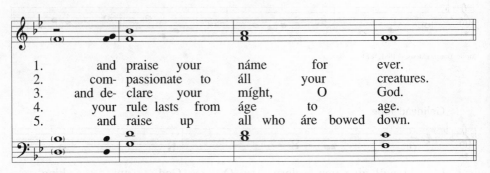

1.   and praise your   náme   for   ever.
2.   com- passionate to   áll   your   creatures.
3.   and de- clare your   míght,   O   God.
4.   your rule lasts from   áge   to   age.
5.   and raise up   all who   áre bowed   down.

Text: Psalm 145:1-2, 8-9, 10-11, 12-13, 13-14; The Grail
Music: Joseph Gelineau, SJ
© 1963, 1993, The Grail, GIA Publications, Inc., agent

195   Psalm 146: O Lord, Come and Save Us

Antiphon I

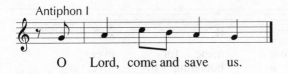

O   Lord,   come and save   us.

Text: *Lectionary for Mass,* © 1969, 1981, ICEL
Music: Robert LeBlanc, © 1975, GIA Publications, Inc.

Antiphon II

Praise   the Lord, my   soul!   Praise the   Lord!

Text: *Lectionary for Mass,* © 1969, 1981, ICEL
Music: Richard Proulx, © 1975, GIA Publications, Inc.

Psalm Tone

Music: Howard Hughes, SM, © 1986, GIA Publications, Inc.

Gelineau Tone

1. It is the Lord who keeps faith for ever,
2. The Lord who gives sight to thè blind,
3. It is the Lord who loves thè just

1. who is just to those who are óp- pressed.
2. who raises up those who are bówed down,
3. but thwarts the path of thé wicked.

1. It is God who gives bread to thè hungry,
2. the Lord, who pro- tects thè stranger
3. The Lord will reign for ever,

1. the Lord, who sets prisonérs free.
2. and up- holds the widow ánd orphan.
3. Zion's God, from age tó age.

Text: Psalm 146:6-7, 8-9, 9-10; The Grail
Music: Joseph Gelineau, SJ
© 1963, 1993, The Grail, GIA Publications, Inc., agent

196 Psalm 146: Happy the Poor

Refrain

Hap-py the poor in spir-it; the king-dom of heav-en is theirs!

Verses

1. It is the Lord who keeps faith for ever,
2. The Lord who gives sight to the blind,
3. The Lord upholds the wid - ow and orphan,

who is just to those who are op - pressed.
who raises up those who are bowed down,
but thwarts the path of the wick - ed.

It is God who gives bread to the hungry,
It is the Lord who loves the just,
The Lord will reign for ever,

D.C.

the Lord, who sets prisoners free.
the Lord, who protects the stran - ger.
Zion's God, from age to age.

Text: Psalm 146:6-7, 8-9, 9-10; © 1963, 1993, The Grail, GIA Publications, Inc., agent; refrain trans. © 1969, ICEL
Music: Michel Guimont, © 1995, GIA Publications, Inc.

Psalm 146: I Will Praise the Lord   197

Refrain
mf

I will praise the Lord all my days, make

mu-sic to my God while I live, make

Last time

mu-sic to my God while I live.

2. It is the
3. It is the

Verse 1
p

1. Put no trust in the pow-er-ful, mere

mor-tals in whom there is no help. Take their

breath, they re-turn to clay, and their

plans that day come to noth-ing. They are

hap-py who are helped by Ja-cob's God, whose

hope is in the Lord their God, who a -

lone made heav - en and earth, the

D.C.

seas and all they con - tain.

Verse 2
mp

(2.) Lord who keeps faith for ev - er, who is

3

just to the op - pressed. It is

God who gives bread to the hun - gry, the

Lord, who sets pris - on - ers free. It is the

Lord who gives sight to the blind, who

rais - es up those who are bowed down, the

Lord who pro-tects the stran - ger, and up -
holds the wid - ow and or - phan.

D.C.

Verse 3

(3.) Lord who loves the just but
thwarts the path of the wick-ed. The
Lord will reign for ev - er, Zi-on's

D.C.

God from age to age.

Text: Psalm 146; © 1963, 1993, The Grail, GIA Publications, Inc., agent
Tune: Michael Joncas, © 1990, GIA Publications, Inc.

198 Psalm 147: Praise the Lord

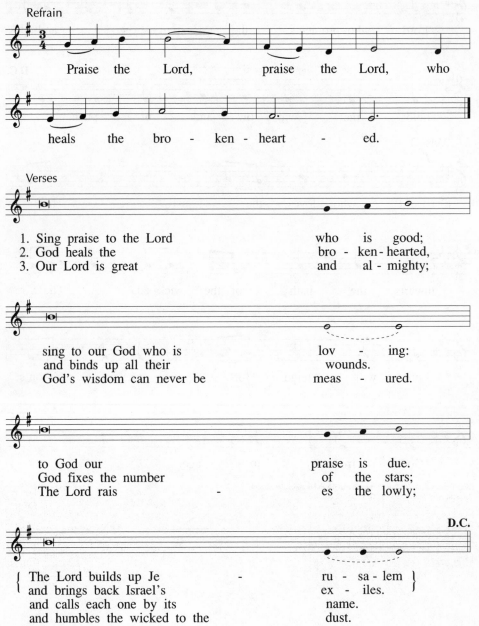

Refrain

Praise the Lord, praise the Lord, who

heals the bro - ken - heart - ed.

Verses

1. Sing praise to the Lord   who is good;
2. God heals the   bro - ken - hearted,
3. Our Lord is great   and al - mighty;

sing to our God who is   lov - ing:
and binds up all their   wounds.
God's wisdom can never be   meas - ured.

to God our   praise is due.
God fixes the number   of the stars;
The Lord rais -   es the lowly;

D.C.

{ The Lord builds up Je -   ru - sa - lem }
{ and brings back Israel's   ex - iles. }
and calls each one by its   name.
and humbles the wicked to the   dust.

Text: Psalm 147:1-2, 3-4, 5-6; © 1963, 1993, The Grail, GIA Publications, Inc., agent; refrain trans. © 1969, ICEL
Music: Michel Guimont, © 1995, GIA Publications, Inc.

Psalm 147: Praise the Lord   199

Antiphon

Praise   the   Lord,   Je - ru - sa - lem.

Text: *Lectionary for Mass,* © 1969, 1981, ICEL
Music: Chrysogonus Waddell, OCSO, © 1986, GIA Publications, Inc.

Psalm Tone

Music: Richard Proulx, © 1975, GIA Publications, Inc.

Gelineau Tone

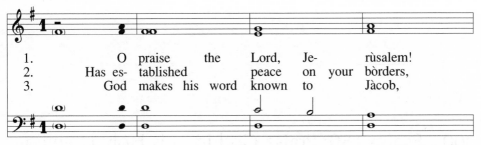

1.   O praise   the   Lord,   Je-   rùsalem!
2.   Has es- tablished   peace   on   your   bòrders,
3.   God   makes   his   word   known   to   Jàcob,

1.   Zí-   on   praise   your   God!
2.   and feeds yóu with   finest   wheat.
3.   to Israel   his   láws   and de-   crees.

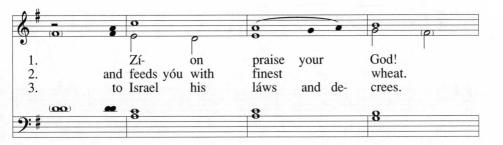

1.   God has   strength-ened   the   bars   of   your   gàtes,
2.   God   sends   out   word   to   the   èarth
3.   God has   not   dealt   thus with oth- er   nàtions;

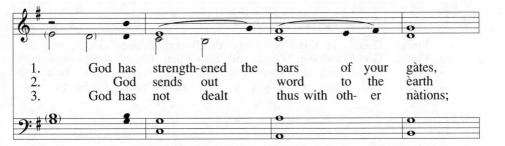

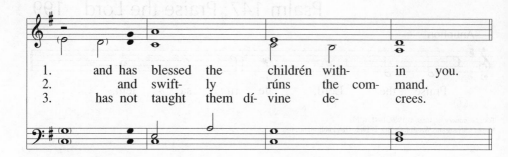

1. and has blessed the childrén with- in you.
2. and swift- ly rúns the com- mand.
3. has not taught them dí- vine de- crees.

Text: Psalm 147:12-13, 14-15, 19-20; The Grail
Music: Joseph Gelineau, SJ
© 1963, 1993, The Grail, GIA Publications, Inc., agent

200 Psalm 150: Praise God in This Holy Dwelling

Al- le - lu - ia, al - le - lu - ia, al- le- lu - ia.

1. Praise God in this ho - ly dwell- ing; Praise God on the
2. Praise God with the blast of trum - pet; Bring praise now with
3. Praise God with re - sound- ing cym - bals; With cym - bals that
4. Praise God, the al - might - y Fa - ther; Praise Christ, his be-

might - y throne; Prais - ing for all won - der-ful deeds;
lyre and harp; Prais - ing with the tim - brel and dance;
crash, give praise; O let ev - 'ry-thing that has breath,
lov - ed Son; Give praise to the Spir - it of love;

Sing praise to our sov - 'reign maj - es - ty.
With the gen - tle sound of string and reed.
Let all liv - ing crea - tures praise the Lord.
For ev - er the Tri - une God be praised.

Al - le - lu - ia, al - le - lu - ia,

1.-3.
al - le - lu - ia.

4.
lu - ia.

Text: Psalm 150:1-2, 3-4, 5-6; adapt. by Omer Westendorf
Music: Jan M. Vermulst
© 1964, World Library Publications, Inc.

201 Exodus 15: Let Us Sing to the Lord

Refrain *with vigor*

Cantor: Let us sing to the Lord; All: Let us sing to the Lord; Cantor: he has

cov-ered him-self in glo-ry; All: he has cov-ered him-self in glo-ry!

Verse 1

Cantor:

1. I will sing to the Lord, for he is gloriously tri - um - phant;

horse and chariot he has cast in - to the sea.

My strength and my courage is the Lord, and he has been my sav-ior.

D.C.

He is my God, I praise him; the God of my father, I ex-tol him.

Verse 2

Cantor:

2. The Lord is a warrior, Lord is his name!

Pharaoh's chariots and army he hurled in - to the sea.

At a breath of your anger the waters piled up,

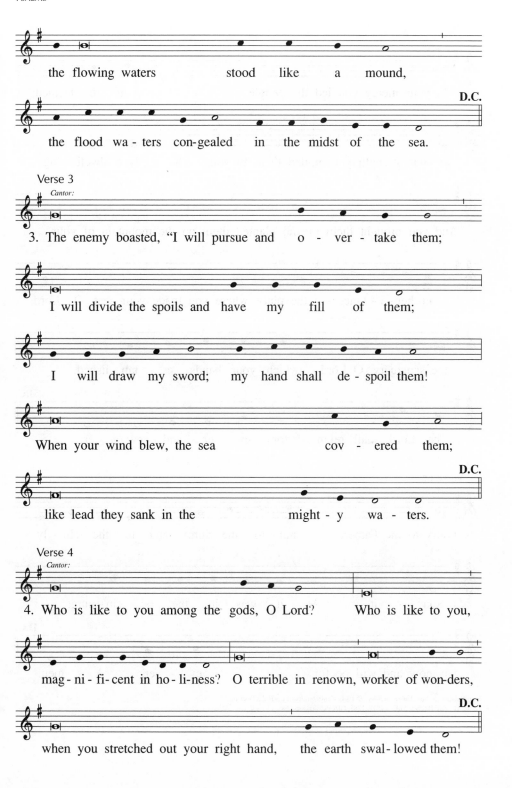

the flowing waters stood like a mound,

D.C.

the flood wa-ters con-gealed in the midst of the sea.

Verse 3

Cantor:

3. The enemy boasted, "I will pursue and o - ver - take them;

I will divide the spoils and have my fill of them;

I will draw my sword; my hand shall de - spoil them!

When your wind blew, the sea cov - ered them;

D.C.

like lead they sank in the might - y wa - ters.

Verse 4

Cantor:

4. Who is like to you among the gods, O Lord? Who is like to you,

mag - ni - fi - cent in ho - li-ness? O terrible in renown, worker of won-ders,

D.C.

when you stretched out your right hand, the earth swal-lowed them!

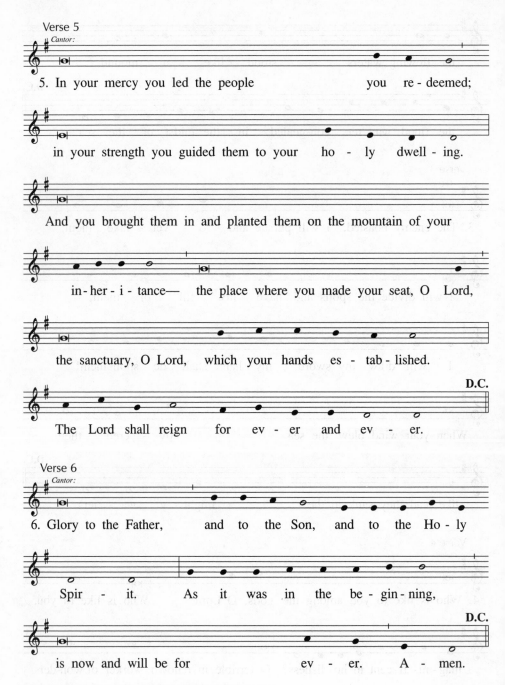

Verse 5

Cantor:

5. In your mercy you led the people   you re - deemed;

in your strength you guided them to your   ho - ly   dwell - ing.

And you brought them in and planted them on the mountain of your

in - her - i - tance—   the place where you made your seat, O   Lord,

the sanctuary, O Lord,   which your hands es - tab - lished.

D.C.

The   Lord   shall   reign   for   ev - er   and   ev - er.

Verse 6

Cantor:

6. Glory to the Father,   and   to   the   Son,   and   to   the   Ho - ly

Spir - it.   As   it   was   in   the   be - gin - ning,

D.C.

is   now   and   will   be   for   ev - er.   A - men.

Text: Exodus 15, *New American Bible,* © 1970, Confraternity of Christian Doctrine
Music: Howard Hughes, SM, © 1979, 1988, GIA Publications, Inc.

Exodus 15: Song at the Sea   202

Refrain

Melody:

Let us sing   to the   Lord   who is

Harmony:

Let us sing,   sing to the   Lord,

cov - ered   in   won - drous   glo   -   ry.

Last time ⌢

Last time ⌢

Verse 1

1. I   will   sing   to   the   Lord,   in   glo - ry   tri -

um - phant;   horse   and   rid - er   are   thrown   to

the   sea.   God   of   strength,   of   song,   of   sal -

va - tion,   God   of   mine,   hear   these   prais - es.

D.C.

Verse 2

2. My   God   is   a   war - rior   whose   name   is   "The

Lord."   Phar - oah's   ar - my   is   thrown   to

the sea. Your right hand is mag - nif - i - cent in

D.C.

pow'r, your right hand has crushed the en - e- my.

Verse 3

3. In your mer - cy you led the

peo - ple you re - deemed. You brought them

to your sa - cred home.

There you will plant them on the moun - tain that is

D.C.

yours. The Lord shall reign for - ev - er!

Text: Exodus 15; Niamh O'Kelly-Fischer
Music: Niamh O'Kelly-Fischer
© 1992, GIA Publications, Inc.

1 Chronicles 29: We Praise Your Glorious Name   203

Antiphon

We praise your glo - ri - ous name, O might - y God!

Text: *Lectionary for Mass,* © 1969, ICEL
Music: Richard Proulx, © 1975, GIA Publications, Inc.

Psalm Tone

Music: Chant tone 8-g; acc. by Richard Proulx, © 1985, GIA Publications, Inc.

Gelineau Tone

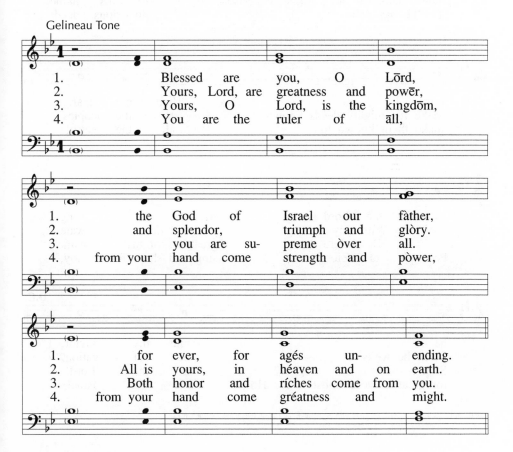

1. Blessed are you, O Lōrd,
2. Yours, Lord, are greatness and powēr,
3. Yours, O Lord, is the kingdōm,
4. You are the ruler of āll,

1.   the God of Israel our fàther,
2.   and splendor, triumph and glòry.
3.   you are su- preme òver all.
4. from your hand come strength and pòwer,

1.   for ever, for agés un- ending.
2. All is yours, in héaven and on earth.
3. Both honor and ríches come from you.
4. from your hand come gréatness and might.

Text: 1 Chronicles 29:10, 11, 11-12, 12
Music: Joseph Gelineau, SJ
© 1963, The Grail, GIA Publications, Inc., agent

204 Isaiah 12: You Will Draw Water

Refrain

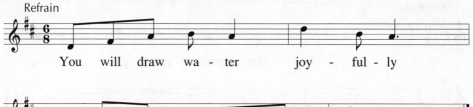

You will draw wa - ter joy - ful - ly

from the springs of sal - va - tion.

Verses

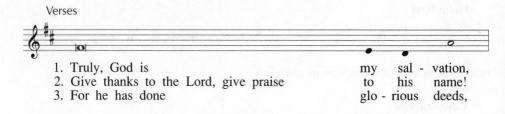

1. Truly, God is — my sal - vation,
2. Give thanks to the Lord, give praise — to his name!
3. For he has done — glo - rious deeds,

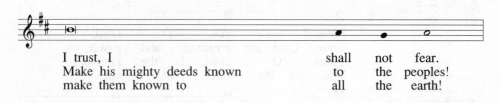

I trust, I — shall not fear.
Make his mighty deeds known — to the peoples!
make them known to — all the earth!

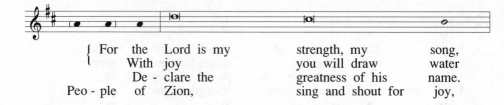

{ For the Lord is my — strength, my song,
With joy — you will draw water
De - clare the — greatness of his name.
Peo - ple of Zion, — sing and shout for joy,

D.C.

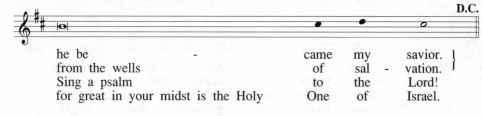

he be - — came my savior. }
from the wells — of sal - vation. }
Sing a psalm — to the Lord!
for great in your midst is the Holy — One of Israel.

Text: Isaiah 12:2-3, 4, 5-6; © 1963, The Grail, GIA Publications, Inc., agent; refrain trans. © 1969, ICEL
Music: Michel Guimont, © 1995, GIA Publications, Inc.

Isaiah 12: Cry Out with Joy and Gladness   205

Antiphon

Cry out with joy and glad - ness: for a -

mong you is the great and Ho - ly One of Is - ra - el.

Text: *Lectionary for Mass,* © 1969, ICEL
Music: Robert J. Batastini, © 1975, GIA Publications, Inc.

Psalm Tone

Music: A. Gregory Murray, OSB, © L. J. Carey & Co., Ltd.

Gelineau Tone

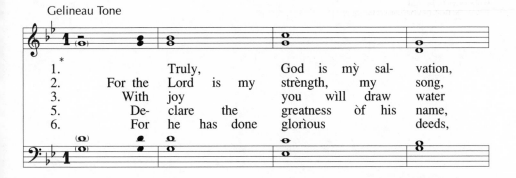

1.*		Truly,	God is mỳ sal-	vation,
2.	For the	Lord is my	strèngth, my	song,
3.	With	joy	you will draw	water
5.	De-	clare the	greatness òf his	name,
6.	For	he has done	glorìous	deeds,

1.		I	trust, I shàll not	fear.
2.		he be-	cáme my	savior.
3.		from the	wells óf sal-	vation.
5.		sing a	psalm tó the	Lord!
6.		make them	known to àll the	earth!

*The antiphon is sung after stanzas 3, 4, and 7.

4.   Give   thanks to the   Lord, give   praise tò his   name!
7.   People of   Zion,   sing   and   shòut   for   joy

(hum)

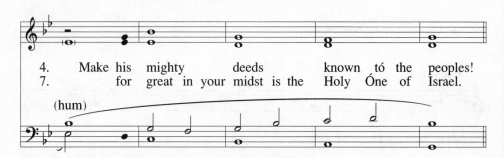

4.   Make his   mighty   deeds   known tó the   peoples!
7.   for   great in your midst is the   Holy Óne of   Israel.

(hum)

Text: Isaiah 12:2-3, 4-5, 5-6
Music: Joseph Gelineau, SJ
© 1963, The Grail, GIA Publications, Inc., agent

Daniel 3:52-57 / Song of the Three Children   206

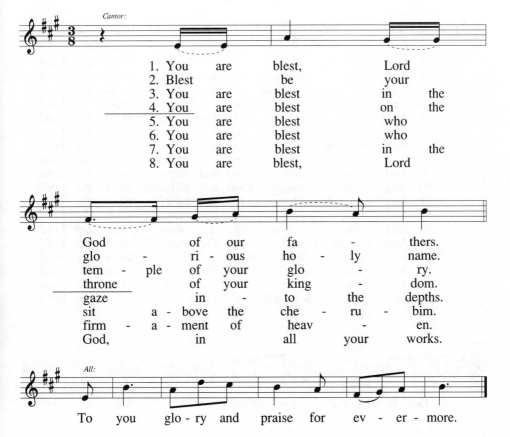

Cantor:

1. You   are   blest,   Lord
2. Blest   be   your
3. You   are   blest   in   the
4. You   are   blest   on   the
5. You   are   blest   who
6. You   are   blest   who
7. You   are   blest   in   the
8. You   are   blest,   Lord

God   of   our   fa   -   thers.
glo   -   ri   -   ous   ho   -   ly   name.
tem   -   ple   of   your   glo   -   ry.
throne   of   your   king   -   dom.
gaze   in   -   to   the   depths.
sit   a - bove   the   che   -   ru   -   bim.
firm   -   a - ment   of   heav   -   en.
God,   in   all   your   works.

All:

To   you   glo - ry   and   praise   for   ev - er - more.

Text: Daniel 2:52-57; The Grail
Music: Joseph Gelineau, SJ
© 1963, The Grail, GIA Publications, Inc., agent

207 Daniel 3:57-88 / Song of the Three Children

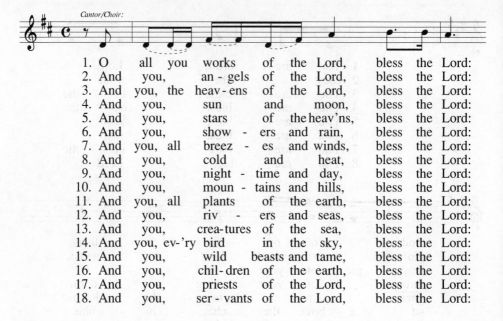

Cantor/Choir:

1. O all you works of the Lord, bless the Lord:
2. And you, an - gels of the Lord, bless the Lord:
3. And you, the heav - ens of the Lord, bless the Lord:
4. And you, sun and moon, bless the Lord:
5. And you, stars of the heav'ns, bless the Lord:
6. And you, show - ers and rain, bless the Lord:
7. And you, all breez - es and winds, bless the Lord:
8. And you, cold and heat, bless the Lord:
9. And you, night - time and day, bless the Lord:
10. And you, moun - tains and hills, bless the Lord:
11. And you, all plants of the earth, bless the Lord:
12. And you, riv - ers and seas, bless the Lord:
13. And you, crea-tures of the sea, bless the Lord:
14. And you, ev-'ry bird in the sky, bless the Lord:
15. And you, wild beasts and tame, bless the Lord:
16. And you, chil-dren of the earth, bless the Lord:
17. And you, priests of the Lord, bless the Lord:
18. And you, ser - vants of the Lord, bless the Lord:

All:

To God be high-est glo - ry and praise for ev - er.

Text: Daniel 3:57-88; The Grail
Music: A. Gregory Murray, OSB
© 1963, The Grail, GIA Publications, Inc., agent

Daniel 3:57-87 / Benedicite 208

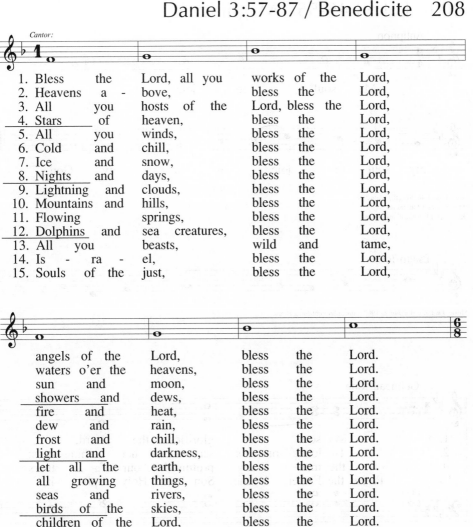

Cantor:

1. Bless the Lord, all you works of the Lord,
2. Heavens a - bove, bless the Lord,
3. All you hosts of the Lord, bless the Lord,
4. Stars of heaven, bless the Lord,
5. All you winds, bless the Lord,
6. Cold and chill, bless the Lord,
7. Ice and snow, bless the Lord,
8. Nights and days, bless the Lord,
9. Lightning and clouds, bless the Lord,
10. Mountains and hills, bless the Lord,
11. Flowing springs, bless the Lord,
12. Dolphins and sea creatures, bless the Lord,
13. All you beasts, wild and tame,
14. Is - ra - el, bless the Lord,
15. Souls of the just, bless the Lord,

angels of the Lord, bless the Lord.
waters o'er the heavens, bless the Lord.
sun and moon, bless the Lord.
showers and dews, bless the Lord.
fire and heat, bless the Lord.
dew and rain, bless the Lord.
frost and chill, bless the Lord.
light and darkness, bless the Lord.
let all the earth, bless the Lord.
all growing things, bless the Lord.
seas and rivers, bless the Lord.
birds of the skies, bless the Lord.
children of the Lord, bless the Lord.
servants of the Lord, bless the Lord.
humble hearts, bless the Lord.

All:

Praise and ex - alt him for ev - er, O

praise and ex - alt him for ev - er.

Text: Daniel 3:57-87, *New American Bible,* © 1970, Confraternity of Christian Doctrine
Music: Robert M. Hutmacher, OFM, © 1984, GIA Publications, Inc.

209 Luke 1:46-55 / Magnificat

Antiphon

My soul re - joic - es,

my soul re - joic - es in my God.

Text: Luke 1:46; Robert J. Batastini
Music: Robert J. Batastini
© 1975, GIA Publications, Inc.

Psalm Tone

Music: *Lutheran Worship,* © 1982, Concordia Publishing House

Gelineau Tone

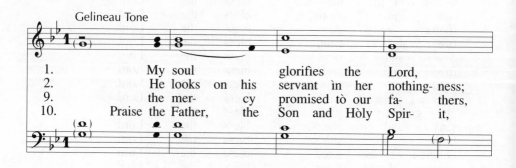

1.   My soul   glorifies   the   Lord,
2.   He looks on his   servant in her   nothing- ness;
9.   the mer-   cy   promised tò our   fa-   thers,
10.   Praise the Father,   the   Son and Hòly   Spir-   it,

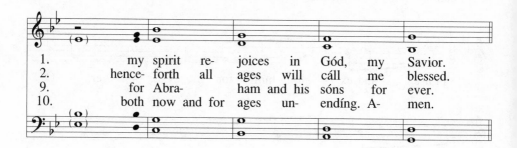

1.   my spirit   re-   joices   in   Gód,   my   Savior.
2.   hence- forth   all   ages   will   cáll   me   blessed.
9.   for Abra-   ham and his   sóns   for   ever.
10.   both now and for   ages   un-   endíng. A-   men.

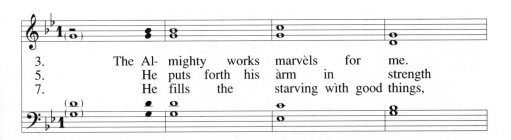

3. The Al- mighty works marvèls for me.
5. He puts forth his àrm in strength
7. He fills the starving with good things,

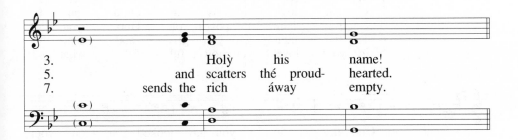

3. Holỳ his name!
5. and scatters thé proud- hearted.
7. sends the rich áway empty.

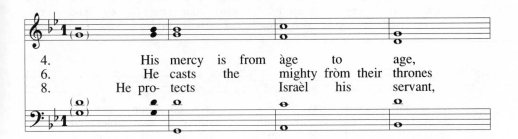

4. His mercy is from àge to age,
6. He casts the mighty fròm their thrones
8. He pro- tects Israèl his servant,

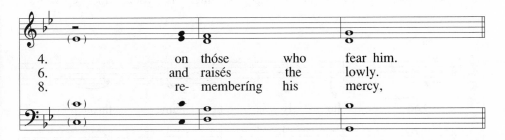

4. on thóse who fear him.
6. and raisés the lowly.
8. re- memberíng his mercy,

Text: Luke 1:46-55; The Grail
Music: Joseph Gelineau, SJ
© 1963, The Grail, GIA Publications, Inc., agent

210 Luke 1:46-55 / Magnificat / Holy Is Your Name

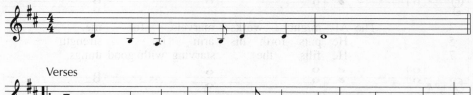

Verses

1. My soul is filled with joy as I
2. I am low - ly as a child, but I
3. I pro - claim the pow'r of God, you do
4. To the hun - gry you give food, send the
5. In your love you now ful - fill what you

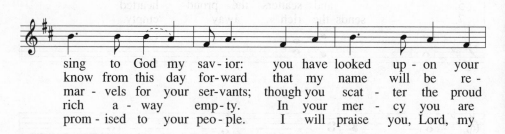

sing to God my sav - ior: you have looked up - on your
know from this day for - ward that my name will be re -
mar - vels for your ser - vants; though you scat - ter the proud
rich a - way emp - ty. In your mer - cy you are
prom - ised to your peo - ple. I will praise you, Lord, my

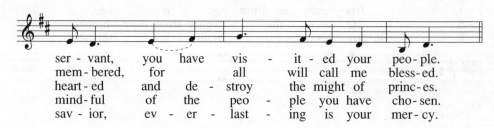

ser - vant, you have vis - it - ed your peo - ple.
mem - bered, for all will call me bless - ed.
heart - ed and de - stroy the might of princ - es.
mind - ful of the peo - ple you have cho - sen.
sav - ior, ev - er - last - ing is your mer - cy.

Refrain

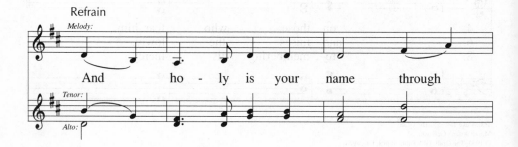

Melody:

And ho - ly is your name through

Tenor:

Alto:

all gen - er - a - tions! Ev - er - last - ing is your

mer - cy to the peo - ple you have cho - sen, and

Final ending

ho - ly is your name.

Text: Luke 1:46-55, David Haas
Music: WILD MOUNTAIN THYME, Irregular; Irish traditional; arr. by David Haas
© 1989, GIA Publications, Inc.

211 Luke 1:46-55 / Magnificat

Refrain

Descant:

Pro - claim the great-ness of God; re-

Melody:

Pro - claim the great-ness of God; re - joice in God, my

joice in God. Re - joice in God, my Sav-ior!

Sav-ior! Re - joice in God, my Sav-ior!

Verses

unis.

1. For he has fa - vored his
2. He fa - vors those who
3. He has cast the might - y
4. He has helped his ser - vant

div.

Melody:

low - ly one, and all shall call me
fear his name, in ev - 'ry gen - er -
from their thrones, and lift - ed up the
Is - ra - el, re - mem - ber - ing his

bless - ed. The al - might - y has done great things for
a - tion. He has shown the might and strength of his
low - ly. He has filled the hun - gry with all good
mer - cy. He prom-ised his mer - cy to A - bra -

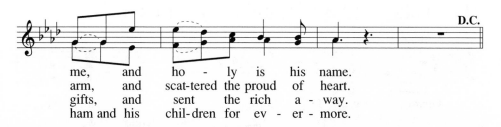

D.C.

me,	and	ho - ly	is	his	name.
arm,	and	scat-tered the	proud	of	heart.
gifts,	and	sent the	rich	a -	way.
ham and his		chil-dren for	ev -	er -	more.

Text: Luke 1:46-55; James J. Chepponis
Music: James J. Chepponis
© 1980, GIA Publications, Inc.

212 Luke 2:29-32 / Canticle of Simeon

Antiphon

Guard us, O Lord, while we
while we

sleep, and keep us in peace.

Text: The Grail
Music: Guy Weitz and A. Gregory Murray, OSB
© 1963, The Grail, GIA Publications, Inc., agent

Psalm Tone

Music: Psalm tone 3-b; acc. by Richard Proulx, © 1975, GIA Publications, Inc.

Gelineau Tone

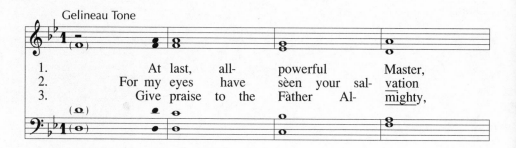

1. At last, all-powerful Master,
2. For my eyes have seen your sal- vation
3. Give praise to the Father Al- mighty,

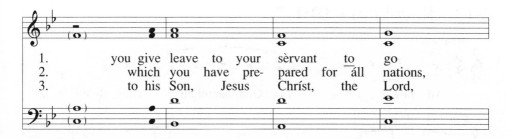

1. you give leave to your sèrvant to go
2. which you have pre- pared for áll nations,
3. to his Son, Jesus Chríst, the Lord,

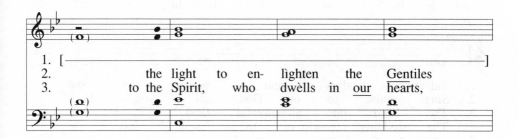

1. [   ]
2. the light to en- lìghten the Gentiles
3. to the Spirit, who dwèlls in our hearts,

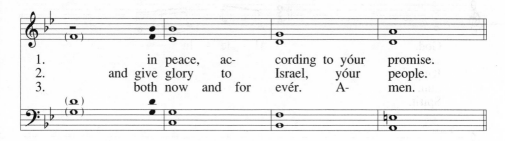

1. in peace, ac- cording to yóur promise.
2. and give glory to Israel, yóur people.
3. both now and for evér. A- men.

Text: Luke 2:29-32; The Grail
Music: Joseph Gelineau
© 1963, The Grail, GIA Publications, Inc., agent

213 Revelation 19:1-7

Antiphon

All pow'r is yours, Lord God, our might-y King, al-le-lu-ia!

Refrain I

Al-le-lu - ia, al-le-lu - ia!

Canticle

Cantor:

1. Salvation, glory and power to our
2. Sing praise to our God, all you his
3. The Lord our all-powerful God is
4. The wedding feast of the Lamb has be-
5. Glory to the Father, and to the Son, and to the Holy

Refrain II

God: Al - le - lu - ia!
servants,
King;
gun,
Spirit,

Cantor:

his judgements are honest and
all who worship him reverently, great and
let us rejoice, sing praise, and give him
and his bride is pre- pared to
as it was in the beginning, is now, and will be for ever. A-

Refrain I

true. Al-le-lu - ia, al-le-lu - ia!
small.
glory.
welcome him.
men.

Text: Revelation 19:1-7; Howard Hughes, SM
Music: Howard Hughes, SM
© 1977, ICEL

Christian Initiation of Adults

The passage of an adult into the Christian community takes place over an extended period of time. The members of the local church, the catechists and sponsors, the clergy and the diocesan bishop take part in the journey from inquiry through the catechumenate to baptism, confirmation and eucharist. The candidates are invited by example to pray, reflect on the scriptures, to fast and to join in the community's practice of charity. They are to learn the way of Jesus from the members of the church.

This journey of the candidates and community is marked by liturgical rites; thus the community publicly acknowledges, encourages and strengthens the candidates. The first of these is the rite of becoming catechumens. It concludes the sometimes lengthy period during which those who have come to ask about the way of the church and the life of a Christian have heard the gospel proclaimed and seen it practiced. Those who then feel called to walk in this way of Christ's church ask to begin the journey toward baptism. If the church judges the inquirers ready, they are accepted into the order of catechumens.

Those who have entered the catechumenate are already part of the household of Christ. During this time the catechumens are to hear and reflect on God's word, to learn the teachings and practices of the church, to become gradually accustomed to the ways of prayer and discipline in the church, to observe and to join in the good works of Christians. Ordinarily the catechumens are present on Sunday for the liturgy of the word and may be dismissed after the homily—to continue prayer and study with their catechists—since they cannot join in the eucharist.

Rites of exorcism and blessing may be celebrated during the catechumenate. Through such rites the church prays that the catechumens will be purified, strengthened against all evil and thus eagerly grow in faith and good works. The very presence of the catechumens—at the Sunday liturgy, in these special rites and in everyday life—is itself a source of strength and blessing to the faithful.

Each year as Lent begins, the bishop, with the help of the local pastor and others involved with the catechumens, is to call those catechumens who are judged ready to prepare themselves for baptism at the Easter Vigil. Thus the catechumens become the "elect", the chosen, and for the forty days of Lent they make preparations: praying, fasting, doing good works. All the faithful join them in this. On several Sundays in Lent the rites of scrutiny take place when the assembled church prays over the elect. During Lent also the catechumens may publicly receive the words of the church's profession of faith (creed) and the Lord's Prayer.

Good Friday and Holy Saturday are days of prayer, fasting and preparation for the rites of the Easter Vigil. On the night between Saturday and Easter Sunday, the church assembles to keep vigil and listen to many readings from scripture. Then the catechumens are called forward for baptism and confirmation. These rites are found in the Easter Vigil.

The newly baptized, now called neophytes, take a special place in the Sunday eucharist throughout the fifty days of Eastertime. This is a time for their full incorporation into the local community.

All of these stages of initiation take place in the midst of the community. In various rites, the faithful affirm their support for the catechumens. The daily lives of the faithful show the Christian life to the inquirers and catechumens. In turn, the faithful are strengthened and challenged in their faith by the presence of the catechumens.

Those who seek to belong to the Roman Catholic church and who are already baptized may take some part in the catechumenate but they are not baptized again. Rather, they are received into the full communion of the Roman Catholic Church by a profession of faith.

215 ACCEPTANCE INTO THE ORDER OF CATECHUMENS

INTRODUCTORY RITES

The priest greets the assembly: candidates, sponsors, members of the parish. The candidates are asked what it is that they seek and each replies. After each candidate has responded, one of the following acclamations may be sung by the assembly:

216

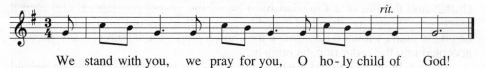

We stand with you, we pray for you, O ho-ly child of God!

Text: David Haas, b.1957
Tune: David Haas, b.1957
© 1988, GIA Publications, Inc.

217

We praise you, Lord, we praise you, Lord,

we praise you, Lord, and we bless you.

Music: Marty Haugen, © 1995, GIA Publications, Inc.

CANDIDATES' FIRST ACCEPTANCE OF THE GOSPEL 218

The priest solemnly asks if the candidates are ready to begin walking this way of the gospel. The sponsors and all present are asked if they stand ready to assist the candidates as they strive to know and follow Christ. All respond: **We are.**

SIGNING OF THE CANDIDATES WITH THE CROSS 219

The sign of the cross marks the candidates for their new way of life. The priest signs each on the forehead saying:

N., receive the cross on your forehead.
It is Christ himself who now strengthens you
with this sign of his love.
Learn now to know him and follow him.

Sponsors and others also sign the candidates. Ears and eyes and other senses may also be signed. The priest prays that the catechumens may share in the saving power of the cross.

One of the following musical settings with assembly acclamations may be used:

220

Priest: Receive the sign of the cross....

Christ will be your strength! Learn to know and fol-low him.

Music: David Haas, © 1988, GIA Publications, Inc.

221

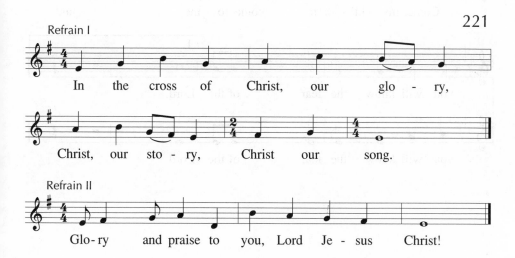

Refrain I

In the cross of Christ, our glo - ry,

Christ, our sto - ry, Christ our song.

Refrain II

Glo- ry and praise to you, Lord Je - sus Christ!

Verses

freely

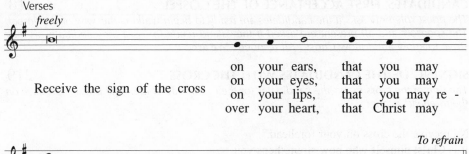

Receive the sign of the cross

on your ears, that you may
on your eyes, that you may
on your lips, that you may re -
over your heart, that Christ may

To refrain

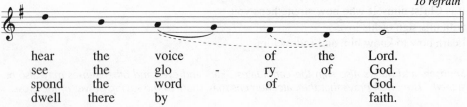

hear	the	voice	of	the	Lord.
see	the	glo - ry	of	God.
spond	the	word	of	God.
dwell	there	by	faith.

Text: Adapt. by Marty Haugen
Music: Marty Haugen
© 1995, GIA Publications, Inc.

222 INVITATION TO THE CELEBRATION OF THE WORD OF GOD

The assembly may go into the church for the liturgy of the word singing the following psalm:

Refrain

Descant:

Come, my chil - dren, come to me, and

Melody:

Come, my chil - dren, come to me, and

1.

you will know the fear of the Lord.

you will know the fear of the Lord.

Text: Psalm 34; adapt. by David Haas
Music: David Haas
© 1988, GIA Publications, Inc.

223 LITURGY OF THE WORD

There may be one or more readings from scripture, together with a responsorial psalm. After the homily, a book containing the scriptures may be given to the new catechumens for their study and prayer throughout the time of the catechumenate.

INTERCESSIONS

All join in prayer for the new catechumens.

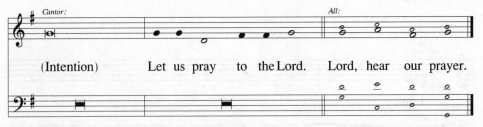

Music: Byzantine chant; harm. by Robert J. Batastini, © 1986, GIA Publications, Inc.

If the eucharist is to be celebrated, the catechumens may be dismissed.

RITES OF THE CATECHUMENATE 224

DISMISSAL OF THE CATECHUMENS

When the catechumens are present at Mass, they are usually dismissed after the homily. Only when they have been baptized are they able to join the faithful in the reception of the eucharist. After their dismissal, the catechumens remain together and are joined by their catechists or others to pray and reflect on the scripture.

One of the following settings may be sung to accompany the dismissal:

225

Priest: Go in peace, and may the Lord remain with you   always.

All: Go now in peace, go now in peace,

Christ will be your way, your truth, your life.

Text: *Rite of Christian Initiation of Adults*, © 1985, ICEL
Music: Lynn Trapp, © 1991, Morning Star Music Publishers

226

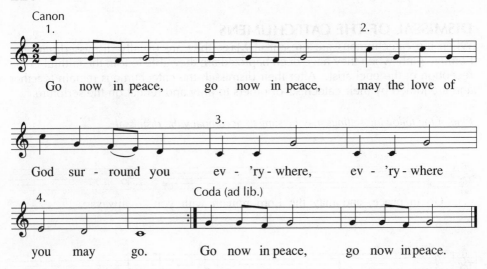

Go now in peace, go now in peace, may the love of
God sur - round you ev - 'ry - where, ev - 'ry - where
you may go. Go now in peace, go now in peace.

Text: Natalie Sleeth, *Sunday Songbook*
Tune: Natalie Sleeth, *Sunday Songbook*
© 1976, Hinshaw Music, Inc.

227 CELEBRATIONS OF THE WORD OF GOD

On Sundays, after the catechetical sessions, before the liturgical seasons and at other times the catechumens and others may join for liturgy: song, reading of scripture, psalmody, prayer and silence are normally part of such a service.

228 MINOR EXORCISMS

At appropriate times during the catechumenate, the catechists or other ministers may lead the community in prayers of exorcism over the catechumens. These prayers acknowledge the struggle against evil and ask that God strengthen the catechumens.

229 BLESSINGS OF THE CATECHUMENS

Prayers of blessing and the laying on of hands may take place whenever the catechumens gather for instruction of other purposes. Catechists or other ministers ask these blessings over the catechumens.

230 ANOINTINGS AND PRESENTATIONS

During the catechumenate or during Lent, the candidates may be anointed with the oil of catechumens as a sign of strength given for their struggle to live the gospel. At some point in this time they are publicly presented with the church's treasury of prayer and faith, the Our Father and the Creed.

231 RITE OF ELECTION OR ENROLLMENT OF NAMES

On the first Sunday of Lent, the following acclamation, with or without verses, may be sung while or immediately after the candidates sign their names in the book:

Text: David Haas
Music: David Haas
© 1988, GIA Publications, Inc.

232 SCRUTINIES

The scrutinies occur on the third, fourth and fifth Sundays of Lent. The elect are called before the community for exorcism and prayer. This rite may conclude with the following song, sung prior to dismissal of the elect:

Refrain

First Scrutiny: God of all pow-er, foun-tain of grace: O liv-ing
Second Scrutiny: God of all mer-cy, re-store our sight: Lead us from
Third Scrutiny: God of the liv-ing, not of the dead: Raise us to

wa-ter, show your face! God of all pow-er, foun-tain of
dark-ness in-to light! God of all mer-cy, re-store our
life be-yond our death! God of the liv-ing, not of the

rit. ⌢ *Last time*

grace: O liv-ing wa-ter, show your face!
sight: Lead us from dark-ness in-to light!
dead: Raise us to life be-yond our death!

Verses

Freely ⌢

First Scrutiny: 1. Come to us, O liv-ing wa-ter, Lord, we thirst for
2. Come to us, God of for-give-ness, foun-tain of our
3. Come to us, God of com-pas-sion, com-fort in our
Second Scrutiny: 1. Come to us, Lord Je-sus, O king-dom of all
2. Come to us, light in our dark-ness, help us all to
3. Come to us, O sav-ing light, burn with-in our
Third Scrutiny: 1. Come to us, O ris-en Christ, prom-ise of new
2. Come to us, O ho-ly one, vic-t'ry from the
3. Come to us, Great God of pow-er, sign to all the

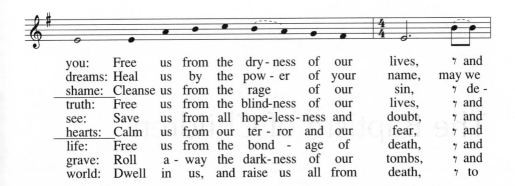

you:	Free	us	from	the	dry-ness	of	our	lives,	ɣ and
dreams:	Heal	us	by	the	pow-er	of	your	name,	may we
shame:	Cleanse	us	from	the	rage	of	our	sin,	ɣ de-
truth:	Free	us	from	the	blind-ness	of	our	lives,	ɣ and
see:	Save	us	from	all	hope-less-ness	and	doubt,	ɣ and
hearts:	Calm	us	from	our	ter-ror	and	our	fear,	ɣ and
life:	Free	us	from	the	bond-age	of	death,	ɣ and
grave:	Roll	a-way	the	dark-ness	of	our	tombs,	ɣ and
world:	Dwell	in	us,	and	raise	us	all	from	death,	ɣ to

pur-i-fy	our	hearts	to	hear	your	word!
drink	of	you	and	nev-er	thirst	a-gain!
liv-er	us,	and	keep	us	in	your	peace!
lead	us	to	the	vi-sion	of	your	light!
o-pen	up	our	eyes	to	fol-low	you!
show	to	us	the	free-dom	of	your	way!
share	with	us	the	hope	of	your	glo-ry!
breathe	in	us	the	won-der	of	new	life!
live,	to	pray,	to	heal,	and	to	for-give!

Text: David Haas
Music: David Haas
© 1988, GIA Publications, Inc.

PREPARATORY RITES 233
Various preparation rites take place during the day on Holy Saturday. These include prayer, recitation of the Creed, and the rite of Ephpheta (opening of ears and mouth).

SACRAMENTS OF INITIATION 234
The sacraments of initiation take place at the Easter Vigil.

PERIOD OF MYSTAGOGIA 235
"Mystagogia" refers to the fifty-day period of postbaptismal celebration when the newly baptized are gradually drawn by the community into the fullness of Christian life and prayer. The newly baptized retain a special place in the assembly and are mentioned in the prayers of intercession. A special celebration, on Pentecost or just before, may mark the conclusion of the whole period of initiation.

The Baptism of Children

236

Children are baptized in the faith of the church: of parents, godparents, the local parish, the church throughout the world, the saints. Bringing their children for baptism, the parents profess their commitment to make a home where the gospel is lived. And the godparents and all members of the community promise to support the parents in this. Thus the children enter the waters of baptism and so are joined to this people, all baptized into the death and resurrection of Christ.

Baptism is celebrated above all at the Easter Vigil, but also on other Sundays, for Sunday is the Lord's day, the day when the church gathers to proclaim the paschal mystery. Although baptism may take place at the Sunday Mass, it is always to be celebrated in an assembly of members of the church.

237 RECEPTION OF THE CHILDREN

The parents and godparents are welcomed by all. The priest/deacon asks the names of the children and questions the parents about their own expectations and willingness to take on the responsibilities this baptism brings. The godparents are asked if they are ready to assist the parents to become Christian mothers and fathers.

With joy, then, the priest/deacon, the parents and godparents make the sign of the cross on the child's forehead: "I claim you for Christ our Savior by the sign of his cross."

All then go in procession to the place where the scriptures will be read. The following antiphon, or a hymn, may be sung during this procession:

Cantor: There is one God and

Text: ICEL, © 1969
Music: Marty Haugen, © 1995, GIA Publications, Inc.

238 LITURGY OF THE WORD

FIRST READINGS

One or more passages from scripture are read. At the conclusion of each:

    Reader: The word of the Lord.

    Assembly: **Thanks be to God.**

RESPONSORIAL PSALM

The following psalm may follow the first reading:

Refrain

The Lord   is my   light   and my sal - va - tion.

Text: *Lectionary for Mass,* © 1969, ICEL
Music: Anthony E. Jackson, © 1984

Verses

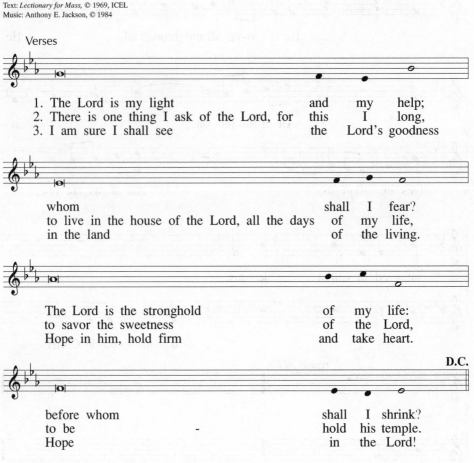

1. The Lord is my light   and   my   help;
2. There is one thing I ask of the Lord, for   this   I   long,
3. I am sure I shall see   the   Lord's goodness

whom   shall I fear?
to live in the house of the Lord, all the days   of my life,
in the land   of the living.

The Lord is the stronghold   of my life:
to savor the sweetness   of the Lord,
Hope in him, hold firm   and take heart.

D.C.

before whom   shall I shrink?
to be   -   hold his temple.
Hope   in the Lord!

Text: Psalm 27:1, 4, 13-14, © 1963, The Grail, GIA Publications, Inc., agent
Music: Cyril Baker, © The Antilles Episcopal Conference

GOSPEL

239

Before the gospel reading, this acclamation is sung:

Al-le-lu-ia, al-le-lu-ia, al-le-lu-ia.

Music: Chant Mode VI; acc. by Richard Proulx, © 1985, GIA Publications, Inc.

During Lent:

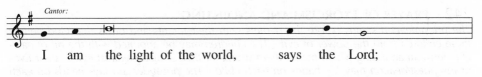

Praise to you, Lord Je-sus Christ, king of end-less glo-ry!

Music: Frank Schoen, © 1970, GIA Publications, Inc.

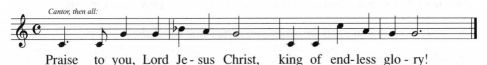

I am the light of the world, says the Lord;

the one who follows me will have the light of life.

Text: ICEL, © 1969
Music: Tone 6F, acc. by Robert J. Batastini, © 1986, GIA Publications, Inc.

Deacon (or priest): The Lord be with you.

Assembly: **And also with you.**

Deacon: A reading from the holy gospel according to N.

Assembly: **Glory to you, Lord.**

After the reading:

Deacon: The gospel of the Lord.

Assembly: **Praise to you, Lord Jesus Christ.**

GENERAL INTERCESSIONS

240

All join in prayer for the church, the needs of the world, the poor, the children to be baptized and their parents.

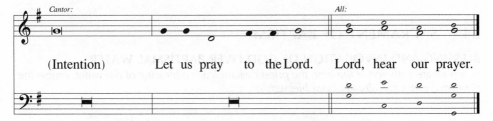

(Intention) Let us pray to the Lord. Lord, hear our prayer.

Music: Byzantine chant; harm. by Robert J. Batastini, © 1986, GIA Publications, Inc.

241

This prayer concludes with the litany of the saints which may include the patron saints of the children and of the local church.

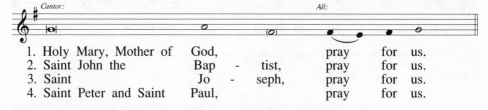

1. Holy Mary, Mother of God,   pray for us.
2. Saint John the Bap - tist,   pray for us.
3. Saint Jo - seph,   pray for us.
4. Saint Peter and Saint Paul,   pray for us.

The names of other saints may be added here. The litany concludes:

5. All you saints of God,   pray for us.

242   PRAYER OF EXORCISM AND ANOINTING

The priest/deacon stands before the parents with their infants and prays that God deliver these children from the power of evil. The children may be anointed with the oil of cate-chumens, an anointing which makes them strong for their struggle against evil in their lives or the priest/deacon may lay hands on each child. The priest/deacon lays hands on each child to show the love and concern the Church has for them. If there is a procession to the baptistry, the following may be sung:

We come to you, Lord Je - sus, fill us with your

1. life. We life. 2. Make us chil - dren of the

Fa - ther and one in you. Make us you.

Music: Ronald Arnatt, © 1984, GIA Publications, Inc.

243   SACRAMENT OF BAPTISM

BLESSING AND INVOCATION OF GOD OVER BAPTISMAL WATER

When all are gathered at the font, the priest/deacon leads a blessing of the water, unless the baptismal water has already been blessed.

RENUNCIATION OF SIN AND PROFESSION OF FAITH

The priest/deacon then questions the parents and godparents, and they make a renunciation of sin and evil and profess their faith. The assembly listens to their responses. The priest/deacon then invites all to give their assent to this profession of faith:

Priest or deacon:

This is our faith. This is the faith of the Church.

We are proud to pro-fess it, in Christ Je-sus our Lord.

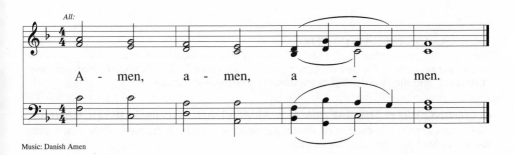

All:

A - men, a - men, a - men.

Music: Danish Amen

BAPTISM   244

One by one, the infants are brought to the font by their parents. There the parents express their desire to have their child baptized in the faith of the church which they have professed. The infant is then immersed in the water three times (or water is poured over the infant's head three times) as the priest/deacon says: "N., I baptize you in the name of the Father, and of the Son, and of the Holy Spirit." All may respond to each baptism with an acclamation.

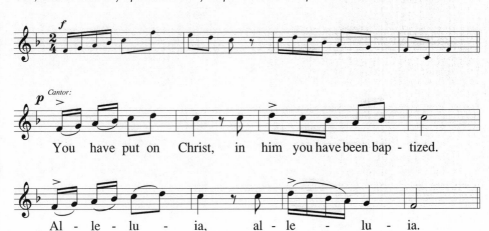

Cantor:

You have put on Christ, in him you have been bap - tized.

Al - le - lu - ia, al - le - lu - ia.

You have put on Christ, in him you have been bap - tized.

Al - le - lu - ia, al - le - lu - ia.

Music: Howard Hughes, SM, © 1977, ICEL

245 ANOINTING WITH CHRISM
The priest/deacon anoints each child on the crown of the head with holy chrism, a mixture of oil and perfume. The word "Christ" means "anointed." The baptized child has been "Christ-ed" and the sweet smell of the anointing reminds all of this.

CLOTHING WITH THE BAPTISMAL GARMENT AND GIVING OF THE CANDLE
The infants are then clothed in baptismal garments and a candle for each of the newly baptized is lighted from the paschal candle.

Optional

The priest/deacon may touch the ears and mouth of each child: "May Jesus soon touch your ears to receive his word, and your mouth to proclaim his faith."

CONCLUSION AND BLESSING
If baptism is celebrated at Mass, the liturgy continues with the eucharist. Otherwise, all process to the altar, carrying lighted candles. The above acclamation may be sung again during this procession. All then pray the Lord's Prayer, the parents are blessed and the liturgy concludes with a hymn of praise and thanksgiving.

Holy Communion Outside Mass

246

When for good reason communion cannot be received at Mass, the faithful may share in the paschal mystery through the liturgy of the word and the reception of holy communion.

INTRODUCTORY RITES
An appropriate hymn or psalm may be sung.

GREETING 247
If the minister is a priest or deacon, the usual form of greeting is used:

Assembly: **And also with you.**

If the minister is not a priest or deacon, another form of greeting may be used:

Assembly: **Blessed be God forever.**

PENITENTIAL RITE
The minister invites silent reflection and repentance. After some silence:

Assembly: **I confess to almighty God,**
and to you, my brothers and sisters,
that I have sinned through my own fault
in my thoughts and in my words,
in what I have done,
and in what I have failed to do;
and I ask blessed Mary, ever virgin,
all the angels and saints,
and you, my brothers and sisters,
to pray for me to the Lord our God.

The forms found at no. 289 may also be used.

248 CELEBRATION OF THE WORD OF GOD

FIRST READINGS
One or more passages from scripture are read. At the conclusion of each:

Reader: The word of the Lord.

Assembly: **Thanks be to God.**

RESPONSORIAL PSALM
The following psalm (or another appropriate psalm) may follow the first reading.

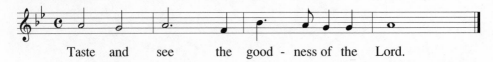

Taste and see the good - ness of the Lord.

Text: *Lectionary for Mass,* © 1969, 1981, ICEL
Music: Richard Proulx, © 1975, GIA Publications, Inc.

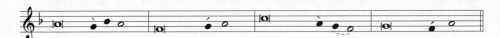

Music: Richard Proulx, © 1986, GIA Publications, Inc.

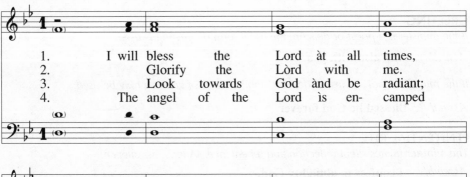

1. I will bless the Lord àt all times,
2. Glorify the Lòrd with me.
3. Look towards God ànd be radiant;
4. The angel of the Lord ìs en- camped

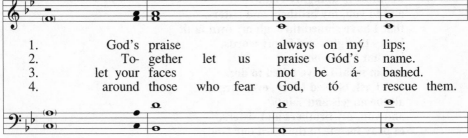

1. God's praise always on mý lips;
2. To- gether let us praise Gód's name.
3. let your faces not be á- bashed.
4. around those who fear God, tó rescue them.

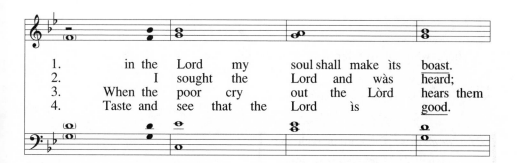

1. in the Lord my soul shall make its boast.
2. I sought the Lord and was heard;
3. When the poor cry out the Lòrd hears them
4. Taste and see that the Lord is good.

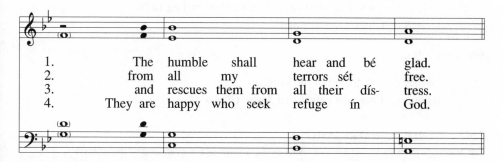

1. The humble shall hear and bé glad.
2. from all my terrors sét free.
3. and rescues them from all their dís- tress.
4. They are happy who seek refuge ín God.

Text: Psalm 34:2-3, 4-5, 6-7, 8-9; The Grail
Music: Joseph Gelineau, SJ
© 1963, 1993, The Grail, GIA Publications, Inc., agent

THE GOSPEL   249

Before the gospel reading, this acclamation is sung:

Cantor, then all:

Al- le- lu-ia,   al - le-lu - ia,   al - le - lu - ia.

Music: Chant Mode VI; acc. by Richard Proulx, © 1985, GIA Publications, Inc.

During Lent:

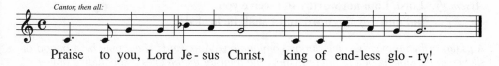

Cantor, then all:

Praise   to you, Lord Je - sus Christ,   king of end-less glo - ry!

Music: Frank Schoen, © 1970, GIA Publications, Inc.

Cantor:

I   am   the living bread from heaven,   says   the   Lord,

those who eat this bread   will live for ev - er.

Text: ICEL, © 1969
Music: Tone 6F, acc. by Robert J. Batastini, © 1986, GIA Publications, Inc.

Priest or deacon: The Lord be with you.
     Assembly: **And also with you.**

     Reader: A reading from the holy gospel according to N.

     Assembly: **Glory to you, Lord.**

After the reading:

     Reader: The gospel of the Lord.

     Assembly: **Praise to you, Lord Jesus Christ.**

250   GENERAL INTERCESSIONS

The assembly joins in prayer for the needs of the world, of the poor and of the church.

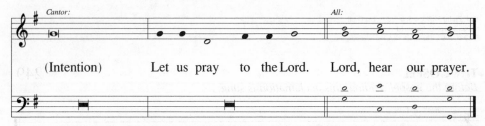

Cantor: All:

(Intention)   Let us pray to the Lord.   Lord, hear our prayer.

Music: Byzantine chant; harm. by Robert J. Batastini, © 1986, GIA Publications, Inc.

251   HOLY COMMUNION

The minister invites all to join in the Lord's Prayer, then to exchange a sign of peace. The minister then raises the eucharistic bread and all respond to the invitation.

Assembly: **Lord, I am not worthy to receive you,**
           but only say the word and I shall be healed.

A psalm or hymn may be sung during communion. Afterwards, there may be a period of silence or the singing of a psalm or hymn. The minister then recites a concluding prayer.

CONCLUDING RITE

All are blessed and dismissed.

Presiding minister: Go in the peace of Christ.

     Assembly: **Thanks be to God.**

Reconciliation of Several Penitents

252

The sacrament of penance, also called the sacrament of reconciliation, may be celebrated with one penitent or with many. The latter form, the communal penance service, is a gathering of a few or a large number of Christians. Together they listen to the scriptures, sing psalms and hymns, pray, individually confess their sins and receive absolution, then praise God whose mercy and love are greater than our evil. In the rite of penance, the members of the church confront the struggle that was entered at baptism. There has been failure, evil done and good undone, but the penitent church comes again and again to name and renounce its sins and to return to the way of the Lord.

INTRODUCTORY RITES

253

An appropriate hymn or psalm may be sung.

GREETING

The priest and people greet each other in these or other words:

> *Priest:* Grace, mercy, and peace be with you from God the Father and
> Christ Jesus our Savior.

Assembly: **And also with you.**

OPENING PRAYER

After silent prayer, the priest concludes the gathering rite with a solemn prayer.

CELEBRATION OF THE WORD OF GOD

254

FIRST READINGS

One or more passages from scripture are read. At the conclusion of each:

> *Reader:* The word of the Lord.

Assembly: **Thanks be to God.**

RESPONSORIAL PSALM

The following psalm may follow the first reading:

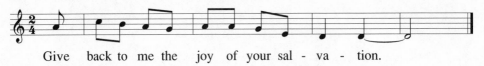

Give back to me the joy of your sal - va - tion.

Text: © 1974, ICEL
Music: Howard Hughes, SM, © 1986, GIA Publications, Inc.

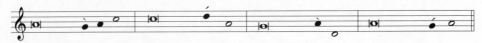

Music: Chrysogonus Waddell, OCSO, © Gethsemani Abbey

1. Have mercy on me, God, in your kind- ness
2. My of- fenses truly I know them;
3. A pure heart cre- ate for mè, O God,
4. Give me a- gain the joy òf your help;

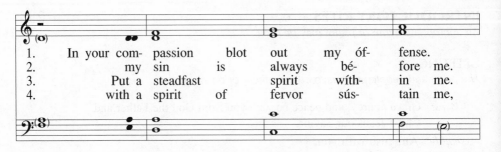

1. In your com- passion blot out my óf- fense.
2. my sin is always bé- fore me.
3. Put a steadfast spirit with- in me.
4. with a spirit of fervor sús- tain me,

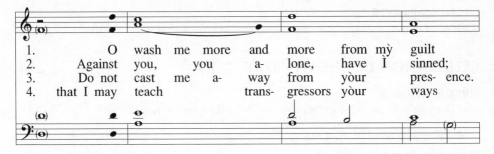

1. O wash me more and more from mỳ guilt
2. Against you, you a- lone, have I sinned;
3. Do not cast me a- way from yòur pres- ence.
4. that I may teach trans- gressors yòur ways

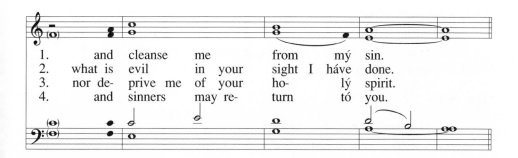

1. and cleanse me from mý sin.
2. what is evil in your sight I háve done.
3. nor de- prive me of your ho- lý spirit.
4. and sinners may re- turn tó you.

Text: Psalm 51:3-4, 5-6, 12-13, 14-15
Music: Joseph Gelineau, SJ
© 1963, The Grail, GIA Publications, Inc., agent

GOSPEL 255

Before the gospel reading, this acclamation is sung:

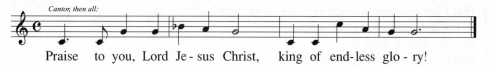

Cantor, then all:

Al- le - lu - ia, al - le - lu - ia, al - le - lu - ia.

Music: Chant Mode VI; acc. by Richard Proulx, © 1985, GIA Publications, Inc.

During Lent:

Cantor, then all:

Praise to you, Lord Je - sus Christ, king of end-less glo - ry!

Music: Frank Schoen, © 1970, GIA Publications, Inc.

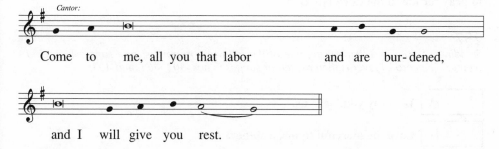

Cantor:

Come to me, all you that labor and are bur- dened,

and I will give you rest.

Text: © 1969, ICEL
Music: Tone 6F, acc. by Robert J. Batastini, © 1986, GIA Publications, Inc.

Deacon (or priest): The Lord be with you.

    Assembly: **And also with you.**

      Deacon: A reading from the holy gospel according to N.

    Assembly: **Glory to you, Lord.**

After the reading:

      Deacon: The gospel of the Lord.

    Assembly: **Praise to you, Lord Jesus Christ.**

HOMILY

EXAMINATION OF CONSCIENCE
In silence or through some other manner all reflect on their lives with sorrow for their sins.

256   SACRAMENT OF PENANCE

GENERAL CONFESSION OF SINS
Kneeling (or with another posture that expresses sorrow,) all join in confession. This form may be used:

**I confess to almighty God,
and to you, my brothers and sisters,
that I have sinned through my own fault
in my thoughts and in my words,
in what I have done,
and in what I have failed to do;
and I ask blessed Mary, ever virgin,
all the angels and saints,
and you, my brothers and sisters,
to pray for me to the Lord our God.**

257
Standing, all join in a litany using one of the following responses, or a song asking God's mercy. The Lord's Prayer is then recited or sung (see nos. 303, 464, and 465).

| A | **We pray you, hear us.** |

| B | **Lord, be merciful to me, a sinner.** |

| C | **Lord, have mercy.** |

258   INDIVIDUAL CONFESSION AND ABSOLUTION
One by one the penitents approach the priest confessors. All confess their sins, accept some fitting act of satisfaction and the counsel of the confessor. Then the priest extends

his hands over the penitent's head and speaks the prayer of absolution, concluding: "Through the ministry of the church may God give you pardon and peace, and I absolve you from your sins in the name of the Father, and of the Son, and of the Holy Spirit." The penitent responds, "Amen." (Note: On those occasions when general absolution is permitted, the rest of the rite remains the same.)

PROCLAMATION OF PRAISE FOR GOD'S MERCY   259

The priest invites all to give thanks and to show by their lives—and in the life of the whole community—the grace of repentance. A psalm, canticle or hymn may be sung to proclaim God's mercy.

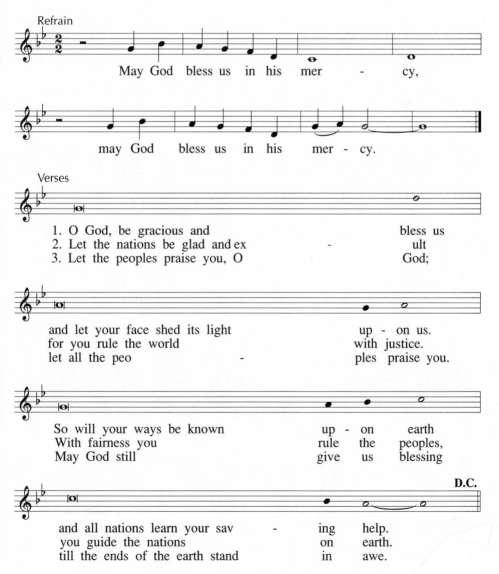

Refrain

May God bless us in his mer - cy,

may God bless us in his mer - cy.

Verses

1. O God, be gracious and   bless us
2. Let the nations be glad and ex -   ult
3. Let the peoples praise you, O   God;

and let your face shed its light   up - on us.
for you rule the world   with justice.
let all the peo -   ples praise you.

So will your ways be known   up - on earth
With fairness you   rule the peoples,
May God still   give us blessing

D.C.

and all nations learn your sav - ing help.
you guide the nations on earth.
till the ends of the earth stand in awe.

Text: Psalm 67:2-3, 5, 6, 6-8; © 1963, 1993, The Grail, GIA Publications, Inc., agent; refrain trans. © 1969, ICEL
Music: Michel Guimont, © 1994, GIA Publications, Inc.

260   CONCLUDING PRAYER OF THANKSGIVING
This prayer is spoken by the priest.

BLESSING AND DISMISSAL
The priest blesses all present and the deacon or other minister dismisses the assembly. All respond:

Thanks be to God.

Marriage

Many rituals of various kinds and origins surround a wedding. These rites of preparation and of celebration are ways for the couple, the families and friends to share
in and to strengthen the making of a marriage. The marriage rite itself is a covenant
made by bride and groom, the consent each gives to and accepts from each other.
The church assembles to witness and bless this union.

LITURGY OF THE WORD

*The Sacrament of Marriage may be celebrated at Mass, or outside of Mass. In either case, the
rite begins with the reading of one or more passages from scripture. The form is similar to that
found in the Order of Mass (nos. 293 to 294).*

SACRAMENT OF MARRIAGE   262

*After the homily, the presiding minister invites the couple to give their consent to each other
freely in the presence of the church. When they have done so, the presiding minister receives
their consent in the name of the church. The wedding rings, a sign of love and fidelity, are
then blessed and exchanged.*

*Mass then continues with the Liturgy of the Eucharist and Communion (nos. 298 to 303).
If Mass is not celebrated, the rite concludes with the General Intercessions, Nuptial Blessing,
Lord's Prayer and Final Blessing.*

Anointing of the Sick

263

The sacrament of anointing is celebrated when a Christian's health is seriously impaired by sickness or old age. If possible, it is celebrated when the sick person is able to take part in the rite. When the sick person is able to receive holy communion, the rite of anointing may be celebrated within the liturgy of the Mass.

Through the anointing with the blessed oil of the sick, the church supports those who struggle against illness or injury and continues the healing work of Christ. The anointing is intended to bring hope and comfort to the one anointed and, to the gathered family and friends, a spirit of support and sharing in the sufferings of our brothers and sisters.

The Mass begins in the usual way; after the greeting the priest welcomes the sick.

264   LITURGY OF THE WORD

FIRST READINGS

One or more passages from scripture are read. At the conclusion of each:

Reader: The word of the Lord.

Assembly: **Thanks be to God.**

RESPONSORIAL PSALM

The following psalm may follow the first reading:

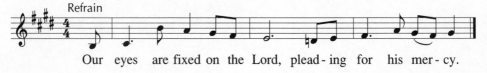

Our eyes are fixed on the Lord, pleading for his mercy.

1. To you I have lifted up my   eyes,
2. Like the eyes of a   servant
3. Have mercy on us Lord, have   mercy.

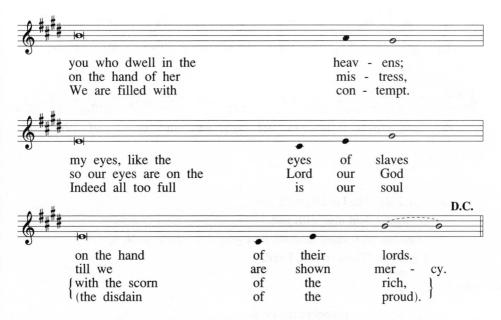

you who dwell in the   heav - ens;
on the hand of her   mis - tress,
We are filled with   con - tempt.

my eyes, like the   eyes   of   slaves
so our eyes are on the   Lord   our   God
Indeed all too full   is   our   soul

D.C.

on the hand   of   their   lords.
till we   are   shown   mer - cy.
{ with the scorn   of   the   rich, }
{ (the disdain   of   the   proud). }

Text: Psalm 123:1-2, 3-4; © 1963, 1993, The Grail, GIA Publications, Inc., agent; refrain trans. © 1969, ICEL
Music: Michel Guimont, © 1994, GIA Publications, Inc.

GOSPEL   265

Before the gospel reading, this acclamation is sung:

Cantor, then all:

Al- le- lu- ia,   al - le- lu- ia,   al - le - lu - ia.

Music: Chant Mode VI; acc. by Richard Proulx, © 1985, GIA Publications, Inc.

During Lent:

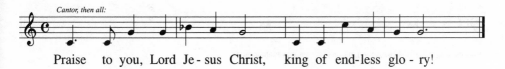

Cantor, then all:

Praise   to you, Lord Je - sus Christ,   king of end-less glo - ry!

Music: Frank Schoen, © 1970, GIA Publications, Inc.

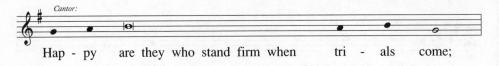

Hap - py are they who stand firm when tri - als come;

they have proven themselves, and will win the crown of life.

Text: ICEL, © 1969
Music: Tone 6F, acc. by Robert J. Batastini, © 1986, GIA Publications, Inc.

Deacon (or priest): The Lord be with you.

Assembly: **And also with you.**

Deacon: A reading from the holy gospel according to N.

Assembly: **Glory to you, Lord.**

After the reading:

Deacon: The gospel of the Lord.

Assembly: **Praise to you, Lord Jesus Christ.**

HOMILY

266 LITURGY OF ANOINTING

LITANY

The assembly joins in prayers for the sick and for those who care for them.

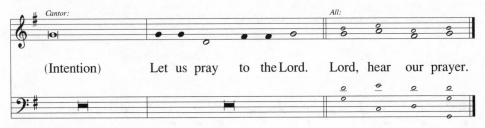

(Intention)   Let us pray   to the Lord.   Lord, hear   our prayer.

Music: Byzantine chant; harm. by Robert J. Batastini, © 1986, GIA Publications, Inc.

LAYING ON OF HANDS

The priest silently lays hands on the head of each sick person in a gesture of prayer, healing and solidarity.

PRAYER OVER THE OIL

If the oil is already blessed, the priest leads a prayer of thanksgiving over it.
After each prayer:

Assembly: **Blessed be God who heals us in Christ.**

If the oil is not blessed, the priest leads the prayer of blessing.

ANOINTING

The priest anoints each sick person on the forehead in a sign of strength and soothing comfort.

> *Priest:* Through this holy anointing may the Lord in his love and mercy help you with the grace of the Holy Spirit.

Assembly: **Amen.**

The priest anoints the hands of each sick person.

> *Priest:* May the Lord who frees you from sin save you and raise you up.

Assembly: **Amen.**

The priest may anoint other parts of the body.

PRAYER AFTER ANOINTING   267
The priest prays for those who have been anointed. Then the liturgy of the eucharist is celebrated with special prayers for the sick.

[If the rite of anointing is celebrated outside of Mass, the liturgy begins with the greeting, rite of sprinkling and penitential rite. After the scripture readings and homily, the liturgy of anointing is celebrated as above. Then the Lord's Prayer is recited or sung and the rite may conclude with holy communion.]

Funeral Mass

268

The rites which surround the death of a Christian extend from the Viaticum (last communion) and final prayers before death through the wake service and funeral Mass to the burial of the body or ashes. In all of this the community affirms its faith in the communion of saints and the resurrection of the dead. The family and friends are helped in their time of sorrow with prayer and song. Thus they express present grief even as they hold to the church's lasting hope. Following is the rite of the funeral Mass.

INTRODUCTORY RITES

269   GREETING

The priest greets the assembly at the door, using these or similar words.

> *Priest:* The grace and peace of God our Father and the Lord Jesus Christ be with you.
>
> *All:* **And also with you.**

The body is sprinkled with holy water.

SONG

As the procession enters the church, an appropriate song is sung.

270 OPENING PRAYER
At the conclusion of the prayer all respond: **Amen.**

LITURGY OF THE WORD

271   READINGS

One or two passages from scripture are read before the gospel reading. At the conclusion of each:

> *Reader:* The word of the Lord.
>
> *All:* **Thanks be to God.**

RESPONSORIAL PSALM

One of the following, or another psalm may follow the first reading.

The Lord is my shep - herd; there is noth - ing I shall want.

Text: *Lectionary for Mass,* © 1969, ICEL
Music: Richard Proulx, © 1975, GIA Publications, Inc.

Omit for 4-line stanza

Music: Richard Proulx, © 1975, GIA Publications, Inc.

1. Lord, you are mỳ shepherd;
2. You guide me a- long the rìght path;
3. You have pre- pared a banquet fòr me
4. Surely goodness and kindness shàll follow me

1. there is nothing Í shall want.
2. You are true tó your name.
3. in the sight óf my foes.
4. all the days óf my life.

1. Fresh and green are thè pastures
2. If I should walk in the valley òf darkness
3. My head you have a- nointed with oil,
4. In the Lord's own house shall Ì dwell

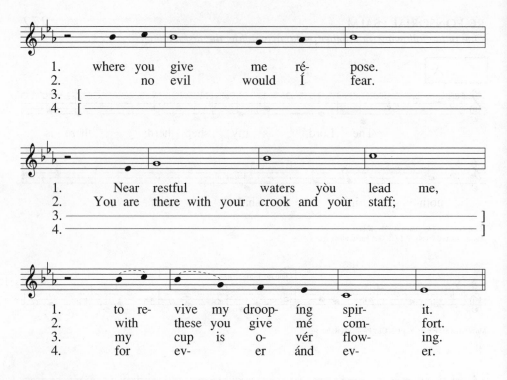

1. where you give me ré- pose.
2. no evil would Í fear.
3. [⸺
4. [⸺

1. Near restful waters yòu lead me,
2. You are there with your crook and yoùr staff;
3. ⸺]
4. ⸺]

1. to re- vive my droop- íng spir- it.
2. with these you give mé com- fort.
3. my cup is o- vér flow- ing.
4. for ev- er ánd ev- er.

Text: Psalm 23; The Grail
Music: Joseph Gelineau, SJ
© 1963, 1993, The Grail, GIA Publications, Inc., agent

B

Refrain

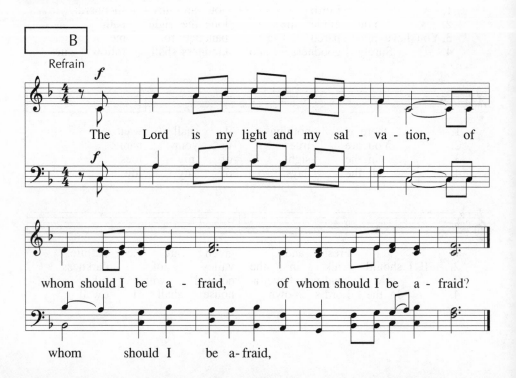

The Lord is my light and my sal- va- tion, of

whom should I be a - fraid, of whom should I be a - fraid?

whom should I be a- fraid,

Verse 1 *mf*

1. The Lord is my light and my help; whom should I fear? The Lord is the strong-hold of my life; be-fore whom should I shrink?

Verse 2 *mf*

2. There is one thing I ask of the Lord; for this I long: to live in the house of the Lord all the days of my life.

Verse 3 *mf*

3. I be-lieve I shall see the good - ness of the Lord in the land of the liv - ing; hope in God, and take heart. Hope in the Lord!

273 GOSPEL

Before the gospel one of the following, or another gospel acclamation is sung.

Cantor, then all:

Al- le- lu- ia,   al - le- lu - ia,   al - le - lu - ia.

Music: Chant Mode VI; acc. by Richard Proulx, © 1985, GIA Publications, Inc.

During Lent:

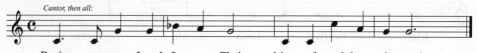

Cantor, then all:

Praise   to you, Lord Je - sus Christ,   king of end- less glo - ry!

Music: Frank Schoen, © 1970, GIA Publications, Inc.

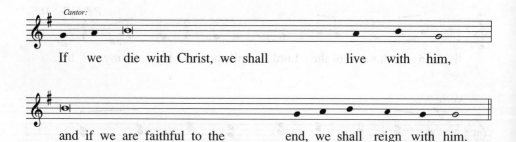

Cantor:

If   we   die with Christ, we shall   live   with   him,

and if we are faithful to the   end, we shall   reign   with him.

Text: ICEL, © 1969
Music: Tone 6F, acc. by Robert J. Batastini, © 1986, GIA Publications, Inc.

The gospel is proclaimed by a deacon or a priest.

Deacon (or priest): The Lord be with you.

All: **And also with you.**

Deacon (or priest): A reading from the holy gospel according to N.

All: **Glory to you, Lord.**

After the gospel is proclaimed:

Deacon (or priest): The gospel of the Lord.

All: **Praise to you, Lord Jesus Christ.**

HOMILY

GENERAL INTERCESSIONS   274

All pray for the Church, the local community, the deceased and those who mourn, using one of the forms below.

Reader: We pray to the Lord. (Let us pray to the Lord.)

> *All:* **Lord, hear our prayer.**

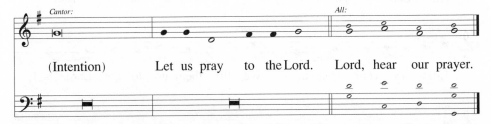

Music: Byzantine chant; harm. by Robert J. Batastini, © 1986, GIA Publications, Inc.

Or:

Reader: Lord, in your mercy:

> *All:* **Hear our prayer.**

The priest concludes the petitions with a prayer and all respond: **Amen.**

LITURGY OF THE EUCHARIST

PREPARATION OF THE ALTAR AND GIFTS   275

As bread and wine are brought to the table, and preparations are made to celebrate the eucharist, a song is sung. If there is no music, the prayers of preparation may be said aloud and all may respond: **Blessed be God for ever.**

The priest then invites everyone to pray.

All: **May the Lord accept the sacrifice at your hands for the praise and glory of his name, for our good, and the good of all his Church.**

PRAYER OVER THE GIFTS

At the conclusion of the prayer over the gifts, all respond: **Amen.**

276 EUCHARISTIC PRAYER

This central prayer of the liturgy begins with the following dialogue:

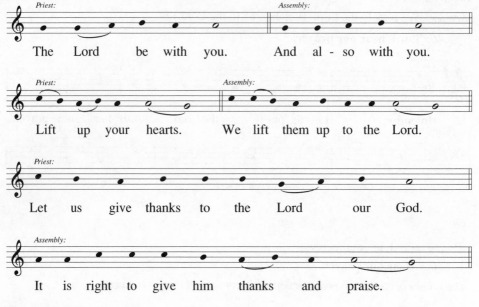

Priest: The Lord be with you. Assembly: And al - so with you.

Priest: Lift up your hearts. Assembly: We lift them up to the Lord.

Priest: Let us give thanks to the Lord our God.

Assembly: It is right to give him thanks and praise.

Music: Sacramentary, 1974

The priest continues with the preface, which concludes with the Sanctus.

277 SANCTUS

Ho - ly, ho - ly, ho - ly Lord, God of pow-er, God of might, heav-en and earth are full of your

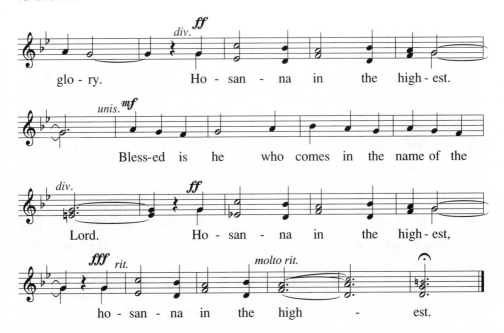

glo - ry. Ho - san - na in the high - est.

Bless-ed is he who comes in the name of the

Lord. Ho - san - na in the high - est,

ho - san - na in the high - est.

Music: *Mass of Creation,* Marty Haugen, © 1984, GIA Publications, Inc.

After the words of institution the priest sings or says: "Let us proclaim the mystery of faith"
and all respond with one of the following acclamations:

MEMORIAL ACCLAMATIONS   278

Let us pro - claim the mys - ter - y of faith:

Christ has died, Christ is ris - en, Christ will come a - gain.

Christ has died, Christ is ris - en, Christ will come a - gain!

Music: *Mass of Creation,* Marty Haugen, © 1984, GIA Publications, Inc.

B

Music: *Mass of Creation*, Marty Haugen, ©1990, GIA Publications, Inc.

Music: Mass of Creation, Marty Haugen, © 1993, GIA Publications, Inc.

Music: *Mass of Creation*, Marty Haugen, © 1993, GIA Publications, Inc.

At the conclusion of the eucharistic prayer the priest sings or says: **279**

Priest: Through him, with him, in him, in the unity of the Ho - ly Spir- it, all

glory and honor is yours, al - might - y Fa - ther, for

ev - er and ev - er.

All:
Descant:
A - men, a - men, a - men!

Melody:
A - men, a - men, a - men!

rit.

Music: *Mass of Creation,* Marty Haugen, © 1984, GIA Publications, Inc.

280 COMMUNION RITE

The priest invites everyone to sing or say the Lord's Prayer.

Our Fa - ther, who art in heav - en, hal - lowed be thy name;

thy king - dom come; thy will be done on earth as it

is in heav - en. Give us this day our dai - ly bread;

and for - give us our tres - pass - es as we for - give

those who tres - pass a - gainst us; and lead us not

in - to temp - ta - tion, but de - liv - er us from e - vil.

Priest: Deliver us, Lord...
for the coming of our Savior, Jesus Christ.

All:
For the king - dom, the pow'r, and the

glo - ry are yours, now and for ev - er.

Music: Traditional chant, adapt. by Robert Snow, 1964; acc. by Robert J. Batastini, © 1975, 1993, GIA Publications, Inc.

SIGN OF PEACE

Following the prayer "Lord Jesus Christ," the priest invites all to exchange a sign of peace.

Priest: The peace of the Lord be with you al - ways. Assembly: And al - so with you.

All exchange a sign of the peace of Christ.

AGNUS DEI   281

Cantor: Lamb of God, All: you take a - way the sins of the world: have mer - cy on us.

Cantor: Lamb of God, All: you take a - way the sins of the world: grant us peace.

Music: Agnus Dei XVIII, Vatican Edition; acc. by Robert J. Batastini, © 1993, GIA Publications, Inc.

COMMUNION   282

The priest invites the assembly to share in holy communion, and all respond:

Lord, I am not worthy to receive you, but only say the word and I shall be healed.

A song is sung during the distribution of communion.

PRAYER AFTER COMMUNION   283

The priest sings or says the prayer and all respond: **Amen.**

If the final commendation is to be celebrated at the place of committal, the procession to the place of committal immediately follows the prayer after communion.

FINAL COMMENDATION

The final commendation begins with an invitation to silent prayer.

SONG OF FAREWELL

The following or another appropriate responsory or song may be sung.

284 **SAINTS OF GOD**

Cantor or choir:
1. Saints of God, come to his/her aid! Has-ten to meet him/her, an - gels of the Lord!

𝄋 Refrain
Cantor or choir: Re - ceive his/her soul, *All:* re - ceive his/her soul, *Cantor or choir:* and pre - sent him/her to God the Most High, *All:* and pre - sent him/her to God the Most High.

To verses 2, 3

Verse 2
Cantor or choir:
2. May Christ, who called you, take you to him - self; may an-gels lead you to the bos - om of A - bra - ham.

D.S.

Verse 3
Cantor or choir:
3. E - ter - nal rest grant un - to him/her, O

Lord, and let per - pet - u - al
light shine up - on him/her.

D.S.

Text: *Order of Christian Funerals*, © 1985, ICEL
Tune: Steven R. Janco, b. 1961, © 1990, GIA Publications, Inc.

B

Cantor or choir:
mp - mf

1. Saints of God, come to her/his aid!
2. May Christ who called you, take you home;
3. Give e - ter - nal rest, O Lord;

Come to meet her/him, an - gels of the Lord!
May an - gels lead you to our par - ents side!
And may your light shine on her/him, for ev - er!

mp ——— *mf*
All:

Re - ceive her/his soul and pre - sent her/him to

God, pre - sent this soul to God most high.

Last time

Text: *Order of Christian Funerals;* para. by David Haas
Music: David Haas
© 1990, GIA Publications, Inc.

C

Cantor:

1. Saints of God, come to his/her aid!
2. May Christ who called you, take you to him - self;
3. Give him/her e - ter - nal rest, O Lord,

Come to meet him,/her, an - gels of the
may an - gels lead you to A - bra - ham's
and may your light shine on him/her for

Lord!
side. Re - ceive his/her soul and pre -
ev - er.

sent him/her to God, to God the Most High.

All:

Re - ceive his/her soul and pre - sent him/her to

God, to God the Most High.

Text: *Order of Christian Funerals;* para. by Richard Proulx
Music: Richard Proulx
© 1975, GIA Publications, Inc.

285 PRAYER OF COMMENDATION
At the conclusion of the prayer all respond: **Amen.**

PROCESSION TO THE PLACE OF COMMITTAL
The deacon or priest says: In peace let us take our brother/sister to his/her place of rest.

SONG

As the assembly leaves the church, the following or another appropriate responsory or song may be sung.

lead you to the bos-om of A-bra-ham; and where Laz-a-rus is

poor no long-er, may you have e-ter-nal rest.

All: May the an-gels lead you in-to

Optional descant: In pa-ra - di - sum

par-a-dise; may the mar-tyrs come to wel-come you and

de - du - cant te an - ge -

take you to the ho-ly cit-y, the new and e-ter-nal Je-

li.

ru - sa - lem.

Text: *Order of Christian Funerals,* © 1985, ICEL
Music: Steven R. Janco, © 1990, GIA Publications, Inc.

The Order of Mass

Each church gathers on the Lord's Day to listen to the Scriptures, to offer prayers, to give thanks and praise to God while recalling God's gifts in creation and saving deeds in Jesus, and to share in holy communion.

In these rites of word and eucharist, the Church keeps Sunday as the Lord's Day, the day of creation and resurrection, the "eighth day" when the fullness of God's kingdom is anticipated. The Mass or eucharistic celebration of the Christian community has rites of gathering, of word, of eucharist, of dismissal. All those who gather constitute the assembly. One member of this assembly who has been ordained to the presbyterate or episcopate—the priesthood—leads the opening and closing prayers and the eucharistic prayer, and presides over the whole assembly. A member ordained to the diaconate may assist, read the gospel, and preach. Other members of the assembly are chosen and trained for various ministries: These are the readers, servers, ushers, musicians, communion ministers. All of these assist the assembly. It is the assembly itself, all those present, that does the liturgy.

The Order of Mass which follows is familiar to all who regularly join in this assembly. It is learned through repetition. This Order of Mass leaves many decisions to the local community and others are determined by the various seasons of the liturgical year.

INTRODUCTORY RITES

The rites which precede the liturgy of the word assist the assembly to gather as a community. They prepare that community to listen to the Scriptures and to celebrate the eucharist together. The procession and entrance song are ways of expressing the unity and spirit of the assembly.

GREETING

All make the sign of the cross.

Priest: In the name of the Father, and of the Son, and of the Holy Spirit.

Assembly: **Amen.**

After the sign of the cross one of the greetings is given.

A   *Priest:*   The grace of our Lord Jesus Christ and the love of God and the fellowship of the Holy Spirit be with you all.

            Assembly: **And also with you.**

B   *Priest:*   The grace and peace of God our Father and the Lord Jesus Christ be with you.

            Assembly: **Blessed be God, the Father of our Lord Jesus Christ.**
                     or: **And also with you.**

C   *Priest:*   The Lord be with you. (*Bishop:* Peace be with you.)

            Assembly: **And also with you.**

288   BLESSING AND SPRINKLING OF HOLY WATER

On Sundays, especially during the season of Easter, instead of the penitential rite below, the blessing and sprinkling of holy water may be done. The following or another appropriate song is sung as the water is sprinkled.

Cleanse us, Lord, from all our sins; wash us and we shall be clean as new snow. Cleanse us, Lord, from all our sins; wash us and we shall be clean as new snow.

Verse 1

Cantor:
1. Springs of wa-ter, bless the Lord; give him glo-ry, glo-ry and praise.

Choir:
Ah_____ Ah_____

Seas and riv-ers, bless the Lord; give him glo-ry, glo-ry and praise!

Ah_____ Ah_____

D.C.

Verse 2

Cantor:
2. Dew and rain, bless the Lord; give him glo-ry, glo-ry and praise.

Choir:
Ah_____ Ah_____

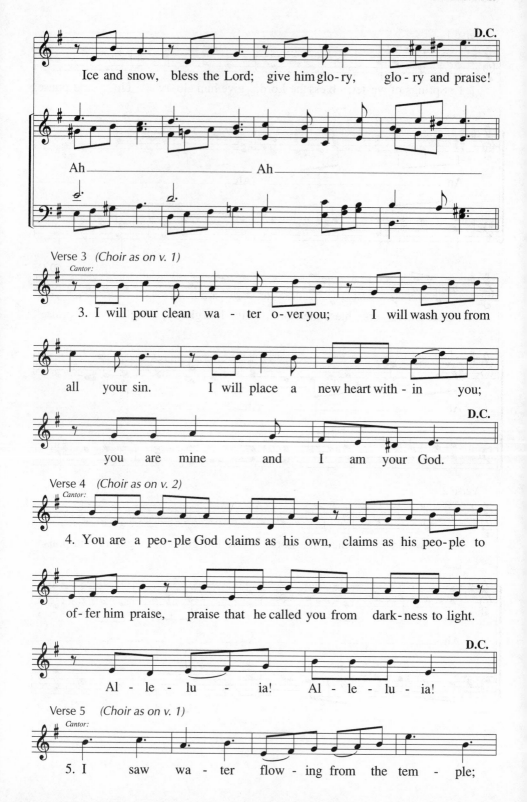

Ice and snow, bless the Lord; give him glo-ry, glo-ry and praise!

D.C.

Ah_____ Ah_____

Verse 3 *(Choir as on v. 1)*
Cantor:

3. I will pour clean wa - ter o-ver you; I will wash you from all your sin. I will place a new heart with - in you; you are mine and I am your God.

D.C.

Verse 4 *(Choir as on v. 2)*
Cantor:

4. You are a peo-ple God claims as his own, claims as his peo-ple to of-fer him praise, praise that he called you from dark-ness to light. Al - le - lu - ia! Al - le - lu - ia!

D.C.

Verse 5 *(Choir as on v. 1)*
Cantor:

5. I saw wa - ter flow - ing from the tem - ple;

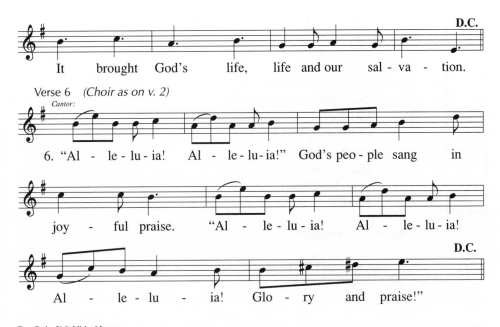

It brought God's life, life and our sal - va - tion.

Verse 6 *(Choir as on v. 2)*

Cantor:

6. "Al - le - lu - ia! Al - le - lu - ia!" God's peo - ple sang in

joy - ful praise. "Al - le - lu - ia! Al - le - lu - ia!

Al - le - lu - ia! Glo - ry and praise!"

D.C.

Text: Psalm 51:9; Michael Joncas
Music: Michael Joncas
© 1988, GIA Publications, Inc.

PENITENTIAL RITE

The priest invites all to be mindful of their sins and of the great mercy of God. After a time of silence, one of the following forms is used.

A | *Assembly:* **I confess to almighty God,**
and to you, my brothers and sisters,
that I have sinned through my own fault
in my thoughts and in my words,
in what I have done,
and in what I have failed to do;
and I ask blessed Mary, ever virgin,
all the angels and saints,
and you, my brothers and sisters,
to pray for me to the Lord our God.

B | *Priest:* Lord, we have sinned against you:
Lord, have mercy.

Assembly: **Lord, have mercy.**

Priest: Lord, show us your mercy and love.

Assembly: **And grant us your salvation.**

C *The priest or another minister makes a series of invocations according to the following pattern.*

> *Priest:* (Invocation)
> Lord, have mercy.
>
> *Assembly:* **Lord, have mercy.**
>
> *Priest:* (Invocation)
> Christ, have mercy.
>
> *Assembly:* **Christ, have mercy.**
>
> *Priest:* (Invocation)
> Lord, have mercy.
>
> *Assembly:* **Lord, have mercy.**

The penitential rite always concludes:

> *Priest:* May almighty God have mercy on us, forgive us our sins, and bring us to everlasting life.
>
> *Assembly:* **Amen.**

290 KYRIE

Unless form C of the penitential rite has been used, the Kyrie follows.

Lord, have mer - cy. Lord, have mer - cy.

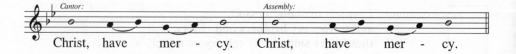

Christ, have mer - cy. Christ, have mer - cy.

Lord, have mer - cy. Lord, have mer - cy.

Music: *A Community Mass,* Richard Proulx, © 1971, 1977, GIA Publications, Inc.

GLORIA

The Gloria is omitted during Advent, Lent, and most weekdays.

Glo-ry to God in the high-est, and peace to his peo-ple on earth. Lord God, heav-en-ly King, al-might-y God and Fa-ther, we wor-ship you, we give you thanks, we praise you for your glo-ry.

Slighty slower

Choir (Congr. ad lib):

Lord Je-sus Christ, on-ly Son of the Fa-ther, Lord God, Lamb of God, you take a-way the sin of the

world: have mer-cy on us; you are

seat-ed at the right hand of the Fa-ther:

re - ceive our prayer.
re - ceive, re-ceive our prayer.
re - ceive our prayer.

All:
ƒ Tempo primo

For you a-lone are the Ho-ly One, you a - lone are the

Lord, you a - lone are the Most High,

Je - sus Christ, with the Ho-ly Spir-it, in the glo-ry of

ff *rit.*

God the Fa-ther. A - men.

Music: *A New Mass for Congregations,* Carroll T. Andrews, © 1970, GIA Publications, Inc.

OPENING PRAYER   292

After the invitation from the priest, all pray for a while. The introductory rites conclude with the proper opening prayer and the Amen of the assembly.

LITURGY OF THE WORD   293

When the Church assembles, the book containing the Scriptures (Lectionary) is opened and all listen as the readers and deacon (or priest) read from the places assigned. The first reading is normally from the Hebrew Scriptures (Old Testament), the second from the letters of the New Testament, and the third from the Book of Gospels. Over a three-year cycle, the Church reads through the letters and gospels and a portion of the Hebrew Scriptures. During the Sundays of Ordinary Time, the letters and gospels are read in order, each Sunday continuing near the place where the previous Sunday's readings ended. During Advent/Christmas and Lent/Easter, the readings are those which are traditional and appropriate to these seasons.

The Church listens to and—through the weeks and years—is shaped by the Scriptures. Those who have gathered for the Sunday liturgy are to give their full attention to the words of the reader. A time of silence and reflection follows each of the two readings. After the first reading, this reflection continues in the singing of the psalm. A homily, bringing together the Scriptures and the life of the community, follows the gospel. The liturgy of the word concludes with the creed, the dismissal of the catechumens and the prayers of intercession. In the latter, the assembly continues its constant work of recalling and praying for the universal Church and all those in need.

This reading and hearing of the word—simple things that they are—are the foundation of the liturgical celebration. The public reading of the Scriptures and the rituals which surround this—silence and psalm and acclamation, posture and gesture, preaching and litany of intercession—gather the Church generation after generation. They gather and sustain and gradually make of us the image of Christ.

READING I
In conclusion:

> *Reader:* The word of the Lord.
> *Assembly:* **Thanks be to God.**

After a period of silence, the responsorial psalm is sung.

READING II
In conclusion:

> *Reader:* The word of the Lord.
> *Assembly:* **Thanks be to God.**

A time of silence follows the reading.

294 GOSPEL

Before the gospel, an acclamation is sung.

Cantor, then all:

Al-le-lu-ia, al - le-lu - ia, al - le - lu - ia.

Music: Chant Mode VI; acc. by Richard Proulx, © 1985, GIA Publications, Inc.

During Lent one of the following acclamations replaces the alleluia.

A

Cantor, then all:

Praise to you, Lord Je - sus Christ, king of end-less glo - ry!

Music: Frank Schoen, © 1970, GIA Publications, Inc.

Tone for verses

Cantor:

D.C.

Music: Tone 6F

Or:

B **Praise and honor to you, Lord Jesus Christ!**

C **Glory and praise to you, Lord Jesus Christ!**

D **Glory to you, Word of God, Lord Jesus Christ!**

Deacon (or priest): The Lord be with you.

Assembly: **And also with you.**

Deacon: A reading from the holy gospel according to N.

Assembly: **Glory to you, Lord.**

After the reading:

Deacon: The gospel of the Lord.

Assembly: **Praise to you, Lord Jesus Christ.**

HOMILY

PROFESSION OF FAITH 295

We believe in one God,
    the Father, the Almighty,
    maker of heaven and earth,
    of all that is seen and unseen.

We believe in one Lord, Jesus Christ,
    the only Son of God,
    eternally begotten of the Father,
    God from God, Light from Light,
    true God from true God,
    begotten, not made, one in Being with the Father.
    Through him all things were made.
    For us men and for our salvation he came down from heaven:

All bow at the following words up to: and became man.

    by the power of the Holy Spirit
        he was born of the Virgin Mary, and became man.
    For our sake he was crucified under Pontius Pilate;
        he suffered, died, and was buried.
        On the third day he rose again
        in fulfillment of the Scriptures;
        he ascended into heaven
        and is seated at the right hand of the Father.
    He will come again in glory to judge the living and the dead,
        and his kingdom will have no end.

We believe in the Holy Spirit, the Lord, the giver of life,
    who proceeds from the Father and the Son.
    With the Father and the Son he is worshiped and glorified.
    He has spoken through the Prophets.
    We believe in one holy catholic and apostolic Church.
    We acknowledge one baptism for the forgiveness of sins.
    We look for the resurrection of the dead,
        and the life of the world to come. Amen.

At Masses with children, the Apostles' Creed may be used: **296**

We believe in God, the Father almighty,
    creator of heaven and earth.

We believe in Jesus Christ, his only Son, our Lord.
    He was conceived by the power of the Holy Spirit
        and born of the Virgin Mary.
    He suffered under Pontius Pilate,
        was crucified, died, and was buried.
    He descended to the dead.
    On the third day he arose again.
    He ascended into heaven,
        and is seated at the right hand of the Father.

He will come again to judge the living and the dead.

We believe in the Holy Spirit,
    the holy catholic Church,
    the communion of saints,
    the forgiveness of sins,
    the resurrection of the body,
    and the life everlasting. Amen.

297   GENERAL INTERCESSIONS

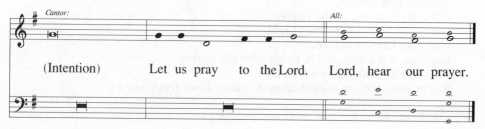

Music: Byzantine chant; harm. by Robert J. Batastini, © 1986, GIA Publications, Inc.

298   LITURGY OF THE EUCHARIST

To celebrate the eucharist means to give God thanks and praise. When the table has been prepared with the bread and wine, the assembly joins the priest in remembering the gracious gifts of God in creation and God's saving deeds. The center of this is the paschal mystery, the death of our Lord Jesus Christ which destroyed the power of death and his rising which brings us life. That mystery into which we were baptized we proclaim each Sunday at the eucharist. It is the very shape of Christian life. We find this in the simple bread and wine which stir our remembering and draw forth our prayer of thanksgiving. "Fruit of the earth and work of human hands," the bread and wine become our holy communion in the body and blood of the Lord. We eat and drink and so proclaim that we belong to one another and to the Lord.

The members of the assembly quietly prepare themselves even as the table is prepared. The priest then invites all to lift up their hearts and join in the eucharistic prayer. All do this by giving their full attention and by singing the acclamations from the "Holy, holy" to the great "Amen." Then the assembly joins in the Lord's Prayer, the sign of peace and the "Lamb of God" litany which accompanies the breaking of bread. Ministers of communion assist the assembly to share the body and blood of Christ. A time of silence and prayer concludes the liturgy of the eucharist.

PREPARATION OF THE ALTAR AND THE GIFTS

Bread and wine are brought to the table and the deacon or priest prepares these gifts. If there is no music, the prayers may be said aloud, and all may respond: **"Blessed be God for ever."** *The priest then invites all to pray.*

Assembly: **May the Lord accept the sacrifice at your hands**
                for the praise and glory of his name,
                for our good, and the good of all his Church.

The priest says the prayer over the gifts and all respond: **Amen.**

EUCHARISTIC PRAYER

The central prayer of the Mass begins with this greeting and invitation between priest and assembly.

Priest: The Lord be with you. Assembly: And al - so with you.

Priest: Lift up your hearts. Assembly: We lift them up to the Lord.

Priest: Let us give thanks to the Lord our God.

Assembly: It is right to give him thanks and praise.

Music: Sacramentary, 1974

300

The Sanctus acclamation is sung to conclude the introduction to the eucharistic prayer.

Ho-ly,
ho-ly, ho-ly Lord, God of pow-er,
God of might, heav-en and earth are full of your
glo-ry. Ho-san-na in the high-est.
Bless-ed is he who comes in the name of the
Lord. Ho-san-na in the high-est,
ho-san-na in the high - est.

Music: *Mass of Creation*, Marty Haugen, © 1984, GIA Publications, Inc.

301

One of the following acclamations follows the priest's invitation: "Let us proclaim the mystery of faith."

Let us pro-claim the mys-ter-y of faith:

Christ has died, Christ is ris-en, Christ will come a-gain.

Christ has died, Christ is ris-en, Christ will come a-gain!

Music: *Mass of Creation,* Marty Haugen, © 1984, GIA Publications, Inc.

B **Dying you destroyed our death, rising you restored our life. Lord Jesus, come in glory.**

C **When we eat this bread, when we drink this cup, we proclaim your death, Lord Jesus, until you come in glory.**

D **Lord, by your cross and resurrection you have set us free. You are the Savior of the world.**

The eucharistic prayer concludes:

302

Priest: Through him, with him, in him, in the unity of the Holy Spirit, all glory and honor is yours, almighty Father, for ever and ever.

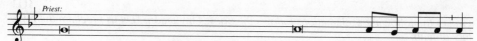

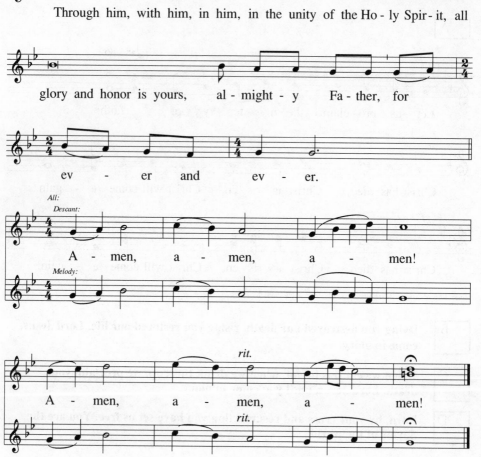

Through him, with him, in him, in the unity of the Ho - ly Spir - it, all

glory and honor is yours, al - might - y Fa - ther, for

ev - er and ev - er.

All:
Descant:
A - men, a - men, a - men!

Melody:

rit.
A - men, a - men, a - men!
rit.

Music: *Mass of Creation,* Marty Haugen, © 1984, GIA Publications, Inc.

COMMUNION RITE

The priest invites all to join in the Lord's Prayer.

Our Fa - ther, who art in heav - en, hal - lowed be thy name;

thy king - dom come; thy will be done on earth as it

is in heav - en. Give us this day our dai - ly bread;

and for - give us our tres - pass - es as we for - give

those who tres - pass a - gainst us; and lead us not

in - to temp - ta - tion, but de - liv - er us from e - vil.

Priest: Deliver us, Lord...for the coming of our Savior, Jesus Christ.

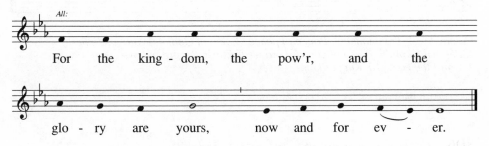

All:

For the king - dom, the pow'r, and the

glo - ry are yours, now and for ev - er.

Music: Traditional chant, adapt. by Robert Snow, 1964; acc. by Robert J. Batastini, © 1975, 1993, GIA Publications, Inc.

Following the prayer "Lord, Jesus Christ," the priest invites all to exchange the sign of peace.

Priest: The peace of the Lord be with you always.

Assembly: **And also with you.**

All exchange a sign of peace.

305 *Then the eucharistic bread is solemnly broken and the consecrated bread and wine are prepared for holy communion. The litany "Lamb of God" is sung during the breaking of the bread.*

Cantor or Choir: *All:*

*Lamb of God, you take a-way the

sins of the world, have mer-cy on us.

To repeat

Last time

grant us peace.

*Alternates: 1. Emmanuel, 2. Prince of peace, 3. Son of God, 4. Word made flesh, 5. Paschal Lamb, 6. Bread of Life, 7. Lord Jesus Christ, 8. Lord of Love, 9. Christ the Lord, 10. King of kings.

Music: *Holy Cross Mass;* David Clark Isele, © 1979, GIA Publications, Inc.

306 *The priest then invites all to share in holy communion.*

> *Priest:* This is the Lamb of God...his supper.
>
> *Assembly:* **Lord, I am not worthy to receive you,**
> **but only say the word and I shall be healed.**

Minister of communion: The body (blood) of Christ.
Communicant: **Amen.**

A song or psalm is ordinarily sung during communion. After communion, a time of silence is observed or a song of thanksgiving is sung. The rite concludes with the prayer after communion to which all respond: **Amen.**

CONCLUDING RITE 307

The liturgy of word and eucharist ends very simply. There may be announcements of events and concerns for the community, then the priest gives a blessing and the assembly is dismissed.

GREETING AND BLESSING

Priest: The Lord be with you.

Assembly: **And also with you.**

Optional

When the bishop blesses the people he adds the following:

Bishop: Blessed be the name of the Lord.

Assembly: **Now and for ever.**

Bishop: Our help is in the name of the Lord.

Assembly: **Who made heaven and earth.**

The blessing may be in a simple or solemn form. All respond to the blessing or to each part of the blessing: **Amen.**

DISMISSAL

The deacon or priest then dismisses the assembly:

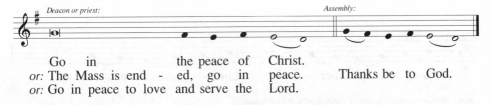

Go in the peace of Christ.
or: The Mass is end - ed, go in peace.   Thanks be to God.
or: Go in peace to love and serve the Lord.

EASTER DISMISSAL

The deacon or priest then dismisses the assembly:

Go in the peace of Christ, al-le-lu - ia, al-le - lu - ia.
Thanks be to God, al-le-lu - ia, al-le - lu - ia.

Setting One

A COMMUNITY MASS

308 KYRIE

Lord, have mer - cy. Lord, have mer - cy.

Christ, have mer - cy. Christ, have mer - cy.

Lord, have mer - cy. Lord, have mer - cy.

Or:

Ky - ri - e e - le - i - son. Ky - ri - e e - le - i - son.

Chri - ste e - le - i - son. Chri - ste e - le - i - son.

Ky - ri - e   e - le - i - son.   Ky - ri - e   e - le - i - son.

Music: Traditional chant; acc. by Richard Proulx, © 1971, GIA Publications, Inc.

GLORIA   309

Glo - ry to God in the high - est,   and   peace to his peo - ple on

earth.   Lord   God,   heav-en - ly   King,   al -

might - y God and   Fa - ther,   We   wor - ship you, we

give   you thanks, we   praise you   for   your   glo - ry.

Music: *A Community Mass,* Richard Proulx, © 1971, 1977, GIA Publications, Inc.

310 SANCTUS

With majesty

Ho-ly, ho-ly, ho - ly Lord, God of pow-er and might, heav'n and earth are full of your glo - ry. Ho - san - na in the high - est, ho - san - na in the high-est. Blest is he who comes in the name of the Lord. Ho - san - na in the

Descant: Ho - san - na, high - est, ho - san - na in the high - est.

Music: *A Community Mass,* by Richard Proulx, © 1971, 1977, GIA Publications, Inc.

311 MEMORIAL ACCLAMATION

♩ = *ca.* 72

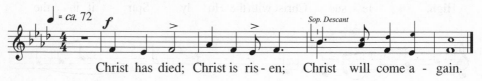

Sop. Descant

Christ has died; Christ is ris - en; Christ will come a - gain.

Music: *A Community Mass,* Richard Proulx, © 1971, 1977, GIA Publications, Inc.

MEMORIAL ACCLAMATION 312

When we eat this bread and drink this cup, we pro -
claim your death, Lord Je-sus, un - til you come in glo - ry.

Music: *A Community Mass,* Richard Proulx, © 1988, GIA Publications, Inc.

AMEN 313

A - men, a - men, a - men.

Music: *A Community Mass,* Richard Proulx, © 1971, 1977, GIA Publications, Inc.

AGNUS DEI 314

Lamb of God, you take a - way the
sins of the world: have mer - cy on us.

Lamb of God, you take a - way the
grant us peace.
sins of the world: grant us peace.

Music: *A Community Mass,* Richard Proulx, © 1971, 1977, GIA Publications, Inc.

Setting Two

MASS OF CREATION

315 **BLESSING AND SPRINKLING OF HOLY WATER**

Refrain

If we have died to our-selves in Je - sus, then

we shall a - rise to new life in him. Al - le -

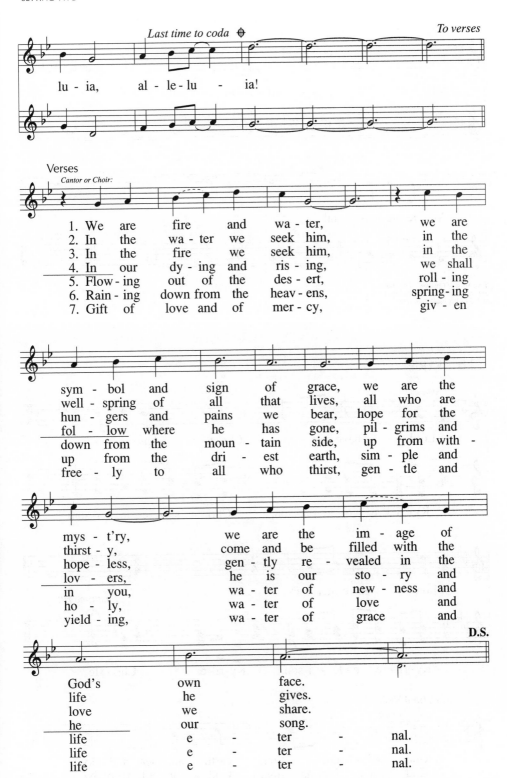

lu - ia, al - le - lu - ia!

Verses
Cantor or Choir:

1. We are fire and wa - ter, we are
2. In the wa - ter we seek him, in the
3. In the fire we seek him, in the
4. In our dy - ing and ris - ing, we shall
5. Flow - ing out of the des - ert, roll - ing
6. Rain - ing down from the heav - ens, spring - ing
7. Gift of love and of mer - cy, giv - en

sym - bol and sign of grace, we are the
well - spring of all that lives, all who are
hun - gers and pains we bear, hope for the
fol - low where he has gone, pil - grims and
down from the moun - tain side, up from with -
up from the dri - est earth, sim - ple and
free - ly to all who thirst, gen - tle and

mys - t'ry, we are the im - age of
thirst - y, come and be filled with the
hope - less, gen - tly re - vealed in the
lov - ers, he is our sto - ry and
in you, wa - ter of new - ness and
ho - ly, wa - ter of love and
yield - ing, wa - ter of grace and

D.S.

God's own face.
life he gives.
love we share.
he our song.
life e - ter - nal.
life e - ter - nal.
life e - ter - nal.

⊕ Coda

ia!   Al - le - lu - ia!

Al - le - lu - ia!   *no rit.*

Text: *Mass of Creation,* Marty Haugen
Music: *Mass of Creation,* Marty Haugen
© 1984, GIA Publications, Inc.

316 KYRIE

Melody:
Lord, have mer - cy.   Christ, have mer - cy.

Harmony:
Ky - ri - e   e - le - i - son.   Chri - ste   e - le - i - son.

Lord, have mer - cy.

Ky - ri - e   e - le - i - son.   Ky - ri - e.   Chri - ste.

Last time rit.

Optional Verses*

Cantor or priest:

1. God   of all cre - a - tion,   earth   and sea and sky,
2. God   of ev - 'ry na - tion,   God   of all who live,
3. God   of our sal - va - tion,   God   of grace and peace,

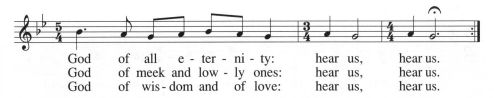

God   of all   e - ter - ni - ty: hear us,   hear us.
God   of meek and low - ly ones: hear us,   hear us.
God   of wis - dom and of love: hear us,   hear us.

*May be sung over ostinato Kyrie, or in alternation with the Kyrie using the same
accompaniment.*

Text: *Mass of Creation,* Marty Haugen
Music: *Mass of Creation,* Marty Haugen
© 1984, GIA Publications, Inc.

GLORIA   317

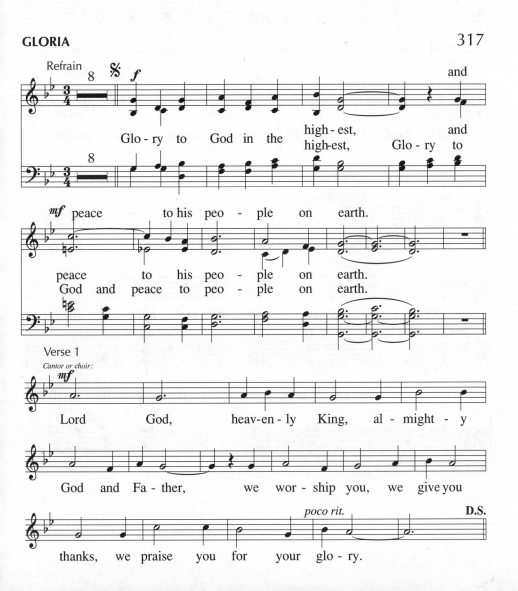

Refrain   and
Glo - ry to   God in the   high - est,   and
                               high - est,   Glo - ry to
peace   to his peo - ple   on   earth.
peace   to his peo - ple   on   earth.
God and peace to peo - ple   on   earth.   Glo - ry to

Verse 1
Cantor or choir:

Lord   God,   heav-en-ly King,   al - might - y
God   and Fa - ther,   we wor - ship you,   we give you

poco rit.   D.S.

thanks, we praise   you   for   your   glo - ry.

Verse 2

Cantor or choir:

Lord Je-sus Christ, on - ly Son of the Fa - ther, Lord

God, Lamb of God, you take a - way the sin of the

cresc.

world: have mer - cy on us; you are seat - ed at the

mf   *poco rit. f* **D.S.**

right hand of the Fa - ther: re - ceive our prayer.

Verse 3

Cantor or choir:

mf

For you a - lone are the Ho- ly One, you a - lone are the

Lord, you a - lone are the Most High,

div. f   *ff*

Je - sus Christ, with the Ho - ly

Spir - it, in the glo - ry of God, the
in the glo - ry of the

poco rit. *to Final refrain*

Fa - ther. A - men! A - men!
Fa - ther. A men! A - men!

A - men! A - men!

Final refrain

a tempo

ff Glo - ry to God, and peace

All:

Glo - ry to God in the high - est, and peace
Glo - ry to God,

to

fff *no rit.*

to his peo - ple on earth.
peace to peo - ple on earth.

Music: *Mass of Creation*, Marty Haugen, © 1984, GIA Publications, Inc.

318 GOSPEL ACCLAMATION

1,5. Praise the God of all cre - a - tion, God of
2. Tree of life and end-less wis - dom, be our
3. Liv - ing wa - ter, we are thirst - ing for the
4. Come, O Spir - it, kin-dle fire in the

mer - cy and com - pas - sion:
root, our growth and glo - ry: Al - le - lu - ia! Al-le -
life that you have prom - ised:
hearts of all your peo - ple:

lu - ia! Praise the Word of truth and life! life!

Alternate Verses

Speak, O Lord, your servant listens, yours the word of life eternal:
To the humble and the lowly you reveal the Kingdom's myst'ry:
Praise the Word who lived among us, made us children of the Kingdom:
You are light, Lord, for our darkness, break upon our waiting spirits:
Gentle shepherd, you who know us, call us all into your presence:
Be our way, Lord, be our truth, Lord, be our hope of life eternal:
We who love you, seek your truth, Lord, come and make your home within us:
We shall watch, Lord, we shall pray, Lord, for we know not when you cometh:

Text: *Mass of Creation,* Marty Haugen
Music: *Mass of Creation,* Marty Haugen
© 1984, GIA Publications, Inc.

LENTEN ACCLAMATION

Refrain

Praise to you, Lord Jesus Christ, king of end-less glo-ry!

Praise to you, Lord Jesus Christ, king of end-less glo-ry!

Verses

Cantor or choir: **mp**

1st Sun.	We	do	not	live	on	bread a - lone,	but we
2nd Sun.	From the	shin - ing	cloud	a	voice	is heard—	"This is
3rd Sun.	"Come,	take	the	wa - ter	that	I give,	if you
4th Sun.	"I		am	the Light	of	all the world,	all who
5th Sun.	"I		am	the Res - ur - rec - tion,			I am
6th Sun.	Christ	was	o - be - dient	un - to death,			e - ven
General	Turn	to	the Lord	with	all	your heart,	for the

D.S.

live on ev-'ry word from our God.
my be-lov-ed Son, hear his words."
drink you will nev-er thirst a - gain."
fol-low me will have the light of life."
life to all who trust in my name."
death on the wood of the cross.
time of sal-va-tion is here.

Music: *Mass of Creation*, Marty Haugen, © 1984, GIA Publications, Inc.

320 GENERAL INTERCESSIONS

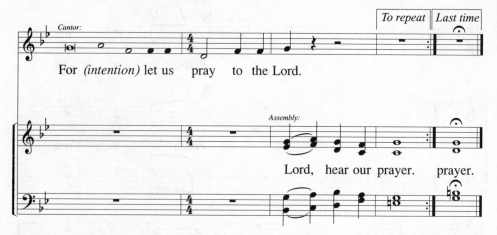

For *(intention)* let us pray to the Lord.

Lord, hear our prayer. prayer.

Music: *Mass of Creation*, Marty Haugen, © 1984, GIA Publications, Inc.

321 EUCHARISTIC PRAYER

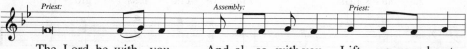

The Lord be with you. And al - so with you. Lift up your hearts.

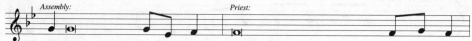

We lift them up to the Lord. Let us give thanks to the Lord, our God.

It is right to give him thanks and praise.

Music: *Mass of Creation*, Marty Haugen, © 1984, GIA Publications, Inc.

322 SANCTUS

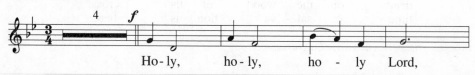

Ho - ly, ho - ly, ho - ly Lord,

God of pow-er, God of might, heav-en and

earth are full of your glo - ry.

div. **ff**

Ho - san - na in the high - est.

unis. **mf**

Bless- ed is he who comes in the name of the

div. **ff**

Lord. Ho - san - na in the high - est,

fff *rit.* *molto rit.*

ho - san - na in the high - est.

Music: *Mass of Creation,* Marty Haugen, © 1984, GIA Publications, Inc.

MEMORIAL ACCLAMATION 323

Priest: ♩=84-86

Let us pro - claim the mys - ter - y of faith:

Music: *Mass of Creation,* Marty Haugen, © 1984, GIA Publications, Inc.

324 MEMORIAL ACCLAMATION

come in glo - ry.

Lord Je - sus, come in glo - ry.

Music: *Mass of Creation*, Marty Haugen, ©1990, GIA Publications, Inc.

MEMORIAL ACCLAMATION 325

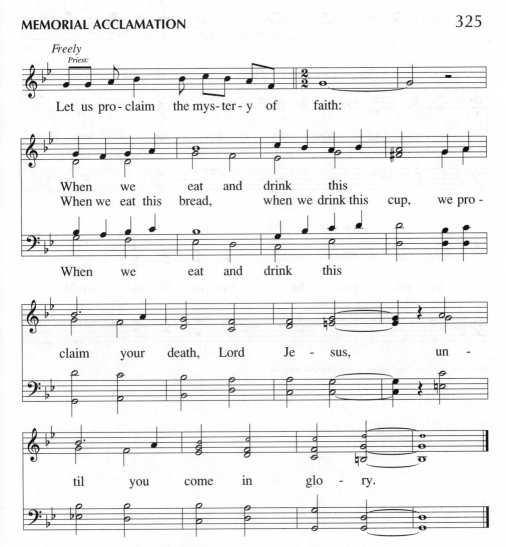

Freely
Priest:

Let us pro-claim the mys-ter-y of faith:

When we eat and drink this
When we eat this bread, when we drink this cup, we pro-

When we eat and drink this

claim your death, Lord Je - sus, un -

til you come in glo - ry.

Music: *Mass of Creation*, Marty Haugen, © 1993, GIA Publications, Inc.

326 MEMORIAL ACCLAMATION

Music: *Mass of Creation*, Marty Haugen, © 1993, GIA Publications, Inc.

AMEN

Through him, with him, in him, in the unity of the Ho - ly Spir- it, all glory and honor is yours, al - might - y Fa - ther, for ev - er and ev - er.

A - men, a - men, a - men!

A - men, a - men, a - men!

Music: *Mass of Creation,* Marty Haugen, © 1984, GIA Publications, Inc.

328 LORD'S PRAYER

Gently ♩=80-84

mf

Our Fa - ther, who art in heav - en,

hal - low - ed be thy name; thy king - dom come; thy

will be done on earth as it is in heav - en.

f

Give us this day our dai - ly bread; and for -

mf   *poco rit.*

give us our tres - pass - es as we for - give those who

329   AGNUS DEI

Cantor or choir:

1. Je - sus, Lamb of God,
2. Je - sus, Bread of Life,   you take a - way the sins of the
3. Je - sus, Prince of Peace,

world: have mer - cy on us.

Last time

Cantor or choir:

Je - sus, Lamb of God; you take a - way the sins of the

world: grant us your peace.

Additional Invocations:

Jesus, Word of God,...   Jesus, Fire of Love,...
Jesus, Tree of Life,...   Jesus, Bread of Peace,...
Jesus, Lord of Lords,...   Jesus, Hope for all,...
Jesus, King of Kings,...

Music: *Mass of Creation*, Marty Haugen, © 1984, GIA Publications, Inc.

Setting Three

MASS OF LIGHT

330 KYRIE

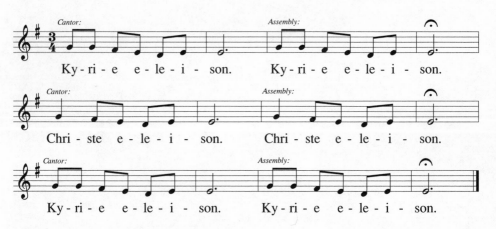

Ky-ri-e e-le-i-son. Ky-ri-e e-le-i-son.

Chri-ste e-le-i-son. Chri-ste e-le-i-son.

Ky-ri-e e-le-i-son. Ky-ri-e e-le-i-son.

Music: *Mass of Light*, David Haas, © 1987, GIA Publications, Inc.

GLORIA

Verse 2

Cantor or choir:

2. Lord Je-sus Christ, on-ly Son of the Fa-ther, Lord

God, Lamb of God, you take a-

way the sin of the world: have mer-cy on us;

Harmony:
Melody:
you are seat-ed at the

D.S.
right hand of the Fa-ther: re-ceive our prayer.

Verse 3

Women:

3. For you a - lone are the Ho - ly

One, you a - lone are the Lord, the

All:
Most High, Je - sus Christ, with the Ho - ly

Spir - it, in the glo-ry of God the Fa - ther.

Final Refrain

Descant:
And sing!

All: *ff*
Glo-ry to God in the high-est, Sing! Glo-ry to

Glo-ry to God in the high-est, and

God! Glo-ry to God in the high-est, and

peace to his peo-ple on earth!

peace to his peo-ple on earth!

Music: *Mass of Light*, David Haas, © 1988, GIA Publications, Inc.

332 ALLELUIA

Refrain
Cantor or choir, then all:

Al- le - lu - ia! Al- le - lu - ia! Al - le - lu - ia!

Verses for Ordinary Time
Verse 1
Cantor:

1. Speak, O Lord, your ser- vant is lis - t'ning:

D.C.

you have the words of ev - er - last - ing life!

Verse 2

2. Your words, O Lord, are spir- it and life,

D.C.

you have the words of ev - er - last - ing life!

Verse 3

3. I am the way, the truth, and the life.

D.C.

No one comes to God, ex - cept through me!

Additional verses may be found in the original published edition of "Mass of Light."

Music: *Mass of Light*, David Haas, © 1988, GIA Publications, Inc.

GOSPEL ACCLAMATION 333

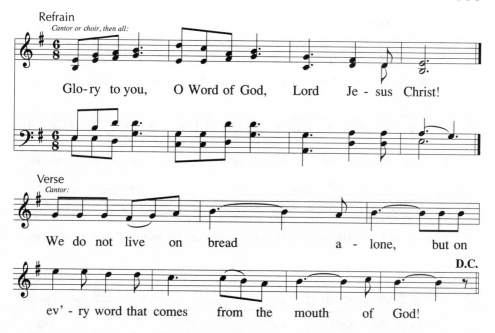

Refrain
Cantor or choir, then all:

Glo-ry to you, O Word of God, Lord Je-sus Christ!

Verse
Cantor:

We do not live on bread a - lone, but on

D.C.

ev' - ry word that comes from the mouth of God!

Additional verses may be found in "Who Calls You by Name", a collection of music for the RCIA, and in the original published edition of "Mass of Light."

Music: *Mass of Light*, David Haas, © 1988, GIA Publications, Inc.

PREFACE DIALOG 334

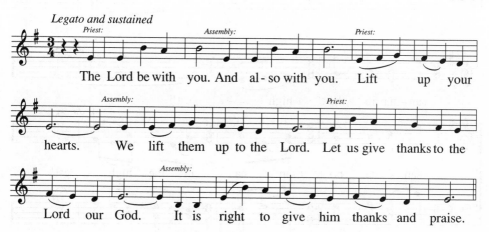

Legato and sustained
Priest: *Assembly:* *Priest:*

The Lord be with you. And al- so with you. Lift up your

Assembly: *Priest:*

hearts. We lift them up to the Lord. Let us give thanks to the

Assembly:

Lord our God. It is right to give him thanks and praise.

Music: *Mass of Light*, David Haas, © 1988, GIA Publications, Inc.

335 **SANCTUS**

Music: *Mass of Light*, David Haas, © 1988, GIA Publications, Inc.

EUCHARISTIC ACCLAMATION I (OPTIONAL) *   336

Ho - san - na in the high - est!

As in the Eucharistic Prayers for Masses with Children.

Music: *Mass of Light*, David Haas, © 1988, GIA Publications, Inc.

MEMORIAL ACCLAMATION   337

Let us proclaim the mys - ter - y of faith: Dy - ing you de -
stroyed our death, ris - ing you re - stored our life. Lord Je - sus come!

Lord Je - sus come in glo - ry!

Lord Je - sus come! Lord Je - sus come in glo - ry!

Music: *Mass of Light*, David Haas, © 1988, GIA Publications, Inc.

338 EUCHARISTIC ACCLAMATION II (OPTIONAL)

Hear us, hear us. Hear us, hear us.

This refrain is repeated continually under the spoken prayer of the priest.

Music: *Mass of Light,* David Haas, © 1988, GIA Publications, Inc.

339 AMEN

With strength

A - men, a - men! A - men,

A - men, a - men! A - men,

a - men!

a - men!

Music: *Mass of Light,* David Haas, © 1988, GIA Publications, Inc.

AGNUS DEI

340

*Lamb of God,
Bread of Life, you take a - way the sins of the world: have
Son of God,

mer - cy on us.

Schola: Have mer - cy on us.

Last time

world: grant us your peace.

Grant us your peace.

*"Lamb of God" is sung the first and last times. Alternate intervening invocations
include: "Saving Cup," "Hope for all," "Prince of Peace," "Wine of Peace," etc.*

Setting Four

MASS OF REMEMBRANCE

341 KYRIE

Refrain

Ky - ri - e   e - le - i-son,   Chri - ste   e - le - i - son,

Lord,   have   mer   -   cy,   Christ,   have   mer   -   cy,

To verses

Ky - ri - e   e - le - i - son.

Lord,   have   mer   -   cy.

son.

cy.

Verses 1, 2
Priest, deacon, or cantor:

1. Lord Je - sus, you came to gath-er the na - tions
2. You come in word and sac - ra - ment to

rit. **D.S.**

in - to the peace of God's King - dom.
strength - en us in ho - li - ness.

Verse 3
Priest, deacon, or cantor:

3. You will come in glo - ry with sal -

rit. **D.S.**

va - tion for your peo - ple.

Music: *Mass of Remembrance,* Marty Haugen, © 1987, GIA Publications, Inc.

342 GLORIA

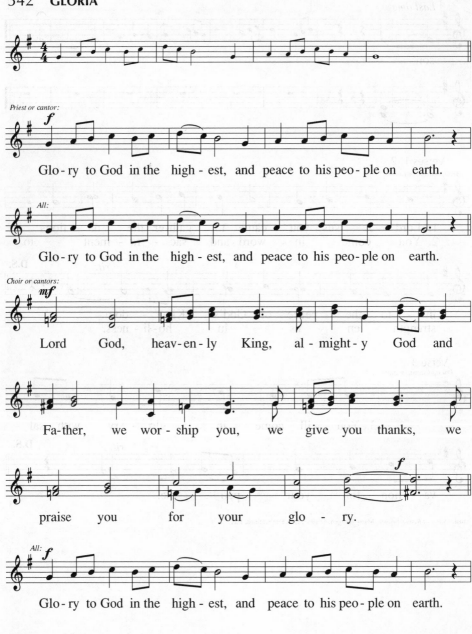

Priest or cantor:

f

Glo-ry to God in the high-est, and peace to his peo-ple on earth.

All:

Glo-ry to God in the high-est, and peace to his peo-ple on earth.

Choir or cantors:

mf

Lord God, heav-en-ly King, al-might-y God and

Fa-ther, we wor-ship you, we give you thanks, we

praise you for your glo-ry.

All: **f**

Glo-ry to God in the high-est, and peace to his peo-ple on earth.

Glo-ry to God in the high-est, and peace to his peo-ple on earth.

Choir or cantors:

Lord Je-sus Christ, on-ly Son of the Fa-ther,

Lord God, Lamb of God, you take a - way the

sin of the world: have mer - cy on us;

you are seat-ed at the right hand of the

Fa - ther: re - ceive our prayer.

Descant:

Glo - ry, glo - ry, and peace on the earth.

All:

Glo-ry to God in the high - est, and peace to his peo-ple on earth.

Glo - ry, glo - ry and peace on the earth.

Glo-ry to God in the high - est, and peace to his peo-ple on earth.

Choir or cantors:

For you a - lone are the Ho-ly One, you a-lone are the

Lord, you a - lone are the Most High,

Je - sus Christ, with the Ho - ly Spir - it, in the

A - men. A -

glo - ry of God the Fa-ther. A - men, a - men.

Descant:

Glo - ry, glo - ry, and

All:

men! A -

Glo - ry to God in the high - est, and

peace on the earth.

men! A -

peace to his peo - ple on earth.

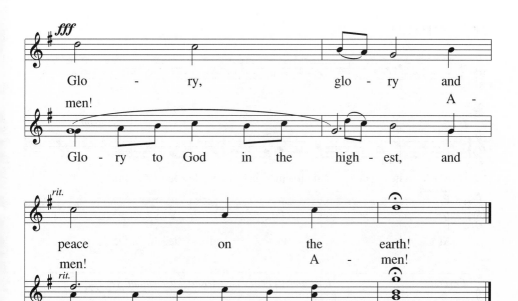

Glo - ry, glo - ry and A -
men!

Glo - ry to God in the high - est, and

peace on the earth!
men! A - men!

peace to his peo - ple on earth!

Music: *Mass of Remembrance,* Marty Haugen, © 1987, GIA Publications, Inc.

343 ALLELUIA

Al - le - lu - ia, al - le - lu - ia, al - le - lu - ia!

Descant:

Al - le - lu - ia, al - le - lu - ia!

To verses ia! ia!

Last time (repeat as needed to finish canon) *ff*

Al - le - lu - ia! Al - le - lu - ia!

ia! ia! Al - le - lu - ia! Al - le - lu - ia!

Verse 1
mf Cantor or schola:

1. Speak, O Lord, your ser - vant is lis - t'ning,
you have the words of ev - er - last - ing life. **D.S.**

Verse 2
mf Cantor or schola:

2. "I am the Light of the world," says the Lord,
"All who fol - low me shall have the light of life." **D.S.**

Verse 3

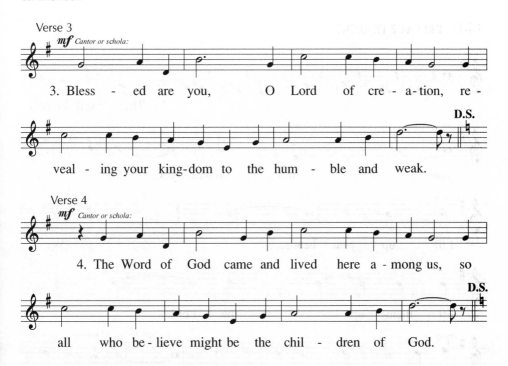

mf Cantor or schola:

3. Bless - ed are you, O Lord of cre - a-tion, re -

D.S.

veal - ing your king-dom to the hum - ble and weak.

Verse 4

mf Cantor or schola:

4. The Word of God came and lived here a - mong us, so

D.S.

all who be - lieve might be the chil - dren of God.

Music: *Mass of Remembrance,* Marty Haugen, © 1987, GIA Publications, Inc.

344   PREFACE DIALOG

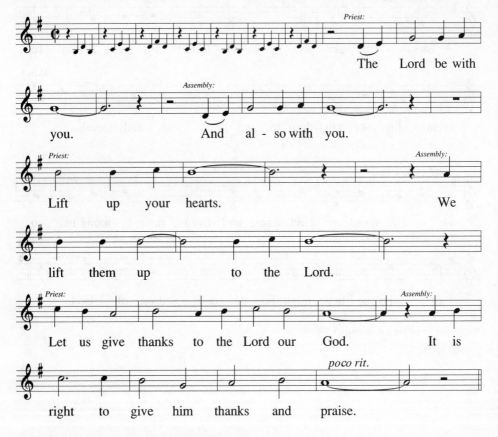

The Lord be with you. And al - so with you.

Priest: Lift up your hearts. Assembly: We lift them up to the Lord.

Priest: Let us give thanks to the Lord our God. Assembly: It is right to give him thanks and praise.

poco rit.

Music: *Mass of Remembrance,* Marty Haugen, © 1987, GIA Publications, Inc.

345   EUCHARISTIC ACCLAMATION IA (OPTIONAL)*

Praise, thanks and glo - ry be to you, O God!

As in the Eucharistic Prayers for Masses with Children.

Music: *Mass of Remembrance,* Marty Haugen, © 1987, GIA Publications, Inc.

SANCTUS

With movement

f

Ho - ly, ho - ly, ho - ly Lord, God of

pow-er and might, heav'n and earth are

Melody: ff

Harmony:

full of your glo-ry. Ho - san - na in the

dim. *mp* *Melody:* *poco a poco cresc.*

high - est. Bless - ed is he who comes in the

Harmony:

Bless - ed is he who

f

name of the Lord. Ho - san - na in the

f

comes in the name of the Lord. Ho -

ff *rit.*

high - est. Ho - san - na in the high - est!

san - na in the high - est, the high - est!

Music: *Mass of Remembrance,* Marty Haugen, © 1987, GIA Publications, Inc.

347 EUCHARISTIC ACCLAMATION IB (OPTIONAL)

Praise, thanks and glo-ry be to you, O Christ!

Music: *Mass of Remembrance*, Marty Haugen, © 1987, GIA Publications, Inc.

348 MEMORIAL ACCLAMATION

Priest:

Let us proclaim the myster-y of faith:

All:

When we eat this bread, when we drink this

Melody:

Harmony:

cup, we pro-claim your death, Lord Je-sus,

un-til you come, un-til you come in

1.

glo - ry!

2. *rit.*

glo - ry!

Music: *Mass of Remembrance*, Marty Haugen, © 1987, GIA Publications, Inc.

EUCHARISTIC ACCLAMATION II (OPTIONAL) 349

We re-mem-ber how you loved us to your death, and still we cel-e-brate, for you are here; and we be-lieve that we will see you when you come in your glo-ry, Lord. We re-mem-ber, we cel-e-brate, we be-lieve.

Music: *Mass of Remembrance,* Marty Haugen, © 1987, GIA Publications, Inc.

350 EUCHARISTIC ACCLAMATION III (OPTIONAL)

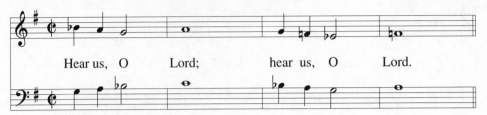

Hear us, O Lord; hear us, O Lord.

Music: *Mass of Remembrance*, Marty Haugen, © 1987, GIA Publications, Inc.

351 AMEN

Through him, with him, in him, in the u-ni-ty of the Ho-ly

Spir-it, all glo-ry and hon-or is yours, al-might-y

Fa-ther, for ev-er and ev-er.

Fa-ther,

Al - le - lu - ia, a - men!
*Praise to you, Lord, a - men!

Al - le - lu - ia,
*Praise to you, Lord,

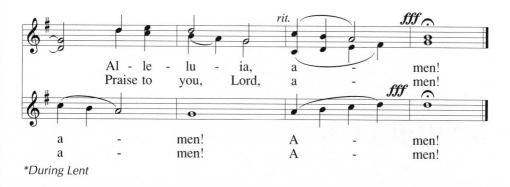

Al - le - lu - ia, a - men!
Praise to you, Lord, a - men!

a - men! A - men!
a - men! A - men!

*During Lent

Music: *Mass of Remembrance*, Marty Haugen, © 1987, GIA Publications, Inc.

AGNUS DEI

352

1. *Lamb of God,
2. Prince of Peace, you take a - way the sins of the
3. Bread of Life,

To repeat

world: have mer - cy on us.

Last time

world: grant us peace, grant us peace.

* "Lamb of God" is sung the first and last times. Alternate intervening invocations
include: Ancient Cup, Bread of Peace, Wine of Hope, Lord of Lords.

Music: *Mass of Remembrance*, Marty Haugen, © 1987, GIA Publications, Inc.

Setting Five

MISSA EMMANUEL
This entire setting is sung unaccompanied.

353 KYRIE

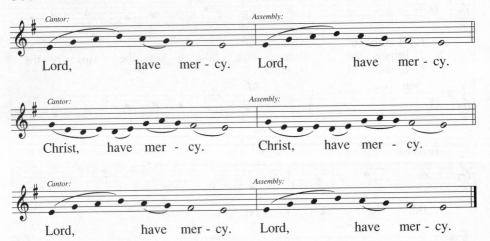

Cantor: Lord, have mer - cy. Assembly: Lord, have mer - cy.

Cantor: Christ, have mer - cy. Assembly: Christ, have mer - cy.

Cantor: Lord, have mer - cy. Assembly: Lord, have mer - cy.

Music: *Missa Emmanuel;* Richard Proulx, © 1991, GIA Publications, Inc.

354 SANCTUS

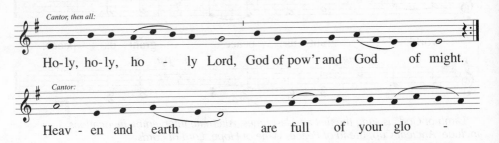

Cantor, then all: Ho-ly, ho-ly, ho - ly Lord, God of pow'r and God of might.

Cantor: Heav - en and earth are full of your glo -

ry.   Ho - san - na in   the   high   -   est,

ho - san - na   in   the   high   -   est.

All:
Ho - san   -   na in   the   high   -   est,

ho - san - na   in   the   high   -   est.

Cantor:
Bless - ed is   he   who   comes   in   the   name

of   the   Lord.   Ho - san - na   in   the

high   -   est,   ho - san - na   in   the

high   -   est.   *All:*   Ho - san - na in   the   high   -

est,   ho - san - na   in   the   high   -   est.

Music: *Missa Emmanuel,* Richard Proulx, © 1991, GIA Publications, Inc.

355 MEMORIAL ACCLAMATION

Christ has died, Christ is ris - en, Christ will come a - gain.

Music: *Missa Emmanuel,* Richard Proulx, © 1991, GIA Publications, Inc.

356 AMEN

A - men, a - men, a - men, a - men.

Music: *Missa Emmanuel,* Richard Proulx, © 1991, GIA Publications, Inc.

357 AGNUS DEI

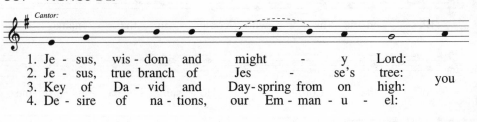

1. Je - sus, wis - dom and might - y Lord:
2. Je - sus, true branch of Jes - se's tree: you
3. Key of Da - vid and Day-spring from on high:
4. De - sire of na - tions, our Em - man - u - el:

1., 2., 3.   Assembly:

take a-way the sins of the world, have mer - cy on us, have

4.   Assembly:

mer - cy on us. grant us peace, grant us peace.

Music: *Missa Emmanuel,* Richard Proulx, © 1991, GIA Publications, Inc.

Setting Six

CORPUS CHRISTI MASS
This entire setting is sung unaccompanied.

KYRIE 358

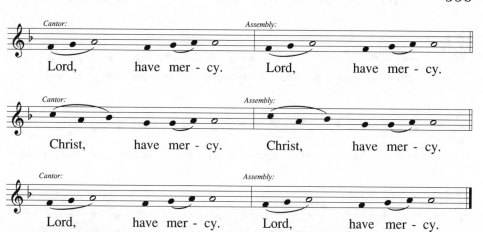

Music: *Corpus Christi Mass,* Kyrie XVI, adapt. by Richard Proulx, © 1992, GIA Publications, Inc.

359 SANCTUS

Ho - ly, ho - ly, ho - ly Lord, God of pow'r and might.

All:

Ho - ly, ho - ly, ho - ly Lord, God of pow'r and might.

Cantor:

Heav'n and earth are full of your glo - ry.

Ho - san - na in the high - est, in the high - est.

All:

Ho - san - na in the high - est, in the high - est.

Cantor:

Blessed is he who comes in the name of the Lord.

Ho - san - na in the high - est, in the high - est.

All:

Ho - san - na in the high - est, in the high - est.

Music: *Corpus Christi Mass, Adoro te devote*, setting by Richard Proulx, © 1992, GIA Publications, Inc.

MEMORIAL ACCLAMATION 360

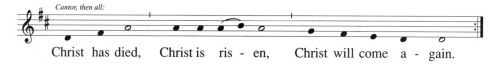

Cantor, then all:

Christ has died, Christ is ris - en, Christ will come a - gain.

Music: *Corpus Christi Mass, Adoro te devote,* setting by Richard Proulx, © 1992, GIA Publications, Inc.

AMEN 361

Cantor, then all:

A - men, a - men, a - men.

Music: *Corpus Christi Mass, Adoro te devote,* setting by Richard Proulx, © 1992, GIA Publications, Inc.

AGNUS DEI 362

Cantor:

1. Je - sus, Lamb of God, Bear - er of our sins,
2. Je - sus, Lamb of God, Sav - ior of the world,
3. Je - sus, Lamb of God, Bread come down from heav'n,
4. Je - sus, Lamb of God, Shep - herd of our souls,

have

Assembly: *repeat as needed*

mer - cy on us, have mer - cy on us.

Cantor:

5. Je - sus, Lamb of God, gen - tle Prince of peace,

grant us peace, grant us peace.

Assembly:

Grant us peace, grant us peace.

Music: *Corpus Christi Mass, Adoro te devote,* setting by Richard Proulx, © 1992, GIA Publications, Inc.

Setting Seven

CANTUS MISSAE

363 **KYRIE**

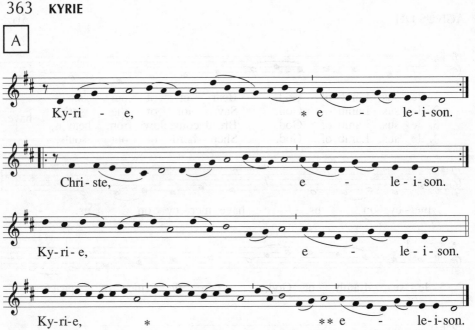

Music: Vatican Edition VIII; acc. by Richard Proulx, © 1995, GIA Publications, Inc.

B

Cantor: Assembly:

Ky - ri - e e - le - i - son. Ky - ri - e e - le - i - son.

Cantor: Assembly:

Chris - te e - le - i - son. Chris - te e - le - i - son.

Cantor: Assembly:

Ky - ri - e e - le - i - son. Ky - ri - e e - le - i - son.

Music: Vatican Edition XVI; acc. by Richard Proulx, © 1995, GIA Publications, Inc.

GLORIA 364

Gló - ri - a in ex - cél - sis De - o. Et in ter - ra pax ho - mí - ni - bus

bo - nae vo - lun - tá - tis. Lau - dá - mus te.

Be - ne - dí - ci - mus te. A - do - rá - mus te.

Glo - ri - fi - cá - mus te. Grá - ti - as á - gi - mus ti - bi

pro - pter ma - gnam gló - ri - am tu - am. Dó - mi - ne De - us, Rex cae -

lé - stis, De - us Pa - ter om - ní - po - tens.

Dó - mi - ne Fi - li u - ni - gé - ni - te, Je - su Chri - ste.

Dó - mi - ne De - us, A - gnus De - i, Fí - li - us Pa - tris.

Qui tol - lis pec - cá - ta mun - di, mi - se - ré - re no - bis.

Qui tol - lis pec - cá - ta mun - di, sú - sci - pe de - pre - ca - ti - ó -

nem no - stram. Qui se - des ad déx - te - ram Pa - tris,

mi - se - ré - re no - bis. Quó - ni - am tu so - lus San - ctus.

Tu so - lus Dó - mi - nus. Tu so - lus Al - tís - si - mus,

Je - su Chri - ste. Cum San - cto Spí - ri - tu,

in gló - ri - a De - i Pa - tris. A - men.

Music: Vatican Edition VIII; acc. by Richard Proulx, © 1995, GIA Publications, Inc.

LITURGY OF THE WORD

THE FIRST READINGS 365

After the first reading:

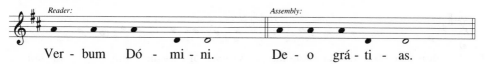

Reader: Ver - bum Dó - mi - ni.
Assembly: De - o grá - ti - as.

After the second reading or if there is only one reading before the gospel:

Reader: Ver - bum Dó - mi - ni.
Assembly: De - o grá - ti - as.

GOSPEL 366

Before the gospel:

Deacon or priest: Dó - mi - nus vo - bís - cum.
Assembly: Et cum spí - ri - tu tu - o.

Deacon: Lé - cti - o sanc - ti E - van - gé - li - i se - cún - dum

N...
Assembly: Gló - ri - a ti - bi, Dó - mi - ne.

After the gospel:

Deacon: Ver - bum Dó - mi - ni.
Assembly: Laus ti - bi, Chri - ste.

367 CREDO

Cre-do in u-num De - um, Pa - trem om - ni - po - tén-tem fa-

ctó-rem cae - li et ter-rae, vi - si - bí - li-um óm - ni - um

et in - vi - si - bí - li-um. Et in u-num Dó - mi - num

Je - sum Chri-stum, Fí - li-um De - i u - ni - gé - ni - tum.

Et ex Pa-tre na - tum an - te óm - ni - a sáe - cu - la.

De-um de De - o, lu-men de lú - mi - ne, De-um ve-rum

de De-o ve-ro. Gé - ni-tum, non fa - ctum, con-sub-stan - ti -

á - lem Pa - tri: per quem óm - ni - a fa - cta sunt.

Qui pro-pter nos hó - mi - nes et pro-pter no-stram sa - lú - tem de-

scén-dit de cae-lis. Et in-car-ná-tus est de Spí - ri - tu

San - cto ex Ma - rí - a Vír-gi - ne, et ho - mo fa - ctus est.

Cru - ci - fí - xus é - ti - am pro no - bis sub

Pón - ti - o Pi - lá - to, pas - sus et se - púl - tus est.

Et re - sur - ré - xit tér - ti - a di - e, se - cún - dum Scri - ptú - ras,

et a - scén - dit in cae - lum, se - det ad déx - te - ram Pa - tris.

Et í - te - rum ven - tú - rus est cum gló - ri -

a, ju - di - cá - re vi - vos et mór - tu - os, cu - jus re - gni non e - rit fi - nis.

Et in Spí - ri - tum San - ctum, Dó - mi - num et vi - vi - fi - cán - tem:

qui ex Pa - tre Fi - li - ó - que pro - cé - dit.

Qui cum Pa - tre et Fi - li - o si - mul a - do - rá - tur, en con - glo -

ri - fi - cá - tur: qui lo - cú - tus est per Pro - phé - tas.

Et u - nam, san - ctam, ca - thó - li - cam et a - po - stó - li - cam Ec - clé - si - am.

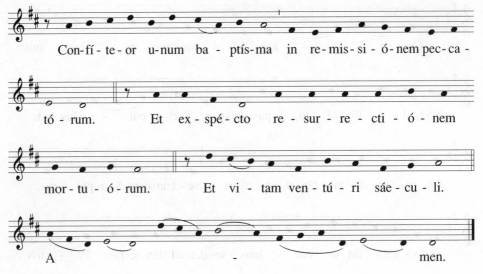

Con-fí - te - or u-num ba - ptís-ma in re-mis-si - ó-nem pec-ca -

tó - rum. Et ex - spé - cto re - sur - re - cti - ó - nem

mor-tu - ó - rum. Et vi - tam ven - tú - ri sáe - cu - li.

A - men.

Music: Vatican Edition III; acc. by Richard Proulx, © 1995, GIA Publications, Inc.

368 GENERAL INTERCESSIONS

After each intention:

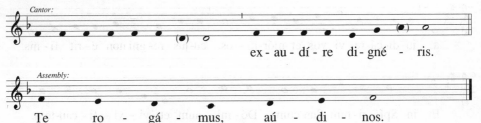

Cantor:

ex - au - dí - re di - gné - ris.

Assembly:

Te ro - gá - mus, aú - di - nos.

LITURGY OF THE EUCHARIST

369 PREFACE DIALOG

Priest:

Dó - mi - nus vo - bí - scum.

Assembly:

Et cum Spír - i - tu tu - o.

Priest:

Sur - sum cor - da.

Assembly:

Ha - bé - mus ad Dó - mi - num.

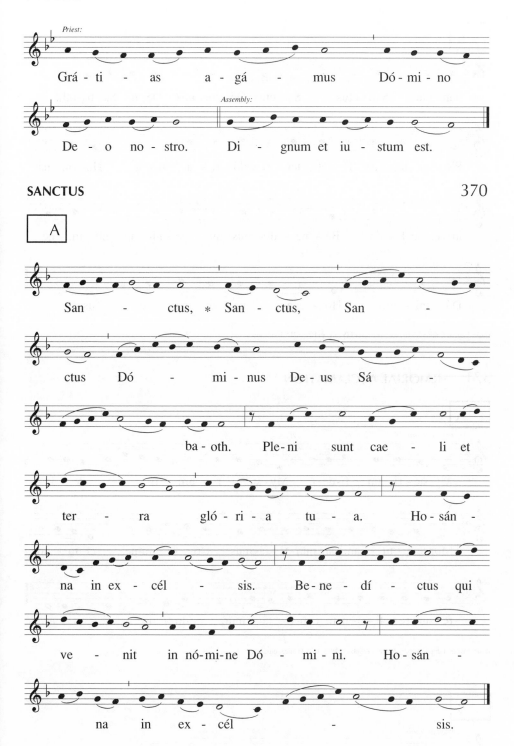

Grá - ti - as   a - gá - mus   Dó - mi - no   De - o   no - stro.   Di - gnum et iu - stum est.

SANCTUS   370

A

San - ctus, * San - ctus, San - ctus Dó - mi - nus De - us Sá - ba - oth. Ple - ni sunt cae - li et ter - ra gló - ri - a tu - a. Ho - sán - na in ex - cél - sis. Be - ne - dí - ctus qui ve - nit in nó - mi - ne Dó - mi - ni. Ho - sán - na in ex - cél - sis.

Music: Vatican Edition VIII; acc. by Richard Proulx, © 1995, GIA Publications, Inc.

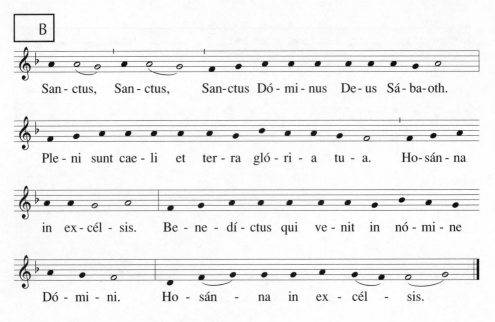

San - ctus, San - ctus, San - ctus Dó - mi - nus De - us Sá - ba - oth.

Ple - ni sunt cae - li et ter - ra gló - ri - a tu - a. Ho - sán - na

in ex - cél - sis. Be - ne - dí - ctus qui ve - nit in nó - mi - ne

Dó - mi - ni. Ho - sán - na in ex - cél - sis.

Music: Vatican Edition XVIII; acc. by Richard Proulx, © 1995, GIA Publications, Inc.

371 MEMORIAL ACCLAMATION

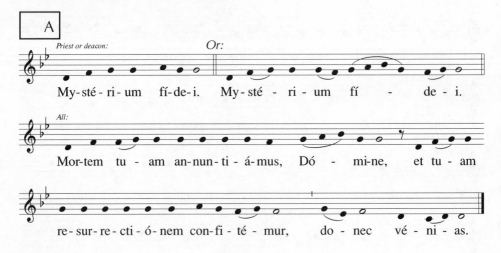

Priest or deacon: *Or:*

My - sté - ri - um fí - de - i. My - sté - ri - um fí - de - i.

All:

Mor - tem tu - am an - nun - ti - á - mus, Dó - mi - ne, et tu - am

re - sur - re - cti - ó - nem con - fi - té - mur, do - nec vé - ni - as.

Music: Vatican Edition; acc. by Richard Proulx, © 1995, GIA Publications, Inc.

Priest or deacon:

My - sté - ri - um fí - de - i.

Mor-tem tu - am an - nun - ti - á - mus, Dó - mi - ne, et re - sur -

re - cti - ó - nem con - fi - té - mur, do - nec vé - ni - as.

Music: Vatican Edition; acc. by Richard Proulx, © 1995, GIA Publications, Inc.

AMEN 372
After the doxology:

Assembly:

per o - mni - a sae-cu - la sae-cu - lo - rum. A - men.

COMMUNION RITE

LORD'S PRAYER 373

Priest:

Prae - cé - ptis sa - lu - tá - ri - bus mó - ni - ti, et de - ví - na

in - sti - tu - ti - ó - ne for-má - ti, au - dé - mus dí - ce - re:

All:

Pa - ter no-ster, qui es in cae-lis: san-cti - fi - cé - tur no - men

tu - um; ad - vé - ni - at re-gnum tu-um; fi - at vo - lún-tas

tu - a, si - cut in cae - lo, et in ter - ra.

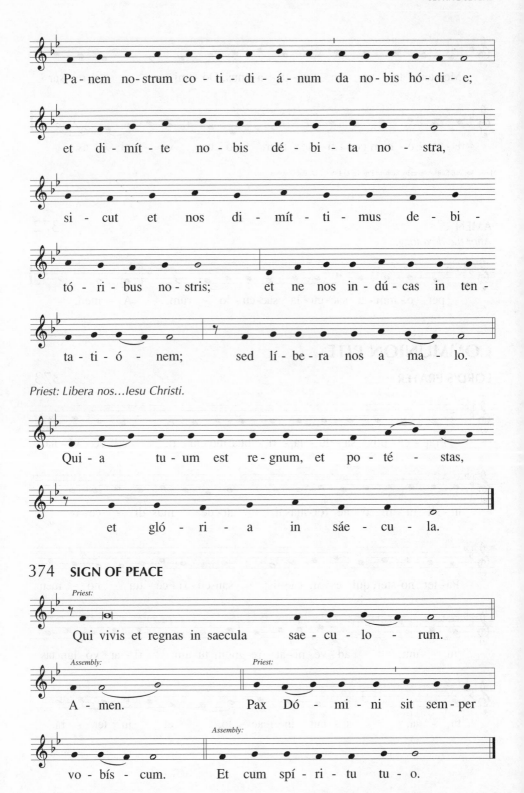

Pa - nem no-strum co - ti - di - á - num da no-bis hó - di - e;

et di - mít - te no - bis dé - bi - ta no - stra,

si - cut et nos di - mít - ti - mus de - bi -

tó - ri - bus no - stris; et ne nos in - dú - cas in ten -

ta - ti - ó - nem; sed lí - be - ra nos a ma - lo.

Priest: Libera nos…Iesu Christi.

Qui - a tu - um est re - gnum, et po - té - stas,

et gló - ri - a in sáe - cu - la.

374 **SIGN OF PEACE**

Priest:

Qui vivis et regnas in saecula sae - cu - lo - rum.

Assembly: *Priest:*

A - men. Pax Dó - mi - ni sit sem - per

Assembly:

vo - bís - cum. Et cum spí - ri - tu tu - o.

AGNUS DEI

A - gnus De - i, ∗ qui tol - lis pec-cá -
ta mun - di, mi-se-ré-re no - bis.
A - gnus De - i, ∗ qui tol - lis pec-cá -
ta mun - di, mi-se-ré-re no - bis.
A - gnus De - i, ∗ qui tol - lis pec-cá -
ta mun - di, do-na no - bis pa - cem.

Music: Vatican Edition VIII; acc. by Richard Proulx, © 1995, GIA Publications, Inc.

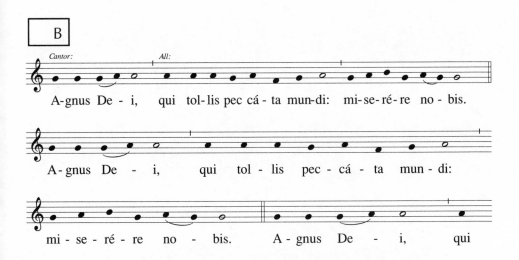

Cantor: All:
A-gnus De - i, qui tol-lis pec cá - ta mun-di: mi-se-ré-re no - bis.
A-gnus De - i, qui tol - lis pec - cá - ta mun - di:
mi - se - ré - re no - bis. A - gnus De - i, qui

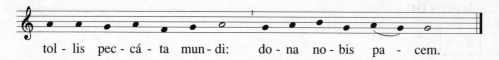

tol - lis pec - cá - ta mun - di: do - na no - bis pa - cem.

Music: Vatican Edition XVIII; acc. by Richard Proulx, © 1995, GIA Publications, Inc.

CONCLUDING RITE

376 DISMISSAL

Priest or deacon, then all:

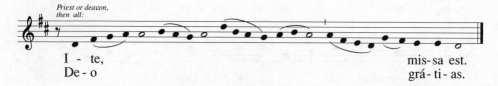

I - te,
De - o

mis- sa est.
grá- ti- as.

Music: Vatican Edition VIII; acc. by Richard Proulx, © 1995, GIA Publications, Inc.

Service Music

Refrain

Moving

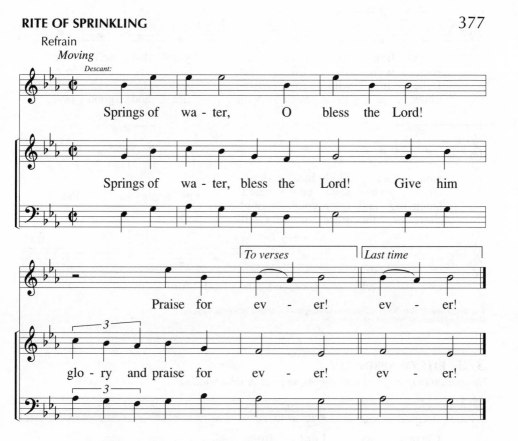

Springs of wa - ter, O bless the Lord!

Springs of wa - ter, bless the Lord! Give him

Praise for ev - er! ev - er!

glo - ry and praise for ev - er! ev - er!

Verses

Cantor:

1. O - ceans of earth, sing glo - ry to God!
2. Riv - ers and lakes, sing glo - ry to God!
3. Brooks of the hills, sing glo - ry to God!
4. Show - ers and springs, sing glo - ry to God!

Praise to the one who formed you!
Praise, all you ponds and bogs!
Praise to the source of life!
Praise, all you liv - ing wa - ters!

Sound from your depths a hymn that tells the
Rich with the life that God cre - ates, now
Danc - ing with joy from peak to val - ley,
Show - er the earth with life and good - ness,

won - ders God has done!
let your song be heard!
laugh-ing and clear your song!
show - er the grace of God!

Oh Bless - ed be God for

All:

ev - er! Bless-ed be God for ev - er!

D.C.

Text: Refrain trans. © 1973, ICEL; additional text by Marty Haugen, © 1994, GIA Publications, Inc.
Music: Marty Haugen, © 1994, GIA Publications, Inc.

378 RITE OF SPRINKLING

This refrain may be used with the Asperges Me, which follows.

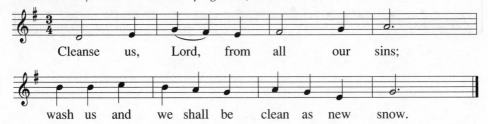

Cleanse us, Lord, from all our sins;

wash us and we shall be clean as new snow.

Text: *Roman Missal*
Music: Howard Hughes, SM, © 1986, GIA Publications, Inc.

RITE OF SPRINKLING

A - spér - ges me, Dó - mi - ne hys -
Cleanse me from sin, O Lord God, wash

só - po, et mun - dá - bor: la - vá - bis me,
me with hys - sop branch - es: cleanse me from guilt,

et su - per ni - vem de - al - bá - bor.
and I shall be clean as the new snow.

Mis - se - ré re me - i, De - us, se - cún -
Have mer - cy on me, O my God, ac - cord -

D.C. *(ad lib.)*

dum magnam miseri - cór - di - am tu - am.
ing to your great com-pas - sion.

Gló - ri - a Patri, et Filio, et Spi - rí - tu - i San - cto:
Glo - ry be to the Father
and to the Son, and to the Ho - ly Spir - it:

Si - cut erat in princípio, et nunc, et sem - per,
As it was in the beginning, is now and ev - er shall be,

D.C.

et in saécula saé - cu - ló - rum. A - men.
world with - out end. A - men.

Text: *Roman Missal*; trans. by Richard Proulx, © 1975, GIA Publications, Inc.
Music: Vatican Edition, adapt. by Richard Proulx, © 1975, GIA Publications, Inc.

380 RITE OF SPRINKLING

Moderately slow

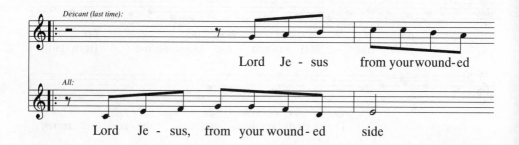

Lord Je - sus from your wound-ed

Lord Je - sus, from your wound - ed side

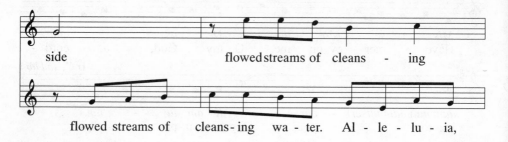

side flowed streams of cleans - ing

flowed streams of cleans - ing wa - ter. Al - le - lu - ia,

wa - ter. The world was washed of

al - le - lu - ia, al - le - lu - ia. The world was

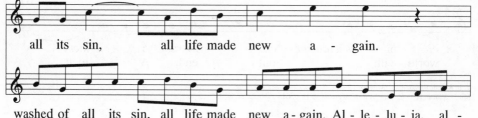

all its sin, all life made new a - gain.

washed of all its sin, all life made new a - gain. Al - le - lu - ia, al -

Music: *Festival Liturgy*, Richard Hillert, © 1983, GIA Publications, Inc.

381　KYRIE

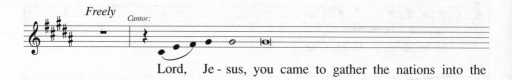

Freely　*Cantor:*

Lord,　Je - sus, you came to gather the nations into the

Cantor, then all:

peace of God's king-dom:　Lord　have mer - cy,　Lord have mer - cy.
**Show us your mer-cy,　be with us　now!

Cantor:

You come in word and　sacrament to strength-en us in　ho - li - ness:

Cantor, then all:

Christ　have mer - cy,　　Christ　have　mer - cy.
Show us your mer - cy,　　be　with　us　now!

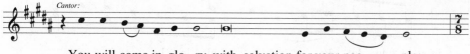

Cantor:

You will come in glo - ry with salvation for your peo - ple:

Cantor, then all:　　　　　　　　　　*Last time* ⌒

Lord　have　mer - cy,　　Lord　have　mer - cy.
Show us your　mer - cy,　　be　with　us　now!

**Alternate text*

Music: Gary Daigle, © 1993, GIA Publications, Inc.

KYRIE

decresc.

mer - cy on us.

p

Lord, have mer - cy, Lord,

cresc. *mf* *rit. to end*

have mer - cy, Lord, have

decresc.

mer - cy, have mer - cy on us.

Music: *Mass of St. Augustine,* Leon C. Roberts, © 1981, GIA Publications, Inc.

KYRIE 383

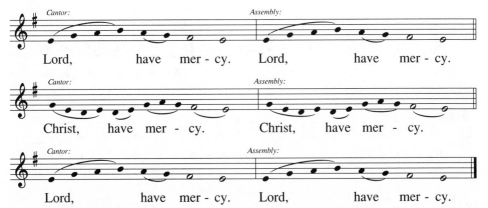

Music: *Kyrie cum jubilo,* Vatican edition; adapt. by Gerard Farrell, OSB, © 1986, GIA Publications, Inc.

384 KYRIE

Cantor or choir, then all:

Ky-ri - e e - le - i - son,

Ky-ri-e e - le-i-son, Ky-ri - e e - le - i - son.

Cantor or choir:

Chris - te e - le - i - son,

Chris - te e - le - i - son,

Chris - te e - le - i - son,

e - le - i - son.

Descant:

Ky - ri - e e - le - i -

Assembly:

Ky - ri - e e - le - i - son, Ky - ri - e e - le - i - son,

son,   Ky - ri - e   e - le - i - son,   Ky - ri - e   e -

Ky - ri - e   e - le - i - son,   e -

le -   i - son.

le - i - son.

Music: *Music for Celebration*, David Hurd, © 1979, GIA Publications, Inc.

KYRIE   385

Ky - ri - e   e - lei - son.   Ky - ri - e   e - lei - son.
Chri - ste   e - lei - son.   Chri - ste   e - lei - son.
Ky - ri - e   e - lei - son.   Ky - ri - e   e - lei - son.

Ky - ri - e   e - lei -   son.
Chri - ste   e - lei -   son.
Ky - ri - e   e - lei -   son.

Music: Russian Orthodox; arr. by John L. Bell, © 1990, Iona Community, GIA Publications, Inc., agent

386 KYRIE

Ky - ri - e,   e - lei - son.   Ky - ri - e   e -
Chri - ste   e - lei - son.   Chri - ste   e -
Ky - ri - e,   e - lei - son.   Ky - ri - e   e -

Ky - ri - e,
Chri - ste,
Ky - ri - e

(Hum)

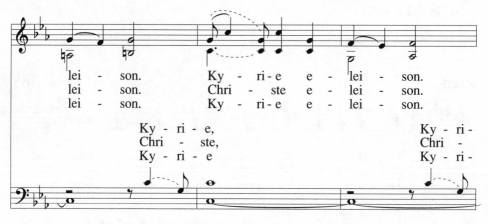

lei - son.   Ky - ri - e   e - lei - son.
lei - son.   Chri - ste   e - lei - son.
lei - son.   Ky - ri - e   e - lei - son.

Ky - ri - e,   Ky - ri -
Chri - ste,   Chri -
Ky - ri - e   Ky - ri -

Ky - ri - e   e - lei - son.
Chri - ste   e - lei - son.
Ky - ri - e   e - lei - son.

e, Ky - ri - e   e - lei - son.
ste, Chri - ste   e - lei - son.
e, Ky - ri - e   e - lei - son.

Music: Dinah Reindorf, © 1987; arr. by John L. Bell, © 1990, Iona Community, GIA Publications, Inc., agent

GLORIA

Glo-ry to God in the high - est, and peace to his peo-ple on earth. Lord God, heav-en-ly, King, Al-might-y, God and Fa - ther, we wor-ship you, we give you thanks, we praise you for your glo - ry. Lord Je - sus Christ, on-ly Son of the Fa - ther, Lord God, Lamb of God, you take a - way the sin of the world: have mer-cy on us; you are seat-ed at the right hand of the Fa - ther: re-ceive our prayer. For you a - lone are the Ho-ly One, you a - lone are the Lord, you a - lone are the Most High, Je - sus Christ, with the Ho-ly Spir - it, in the glo - ry of God the Fa - ther. A - men.

Music: *New Plainsong*, David Hurd, © 1981, GIA Publications, Inc.

388 **GLORIA**

mer - cy on us; you are seat - ed at the right hand of the

Fa - ther: re - ceive our prayer, re - ceive our prayer.

Glo - ry to God, glo - ry in the high - est.

Peace to his peo - ple, peace on earth. For you a - lone are the

Ho - ly One, you a - lone are the Lord, you a -

lone are the Most High, Je - sus Christ, with the Ho - ly

Spir - it, in the glo - ry of God, the

glo - ry of God the Fa - ther. Glo - ry to God,

glo - ry in the high - est. Peace to his peo - ple, peace on earth.

A - men, a - men.

Music: Peter Jones, © 1981, 1982
Published by OCP Publications

389 GLORIA

Cantor, then all:

Glo-ry to God in the high-est, and peace to his peo-ple on

earth. earth.

Choir or cantor:

Lord God, heav-en-ly King,

al-might-y God and Fa-ther, we wor-ship you,

We wor-ship

we give you thanks, we praise you for your glo-ry.

you, we give you thanks for your glo-ry.

+ Assembly:

Glo-ry to God in the high-est, and peace to his peo-ple on earth.

Choir or cantor:

Lord Je-sus Christ, on-ly Son of the Fa - ther,

Lord God, you take a-way sin,

Lamb of God, sin of the

have mer-cy on us; you are seat-ed,

world, have mer-cy on us; at the right

hand of the Fa-ther, re-ceive our prayer.

hand, re-ceive our prayer, re-ceive our

Music: *Assembly Mass,* Thomas Porter, © 1987, GIA Publications, Inc.

390 **GLORIA**

Joyfully
Refrain

Glo - ry to God in the high - est, and

last time to Coda ⊕

peace to his peo - ple on earth.

Verse 1

1. Lord God, heav - en - ly King, al -

D.C.

might - y God and Fa - ther.

Verse 2

2. We wor - ship you, we give you

thanks, we praise you, we

D.C.

praise you for your glo - ry.

Verse 3 *expressively, slower*

3. Lord Je - sus Christ, on - ly

Son of the Fa - ther, Lord God,

Lamb of God, you take a-way the sin of the world: have

mer - cy on us; you are

seat - ed at the right hand of the Fa - ther: re -

D.C.

ceive, re - ceive our prayer.

Verse 4

4. For you a-lone are the Ho- ly One, you a - lone are the

Lord, you a - lone are the Most High,

Je - sus Christ, with the Ho - ly Spir-it in the

D.C.

glo - ry of God the Fa - ther.

Coda

Descant:

Glo - ry to God, A - men.

Glo - ry to God in the high - est, and

A - men!

peace to his peo- ple on earth.

Music: *Melodic Gloria,* James J. Chepponis, © 1986, GIA Publications, Inc.

391 **GLORIA**

Refrain

Glo-ry to God in the high - est, and peace to his

To verses | Last time

peo-ple on earth. peo-ple on earth.

Verse 1

1. Lord God, heav-en-ly King, al - might - y God and

Fa - ther, we wor - ship you, we

D.C.

give you thanks, we praise you for your glo - ry.

Verse 2

2. Lord Je - sus Christ, on - ly Son of the Fa - ther,

Lord God, Lamb of God, you take a - way the

sin of the world: have mer - cy on us; you are

seat - ed at the right hand of the

D.C.

Fa - ther: re - ceive our prayer.

Verse 3

3. For you a-lone are the Ho - ly One, you a-lone are the

Lord, you a - lone are the Most High,

Je - sus Christ, with the Ho - ly Spir -

it, in the glo - ry of God the Fa - ther.

D.C.

A - men.

Music: *Mass of Hope;* Becket Senchur, OSB, © 1992, GIA Publications, Inc.

392 GLORIA

I *(Cantor/choir)*

Glo-ry to God in the high - est, and peace to his peo-ple on earth.

II *(Assembly)*

Lord God, heav'n-ly King, al-might-y God and Fa - ther.

I

We wor-ship you, we give you thanks, we praise you for your glo - ry.

II

Lord Je - sus Christ, on - ly Son of the Fa - ther,

I

Lord God, Lamb of God, you take a - way the sin of the world:

II

have mer-cy on us; you are seat-ed at the right hand of the

Fa - ther: re - ceive our prayer.

I

For you a - lone are the Ho - ly One,

you a - lone are the Lord, you a -

lone are the Most High, Je-sus Christ, with the Ho-ly Spir - it,

in the glo-ry of God the Fa-ther. A - men.

Music: *Congregational Mass;* John Lee, © 1970, GIA Publications, Inc.

GLORIA

393

Glo-ry to God in the high-est, and peace to his peo-ple on

earth. Glo-ry to God in the high-est, and

peace to his peo-ple on earth. Lord God,

heav-en-ly King, al-might-y God and Fa - ther.

Glo-ry to God in the high-est, and peace to his peo-ple on

earth. We wor-ship you, we give you thanks,

394 ALLELUIA

Refrain

Al - le - lu - ia, al - le - lu - ia,

al - le - lu - ia, al-le-lu-ia, al-le - lu - ia.

Verse

We will hear your word, one in love; we will live your word, one in

D.C.

love; we will spread your word, one in love.

Music: Joe Wise; acc. by Kelly Dobbs Mickus, © 1966, 1973, 1986, GIA Publications, Inc.

395 ALLELUIA

Refrain

Descant:

Al - le - lu - ia, al - le - lu - ia!

Melody:

Al - le - lu - ia, al - le - lu - ia!

Verses
1. The Word of the Lord lasts for ev - er.
2. The Word of the Lord is a - live, the
3. “Fa - ther of all you are bless-ed, cre -
4. “I call you friends,” says the Lord,
5. “The sheep of my flock,” says the Lord,
6. “E - ven if you have to die,
7. Give thanks to the Lord, who is good. The
8. The right hand of God raised me up. The
9. The stone which the build - ers re - ject - ed be -
What is the Word that is liv - ing? It is
Word of God is ac - tive— it can
a - tor of earth and heav - en, for the
“you who are my dis - ci - ples. I make
“hear - ing my voice, they will lis - ten; they will
close to my Word keep faith - ful; for your
love of the Lord knows no end - ing. All in
hand of the Lord has tri - umphed. I shall
comes the cor - ner - stone chos - en. Praise the
D.C.
brought to us through God’s Son, Je - sus Christ.
judge our thoughts, bring us clos - er to the Fa - ther.
mys - ter - ies of the king - dom shown to chil - dren.”
known to you all I’ve learned from my Fa - ther.”
fol - low me, for I know them, they are mine.”
faith - ful - ness I will give you the crown of life.”
Is - ra - el, say: “God’s love has no end.”
nev - er die— I shall live tell - ing God’s deeds.
work of God for this mar - vel in our eyes!

Text: *Celtic Alleluia*, Christopher Walker
Music: Fintan O’Carroll and Christopher Walker
© 1985, Fintan O’Carroll and Christopher Walker, published by OCP Publications

396 ALLELUIA

Gospel Verse*
Ordinary time verses:

1. Oh God to whom shall we go? You a - lone have the
2. My sheep hear my voice, says the Lord. When I call them, they

words of life. Let your words be our prayer and the
fol - low me. I will lead them to rest by the

song we sing: Hal-le - lu-jah, hal - le - lu - jah.
rest - ful streams:

3. I am the light of the world says the Lord. Walk in the

light of life. All who fol - low my words shall have

life in - deed: Hal - le - lu-jah, hal - le - lu - jah.

Easter verse:

4. Now Christ is raised up from death, he will nev - er

die a - gain. All who fol - low his way shall have

life in him: Hal - le - lu-jah, hal - le - lu - jah.

Verse is sung over the instrumental refrain, with optional humming.

Music: Traditional Carribean, arr. by John L. Bell, © 1990, Iona Community, GIA Publications, Inc., agent; verses and acc. by Marty Haugen
© 1993, GIA Publications, Inc.

397 ALLELUIA

Al - le - lu - ia, al - le -

(Al - le - lu - ia)

lu - ia, al - le - lu - ia! (hum)

D.S.

Music: Alleluia II, Jacques Berthier, © 1984, Les Presses de Taizé, GIA Publications, Inc., agent

398 ALLELUIA

Al - le - lu - ia, al - le - lu - ia, al - le - lu - ia.

Music: A. Gregory Murray, OSB, © 1958, The Grail, GIA Publications, Inc., agent

Tone for verses

D.C.

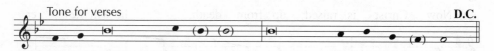

Music: tone VIII-g; acc. by Richard Proulx, © 1975, GIA Publications, Inc.

399 ALLELUIA

Cantor:

f Assembly:

Cantor:

Al - le - lu - ia. Al - le - lu - ia. Al - le - lu - ia.

Music: *Alleluia in C,* Howard Hughes, SM © 1973, 1982, GIA Publications, Inc.

ALLELUIA

400

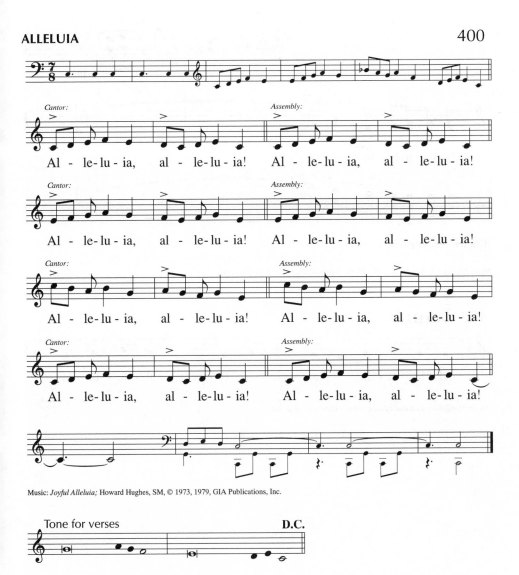

Music: *Joyful Alleluia;* Howard Hughes, SM, © 1973, 1979, GIA Publications, Inc.

Music: *Lutheran Book of Worship,* © 1978, Augsburg Publishing House

401 ALLELUIA

Al-le - lu - ia, al-le - lu-ia, al-le - lu - ia. Al-le - lu-ia, al-le -

Cantor:
freely

Al-le-lu - ia!

Last time

lu - ia, al-le - lu - ia!

Last time

*Choose either part

Music: Alleluia 7; Jacques Berthier, © 1984, Les Presses de Taizé, GIA Publications, Inc., agent

402 ALLELUIA

Al - le - lu - ia, al - le - lu - ia, al - le - lu - ia.

Music: Mode II; acc. by Richard Proulx, © 1986, GIA Publications, Inc.

ALLELUIA

Christmas: 1. Glo - ry, to God in heav - en, peace and grace to his peo - ple on earth.
Easter: 2. Christ has ris - en and shines up - on us, whom he has re - deemed by his blood.
Ordinary: 3. Speak, O Lord, your ser - vant is list - en - ing. You have the words of e - ter - nal life.
Last Week: 4. Lift up your heads and see: your re - demp-tion is near at hand.
Weddings: 5. If we love one an - oth - er, God will live in us in per - fect love.

Al - le - lu - ia. Al - le - lu - ia.

Text: Adapt. by Ralph C. Verdi, CPPS
Music: Ralph C. Verdi, CPPS
© 1977, GIA Publications, Inc.

404 ALLELUIA

Al - le - lu - ia, al - le -

lu - ia, al - le - lu - ia, al - le - lu - ia,

al - le - lu - ia.

Tone for verses

Music: Richard Proulx, © 1980 ICEL

405 ALLELUIA

Broadly

f

Al - le - lu - ia, al - le - lu - ia, al - le - lu - ia,

al - le - lu - ia, al - le - lu - ia.

Tone for verses

Music: Richard Proulx, © 1975, GIA Publications, Inc.

LENTEN ACCLAMATION

Refrain

mf Cantor:

Al - le - lu - ia!   Al - le - lu - ia!
*Praise to you, Lord Je - sus Christ,

Al - le - lu - ia, al - le - lu - ia!
King of end - less glo - ry!

f All:

Al - le - lu - ia!   Al - le - lu - ia!
*Praise to you, Lord Je - sus Christ,

Al - le - lu - ia, al - le - lu - ia!
King of end - less glo - ry!

Tone for verses

freely

Speak, O Lord, your   ser - vant is list-ning;
*If today you hear God's voice,

* Lent

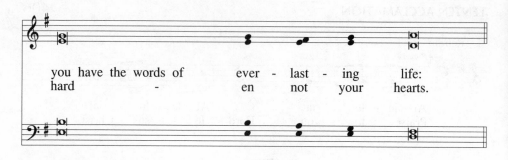

you have the words of ever - last - ing life:
hard - en not your hearts.

Final Refrain
a tempo
Descant (outside Lent):

Al - le - lu - ia!

Al - le - lu - ia! Al - le - lu - ia!
*Praise to you, Lord Je - sus Christ,

Al - le - lu - ia, al - le - lu - ia!
Al - le - lu - ia, al - le - lu - ia!
King of end - less glo - ry!

Music: *Mass for John Carroll*, Michael Joncas, © 1990, GIA Publications, Inc.

LENTEN ACCLAMATION

Refrain

Praise to you, Lord Je-sus, king of end - less glo-ry,

Sav-ior of the world, Sav-ior of the world. world.

1.- 7. *To verses* 8.
accel.

Verses *a bit faster*

1. Turn	to	the Lord		with	all your	heart,	for the
2. We	do	not live		by	bread a -	lone,	but we
3. Fol - low	the Lord		in	hum-ble -	ness,	that God's
4. Out	of	the cloud		a	voice is	heard	say-ing:
5. Give	us	the liv -	ing	wa -	ter,	that we
6. Je - sus,	the Light,		is	call-ing	us,	he will
7. "I	am	the res-ur-rec-tion	and the	life,	if you
8. Christ was	o - be -	dient	un - to	death,	e - ven

rit. **D.C.**

time	of	sal - va - tion	is	here.
live	by	the	words of	our	God.
glo - ry	might	shine from	your	hearts.
"Here	is	my	voice in	the	world."
nev - er	be	thirst - y	a -	gain.
o - pen	the	eyes of	our	soul.
live in	me	you	live for	all	time.
death	on	the	wood of	the	cross.

Text: Marty Haugen
Music: Marty Haugen
© 1983, GIA Publications, Inc.

408 LENTEN ACCLAMATION

Descant:

Glo - ry to you, O Word of God, Lord Je - sus Christ!

Melody:

Glo - ry to you, O Word of God, Lord Je - sus Christ!

Tone for verses

Music: Richard Proulx, © 1975, GIA Publications, Inc.

409 GENERAL INTERCESSIONS

Moderately slow with rhythmic refrain

Priest:

God is a good God,
Lord of heaven and earth.
Let us humbly bring our
cares before God's throne...

Let us pray to the Lord.

(hum)

O Lord, hear our prayer.
1. For the bishop of Rome,
2. God watch over our land,
3. Wa-ter our faith, Lord,
4. Nour-ish your people, Lord,
5. Bring us justice, Lord,
6. Watch o'er our dead, O Lord,

O Lord, hear our prayer. (hum)

for our shepherds and teach-ers, let us pray to the Lord.
give our leaders com-pas-sion,
make it bloom in works of love,
hun-gry for your Word and bread,
send your mer - cy and peace,
guard them in the shadow of your wings,

Text: Ray East
Music: Ray East
© 1987, GIA Publications, Inc.

GENERAL INTERCESSIONS   410

Refrain

O God, hear us; hear our prayer.

Text: Bob Hurd, © 1984
Music: Bob Hurd, © 1984; acc. by Dominic MacAller, © 1989, OCP Publications
Published by OCP Publications

411 GENERAL INTERCESSIONS

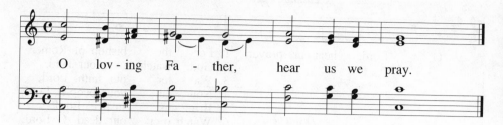

O lov-ing Fa - ther, hear us we pray.

Music: James Moore, © 1983, GIA Publications, Inc.

412 GENERAL INTERCESSIONS

Lord, we ask you, hear our prayer.

Music: From the *Litany of the Saints*

413 GENERAL INTERCESSIONS

Gra-cious Lord, hear us we pray.

Music: Ronald F. Krisman, © 1977, GIA Publications, Inc.

414 GENERAL INTERCESSIONS

Refrain

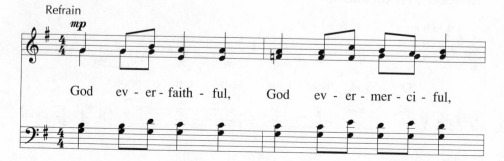

God ev - er - faith - ful, God ev - er - mer - ci - ful,

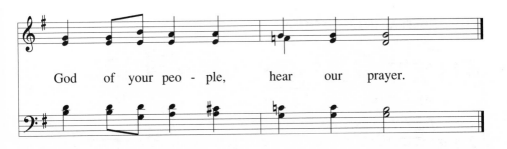

God of your peo - ple, hear our prayer.

Verses

1. For	those	who	lead	and	guide the Church of Christ;
2. For	faith - ful	wit -	ness,	fel - low - ship	in	love;
3. For	those	who	guide	the	na - tions	of	the earth;
4. For	those	who	seek	and	serve the com - mon good;
5. For	neigh - bors' needs,	for	shel - ter	from the storm;
6. For	those	in	sor -	row,	an - guish, and	de - spair;
7. For	those	op - pressed,	for	those who live	in	fear;
8. For	all	the	sick,	the	dy - ing,	and	the dead,
9. That	we	might	live	in	peace from	day	to day;
10. That	we	stay	faith -	ful,	o - pen	to	your Word;
11. For	all	the	dreams	held	deep with - in	our hearts;
12. En - trust - ing	all	we	are	in - to	your hands,

D.C.

for	lov - ing care,	we	pray to you, O Lord:
for	liv - ing hope,	we	pray to you, O Lord:
that	wis - dom reign,	we	pray to you, O Lord:
that	jus - tice reign,	we	pray to you, O Lord:
for	homes of peace,	we	pray to you, O Lord:
that	they find hope,	we	pray to you, O Lord:
that	they be freed,	we	pray to you, O Lord:
be	life and grace,	we	pray to you, O Lord:
that	wars will cease,	we	pray to you, O Lord:
your	King - dom come!	we	pray to you, O Lord:
for	all our needs,	we	pray to you, O Lord:
we	call your name,	and	pray to you, O Lord:

Text: Michael Joncas
Music: Michael Joncas
© 1990, GIA Publications, Inc.

415 GENERAL INTERCESSIONS

Ky - ri - e, Ky - ri - e, e - le - i - son;

Ky - ri - e, Ky - ri - e, e - le - i - son;

Ky - ri - e, Ky - ri - e, e - le - i - son.

Ky - ri - e, Ky - ri - e, e - le - i - son.

(Intention) Chri - ste, ex - au - di - nos.
O Lord, hear our prayer.

(hum)

Music: Jacques Berthier, © 1980, Les Presses de Taizé, GIA Publications, Inc., agent

GENERAL INTERCESSIONS

416

Ky - ri - e,   Ky - ri - e,   e - le - i - son.   (hum)

*Descant ad lib. 2nd time only

Music: Jacques Berthier, © 1980, Les Presses de Taizé, GIA Publications, Inc., agent

PREFACE DIALOG

417

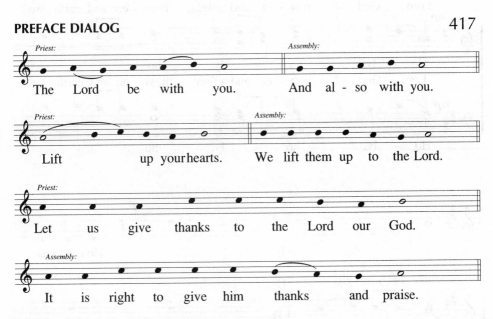

Priest: The Lord be with you.   Assembly: And al - so with you.

Priest: Lift up your hearts.   Assembly: We lift them up to the Lord.

Priest: Let us give thanks to the Lord our God.

Assembly: It is right to give him thanks and praise.

Music: *Sacramentary,* 1966

418 SANCTUS—PSALLITE MASS

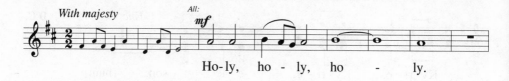

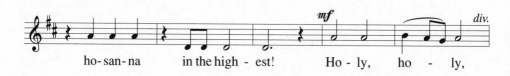

419 MEMORIAL ACCLAMATION

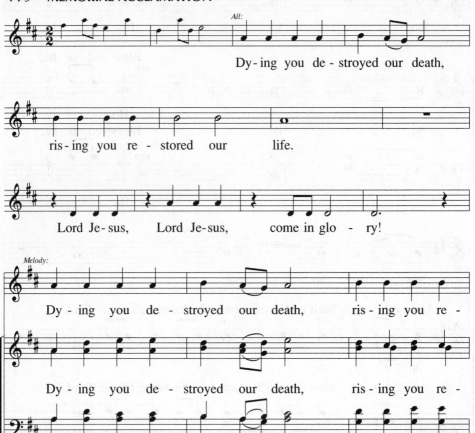

Dy-ing you de-stroyed our death,

ris-ing you re-stored our life.

Lord Je-sus, Lord Je-sus, come in glo - ry!

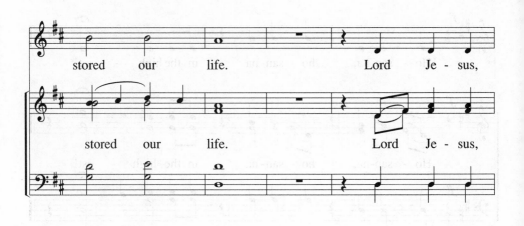

Melody:

Dy - ing you de - stroyed our death, ris - ing you re-

Dy - ing you de - stroyed our death, ris - ing you re-

stored our life. Lord Je - sus,

stored our life. Lord Je - sus,

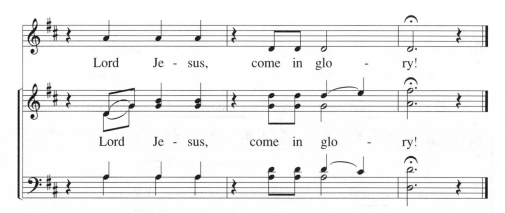

Music: *The Psallite Mass,* Michael Joncas, © 1988, GIA Publications, Inc.

AMEN

420

Music: *The Psallite Mass,* Michael Joncas, © 1988, GIA Publications, Inc.

SANCTUS—AGAPÉ

The introduction is omitted when the connecting pattern is played.

422 MEMORIAL ACCLAMATION

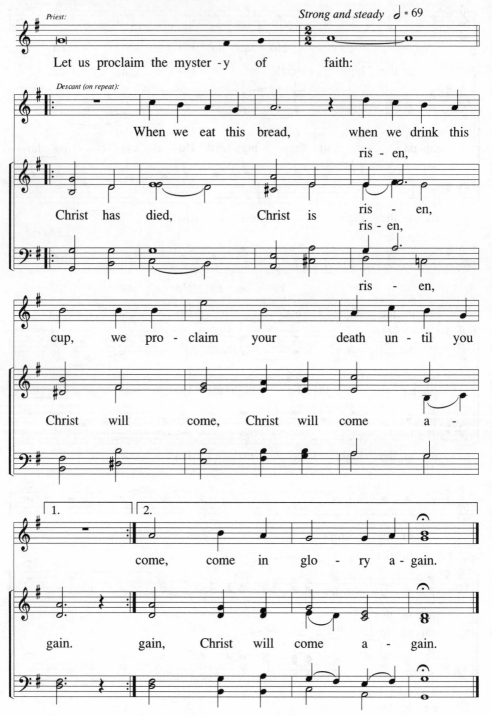

Music: *Agapé*, Marty Haugen, © 1993, GIA Publications, Inc.

DOXOLOGY AND GREAT AMEN

Freely

Through him, with him, in him, in the unity of the Ho-ly Spir-it, all

glory and honor is yours, al-might-y Fa-ther, for ev-er and ev - er.

Descant I (on repeat):

A-men! Al - le - lu - ia! A-men! Al - le -

Descant II (on repeat):

Al - le - lu - ia! Al - le - lu - ia!

ff

A - men! Al - le - lu - ia!

lu - ia! A-men! Al-le-lu -

Al - le - lu - ia! Al - le - lu -

A - men! Al - le - lu - ia!

During Lent, substitute "Praise to you, Lord" for "Alleluia" and do not use descants. The descants may be used separately or together.

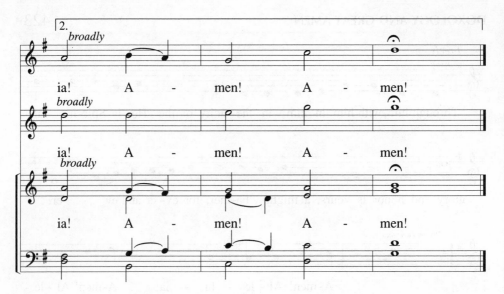

ia! A - men! A - men!

ia! A - men! A - men!

ia! A - men! A - men!

Music: *Agapé*, Marty Haugen, © 1993, GIA Publications, Inc.

424 PREFACE DIALOG—EUCHARISTIC PRAYER FOR CHILDREN

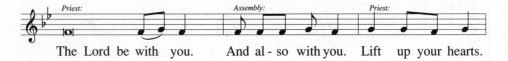

The Lord be with you. And al - so with you. Lift up your hearts.

We lift them up to the Lord. Let us give thanks to the Lord, our God.

It is right to give him thanks and praise.

Music: *Mass of Creation*, Marty Haugen, © 1984, GIA Publications, Inc.

CHILDREN'S ACCLAMATION 1 — 425

Ho - san - na in the high - est,

ho - san - na in the high - est!

Music: Eucharistic Prayer for Children, *Mass of Creation*, Marty Haugen, adapt by Rob Glover, © 1989, GIA Publications, Inc.

SANCTUS — 426

f

Ho - ly,

ho - ly, ho - ly Lord, God of pow-er,

God of might, heav-en and earth are full of your

div. *ff*

glo - ry. Ho - san - na in the high - est.

unis. *mf*

Bless-ed is he who comes in the name of the

div. *ff*

Lord. Ho - san - na in the high - est,

fff *rit.* *molto rit.*

ho - san - na in the high - est.

Music: *Mass of Creation*, Marty Haugen, © 1984, GIA Publications, Inc.

427 CHILDREN'S ACCLAMATION 2

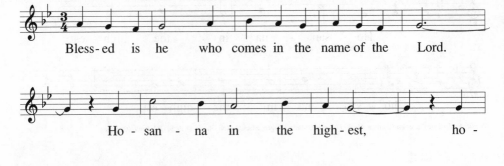

Bless-ed is he who comes in the name of the Lord.

Ho - san - na in the high - est, ho -

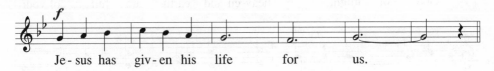

san - na in the high - est!

Music: Eucharistic Prayer for Children, *Mass of Creation,* Marty Haugen, adapt. by Rob Glover, © 1989, GIA Publications, Inc.

428 CHILDREN'S ACCLAMATION 3

mf

Je - sus has giv-en his life for us;

f

Je - sus has giv-en his life for us.

Music: Eucharistic Prayer for Children, *Mass of Creation,* Marty Haugen, adapt. by Rob Glover, © 1989, GIA Publications, Inc.

429 CHILDREN'S ACCLAMATION 4

We

praise you, we bless you, we thank you. We

praise you, we bless you, we thank you.

Music: Eucharistic Prayer for Children, *Mass of Creation,* Marty Haugen, adapt. by Rob Glover, © 1989, GIA Publications, Inc.

DOXOLOGY AND GREAT AMEN

430

Priest:

Through him, with him, in him, in the unity of the Ho - ly Spir- it, all

glory and honor is yours, al - might - y Fa - ther, for

ev - er and ev - er.

All:
Descant:

A - men, a - men, a - men!

Melody:

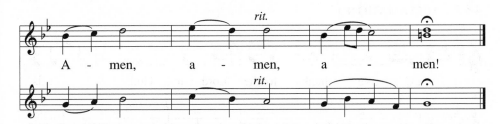

A - men, a - men, a - men!

rit.

Music: *Mass of Creation,* Marty Haugen, © 1984, GIA Publications, Inc.

431 PREFACE DIALOG—EUCHARISTIC PRAYER II

Priest: The Lord be with you. *Assembly:* And al - so with

you. *Priest:* Lift up your hearts. *Assembly:* We lift them up to the Lord.

Priest: Let us give thanks to the Lord our God. *Assembly:* It is

right to give him thanks and praise. *poco rit.*

Music: *Eucharistic Prayer II,* Marty Haugen, © 1990, GIA Publications, Inc.

432 ACCLAMATION 1

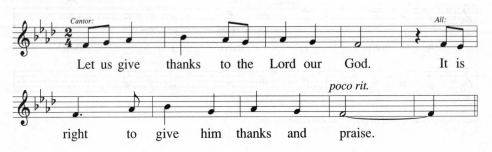

Cantor: Let us give thanks to the Lord our God. *All:* It is

right to give him thanks and praise. *poco rit.*

Music: *Eucharistic Prayer II,* Marty Haugen, © 1990, GIA Publications, Inc.

SANCTUS

433

Ho - ly, ho - ly, ho - ly

Lord, God of pow-er and might;

Ho - ly, ho - ly, God of pow-er and

heav - en and earth are full of your glo - ry: Ho -

might

san - na in the high - est! Bless - ed is

he, bless-ed is he who comes in the name of the

Lord. Ho - san - na in the high - est!

Ho - san - na in the high - est!

Music: *Eucharistic Prayer II,* Marty Haugen, © 1990, GIA Publications, Inc.

434 ACCLAMATION 2

Cantor:
Lord, you are ho - ly in - deed,

Assembly:
Lord, you are

the foun - tain of all ho - li - ness.

ho - ly in - deed, the

foun - tain of all ho - li - ness.

Music: *Eucharistic Prayer II,* Marty Haugen, © 1990, GIA Publications, Inc.

ACCLAMATION 3 435

Glo-ry and praise to you, O Christ! Sav - ior
of the world! Glo-ry and praise to
you, O Christ! Sav - ior of the world!

Music: *Eucharistic Prayer II,* Marty Haugen, © 1990, GIA Publications, Inc.

MEMORIAL ACCLAMATION 436

Freely

Let us pro - claim the mys-ter-y of faith:
Dy - ing, you de -
Dy - ing, you de - stroyed our death,
stroyed our death, ris - ing you re -
ris - ing you re - stored our life;
stored our life; Lord Je - sus,

opt. harm.

Lord Je - sus, come in glo - ry.

come in glo - ry.

Music: *Eucharistic Prayer II,* Marty Haugen, © 1990, GIA Publications, Inc.

437   ACCLAMATION 4

Cantor:

Good and gra - cious God, hear and re -

All:

mem - ber us. Good and gra - cious God,

opt. harm.

hear and re - mem - ber us.

Music: *Eucharistic Prayer II,* Marty Haugen, © 1990, GIA Publications, Inc.

438   DOXOLOGY AND GREAT AMEN

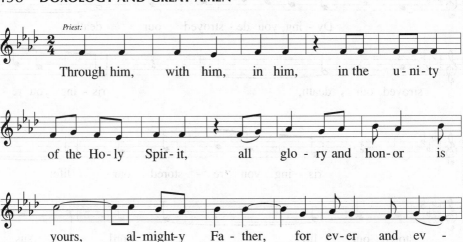

Priest:

Through him, with him, in him, in the u - ni - ty

of the Ho - ly Spir - it, all glo - ry and hon - or is

yours, al - might - y Fa - ther, for ev - er and ev -

* During Lent

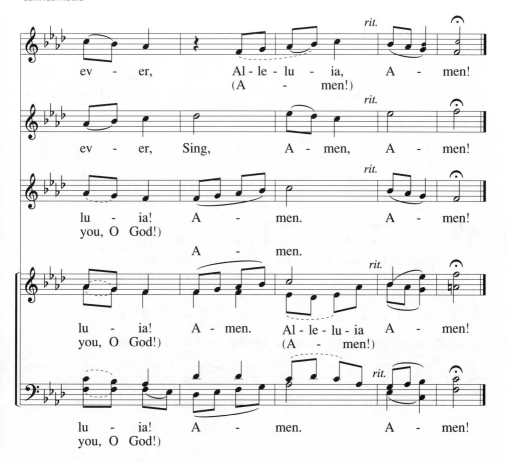

Music: *Eucharistic Prayer II,* Marty Haugen, © 1990, GIA Publications, Inc.

439 SANCTUS—ST. LOUIS JESUITS MASS

Ho - ly, ho - ly, ho - ly Lord, God of pow'r and

might, heav - en and earth are full of your glo -

ry. Ho - san - na, ho - san - na on high.

Descant:
Bless - ed is he who comes in the name of the Lord.

Melody:
Bless - ed is he who comes in the name of the Lord. Ho -

Ho - san - na, ho - san - na, ho -

san - na in the high - est, ho - san - na in the high - est, ho -

div.
san - na, ho - san - na on high.

san - na, ho - san - na on high.

Music: *St. Louis Jesuits Mass,* Robert J. Dufford, SJ, and Daniel L. Schutte, © 1973, administered by New Dawn Music; acc. by Diana Kodner, © 1993, GIA Publications, Inc.

WHEN WE EAT THIS BREAD

Priest: Let us pro-claim the mys-ter-y of faith:

All: When we eat this bread of life, when we drink of this ho-ly cup, we pro-claim your death, O Lord,

1. till you come a-gain.

2. till you come a-gain!

Music: *St. Louis Jesuits Mass*, Robert J. Dufford, SJ, and Daniel L. Schutte, © 1977, 1979, administered by New Dawn Music

441 AMEN

Freely

Priest:

Through him, with him, and in him, in the u-ni-ty of the Ho-ly

Spir-it, all glo-ry and hon-or is yours, al-might-y

a tempo

Fa-ther, for ev-er and ev-er.

All:
Descant:

A - men, al-le-lu - ia.

Melody:

A - men, al-le-lu - ia, for

A - men, a - men. Al - le - lu - ia, for

ev-er and ev-er, for ev - er, al-le-lu - ia, for

ev-er and ev-er. A - men.

ev-er and ev-er. A - men.

Music: *St. Louis Jesuits Mass,* Robert J. Dufford, SJ, and Daniel L. Schutte, © 1973, administered by New Dawn Music; acc. by Diana Kodner, © 1993,
    GIA Publications, Inc.

SANCTUS—LAND OF REST 442

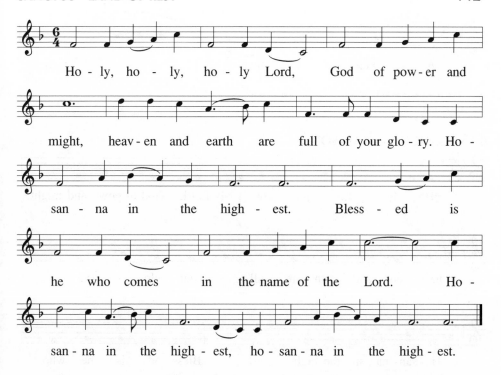

Ho - ly, ho - ly, ho - ly Lord, God of pow-er and
might, heav - en and earth are full of your glo - ry. Ho -
san - na in the high - est. Bless - ed is
he who comes in the name of the Lord. Ho -
san - na in the high - est, ho - san - na in the high - est.

Music: *Land of Rest,* adapt. by Marcia Pruner, © 1980, Church Pension Fund; acc. by Richard Proulx, © 1986, GIA Publications, Inc.

MEMORIAL ACCLAMATION 443

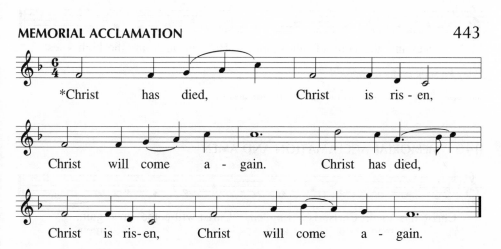

*Christ has died, Christ is ris - en,
Christ will come a - gain. Christ has died,
Christ is ris-en, Christ will come a - gain.

For a shorter version of this acclamation, sing the first two measures and the last two measures.

Music: *Land of Rest,* adapt. by Richard Proulx, © 1986, GIA Publications, Inc.

444 AMEN

A - men, a - men, a - men.

Music: *Land of Rest,* adapt. by Richard Proulx, © 1986, GIA Publications, Inc.

445 SANCTUS—PLAINSONG

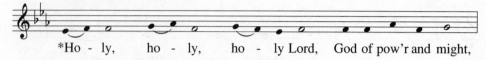

*Ho - ly, ho - ly, ho - ly Lord, God of pow'r and might,

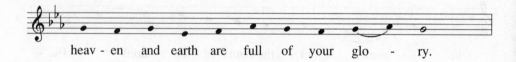

heav - en and earth are full of your glo - ry.

Ho - san - na in the high - est. Bless - ed is he who

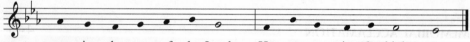

comes in the name of the Lord. Ho - san - na in the high - est.

May be sung unaccompanied.

Music: *Sacramentary,* 1974; adapt. by Robert J. Batastini, © 1975, GIA Publications, Inc.

446 MEMORIAL ACCLAMATION AND AMEN

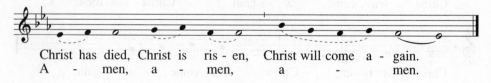

Christ has died, Christ is ris - en, Christ will come a - gain.
A - men, a - men, a - men.

Music: *Sacramentary,* 1974; adapt. by Robert J. Batastini, © 1980, GIA Publications, Inc.

SANCTUS—DEUTSCHE MESSE

Slowly ♩ = ca. 72

Ho - ly, ho - ly, ho - ly Lord, God of pow'r and might. Ho - ly, ho - ly, ho - ly Lord, God of pow'r and might. Heav - en and earth are full, full of your glo - ry. Ho -

Music: *Deutsche Messe,* Franz Schubert, 1797-1828; adapt. by Richard Proulx, © 1985, 1989, GIA Publications, Inc.

MEMORIAL ACCLAMATION 448

Christ has died, Christ is ris - en, Christ will come a - gain. Christ has died, Christ is ris - en, Christ will come a - gain.

Music: *Deutsche Messe,* Franz Schubert, 1797-1828; adapt. by Richard Proulx, © 1985, 1995, GIA Publications, Inc.

AMEN 449

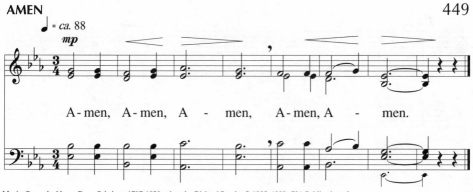

A - men, A - men, A - men, A - men, A - men.

Music: *Deutsche Messe,* Franz Schubert, 1797-1828, adapt. by Richard Proulx, © 1985, 1989, GIA Publications, Inc.

450 SANCTUS—A FESTIVAL EUCHARIST

MEMORIAL ACCLAMATION 451

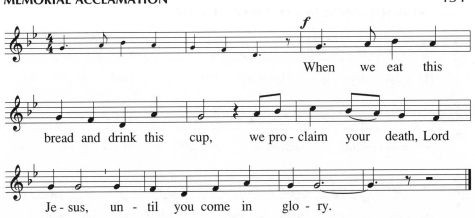

When we eat this bread and drink this cup, we pro - claim your death, Lord Je - sus, un - til you come in glo - ry.

Music: *A Festival Eucharist,* Richard Proulx, © 1975, GIA Publications, Inc.

AMEN 452

Descant:
A - men, a -

Assembly and choir:
A - men, a -

men, a - men, a - men.

men, a - men, a - men.

Music: *A Festival Eucharist,* Richard Proulx, © 1975, GIA Publications, Inc.

453 SANCTUS—MASS IN HONOR OF ST. PAUL

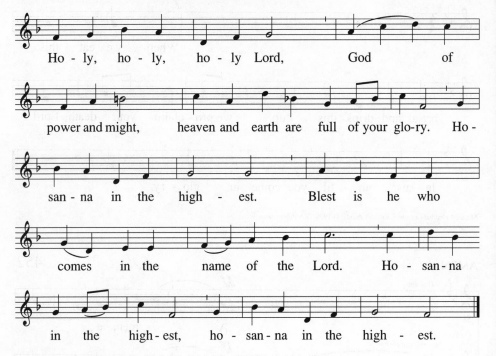

Ho - ly, ho - ly, ho - ly Lord, God of power and might, heaven and earth are full of your glo-ry. Ho-san-na in the high - est. Blest is he who comes in the name of the Lord. Ho - san-na in the high - est, ho - san - na in the high - est.

Music: *Mass in Honor of St. Paul*, Kevin Vogt, © 1995, GIA Publications, Inc.

454 MEMORIAL ACCLAMATION

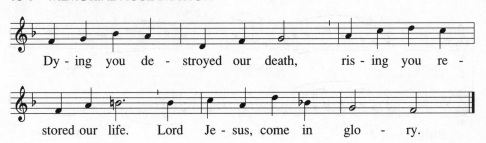

Dy - ing you de - stroyed our death, ris - ing you re - stored our life. Lord Je - sus, come in glo - ry.

Music: *Mass in Honor of St. Paul*, Kevin Vogt, © 1995, GIA Publications, Inc.

AMEN

455

A - men, a -

men, a - men.

Music: *Mass in Honor of St. Paul,* Kevin Vogt, © 1995, GIA Publications, Inc.

SANCTUS—PEOPLE'S MASS

456

Ho - ly, ho - ly, ho - ly Lord, God of pow-er and

Ho - ly, ho - ly, ho - ly Lord, God of pow-er and

might, heav - en and earth are full of your glo -

might, heav - en and earth are full of your glo -

Music: *People's Mass*, Jan Vermulst, 1925-1994, acc. by Richard Proulx, © 1970, World Library Publications

MEMORIAL ACCLAMATION 457

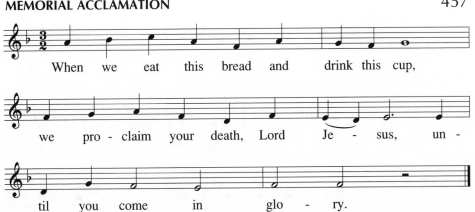

Music: *Danish Amen Mass*, Charles G. Frischmann and David Kraehenbuehl, © 1973, World Library Publications

AMEN 458

Music: Danish Amen

459 SANCTUS—MASS FOR THE CITY

Music: *Mass for the City*, Richard Proulx, © 1991, GIA Publications, Inc.

460 MEMORIAL ACCLAMATION 1

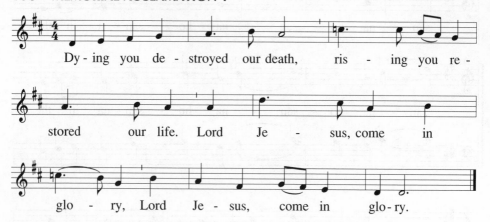

Dy-ing you de-stroyed our death, ris-ing you re-

stored our life. Lord Je-sus, come in

glo-ry, Lord Je-sus, come in glo-ry.

Music: *Mass for the City,* Richard Proulx, © 1995, GIA Publications, Inc.

461 MEMORIAL ACCLAMATION 2

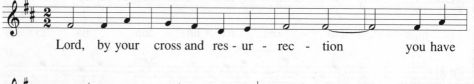

Lord, by your cross and res-ur-rec-tion you have

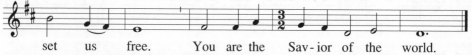

set us free. You are the Sav-ior of the world.

Music: *Mass for the City,* Richard Proulx, © 1995, GIA Publications, Inc.

462 AMEN

A - men, a - men, a - men.

Music: *Mass for the City,* Richard Proulx, © 1995, GIA Publications, Inc.

463 MEMORIAL ACCLAMATION

Christ has died, al-le-lu-ia. Christ is ris-en,

al-le - lu - ia. Christ will come a - gain, al-le -

lu - ia, al - le - lu - ia.

Music: Joe Wise; acc. by T.F. and R.P., © 1971, 1972, GIA Publications, Inc.

LORD'S PRAYER 464

mp

Our Fa - ther, who art in heav-en,

hal-lowed be thy name; thy king - dom come; thy

will be done on earth as it is in heav - en.

Give us this day our dai - ly bread; and for - give us our

tres - pass-es as we for - give those who

tres - pass a - gainst us; and lead us not in - to temp-

ta - tion, but de - liv - er us from e - vil.

After the prayer "Deliver Us":

For the king-dom, the pow-er, and the glo - ry are yours, now and for ev - er.

Music: *A Festival Eucharist,* Richard Proulx, © 1975, GIA Publications, Inc.

465 LORD'S PRAYER—LYRIC LITURGY

With simplicity

Priest:

Let us pray with con - fi-dence to the Fa - ther in the words our Sav - ior gave us:

Expressively

All:

Our Fa - ther, who art in heav - en, hal-lowed be thy name; thy king-dom come; thy will be done on earth as it is in heav-en. Give us this day our dai - ly bread; and for - give us our tres - pass - es as we for -

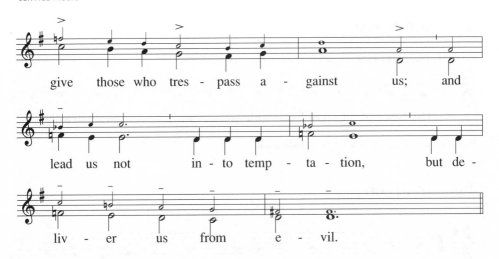

give those who tres - pass a - gainst us; and

lead us not in - to temp - ta - tion, but de -

liv - er us from e - vil.

Music: *Lyric Liturgy,* Alexander Peloquin, © 1974, GIA Publications, Inc.

After the prayer "Deliver Us": 466

With grandeur

A - men!

For the king - dom, the pow - er, the

A - men!

For the king - dom, the pow - er, the

A - men!

glo - ry are yours, now and for ev - er.

A - men! now and for ev - er.

glo - ry are yours, now and for ev - er.

Music: *Lyric Liturgy,* Alexander Peloquin, © 1974, GIA Publications, Inc.

467 RITE OF PEACE

Priest: Lord, Jesus Christ... for ever and ever. *All:* **Amen.**

The peace of the Lord be with you al - ways. And al - so with you.

Music: *Lyric Liturgy,* Alexander Peloquin, © 1974, GIA Publications, Inc.

468 AGNUS DEI

Lamb of God, you take a-way the sins of the world:

have mer - cy on us.

Lamb of God, you take a-way the sins of the world:

Lamb of God, Lamb of God,

have mer - cy on us.

have mer - cy on us.

Lamb of God, you take a-way the sins of the world:

have mer - cy on us.

Music: *Lyric Liturgy,* Alexander Peloquin, © 1974, GIA Publications, Inc.

LAMB OF GOD

First Invocation

Je-sus, Lamb of God, you take a-way the sins of the world: have

you take a-way the sins of the world: have

mer - cy, have mer - cy on us.

mer - cy, have mer - cy on us, have mer - cy.

Invocations

1. Bread of life and sav - ing cup,
2. King of kings and Lord of lords, you take a-way the
3. Lov - ing Sav - ior, Prince of peace,

Ah, you take a-way the

Alternate Invocations

General II:
1. Jesus, food for hungry hearts,
2. Jesus, God's own Promised One,
3. Jesus, at our kingdom-feast,

General III:
1. Jesus, Way that leads to God,
2. Jesus, Truth that comes from God,
3. Jesus, Life bestowed in God,

Advent:
1. Hope for all of humankind,
2. Dawn in darkness, Morning Star,
3. Key of David, Lord of might,

Christmas:
1. Son of God and Son of Man,
2. King, Messiah, David's Son,
3. Holy Child of Bethlehem,

Lent:
1. Jesus, light for blinded eyes,
2. Jesus, hope for haunted lives,
3. Jesus, servant of our God,

Eastertide:
1. Jesus, risen from the tomb,
2. Jesus, victor over death,
3. Jesus, future of our lives,

Music: *The Psallite Mass,* Michael Joncas, © 1988, GIA Publications, Inc.

LAMB OF GOD 470

1. Lamb of God, you take a - way the sins of the world;
2. Lamb of God, you break the chains of ha - tred and fear;
3. Lamb of God, you are the way of jus - tice and peace:
4. Lamb of God, you are the way of mer - cy and love:

have mer-cy on us, mer-cy on us,

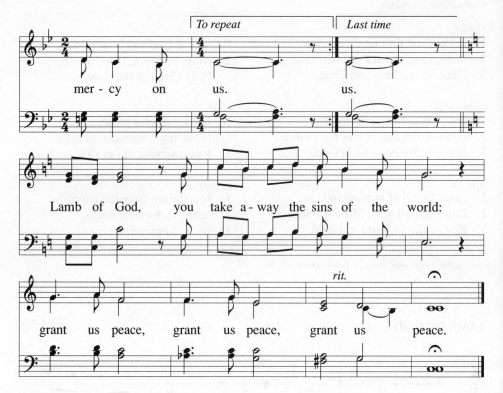

mer - cy on us. us.

Lamb of God, you take a - way the sins of the world:

grant us peace, grant us peace, grant us peace.

Text: ICET; additional text by Marty Haugen, © 1990, GIA Publications, Inc.
Music: *Now the Feast and Celebration,* Marty Haugen, © 1990, GIA Publications, Inc.

471 LAMB OF GOD

With quiet dignity

1. Je - sus, Lamb of God you take a - way the
2. Je - sus, Pas - chal vic - tim

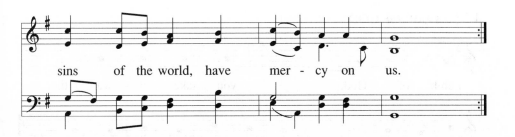

sins   of the world, have   mer - cy on   us.

Optional Interlude (before last time)

Je - sus, Lamb of God   you take a - way the   sins of the world,

grant   us   peace,   grant   us   peace.

Additional Invocations:

3. Jesus, Food of Pilgrims...
4. Jesus, True Bread from Heaven...
5. Jesus, Wine of Peace...
6. Jesus, Good Shepherd...

Music: Tony Way, © 1995, GIA Publications, Inc.

472 LAMB OF GOD

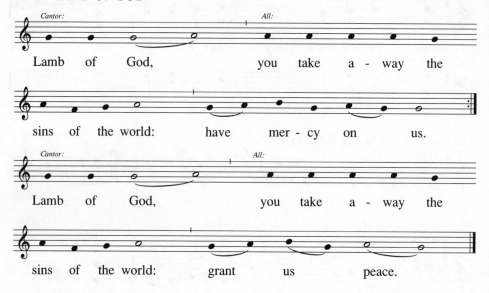

Lamb of God, you take a - way the sins of the world: have mer - cy on us.

Lamb of God, you take a - way the sins of the world: grant us peace.

Music: Agnus Dei XVIII, Vatican Edition; acc. by Robert J. Batastini, © 1993, GIA Publications, Inc.

473 LAMB OF GOD

Lamb of God, you take a - way the sins of the world: have mer - cy on us. Have mer - cy on us.

*Lamb of God, you take a - way the sins of the world: have mer - cy on us. Have mer - cy on us.

*Other titles, e.g., Bread of Life, Lord of Love, may be used.

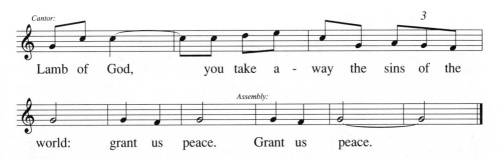

Cantor:

3

Lamb of God, you take a - way the sins of the

Assembly:

world: grant us peace. Grant us peace.

Music: Howard Hughes, SM, © 1981, GIA Publications, Inc.

LAMB OF GOD

474

Lamb of God, you take a- way the

sins of the world: have mer - cy on us.

Optional descant:

Lamb of God, you take a- way the sins of the

Lamb of God, you take a- way the sins of the

world: grant us peace, grant us peace.

world: grant us peace, grant us peace.

Music: Richard Proulx, © 1975, GIA Publications, Inc.

475 LAMB OF GOD

Choir or cantor:

*Lamb of God,

Descant:

To repeat

you take a - way the sins of the world, have

All:

you take a - way the sins of the world, have

Last time

mer - cy on us. world. grant

mer - cy on us. world. grant

rall.

us, grant us peace.

rall.

us peace.

*Alternates: 1. Bread of life, 2. Prince of peace, 3. King of kings.

Music: *Festival Liturgy,* Richard Hillert, © 1983, GIA Publications, Inc.

LAMB OF GOD: MAY WE BE ONE

Cantor(s):

1. Lamb of God, you take a - way the sins of the world:
2. Lamb of God, un - blem - ished of - f'ring made for our sin:
3. Lamb of God, de - stroyed that all who eat might be healed:
4. Lamb of God, whose blood will save your peo - ple from death:
5. Lamb of God, our com - mon mem - 'ry, cov - e - nant feast:
6. Lamb of God, our free - dom won, re - mem - bered for ev - er:

Repeat as needed

All:

have mer - cy on us, have mer - cy on us.

Tenor:
Alto:

have mer - cy, have mer - cy on us, have mer - cy on us.

Last time
Cantor(s):

Lamb of God, you take a - way the sins of the world,

All:

grant us peace, grant us peace.

rit.

grant us, grant us peace, grant us peace.

rit.

Additional invocations:

Lamb of God, the shepherd of all who hunger and thirst...
Lamb of God, joy of the martyrs, song of the saints...
Lamb of God, all peoples will sing your victory song...
Lamb of God, unconquered light of the city of God...
Lamb of God, how blessed are those who are called to your feast...

Text: *Agnus Dei;* additional text by Rory Cooney
Music: Gary Daigle
© 1993, GIA Publications, Inc.

477   MAY WE BE ONE (COMMUNION HYMN)

Refrain

When we eat this bread and drink this cup,

we pro-claim your death, Lord Je - sus. So as we

may we be - come

share this feast may we be - come, may we be - come heal-ing and

may we be - come

To verses | Last time

light and peace. May we be one. one.

Verses

1. This is the bread of Is - ra - el's
2. This is the bread of rain and of
3. This is the bless - ing cup of the
4. This is the wine of plant - ing and
5. This is a peo - ple home - less and
6. This is a bread we pass as for -

wan - d'ring.   The
sun - light.   The
Sab - bath.   The
prun - ing.   The
wan - d'ring.   A
give - ness.   A

All:

A - men, a - men.

A - men, a - men, a - men.

A - men, a - men.

bread that strength-ened E - li - jah.   The
bread of earth's fer - tile boun - ty.   The
cup of Ca - na's a - maze-ment.   The
cup of bur - geon-ing vine-yards.   The
peo - ple at home with each oth - er,   A
cup we share as our wel-come.   A

A - men, a - men.

bread   that   fed   man - y   thou - sands.
bread   of   wheat   and   of   bar - ley.
cup   that   would   not   pass   from you.
grapes   now   crushed   in   the   wine - press.
peo - ple   gath - ered   at   ta - ble,
ta - ble   o - pen   to   stran - gers.

A - men, a -

This   is   the   bread   of   Ju - das' be - tray - al.
This   is   the   bread   of   earth's man - y   col - ors.
This   is   the   cup   now   shared in   your   mem - 'ry.
This   is   the   wine   of   wait - ing   in   dark - ness.
This   is   a   peo - ple   grate - ful for   bless - ing.
This   is   a   ban - quet of   rest   for   the   wea - ry.

men.

men,   a - men.

A -

men.

Take and eat; this
Take and eat; this
Take and drink; this
Take and drink; this
And deep with - in all
And deep with - in all

men, a - men.

D.C.

bread is the life of God.
bread is the life of God.
cup is the life of God.
cup is the life of God.
peo - ple the breath of God.
peo - ple the breath of God.

Text: Rory Cooney, b.1952
Tune: Gary Daigle, b.1957
© 1993, GIA Publications, Inc.

A Message Came to a Maiden Young 478

1. A mes - sage came to a maid - en young; The
2. No great - er news could a mes-sen - ger bring; For
3. He came, God's Word to the world here be-low; And
4. And some - times trum - pets from Si - on ring out, And

an - gel stood be - side her In shin - ing robes, and with
'twas from that young moth - er He came, who walked on the
round him there did gath - er A band who found that this
tramp - ing comes, and drum-ming; "Thy king - dom come," so we

gold - en tongue He told what should be - tide her:
earth as a king, And yet to all a broth - er:
teach - er to know Was e'en to know the Fa - ther:
cry; and they shout, "It comes!" and still 'tis com - ing.

The maid was lost in won - der; Her world was
His truth has spread like leav - en; 'Twill mar - ry
He healed the sick who sought him, For - gave the
Far, far a - head, to win us, Yet with us,

rent a - sun - der; Ah! how could she Christ's moth-er
earth to heav - en, Till all a - gree In char - i -
foes who fought him; Be - side the sea Of Gal - i -
nay with - in us; Till all shall see That King is

be By God's most high de - cree!
ty To dwell from sea to sea.
lee He set the na - tions free.
he, The Love from Gal - i - lee!

Text: St. 1, Dutch; para. E.B.G., 1928; sts. 2-4, Percy Dearmer, 1867-1936, © Oxford University Press
Tune: ANNUNCIATION, Irregular; traditional Dutch melody, © 1896; harm. by David McK. Williams, b.1940

479 O Come, Divine Messiah

1. O come, Di - vine Mes - si - ah, The world in si - lence waits the day When hope shall sing its tri - umph, And sad - ness flee a - way.

2. O come De - sired of na - tions, Whom priest and proph - et long fore - told, Will break the cap - tive fet - ters, Re - deem the long - lost fold.

3. O come in peace and meek - ness, For low - ly will your cra - dle be: Though clothed in hu - man weak - ness We shall your God - head see.

Text: *Venez, divin Messie;* Abbé Simon-Joseph Pellegrin, 1663-1745; tr. by S. Mary of St. Philip, 1877
Tune: VENEZ, DIVIN MESSIE, 7 8 7 6 with refrain; French Noël, 16th C.; harm. by Healey Willan, 1880-1968. © 1958,
Ralph Jusko Publications, Inc.

480 Savior of the Nations, Come

1. Sav - ior of the na - tions, come; Show the glo - ry
2. Not by hu - man flesh and blood, By the Spir - it
3. Won - drous birth! O won - drous child Of the Vir - gin
4. God Cre - a - tor is his source, Back to God he
5. Now your low - ly man - ger bright Hal - lows night with

of the Son! Mar - vel now, O heav'n and earth,
of our God Was the word of God made flesh—
un - de - filed! Might - y God and man in one,
runs his course, Down to death and hell de - scends,
new - born light; Let no night this light sub - due,

That our Lord chose such a birth.
Wom - an's off - spring, pure and fresh.
Ea - ger now his race to run!
God's high throne he re - as - cends.
Let our faith shine ev - er new.

Text: *Veni, Redemptor gentium;* ascr. to St. Ambrose, 340-397; tr. sts. 1-3a, William Reynolds, 1812-1876; sts. 3b-5, Martin L. Seltz, 1909-1967, alt.
Tune: NUN KOMM DER HEIDEN HEILAND, 77 77; *Geystliche gesangk Buchleyn,* Wittenberg, 1524

Each Winter As the Year Grows Older 481

1. Each win-ter as the year grows old-er, We
2. When race and class cry out for trea-son, When
3. Yet I be-lieve be-yond be-liev-ing, That
4. So e-ven as the sun is turn-ing, To
5. O Child of ec-sta-sy and sor-rows, O

each grow old - er too. The
si - rens call for war, They
life can spring from death; That
jour - ney to the north, The
Prince of peace and pain, Bright-

chill sets in a lit - tle cold - er; The
o - ver-shout the voice of rea - son, And
growth can flow - er from our griev - ing; That
liv - ing flame, in se - cret burn - ing, Can
en to - day's world by to - mor - row's, Re -

ver - i - ties we knew Seem shak-en and un -
scream till we ig - nore All we held dear be -
we can catch our breath And turn trans-fixed by
kin - dle on the earth, And bring God's love to
new our lives a - gain; Lord Je - sus, come and

1.- 4.

true.
fore.
faith.
birth.

5.

reign!

Text: William Gay, fl. 1969, © 1971, United Church Press
Tune: CAROL OF HOPE, 9 6 9 6 6; Annabeth Gay, b.1925, © 1971, United Church Press; acc. by Marty Haugen, b.1950, alt.,
© 1987, GIA Publications, Inc.

482 People, Look East

1. Peo - ple, look East. The time is near Of the crown - ing of the year. Make your house fair as you are
2. Fur - rows, be glad. Though earth is bare. One more seed is plant - ed there: Give up your strength the seed to
3. Birds, though you long have ceased to build, Guard the nest that must be build, E - ven the hour when wings are
4. Stars, keep the watch. When night is dim One more light the bowl shall brim, Shin - ing be - yond the frost - y
5. An - gels an - nounce with shouts of mirth Him who brings new life to earth. Set ev - 'ry peak and val - ley

a - ble,
nour - ish,
fro - zen
weath - er,
hum - ming

Trim the hearth and set the
That in course the flow'r may
He for fledg - ing time has
Bright as sun and moon to -
With the word, the Lord is

Peo - ple look East and sing to -

ta - ble.
flour - ish.
cho - sen.
geth - er.
com - ing.

Peo - ple look East:

Peo - ple look

day:

East:

Love the Guest is on the way.
Love the Rose is on the way.
Love the Bird is on the way.
Love the Star is on the way.
Love the Lord is on the way.
Love is on the way.

Text: Eleanor Farjeon, 1881-1965, © David Higham Assoc. Ltd.
Tune: BESANCON, 87 98 87; French traditional; harm. by Martin Shaw, 1875-1958, © Oxford University Press

483 Creator of the Stars of Night

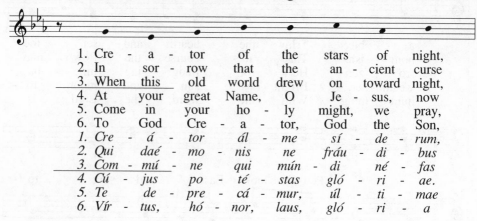

1. Cre - a - tor of the stars of night,
2. In sor - row that the an - cient curse
3. When this old world drew on toward night,
4. At your great Name, O Je - sus, now
5. Come in your ho - ly might, we pray,
6. To God Cre - a - tor, God the Son,

1. *Cre - á - tor ál - me sí - de - rum,*
2. *Qui daé - mo - nis ne fráu - di - bus*
3. *Com - mú - ne qui mún - di né - fas*
4. *Cú - jus po - té - stas gló - ri - ae.*
5. *Te de - pre - cá - mur, úl - ti - mae*
6. *Vír - tus, hó - nor, laus, gló - ri - a*

Your peo - ple's ev - er - last - ing light,
Should doom to death a u - ni - verse,
You came; but not in splen - dor bright,
All knees must bend, all hearts must bow:
Re - deem us for e - ter - nal day;
And God the Spir - it, Three in One,

Ae - tér - na lux cre - dén - ti - um,
Per - í - ret ór - bis ím - pe - tu
Ut ex - pi - á - res, ad crú - cem
No - mén - que cum prí - mum só - nat,
Má - gnum di - é - i Jú - di - cem,
Dé - o Pá - tri cum Fí - li - o,

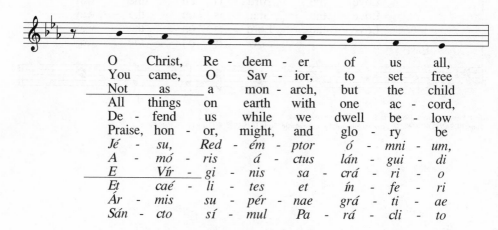

O Christ, Re - deem - er of us all,
You came, O Sav - ior, to set free
Not as a mon - arch, but the child
All things on earth with one ac - cord,
De - fend us while we dwell be - low
Praise, hon - or, might, and glo - ry be

Jé - su, Red - ém - ptor ó - mni - um,
A - mó - ris á - ctus lán - gui - di
E Vír - gi - nis sa - crá - ri - o
Et caé - li - tes et ín - fe - ri
Ár - mis su - pér - nae grá - ti - ae.
Sán - cto sí - mul Pa - rá - cli - to

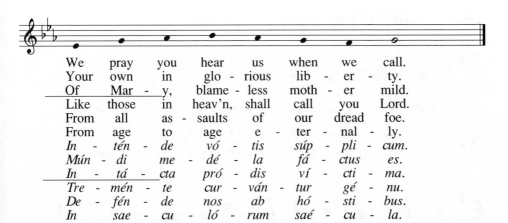

We	pray	you	hear	us	when	we	call.
Your	own	in	glo -	rious	lib -	er -	ty.
Of	Mar -	y,	blame -	less	moth -	er	mild.
Like	those	in	heav'n,	shall	call	you	Lord.
From	all	as -	saults	of	our	dread	foe.
From	age	to	age	e -	ter -	nal -	ly.
In -	*tén -*	*de*	*vó -*	*tis*	*súp -*	*pli -*	*cum.*
Mún -	*di*	*me -*	*dé -*	*la*	*fá -*	*ctus*	*es.*
In -	*tá -*	*cta*	*pró -*	*dis*	*ví -*	*cti -*	*ma.*
Tre -	*mén -*	*te*	*cur -*	*ván -*	*tur*	*gé -*	*nu.*
De -	*fén -*	*de*	*nos*	*ab*	*hó -*	*sti -*	*bus.*
In	*sae -*	*cu -*	*ló -*	*rum*	*saé -*	*cu -*	*la.*

Text: *Conditor alme siderum,* Latin 9th C., alt. 1632; tr. *The Hymnal 1982,* © 1985, The Church Pension Fund
Tune: CONDITOR ALME SIDERUM, LM; Mode IV; acc. by Gerard Farrell, OSB, b.1919, © 1986, GIA Publications, Inc.

484 Wait for the Lord

Ostinato Response

Wait for the Lord, whose day is near.

*To verse ***

Wait for the Lord: be strong, take heart!

*Verses

Cantor:

1. Pre - pare the way for the

2. The glo - ry of the

3. All the

4. Re - joice in the Lord

5. Seek first the king - dom of

Choir or keyboard:

...heart!   *(hum)*

*If verses are sung, the response is not repeated as an ostinato, but the response and verses are sung one after the other.

ADVENT

Text: Isaiah 40, Philippians 4, Matthew 6-7; Taizé Community, 1984
Tune: Jacques Berthier, 1923-1994
© 1984, Les Presses de Taizé, GIA Publications, Inc., agent

485   A Voice Cries Out

Refrain

A voice cries out in the wil - der - ness: Pre - pare a way for the Lord! A voice cries out in the wil - der -

Last time

ness: Make straight a high - way for God!

Verse 1

1. Con - sole my peo - ple, the ones dear to me: speak to the heart of Je - ru - sa - lem: the time of your mourn - ing is

D.C.

end - ed now, the Lord of life will come.

Verse 2

2. Ev - 'ry val - ley is made a plain, ev - 'ry moun - tain is lev - eled the glo - ry of God shall

D.C.

then be re - vealed, and the na - tions will sing in praise.

Verse 3

3. A voice shouts: "Cry!" O what shall I cry? All flesh is like grass and its flow-ers: the grass may with-er, the flow-er may fade, but the Word of the Lord is for - ev - er.

D.C.

Verse 4

4. Zi - on, shout from the moun-tain top, lift up your voice O Je - ru - sa - lem, and say to the peo-ple of God's own land, "Be - hold, be - hold your God!"

D.C.

Verse 5

5. The Lord will ap - pear as a shep - herd, hold-ing his lambs in his arms, keep-ing his flock so close to his heart lead-ing them all, old and young.

D.C.

Text: Isaiah 40:1-11; Michael Joncas, b.1951
Tune: Michael Joncas, b.1951
© 1981, 1982, Michael Joncas, published by Cooperative Ministries, Inc., OCP Publications, exclusive agent

486 City of God, Jerusalem

1. Cit-y of God, Je - ru - sa - lem, Where he has set his
love; Church of Christ that is one on earth With Je -
ru - sa - lem a - bove: Here as we walk this
chang-ing world Our joys are mixed with tears, But the
day will be soon when the Sav - ior re - turns And his
voice will ban - ish our fears.

2. Sing and be glad, Je - ru - sa - lem, For God does not for -
get; He who said he would come to save Nev - er
failed his peo - ple yet. Though we are tempt - ed
by de - spair And daunt - ed by de - feat, Our in -
vin - ci - ble Lord will be seen in his strength, And his
tri - umph will be com - plete.

3. Sor - row no more, Je - ru - sa - lem, Dis - card your rags of
shame! Take your crown as a gift from God Who has
called you by his name. Put off your sin, and
wear the robe Of glo - ry in its place; You will
shine in his light, you will share in his joy, You will
praise his won - der - ful grace.

4. Look all a - round, Je - ru - sa - lem, Sur - vey from west to
east; Sons and daugh - ters of God the king Are in -
vit - ed to his feast. Out of their ex - ile
far a - way His scat-tered fam - 'ly come, And the
streets will re - sound with the song of the saints When the
Sav - ior wel-comes us home.

1.-3.   4.

Text: Baruch 4-5; Christopher Idle, b.1938, © 1982, Hope Publishing Co.
Tune: PURPOSE, 8 6 8 7 8 6 12 8; Martin Shaw, 1875-1958, © Oxford University Press

When the King Shall Come Again   487

1. When the King shall come a-gain All his pow'r re-
2. In the des-ert trees take root Fresh from his cre-
3. Strength-en fee-ble hands and knees, Faint-ing hearts, be
4. There God's high-way shall be seen Where no roar-ing

veal - ing, Splen - dor shall an - nounce his reign,
a - tion; Plants and flow'rs and sweet - est fruit
cheer - ful! God who comes for such as these
li - on, Noth - ing e - vil or un - clean

Life and joy and heal - ing; Earth no
Join the cel - e - bra - tion; Riv - ers
Seeks and saves the fear - ful; Deaf ears,
Walks the road to Zi - on: Ran - somed

long - er in de - cay, Hope no more frus - trat - ed;
spring up from the earth, Bar - ren lands a - dorn - ing;
hear the si - lent tongues Sing a - way their weep - ing;
peo - ple home - ward bound All your prais - es voic - ing,

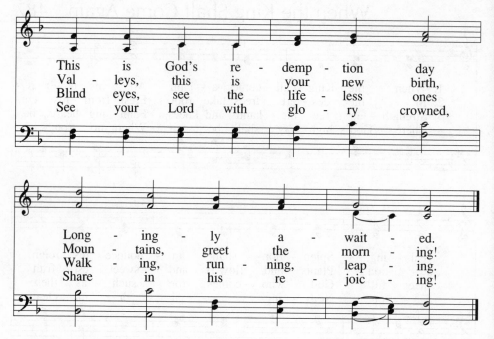

This   is   God's   re - demp - tion   day
Val - leys,   this   is   your   new   birth,
Blind   eyes,   see   the   life - less   ones
See   your   Lord   with   glo - ry   crowned,

Long - ing - ly   a - wait - ed.
Moun - tains,   greet   the   morn - ing!
Walk - ing,   run - ning,   leap - ing.
Share   in   his   re - joic - ing!

Text: Isaiah 35; Christopher Idle, b.1938, © 1982, Hope Publishing Co.
Tune: GAUDEAMUS PARITER, 7 6 7 6 D; Johann Horn, c. 1495-1547

488   Comfort, Comfort, O My People

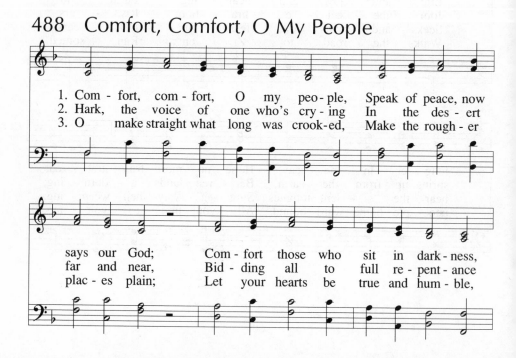

1. Com - fort, com - fort, O my peo - ple,   Speak of peace, now
2. Hark, the voice of one who's cry - ing   In the des - ert
3. O make straight what long was crook - ed,   Make the rough - er

says our God;   Com - fort those who sit in dark - ness,
far and near,   Bid - ding all to full re - pent - ance
plac - es plain;   Let your hearts be true and hum - ble,

Mourn - ing 'neath their sor - row's load. Speak un - to Je -
Since the king - dom now is here. O that warn - ing
As be - fits his ho - ly reign. For the glo - ry

ru - sa - lem Of the peace that waits for them;
cry o - bey! Now pre - pare for God a way;
of the Lord Now o'er earth is shed a - broad;

Tell of all the sins I cov - er, And that war - fare now is o - ver.
Let the val - leys rise to meet him And the hills bow down to greet him.
And all flesh shall see the to - ken That his word is nev - er bro - ken.

Text: Isaiah 40:1-8; *Tröstet, tröstet, meine Lieben;* Johann Olearius, 1611-1684; tr. by Catherine Winkworth, 1827-1878, alt.
Tune: GENEVA 42, 8 7 8 7 77 88; *Genevan Psalter,* 1551; harm. adapt. from Claude Goudimel, 1505-1572

489 Wake, O Wake, and Sleep No Longer

1. Wake, O wake, and sleep no long - er, For
2. Zi - on hears the sound of sing - ing; Our
3. Glo - ry, glo - ry, sing the an - gels, While

he who calls you is no stran - ger: A -
hearts are thrilled with sud - den long - ing: She
mu - sic sounds from strings and cym - bals; All

wake, God's own Je - ru - sa - lem! Hear, the mid - night
stirs, and wakes, and stands pre-pared. Christ, her friend, and
hu - man - kind, with songs a - rise! Twelve the gates in -

bells are chim - ing The sig - nal for his roy - al com -
lord, and lov - er, Her star and sun and strong re - deem -
to the cit - y, Each one a pearl of shin-ing beau -

ing: Let voice to voice an - nounce his name! We
er— At last his might - y voice is heard. The
ty; The streets of gold ring out with praise. All

feel his foot-steps near, The Bride-groom at the door—
Son of God has come To make with us his home:
crea - tures round the throne A - dore the ho - ly One

Al - le - lu - ia! The lamps will shine With light di - vine
Sing Ho - san - na! The fight is won, The feast be - gun;
With re - joic - ing: A - men be sung By ev - 'ry tongue

As Christ the Sav - ior comes to reign.
We fix our eyes on Christ a - lone.
To crown their wel - come to the King.

Text: Matt. 25:1-13; *Wachet auf, ruft uns die Stimme*, Philipp Nicolai, 1556-1608; tr. and adapt. by Christopher Idle, b. 1938, © 1982, Hope
    Publishing Co.
Tune: WACHET AUF, 89 8 89 8 66 4 44 8; Philipp Nicolai, 1556-1608; harm. by J.S. Bach, 1685-1750

490 On Jordan's Bank

1. On Jordan's bank the Baptist's cry An-
2. Then cleansed be every heart from sin; Make
3. For you are our salvation, Lord, Our
4. To heal the sick stretch out your hand, And
5. All praise the Son eternally, Whose

nounces that the Lord is nigh; Awake and hearken,
straight the way of God within, And let each heart pre-
refuge, and our great reward; Without your grace we
bid the fallen sinner stand; Shine forth, and let your
advent sets his people free; Whom with the Father

for he brings Glad tidings of the King of kings.
pare a home Where such a mighty guest may come.
waste away Like flow'rs that wither and decay.
light restore Earth's own true loveliness once more.
we adore And Spirit blest for evermore.

Text: *Jordanis oras praevia;* Charles Coffin, 1676-1749; tr. by John Chandler, 1806-1876
Tune: WINCHESTER NEW, LM; adapt. from *Musikalisches Handbuch,* Hamburg, 1690

Prepare the Way of the Lord   491

Canon

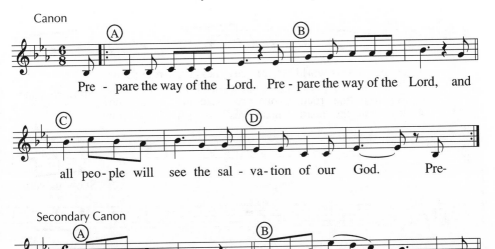

Pre - pare the way of the Lord. Pre - pare the way of the Lord, and

all peo - ple will see the sal - va - tion of our God. Pre-

Secondary Canon

Al - le - lu - ia.   Al - le - lu - ia.   Al - le -

lu - ia.   Al - le - lu - ia.

Text: Luke 3:4,6; Taizé Community, 1984
Tune: Jacques Berthier, 1923-1994, © 1984, Les Presses de Taizé, GIA Publications, Inc., agent

492 Advent Gathering

Verses

Cantor:

Assembly:

1. Here in this world where dark-ness sur - rounds us,
2. Where is the peace you prom-ised the wid - ow?
3. Where is the road you prom-ise the ex - ile?
4. Where is the heart whose "yes" is sal - va - tion?

Show us your

Show us your

Cantor:

face, O prom-ise of dawn.
We seek a sign that you are a-
Where is the home you prom - ised the
Where is the good news preached to the
Where is the child whose life is our

face, O prom-ise of dawn.

Assembly:

mong us.
or - phan?
low - ly? Show us your face, O Lord Je-sus come.
fu - ture?

unis.

Show us your face, O Lord Je-sus come.

div.

Refrain

Cantor:

Come, O hope of your peo-ple. Come a-mong us and

Choir and assembly:

Come, O hope of your peo-ple.

unis.

stay. Lead us in mer-cy up from the

Come a - mong us and stay.

shad-ows, Shine in our dark - ness, be here to - day.

Shine in our dark - ness, be here to - day.

div.

Text: Rory Cooney, b.1952
Tune: Gary Daigle, b.1957
© 1993, GIA Publications, Inc.

493 O Come, O Come, Emmanuel

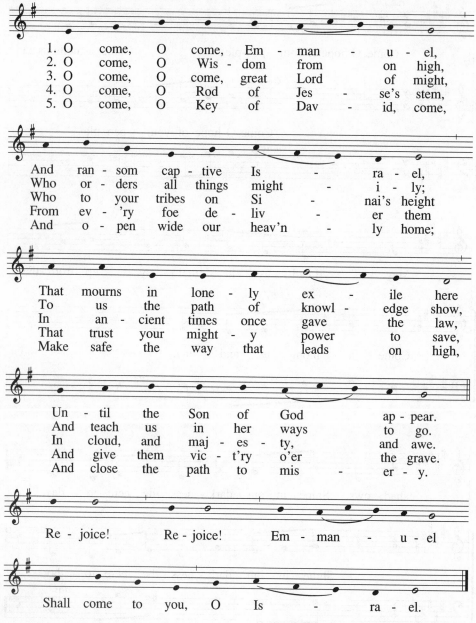

1. O come, O come, Em - man - u - el,
2. O come, O Wis - dom from on high,
3. O come, O come, great Lord of might,
4. O come, O Rod of Jes - se's stem,
5. O come, O Key of Dav - id, come,

And ran - som cap - tive Is - ra - el,
Who or - ders all things might - i - ly;
Who to your tribes on Si - nai's height
From ev - 'ry foe de - liv - er them
And o - pen wide our heav'n - ly home;

That mourns in lone - ly ex - ile here
To us the path of knowl - edge show,
In an - cient times once gave the law,
That trust your might - y power to save,
Make safe the way that leads on high,

Un - til the Son of God ap - pear.
And teach us in her ways to go.
In cloud, and maj - es - ty, and awe.
And give them vic - t'ry o'er the grave.
And close the path to mis - er - y.

Re - joice! Re - joice! Em - man - u - el

Shall come to you, O Is - ra - el.

6. O come, O Dayspring from on high
And cheer us by your drawing nigh;
Disperse the gloomy clouds of night,
And death's dark shadow put to flight.

7. O come, Desire of nations, bind
In one the hearts of humankind;
O bid our sad divisions cease,
And be for us our King of Peace.

Text: *Veni, veni Emmanuel;* Latin 9th C.; tr. by John M. Neale, 1818-1866, alt.
Tune: VENI VENI EMMANUEL, LM with refrain; Mode I; adapt. by Thomas Helmore, 1811-1890; acc. by Richard Proulx, b.1937, © 1975, GIA Publications, Inc.

Awake! Awake, and Greet the New Morn   494

1. A - wake! a - wake, and greet the new morn, For
2. To us, to all in sor - row and fear, Em -
3. In dark - est night his com - ing shall be, When
4. Re - joice, re - joice, take heart in the night, Though

an - gels her - ald its dawn - ing, Sing out your joy, for
man - u-el comes a - sing - ing, His hum - ble song is
all the world is de - spair - ing, As morn - ing light so
dark the win - ter and cheer-less, The ris - ing sun shall

soon he is born, Be - hold! the Child of our long - ing.
qui - et and near, Yet fills the earth with its ring - ing;
qui - et and free, So warm and gen - tle and car - ing.
crown you with light, Be strong and lov - ing and fear - less;

Come as a ba - by weak and poor, To bring all hearts to -
Mu - sic to heal the bro - ken soul And hymns of lov - ing
Then shall the mute break forth in song, The lame shall leap in
Love be our song and love our prayer, And love, our end - less

geth - er, He o - pens wide the heav'n - ly door And
kind - ness, The thun - der of his an - thems roll To
won - der, The weak be raised a - bove the strong, And
sto - ry, May God fill ev - 'ry day we share, And

1.-3.   4.

lives now in - side us for ev - er.
shat - ter all ha - tred and blind - ness.
weap-ons be bro - ken a - sun - der.
bring us at last in - to glo - ry.

Text: Marty Haugen, b.1950
Tune: REJOICE, REJOICE, 9 8 9 8 8 7 8 9; Marty Haugen, b.1950
© 1983, GIA Publications, Inc.

495 My Soul in Stillness Waits

Refrain

For you, O Lord, my soul in still-ness waits,

To verses | *Last time*

tru - ly my hope is in you. you.

Verses

1. O Lord of Light, our on - ly hope of
2. O Spring of Joy, rain down up - on our
3. O Root of Life, im - plant your seed with -
4. O Key of Knowl - edge, guide us in our
5. Come, let us bow be - fore the God who
6. Here we shall meet the Mak - er of the

glo - ry, your ra - diance shines in all who look to
spir - its, our thirst - y hearts are yearn - ing for your
in us, and in your ad - vent, draw us all to
pil - grim - age, we ev - er seek, yet un - ful - filled re -
made us, let ev - 'ry heart be o - pened to the
heav - ens, Cre - a - tor of the moun - tains and the

you, come, light the hearts of all in dark and shad - ow.
Word, come, make us whole, be com - fort to our hearts.
you, our hope re - born in dy - ing and in ris - ing.
main, o - pen to us the path - way of your peace.
Lord, for we are all the peo - ple of his hand.
seas, Lord of the stars, and pres - ent to us now.

D.C.

Text: Psalm 95 and "O" Antiphons; Marty Haugen, b.1950
Tune: Marty Haugen, b.1950
© 1982, GIA Publications, Inc.

Come, O Long Expected Jesus   496

1. Come, O long ex - pect - ed Je - sus, Born to set your
2. Born your peo - ple to de - liv - er; Born a child and

peo - ple free; From our fears and sins re - lease us;
yet a king! Born to reign in us for ev - er,

Free us from cap - tiv - i - ty. Is - rael's strength and
Now your gra - cious king - dom bring. By your own e -

con - so - la - tion, You, the hope of all the earth,
ter - nal Spir - it Rule in all our hearts a - lone;

Dear de - sire of ev - 'ry na - tion,
By your all suf - fi - cient mer - it

Come, and save us by your birth.
Raise us to your glo - rious throne.

Text: Haggai 2:7; Charles Wesley, 1707-1788, alt.
Tune: JEFFERSON, 8 7 8 7 D; William Walker's *Southern Harmony,* 1855; acc. by Theophane Hytrek, OSF, 1915-1992, © 1981, ICEL

497 The King Shall Come When Morning Dawns

1. The King shall come when morning dawns And light tri - um - phant breaks. When beau - ty gilds the east - ern hills And life to joy a - wakes.
2. Not, as of old, a lit - tle child, To suf - fer and to die, But crowned with glo - ry like the sun That lights the morn - ing sky.
3. The King shall come when morning dawns And earth's dark night is past; O haste the ris - ing of that morn Whose day shall ev - er last.
4. And let the end - less bliss be - gin, By wea - ry saints fore - told, When right shall tri - umph of wrong, And truth shall be ex - tolled.
5. The King shall come when morning dawns And light and beau - ty brings. Hail, Christ, the Lord! Your peo - ple pray: Come quick - ly, King of kings.

Text: John Brownlie, 1857-1925
Tune: MORNING SONG, CM; John Wyeth, 1770-1858; arr. by Robert J. Batastini, b.1942, © 1994, GIA Publications, Inc.

It Came upon the Midnight Clear   498

1. It came up-on the mid - night clear, That
2. Still through the clo - ven skies they come, With
3. Yet with the woes of sin and strife, The
4. For, lo, the days are has - tening on, By

glo - rious song of old, From
peace - ful wings un - furled, And
world has suf - fered long; Be -
proph - ets seen of old, When

an - gels bend - ing near the earth To
still their heav'n - ly mu - sic floats O'er
neath the heav'n - ly hymn have rolled Two
with the ev - er - cir - cling years Shall

touch their harps of gold: "Peace
all the wea - ry world: A -
thou - sand years of wrong; And
come the time fore - told, When

on the earth, good will to all From
bove its sad and low - ly plains They
war - ring hu - man - kind hears not The
peace shall o - ver all the earth Its

heaven's all gra - cious King"; The
bend on hov - 'ring wing, And
tid - ings which they bring; O
an - cient splen - dors fling, And

world in sol - emn still - ness lay, To
ev - er o'er its Ba - bel sounds The
hush the noise and cease your strife And
all the world give back the song Which

hear the an - gels sing.
bless - ed an - gels sing.
hear the an - gels sing.
now the an - gels sing.

Text: Edmund H. Sears, 1810-1876, alt.
Tune: CAROL, CMD; Richard S. Willis, 1819-1900

O Come, All Ye Faithful / Adeste Fideles   499

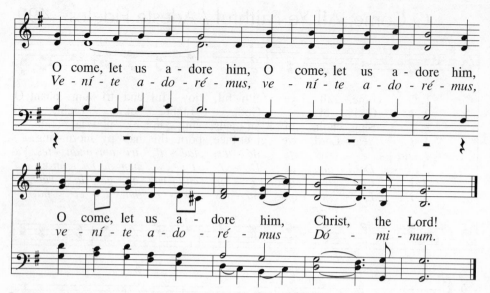

O come, let us a-dore him, O come, let us a-dore him,
Ve - ní - te a - do - ré - mus, ve - ní - te a - do - ré - mus,

O come, let us a-dore him, Christ, the Lord!
ve - ní - te a - do - ré - mus Dó - mi - num.

Text: *Adeste fideles;* John F. Wade, c.1711-1786; tr. by Frederick Oakeley, 1802-1880, alt.
Tune: ADESTE FIDELES, Irregular with refrain; John F. Wade, c.1711-1786

500 A Child Is Born in Bethlehem

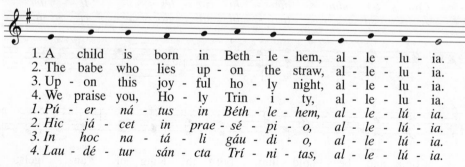

1. A child is born in Beth - le - hem, al - le - lu - ia.
2. The babe who lies up - on the straw, al - le - lu - ia.
3. Up - on this joy - ful ho - ly night, al - le - lu - ia.
4. We praise you, Ho - ly Trin - i - ty, al - le - lu - ia.
1. *Pú - er ná - tus in Béth - le - hem, al - le - lú - ia.*
2. *Hic já - cet in prae - sé - pi - o, al - le - lú - ia.*
3. *In hoc na - tá - li gáu - di - o, al - le - lú - ia.*
4. *Lau - dé - tur sán - cta Trí - ni - tas, al - le - lú - ia.*

There - fore re - joice Je - ru - sa - lem, al - le - lu - ia,
Will rule the world for ev - er - more, al - le - lu - ia,
We bless your Name, O Lord of Light, al - le - lu - ia,
A - dor - ing you e - ter - nal - ly, al - le - lu - ia,
Un - de gáu - det Je - rú - sa - lem, al - le - lú - ia,
Qui ré - gnat sí - ne tér - mi - no, al - le - lú - ia,
Be - ne - di - cá - mus Dó - mi - no, al - le - lú - ia,
Dé - o di - cá - mus grá - ti - as, al - le - lú - ia,

al - le - lu - ia. Our joy-ful hearts we raise, Christ is born, O
al - le - lú - ia. In cór - dis jú - bi - lo Chrí - stum ná - tum

come a - dore him In new - found songs of praise.
a - do - ré - mus Cum nó - vo cán - ti - co.

Text: *Puer natus in Bethlehem;* Latin 14th C.; tr. by Ruth Fox Hume, b.1922, © 1964, GIA Publications, Inc.
Tune: PUER NATUS, 8 8 with alleluias and refrain; Mode I; acc. by Richard Proulx, b.1937, © 1986, GIA Publications, Inc.

The Virgin Mary Had a Baby Boy 501

1. The vir - gin Mar - y had a ba - by boy, the
2. The an - gels sang when the ba - by born, the
3. The wise men saw where the ba - by born, the

vir - gin Mar - y had a ba - by boy, the
an - gels sang when the ba - by born, the
wise men saw where the ba - by born, the

vir - gin Mar - y had a ba - by boy, and they
an - gels sang when the ba - by born, and they
wise men went where the ba - by born, and they

say that his name was Je - sus.
say that his name was Je - sus.
say that his name was Je - sus.

He come from the glo - ry, he come from the

glo - rious king - dom. Oh, yes! be - liev - er!

Oh, yes! be - liev - er! He come from the

glo - ry, he come from the glo - rious king-dom.

502 Hark! The Herald Angels Sing

1. Hark! the her - ald an - gels sing, "Glo - ry to the
2. Christ, by high - est heaven a - dored, Christ the ev - er-
3. Hail the heav'n - born Prince of Peace! Hail the Sun of

new - born King; Peace on earth, and mer - cy mild
last - ing Lord: Late in time be - hold him come,
Right-eous-ness! Light and life to all he brings,

God and sin - ners rec - on - ciled!"   Joy - ful, all you
Off - spring of the Vir - gin's womb.   Veiled in flesh the
Ris'n with heal - ing in his wings.   Mild he lays his

na - tions, rise,   Join the tri - umph of the skies;
God - head see: Hail the in - car - nate De - i - ty,
glo - ry by,   Born that we no more may die,

With the an - gel - ic host pro-claim,   "Christ is born in Beth - le - hem!"
Pleased as man with us to dwell,   Je - sus, our Em - man - u - el.
Born to raise us from the earth,   Born to give us sec - ond birth.

Org.

Hark! the her - ald an - gels sing,   "Glo - ry to the new-born King!"

Org. Ped.

Text: Charles Wesley, 1707-1788, alt.
Tune: MENDELSSOHN 77 77 D with refrain; Felix Mendelssohn, 1809-1847

503 God Rest You Merry, Gentlemen

1. God rest you mer - ry, gen - tle - men, Let
2. In Beth - le - hem in Ju - dah This
3. From God our great Cre - a - tor A
4. The shep - herds at those tid - ings Re -
5. Now to the Lord sing prais - es, All

noth - ing you dis - may, For Je - sus Christ our
bless - ed babe was born, And laid with - in a
bless - ed an - gel came, And un - to cer - tain
joic - ed much in mind, And left their flocks a -
you with - in this place, And with true love and

Sav - ior Was born up - on this day,
man - ger Up - on this bless - ed morn:
shep - herds Brought tid - ings of the same,
feed - ing In tem - pest, storm, and wind,
char - i - ty Each oth - er now em - brace;

To save us all from Sa - tan's power When
For which his moth - er Mar - y Did
How that in Beth - le - hem was born The
And went to Beth - le - hem straight - way, The
This ho - ly tide of Christ - mas All

we   were   gone   a   -   stray.
noth - ing   take   in   scorn.
Son   of   God   by   name.
bless - ed   babe   to   find.
oth - ers   shall   re   -   place.

O   tid - ings   of   com - fort   and   joy,   com - fort   and
joy;   O   tid - ings   of   com - fort   and   joy!

Text: English carol, 18th C.
Tune: GOD REST YOU MERRY, 8 6 8 6 8 6 with refrain; English 18th C.; harm by John Stainer, 1840-1901

504 Angels We Have Heard on High

1. An - gels we have heard on high
2. Shep - herds, why this ju - bi - lee?
3. Come to Beth - le - hem and see
4. See him in a man - ger laid,

Sweet - ly sing - ing o'er the plains,
Why your joy - ous strains pro - long?
Him whose birth the an - gels sing;
Whom the choirs of an - gels praise;

And the moun - tains in re - ply
Say what may the tid - ings be,
Come a - dore, on bend - ed knee,
Mar - y, Jo - seph, lend your aid,

Ech - o back their joy - ous strains.
Which in - spire your heav'n - ly song.
Christ, the Lord, the new - born King.
While our hearts in love we raise.

Glo - - - ri - a in ex- cel- sis De - o, Glo - - - ri - a in ex- cel- sis De - o.

Text: *Les anges dans nos campagnes;* French, c. 18th C.; tr. from *Crown of Jesus Music,* London, 1862
Tune: GLORIA, 7 7 7 7 with refrain; French traditional

505 Rise Up, Shepherd, and Follow

Choir may hum or sing "oo" or "ah" when leader is singing.

Refrain

Fol - low, fol - low, Rise up, shep - herd, and

fol - low, Fol - low the Star of Beth - le - hem,

Rise up, shep - herd, and fol - low.

Text: Traditional
Tune: African-American spiritual

506 Child of Mercy

Refrain

Descant:

Glo - - ri - a

Child of mer - cy, child of peace, Je - sus, Bread of life,

in ex - cel - sis De - o, Glo - - -

food to fill our long - ing. Child of jus - tice, child of light,

| 1.- 4. | 5. |

- ri - a in ex - cel - sis De - o.

Je - sus, sav - ing cup, Em - man - u - el, God with us.

Verses

1. All who walk in dark - ness have
2. 𝄾 A child is born to us, a
3. 𝄾 We name him: "Won - der, coun - s'lor,
4. We pro - claim good news to you, great

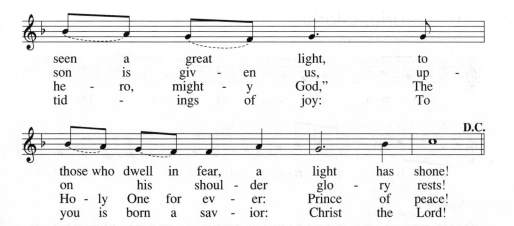

seen   a   great   light,   to
son   is   giv - en   us,   up -
he - ro,   might - y   God,"   The
tid - ings   of   joy: To

those who dwell   in   fear,   a   light   has   shone!
on   his   shoul - der   glo - ry   rests!
Ho - ly   One   for   ev - er: Prince   of   peace!
you   is   born   a   sav - ior: Christ   the   Lord!

Text: Isaiah 9:1, 5; David Haas, b.1957
Tune: David Haas, b.1957
© 1991, GIA Publications, Inc.

507 Gloria, Gloria

Refrain/Canon—*4 voices*

1. Glo - ri - a, glo - ri - a, 2. in ex - cel - sis De - o!

3. Glo - ri - a, glo - ri - a, 4. al - le - lu - ia, al - le - lu - ia!

Verse 1

Cantor or choir:

1. Glo - ry to God in the high - est, and

peace to his peo - ple on earth.

Lord God, heav - en - ly King, al - might - y God and

Fa - ther, we wor - ship you, we give you thanks,

Refrain ad lib.

we praise you for your glo - ry.

Verse 2

2. Lord Je - sus Christ, on - ly Son of the Fa - ther,

Lord God, Lamb of God, you take a - way the

*The refrain may be sung as an ostinato throughout all or part of the text, or it may be sung as a response at the beginning and after each section of the text.

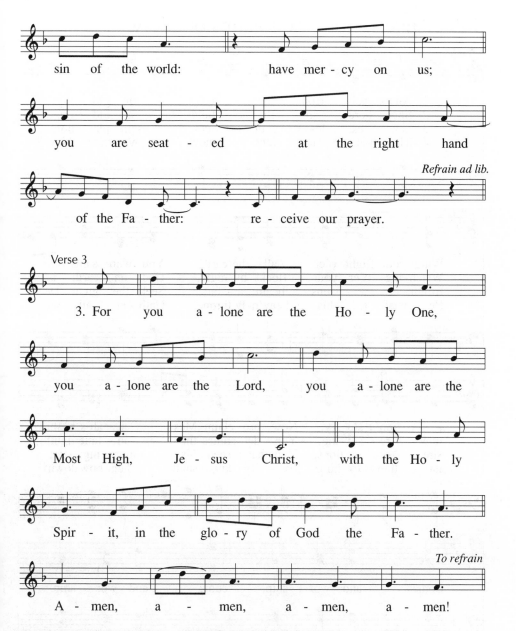

Refrain ad lib.

sin of the world: have mer - cy on us; you are seat - ed at the right hand of the Fa - ther: re - ceive our prayer.

Verse 3

3. For you a - lone are the Ho - ly One, you a - lone are the Lord, you a - lone are the Most High, Je - sus Christ, with the Ho - ly Spir - it, in the glo - ry of God the Fa - ther.

To refrain

A - men, a - men, a - men, a - men!

Tune: Jacques Berthier, © 1979, 1988, Les Presses de Taizé, GIA Publications, Inc., agent

508 Angels, from the Realms of Glory

1. An - gels, from the realms of glo - ry,
2. Shep - herds, in the fields a - bid - ing,
3. Sag - es, leave your con - tem - pla - tions,
4. Though an in - fant now we view him,

Wing your flight o'er all the earth; You who sang cre -
Watch-ing o'er your flocks by night, God on earth is
Bright - er vi - sions beam a - far; Seek the great De -
He shall fill his heav'n-ly throne, Gath - er all the

a - tion's sto - ry, Now pro - claim Mes - si - ah's birth:
now re - sid-ing, Yon - der shines the in - fant light:
sire of na-tions, You have seen his morn-ing star:
na - tions to him; Ev - 'ry knee shall then bow down:

Come and wor - ship, come and wor - ship,

Wor - ship Christ, the new - born King.

Text: Sts. 1-3, James Montgomery, 1771-1854; st. 4, *Christmas Box,* 1825
Tune: REGENT SQUARE, 8 7 8 7 8 7; Henry Smart, 1813-1879

Infant Holy, Infant Lowly 509

1. In - fant ho - ly, In - fant low - ly, For his bed a cat - tle stall; Ox - en low - ing, Lit - tle know - ing Christ the babe is Lord of all. Swift are wing - ing An - gels sing - ing, No - els ring - ing, Tid - ings bring - ing: Christ the babe is Lord of all.

2. Flocks were sleep - ing: Shep - herds keep - ing Vi - gil till the morn - ing new. Saw the glo - ry, Heard the sto - ry, Tid - ings of a gos - pel true. Thus re - joic - ing, Free from sor - row, Prais - es voic - ing Greet the mor - row: Christ the babe was born for you.

Text: Polish carol; para. by Edith M.G. Reed, 1885-1933
Tune: W ZLOBIE LEZY, 44 7 44 7 4444 7; Polish carol; harm. by A.E. Rusbridge, 1917-1969, © Horfield Baptist Housing Assoc., Ltd.

510 Of the Father's Love Begotten

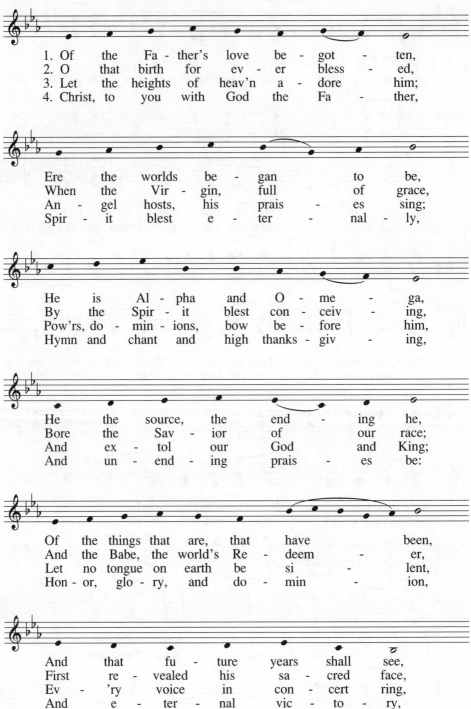

1. Of the Fa - ther's love be - got - ten,
2. O that birth for ev - er bless - ed,
3. Let the heights of heav'n a - dore him;
4. Christ, to you with God the Fa - ther,

Ere the worlds be - gan to be,
When the Vir - gin, full of grace,
An - gel hosts, his prais - es sing;
Spir - it blest e - ter - nal - ly,

He is Al - pha and O - me - ga,
By the Spir - it blest con - ceiv - ing,
Pow'rs, do - min - ions, bow be - fore him,
Hymn and chant and high thanks - giv - ing,

He the source, the end - ing he,
Bore the Sav - ior of our race;
And ex - tol our God and King;
And un - end - ing prais - es be:

Of the things that are, that have been,
And the Babe, the world's Re - deem - er,
Let no tongue on earth be si - lent,
Hon - or, glo - ry, and do - min - ion,

And that fu - ture years shall see,
First re - vealed his sa - cred face,
Ev - 'ry voice in con - cert ring,
And e - ter - nal vic - to - ry,

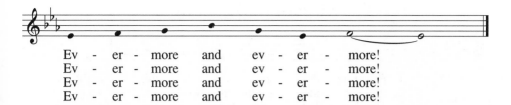

Ev - er - more and ev - er - more!
Ev - er - more and ev - er - more!
Ev - er - more and ev - er - more!
Ev - er - more and ev - er - more!

Text: *Corde natus ex Parentis;* Aurelius Prudentius, 348-413; tr. by John M. Neale, 1818-1866 and Henry W. Baker, 1821-1877
Tune: DIVINUM MYSTERIUM, 8 7 8 7 8 7 7; 12th C.; Mode V; acc. by Richard Proulx, b. 1937, © 1985, GIA Publications, Inc.

Gloria 511

¡Glo - ria, glo - ria, glo - ria   en   las al - tur - as   a Dios!
Glo - ry, glo - ry, glo - ry,   glo - ry be to God on high!

Y en la tie - rra paz   pa - ra a - que - llos   que a - ma el Se - ñor.
And on earth   peace   to the peo - ple in whom God is well   pleased.

Text: Luke 2:14
Tune: Pablo Sosa, © 1990

512 Before the Marvel of This Night

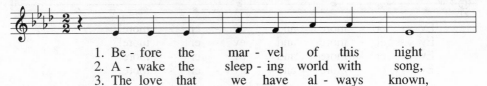

1. Be - fore the mar - vel of this night
2. A - wake the sleep - ing world with song,
3. The love that we have al - ways known,

A - dor - ing, fold your wings and bow,
This is the day the Lord has made.
Our con - stant joy and end - less light,

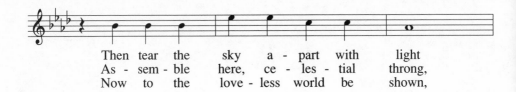

Then tear the sky a - part with light
As - sem - ble here, ce - les - tial throng,
Now to the love - less world be shown,

And with your news the world en - dow.
In roy - al splen - dor come ar - rayed.
Now break up - on its death - ly night.

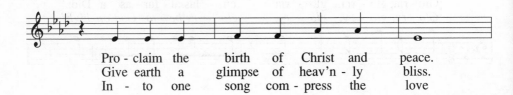

Pro - claim the birth of Christ and peace.
Give earth a glimpse of heav'n - ly bliss.
In - to one song com - press the love

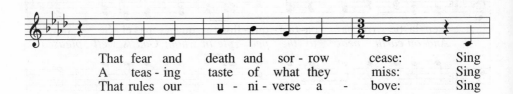

That fear and death and sor - row cease: Sing
A teas - ing taste of what they miss: Sing
That rules our u - ni - verse a - bove: Sing

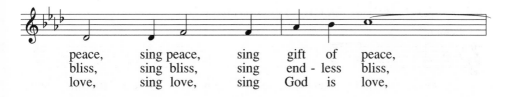

peace,   sing peace,   sing   gift   of   peace,
bliss,   sing bliss,   sing   end - less   bliss,
love,   sing love,   sing   God   is   love,

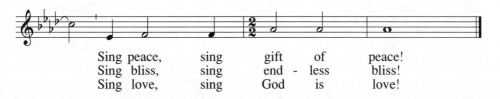

Sing peace,   sing   gift   of   peace!
Sing bliss,   sing   end - less   bliss!
Sing love,   sing   God   is   love!

Text: Jaroslav J. Vajda, b.1919, © 1981
Tune: MARVEL, 8 8 8 8 8 8 8 6; Carl F. Schalk, b.1929, © 1981, GIA Publications, Inc.

Christ Was Born on Christmas Day   513

1. Christ was born   on Christ-mas day: Wreathe the hol - ly,
2. He   is born   to   set   us   free,   He   is born   our
3. Let   the bright   red ber - ries glow   Ev - 'ry-where   in
4. Chris - tians all,   re - joice and sing,   'Tis   the birth - day

twine the bay,   *Chri - stus na - tus   ho - di - e:*   The
Lord to be,   *Ex Ma - ri - a   Vir - gi - ne:*   The
good - ly show: *Chri - stus na - tus   ho - di - e:*   The
of   a   King,   *Ex Ma - ri - a   Vir - gi - ne:*   The

Babe, the Son, the   Ho - ly One of   Mar - y.
God, the Lord, by   all   a - dored for   ev - er.
Babe, the Son, the   Ho - ly One of   Mar - y.
God, the Lord, by   all   a - dored for   ev - er.

Text: Traditional
Tune: RESONET IN LAUDIBUS, 777 11; German, 16th C.; harm. by Ralph Vaughan Williams, 1872-1958, © Oxford University Press

514 Go Tell It on the Mountain

Refrain

Go tell it on the moun - tain, O - ver the hills and ev - 'ry - where; Go tell it on the moun - tain That Je - sus Christ is born!

Verses

1. While shep - herds kept their watch - ing O'er si - lent flocks by night, Be - hold through - out the heav - ens There shone a ho - ly light.
2. The shep - herds feared and trem - bled When lo! a - bove the earth Rang out the an - gel cho - rus That hailed our Sav - ior's birth.
3. Down in a low - ly man - ger The hum - ble Christ was born, And God sent us sal - va - tion That bless - ed Christ - mas morn.

D.C.

Text: African-American spiritual; adapt. by John W. Work, Jr., 1871-1925, © Mrs. John W. Work, III
Tune: GO TELL IT ON THE MOUNTAIN, 7 6 7 6 with refrain; African-American spiritual; harm. by Robert J. Batastini, b.1942, © 1995, GIA
Publications, Inc.

Away in a Manger 515

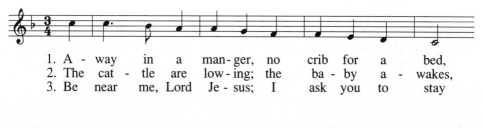

1. A - way in a man-ger, no crib for a bed,
2. The cat - tle are low-ing; the ba - by a - wakes,
3. Be near me, Lord Je - sus; I ask you to stay

The lit - tle Lord Je - sus laid down his sweet head.
But lit - tle Lord Je - sus, no cry - ing he makes.
Close by me for - ev - er, and love me, I pray.

The stars in the bright sky looked down where he lay,
I love you, Lord Je - sus, look down from the sky,
Bless all the dear chil - dren in your ten - der care,

The lit - tle Lord Je - sus, a - sleep on the hay.
And stay by my cra - dle till morn-ing is nigh.
And fit us for heav - en to live with you there.

Text: St. 1-2, anonymous, st. 3, John T. McFarland, 1851-1913
Tune: MUELLER, 11 11 11 11; James R. Murray, 1841-1905; harm. by Robert J. Batastini, b. 1942, © 1994, GIA Publications, Inc.

516 Carol at the Manger

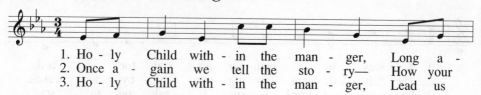

1. Ho - ly   Child with - in   the   man - ger,   Long a -
2. Once a - gain   we   tell   the   sto - ry—   How your
3. Ho - ly   Child with - in   the   man - ger,   Lead us

go   yet   ev - er   near;   Come as   friend   to   ev - 'ry
love   for   us was   shown,   When the   Im - age of your
ev - er   in your   way,   So   we   see   in   ev - 'ry

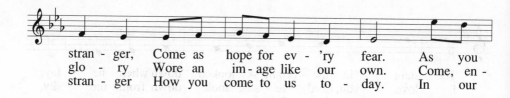

stran - ger,   Come as   hope for ev - 'ry   fear.   As   you
glo - ry   Wore an   im - age like   our   own.   Come, en -
stran - ger   How you   come to   us   to - day.   In   our

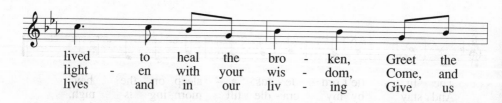

lived   to   heal   the   bro - ken,   Greet   the
light - en   with   your   wis - dom,   Come, and
lives   and   in   our   liv - ing   Give   us

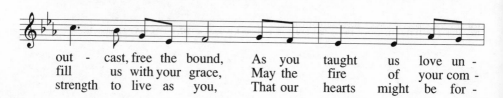

out - cast, free the bound,   As you   taught   us   love un -
fill   us with your grace,   May the   fire   of   your com -
strength   to live as   you,   That our   hearts   might   be   for -

spo - ken,   Teach us   now where you   are   found.
pas - sion   Kin - dle   ev - 'ry   land   and   race.
giv - ing   And our   spir - its   strong   and   true.

Text: Marty Haugen, b.1950
Tune: JOYOUS LIGHT, 8 7 8 7 D; Marty Haugen, b.1950
© 1987, GIA Publications, Inc.

Where Shepherds Lately Knelt   517

1. Where shep-herds late - ly knelt and kept the an - gel's
2. like - ly place I find him as they
3. not have known I - sa - iah would be
4. I for - get how love was born and

word, I come in half - be - lief, a
said: Sweet, new - born babe, how frail, and
there, His proph - e - cies ful - filled? With
burned Its way in - to my heart: un -

pil - grim strange - ly stirred; But there is room and
in a man - ger bed: A still, small voice to
pound-ing heart, I stare: A Child, a Son, the
asked, un - forced, un - earned. To die, to live, and

wel - come there for me,
cry one day for me,
Prince of Peace for me,
not a - lone for me,

But there is room and wel - come there for
A still small voice to cry one day for
A Child, a Son, the Prince of Peace for
To die, to live, and not a - lone for

1.- 3. | 4.

me. | 2. In that un -
me. | 3. How should I
me. | 4. Can I, will
me.

Text: Jaroslav J. Vajda, b.1919, © 1986
Tune: MANGER SONG, 12 12 10 10; Carl F. Schalk, b.1929, © 1986, GIA Publications, Inc.

518 Good Christian Friends, Rejoice

1. Good Chris-tian friends, re - joice With heart and soul and voice; O give heed to what we say: Je - sus Christ is born to - day! Ox and ass be - fore him bow, And he is in the man-ger now.

2. Good Chris-tian friends, re - joice With heart and soul and voice; Now you hear of end-less bliss: Je - sus Christ was born for this! He has o - pened heav-en's door, And we are blest for ev - er - more.

3. Good Chris-tian friends, re - joice With heart and soul and voice; Now you need not fear the grave: Je - sus Christ was born to save! Calls you one and calls you all To gain his ev - er - last-ing hall.

1. Good Chris-tian friends, re - joice With heart and soul and voice! Raise your wea - ry hearts and see: Je - sus Christ has come to free! When the cap - tives find re - lease, In feet that bring the word of peace,

2. Good Chris-tian friends, re - joice With heart and soul and voice! In the kind and just and true Je - sus Christ is born a - new! In the low - ly, weak and poor, The hum - ble stran - ger at our door,

3. Good Chris-tian friends, re - joice With heart and soul and voice! Still be - fore us on the way, Je - sus Christ is here to - day! In the break-ing of the bread, In life that cries out to the dead,

Christ is born to - day!   Christ is born to - day!
Christ was born for this!   Christ was born for this!
Christ was born to save!   Christ was born to save!
Christ has come to free!   *Christ has come to free!*
Christ is born a - new!   *Christ is born a - new!*
Christ is born to - day!   *Christ is born to - day!*

Text: *In dulci jubilo;* Latin and German, 14th C.: tr. by John M. Neale, 1818-1866; alternate verses, Marty Haugen, b.1950;
    © 1992, GIA Publications, Inc.
Tune: IN DULCI JUBILO, 66 77 78 55; Klug's *Geistliche Lieder,* Wittenberg, 1535; harm. by Robert L. Pearsall, 1795-1856

He Came Down   519

He came down that we may have *love; He

came down that we may have love; He came down that we may

have love, Hal - le - lu - jah for ev - er - more.

Cantor: Why did he come?

Substitute peace, joy, hope, life, etc.

Text: Cameroon traditional

520 O Little Town of Bethlehem

1. O lit - tle town of Beth - le - hem, How
2. For Christ is born of Mar - y, And
3. How si - lent - ly, how si - lent - ly, The
4. O ho - ly Child of Beth - le - hem! De -

still we see thee lie! A - bove thy deep and
gath - ered all a - bove, While mor - tals sleep, the
won - drous gift is giv'n! So God im - parts to
scend to us we pray; Cast out our sin and

dream - less sleep The si - lent stars go by;
an - gels keep Their watch of won - d'ring love.
hu - man hearts The bless - ings of his heav'n.
en - ter in, Be born in us to - day.

Yet in the dark streets shin - eth The ev - er - last - ing
O morn - ing stars, to - geth - er Pro - claim the ho - ly
No ear may hear his com - ing, But in this world of
We hear the Christ - mas an - gels The great glad tid - ings

Light;   The   hopes   and   fears   of
birth!   And   prais - es   sing   to
sin,   Where meek   souls   will   re -
tell;   O   come   to   us,   a -

all   the   years   Are   met   in   thee   to - night.
God   the   King,   And   peace to   all   on   earth.
ceive him,   still   The   dear   Christ en - ters in.
bide   with   us,   Our   Lord   Em -   man - u - el!

Text: Phillips Brooks, 1835-1893
Tune: ST. LOUIS, 8 6 8 6 7 6 8 6; Lewis H. Redner, 1831-1908

521 Nativity Carol

Verses

1. Si - lent, in the chill of mid - night,
2. "Fear not," said an - gel - ic voic - es;
3. Je - sus, Lord of all cre - a - tion,

star - light shines up - on a low - ly man - ger.
"tid - ings of a won - drous love we bring you.
sleep now close be - side your moth - er, Mar - y.

Won - der, won - der of the a - ges;
Go now, find him in a man - ger;
Bring us light a - mid the dark - ness,

heav - en breaks forth on the earth.
vis - it God's home on the earth."
prom - ise of life with - out end.

Refrain

For a child is born, the world re -

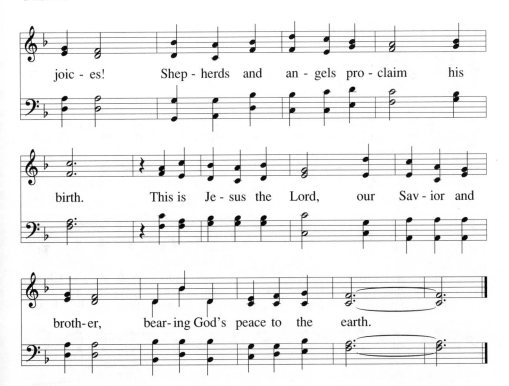

joic - es! Shep - herds and an - gels pro - claim his
birth. This is Je - sus the Lord, our Sav - ior and
broth - er, bear- ing God's peace to the earth.

Text: Francis Patrick O'Brien, b.1958
Tune: Francis Patrick O'Brien, b.1958
© 1992, GIA Publications, Inc.

522 Silent Night, Holy Night

1. Si - lent night, ho - ly night, All is calm,
2. Si - lent night, ho - ly night, Shep - herds quake
3. Si - lent night, ho - ly night, Son of God,

all is bright Round yon Vir - gin Moth - er and Child,
at the sight; Glo - ries stream from heav - en a - far,
love's pure light Ra - diant beams from thy ho - ly face,

Ho - ly In - fant so ten - der and mild, Sleep in heav - en - ly
Heav'n - ly hosts sing al - le - lu - ia; Christ, the Sav - ior, is
With the dawn of re - deem - ing grace, Je - sus, Lord, at thy

peace, Sleep in heav - en - ly peace.
born! Christ, the Sav - ior, is born!
birth, Je - sus, Lord, at thy birth.

Text: *Stille Nacht, heilige Nacht;* Joseph Mohr, 1792-1849; tr. John F. Young, 1820-1885
Tune: STILLE NACHT, 66 89 66; Franz X. Gruber, 1787-1863

Night of Silence   523

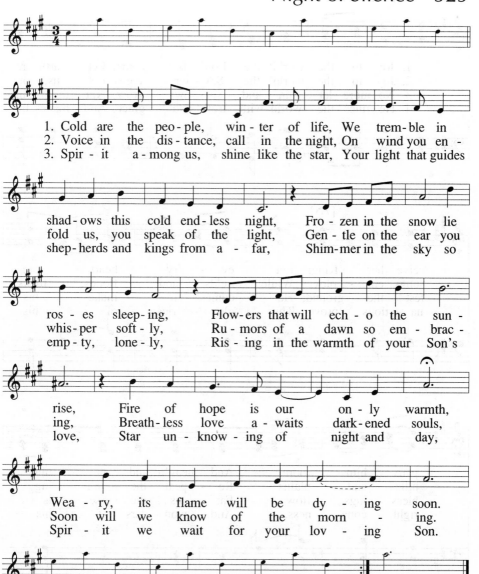

1. Cold are the peo - ple, win - ter of life, We trem - ble in
2. Voice in the dis - tance, call in the night, On wind you en -
3. Spir - it a - mong us, shine like the star, Your light that guides

shad - ows this cold end - less night, Fro - zen in the snow lie
fold us, you speak of the light, Gen - tle on the ear you
shep - herds and kings from a - far, Shim - mer in the sky so

ros - es sleep - ing, Flow - ers that will ech - o the sun -
whis - per soft - ly, Ru - mors of a dawn so em - brac -
emp - ty, lone - ly, Ris - ing in the warmth of your Son's

rise, Fire of hope is our on - ly warmth,
ing, Breath - less love a - waits dark - ened souls,
love, Star un - know - ing of night and day,

Wea - ry, its flame will be dy - ing soon.
Soon will we know of the morn - ing.
Spir - it we wait for your lov - ing Son.

"Night of Silence" was written to be sung simultaneously with "Silent Night." It is suggested that selected voices hum "Silent Night" while the remaining voices sing the final verse of "Night of Silence". Likewise, the song "Silent Night" may be sung by the choir and congregation as the instruments play "Night of Silence".

Text: Daniel Kantor, b.1960
Tune: Daniel Kantor, b.1960
© 1984, GIA Publications, Inc.

524 Joy to the World

1. Joy to the world! the Lord is come: Let earth re-
2. Joy to the world! the Sav - ior reigns: Let us, our
3. No more let sin and sor - rows grow, Nor thorns in -
4. He rules the world with truth and grace, And makes the

[𝄐]

ceive her King; Let ev - 'ry heart pre -
songs em - ploy; While fields and floods, rocks,
fest the ground; He comes to make his
na - tions prove The glo - ries of his

pare him room, And heav'n and na - ture
hills and plains Re - peat the sound - ing
bless - ings flow Far as the curse is
right - eous - ness, And won - ders of his

And
Re -
Far
And

Text: Psalm 98; Isaac Watts, 1674-1748
Tune: ANTIOCH, CM; arr. from George F. Handel, 1685-1759, in T. Hawkes' *Collection of Tunes*, 1833

525　The Aye Carol

1. Who is the ba-by an hour or two old
2. Who is the wom-an with child at her breast,
3. Who is the man who looks on at the door,
4. Who are the peo-ple come in from the street,
5. Will you come with me, ev'n though I feel shy,

Looked for by shep-herds far strayed from their fold,
Giv-ing her milk to earth's heav-en-ly guest,
Wel-com-ing stran-gers, some rich but most poor,
Some to bring pres-ents and some just to meet,
Come to his cra-dle and come to his cry,

Lost in the world though more pre-cious than gold?
Tell-ing her mind to be calm and at rest?
Scan-ning the world as if some-how un-sure?
Join-ing their song to what an-gels re-peat?
Give him your nod or your "yes" or your "aye,"

Final ending

This is God with us in Je-sus.
Mar-y, the moth-er of Je-sus.
Jo-seph, the fa-ther of Je-sus.
These are the new friends of Je-sus.
Give what you can give to Je-sus?

Text: John L. Bell, b.1949
Tune: AYE CAROL, 10 10 10 8; John L. Bell, b.1949
© 1987, Iona Community, GIA Publications, Inc., agent

Once in Royal David's City   526

1. Once in roy - al Da - vid's cit - y Stood a
2. He came down to earth from heav - en Who is
3. And through all his won - drous child - hood He would
4. For he is our child - hood's pat - tern, Day by
5. And our eyes at last shall see him, Through his

low - ly cat - tle shed, Where a moth - er laid her
God and Lord of all, And his shel - ter was a
hon - or and o - bey, Love and watch the low - ly
day like us he grew; He was lit - tle, weak, and
own re - deem - ing love; For that child so dear and

ba - by In a man - ger for his bed. Mar - y
sta - ble, And his cra - dle was a stall. With the
maid - en In whose gen - tle arms he lay. Chris - tian
help - less, Tears and smiles like us he knew: And he
gen - tle Is our Lord in heav'n a - bove: And he

was   that moth - er   mild,   Je - sus
poor   and mean and low - ly   Lived on
chil - dren all should be   Kind, o -
feels   for all   our sad - ness, And he
leads   his chil - dren on   To the

Christ   her lit - tle   Child.
earth   our Sav - ior ho - ly.
be - dient, good as   he.
shares in all   our glad - ness.
place where he has   gone.

Text: Cecil Frances Alexander, 1818-1895
Tune: IRBY, 8 7 8 7 77; Henry J. Gauntlett, 1805-1876; harm. by Arthur H. Mann, 1850-1929. © 1957, Novello and Co. Ltd.

527 Virgin-born, We Bow before You

1. Vir - gin - born, we bow be - fore you: Bless - ed was the
2. Bless - ed she by all cre - a - tion, Who brought forth the

womb that bore you; Mar - y, Moth - er meek and mild,
world's sal -va - tion. Bless - ed they who ev - er blest,

Bless - ed was she in her Child. Bless - ed
Love you most and serve you best. Vir - gin -

was the breast that fed you; Bless - ed was the
born, we bow be - fore you; Bless - ed was the

hand that led you; Bless - ed was the moth - er's
womb that bore you; Mar - y, Moth - er meek and

eye Watch - ing o'er your in - fan - cy.
mild, Bless - ed was she in her Child.

Text: Reginald Herber, 1783-1826, alt.
Tune: MON DIEU PRETE-MOI L'OREILLE, 88 77 D; attr. to Louis Bourgeois, c.1510-1561; harm. by Claude Goudimel, 1505-1572, alt.

528 Sing of Mary, Meek and Lowly

1. Sing of Mar - y meek and low - ly, Vir - gin - moth - er
2. Sing of Je - sus, son of Mar - y, In the home at
3. Glo - ry be to God the Fa - ther; Glo - ry be to

pure and mild, Sing of God's own Son most ho - ly,
Naz - a - reth. Toil and la - bor can - not wea - ry
God the Son; Glo - ry be to God the Spir - it;

Who be - came her lit - tle child. Fair - est child of
Love en - dur - ing un - to death. Con - stant was the
Glo - ry to the Three in One. From the heart of

fair - est moth-er, God the Lord who came to earth,
love he gave her, Though he went forth from her side,
bless - ed Mar - y, From all saints the song as - cends,

Word made flesh, our ver - y broth - er,
Forth to preach, and heal, and suf - fer,
And the church the strain re - ech - oes

Takes our na - ture by his birth.
Till on Cal - va - ry he died.
Un - to earth's re - mot - est ends.

Text: Roland F. Palmer, 1891-1985
Tune: PLEADING SAVIOR, 8 7 8 7 D; *Christian Lyre*, 1830; harm. by Richard Proulx, b.1937. © 1986, GIA Publications, Inc.

Songs of Thankfulness and Praise   529

1. Songs of thank-ful - ness and praise, Je - sus, Lord, to
2. Man - i - fest at Jor - dan's stream, Proph-et, Priest, and
3. Man - i - fest in mak - ing whole Pal - sied limbs and
4. Grant us grace to see you, Lord, Mir - rored in your

you we raise, Man - i - fest - ed by the star
King su-preme; And at Ca - na, wed - ding guest,
faint - ing soul; Man - i - fest in val - iant fight,
ho - ly word; May we im - i - tate you now,

To the sag - es from a - far; Branch of roy - al
In your God - head man - i - fest; Man - i - fest in
Quell - ing all the dev - il's might; Man - i - fest in
And on us your grace en - dow; That we like to

Da - vid's stem In your birth at Beth - le - hem;
pow'r di - vine, Chang - ing wa - ter in - to wine;
gra - cious will, Ev - er bring - ing good from ill;
you may be At your great e - piph - a - ny;

Anthems be to you ad - drest, God in flesh made man - i - fest.
Anthems be to you ad - drest, God in flesh made man - i - fest.
Anthems be to you ad - drest, God in flesh made man - i - fest.
And may praise you ev - er blest, God in flesh made man - i - fest.

Text: Christopher Wordsworth, 1807-1885
Tune: SALZBURG, 77 77 D; Jakob Hintze, 1622-1702, alt; harm. by J.S. Bach, 1685-1750

530 What Child Is This

1. What child is this, who, laid to rest, On
2. Why lies he in such mean es - tate Where
3. So bring him in - cense, gold and myrrh, Come

Mar - y's lap is sleep - ing? Whom an - gels greet with
ox and ass are feed - ing? Good Chris - tian, fear; for
peas - ant, king to own him; The King of kings sal -

an - thems sweet, While shep - herds watch are keep - ing?
sin - ners here The si - lent Word is plead - ing.
va - tion brings, Let lov - ing hearts en - throne him.

This, this is Christ the King, Whom shep - herds guard and an - gels sing;

Haste, haste to bring him laud, The babe, the son of Mar - y.

Text: William C. Dix, 1827-1898
Tune: GREENSLEEVES, 8 7 8 7 with refrain; English Melody, 16th C.; harm. by John Stainer, 1840-1901

531 What Star Is This

1. What star is this with beams so bright, More love-ly
than the noon-day light? 'Tis sent to an-nounce a
new-born king, Glad tid-ings of our God to bring.

2. 'Tis now ful-filled what God de-creed, "From Ja-cob
shall a star pro-ceed"; And lo! the east-ern
sag-es stand, To read in heaven the Lord's com-mand.

3. O Je-sus, while the star of grace Im-pels us
on to seek your face, Let not our sloth-ful
hearts re-fuse The guid-ance of your light to use.

4. To God Cre-a-tor, heav'n-ly light, To Christ, revealed in earth-ly night, To God the Spir-it
blest we raise An end-less song of thank-ful praise!

Text: *Quem stella sole pulchrior*, Charles Coffin, 1676-1749; tr. by John Chandler, 1806-1876, alt.
Tune: PUER NOBIS, LM; adapt. by Michael Praetorius, 1571-1621

Sion, Sing 532

Refrain
Cantor, then all:

Si - on, sing, break in - to song!

For with - in you is the Lord with sav - ing pow'r.

Verses
Cantor:

1. Rise and shine forth, for your   light   has come,
2. Wonder and thanksgiving   shall fill your heart,

and upon you breaks the glory   of   the   Lord;
As the wealth of nations en - rich - es   you;

For the   darkness   covers the   earth,
You shall be   called the   City of the   Lord,

D.C.

and the   thick   clouds, the   peo - ple.
Dear to   the   Holy One of   Is - ra - el.

Text: Refrain, Zephaniah 3:14-17, Luke 1:28-35; verses, Isaiah 60:1-5, 14
Music: Lucien Deiss, CSSp, b.1921
© 1965, World Library Publications, Inc.

533 Brightest and Best

1. Bright - est and best of the stars of the morn - ing,
2. Cold on his cra - dle the dew - drops are shin - ing,
3. Shall we then yield him, in cost - ly de - vo - tion,
4. Vain - ly we of - fer each am - ple o - bla - tion,
5. Bright - est and best of the stars of the morn - ing,

Dawn on our dark - ness, and lend us thine aid;
Low lies his head with the beasts of the stall;
O - dors of E - dom, and of - f'rings di - vine,
Vain - ly with gifts would his fa - vor se - cure,
Dawn on our dark - ness, and lend us thine aid;

Star of the east, the ho - ri - zon a - dorn - ing,
An - gels a - dore him in slum - ber re - clin - ing,
Gems of the moun - tain, and pearls of the o - cean,
Rich - er by far is the heart's ad - o - ra - tion,
Star of the east, the ho - ri - zon a - dorn - ing,

Guide where our in - fant Re - deem - er is laid.
Mak - er and Mon - arch and Sav - ior of all.
Myrrh from the for - est, and gold from the mine?
Dear - er to God are the pray'rs of the poor.
Guide where our in - fant Re - deem - er is laid.

Bright-est and best of the stars of the morn-ing, Dawn on our

dark - ness, and lend us thine aid; Star of the east, the ho -

ri - zon a - dorn - ing, Guide where our in - fant Re - deem-er is laid.

Text: Reginald Heber, 1783-1826, alt.
Tune: STAR IN THE EAST, 11 10 11 10 with refrain; *Southern Harmony,* 1835; harm. by Marty Haugen, b.1950, © 1987, GIA Publications, Inc.

As with Gladness Men of Old 534

1. As with glad-ness men of old Did the guid-ing
2. As with joy-ful steps they sped To that low-ly
3. As they of-fered gifts most rare At that man-ger
4. Christ Re-deem-er, with us stay, Help us live your
5. In the heav'n-ly cit-y bright None shall need cre-

star be-hold; As with joy they hailed its light,
man-ger-bed, There to bend the knee be-fore
crude and bare; So may we this ho-ly day,
ho-ly way; And when earth-ly things are past,
a-ted light; You, its light, its joy, its crown,

Lead-ing on-ward, beam-ing bright; So, most gra-cious
Christ whom heav'n and earth a-dore; So may we with
Drawn to you with-out de-lay, All our cost-liest
Bring our ran-somed souls at last Where they need no
You, its sun which goes not down; There for ev-er

Lord, may we Ev-er-more your splen-dor see.
hur-ried pace Run to seek your throne of grace.
treas-ures bring, Christ, to you, our heav'n-ly King.
star to guide, Where no clouds your glo-ry hide.
may we sing Al-le-lu-ias to our King.

Text: William C. Dix, 1837-1898
Tune: DIX, 77 77 77; arr. from Conrad Kocher, 1786-1872, by William H. Monk, 1823-1889

535 We Three Kings of Orient Are

1. We three kings of O - ri - ent are,
2. Born a babe on Beth - le - hem's plain,
3. Frank - in - cense to of - fer have I;
4. Myrrh is mine: its bit - ter per - fume
5. Glo - rious now be - hold him rise,

Bear - ing gifts we trav - erse a - far
Gold we bring to crown him a - gain;
In - cense owns a De - i - ty nigh,
Breathes a life of gath - 'ring gloom;
King and God and sac - ri - fice:

Field and foun - tain, Moor and
King for - ev - er, Ceas - ing
Prayer and prais - ing Glad - ly
Sor - rowing, sigh - ing, Bleed - ing
Heav'n sings, "Hal - le - lu - jah!"

moun - tain, Fol - low - ing yon - der star.
nev - er, O - ver us all to reign.
rais - ing, Wor - ship - ing God on high.
dy - ing, Sealed in the stone cold tomb.
"Hal - le - lu - jah!" earth re - plies.

O star of won - der, star of night, Star with

roy - al beau - ty bright, West - ward lead - ing,

still pro - ceed - ing, Guide us to the per - fect Light.

Text: Matthew 2:1-11; John H. Hopkins, Jr., 1820-1891
Tune: KINGS OF ORIENT, 88 44 6 with refrain; John H. Hopkins, Jr., 1820-1891

536   Lord, Today

Refrain

Lord, to - day we have seen your glo - ry, dawn
fol - lows the night. We, your peo - ple who
walked in dark - ness now have seen a great light.

To verses   Last time

Verses

1. A child is born, a Son giv - en us,
2. The Lord is king, the na - tions re - joice,
3. O Beth - le - hem, you are from of old,
4. The days will come, the Lord prom - ised us,
5. New light has dawned up - on all the just,

on him do - min - ion shall rest.
let all God's peo - ple be glad.
too small a - mong Ju - dah's clans.
when God would raise up a shoot
glad - ness for up - right of heart.

His name shall
The heav - ens pro -
From you shall
to rule the
Re - joice in the

Melody:

be Won - der - ful God,
claim jus - tice for all.
come a rul - er this day,
land, reign as a king,
Lord, you faith - ful ones.

Coun - sel - or,
Glo - ry has
shep - herd to
whose name is
Give thanks to

Harmony:

D.C.

Prince of Peace.
filled the land.
guide the land.
Lord the Just.
God's great name.

Text: Mike Balhoff, b.1946
Tune: Darryl Ducote, b.1945, Gary Daigle, b.1957
© 1978, Damean Music. Distributed by GIA Publications, Inc.

537 The First Nowell

1. The first Now - ell, the an - gel did say, Was to
2. They look - ed up and saw a star Shin - ing
3. And by the light of that same star Three
4. This star drew nigh to the north - west, O'er
5. Then en - tered in those wise men three, Full
6. Then let us all with one ac - cord Sing

cer - tain poor shep-herds in fields as they lay; In
in the east, be - yond them far, And
wise men came from coun - try far; To
Beth - le - hem it took its rest; And
rev - 'rent - ly up - on their knee, And
prais - es to our heav - 'nly Lord; Who

fields where they lay keep-ing their sheep, On a
to the earth it gave great light, And
seek for a king was their in - tent, And to
there it did both stop and stay, Right
of - fered there, in his pres - ence, Their
with the Fa - ther we a - dore And

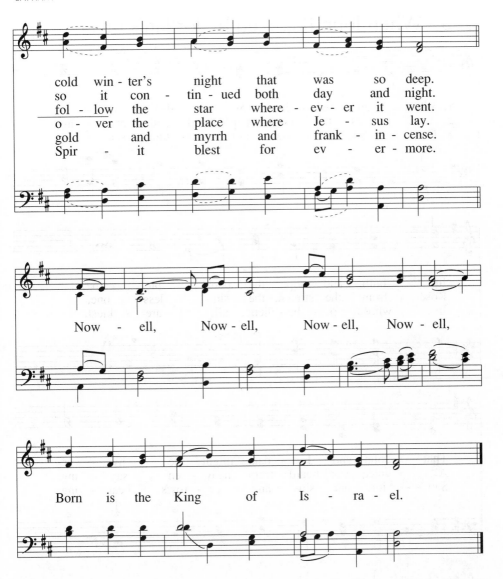

cold win - ter's night that was so deep.
so it con - tin - ued both day and night.
fol - low the star where - ev - er it went.
o - ver the place where Je - sus lay.
gold and myrrh and frank - in - cense.
Spir - it blest for ev - er - more.

Now - ell, Now - ell, Now - ell, Now - ell,

Born is the King of Is - ra - el.

Text: English Carol, 17th C.
Tune: THE FIRST NOWELL, Irregular; English Melody; harm. from *Christmas Carols New and Old*, 1871

538 When John Baptized by Jordan's River

1. When John bap - tized by Jor - dan's riv - er
2. There as the Lord, bap - tized and pray - ing,
3. O Son of Man, our na - ture shar - ing,

In faith and hope the peo - ple came,
Rose from the stream, the sin - less one,
In whose o - be - dience all are blest,

That John and Jor - dan might de - liv - er
A voice was heard from heav - en say - ing,
Sav - ior, our sins and sor - rows bear - ing,

Their trou - bled souls from sin and shame.
"This is my own be - lov - ed Son."
Hear us and grant us this re - quest:

They came to seek a new be - gin - ning,
There as the Fa - ther's word was spo - ken,
Dai - ly to grow, by grace de - fend - ed,

The hu - man spir - it's age - less quest,
Not in the pow'r of wind and flame,
Filled with the Spir - it from a - bove;

Re - pent - ance, and an end of sin - ning,
But of his love and peace the to - ken,
In Christ bap - tized, be - loved, be - friend - ed,

Re - nounc - ing ev - 'ry wrong con - fessed.
Seen as a dove, the Spir - it came.
Chil - dren of God in peace and love.

Text: Timothy Dudley-Smith, b.1926, © 1984, Hope Publishing Co.
Tune: RENDEZ À DIEU, 9 8 9 8 D; Louis Bourgeois, c.1510-1561

539 Dust and Ashes

lead us through the des - ert sands,

lead us, lead us through the des - ert

bring us liv - ing wa - ter,

sands, bring us liv - ing

Ho - ly Spir - it, come.

wa - ter, Ho - ly Spir - it, come.

1.-2. 3.

Text: Brian Wren, b.1936, © 1989, Hope Publishing Co.
Tune: David Haas, b.1957, © 1991, GIA Publications, Inc.

540 Seek the Lord

Refrain

Descant:

Seek the Lord while he may be found;

Melody:

Seek the Lord while he may be found;

Bass:

call to him while he is still near.

1.- 3. | Last time

call to him while he is still near.

call to him while he is still near.

Verses 1, 2

Melody:

1. To - day is the day and now the pro- per hour to for-
2. As high as the sky is a - bove the earth, so

Harmony:

sake our sin - ful lives and turn to the Lord.
high a- bove our ways, the ways of the Lord.

D.C.

Verse 3

3. Find-ing the Lord, let us cling to him. His words, his ways lead us to life.

Verse 4

4. Some day we'll live in the house of God; gaze on his face and praise his name.

Text: Isaiah 55:6-9; Roc O'Connor, SJ, b.1949
Tune: Roc O'Connor, SJ, b.1949; arr. by Peter Felice, alt.
© 1976, Robert F. O'Connor, SJ, and New Dawn Music

541   Tree of Life

1. Tree   of   Life   and   awe - some   mys - t'ry,   In   your
2. Seed   that   dies   to   rise   in   glo - ry,   May   we
3. We   re - mem - ber   truth   once   spo - ken,   Love passed
4. Gen - tle   Je - sus,   might - y   Spir - it,   Come   in -
*5. Christ, you   lead   and   we   shall   fol - low,   Stum - bling

death   we   are   re - born,   Though you   die   in   all   of
see   our - selves   in   you,   If   we   learn   to   live your
on   through act   and   word,   Ev - 'ry   per - son lost and
flame   our   hearts   a - new,   We   may   all   your joy in -
though our   steps   may   be,   One   with   you   in   joy and

his - t'ry,   Still   you   rise with   ev - 'ry   morn,   Still   you
sto - ry,   We   may   die to   rise   a - new,   We   may
bro - ken   Wears the   bod - y   of   our   Lord,   Wears the
her - it   If   we   bear the   cross with   you,   If   we
sor - row,   We   the   riv - er,   you   the   sea,   We   the

Last time

rise with ev - 'ry   morn.
die to rise a -   new.
bod - y   of   our   Lord.
bear the cross with   you.
riv - er, you the   sea.

The refrain "Adoramus Te Christe" can be used as a descant to the final stanza of this hymn.

Lenten Verses:

General: Light of life beyond conceiving, Mighty Spirit of our Lord;
Give new strength to our believing, Give us faith to live your word.

1st Sunday: From the dawning of creation, You have loved us as your own;
Stay with us through all temptation, Make us turn to you alone.

2nd Sunday: In our call to be a blessing, May we be a blessing true;
May we live and die confessing Christ as Lord of all we do.

3rd Sunday: Living Water of salvation, Be the fountain of each soul;
Springing up in new creation, Flow in us and make us whole.

4th Sunday: Give us eyes to see you clearly, Make us children of your light;
Give us hearts to live more nearly As your gospel shining bright.

5th Sunday: God of all our fear and sorrow, God who lives beyond our death;
Hold us close through each tomorrow, Love as near as every breath.

Text: Marty Haugen, b.1950
Tune: THOMAS, 8 7 8 77; Marty Haugen, b.1950
© 1984, GIA Publications, Inc.

Adoramus Te Christe 542

* *This refrain can be used as descant to the final verse of "Tree of Life."*

Text: Antiphon from Good Friday Liturgy; *We adore you, O Christ, and we bless you, because by your holy cross you have redeemed the world.*
Tune: Marty Haugen, b.1950, © 1984, GIA Publications, Inc.

543 By the Babylonian Rivers

1. By the Bab-y-lo-nian riv-ers We sat
2. There our cap-tors in de-ri-sion Did re-
3. How shall we sing the Lord's song In a
4. Let the Cross be ben-e-dic-tion For those

down in grief and wept; Hung our harps up-on the
quire of us a song; So we sat with star-ing
strange and bit-ter land; Can our voic-es veil the
bound in tyr-an-ny; By the power of res-ur-

wil-low, Mourned for Zi-on when we slept.
vi-sion, And the days were hard and long.
sor-row? Lord God, hold your ho-ly band.
rec-tion Loose them from cap-tiv-i-ty.

Text: Psalm 137; Ewald Bash, b.1924
Tune: KAS DZIEDAJA, 8 7 8 7; Latvian Folk Melody; acc. by Robert J. Batastini, b.1942, © 1995, GIA Publications, Inc.

544 O Sun of Justice

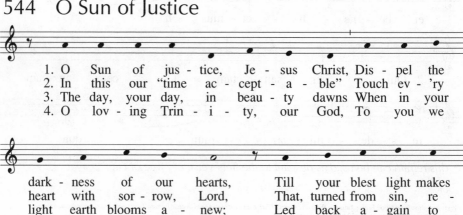

1. O Sun of jus-tice, Je-sus Christ, Dis-pel the
2. In this our "time ac-cept-a-ble" Touch ev-'ry
3. The day, your day, in beau-ty dawns When in your
4. O lov-ing Trin-i-ty, our God, To you we

dark-ness of our hearts, Till your blest light makes
heart with sor-row, Lord, That, turned from sin, re-
light earth blooms a-new; Led back a-gain to
bow through end-less days, And in your grace new-

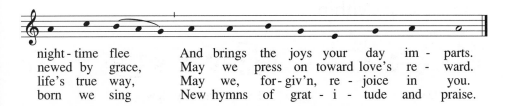

night - time flee	And	brings	the	joys	your	day	im -	parts.
newed by grace,	May	we	press	on	toward	love's	re -	ward.
life's true way,	May	we,	for-giv'n,	re -	joice	in	you.
born we sing	New	hymns	of	grat - i -	tude	and	praise.

Text: *Jam Christe sol justitiae;* Latin, 6th C.; tr. by Peter J. Scagnelli, b.1949, ©
Tune: JESU DULCIS MEMORIA, LM; Mode I; acc. by Richard Proulx, b.1937, © 1975, GIA Publications, Inc.

The Glory of These Forty Days   545

1. The	glo -	ry	of	these	for -	ty	days	We
2. A -	lone	and	fast -	ing,	Mo -	ses	saw	The
3. So	Dan -	iel	trained	his	mys -	tic	sight,	De -
4. Then	grant	that	we	like	them	be	true,	Con -

cel - e - brate with	songs	of	praise;	For	Christ,	by	whom	all
lov - ing God who	gave	the	law;	And	to	E -	li -	jah,
liv - ered from the	li - on's might;	And	John,	the	Bride-groom's
sumed in fast and	prayer	with	you;	Our	spir -	its	strength-en

things	were	made,	Him -	self	has	fast - ed	and	has prayed.
fast -	ing,	came	The	steeds	and	char - i -	ots	of flame.
friend,	be -	came	The	her -	ald	of Mes -	si -	ah's name.
with	your	grace,	And	give	us	joy	to	see your face.

Text: *Clarum decus jejunii;* ascr. to Gregory the Great, c.540-604; tr. by Maurice F. Bell, 1862-1947, © Oxford University Press
Tune: ERHALT UNS HERR, LM; Klug's *Geistliche Lieder,* 1543; harm. by J.S. Bach, 1685-1750

546 Deep Within

Refrain

Deep with-in I will plant my law,
not on stone, but in your heart.
Fol-low me, I will bring you back, you will
be my own, and I will be your God.

Verses

1. I will give you a new heart, a new spir - it with-
2. Seek my face, and see your
3. Re - turn to me, with all your

D. C.

in you, for I will be your strength.
God, for I will be your hope.
heart, and I will bring you back.

Text: Jeremiah 31:33, Ezekiel 36:26, Joel 2:12; David Haas, b.1957
Tune: David Haas, b.1957; acc. by Jeanne Cotter, b.1964
© 1987, GIA Publications, Inc.

Somebody's Knockin' at Your Door 547

Some-bod - y's knock-in' at your door; Some-bod - y's knock-in' at your door; O sin-ner, why don't you an-swer? Some-bod - y's knock-in' at your door.

Solo:
1. Knocks like Je - sus,
2. Can't you hear him?
3. Je - sus calls you,
4. Can't you trust him?

All:
Some-bod - y's knock-in' at your door.

Solo:
Knocks like Je - sus,
Can't you hear him?
Je - sus calls you,
Can't you trust him?

All:
Some-bod - y's knock-in' at your door.

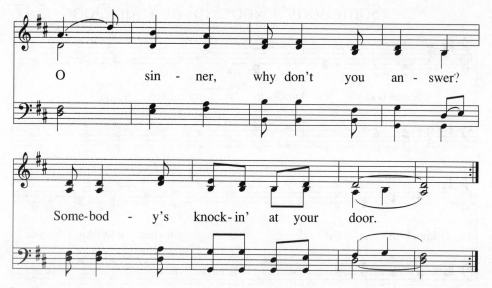

O sin - ner, why don't you an - swer?

Some-bod - y's knock- in' at your door.

Text: African-American spiritual
Tune: SOMEBODY'S KNOCKIN', Irregular; African-American spiritual; harm. by Richard Proulx, b.1937, © 1986, GIA Publications, Inc.

548 Jesus, Tempted in the Desert

1. Je - sus, tempt - ed in the des - ert,
2. Je - sus, tempt - ed at the tem - ple,
3. Je - sus, tempt - ed on the moun - tain,
4. When we face temp - ta - tion's pow - er,

Lone - ly, hun - gry, filled with dread:
High a - bove its an - cient wall:
By the lure of vast do - main:
Lone - ly, strug - gling, filled with dread,

"Use your pow'r," the tempt - er tells him;
"Throw your - self from loft - y tur - ret;
"Fall be - fore me! Be my ser - vant!
Christ, who knew the tempt - er's ho - ur,

"Turn these bar - ren rocks to bread!"
An - gels wait to break your fall!"
Glo - ry, fame, you're sure to gain!"
Come and be our liv - ing bread.

"Not a - lone by bread," he an - swers,
Je - sus shuns such emp - ty mar - vels,
Je - sus sees the daz - zling vi - sion,
By your grace, pro - tect, pre - serve us

"Can the hu - man heart be filled.
Feats that fick - le crowds re - quest:
Turns his eyes an - oth - er way:
Lest we fall, your trust be - tray.

On - ly by the Word that calls us
"God, whose grace pro - tects, pre - serves us,
"God a - lone de - serves our hom - age!
Yours, a - bove all oth - er voic - es,

Is our deep - est hun - ger stilled!"
We must nev - er vain - ly test."
God a - lone will I o - bey!"
Be the Word we hear, o - bey.

Text: Matthew 4:1-11, Luke 4:1-13; Herman Stuempfle, b.1923, © 1993, GIA Publications, Inc.
Tune: EBENEZER, 8 7 8 7 D; Thomas J. Williams, 1869-1944

549 Parce Domine

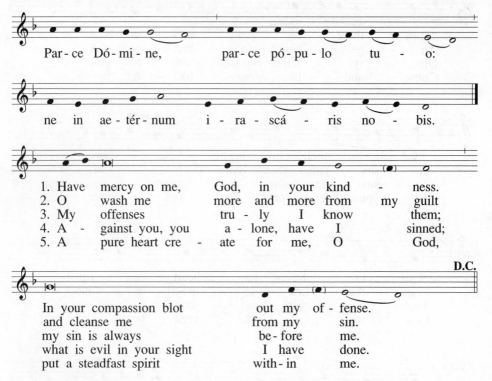

Par - ce Dó - mi - ne, par - ce pó - pu - lo tu - o:

ne in ae - tér - num i - ra - scá - ris no - bis.

1. Have mercy on me, God, in your kind - ness.
2. O wash me more and more from my guilt
3. My offenses tru - ly I know them;
4. A - gainst you, you a - lone, have I sinned;
5. A pure heart cre - ate for me, O God,

D.C.

In your compassion blot out my of - fense.
and cleanse me from my sin.
my sin is always be - fore me.
what is evil in your sight I have done.
put a steadfast spirit with - in me.

Text: *Spare your people, Lord, lest you be angry for ever,* Joel 2:17, Psalm 51:3-6, 12; tr. The Grail, © 1963, GIA Publications, Inc., agent
Tune: PARCE DOMINE, Irregular; Mode I with Tonus Peregrinus; acc. by Robert LeBlanc, OSB, b.1948, © 1986, GIA Publications, Inc.

550 Remember Your Love

Refrain

Descant:

Re - mem - ber your love and your faith - ful - ness, O

Melody:

Lord. Re - mem - ber your peo - ple and have mer - cy on us, Lord. Lord.

To verses | Last time

1. The
2. If you
3. O
4. As
5. Be -

Verses

Lord is my light and my sal - va - tion, whom should I
dwelt, O Lord, up - on our sin - ful-ness, then who could
Lord, hear the sound of my call and an - swer
watch - man who waits up - on the day - light, wait for the
fore all the moun - tains were be - got - ten and earth took

fear? The Lord is my life and my
stand? But with you there is mer - cy and for -
me. My heart cries out for your
Lord. I trust in your kind-ness and re -
shape, e - ven then, O Lord, you were our

D.C.

ref - uge, when I call God hears.
give - ness and a guid - ing hand.
pres - ence; it is you I seek.
demp - tion; and your faith - ful word.
ref - uge through-out ev - 'ry age.

Text: Psalm 27; Mike Balhoff, b.1946
Tune: Darryl Ducote, b.1945, and Gary Daigle, b.1957
© 1978, Damean Music. Distributed by GIA Publications, Inc.

551 At the Cross Her Station Keeping

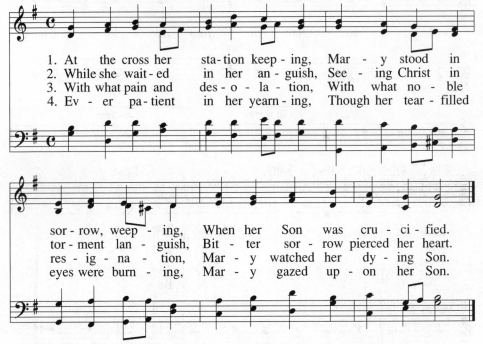

1. At the cross her sta-tion keep-ing, Mar-y stood in
2. While she wait-ed in her an-guish, See-ing Christ in
3. With what pain and des-o-la-tion, With what no-ble
4. Ev-er pa-tient in her yearn-ing, Though her tear-filled

sor-row, weep-ing, When her Son was cru-ci-fied.
tor-ment lan-guish, Bit-ter sor-row pierced her heart.
res-ig-na-tion, Mar-y watched her dy-ing Son.
eyes were burn-ing, Mar-y gazed up-on her Son.

5. Who, that sorrow contemplating,
   On that passion meditating,
      Would not share the Virgin's grief?

6. Christ she saw, for our salvation,
   Scourged with cruel acclamation,
      Bruised and beaten by the rod.

7. Christ she saw with life-blood failing,
   All her anguish unavailing,
      Saw him breathe his very last.

8. Mary, fount of love's devotion,
   Let me share with true emotion
      All the sorrow you endured.

9. Virgin, ever interceding,
   Hear me in my fervent pleading:
      Fire me with your love of Christ.

10. Mother, may this prayer be granted:
    That Christ's love may be implanted
       In the depths of my poor soul.

11. At the cross, your sorrow sharing,
    All your grief and torment bearing,
       Let me stand and mourn with you.

12. Fairest maid of all creation,
    Queen of hope and consolation,
       Let me feel your grief sublime.

13. Virgin, in your love befriend me,
    At the Judgment Day defend me.
       Help me by your constant prayer.

14. Savior, when my life shall leave me
    Through your mother's prayers
       receive me
    With the fruits of victory.

15. Let me to your love be taken,
    Let my soul in death awaken
       To the joys of Paradise.

Text: *Stabat mater dolorosa*; Jacopone da Todi, 1230-1306; trans. by Anthony G. Petti, 1932-1985, © 1971, Faber Music, Ltd.
Tune: STABAT MATER, 88 7; *Mainz Gesangbuch*, 1661; harm. by Richard Proulx, b.1937, © 1986, GIA Publications, Inc.

Hear Us, Almighty Lord / Attende Domine   552

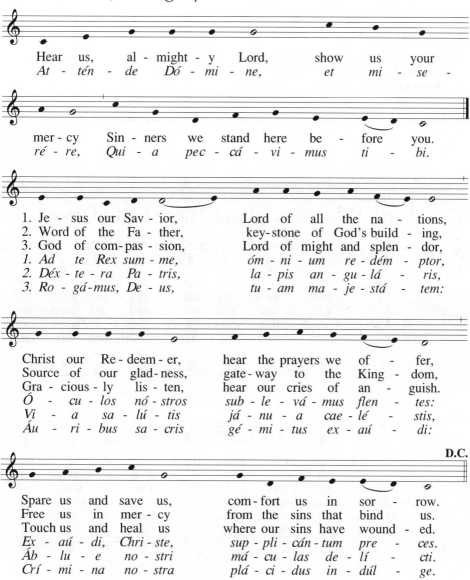

Hear us, al - might - y Lord, show us your
At - tén - de Dó - mi - ne, et mi - se -

mer - cy Sin - ners we stand here be - fore you.
ré - re, Qui - a pec - cá - vi - mus ti - bi.

1. Je - sus our Sav - ior, Lord of all the na - tions,
2. Word of the Fa - ther, key-stone of God's build - ing,
3. God of com-pas - sion, Lord of might and splen - dor,
1. *Ad te Rex sum - me, óm - ni - um re - dém - ptor,*
2. *Déx - te - ra Pa - tris, la - pis an - gu - lá - ris,*
3. *Ro - gá-mus, De - us, tu - am ma - je - stá - tem:*

Christ our Re - deem - er, hear the prayers we of - fer,
Source of our glad-ness, gate-way to the King - dom,
Gra - cious - ly lis - ten, hear our cries of an - guish.
Ó - cu - los nó - stros sub - le - vá - mus flen - tes:
Vi - a sa - lú - tis já - nu - a cae - lé - stis,
Áu - ri - bus sa - cris gé - mi - tus ex - aú - di:

D.C.

Spare us and save us, com - fort us in sor - row.
Free us in mer - cy from the sins that bind us.
Touch us and heal us where our sins have wound - ed.
Ex - aú - di, Chri - ste, sup - pli - cán - tum pre - ces.
Áb - lu - e no - stri má - cu - las de - lí - cti.
Crí - mi - na no - stra plá - ci - dus in - dúl - ge.

4. Humbly confessing that we have offended,
   Stripped of illusions, naked in our sorrow,
   Pardon, Lord Jesus, those your blood has ransomed.

5. Innocent captive, you were led to slaughter,
   Sentenced by sinners when they brought false witness.
   Keep from damnation those your death has rescued.

4. *Tibi fatémur, crímina admíssa:*
   Contríto corde pándimus occúlta:
   Túa redémptor, píetas ignóscat.

5. *Innocens captus, nec repúgnans ductus,*
   Téstibus falsis, pro ímpiis damnátus:
   Quos redemísti, tu consérva, Christe.

Text: Latin, 10th C.; tr. by Ralph Wright, OSB, b.1938, © 1980, ICEL
Tune: ATTENDE DOMINE, 11 11 11 with refrain; Mode V; acc. by Richard Proulx, b.1937, © 1975, GIA Publications, Inc.

553 Lord, Who throughout These Forty Days

1. Lord, who through - out these for - ty days, For us did fast and pray, Teach us to o - ver - come our sins, And close by you to stay.
2. As you with Sa - tan did con - tend, And did the vic - t'ry win, O give us strength in you to fight, In you to con - quer sin.
3. As you did hun - ger and did thirst, So teach us, gra - cious Lord, To die to self, and so to live By your most ho - ly word.
4. And through these days of pen - i - tence, And through your Pas - sion - tide, For ev - er - more, in life and death, O Lord! with us a - bide.
5. A - bide with us, that through this life Of doubts and hope and pain, An East - er of un - end - ing joy We may at last at - tain!

Text: Claudia F. Hernaman, 1838-1898, alt.
Tune: ST. FLAVIAN, CM; *John's Day Psalter*, 1562; harm. based on the original *faux-bourdon* setting

Eternal Lord of Love 554

1. E - ter - nal Lord of love, be - hold your Church,
2. So dai - ly dy - ing to the way of self,
3. If dead in you, so in you we a - rise,

Walk - ing once more the pil - grim way of Lent,
So dai - ly liv - ing to your way of love,
You the first - born of all the faith - ful dead;

Led by your cloud by day, by night your fire,
We walk the road, Lord Je - sus, that you trod,
And as through ston - y ground the green shoots break,

Moved by your love and t'ward your pres - ence bent:
Know - ing our - selves bap - tized in - to your death:
Glo - rious in spring - time dress of leaf and flower,

Far off yet here the goal of all de - sire.
So we are dead and live with you in God.
So in the Fa - ther's glo - ry shall we wake.

Text: Thomas H. Cain, b.1931, © 1982
Tune: FENN HOUSE, 10 10 10 10 10 10; Michael Joncas, b.1951, © 1988, GIA Publications, Inc.

555　Return to God

Refrain

Re - turn to God with all your heart, the source of grace and

mer - cy; come seek the ten - der faith - ful - ness of

1.
God.

2.
Last time
God.

Verse 1

1. Now the time of grace has come, the day of sal -

D.C.

va - tion; come and learn now the way of our God.

Verse 2

2. I will take your heart of stone and place a heart with -

D.C.

in you, a heart of com - pas - sion and love.

Verse 3*

3. If you break the chains of op - pres - sion, if you
if you share your bread with the hun - gry, give pro -
give a shel - ter to the home - less, clothe the

1., 2. | 3.

set the pris - 'ner free;
tec - tion to the lost;
na - ked in your midst, then your light shall break

D.C.

forth like the dawn.

*Soprano alone first time through repeated section, sopranos and tenors second time,
all third time.*

Text: Marty Haugen, b.1950
Tune: Marty Haugen, b.1950
© 1990, 1991, GIA Publications, Inc.

556 This Is the Time

Refrain
Cantor or choir, then all:

This is the time of ful-fill-ment! The reign of God is at hand! hand!

Verses—Cycle A
Cantor or choir:

1st Sun.:	O	live	by the	word	from	the
2nd Sun.:	Come,	be	trans -	formed	by	the
3rd Sun.:	Come,	drink	the	liv -	ing	
4th Sun.:	Come,	o -	pen your	eyes	to	the
5th Sun.:	Be -	lieve	the	prom -	ise	of

mouth of God, the mouth of God.
glo - ry of God, the glo - ry of God.
wa - ter of life, the wa - ter of life.
light of the world, the light of the world.
last - ing life, of last - ing life.

Verses—Cycle B
Cantor or choir:

1st Sun.:	Re -	form	your	lives	and	be -
2nd Sun.:	Come,	be	trans -	formed	by	the
3rd Sun.:	Come	wor -	ship	the Lord	who	was
4th Sun.:	Be -	lieve	in the	name	of	God's
5th Sun.:	O	serve	the	Lord	and	

lieve the Good News, be - lieve the Good News.
glo - ry of God, the glo - ry of God.
raised from the dead, was raised from the dead.
on - ly Son, God's on - ly Son.
fol - low his way, and fol - low his way.

Verses—Cycle C

Cantor or choir:

1st Sun.:	O	live	by	the	word	from	the
2nd Sun.:	Come,	be	trans -	formed	by	the
3rd Sun.:	Re -	form	your	lives,	and	bear
4th Sun.:	Re -	turn	to	the	Lord	with	re -
5th Sun.:	O	turn	from	sin,	and	be

mouth of God, the mouth of God.
glo - ry of God, the glo - ry of God.
fruit in God's sight, bear fruit in God's sight.
pen - tant hearts, re - pen - tant hearts.
filled with new life, be filled with new life.

Final Refrain

+ Assembly:

This is the time of ful - fill - ment! The

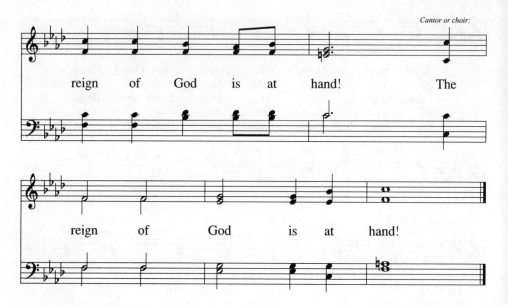

Cantor or choir:

reign of God is at hand! The

reign of God is at hand!

Text: James J. Chepponis, b.1956
Tune: James J. Chepponis, b.1956
© 1994, GIA Publications, Inc.

557 Jesus Walked This Lonesome Valley

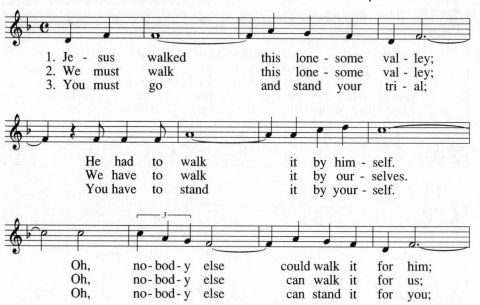

1. Je - sus walked this lone - some val - ley;
2. We must walk this lone - some val - ley;
3. You must go and stand your tri - al;

He had to walk it by him - self.
We have to walk it by our - selves.
You have to stand it by your - self.

Oh, no - bod - y else could walk it for him;
Oh, no - bod - y else can walk it for us;
Oh, no - bod - y else can stand it for you;

He had to walk   it by him - self.
We have to walk   it by our - selves.
You have to stand   it by your - self.

Text: American Folk Hymn
Tune: LONESOME VALLEY, 8 8 10 8; American folk hymn; harm. by Richard Proulx, b.1937, © 1975, GIA Publications, Inc.

Grant to Us, O Lord   558

Refrain
Cantor, then all:

Grant to us, O Lord, a heart re - newed;

re - cre - ate in us your own Spir - it, Lord!

Verse 1
Cantor:

1. Be - hold, the days are com - ing, says the Lord our God, when I will

D.C.

make a new cov-e-nant with the house of Is - ra - el.

Verse 2

2. Deep with - in their be - ing I will im - plant my law; I will write it in their hearts.

D.C.

Verse 3

3. I will be their God, and they shall be my peo-ple.

D.C.

Verse 4

4. And for all their faults I will grant for - give-ness; nev - er - more will I re - mem - ber their sins.

D.C.

Text: Jeremiah 31:31-34
Tune: Lucien Deiss, CSSp, b.1921

Again We Keep This Solemn Fast   559

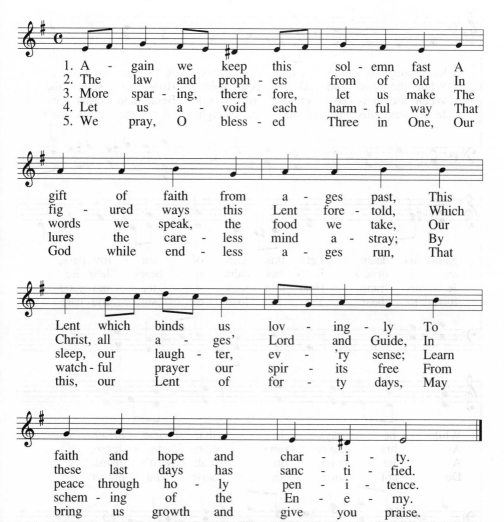

1. A - gain we keep this sol - emn fast A
2. The law and proph - ets from of old In
3. More spar - ing, there - fore, let us make The
4. Let us a - void each harm - ful way That
5. We pray, O bless - ed Three in One, Our

gift of faith from a - ges past, This
fig - ured ways this Lent fore - told, Which
words we speak, the food we take, Our
lures the care - less mind a - stray; By
God while end - less a - ges run, That

Lent which binds us lov - ing - ly To
Christ, all a - ges' Lord and Guide, In
sleep, our laugh - ter, ev - 'ry sense; Learn
watch - ful prayer our spir - its free From
this, our Lent of for - ty days, May

faith and hope and char - i - ty.
these last days has sanc - ti - fied.
peace through ho - ly pen - i - tence.
schem - ing of the En - e - my.
bring us growth and give you praise.

Text: *Ex more docti mystico;* ascr. to Gregory the Great, c.540-604; tr. by Peter J. Scagnelli, b.1949, ©
Tune: ERHALT UNS HERR, LM; Klug's *Geistliche Lieder*, 1543; harm. by J.S. Bach, 1685-1750

560 Stations of the Cross

```
    *  Kneel-ing   in    the     gar - den grass,   Je -  sus   groans   a -
    1. While the  court  and   priests  con - spire  How   to    slant    the
    2. When the   mas - sive  cross  of    wood   Bends and  bruis - es
    3. Je - sus   falls  be - neath  the   weight  Of    the   cross  he's
```

```
    gainst his    death,   Let   this   cup   of    sor -  row pass,
    ev - i - dence         Je -  sus   calm - ly    bears  their ire
    Je - sus' frame        Hear  him   seek  e  -   ter -  nal good
    forced to     bear     Yet   its    load  of    sin    and hate
```

```
    While      he     prays   in          that   same   breath:
    As         his    prayer  grows       more   in  -  tense:
    As         he     prays   in          Yah -  weh's  name:
    Do         not    crush   his         hope   and    prayer:
```

```
    Not        my     will    but    yours    be    done.
```

This stanza begins the devotions. Stanzas 1-14 accompany each station.

1. **Jesus is condemned to death**

2. **Jesus carries his Cross**

3. **Jesus falls the first time**

4. **Jesus meets his afflicted mother**
   Jesus reads in Mary's eyes
   all the sorrow mothers bear,
   and he prays his friend supplies
   grace to strengthen her own prayer:
   > Not my will but yours be done.

5. **Simon of Cyrene helps Jesus to**
   carry his Cross
   We with Simon of Cyrene
   help the Savior bear the cross.
   Step by step we slowly glean
   what true faith and prayer will cost:
   > Not my will but yours be done.

6. **Veronica wipes the face of Jesus**
   Seek the courage and the grace
   that Veronica displays
   when she wipes the bleeding face
   of the one who bravely prays:
   > Not my will but yours be done.

7. **Jesus falls the second time**
   Jesus trips and falls again
   as he struggles through the street
   where the mob's unceasing din
   mocks the prayer his lips repeat:
   > Not my will but yours be done.

8. **Jesus meets the women of Jersusalem**
   Christ directs the women's tears
   toward the coming judgment day
   when God weighs our faithless years
   with our willingness to pray:
   > Not my will but yours be done.

9. **Jesus falls a third time**
   Jesus stumbles one last time
   nearly broken by the load
   yet by prayer finds strength to climb
   Calvary's final stretch of road:
   > Not my will but yours be done.

10. **Jesus is stripped of his clothes**
    Naked to the sun and clouds
    and the jeers and gawking stare
    of the soldiers and the crowds
    Christ continues with his prayer:
    > Not my will but yours be done.

11. **Jesus is nailed to the Cross**
    While the soldiers throw their dice
    they ignore their victim's groans,
    lost to them the sacrifice
    and the prayer that Jesus moans:
    > Not my will but yours be done.

12. **Jesus dies on the Cross**
    Jesus gives one loud last cry
    at the moment of his death
    while his prayer moves heaven's sky
    with his final, parting breath:
    > Not my will but yours be done.

13. **The body of Jesus is taken**
    down from the Cross
    As they take the body down
    and they wrap it in a sheet
    in their hearts they hear the sound
    that his lips no more repeat:
    > Not my will but yours be done.

14. **Jesus is laid in the tomb**
    Quiet is the hollowed cave.
    Peace and tears and grief descend.
    Mourners offer at the grave
    what they learned from Christ their friend:
    > Not my will but yours be done.

Text: Thomas Troeger, © 1993, Oxford University Press
Tune: VIA CRUCIS, 77 77 with refrain; William P. Rowan, © 1995, GIA Publications, Inc.

561 From Ashes to the Living Font

1. From ash - es to the liv - ing font Your
2. Through fast - ing, prayer, and char - i - ty Your
3. *(below)*
4. From ash - es to the liv - ing font, Your

Church must jour - ney, Lord, Bap - tized in grace, in
voice speaks deep with - in, Re - turn - ing us to

Church must jour - ney still, Through cross and tomb to

grace re - newed By your most ho - ly word.
ways of truth And turn - ing us from sin.

Eas - ter joy, In Spir - it - fire ful - filled.

Sundays I & II

3. From desert to the mountaintop
In Christ our way we see,
So, tempered by temptation's might
We might transfigured be.

Sunday IV

3. We sit beside the road and plead,
"Come, save us, David's son!"
Now with your vision heal our eyes,
The world's true Light alone.

Sunday III

3. For thirsting hearts let waters flow
Our fainting souls revive;
And at the well your waters give
Our everlasting life.

Sunday V

3. Our graves split open, bring us back,
Your promise to proclaim;
To darkened tombs call out, "Arise!"
And glorify your name.

Text: Alan J. Hommerding, b.1956, © 1994, World Library Publications, Inc.
Tune: ST. FLAVIAN, CM; *John's Day Psalter*, 1562; harm. based on the original *faux-bourdon* setting

Ride On, Jesus, Ride 562

Ride on, Je - sus, ride. Ride on, Je - sus, ride.
Ride on, Je - sus, con - quering King, Ride on, Je - sus ride.
1. King Je - sus rides on a milk white horse. Ride on, Je - sus,
2. My Je - sus lift - ed his throne a - bove. Ride on, Je - sus,
3. The chil - dren of Je - ru - sa - lem, Ride on, Je - sus,
4. "Bless - ings on the Ho - ly One!" Ride on, Je - sus,
5. Ride so hum - ble, ride so true, Ride on, Je - sus,
6. Ride to set your peo - ple free, Ride on, Je - sus,
7. Ride o - be - dient un - to death, Ride on, Je - sus,
8. Ride a - gain in the hearts of us, Ride on, Je - sus,
9. Now be - yond all time and space, Ride on, Je - sus,
ride. The riv - er Jor - dan he did cross.
ride. See his mer - cy and his love.
ride, strewed their branch - es on his way.
ride. "Bless - ings on the Sav - ing One!"
ride. Ride to bring the world to you, Ride on, Je - sus,
ride. Ride the road to Cal - va - ry,
ride. Ride to break the chains of death,
ride. Ride a - gain in the hands of us,
ride. Now in ev - 'ry land and race,

ride. Ride on, Je-sus, con-quering King. Ride on, Je-sus ride.

Text: African-American spiritual; verses 3-9, Marty Haugen, b.1950, © 1991, GIA Publications, Inc.
Tune: African-American spiritual; harm. by Barbara Jackson Martin, © 1987, GIA Publications, Inc.

563 All Glory, Laud, and Honor

All glo-ry, laud, and hon - or To you, Re-deem-er, King!

To whom the lips of chil - dren Made sweet ho-san-nas ring.

1. You are the King of Is - ra - el, And Da - vid's roy - al Son,
2. The com-pa - ny of an - gels Are prais - ing you on high;
3. The peo-ple of the He - brews With palms be - fore you went:
4. To you be-fore your pas - sion They sang their hymns of praise:
5. Their prais-es you ac - cept - ed, Ac - cept the prayers we bring,

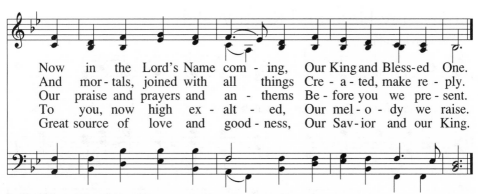

Now   in   the   Lord's Name com - ing,   Our King and Bless-ed   One.
And   mor - tals, joined with   all   things Cre - a - ted, make re - ply.
Our   praise of   prayers and   an - thems Be - fore you   we pre - sent.
To   you, now high   ex - alt - ed,   Our mel - o - dy we raise.
Great source of   love   and   good - ness, Our Sav-ior and our King.

Text: *Gloria, laus et honor*; Theodulph of Orleans, c. 760-821; tr. by John M. Neale, 1818-1866, alt.
Tune: ST. THEODULPH, 7 6 7 6 D; Melchior Teschner, 1584-1635

Jesu, Jesu   564

Refrain

Je - su   Je - su   fill   us with your love, show

us how to serve   the   neigh - bors we have   from you.

Verses

1. Kneels   at   the   feet   of   his   friends,
2. Neigh - bors   are   rich   and   poor,
3. These   are   the   ones   we   should   serve,
4. Kneel   at   the   feet   of   our   friends,

Si - lent - ly   wash - es   their   feet,
Neigh-bors   are   black   and   white,
These are   the   ones   we   should   love.
Si - lent - ly   wash - ing   their   feet,

D.C.

Mas - ter   who pours out him - self   for   them.
Neigh-bors are   near   and   far   a - way.
All   are   neigh-bors to   us   and   you.
This is   the   way   we should   live   with   you.

Text: John 13:3-5; Ghana folk song; tr. by Tom Colvin, b.1925
Tune: CHEREPONI, Irregular; Ghana folk song; Tom Colvin, b.1925; acc. by Jane M. Marshall, b.1924, © 1982, Hope Publishing Co.

565 Stay Here and Keep Watch

Ostinato Refrain

Stay here and keep watch with me. The hour has come.

Stay here and keep watch with me. Watch and pray.

Verses

Cantor:

1. My heart is near-ly bro-ken with sor - row. Re-main here, re - main here and stay a-wake with me.

2. Fa - ther, if it is pos - si - ble, let this cup pass me by.

3. Fa - ther, if this can not pass me by with-out my drink-ing it, then your will be done.

Text: from Matthew 26; Taizé Community
Tune: Jacques Berthier, 1923-1994
© 1984, Les Presses de Taizé, GIA Publications, Inc., agent

Jesus Took a Towel 566

Refrain

Je-sus took a tow-el and he gird-ed him-self, Then he

washed my feet, yes, he washed my feet, Je-sus took a ba-sin and he

knelt him-self down, And he washed, yes, he washed my feet.

Verses 1,2

1. The heav-ens are the Lord's, and the earth is his, The
2. The hour had come, the Pasch was near;

clouds are his char-iot, glo-ry his cloak; He
Je-sus loved his own, loved them to the end. O

made the moun-tains, set the lim-its of the sea; And he
Lord, let me see, let me un-der-stand Why you

D.C.

stooped and washed my feet.
stooped and washed my feet.

Verses 3-5

3. Je-sus came to Pe-ter;
4. Je-sus said to Pe-ter, "Don't you
5. He is King of kings and

Peter said to him, "Do you wash my feet? Lord, do you
un - der - stand? If you want to be mine, I must
Lord of lords, Who dwells in light in - ac -

wash my feet?" Je - sus knelt down, but
wash your feet." "Then not just my feet, but my
ces - si - ble; No one has seen him where he

D.C.

Pe - ter cried out, "Lord, you'll nev - er wash my feet!"
head and my hands! O Lord, I want to be yours."
sits on high, Yet he stooped to wash my feet.

Verses 6-9

6. "Do you know, lit - tle chil - dren, what I've
7. Now friends, let's be glad, let our
8. Who is like you, Lord, now en -
9. O the path is rug - ged, and the

done for you? You call me Mas - ter, and you
joy be full. For God is love, and he a -
throned on high, Where you look up - on the heav - ens and the
go - ing is rough, The jour - ney is long to our

call me Lord. If I am your Mas - ter, and if
bides in us. He washed our feet, he
earth be - low? Be - fore your face the earth
heav'n - ly home, Our feet are wea - ry and

D.C.

I am your Lord, Then, what I've done, you must do."
wash - es them still When we do what he once did.
trem - bles and quakes, Yet you stoop to wash my feet!
cov - ered with mud, So the Lord still wash - es our feet.

Text: John 13; Chrysogonus Waddell, OSCO, b.1930
Tune: JESUS TOOK A TOWEL, Irregular; Chrysogonus Waddell, OCSO, b.1930

All You Who Pass This Way 567

Refrain

All you who pass this way, look and see. see.

Verse 1
1. Is an-y sor-row like the sor-row that af-flicts me?

Verse 2
2. Wom-en of Je-ru-sa-lem! Do not weep for me, but for your-selves, and for your chil-dren.

Verse 3
3. Fa-ther, for-give them! They know not what they do.

Verse 4
4. My God, my God, why have you a-ban-doned me?

Verse 5
5. To-day you will be with me in par-a-dise.

Verse 6
6. I am thirst-y.

Verse 7
7. Fa-ther, in-to your hands I com-mend my spir-it.

Text: From the Passion Gospels; Taizé Community, 1984
Tune: Jacques Berthier, 1923-1994
© 1984, Les Presses de Taizé, GIA Publications, Inc., agent

568 Calvary

Refrain

Cal - va - ry, Cal - va - ry, Cal - va -
ry, Cal - va - ry, Cal - va - ry,
Cal - va - ry, Sure - ly he died on Cal - va - ry.

Verses

1. Ev - 'ry time I think a - bout Je - sus, Ev - 'ry
2. Sin - ner, do you love my Je - sus? Sin - ner,
3. We are climb - ing Ja - cob's lad - der, We are
4. Ev - 'ry round goes high - er and high - er, Ev - 'ry

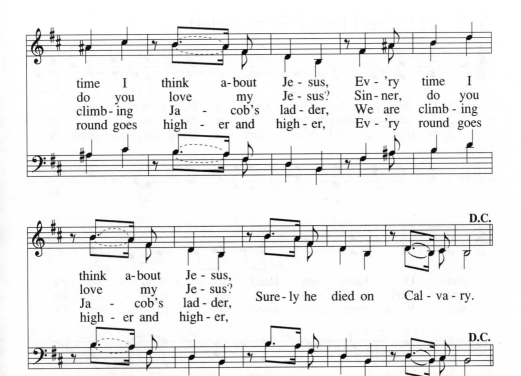

time I   think a-bout   Je - sus,   Ev - 'ry   time   I
do   you   love   my   Je - sus?   Sin - ner,   do   you
climb - ing   Ja - cob's   lad - der,   We are   climb - ing
round goes   high - er and   high - er,   Ev - 'ry   round goes

think   a-bout   Je - sus,
love   my   Je - sus?
Ja - cob's   lad - der,   Sure - ly he   died on   Cal - va - ry.
high - er and   high - er,

Text: African-American spiritual
Tune: African-American spiritual

569 O Sacred Head Surrounded

1. O Sa - cred Head sur - round - ed By crown of pierc - ing
2. I see your strength and vig - or All fad - ing in the
3. In this, your bit - ter pas - sion, Good Shep - herd, think of

thorn! O bleed - ing Head, so wound - ed, Re -
strife, And death with cru - el rig - or, Be -
me With your most sweet com - pas - sion, Un -

viled and put to scorn! The pow'r of death comes
reav - ing you of life; O ag - o - ny and
worth - y though I be: Be - neath your cross a -

o'er you, The glow of life de - cays, Yet
dy - ing! O love to sin - ners free! Je -
bid - ing For ev - er would I rest, In

an - gel hosts a - dore you, And trem - ble as they gaze.
sus, all grace sup - ply - ing, O turn your face on me.
your dear love con - fid - ing, And with your pres - ence blest.

Text: *Salve caput cruentatum;* ascr. to Bernard of Clairvaux, 1091-1153; tr. by Henry Baker, 1821-1877
Tune: PASSION CHORALE, 7 6 7 6 D; Hans Leo Hassler, 1564-1612; harm. by J. S. Bach, 1685-1750

570 Were You There

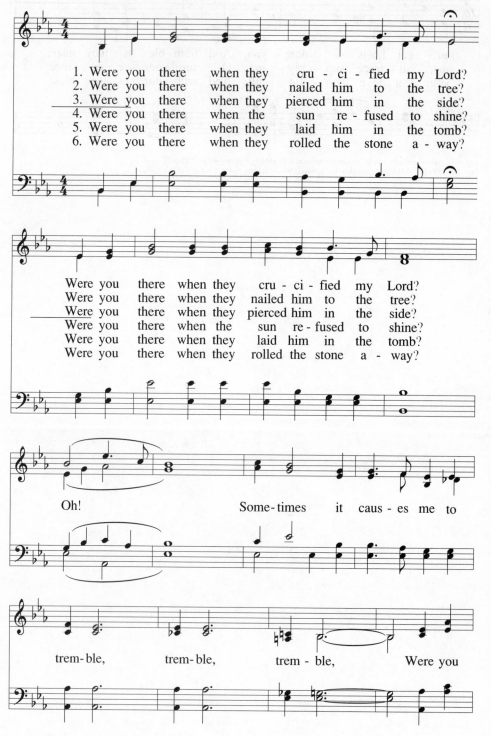

1. Were you there when they cru - ci - fied my Lord?
2. Were you there when they nailed him to the tree?
3. Were you there when they pierced him in the side?
4. Were you there when the sun re - fused to shine?
5. Were you there when they laid him in the tomb?
6. Were you there when they rolled the stone a - way?

Were you there when they cru - ci - fied my Lord?
Were you there when they nailed him to the tree?
Were you there when they pierced him in the side?
Were you there when the sun re - fused to shine?
Were you there when they laid him in the tomb?
Were you there when they rolled the stone a - way?

Oh! Some - times it caus - es me to

trem - ble, trem - ble, trem - ble, Were you

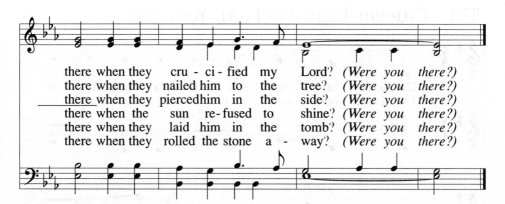

there when they cru - ci - fied my Lord? *(Were you there?)*
there when they nailed him to the tree? *(Were you there?)*
there when they pierced him in the side? *(Were you there?)*
there when the sun re - fused to shine? *(Were you there?)*
there when they laid him in the tomb? *(Were you there?)*
there when they rolled the stone a - way? *(Were you there?)*

Text: African-American spiritual
Tune: WERE YOU THERE, 10 10 with refrain; African-American spiritual; harm. by Robert J. Batastini, b.1942, © 1987, GIA Publications, Inc.

571 Crucem Tuam / O Lord, Your Cross

Cru - cem tu - am a - do - ra - mus Do - mi -
O Lord, your cross, we a - dore and glo - ri -

ne, re - sur - re - cti - o - nem tu - am lau - da - mus Do - mi -
fy, for your ho - ly res - ur - rec - tion, we praise you Lord of

ne. Lau - da - mus et glo - ri - fi - ca - mus.
life. We praise you and we glo - ri - fy you.

Re - sur - re - cti - o - nem tu - am lau - da - mus Do - mi - ne.
For your ho - ly res - ur - rec - tion, we praise you Lord of life.

Text: Taizé Community, 1991
Tune: Jacques Berthier, 1923-1994
© 1991, Les Presses de Taizé, GIA Publications, Inc., agent

My Song Is Love Unknown 572

1. My song is love un - known, My Sav - ior's love for me, Love to the love - less shown That they might love - ly be. O
2. He came from his blest throne, Sal - va - tion to be - stow, But all made strange, and none The longed - for Christ would know. But
3. Some - times they strew his way And his sweet prais - es sing, Re - sound - ing all the day Ho - san - nas to their King. Then
4. Why, what has my Lord done'? What makes this rage and spite? He made the lame to run, He gave the blind their sight. Sweet
5. They rise and needs will have My dear Lord made a - way; A mur - der - er they save: The prince of life they slay. Yet
6. In life, no house, no home My Lord on earth might have; In death, no friend - ly tomb But what a stran - ger gave. What
7. Here might I stay and sing, No sto - ry so di - vine; Nev - er was love, dear King, Nev - er was grief like thine. This

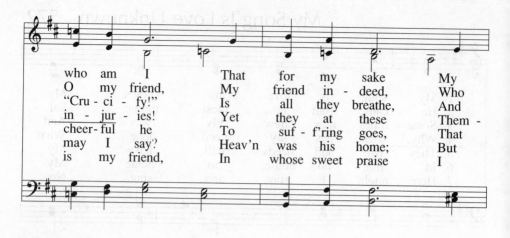

who am I   That for my sake   My
O my friend,   My friend in - deed,   Who
"Cru - ci - fy!" Is all they breathe, And
in - jur - ies! Yet they at these   Them -
cheer- ful he   To suf - f'ring goes,   That
may I say?   Heav'n was his home;   But
is my friend,   In whose sweet praise   I

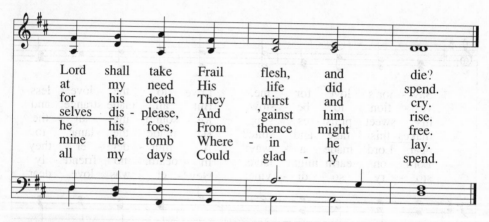

Lord shall take   Frail flesh, and   die?
at my need   His life did   spend.
for his death   They thirst and   cry.
selves dis - please, And 'gainst him   rise.
he his foes,   From thence might   free.
mine the tomb   Where - in he   lay.
all my days   Could glad - ly   spend.

Text: Samuel Crossman, c.1624-1683
Tune: LOVE UNKNOWN, 6 6 6 6 4 44 4; John Ireland, 1879-1962, © John Ireland Trust

Sing, My Tongue, the Song of Triumph   573

1. Sing, my tongue, the song of tri - umph,
2. He en - dured the nails, the spit - ting,
3. Faith - ful Cross, a - bove all oth - er,
4. Bend your boughs, O Tree of glo - ry!

Tell the sto - ry far and wide;
Vin - e - gar and spear and reed;
One and on - ly no - ble tree,
All you rig - id branch - es, bend!

Tell of dread and fi - nal bat - tle,
From that ho - ly bod - y bro - ken
None in fo - liage, none in blos - som,
For a while the an - cient tem - per

Sing of Sav - ior cru - ci - fied;
Blood and wa - ter forth pro - ceed:
None in fruit your peer may be;
That your birth be - stowed, sus - pend;

How up - on the cross a vic - tim
Earth and stars and sky and o - cean
Sweet the wood and sweet the i - ron
And the King of earth and heav - en

Van - quish - ing in death he died.
By that flood from stain are freed.
And your load, most sweet is he.
Gent - ly on your bos - om tend.

Text: *Pange, lingua, gloriosi lauream certaminis;* Venantius Fortunatus, c.530-609; tr. from *The Three Days,* 1981
Tune: PICARDY, 8 7 8 7 8 7; French Carol; harm. by Richard Proulx, b.1937, © 1986, GIA Publications, Inc.

574 Jesus, the Lord

Refrain

Descant:
Je - sus.   Je - sus.

Melody:

Let all cre - a - tion bend the knee   to the

Lord.   1.-3.   *To verses*   4.

Verse 1

1. In him we live,   we move and have our be-ing;   in   him the

Christ, in   him the   King.   Je - sus,   the Lord.   *D.C.*

Verses 2, 3

2. Though Son,   he did not cling to god - li - ness; but emp-tied him-
3. He   lived   o - be-dient-ly   his Fa-ther's will   ac - cept-ing his

self, be - came ⌐3⌐ a   slave!   Je - sus,   the Lord.   *D.C.*
death,   death on a   tree!

Text: *Jesus Prayer,* Philippians 2:5-11; Acts 17:28; Roc O'Connor, SJ, b.1949
Tune: Roc O'Connor, SJ, b.1949; arr. by Rick Modlin
© 1981, Robert F. O'Connor, SJ, and New Dawn Music

Come, Ye Faithful, Raise the Strain 575

1. Come, ye faith - ful raise the strain Of tri - um - phant
2. 'Tis the spring of souls to - day; Christ has burst the
3. Now the queen of sea - sons, bright With the day of
4. Nei - ther could the gates of death, Nor the tomb's dark
5. "Al - le - lu - ia!" now we cry To our King im -

glad - ness; God has brought his Is - ra - el
pris - on, And from three days' sleep in death
splen - dor, With the roy - al feast of feasts,
por - tal, Nor the watch - ers, nor the seal
mor - tal, Who, tri - um - phant, burst the bars

In - to joy from sad - ness; Loosed from
As a sun has ris - en; All the
Comes its joy to ren - der; Comes to
Hold him as a mor - tal; For to -
Of the tomb's dark por - tal; "Al - le -

Phar - aoh's bit - ter yoke Ja - cob's sons and
win - ter of our sins, Long and dark is
glad - den faith - ful hearts Who with true af -
day a - mong the Twelve Christ ap - peared be -
lu - ia!" with the Son, God the Fa - ther

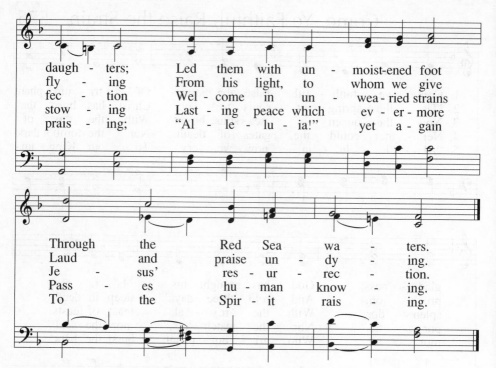

daugh - ters;   Led them with un - moist-ened foot
fly - ing   From his light, to whom we give
fec - tion   Wel - come in un - wea - ried strains
stow - ing   Last - ing peace which ev - er - more
prais - ing;   "Al - le - lu - ia!" yet a - gain

Through the Red Sea wa - ters.
Laud and praise un - dy - ing.
Je - sus' res - ur - rec - tion.
Pass - es hu - man know - ing.
To the Spir - it rais - ing.

Text: Exodus 15; Ασωμεν παντεζ λαοι; John of Damascus, c.675-c.749; tr. by John M. Neale, 1818-1886, alt.
Tune: GAUDEAMUS PARITER, 7 6 7 6 D; Johann Horn, c. 1495-1547

576   This Is the Day

Refrain

This is the day the Lord has made; let us re - joice and be

glad. This is the day the Lord has made;

To verses | *Last time*

let us re - joice and be glad.

Verse 1

1. Give thanks to the Lord for he is good, his

mer - cy en - dures for - ev - er; let the

house of Is - ra-el say: "His

D.C.

mer - cy en - dures for - ev - er."

Verse 2

2. The Lord's right hand has struck with pow'r, the

Lord's right hand is ex - alt - ed;

I shall not die, but live and de -

D.C.

clare the works of the Lord.

Verse 3

3. The stone which the build - ers re - ject - ed has be -

come the cor - ner - stone. By the Lord has this been

D.C.

done; it is won - der - ful in our eyes!

Text: Psalm 118, refrain trans. © 1969, ICEL; verses © Confraternity of Christian Doctrine, alt.
Tune: Michael Joncas, b.1951, © 1981, 1982; published by Cooperative Ministries, Inc. Exclusive agent: OCP Publications

577   Surrexit Christus

Ostinato Refrain

(hum) Sur - re - xit Chri-stus, al-le-lu - ia!

(hum) Can - ta - te Do - mi - no, al-le-lu - ia!

Verses

Cantor:

1. All you heav-ens, bless the Lord.

Stars of the heav-ens bless the Lord.

2. Sun and moon, bless the Lord. And

you, night and day, bless the Lord.

3. Frost and cold, bless the Lord.

Ice and snow, bless the Lord.

*Choose either part

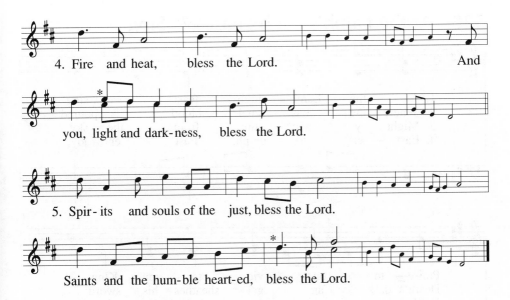

4. Fire and heat, bless the Lord. And
you, light and dark-ness, bless the Lord.

5. Spir-its and souls of the just, bless the Lord.
Saints and the hum-ble heart-ed, bless the Lord.

Text: *Christ is risen, sing to the Lord;* Daniel 3; Taizé Community, 1984
Tune: Jacques Berthier, 1923-1994
© 1984, Les Presses de Taizé, GIA Publications, Inc., agent

578 At the Lamb's High Feast We Sing

1. At the Lamb's high feast we sing
2. Where the Pas - chal blood is poured,
3. Might - y vic - tim from the sky,
4. East - er tri - umph, East - er joy,

Praise to our vic - to - rious King.
Death's dark an - gel sheathes his sword;
Hell's fierce powers be - neath you lie;
This a - lone can sin de - stroy;

Who has washed us in the tide
Is - rael's hosts tri - umph - ant go
You have con - quered in the fight,
From sin's power, Lord, set us free

Flow - ing from his pierc - ed side;
Through the wave that drowns the foe.
You have brought us life and light:
New - born souls in you to be.

Praise we him, whose love di - vine
Praise we Christ, whose blood was shed,
Now no more can death ap - pall,
Fa - ther, who the crown shall give,

Gives his sa - cred Blood for wine,
Pas - chal vic - tim, Pas - chal bread;
Now no more the grave en - thrall;
Sav - ior, by whose death we live,

Gives his Bod - y for the feast,
With sin - cer - i - ty and love
You have o - pened par - a - dise,
Spir - it, guide through all our days,

Christ the vic - tim, Christ the priest.
Eat we man - na from a - bove.
And in you your saints shall rise.
Three in One, your name we praise.

Text: *Ad regias agni dapes;* Latin, 4th C.; tr. by Robert Campbell, 1814-1868
Tune: SALZBURG, 77 77 D; Jakob Hintze, 1622-1702; harm. by J.S. Bach, 1685-1750

579 O Sons and Daughters

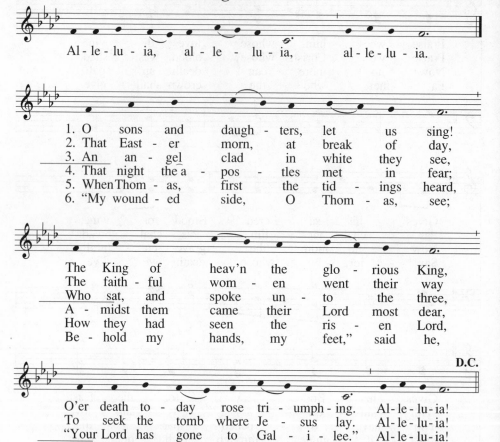

Al - le - lu - ia,   al - le - lu - ia,   al - le - lu - ia.

1. O   sons   and   daugh - ters,   let   us   sing!
2. That   East - er   morn,   at   break   of   day,
3. An   an - gel   clad   in   white   they   see,
4. That   night the a -   pos -   tles   met   in   fear;
5. When Thom - as,   first   the   tid -   ings   heard,
6. "My   wound - ed   side,   O   Thom - as,   see;

The   King   of   heav'n the   glo -   rious   King,
The   faith - ful   wom - en   went   their   way
Who   sat,   and   spoke   un -   to   the   three,
A -   midst them   came   their   Lord   most   dear,
How   they   had   seen   the   ris -   en   Lord,
Be - hold   my   hands, my   feet," said   he,

D.C.

O'er   death to - day   rose   tri - umph - ing.   Al - le - lu - ia!
To   seek   the   tomb   where Je -   sus   lay.   Al - le - lu - ia!
"Your Lord has   gone   to   Gal - i - lee."   Al - le - lu - ia!
And   said, "My   peace   be   on   all   here." Al - le - lu - ia!
He   doubt - ed the   dis - ci - ples' word.   Al - le - lu - ia!
"Not faith - less, but   be - liev - ing   be."   Al - le - lu - ia!

7. No longer Thomas then denied,
   He saw the feet, the hands, the side;
   "You are my Lord and God," he cried. Alleluia!

8. How blest are they who have not seen,
   And yet whose faith has constant been,
   For they eternal life shall win. Alleluia!

9. On this most holy day of days,
   To God your hearts and voices raise,
   In laud, and jubilee and praise. Alleluia!

Text: *O filii et filiae;* Jean Tisserand, d.1494; tr. by John M. Neale, 1818-1866, alt.
Tune: O FILII ET FILIAE, 888 with alleluias; Mode II; acc. by Richard Proulx, b.1937, © 1975, GIA Publications, Inc.

Resucitó 580

Refrain

Descant:

Re - su - ci - tó, re - su - ci - tó,
A - le - lu - ya, a - le - lu - ya,

Melody:

Last time to coda

re - su - ci - tó, a - le - lu - ya.
a - le - lu - ya, re - su - ci - tó.

Verses

1.   La   muer - te   ¿dón-de_es - tá   la
2.   Gra-cias se - an   da -   das   al
3.   A - le - grí - a,   a - le - grí-a_her -
4. Si con Él mo - ri - mos   y con Él vi -

1.   And   death   now,   van-ished is   the
2.   The   king - dom,   praise to God, the
3.   Our   glad - ness,   bliss - ful in our
4.   With   him   then,   die   and live with

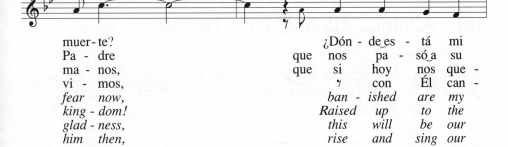

muer - te?   ¿Dón - de_es - tá mi
Pa - dre   que   nos   pa - só_a su
ma - nos,   que   si   hoy nos que -
vi - mos,   y   con   Él can -

fear   now,   ban - ished are my
king - dom!   Raised up   to   the
glad - ness,   this   will be   our
him   then,   rise   and sing our

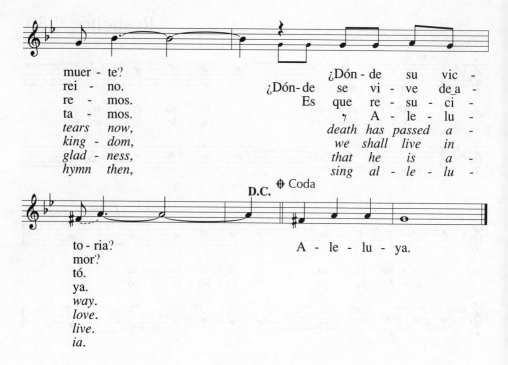

muer - te?
rei - no.
re - mos.
ta - mos.
tears *now,*
king - *dom,*
glad - *ness,*
hymn *then,*

¿Dón - de su vic -
¿Dón - de se vi - ve de_a -
Es que re - su - ci -
⁊ A - le - lu -
death *has* *passed* *a* -
we *shall* *live* *in*
that *he* *is* *a* -
sing *al* - *le* - *lu* -

D.C. ✛ Coda

to - ria?
mor?
tó.
ya.
way.
love.
live.
ia.

A - le - lu - ya.

Text: Kiko Argüello, © 1972, Ediciones Musical PAX, U.S. agent: OCP Publications; trans. by Robert C. Trupia, © 1988, OCP Publications
Tune: Kiko Argüello, © 1972, Ediciones Musical PAX, U.S. agent: OCP Publications; acc. by Diana Kodner, © 1993, GIA Publications, Inc.

581 Alleluia, Alleluia, Give Thanks

Refrain

Descant:

Al - le - lu - ia, al - le -

Melody:

Al - le - lu - ia, al - le - lu - ia, give thanks to the

lu - ia, al - le - lu - ia,

ris - en Lord. Al - le - lu - ia, al - le - lu - ia, give

|1.-5.   *To verses* |6.

praise to his Name.   Name.

Verses

1. Je - sus is Lord of all the earth.
2. Spread the good news o'er all the earth:
3. We have been cru - ci - fied with Christ.
4. God has pro - claimed his gra - cious gift:
5. Come, let us praise the liv - ing God,

D.C.

He is the King of cre - a - tion.
Je - sus has died and has ris - en.
Now we shall live for ev - er.
Life e - ter - nal for all who be - lieve.
Joy - ful - ly sing to our Sav - ior.

Text: Donald Fishel, b.1950, © 1973, Word of God Music
Tune: ALLELUIA NO. 1, 8 8 with refrain; Donald Fishel, b.1950, © 1973, Word of God Music; descant harm. by Betty Pulkingham, b.1929,
   Charles Mallory, b.1953, and George Mims, b.1938, © 1979, Celebration

582 I Know That My Redeemer Lives

1. I know that my Re - deem - er lives;
2. He lives, to bless me with his love;
3. He lives, and grants me dai - ly breath;
4. He lives, all glo - ry to his name;

What joy the blest as - sur - ance gives!
He lives, to plead for me a - bove;
He lives, and I shall con - quer death;
He lives, my Sav - ior still the same;

He lives, he lives, who once was dead;
He lives, my hun - gry soul to feed;
He lives, my man - sion to pre - pare;
What joy the blest as - sur - ance gives;

He lives, my ev - er - last - ing Head!
He lives, to help in time of need.
He lives, to bring me safe - ly there.
I know that my Re - deem - er lives!

Text: Samuel Medley, 1738-1799
Tune: DUKE STREET, LM; John Hatton, c.1710-1793

This Is the Feast of Victory   583

This is the feast of vic-to-ry for our God. Al-le -

lu-ia, al-le-lu-ia, al-le-lu - ia.   lu - ia.

To verses   Last time

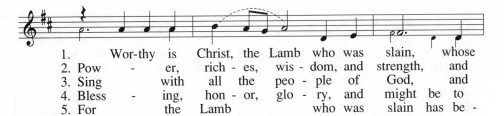

1.   Wor-thy is Christ, the Lamb who was slain, whose
2. Pow - er, rich - es, wis-dom, and strength, and
3. Sing with all the peo - ple of God, and
4. Bless - ing, hon - or, glo - ry, and might be to
5. For the Lamb who was slain has be -

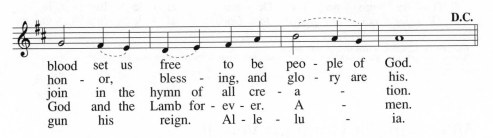

D.C.

blood set us free to be peo - ple of God.
hon - or, bless - ing, and glo - ry are his.
join in the hymn of all cre - a - tion.
God and the Lamb for - ev - er. A - men.
gun his reign. Al - le - lu - ia.

Text: Based on Revelation 5, © 1978, *Lutheran Book of Worship*
Tune: FESTIVAL CANTICLE, Irregular; Richard Hillert, b.1923, © 1975, 1988, Richard Hillert

584 Regina Caeli / O Queen of Heaven

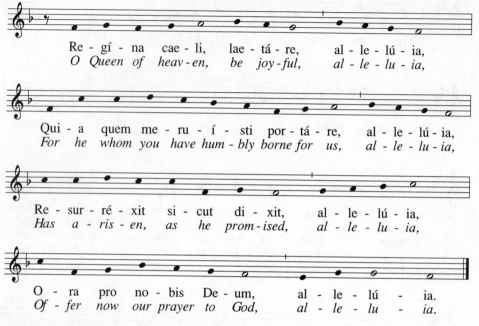

Re - gí - na cae - li, lae - tá - re, al - le - lú - ia,
O Queen of heav-en, be joy-ful, al - le - lu - ia,

Qui - a quem me - ru - í - sti por - tá - re, al - le - lú - ia,
For he whom you have hum - bly borne for us, al - le - lu - ia,

Re - sur - ré - xit si - cut di - xit, al - le - lú - ia,
Has a - ris - en, as he prom - ised, al - le - lu - ia,

O - ra pro no - bis De - um, al - le - lú - ia.
Of - fer now our prayer to God, al - le - lu - ia.

Text: Latin, 12th C.; tr. by C. Winfred Douglas, 1867-1944, alt.
Tune: REGINA CAELI, Irregular; Mode VI; acc. by Robert LeBlanc, OSB, b.1948, © 1986, GIA Publications, Inc.

585 Surrexit Dominus Vere II

Canon—*4 voices*

1. Sur - re - xit Do - mi - nus ve - re.

2. Al - le - lu - ia, al - le - lu - ia.

3. Sur - re - xit Chri - stus ho - di - e,

4. Al - le - lu - ia, al - le - lu - ia.

Text: *The Lord is truly risen! Christ is risen today!* Taizé Community, 1978
Tune: Jacques Berthier, 1923-1994
© 1978, Les Presses de Taizé, GIA Publications, Inc., agent

Good Christians All   586

1. Good Chris - tians all, re - joice and sing!
2. The Lord of life is ris'n to - day!
3. Praise we in songs of vic - to - ry
4. Your Name we bless, O ris - en Lord,
5. To God the Fa - ther, God the Son,

Now is the tri - umph of our King!
Sing songs of praise a - long his way;
That love, that life which can - not die,
And sing to - day with one ac - cord
To God the Spir - it, al - ways One,

To all the world glad news we bring:
Let all the earth re - joice and say:
And sing with hearts up - lift - ed high:
The life laid down, the life re - stored:
We sing for life in us be - gun:

Al - le - lu - ia, al - le - lu - ia, al - le - lu - ia!

Text: Cyril A. Alington, 1872-1955, alt., © 1956, Hymns Ancient and Modern, Ltd.; St. 5, Norman Mealy, b.1923, © 1971, Walton Music Corporation
Tune: GELOBT SEI GOTT, 888 with alleluias; Melchior Vulpius, c.1560-1616; acc. Robert J. Batastini, b.1942, © 1987, GIA Publications, Inc.

587 The Strife Is O'er

Al-le-lu - ia! Al-le-lu - ia! Al-le-lu - ia!

1. The strife is o'er, the bat - tle done; Now is the
2. Death's might - iest pow'rs have done their worst, And Je - sus
3. He closed the yawn - ing gates of hell; The bars from
4. On the third morn he rose a - gain, Glo - rious in

Vic - tor's tri - umph won; Now be the song of
has his foes dis - persed; Let shouts of praise and
heav'n's high por - tals fell; Let hymns of praise his
maj - es - ty to reign; O let us swell the

praise be - gun: Al - le - lu - ia!
joy out - burst: Al - le - lu - ia!
tri - umph tell: Al - le - lu - ia!
joy - ful strain: Al - le - lu - ia!

D.C.

Text: *Finita iam sunt praelia;* Latin, 12th C.; tr. by Francis Pott, 1832-1909, alt.
Tune: VICTORY, 888 with alleluias; Giovanni da Palestrina, 1525-1594; adapt. by William H. Monk, 1823-1889

Hail Thee, Festival Day   588

Hail thee, fes-ti-val day! Blest day that art hal-lowed for ev - er;

Day when our Lord was raised, break-ing the king-dom of death.

1. All the fair beau - ty of earth from the
3. God the Al - might - y, the Lord, the
5. Spir - it of life and of pow'r, now

death of the win - ter a - ris - ing! Ev - 'ry good
rul - er of earth and the heav - ens, Guard us from
flow in us, fount of our be - ing, Light that en -

D.C.

gift of the year now with its mas - ter re - turns.
harm with - out; cleanse us from e - vil with - in.
light - ens us all, life that in all may a - bide.

2. Rise from the grave now, O Lord, the au - thor of
4. Je - sus, the health of the world, en - light - en our
6. Praise to the giv - er of good! O Lov - er and

life and cre - a - tion. Tread - ing the path - way of
minds great Re - deem - er. Son of the Fa - ther su -
Au - thor of con - cord, Pour out your balm on our

D.C.

death, new life you give to us all.
preme, on - ly be - got - ten of God.
days; or - der our ways in your peace.

Text: *Salve festa dies;* Venantius Fortunatus, c.530-609; tr. composite
Tune: SALVE FESTA DIES, Irregular with refrain; Ralph Vaughan Williams, 1872-1958
© Oxford University Press

589 Up from the Earth

1. Up from the earth, and surg-ing like a wave,
2. Up from the cross a bil-lion voic-es strain,
3. Up from the night Christ Morn-ing-star a-wakes.
4. Up from the tomb of all the past con-ceals!
5. Cry to the cross where ty-rants work their dread!

Rise up, O Christ! Your God de-fies the grave.
Cry for a hand to lift them from their pain.
O what a light up-on earth's dark-ness breaks!
See how our God a bright-er day re-veals.
Shout to the tombs where par-ents mourn their dead!

Up from the earth push blade and leaf and stem. They
Up from the cross but scarred in limbs and side, A
Up from the night Christ sows his life like wheat, And
Up from the tomb! Though death had bound us tight, Like
Sing to the earth, for God all new-ness gives! Al-

Last time

D.S.

rise for Christ, and we shall rise with them!
wound-ed church brings heal-ing far and wide!
death it-self lies fal-low at his feet!
Laz-a-rus, we stum-ble in-to light!
le-lu-ia! Christ Lib-er-a-tor lives!

Text: Rory Cooney, b.1952
Tune: LIBERATOR, 10 10 10 10; Rory Cooney, b.1952
© 1987, North American Liturgy Resources

590 Sing to the Mountains

𝄋 Refrain

Descant:

Sing to the moun-tains, sing to the sea. Raise your

Melody:

voic - es, lift your hearts. This is the day the

Lord has made. Let all the earth re - joice.

1.-3.   To verses

Last time

joice. Let all the earth re - joice.

Verse 1

1. I will give thanks to you, my Lord. You have

an-swered my plea. You have saved my soul from

D.S.

death. You are my strength and my song.

Verse 2

2. Ho - ly, ho - ly, ho - ly Lord, heav - en and earth are full of your glo - ry.

Verse 3

Descant:

3. This is the day that the Lord has made. Let us be glad and re - joice. He has turned all death to life. Sing of the glo - ry of God.

Melody:

Text: Psalm 118; Bob Dufford, SJ, b.1943
Tune: Bob Dufford, SJ, b.1943; acc. by Randall DeBruyn
© 1975, 1979, Robert J. Dufford, SJ and New Dawn Music

The Head That Once Was Crowned with Thorns   591

1. The head that once was crowned with thorns Is crowned with glo-ry now; A roy-al di-a-dem a-dorns The might-y vic-tor's brow.
2. The high-est place that heav'n af-fords Be-longs to him by right; The King of kings, and Lord of lords, And heav'n's e-ter-nal light.
3. The joy of all who dwell a-bove, The joy of all be-low, To whom he man-i-fests his love, And grants his name to know.
4. To them the cross with all its shame, With all its grace, is giv'n; Their name an ev-er-last-ing name; Their joy the joy of heav'n.
5. They suf-fer with their Lord be-low; They reign with him a-bove; Their prof-it and their joy to know The mys-t'ry of his love.
6. The cross he bore is life and health, Though shame and death to him, His peo-ple's hope, his peo-ple's wealth, Their ev-er-last-ing theme.

Text: Hebrews 2:9-10; Thomas Kelly, 1769-1855
Tune: ST. MAGNUS, CM; Jeremiah Clarke, 1670-1707

592 Easter Alleluia

Refrain

Last time to coda

Al - le - lu - ia, al - le - lu - ia,

al - le - lu - ia!

Verses

1. Glo - ry to God who does won - drous things,
2. See how sal - va - tion for all has been won,
3. Now in our pres - ence the Lord will ap - pear,
4. Call us, Good Shep - herd, we lis - ten for you,
5. Lord, we are o - pen to all that you say,
6. If we have love, then we dwell in the Lord,

Let all the peo - ple God's prais - es now sing,
Up from the grave our new life has be - gun,
Shine in the fac - es of all of us here,
Want - ing to see you in all that we do,
Read - y to lis - ten and fol - low your way,
God will pro - tect us from fire and sword,

All of cre - a - tion in splen - dor shall ring:
Life now per - fect - ed in Je - sus, the Son:
Fill us with joy and cast out all our fear:
We would the gate of sal - va - tion pass through:
You are the pot - ter and we are the clay:
Fill us with love and the peace of his word:

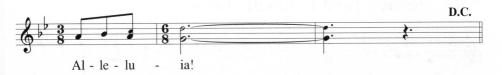

D.C.

Al - le - lu - ia!

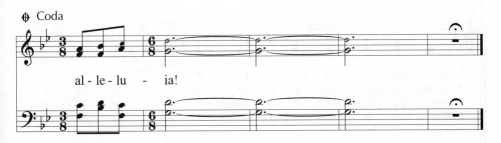

Coda

al - le - lu - ia!

Text: Marty Haugen, b.1950
Tune: O FILII ET FILIAE; 10 10 10 with alleluias; adapt. by Marty Haugen, b.1950
© 1986, GIA Publications, Inc.

593 Jesus Christ Is Risen Today

Descant, verse 4:

4. Sing we to our God a - bove, Al - le - lu - ia!

1. Je - sus Christ is ris'n to - day, Al - le - lu - ia!
2. Hymns of praise then let us sing, Al - le - lu - ia!
3. But the pains which he en - dured, Al - le - lu - ia!
4. Sing we to our God a - bove, Al - le - lu - ia!

Praise e - ter - nal as his love; Al - le - lu - ia!

Our tri - um - phant ho - ly day, Al - le - lu - ia!
Un - to Christ, our heav'n - ly King, Al - le - lu - ia!
Our sal - va - tion have pro - cured; Al - le - lu - ia!
Praise e - ter - nal as his love; Al - le - lu - ia!

Praise him, now his might con-fess, Al - le - lu - ia!

Who did once up - on the cross, Al - le - lu - ia!
Who en-dured the cross and grave, Al - le - lu - ia!
Now a - bove the sky he's King, Al - le - lu - ia!
Praise him, now his might con-fess, Al - le - lu - ia!

Fa - ther, Son, and Spir - it blest. Al - le - lu - ia!

Suf - fer to re - deem our loss. Al - le - lu - ia!
Sin - ners to re - deem and save. Al - le - lu - ia!
Where the an - gels ev - er sing. Al - le - lu - ia!
Fa - ther, Son, and Spir - it blest. Al - le - lu - ia!

Text: St. 1, *Surrexit Christus hodie*, Latin, 14th C.; para. in *Lyra Davidica*, 1708, alt.; st. 2, 3, *The Compleat Psalmodist*, c.1750, alt.; st. 4, Charles
    Wesley, 1707-1788
Tune: EASTER HYMN, 77 77 with alleluias; *Lyra Davidica*, 1708

594   Christ the Lord Is Risen Today

1. Christ the Lord is ris'n to - day;
2. For the sheep the Lamb has bled,
3. Christ, the Vic - tim un - de - filed,
4. Chris - tians, on this hap - py day,
5. Hal - lowed, cho - sen dawn of praise,

Chris - tians, haste your vows to pay;
Sin - less in the sin - ner's stead;
God and sin - ners rec - on - ciled,
Raise your hearts with joy and say:
East - er, queen of all our days:

Make your joy and prais - es known;
Christ the Lord is ris'n on high;
When in fierce and blood - y strife
Christ the Lord is ris'n on high;
Zi - on's chil - dren now come forth;

At the Pas - chal Vic - tim's throne.
Now he lives no more to die.
Met to - geth - er death and life.
Now he lives no more to die.
East to west and south to north.

Al - le - lu - ia. Al - le - lu - ia. Al -
le - lu - ia. Al - le - lu - ia.

6. Let the people praise you, Lord,
   Be, by all that is adored:
   Let the nations shout and sing;
   Glory to their Paschal King.

7. Hymns of glory, songs of praise,
   God on high, to you we raise:
   Risen Lord, we now adore,
   With the Spirit ever more.

Text: *Victimae paschali laudes;* ascr. to Wipo of Burgundy, d.1048; tr. by Jane E. Leeson, 1809-1881, alt.
Tune: SURGIT IN HAEC DIES, 77 77 with alleluias; 12th C.; acc. by Richard Proulx, b.1937, © 1980, GIA Publications, Inc.

Sing with All the Saints in Glory   595

1. Sing with all the saints in glo-ry, Sing the res-ur-
2. O what glo-ry, far ex-ceed-ing All that eye has
3. Life e-ter-nal! heav'n re-joic-es: Je-sus lives who
4. Life e-ter-nal! O what won-ders Crowd on faith; what

rec-tion song! Death and sor-row, earth's dark sto-ry,
yet per-ceived! Ho-liest hearts for a-ges plead-ing,
once was dead; Shout with joy, O death-less voic-es!
joy un-known, When, a-midst earth's clos-ing thun-ders,

To the for-mer days be-long. All a-round the
Nev-er that full joy con-ceived. God has prom-ised,
Child of God, lift up your head! Pa-tri-archs from
Saints shall stand be-fore the throne! O to en-ter

clouds are break-ing, Soon the storms of time shall cease;
Christ pre-pares it, There on high our wel-come waits;
dis-tant a-ges, Saints all long-ing for their heav'n,
that bright por-tal, See that glow-ing fir-ma-ment,

In God's like - ness, we a - wak - en,
Ev - 'ry hum - ble spir - it shares it,
Proph - ets, psalm - ists, seers, and sag - es,
Know, with you, O God im - mor - tal,

Know - ing ev - er - last - ing peace.
Christ has passed the e - ter - nal gates.
All a - wait the glo - ry giv'n.
Je - sus Christ whom you have sent!

Text: 1 Corinthians 15:20; William J. Irons, 1812-1883, alt.
Tune: HYMN TO JOY, 8 7 8 7 D; arr. from Ludwig van Beethoven, 1770-1827, by Edward Hodges, 1796-1867

Darkness Is Gone 596

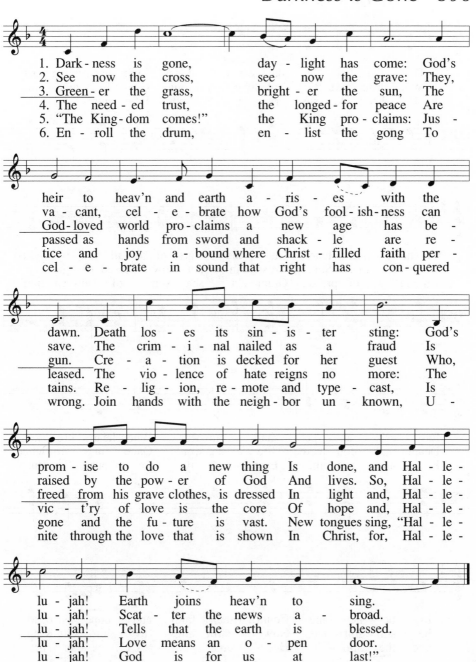

1. Dark-ness is gone, day-light has come: God's
2. See now the cross, see now the grave: They,
3. Green-er the grass, bright-er the sun, The
4. The need-ed trust, the longed-for peace Are
5. "The King-dom comes!" the King pro-claims: Jus-
6. En-roll the drum, en-list the gong To

1. heir to heav'n and earth a-ris-es with the
2. va-cant, cel-e-brate how God's fool-ish-ness can
3. God-loved world pro-claims a new age has be-
4. passed as hands from sword and shack-le are re-
5. tice and joy a-bound where Christ-filled faith per-
6. cel-e-brate in sound that right has con-quered

1. dawn. Death los-es its sin-is-ter sting: God's
2. save. The crim-i-nal nailed as a fraud Is
3. gun. Cre-a-tion is decked for her guest Who,
4. leased. The vio-lence of hate reigns no more: The
5. tains. Re-lig-ion, re-mote and type-cast, Is
6. wrong. Join hands with the neigh-bor un-known, U-

1. prom-ise to do a new thing Is done, and Hal-le-
2. raised by the pow-er of God And lives. So, Hal-le-
3. freed from his grave clothes, is dressed In light and, Hal-le-
4. vic-t'ry of love is the core Of hope and, Hal-le-
5. gone and the fu-ture is vast. New tongues sing, "Hal-le-
6. nite through the love that is shown In Christ, for, Hal-le-

1. lu-jah! Earth joins heav'n to sing.
2. lu-jah! Scat-ter the news a-broad.
3. lu-jah! Tells that the earth is blessed.
4. lu-jah! Love means an o-pen door.
5. lu-jah! God is for us at last!"
6. lu-jah! Christ is our Lord a-lone.

Text: John L. Bell, b.1949
Tune: DAYLIGHT, Irregular; John L. Bell, b.1949

597 Daylight Fades

1. Day - light fades in days when death-less Light has robbed earth's
2. Won - drous mys - t'ry of love's giv - ing! Our for - giv - ing
3. O Lord Je - sus, ris - en Sav - ior, Hear our joy - ful

night of fear; On the edge of all our twi-lights
Fa - ther's Son. Crushed in sor - row, raised to glo - ry
hymn of praise; Grant a sea - son of sal - va - tion,

East - er's an - gel shall ap-pear; When hearts bro - ken
Death had con - quered; life has won! Once in si - lence
Peace, and joy these East - er days. To our Fa - ther

by be - liev - ing Count their faith and hope as dead,
he sub - mit - ted, Now earth sings to him, our King;
and the Spir - it E - qual prais - es ev - er be;

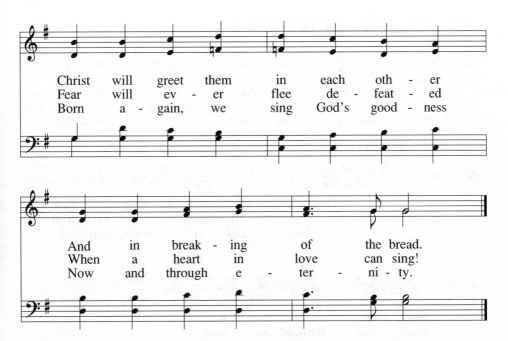

Christ will greet them in each oth - er
Fear will ev - er flee de - feat - ed
Born a - gain, we sing God's good - ness

And in break - ing of the bread.
When a heart in love can sing!
Now and through e - ter - ni - ty.

Text: Luke 24:28-35; Peter J. Scagnelli, b.1949, ©
Tune: HYMN TO JOY, 8 7 8 7 D; arr. from Ludwig van Beethoven, 1770-1827, by Edward Hodges, 1796-1867

598 This Joyful Eastertide

1. This joy-ful East-er-tide A-way with sin and
2. My flesh in hope shall rest And for a sea-son
3. Death's flood has lost its chill Since Je - sus crossed the

sor - row! My love, the Cru-ci-fied,
slum - ber Till trump from east to west
riv - er; Lov-er of souls, from ill

Has sprung to life this mor - row:
Shall wake the dead in num - ber:
My pass - ing soul de-liv - er:

Had Christ, who once was slain, Not burst his three-day pris - on,

Our faith had been in vain: But now has Christ a-ris-en,

a-ris-en, a-ris-en; a-ris - en!

Text: George R. Woodward, 1848-1934
Tune: VRUECHTEN, 6 7 6 7 D; Melody in Oudaen's *David's Psalmen*, 1685; harm. by Paul G. Bunjes, b.1914, © 1969, Concordia Publishing House

That Easter Day with Joy Was Bright 599

1. That Eas-ter day with joy was bright, The sun shone out with fair-er light, When to their long-ing eyes re-stored, The a-pos-tles saw their ris-en Lord.

2. His ris-en flesh with ra-diance glowed; His wound-ed hands and feet he showed; Those scars their sol-emn wit-ness gave That Christ was ris-en from the grave.

3. O Je-sus, King of gen-tle-ness, Who with your grace our hearts pos-sess That we may give you all our days The will-ing trib-ute of our praise.

4. O Lord of all, with us a-bide In this our joy-ful East-er-tide; From ev-'ry weap-on death can wield Your own re-deemed for ev-er shield.

5. All praise, to you, O ris-en Lord, Now both by heaven and earth a-dored; To God the Fa-ther e-qual praise, And Spir-it blest, our songs we raise.

Text: *Claro paschali gaudio;* Latin 5th C.; tr. by John M. Neale, 1818-1866, alt.
Tune: PUER NOBIS, LM; adapt. by Michael Praetorius, 1571-1621

600   Christ the Lord Is Risen

1. Christ the Lord is ris'n! Christ the Lord is ris'n!
2. He has con-quered death. He has con-quered death.
3. Sin has done its worst. Sin has done its worst.
4. He is King of kings. He is King of kings.
5. He is Lord of lords. He is Lord of lords.
6. All the world is his. All the world is his.
7. Come and wor-ship him. Come and wor-ship him.
8. Christ our Lord is ris'n! Christ our Lord is ris'n!
9. Hal-le-lu-jah! Hal-le-lu-jah!

Je-su.   Christ the Lord is ris'n!
Je-su.   He has con-quered death.
Je-su.   Sin has done its worst.
Je-su.   He is King of kings.
Je-su.   He is Lord of lords.
Je-su.   All the world is his.
Je-su.   Come and wor-ship him.
Je-su.   Christ our Lord is ris'n!
Je-su.   Hal-le-lu-jah!

Christ the Lord is ris'n!   Je-su.
He has con-quered death.   Je-su.
Sin has done its worst.   Je-su.
He is King of kings.   Je-su.
He is Lord of lords.   Je-su.
All the world is his.   Je-su.
Come and wor-ship him.   Je-su.
Christ our Lord is ris'n!   Je-su.
Hal-le-lu-jah!   Je-su.

Text: Tom Colvin, b.1925
Tune: Garu, Ghanian folk song, arr. by Kevin R. Hackett
© 1969, Hope Publishing Company

Christ Is Alive 601

1. Christ is a - live! Let Chris - tians sing.
2. Christ is a - live! No long - er bound
3. In ev - 'ry in - sult, rift, and war,
4. Wom - en and men, in age and youth,
5. Christ is a - live, and comes to bring

The cross stands emp - ty to the sky.
To dis - tant years in Pal - es - tine,
Where col - or, scorn or wealth di - vide,
Can feel the Spir - it, hear the call,
Good news to this and ev - 'ry age,

Let streets and homes with prais - es ring.
But sav - ing, heal - ing, here and now,
Christ suf - fers still, yet loves the more,
And find the way, the life, the truth,
Till earth and sky and o - cean ring

Love, drowned in death, shall nev - er die.
And touch - ing ev - 'ry place and time.
And lives, where ev - en hope has died.
Re - vealed in Je - sus, freed for all.
With joy, with jus - tice, love and praise.

Text: Romans 6:5-11; Brian Wren, b.1936, © 1975, Hope Publishing Co.
Tune: TRURO, LM; Williams' *Psalmodia Evangelica*, 1789

602 Christ the Lord Is Risen Today

1. Christ the Lord is ris'n to - day, Al - le - lu - ia! All on earth with an - gels say, Al - le - lu - ia! Raise your joys and tri - umphs high, Al - le - lu - ia!
2. Lives a - gain our glo - rious King; Al - le - lu - ia! Where, O death, is now your sting? Al - le - lu - ia! Once he died our souls to save, Al - le - lu - ia!
3. Love's re - deem - ing work is done, Al - le - lu - ia! Fought the fight, the bat - tle won. Al - le - lu - ia! Death in vain for - bids him rise; Al - le - lu - ia!
4. Soar we now where Christ has led, Al - le - lu - ia! Fol - l'wing our ex - alt - ed head; Al - le - lu - ia! Made like him, like him we rise, Al - le - lu - ia!

Sing,   O   heav'ns,   and   earth   re - ply,
Where   your   vic - to - ry,   O   grave?
Christ   has   o - pened   par - a - dise.
Ours   the   cross,   the   grave,   the   skies.

Al - le - lu - ia!

Text: Charles Wesley, 1707-1788
Tune: LLANFAIR, 77 77 with alleluias; Robert Williams, 1781-1821

603 I Will Be with You

Refrain

"I will be with you!" That is my prom-ise.

"I will be with you for ev-er-more." Trust in my love. Bring me all your cares, for I will be with you for ev-er-more.

prom - ise.

Verses

1. You are my peo-ple, and I am your
2. You have re-ceived me, now go and spread my

God.   I made you a   prom-ise,   to   be with you al -
word.   ⁊ You are with - in   me   and   I   am in

ways,   be-cause I   real-ly   love you.   I   real-ly
you,

D.S.

love you,   and   I   will be with you   for ev - er - more.

Text: James E. Moore, Jr., b.1951
Tune: James E. Moore, Jr., b.1951
© 1983, GIA Publications, Inc.

604 Go

1. Go ye there-fore and teach all na - tions, go,
2. If you love me, real - ly love me, feed

go, go. Go ye there-fore and teach all
my sheep. If you love me, real - ly

na - tions, go, go, go.
love me, feed my sheep. And

Bap - tiz - ing them in the name of the Fa - ther and
lo, I'll be with you for ev - er and ev - er un -

Son and Ho - ly Ghost. Go,
til the ends of the world, go,

Last time

go, go.
go, go.

Text: Leon Patillo
Tune: Leon Patillo
© 1981, 1982, Word Music, Inc.

Hail the Day That Sees Him Rise   605

1. Hail the day that sees him rise   Al - le - lu - ia!
2. There for him high tri - umph waits;   Al - le - lu - ia!
3. High-est heav'n its Lord re - ceives,   Al - le - lu - ia!
4. See, he lifts his hands a - bove.   Al - le - lu - ia!
5. Still for us he in - ter - cedes,   Al - le - lu - ia!
6. There we shall with him re - main,   Al - le - lu - ia!

To his throne a - bove the skies;   Al - le - lu - ia!
Lift your heads, e - ter - nal gates;   Al - le - lu - ia!
Yet he loves the earth he leaves: Al - le - lu - ia!
See, he shows the prints of love.   Al - le - lu - ia!
His pre - vail - ing death he pleads,   Al - le - lu - ia!
Part-ners of his end - less reign;   Al - le - lu - ia!

Christ, a - while to mor - tals given, Al - le - lu - ia!
He has con-quered death and sin; Al - le - lu - ia!
Though re - turn - ing to his throne, Al - le - lu - ia!
Hark, his gra - cious lips be - stow, Al - le - lu - ia!
Near him - self pre - pares our place, Al - le - lu - ia!
There his face un - cloud - ed see, Al - le - lu - ia!

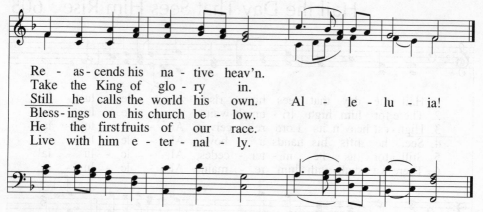

Re - as - cends his na - tive heav'n.
Take the King of glo - ry in.
Still he calls the world his own. Al - le - lu - ia!
Bless - ings on his church be - low.
He the firstfruits of our race.
Live with him e - ter - nal - ly.

Text: Charles Wesley, 1707-1788, alt.
Tune: LLANFAIR, 77 77 with alleluias; Robert Williams, 1781-1821

A Hymn of Glory Let Us Sing   606

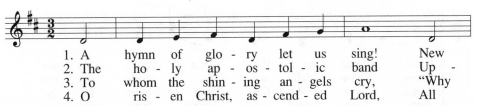

1. A hymn of glo - ry let us sing! New
2. The ho - ly ap - os - tol - ic band Up -
3. To whom the shin - ing an - gels cry, "Why
4. O ris - en Christ, as - cend - ed Lord, All

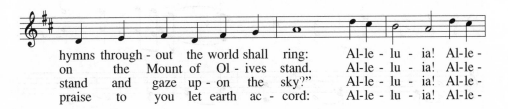

hymns through - out the world shall ring: Al-le - lu - ia! Al-le -
on   the   Mount of Ol - ives stand.   Al-le - lu - ia! Al-le -
stand and   gaze up - on the sky?"   Al-le - lu - ia! Al-le -
praise to   you let earth ac - cord: Al-le - lu - ia! Al-le -

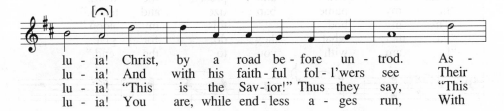

lu - ia! Christ, by a road be - fore un - trod.   As -
lu - ia! And with his faith - ful fol - l'wers see   Their
lu - ia! "This is the Sav-ior!" Thus they say,   "This
lu - ia! You are, while end - less a - ges run,   With

cends un - to   the throne of   God.
Lord as - cend in maj - es - ty.   Al-le - lu - ia! Al-le -
is his glo - rious tri - umph day!"
Fa - ther and with Spir - it   one.

lu - ia! Al-le - lu - ia! Al-le - lu - ia! Al-le - lu - ia!

Text: *Hymnum canamus gloria;* Venerable Bede, 673-735; tr. *Lutheran Book of Worship,* © 1978
Tune: LASST UNS ERFREUEN, LM with alleluias; *Geistliche Kirchengasange,* Cologne, 1623; harm. by Ralph Vaughan Williams, 1872-1958,
   © Oxford University Press

607 Lord, You Give the Great Commission

1. Lord, you give the great com - mis - sion:
2. Lord, you call us to your serv - ice:
3. Lord, you make the com - mon ho - ly:
4. Lord, you show us love's true meas - ure:
5. Lord, you bless with words as - sur - ing:

"Heal the sick and preach the word."
"In my name bap - tize and teach."
"This my bod - y, this my blood."
"Fa - ther, what they do, for - give."
"I am with you to the end."

Lest the Church ne - glect its mis - sion,
That the world may trust your prom - ise,
Let us all, for earth's true glo - ry,
Yet we hoard as pri - vate treas - ure
Faith and hope and love re - stor - ing,

And the Gos - pel go un - heard,
Life a - bun - dant meant for each,
Dai - ly lift life heav - en - ward,
All that you so free - ly give.
May we serve as you in - tend,

Help us wit - ness to your pur - pose
Give us all new fer - vor, draw us
Ask - ing that the world a - round us
May your care and mer - cy lead us
And, a - mid the cares that claim us,

With re - newed in - teg - ri - ty;
Clos - er in com - mun - i - ty;
Share your chil - dren's lib - er - ty;
To a just so - ci - e - ty;
Hold in mind e - ter - ni - ty;

With the Spir - it's gifts em - power us

For the work of min - is - try.

Text: Jeffery Rowthorn, b.1934, © 1978
Tune: ABBOT'S LEIGH, 8 7 8 7 D; Cyril V. Taylor, 1907-1991, © 1942, 1970, Hope Publishing Co.

608 Go to the World

1. Go to the world! Go in-to all the earth. Go preach the cross where Christ re-news life's worth, bap-tis-ing as the sign of our re-birth. Al-le-lu-ia. Al-le-lu-ia.

2. Go to the world! Go in-to ev-'ry place. Go live the Word of God's re-deem-ing grace. Go as the pres-ence in each time and space. Al-le-lu-ia. Al-le-lu-ia.

3. Go to the world! Go strug-gle, bless and pray; the nights of tears give way to joy-ous day, As ser-vant Church, you fol-low Christ's own way. Al-le-lu-ia. Al-le-lu-ia.

4. Go to the world! Go as the ones I send, for I am with you 'til the age shall end, When all the hosts of glo-ry cry "A-men!" Al-le-lu-ia. Al-le-lu-ia.

Text: Sylvia G. Dunstan, 1955-1993, ©1991, GIA Publications, Inc.
Tune: SINE NOMINE, 10 10 10 with alleluias; Ralph Vaughan Williams, 1872-1958, © Oxford University Press

Praise the Spirit in Creation 609

1. Praise the
2. Praise the
3. Praise the
4. Tell of
5. Pray we

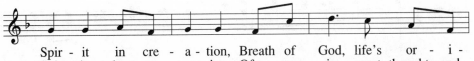

Spir - it   in   cre - a - tion,   Breath of   God, life's   or - i -
Spir - it,   close com - pan - ion   Of   our   in - most thoughts and
Spir - it,   who en - light-ened   Priests and   pro - phets   with   the
how the as-cend - ed   Je - sus   Armed a   peo - ple   for   his
then,   O   Lord the   Spir - it,   On   our   lives de - scend   in

gin: Spir - it   mov - ing   on   the   wa - ters   Quick - 'ning
ways;   Who, in   show - ing   us   God's   won - ders,   Is   him -
word;   His   the   truth be - hind   the   wis - doms   Which   as
own;   How   a   hun - dred men   and   wom - en   Turned   the
might;   Let   your   flame break out   with - in   us,   Fire   our

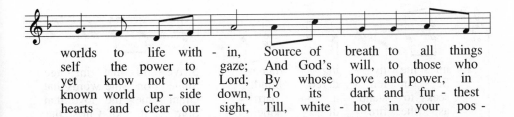

worlds   to   life   with - in,   Source of   breath to   all   things
self   the   power to   gaze;   And God's   will,   to   those who
yet   know   not   our   Lord;   By   whose   love and power,   in
known world   up - side   down,   To   its   dark and   fur - thest
hearts   and   clear our   sight,   Till,   white - hot   in   your   pos -

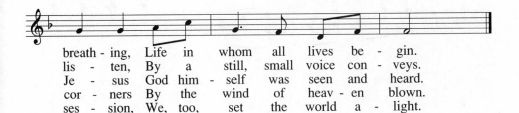

breath - ing,   Life   in   whom   all   lives   be - gin.
lis - ten,   By   a   still,   small   voice   con - veys.
Je - sus   God him - self   was   seen   and   heard.
cor - ners   By   the   wind   of   heav - en   blown.
ses - sion,   We, too,   set   the   world   a - light.

Text: Michael Hewlett, b.1916, alt., © Oxford University Press
Tune: JULION, 8 7 8 7 8 7; David Hurd, b.1950, © 1983, GIA Publications, Inc.

610 Spirit of God within Me

1. Spir - it of God with - in me, Pos - sess my hu - man frame;
2. Spir - it of truth with - in me, Pos - sess my thought and mind;
3. Spir - it of love with - in me, Pos - sess my hands and heart;
4. Spir - it of life with - in me, Pos - sess this life of mine;

1. Fan the dull em - bers of my heart, Stir up the liv - ing flame:
2. Light - en a - new the in - ward eye By Sa - tan ren - dered blind:
3. Break through the bonds of self - con - cern That seeks to stand a - part:
4. Come as the wind of heav - en's breath, Come as the fire di - vine!

1. Strive till that im - age
2. Shine on the words that
3. Grant me the love that
4. Spir - it of Christ, the

A - dam lost, New mint - ed and re -
wis - dom speaks And grant me pow'r to
suf - fers long, That hopes, be - lieves and
liv - ing Lord, Reign in this house of

stored, In shin - ing splen - dor bright - ly
see The truth made known to all in
bears; The love ful - filled in sac - ri -
clay, Till from its dust with Christ I

bears The like - ness of the Lord.
Christ, And in that truth be free.
fice, That cares as Je - sus cares.
rise To ev - er - last - ing day.

Text: Timothy Dudley-Smith, b.1926, © 1968, Hope Publishing Co.
Tune: WILLOW RIVER, 7 6 8 6 8 6 8 6; Michael Joncas, b.1951, © 1985, 1988, GIA Publications, Inc.

611 Come, Holy Ghost

1. Come, Ho - ly Ghost, Cre - a - tor blest, And in our
2. O Com - fort - er, to thee we cry, Thou heav'n - ly
3. O Ho - ly Ghost, Through thee a - lone, Know we the
4. Praise we the Lord, Fa - ther and Son, And Ho - ly

hearts take up thy rest; Come with thy grace
gift of God most high; Thou fount of life,
Fa - ther and the Son; Be this our firm
Spir - it with them one; And may the Son

and heav'n - ly aid To fill the hearts which thou hast
and fire of love, And sweet a - noint - ing from a -
un - chang - ing creed, That thou dost from them both pro -
on us be - stow All gifts that from the Spir - it

made, To fill the hearts which thou hast made.
bove, And sweet a - noint - ing from a - bove.
ceed, That thou dost from them both pro - ceed.
flow, All gifts that from the Spir - it flow.

Text: *Veni, Creator Spiritus;* attr. to Rabanus Maurus, 776-856; tr. by Edward Caswall, 1814-1878, alt.
Tune: LAMBILLOTTE, LM with repeat; Louis Lambillotte, SJ, 1796-1855, harm. by Richard Proulx, b. 1937, © 1986, GIA Publications, Inc.

Send Us Your Spirit 612

Refrain

Come Lord Je-sus, send us your Spir-it, re - new the face of the earth. Come Lord Je-sus, send us your Spir-it, re - new the face of the earth.

To verses | *Final ending*

Verses

1. Come to us, Spir - it of God, breathe in us
2. Fill us with the fire of your love, burn in us
3. Send us the wings of new birth, fill all the

now, we sing to - geth - er.
now, bring us to - geth - er.
earth with the love you have taught us. Let

Spir - it of hope and of light, fill our
Come to us, dwell in us, change our lives, O
all cre - a - tion now be shak - en with

lives, come to us, Spir - it of God.
Lord, come to us, Spir - it of God.
love, come to us, Spir - it of God.

D.C.

*May be sung in canon.

Text: David Haas, b.1957
Tune: David Haas, b.1957; acc. by Jeanne Cotter b.1964
© 1981, 1982, 1987, GIA Publications, Inc.

613 When God the Spirit Came

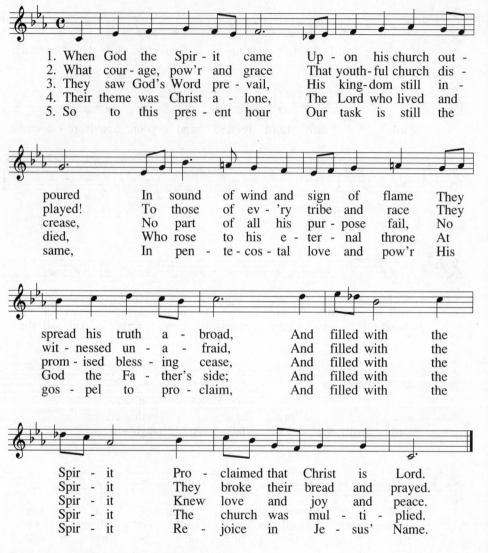

1. When God the Spir - it came Up - on his church out -
2. What cour - age, pow'r and grace That youth - ful church dis -
3. They saw God's Word pre - vail, His king - dom still in -
4. Their theme was Christ a - lone, The Lord who lived and
5. So to this pres - ent hour Our task is still the

poured In sound of wind and sign of flame They
played! To those of ev - 'ry tribe and race They
crease, No part of all his pur - pose fail, No
died, Who rose to his e - ter - nal throne At
same, In pen - te - cos - tal love and pow'r His

spread his truth a - broad, And filled with the
wit - nessed un - a - fraid, And filled with the
prom - ised bless - ing cease, And filled with the
God the Fa - ther's side; And filled with the
gos - pel to pro - claim, And filled with the

Spir - it Pro - claimed that Christ is Lord.
Spir - it They broke their bread and prayed.
Spir - it Knew love and joy and peace.
Spir - it The church was mul - ti - plied.
Spir - it Re - joice in Je - sus' Name.

Text: Acts 2; Timothy Dudley-Smith, b.1926, © 1984, Hope Publishing Co.
Tune: VINEYARD HAVEN, 6 6 8 6 6 6; Richard Dirksen, b.1921, © 1974, 1986, Harold Flammer, Inc.

Fire of God, Undying Flame 614

1. Fire of God, un - dy - ing flame, Spir - it who in
2. Breath of God, that swept in power In the Pen - te -
3. Strength of God, your might with - in Con - quers sor - row,
4. Truth of God, your pierc - ing rays Pen - e - trate my
5. Love of God, your grace pro - found Knows not ei - ther

splen - dor came, Let your heat my soul re - fine,
cos - tal hour, Ho - ly breath, be now in me
pain and sin; For - ti - fy from e - vil art
se - cret ways, May the light that shames my sin
age or bound; Come, my heart's own guest to be,

Till it glows with love di - vine.
Source of vi - tal en - er - gy.
All the gate - ways of my heart.
Guide me ho - lier paths to win.
Dwell for ev - er - more in me.

Text: Albert F. Bayly, 1901-1984, alt., © Oxford University Press
Tune: NUN KOMM DER HEIDEN HEILAND, 77 77; *Geystliche Gesangk Buchleyn,* Wittenberg, 1524; harm. by Melchior Vulpius, c.1560-1616

615 Veni Sancte Spiritus

Ostinato Refrain

As the ostinato continues, vocal and instrumental verses are sung or played as desired with some space always left between the verses (after the cantor's "Veni Sancte Spiritus").

Verses

Cantor:
1. Come, Ho-ly Spir-it, from heav-en shine forth with your glo-rious light. Ve-ni San-cte Spi-ri-tus.

2. Come, Fa-ther of the poor, come, gen-er-ous Spir-it, come, light of our hearts. Ve-ni San-cte Spi-ri-tus.

Text: *Come Holy Spirit;* Verses drawn from the Pentecost Sequence; Taizé Community, 1978
Tune: Jacques Berthier, 1923-1994
© 1979, Les Presses de Taizé, GIA Publications, Inc., agent

O Holy Spirit, by Whose Breath   616

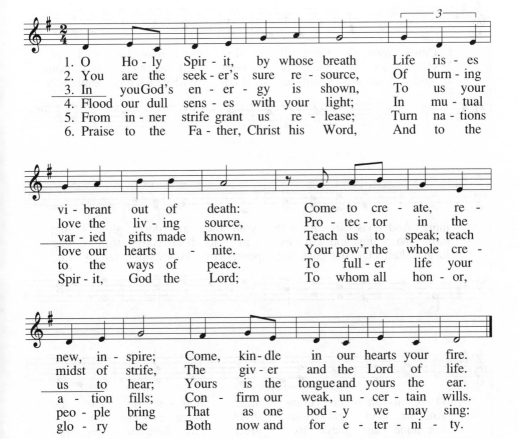

1. O   Ho - ly   Spir - it,   by whose breath   Life   ris - es
2. You   are the   seek - er's   sure   re - source,   Of   burn - ing
3. In   youGod's en - er - gy   is   shown,   To   us   your
4. Flood our dull sens - es   with your   light;   In   mu - tual
5. From in - ner strife grant   us   re - lease;   Turn   na - tions
6. Praise to the Fa - ther, Christ his   Word,   And   to   the

vi - brant   out   of   death: Come to   cre - ate,   re -
love the   liv - ing   source,   Pro - tec - tor   in   the
var - ied   gifts made   known.   Teach us   to   speak; teach
love our   hearts u - nite.   Your pow'r the   whole   cre -
to the   ways of   peace.   To   full - er   life   your
Spir - it,   God the   Lord;   To   whom all   hon - or,

new,   in - spire;   Come,   kin - dle   in   our hearts your   fire.
midst of strife,   The   giv - er   and the   Lord   of   life.
us   to   hear;   Yours   is the   tongueand yours   the   ear.
a - tion   fills;   Con - firm our   weak, un - cer - tain   wills.
peo - ple bring   That   as one   bod - y   we may   sing:
glo - ry   be   Both   now and   for e - ter - ni - ty.

Text: *Veni, Creator Spiritus;* attr. to Rabanus Maurus, 776-865; tr. by John W. Grant, b.1919, © 1971
Tune: VENI CREATOR SPIRITUS, LM; Mode VIII; setting by Richard J. Wojcik, b.1923, © 1975, GIA Publications, Inc.

617 Come Down, O Love Divine

1. Come down, O Love di - vine, Seek now this soul of
2. O let it free - ly burn, Till earth - ly pas - sions
3. And so the yearn - ing strong, With which the soul will

mine, And vis - it it with your own ar - dor glow - ing;
turn To dust and ash - es in its heat con - sum - ing;
long, Shall far out-pass the power of hu - man tell - ing;

O Com - fort - er, draw near, With - in my heart ap -
And let your glo - rious light Shine ev - er on my
For none can guess its grace, Till love cre - ates the

pear, And kin - dle it, your ho - ly flame be - stow - ing.
sight, And clothe me round, the while my path il - lum - ing.
place Where - in the Ho - ly Spir - it makes its dwell - ing.

Text: *Discendi, Amor Santo;* Bianco da Siena, d.c.1434; tr. by Richard F. Littledale, 1833-1890
Tune: DOWN AMPNEY, 66 11 D; Ralph Vaughan Williams, 1872-1958, © Oxford University Press

How Wonderful the Three-in-One 618

1. How won - der - ful the Three - in -
2. Be - fore the flow of dawn and
3. The Lov - er's own Be - lov'd, in
4. Their E - qual Friend all life sus -
5. How won - der - ful the Liv - ing

One, Whose en - er - gies of danc - ing
dark, Cre - a - tion's Lov - er dreamed of
time, Be - tween a cra - dle and a
tains With green - ing pow'r and lov - ing
God: Di - vine Be - lov'd Em - pow'r - ing

light Are un - di - vid - ed, pure and
earth, And with a car - ing deep and
cross, At home in flesh, gave love and
care, And calls us, born a - gain by
Friend, E - ter - nal Lov - er, Three - in -

good, Com - mun - ing love in shared de -
wise, All things con - ceived and brought to
life To heal our bro - ken - ness and
grace, In Love's com - mun - ing life to
One, Our hope's be - gin - ning, way and

1.- 4. ‖ *Final ending* rit.

light.
birth.
loss.
share.

end.

Text: Brian Wren, b.1936, © 1989, Hope Publishing Co.
Tune: PROSPECT, 8 8 8 8; *Southern Harmony*; arr. by Marty Haugen, b.1950, © 1991, GIA Publications, Inc.

619 God, Whose Almighty Word

1. God, whose al - might - y word
2. Sav - ior, you came to give
3. Spir - it of truth and love,
4. Gra - cious and ho - ly Three,

Cha - os and
Those who in
Life - giv - ing,
Glo - ri - ous

dark - ness heard, And took their flight:
dark - ness live Heal - ing and sight,
ho - ly dove, Speed on your flight!
Trin - i - ty, Wis - dom, love, might:

Hear us, we hum - bly pray, And where the gos - pel - day
Health to the sick in mind, Sight to the in - ward blind:
Move on the wa - ter's face Bear - ing the lamp of grace
Bound-less as o - cean's tide Roll - ing in full - est pride

Sheds not its glo - rious ray, Let there be light!
Now to all hu - man - kind Let there be light!
And, in earth's dark - est place, Let there be light!
Through the world far and wide, Let there be light!

Text: John Marriott, 1780-1825, alt.
Tune: ITALIAN HYMN, 66 4 666 4; Felice de Giardini, 1716-1796

Sing Praise to Our Creator   620

1. Sing praise to our Cre - a - tor, Re - deemed of A - dam's race; God's chil - dren by a - dop - tion, Bap - tized in liv - ing grace.

2. To Je - sus Christ give glo - ry, God's co - e - ter - nal Son; As mem - bers of his bod - y We are in Christ made one.

3. Now praise the Ho - ly Spir - it Poured forth up - on the earth, Who sanc - ti - fies and guides us, Con - firmed in our re - birth.

O most ho - ly Trin - i - ty, Un - di - vid - ed u - ni - ty; Ho - ly God, might - y God, God im - mor - tal, be a - dored!

Text: Omer Westendorf, b.1916; © 1962, World Library Publications, Inc.
Tune: GOTT VATER SEI GEPRIESEN, 76 76 with refrain; *Limburg Gesangbuch*, 1838; harm. by Healey Willan, 1880-1968, © 1958, Ralph Jusko Publications, Inc.

621 This Holy Covenant Was Made

1. This ho - ly cov - e - nant was made: God our De - liv -
2. This ho - ly cov - e - nant was new At ta - ble with
3. This ho - ly cov - e - nant of flame Sears in our hearts

'rance was o - beyed. Seas were part - ed; free-dom
Christ's gath - ered few. Bless-ing spo - ken; bod - y
the sav - ing name. Spir - it's fi - re, our de -

start - ed. By cloud and fi - re we were led. By
bro - ken. By lift - ed cup our God for - gives. By
si - re. By wind and tongue the Church is sealed. By

quail and man - na we were fed.
Je - sus' grace a - lone we live. Al - le -
might and pow - er here re - vealed.

lu - ia, Al - le - lu - ia. Al - le - lu - ia, Al - le -

lu - ia, Al - le - lu - ia!

Text: Sylvia Dunstan, 1955-1993, © 1991, GIA Publications, Inc.
Tune: LASST UNS ERFREUEN, LM with alleluias; *Geistliche Kirchengesänge*, 1623; harm. by Ralph Vaughan Williams, 1872-1958, © Oxford University Press

Stand Up, Friends   622

Verses

1. Praise the God who chang - es plac-es, Leaves the loft-y seat,
2. Praise the Rab - bi, speak-ing, do-ing All that God in-tends,
3. Praise the Breath of Love, whose free-dom Spreads our wak-ing wings,
4. Praise, un - til we join the sing-ing Far be-yond our sight,

Wel-comes us with warm em-brac-es, Stoops to wash our feet.
Dy - ing, ris-ing, faith re-new-ing, Cal - ling us his friends.
Lift - ing ev - 'ry blight and bur-den Till the spir - it sings;
With the End-ing and Be-gin-ning Danc-ing in the light.

Refrain

Stand up, friends! Hold your heads high! Free-dom is our song! Al-

le - lu - ia! Free-dom is our song! Al - le - lu - ia!

1.

2. ia!

D.C. Final ending

Text: Brian Wren, b. 1936, © 1986, Hope Publishing Co.
Tune: David Haas, b. 1957, © 1993, GIA Publications, Inc.

623 God Is One, Unique and Holy

1.,4. God is One, u - nique and ho - ly,
2. God is One - ness - by - Com - mun - ion,
3. Through the pain that lov - ing Wis - dom

end - less dance of love and light,
nev - er dis - tant or a - lone,
could fore - see, but not fore - stall,

on - ly source of mind and bod - y,
at the heart of all be - long-ing:
God is One, though torn and an-guished

star - cloud, a - tom, day and night:
loy - al friend - ship, lov - ing home,
in the Christ's for - sa - ken call;

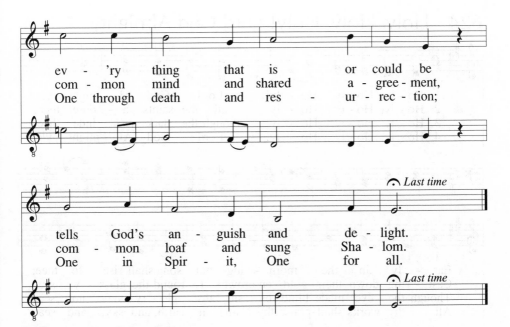

ev - 'ry thing that is or could be
com - mon mind and shared a - gree - ment,
One through death and res - ur - rec - tion;

Last time

tells God's an - guish and de - light.
com - mon loaf and sung Sha - lom.
One in Spir - it, One for all.

Last time

Text: Brian Wren, b.1936, © 1983, Hope Publishing Co.
Tune: Gary Daigle, b.1957, © 1994, GIA Publications, Inc.

624 Holy, Holy, Holy! Lord God Almighty

1. Ho - ly, Ho - ly, Ho - ly! Lord God Al - might - y!
2. Ho - ly, Ho - ly, Ho - ly! all the saints a - dore thee,
3. Ho - ly, Ho - ly, Ho - ly! though the dark-ness hide thee,
4. Ho - ly, Ho - ly, Ho - ly! Lord God Al - might - y!

Ear - ly in the morn - ing our song shall rise to thee:
Cast - ing down their gold - en crowns a - round the glass - y sea;
Though the eye made blind by sin thy glo - ry may not see,
All thy works shall praise thy Name in earth, and sky, and sea;

Ho - ly, Ho - ly, Ho - ly! mer - ci - ful and might - y,
Cher - u - bim and ser - a - phim fall - ing down be - fore thee,
On - ly thou art ho - ly; there is none be - side thee,
Ho - ly, Ho - ly, Ho - ly! mer - ci - ful and might - y,

God in three Per - sons, bless - ed Trin - i - ty.
God ev - er - last - ing through e - ter - ni - ty.
Per - fect in power, in love, and pu - ri - ty.
God in three Per - sons, bless - ed Trin - i - ty.

Text: Reginald Heber, 1783-1826, alt.
Tune: NICAEA, 11 12 12 10; John Bacchus Dykes, 1823-1876

Alleluia, Sing! 625

Cantor:

1. Bless-ed be our God! Bless-ed be our
2. Gift of love and peace! Gift of love and
3. Come, O Spir-it of truth! Come, O Spir-it of

Cantor:

God! Joy of our hearts, source of all life and
peace! Je - sus the Christ, Je - sus our hope and
truth! Prom - ise of hope, kind - ness and mer -

love! God of heav - en and earth!
light! A flame of faith in our hearts! A
cy! Come and dwell in our hearts!

All: Cantor:

God of heav-en and earth! Dwell - ing with - in,
flame of faith in our hearts! Pro - claim - ing the day,
Come and dwell in our hearts! Jus - tice and peace, the

call - ing us all by name!
shin - ing through-out the night!
king - dom of God in us!

All:

Al - le - lu - ia, sing! Al - le - lu - ia, sing!

1.-2. 3.

Text: David Haas, b.1957
Tune: David Haas, b.1957
© 1988, GIA Publications, Inc.

626 Crown Him with Many Crowns

1. Crown him with man - y crowns, The Lamb up - on his throne; Hark! how the heav'n - ly an - them drowns All mu - sic but its own. A - wake, my soul, and sing Of
2. Crown him the Lord of life, Who tri - umphed o'er the grave, And rose vic - to - rious in the strife For those he came to save. His glo - ries now we sing, Who
3. Crown him the Lord of love, Be - hold his hands and side, Rich wounds yet vis - i - ble a - bove In beau - ty glo - ri - fied. No an - gel in the sky Can
4. Crown him the Lord of peace, Whose power a scep - ter sways From pole to pole, that wars may cease, Ab - sorbed in prayer and praise. His reign shall know no end, And
5. Crown him the Lord of years, The ris - en Lord sub - lime, Cre - a - tor of the roll - ing spheres, The Mas - ter of all time. All hail, Re - deem - er, hail! For

him who set us free, And hail him as your
died and rose on high, Who died, e - ter - nal
ful - ly bear that sight, But down - ward bends his
round his pierc - ed feet Fair flow'rs of Par - a -
you have died for me; Your praise and glo - ry

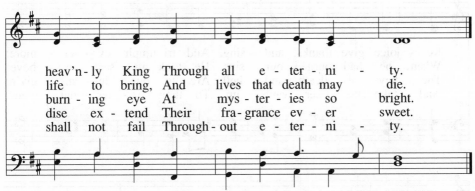

heav'n - ly King Through all e - ter - ni - ty.
life to bring, And lives that death may die.
burn - ing eye At mys - ter - ies so bright.
dise ex - tend Their fra - grance ev - er sweet.
shall not fail Through - out e - ter - ni - ty.

Text: Revelation 19:12; St. 1, 3-5, Matthew Bridges, 1800-1894; St. 2, Godfrey Thring, 1823-1903
Tune: DIADEMATA, SMD.; George J. Elvey, 1816-1893

627 Rejoice, the Lord Is King

1. Re - joice, the Lord is King! Your Lord and King a - dore!
2. The Lord, our Sav - ior, reigns, The God of truth and love;
3. His king-dom can - not fail, He rules o'er earth and heav'n;
4. Re - joice in glo-rious hope! Our Lord the judge shall come

Re - joice, give thanks, and sing, And tri-umph ev - er - more:
When he had purged our sins, He took his seat a - bove:
The keys of death and hell Are to our Je - sus giv'n:
And take his ser - vants up To their e - ter - nal home:

Lift up your heart, lift up your voice!

Re - joice, a - gain I say, re - joice!

Text: Charles Wesley, 1707-1788
Tune: DARWALL'S 148TH, 6 6 6 6 88; John Darwall, 1731-1789; harm. from *The Hymnal 1940*

The King of Glory   628

The King of glo - ry comes, the na - tion re - joic - es.

Last time

O - pen the gates be - fore him, lift up your voic - es.

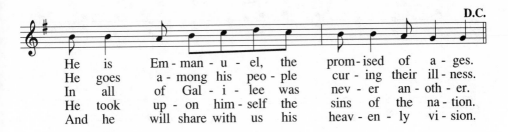

1. Who is the king of glo - ry; how shall we call him?
2. In all of Gal - i - lee, in cit - y or vil - lage,
3. Sing then of Da - vid's Son, our Sav - ior and broth - er;
4. He gave his life for us, the pledge of sal - va - tion,
5. He con - quered sin and death; he tru - ly has ris - en.

D.C.

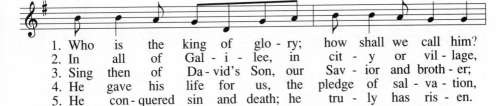

He is Em - man - u - el, the prom - ised of a - ges.
He goes a - mong his peo - ple cur - ing their ill - ness.
In all of Gal - i - lee was nev - er an - oth - er.
He took up - on him - self the sins of the na - tion.
And he will share with us his heav - en - ly vi - sion.

Text: Willard F. Jabusch, b. 1930, © 1966, 1984
Tune: KING OF GLORY, 12 12 with refrain; Israeli; harm. by Richard Proulx, b.1937, © 1986, GIA Publications, Inc.

629 To Jesus Christ, Our Sovereign King

1. To Jesus Christ, our sov - 'reign King, Who
2. Your reign ex - tend, O King be - nign, To
3. To you, and to your church, great King, We

is the world's sal - va - tion, All praise and hom - age
ev - 'ry land and na - tion; For in your King - dom,
pledge our heart's ob - la - tion; Un - til be - fore your

do we bring And thanks and ad - o - ra - tion.
Lord di - vine, A - lone we find sal - va - tion.
throne we sing In end - less ju - bi - la - tion.

Christ Je - sus, Vic - tor! Christ Je - sus, Rul - er!

Christ Je - sus, Lord and Re - deem - er!

Text: Martin B. Hellrigel, 1891-1981, alt., © 1941, Irene C. Mueller
Tune: ICH GLAUB AN GOTT, 8 7 8 7 with refrain; *Mainz Gesangbuch*, 1870; harm. by Richard Proulx, b.1937, © 1986, GIA Publications, Inc.

630 Christ Is the King!

1. Christ is the King! O friends, re - joice:
2. O mag - ni - fy the Lord, and raise
3. They with a faith for ev - er new
4. O Chris - tian wom - en, Chris - tian men,
5. Christ through all a - ges is the same:

Broth - ers and sis - ters, with one voice
An - thems of joy and ho - ly praise
Fol - lowed the King, and round him drew
All the world o - ver, seek a - gain
Place the same hope in his great name,

Let the world know he is your choice.
For Christ's brave saints of an - cient days.
Thou - sands of men and wom - en true.
The Way dis - ci - ples fol - lowed then.
With the same faith his word pro - claim.

Al - le - lu - ia, al - le - lu - ia, al - le - lu - ia.

6. Let love's all reconciling might
Your scattered companies unite
In service to the Lord of light.
Alleluia, alleluia, alleluia.

7. So shall God's will on earth be done,
New lamps be lit, new tasks begun,
And the whole Church at last be one.
Alleluia, alleluia, alleluia.

Text: George K. A. Bell, 1883-1958, alt., © Oxford University Press
Tune: GELOBT SEI GOTT, 888 with alleluias; Melchior Vulpius, c. 1560-1616

Jesus Shall Reign   631

1. Je - sus shall reign wher - e'er the sun
2. To him shall end - less prayer be made,
3. Peo - ple and realms of ev - 'ry tongue
4. Bless - ings a - bound wher - e'er he reigns;
5. Let ev - 'ry crea - ture rise and bring

Does his suc - ces - sive jour - neys run;
And prais - es throng to crown his head;
Dwell on his love with sweet - est song;
The pris - 'ner leaps to lose his chains;
Bless - ing and hon - or to our King;

His king - dom stretch from shore to shore,
His Name like sweet per - fume shall rise
And in - fant voic - es shall pro - claim
The wea - ry find e - ter - nal rest,
An - gels de - scend with songs a - gain,

Till moons shall wax and wane no more.
With ev - 'ry morn - ing sac - ri - fice.
Their ear - ly bless - ings on his Name.
And all who suf - fer want are blest.
And earth re - peat the loud A - men.

Text: Isaac Watts, 1674-1748, alt.
Tune: DUKE STREET, LM; John Hatton, c.1710-1793

632 All Hail the Power of Jesus' Name

1. All hail the pow'r of Je - sus' name! Let
2. Crown him, ye mar - tyrs of our God, Who
3. Ye cho - sen seed of Is - rael's race, A
4. O that, with yon - der sa - cred throng, We

an - gels pros - trate fall; Bring forth the roy - al
from his al - tar call; Ex - tol the stem of
rem - nant weak and small, Hail him who saved you
at his feet may fall, Join in the ev - er -

di - a - dem, And crown him Lord of
Jes - se's rod, And crown him Lord of
by his grace, And crown him Lord of
last - ing song, And crown him Lord of

all, And crown him Lord of all, And
all, And crown him Lord of all, And
all, And crown him Lord of all, And
all, And crown him Lord of all, And

crown him Lord of all. Bring forth the roy - al
crown him Lord of all. Ex - tol the stem of
crown him Lord of all. Hail him who saved you
crown him Lord of all. Join in the ev - er -

di - a - dem, And crown him Lord of all.
Jes - se's rod, And crown him Lord of all.
by his grace, And crown him Lord of all.
last - ing song, And crown him Lord of all.

Text: Edward Perronet, 1726-1792; alt. by John Rippon, 1751-1836, alt.
Tune: DIADEM, CM with repeats; from the *Primitive Baptist Hymn and Tune Book*, 1902; harm. by Robert J. Batastini, b.1942, © 1995,
    GIA Publications, Inc.

I Sing the Mighty Power of God   633

1. I sing the might-y pow'r of God That made the moun-tains rise, That spread the flow-ing seas a-broad, And built the loft-y skies. I sing the wis-dom that or-dained The

2. I sing the good-ness of the Lord That filled the earth with food; That formed cre-a-tion with a word, And then pro-nounced it good. Lord, how your won-ders are dis-played Wher-

3. There's not a plant or flow'r be-low But makes your glo-ries known; And clouds a-rise, and tem-pests blow, By or-der from your throne; While all that bor-rows life from you Is

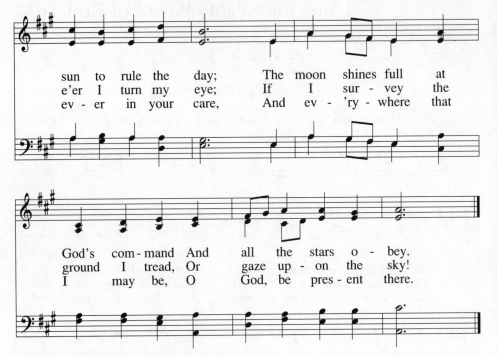

sun to rule the day; The moon shines full at
e'er I turn my eye; If I sur - vey the
ev - er in your care, And ev - 'ry - where that

God's com - mand And all the stars o - bey.
ground I tread, Or gaze up - on the sky!
I may be, O God, be pres - ent there.

Text: Isaac Watts, 1674-1748, alt.
Tune: ELLACOMBE, CMD; *Gesangbuch der Herzogl*, Wirtemberg, 1784

God, beyond All Names 634

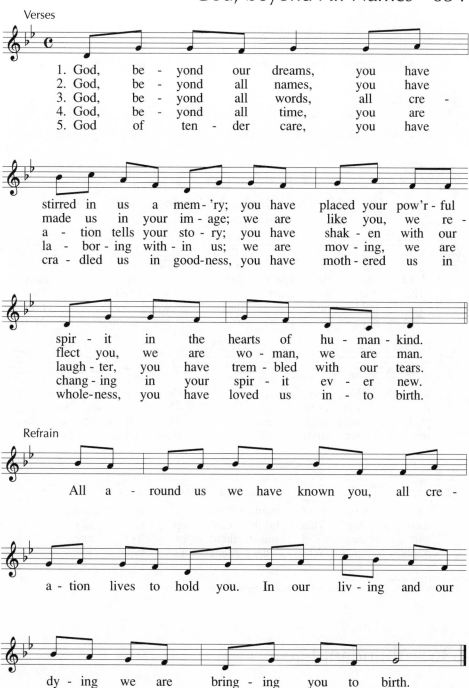

Verses

1. God, be - yond our dreams, you have
2. God, be - yond all names, you have
3. God, be - yond all words, all cre -
4. God, be - yond all time, you are
5. God of ten - der care, you have

stirred in us a mem - 'ry; you have placed your pow'r - ful
made us in your im - age; we are like you, we re -
a - tion tells your sto - ry; you have shak - en with our
la - bor - ing with - in us; we are mov - ing, we are
cra - dled us in good-ness, you have moth - ered us in

spir - it in the hearts of hu - man - kind.
flect you, we are wo - man, we are man.
laugh - ter, you have trem - bled with our tears.
chang - ing in your spir - it ev - er new.
whole-ness, you have loved us in - to birth.

Refrain

All a - round us we have known you, all cre -

a - tion lives to hold you. In our liv - ing and our

dy - ing we are bring - ing you to birth.

Text: Bernadette Farrell, b.1957
Tune: Bernadette Farrell, b.1957
© 1990, Bernadette Farrell, published by OCP Publications

635 All Things Bright and Beautiful

Refrain

All things bright and beau - ti - ful, All
crea - tures great and small, All things wise and
won - der - ful, The Lord God made them all.

Verses

1. Each lit - tle flow'r that o - pens, Each
2. The pur - ple - head - ed moun - tain, The
3. The cold wind in the win - ter, The
4. God gave us eyes to see them, And

lit - tle bird that sings, God made their glow - ing
riv - er run - ning by, The sun - set, and the
pleas-ant sum - mer sun, The ripe fruits in the
lips that we might tell How great is God Al -

D.C.

col - ors, God made their ti - ny wings.
morn - ing That bright - ens up the sky.
gar - den, God made them ev - 'ry one.
might - y, Who has made all things well.

Text: Cecil F. Alexander, 1818-1895, alt.
Tune: ROYAL OAK, 7 6 7 6 with refrain; English Melody; adapted by Martin Shaw, 1875-1958

636 Abundant Life

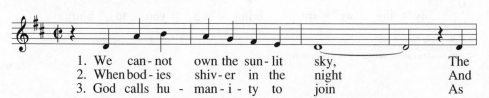

1. We can - not own the sun - lit sky, The
2. When bod - ies shiv - er in the night, And
3. God calls hu - man - i - ty to join As

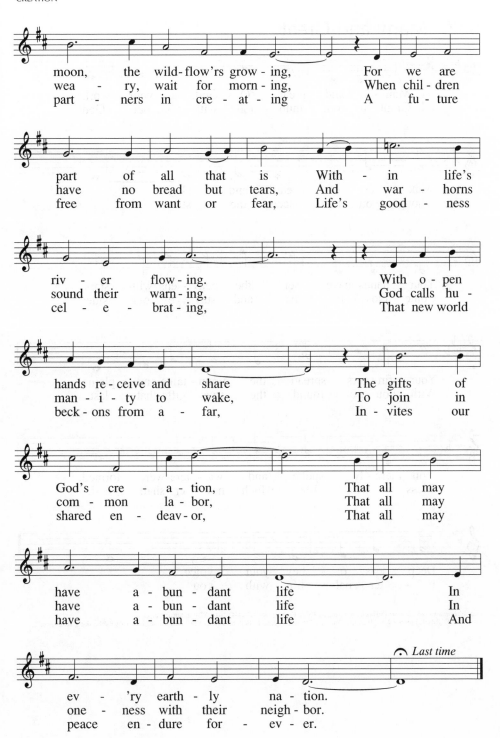

moon, the wild-flow'rs grow-ing, For we are
wea - ry, wait for morn-ing, When chil-dren
part - ners in cre-at-ing A fu - ture

part of all that is With - in life's
have no bread but tears, And war - horns
free from want or fear, Life's good - ness

riv - er flow-ing. With o - pen
sound their warn-ing, God calls hu -
cel - e - brat-ing, That new world

hands re-ceive and share The gifts of
man-i-ty to wake, To join in
beck-ons from a - far, In - vites our

God's cre - a - tion, That all may
com - mon la-bor, That all may
shared en - deav-or, That all may

have a - bun - dant life In
have a - bun - dant life In
have a - bun - dant life And

Last time

ev - 'ry earth - ly na - tion.
one - ness with their neigh - bor.
peace en - dure for - ev - er.

Text: Ruth Duck, b.1947, © 1992, GIA Publications, Inc.
Tune: LA GRANGE, 8 7 8 7 D; Marty Haugen, b.1950, © 1994, GIA Publications, Inc.

637 Many and Great

1. Man - y and great, O God, are your works,
2. Grant us com - mun - ion with you, our God,

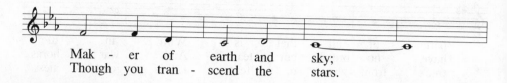

Mak - er of earth and sky;
Though you tran - scend the stars.

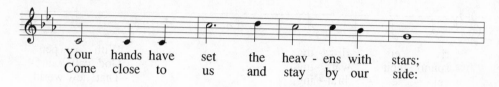

Your hands have set the heav - ens with stars;
Come close to us and stay by our side:

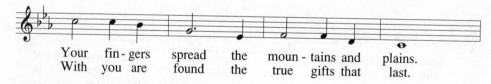

Your fin - gers spread the moun - tains and plains.
With you are found the true gifts that last.

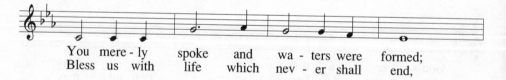

You mere - ly spoke and wa - ters were formed;
Bless us with life which nev - er shall end,

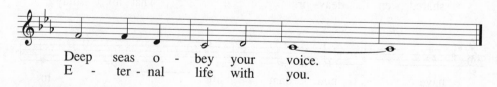

Deep seas o - bey your voice.
E - ter - nal life with you.

Text: *Wakantanka tuku nitawa;* Dakota hymn; para. by Philip Frazier, 1892-1964, © 1916, Walton Music Corp.
Tune: LACQUIPARLE, 9 6 9 9 9 6; *Dakota Odowan,* 1879; acc. by John L. Bell, b.1949, © 1993, Iona Community, GIA Publications, Inc., agent

Canticle of the Sun   638

Refrain

The heav-ens are tell-ing the glo-ry of God, and

all cre - a-tion is shout-ing for joy. Come, dance in the

for - est, come, play in the field, and sing,

sing to the

1.- 6.

To verses

sing the glo - ry of the Lord.

7.

Lord.   Sing, sing to the glo - ry

of the Lord.

Verses

1. Praise for the sun, the bring - er of day, He
2. Praise for the wind that blows through the trees, The
3. Praise for the rain that wa - ters our fields, And
4. Praise for the fire who gives us his light, The
5. Praise for the earth who makes life to grow, The
6. Praise for our death that makes our life real, The

car - ries the light of the Lord in his rays; The
seas might - y storms, 𝄿 the gen - tl - est breeze; They
bless - es our crops 𝄿 so all the earth yields; From
warmth of the sun 𝄿 to bright - en our night; He
crea - tures you made 𝄿 to let your life show; The
know - ledge of loss 𝄿 that helps us to feel; The

moon and the stars who light up the way Un -
blow where they will, they blow where they please To
death un - to life her mys - t'ry re - vealed Springs
danc - es with joy, his spir - it so bright, He
flow - ers and trees that help us to know The
gift of your - self, your pres - ence re - vealed To

D.C.

to your throne.
please the Lord.
forth in joy.
sings of you.
heart of love.
lead us home.

Text: Marty Haugen, b.1950
Tune: Marty Haugen, b.1950
© 1980, GIA Publications, Inc.

The Stars Declare His Glory   639

1. The stars de - clare his glo - ry; The
2. The dawn re - turns in splen - dor, The
3. So shine the Lord's com - mand - ments To
4. So or - der too this life of mine, Di -

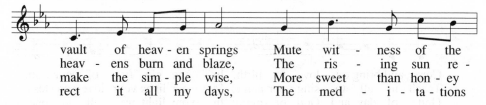

vault of heav - en springs Mute wit - ness of the
heav - ens burn and blaze, The ris - ing sun re -
make the sim - ple wise, More sweet than hon - ey
rect it all my days, The med - i - ta - tions

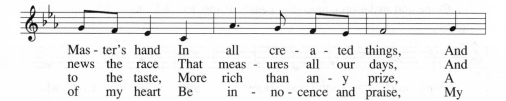

Mas - ter's hand In all cre - a - ted things, And
news the race That meas - ures all our days, And
to the taste, More rich than an - y prize, A
of my heart Be in - no - cence and praise, My

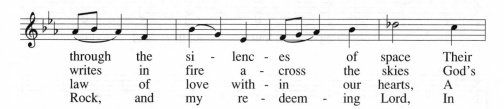

through the si - lenc - es of space Their
writes in fire a - cross the skies God's
law of love with - in our hearts, A
Rock, and my re - deem - ing Lord, In

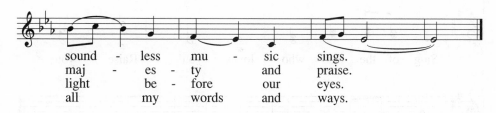

sound - less mu - sic sings.
maj - es - ty and praise.
light be - fore our eyes.
all my words and ways.

Text: Psalm 19; Timothy Dudley-Smith, b.1926, © 1981, Hope Publishing Co.
Tune: ALDINE, 7 6 8 6 8 6; Richard Proulx, b.1937, © 1986, GIA Publications, Inc.

640 Sing Out, Earth and Skies

Verses

1. Come, O God of all the earth: Come to us, O Right-eous One;
2. Come, O God of wind and flame: Fill the earth with right-eous-ness;
3. Come, O God of flash-ing light: Twin-kling star and burn-ing sun;
4. Come, O God of snow and rain: Show - er down up - on the earth;
5. Come, O Jus-tice, Come, O Peace: Come and shape our hearts a - new;

Come, and bring our love to birth: In the glo - ry of your Son.
Teach us all to sing your name: May our lives your love con - fess.
God of day and God of night: In your light we all are one.
Come, O God of joy and pain: God of sor-row, God of mirth.
Come and make op - pres-sion cease: Bring us all to life in you.

Refrain

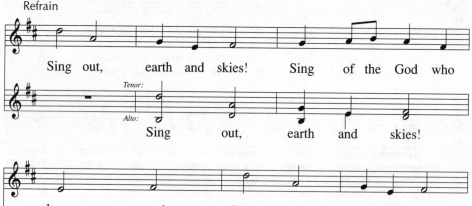

Sing out, earth and skies! Sing of the God who

Tenor:

Alto:

Sing out, earth and skies!

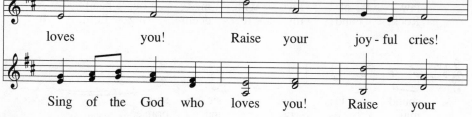

loves you! Raise your joy - ful cries!

Sing of the God who loves you! Raise your

Dance to the life a - round you!

dance to the life a - round you!

Text: Marty Haugen, b.1950
Tune: SING OUT, 77 77 with refrain; Marty Haugen, b.1950
© 1985, GIA Publications, Inc.

I Have Loved You   641

Refrain

I have loved you with an ev-er-last-ing love, I have
called you and you are mine; I have loved you with an
ev-er-last-ing love, I have called you and you are mine.

him: He will   bring   you his light   and his   peace.
him: He will   bring   you his joy   and his   hope.
him: He will   bring   you his care   and his   love.

Text: Jeremiah 31:3, Psalm 24:3; Michael Joncas, b.1951
Tune: Michael Joncas, b.1951
© 1979, New Dawn Music

642 Come to the Feast

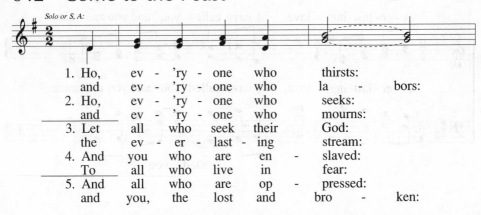

1. Ho,   ev - 'ry - one   who   thirsts:
   and   ev - 'ry - one   who   la - bors:
2. Ho,   ev - 'ry - one   who   seeks:
   and   ev - 'ry - one   who   mourns:
3. Let   all   who   seek   their   God:
   the   ev - er - last - ing   stream:
4. And   you   who   are   en - slaved:
   To   all   who   live   in   fear:
5. And   all   who   are   op - pressed:
   and   you,   the   lost   and   bro - ken:

Text: Isaiah 55; Marty Haugen, b.1950
Tune: Marty Haugen, b.1950
© 1991, GIA Publications, Inc.

You Are All We Have   643

Verse 2

Melody:

Harmony:

2. How won-der-ful   are your gifts to   me,   how

good they   are!   I   praise the Lord   who

D.C.

guides   me and teach-es me the   way of truth   and   life.

Verse 3

3. You are near,   the   God I seek.

Noth-ing   can take me from your   side.   All my days   I

D.C.

rest se-cure;   you will show me   the   path that leads to   life.

Text: Francis Patrick O'Brien, b.1958
Tune: Francis Patrick O'Brien, b.1958
© 1992, GIA Publications, Inc.

All You Who Are Thirsty   644

Refrain

All you who are thirst-y, come to the wa-ter;

All you who hun-ger, come, re-ceive grain; All with-out mon-ey,

come with-out pay-ing; All you who heed me, come for rich fare.

Verses

Cantor or choir:

1. Come now and lis-ten that you may have life; my
2. Why spend your mon-ey for what is not bread, your
3. Drink of this wa-ter a - bun-dant with life and

cov - e - nant I will re - new.   This
wag - es for what fails to sat - is - fy?
eat of the bread I pro - vide.

cov - e - nant shall be e - ter - nal
Heed my com - mand-ments and you shall eat well;
I am the bread, and the wa - ter am I;   put

D.C.

as   I prom - ised to Da - vid.
you shall de - light in rich fare.
thirst - ing and hun - ger a - side.

Text: Isaiah 55; adapt. by Michael Connolly, b.1955
Tune: Michael Connolly, b.1955
© 1982, 1988, GIA Publications, Inc.

645 Who Can Measure Heaven and Earth

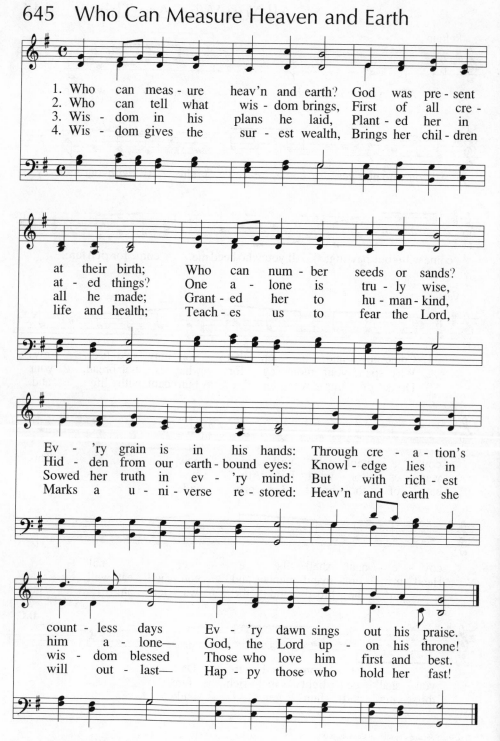

1. Who can meas - ure heav'n and earth? God was pre - sent at their birth; Who can num - ber seeds or sands? Ev - 'ry grain is in his hands: Through cre - a - tion's count - less days Ev - 'ry dawn sings out his praise.

2. Who can tell what wis - dom brings, First of all cre - at - ed things? One a - lone is tru - ly wise, Hid - den from our earth - bound eyes: Knowl - edge lies in him a - lone— God, the Lord up - on his throne!

3. Wis - dom in his plans he laid, Plant - ed her in all he made; Grant - ed her to hu - man - kind, Sowed her truth in ev - 'ry mind: But with rich - est wis - dom blessed Those who love him first and best.

4. Wis - dom gives the sur - est wealth, Brings her chil - dren life and health; Teach - es us to fear the Lord, Marks a u - ni - verse re - stored: Heav'n and earth she will out - last— Hap - py those who hold her fast!

Text: Ecclesiastes 1; Christopher Idle, b.1938, © 1982, Hope Publishing Co.
Tune: DIX, 77 77 77; arr. from Conrad Kocher, 1786-1872, by William H. Monk, 1823-1889

God Is Working His Purpose Out 646

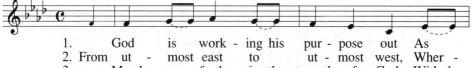

1. God is work - ing his pur - pose out As
2. From ut - most east to ut - most west, Wher -
3. March we forth in the strength of God, With the
4. All we can do is worth - less toil Un -

year suc - ceeds to year: ‹ God is work - ing his
ev - er foot has trod, By the mouth of man - y
ban-ner of Christ un - furled, That the light of the glo - rious
less God bless-es the deed; ‹ Vain - ly we hope for the

pur - pose out, And the time is draw - ing near;
mes - sen - gers Goes forth the voice of God;
gos - pel of truth May shine through- out the world:
har - vest - tide Till God gives life to the seed; Yet

Near - er and near - er draws the time, The time that shall sure - ly
Give ear to me, you con - ti - nents, You isles, give ear to
Fight we the fight with sor-row and sin To set their cap-tives
near - er and near - er draws the time, The time that shall sure - ly

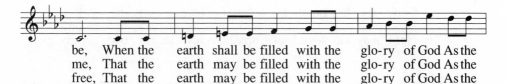

be, When the earth shall be filled with the glo-ry of God As the
me, That the earth may be filled with the glo-ry of God As the
free, That the earth may be filled with the glo-ry of God As the
be, When the earth shall be filled with the glo-ry of God As the

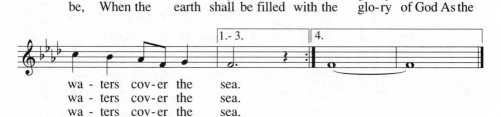

1.- 3. | 4.

wa - ters cov-er the sea.
wa - ters cov-er the sea.
wa - ters cov-er the sea.
wa - ters cov-er the sea.

Text: Habakkuk 1:14; Arthur C. Ainger, 1841-1919, alt.
Tune: PURPOSE, Irregular; Martin Shaw, 1875-1958, © Oxford University Press

647 Light of Christ / Exsultet

Refrain

All:

The light of Christ sur- rounds us, the love of Christ en- folds us, the pow'r of Christ pro- tects us, the pres- ence of Christ watch- es o- ver us.

To verses

Last time

us, for ev- er, and ev- er, for ev- er, and ev- er. A- men.

Verses 1, 2, 3

Cantor or schola:

1. All the earth is a- blaze with the glo- ry of
2. Let us fill ev- 'ry space with the sound of our
3. As this can- dle shines out through the dark- ness of

D.C.

God, for the Light has come to burn a- way the dark- ness.
joy, prais- ing Christ, who is liv- ing now a- mong us.
night, may the love of Christ burn ev- er in our hearts.

Verse 4

slower

4. In the east, the Morn- ing Star ris- es bright up- on you,

D.C.

in its peace- ful light shines the glo- ry of the Lord.

Text: Based on a prayer by James Dillet Freeman and the *Exsultet;* Marty Haugen, b.1950
Tune: Marty Haugen, b.1950
© 1987, GIA Publications, Inc.

We Are Marching   648

We are march - ing* in the light of God, we are

march - ing   in   the   light   of   God.   We are

march   -   ing   in   the   light   of   God,   we   are

march - ing   in   the   light   of   God,   we   are

march - ing   in   the   light   of   the light   of   God,   we   are

march - ing   in   the   light   of   God,

Alternate text: dancing, singing, praying

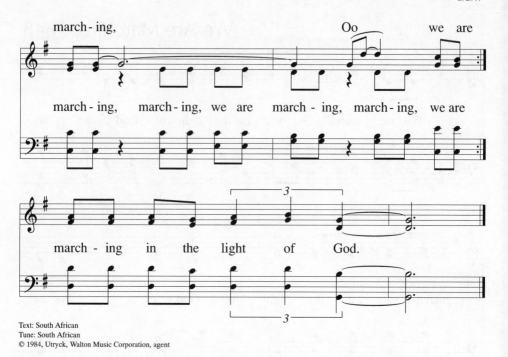

Text: South African
Tune: South African
© 1984, Utryck, Walton Music Corporation, agent

649 The Lord Is My Light

The themes may be sung separately or together, in unison or in canon.

Text: Taizé Community
Tune: Jacques Berthier, 1923-1994
© 1982, Les Presses de Taizé, GIA Publications, Inc., agent

Awake, O Sleeper 650

Refrain

Descant:

A - wake,   O   sleep - er,   a - rise   from   death,   a -

Melody:

ban - don the   shad - ows   of   night;   the   wind   of the

spir - it   shall   be   your   breath,   and   Christ   will

| 1.-3. | *To verses* |

fill   you   with   light.

Last time

light,   and   Christ   will   fill   you   with   light!

Verses 1, 2

1. Once   you   were   dark - ness,   once   you   were   lost   in   the
2. Live   as   God's   peo - ple,   live   as   God's   jus - tice   and

shad - ows.
mer - cy,

Once you were dark - ness,
filled with com - pas - sion,

D.C.

now   you are chil-dren of   light.
filled with the pow - er of   love.

Verse 3

3. Shine   out with the splen - dor of   love,   shine with

right-eous - ness.

jus - tice and right - eous - ness.   Sing the   mu - sic your

spir - it has heard,   the   songs   of   glo - ry and

D.C.

light.

Text: Ephesians 5; Marty Haugen, b.1950
Tune: Marty Haugen, b.1950
© 1987, GIA Publications, Inc.

I Want to Walk as a Child of the Light   651

1. I want to walk as a child of the light.
2. I want to see the bright-ness of God.
3. I'm look-ing for the com-ing of Christ.

I want to fol - low Je - sus.
I want to look at Je - sus.
I want to be with Je - sus.

God set the stars to give light to the world. The
Clear sun of right-eous-ness shine on my path, And
When we have run with pa-tience the race, We

star of my life is Je - sus.
show me the way to the Fa - ther.
shall know the joy of Je - sus.

In him there is no dark - ness at all. The

night and the day are both a - like. The

Lamb is the light of the cit - y of God.

Shine in my heart, Lord Je - sus.

Text: Ephesians 5:8-10, Revelation 21:23, John 12: 46, 1 John 1:5, Hebrews 12:1; Kathleen Thomerson, b.1934, © 1970, 1975, Celebration
Tune: HOUSTON, 10 7 10 8 9 9 10 7; Kathleen Thomerson, b.1934, © 1970, 1975, Celebration; acc. by Robert J. Batastini, b.1942, © 1987, GIA
Publications, Inc.

652 Praise to You, O Christ, Our Savior

Refrain

Praise to you, O Christ, our Sav-ior, Word of the Fa - ther,

call-ing us to life; Son of God who leads us to free-dom:

To verses *Last time*

glo - ry to you, Lord Je - sus Christ! Christ!

Verses

1. You are the Word who calls us out of dark - ness;
2. You are the one whom proph-ets hoped and longed for;
3. You are the Word who calls us to be ser - vants;
4. You are the Word who binds us and u - nites us;

You are the Word who leads us in - to light;
You are the one who speaks to us to - day;
You are the Word whose on - ly law is love;
You are the Word who calls us to be one;

You are the Word who brings us through the des - ert:
You are the one who leads us to our fu - ture:
You are the Word made flesh who lives a - mong us:
You are the Word who teach - es us for - give - ness:

D.C.

Glo - ry to you, Lord Je - sus Christ!
Glo - ry to you, Lord Je - sus Christ!
Glo - ry to you, Lord Je - sus Christ!
Glo - ry to you, Lord Je - sus Christ!

Text: Bernadette Farrell, b.1957
Tune: Bernadette Farrell, b.1957
© 1986, Bernadette Farrell, published by OCP Publications

Word of God, Come Down on Earth 653

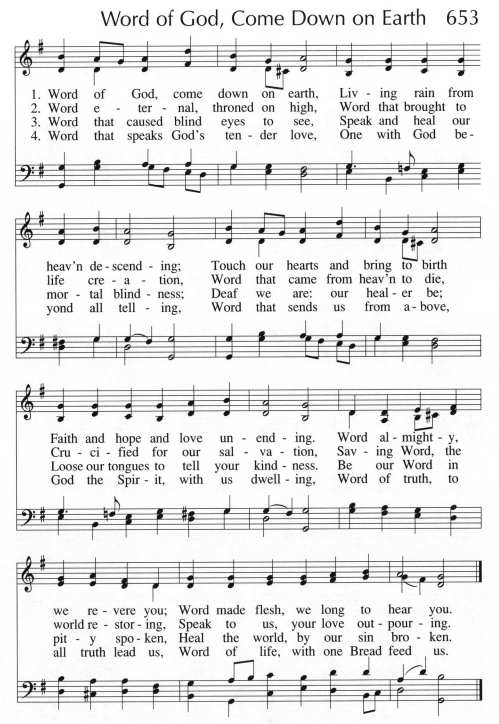

1. Word of God, come down on earth, Liv-ing rain from heav'n de-scend-ing; Touch our hearts and bring to birth Faith and hope and love un-end-ing. Word al-might-y, we re-vere you; Word made flesh, we long to hear you.

2. Word e-ter-nal, throned on high, Word that brought to life cre-a-tion, Word that came from heav'n to die, Cru-ci-fied for our sal-va-tion, Sav-ing Word, the world re-stor-ing, Speak to us, your love out-pour-ing.

3. Word that caused blind eyes to see, Speak and heal our mor-tal blind-ness; Deaf we are: our heal-er be; Loose our tongues to tell your kind-ness. Be our Word in pit-y spo-ken, Heal the world, by our sin bro-ken.

4. Word that speaks God's ten-der love, One with God be-yond all tell-ing, Word that sends us from a-bove, God the Spir-it, with us dwell-ing, Word of truth, to all truth lead us, Word of life, with one Bread feed us.

Text: James Quinn, SJ, b.1919, © 1969. Used by permission of Selah Publishing Co., Inc., Kingston, N.Y.
Tune: LIEBSTER JESU, 7 8 7 8 88; Johann R. Ahle, 1625-1673; harm. by George H. Palmer, 1846-1926

654 God Has Spoken by His Prophets

1. God has spo - ken by his proph - ets, Spo - ken
2. God has spo - ken by Christ Je - sus, Christ, the
3. God is speak - ing by his Spir - it, Speak - ing

his un - chang - ing Word; Each from
ev - er - last - ing Son, Bright - ness
to the hearts of all, In the

age to age pro - claim - ing God, the
of the Fa - ther's glo - ry, With the
age - less Word ex - pound - ing God's own

one the right - eous, Lord. In the
Fa - ther ev - er one; Spo - ken
mes - sage for us all. Through the

world's de - spair and tur - moil, One firm
by the Word In - car - nate, God of
rise and fall of na - tions One sure

an - chor holds us fast; God is
God, be - fore time was; Light of
faith yet stand - ing fast; God a -

king, his throne e - ter - nal; God the
Light, to earth de - scend - ing, He re -
bides, his Word un - chang - ing; God the

first, and God the last.
veals our God to us.
first, and God the last.

Text: George W. Briggs, 1875-1959, alt., © 1953, 1981, Hymn Society of America
Tune: RUSTINGTON, 8 7 8 7 D; Charles H. H. Parry, 1848-1918

655 Your Word Went Forth

1. Your Word went forth and light a - woke. The dark-ness
2. Your Word went forth and shot a flame Of light from
3. Your Word goes forth and light e - rupts From kin - dled
4. Send forth your Word; your si - lence break. Shine in this

fled; Bright day was born And swift - ly sped A - cross pri -
light. Our flesh it wore And walked a - mong Us in this
speech And an - cient page, Your Spir - it's fire Ig - nit - ing
time In which our night Is ter - ror - torn By dreams of

me - val earth. It was cre - a - tion's morn.
dark - ened world Cre - a - tion to re - store.
hu - man words To light - en ev - 'ry age.
fier - y death. Come, be our life, our light.

Text: Psalm 119:130; Herman Stuempfle, b.1923
Tune: AWAKENING WORD, 8 4 4 4 6 6; Randall Sensmeier, b.1948
© 1993, GIA Publications, Inc.

Magnificat 656

1. My soul gives glo - ry to the Lord, In
2. His mer - cy goes to all who fear, From
3. He raised his ser - vant Is - ra - el, Re -

God my Sav - ior I re - joice. My low - li -
age to age and to all parts. His arm of
mem - b'ring his e - ter - nal grace, As from of

ness he did re - gard, Ex - alt - ing me by
strength to all is near; He scat - ters those who
old he did fore - tell To A - bra - ham and

his own choice. From this day all shall call me
have proud hearts. He casts the might - y from their
all his race. O Fa - ther, Son and Spir - it

blest, For he has done great things for me, Of
throne And rais - es those of low de - gree; He
blest, In three - fold Name are you a - dored, To

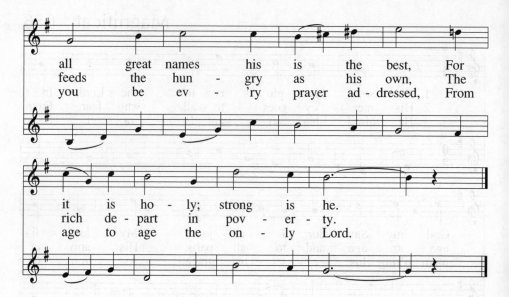

all great names his is the best, For
feeds the hun - gry as his own, The
you be ev - 'ry prayer ad - dressed, From

it is ho - ly; strong is he.
rich de - part in pov - er - ty.
age to age the on - ly Lord.

Text: Luke 1:46-55; J.T. Mueller, 1885-1967, alt.
Tune: MAGNIFICAT, LMD; Michael Joncas, b.1951, © 1979, 1988, GIA Publications, Inc.

Holy God, We Praise Thy Name   657

1. Ho - ly God, we praise thy name!
2. Hark! the loud ce - les - tial hymn
3. Ho - ly Fa - ther, Ho - ly Son,

Lord of all, we bow be - fore thee;
An - gel choirs a - bove are rais - ing;
Ho - ly Spir - it, Three we name thee,

All on earth thy scep - ter claim,
Cher - u - bim and Ser - a - phim
While in es - sence on - ly One,

All in heav'n a - bove a - dore thee;
In un - ceas - ing cho - rus prais - ing,
Un - di - vid - ed God we claim thee,

Optional repeat of last eight measures

Text: *Grosser Gott, wir loben dich;* ascr. to Ignaz Franz, 1719-1790; tr. by Clarence Walworth, 1820-1900
Tune: GROSSER GOTT, 7 8 7 8 77; *Katholisches Gesangbuch,* Vienna, c.1774

Let All Mortal Flesh Keep Silence   658

1. Let all mor - tal flesh keep si - lence,
2. King of kings, yet born of Mar - y,
3. Rank on rank the host of heav - en
4. At his feet the six - winged ser - aph,

And with fear and trem - bling stand;
As of old on earth he stood,
Spreads its van - guard on the way,
Cher - u - bim with sleep - less eye,

Pon - der noth - ing earth - ly mind - ed,
Lord of lords in hu - man ves - ture,
As the Light of Light de - scend - ing
Veil their fac - es to the Pres - ence,

For with bless - ing in his hand
In the Bod - y and the Blood
From the realms of end - less day,
As with cease - less voice they cry,

Christ our God to earth de - scend -
He will give to all the faith -
That the pow'rs of hell may van -
"Al - le - lu - ia, al - le - lu -

ing, Our full hom - age to de - mand.
ful His own self for heav'n - ly food.
ish As the dark - ness clears a - way.
ia, Al - le - lu - ia, Lord, most high!"

Text: Liturgy of St. James 5th C.; para. by Gerard Moultrie, 1829-1885
Tune: PICARDY, 8 7 8 7 8 7; French Carol; harm. by Richard Proulx, b.1937, © 1986, GIA Publications, Inc.

659 You Are the Voice

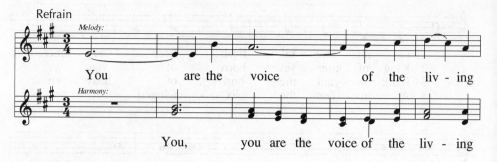

Refrain

Melody:

You are the voice of the liv-ing

Harmony:

You, you are the voice of the liv-ing

God, call-ing us now to live in your

God, call-ing us now to live,

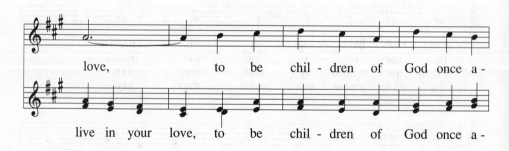

love, to be chil-dren of God once a-

live in your love, to be chil-dren of God once a-

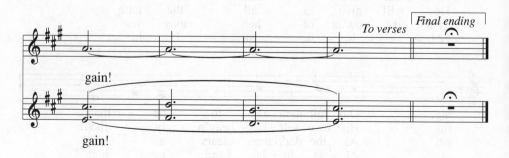

gain!

To verses | **Final ending**

gain!

Verses

1. Praise for the light that shines through the night, from
2. Praise for the wa-ter that springs from the sea, the
3. Praise for the sing-ing and praise for the dance, with

dark - ness to light, from death to new life, and
seed that gives life to all who be - lieve, God's
new heart and voice, all raise the song of

praise to the morn - ing that brings forth the sun, to
love o - ver - flow - ing, our hearts know the joy to be
praise to cre - a - tion; all heav - en and earth, come

All:

o - pen our eyes to the Lord! To o - pen our
daugh - ters and sons of the Lord! To be daugh-ters and
sing of the glo - ry of God! Come sing of the

D.C.

eyes to the Lord! For
sons of the Lord! For
glo - ry of God! For

Text: David Haas, b.1957
Tune: David Haas, b.1957; acc. by Jeanne Cotter, b.1964
© 1983, 1987, GIA Publications, Inc.

660 Laudate Dominum

Ostinato Refrain

Lau-da-te Do-mi-num, lau-da-te Do-mi-num om-nes gen-tes, al-le-lu-ia. al-le-lu-ia.

Verses
Cantor:

Praise the Lord, all you na-tions, praise him all you peo-ples. Al - le - lu - ia.

Strong is his love and mer-cy. He is faith-ful for ev-er. Al - le - lu - ia. Al-le-lu - ia, al-le-lu - ia. Let ev-'ry thing liv-ing give praise to the Lord. Al-le- praise to the Lord.

*Choose either part

Text: Psalm 117, *Praise the Lord, all you peoples;* Taizé Community, 1980
Tune: Jacques Berthier, 1923-1994
© 1980. Les Presses de Taizé, GIA Publications, Inc., agent

Heavenly Hosts in Ceaseless Worship 661

1. Heaven-ly hosts in cease-less wor-ship, "Ho-ly, ho-ly,
2. All cre-a-tion, all re-demp-tion, Join to sing the

ho-ly" cry; "He who is, who was and will be,
Sav-ior's worth; Lamb of God whose blood has bought us,

God, Al-might-y, Lord most high." Praise and hon-or,
Kings and priests, to reign on earth. Wealth and wis-dom,

pow'r and glo-ry, Be to Him who reigns a-lone;
pow'r and glo-ry, Hon-or, might, do-min-ion, praise,

We, with all his hands have fash-ioned,
Now be his from all his crea-tures

Fall be-fore the Fa-ther's throne.
And to ev-er-last-ing days.

Text: Revelation 4-5; Timothy Dudley-Smith, b.1926, © 1975, Hope Publishing Co.
Tune: HEAVENLY HOSTS, 8 7 8 7 D; Noel H. Tredinnick, b.1949, © 1973, Hope Publishing Co.

662 Alabaré

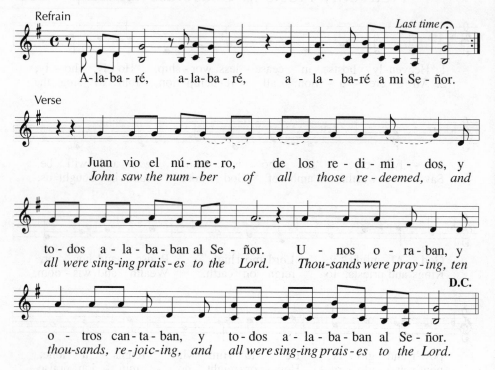

Refrain

A-la-ba - ré, a-la-ba - ré, a - la - ba-ré a mi Se - ñor.

Verse

Juan vio el nú-me-ro, de los re - di - mi - dos, y
John saw the num - ber of all those re - deemed, and

to - dos a - la - ba-ban al Se - ñor. U - nos o - ra-ban, y
all were sing-ing prais - es to the Lord. Thou-sands were pray - ing, ten

o - tros can-ta-ban, y to - dos a - la - ba-ban al Se - ñor.
thou-sands, re - joic-ing, and all were sing-ing prais - es to the Lord.

Text: *I will praise the Lord;* Manuel José Alonso, José Pagán, © 1979 and Ediciones Musical PAX, published by OCP Publications; trans. unknown
Tune: Manuel José Alonso, José Pagán, © 1979 and Ediciones Musical PAX, published by OCP Publications; acc. by Diana Kodner,
    © 1994, GIA Publications, Inc.

How Great Thou Art   663

1. O Lord my God, when I in awe-some
2. When thru the woods and for-est glades I
3. And when I think that God, His Son not
4. When Christ shall come with shout of ac-cla-

won-der Con-sid-er all the worlds Thy hands have
wan-der And hear the birds sing sweet-ly in the
spar-ing, Sent Him to die, I scarce can take it
ma-tion And take me home, what joy shall fill my

made, I see the stars, I hear the roll-ing
trees, When I look down from loft-y moun-tain
in That on the cross, my bur-den glad-ly
heart! Then I shall bow in hum-ble ad-o-

thun-der, Thy pow'r thru-out the un-i-verse dis-played!
gran-deur And hear the brook and feel the gen-tle breeze.
bear-ing, He bled and died to take a-way my sin!
ra-tion And there pro-claim, my God, how great Thou art!

Then sings my soul, my Sav-ior God, to Thee; How great Thou art, how great Thou art! Then sings my soul, my Sav-ior God, to Thee; How great Thou art, How great Thou art!

Text: Stuart K. Hine, 1899-1989
Tune: O STORE GUD, 11 10 11 10 with refrain; Stuart K. Hine, 1899-1989

Cantemos al Señor / Let's Sing unto the Lord   664

1. Can - te - mos al Se - ñor   Un him - no de a - le - grí - a,   Un
2. Can - te - mos al Se - ñor   Un him - no de a - la - ban - za   Que ex-
1. *Let's sing un - to the Lord*   *A hymn of glad re - joic - ing,*   *Let's*
2. *Let's sing un - to the Lord*   *A hymn of a - do - ra - tion,*   *Ex -*

cán - ti - co de a - mor   Al na - cer   el nue - vo dí - a.   El
pre - se nues-tro a - mor,   Nues-tra fe y nues-tra es - pe - ran - za,   En
sing a hymn of love,   *Join - ing hearts and hap - py voic - es.*   *God*
press un - to the Lord   *Our   songs   of faith and hope.*   *Cre -*

hi - zo el cie - lo el mar,   El sol y las es - tre - llas   Y
to - da   la crea - ción   Pre - go - na su gran - de - za,   A -
made the sky a - bove,   *The stars, the sun, the   o - ceans.*   *Their*
a - tion's broad dis - play   *Pro-claims the work of gran-deur,*   *The*

vio en e - llos bon - dad,   Pues sus o - bras e - ran be - llas.
sí   nues - tro can - tar   Va a - nun - cian - do su be - lle - za.
good - ness does pro - claim   *The   glo - ry of God's name.*
bound - less love of   One   Who   bless - es us with beau - ty.

¡A - le - lu - ya!   ¡A - le - lu - ya!   Can -
Al - le - lu - ia!   *Al - le - lu - ia!*   *Let's*

| 1. | | 2. |

te - mos al Se - ñor.   ¡A - le - lu - ya!   lu - ya!
sing un - to the Lord.   *Al - le - lu - ia!*   *lu - ia!*

Text: Based on Psalm 19; Carlos Rosas, b.1939; trans. by Roberto Escamilla, Elise Eslinger, and George Lockwood, 1983,
© 1976, Resource Publications, Inc.
Tune: ROSAS, 6 7 6 8 D with refrain; Carlos Rosas, b.1939, © 1976, Resource Publications, Inc.; acc. by Diana Kodner, b.1957,
© 1993, GIA Publications, Inc.

665 When, in Our Music, God Is Glorified

1. When, in our mu - sic, God is glo - ri - fied,
2. How of - ten, mak - ing mu - sic, we have found
3. So has the Church, in lit - ur - gy and song,
4. And did not Je - sus sing a psalm that night
5. Let ev - 'ry in - stru-ment be tuned for praise!

And ad - o - ra - tion leaves no room for pride,
A new di - men - sion in the world of sound,
In faith and love, through cen - tu - ries of wrong,
When ut - most e - vil strove a - gainst the Light?
Let all re - joice who have a voice to raise!

It is as though the whole cre - a - tion cried:
As wor - ship moved us to a more pro - found
Borne wit - ness to the truth in ev - 'ry tongue:
Then let us sing, for whom he won the fight:
And may God give us faith to sing al - ways:

Al - le - lu - ia!

Text: Mark 14:26; Fred Pratt Green, b.1903, © 1972, Hope Publishing Co.
Tune: ENGELBERG, 10 10 10 with alleluia; Charles V. Stanford, 1852-1924

To God with Gladness Sing 666

1. To God with glad - ness sing, Your Rock and Sav - ior bless; With - in God's tem - ple bring Your songs of thank - ful - ness! O Lord of might, To you we sing, En - throned as King On heav - en's height!

2. God cra - dles in his hand The heights and depths of earth; God made the sea and land, And brought the world to birth! O Lord most high, We are your sheep, On us you keep Your Shep - herd's eye!

3. Your heav'n - ly Fa - ther praise, Ac - claim his on - ly Son, Your voice in hom - age raise To him who makes all one! O Dove of peace, On us de - scend, That us strife may end And joy in - crease!

Text: Psalm 95; James Quinn, SJ, b.1919, © 1969. Used by permission of Selah Publishing., Inc., Kingston, N.Y.
Tune: CYMBALA, 66 66 4 44 4; Michael Joncas, b.1951, © 1979, GIA Publications, Inc.

667 Jubilate Servite

Canon—*2 voices*

Ju – bi – la – te De – o om – nis ter – ra.

Ser – vi – te Do – mi – no in lae – ti – ti – a.

Al – le – lu – ia, al – le – lu – ia, in lae – ti – ti – a.

Al – le – lu – ia, al – le – lu – ia, in lae – ti – ti – a!

Text: Psalm 100, *Rejoice in God, all the earth, Serve the Lord with gladness;* Taizé Community, 1978
Tune: Jacques Berthier, 1923-1994
© 1979, Les Presses de Taizé, GIA Publications, Inc., agent

668 Too Splendid for Speech

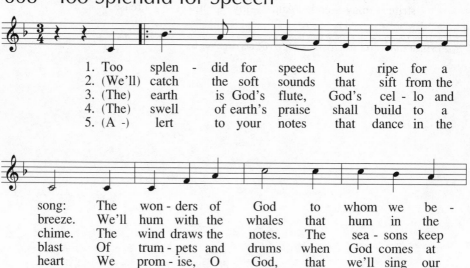

1. Too splen - did for speech but ripe for a
2. (We'll) catch the soft sounds that sift from the
3. (The) earth is God's flute, God's cel - lo and
4. (The) swell of earth's praise shall build to a
5. (A -) lert to your notes that dance in the

song: The won - ders of God to whom we be -
breeze. We'll hum with the whales that hum in the
chime. The wind draws the notes. The sea - sons keep
blast Of trum - pets and drums when God comes at
heart We prom - ise, O God, that we'll sing our

long!   What tune   can we   sing? What rich   chords can we
seas.   The   wa -   ters that tick - le   the   earth in - to
time.   At   dusk   and at   night, from the   sun - rise past
last   To   hear   if   our   lives, like the   heav - ens a -
part   And   pray   that the   song which your   song shall in -

play   To   hon - or the   pot - ter who   made us from
spring   Will teach us   the   lilt - ing new
noon   God's play - ing and sing - ing a   rav - ish - ing
bove,   Are   filled with the mu - sic   of
spire   Will lead ev - 'ry   na - tion   to

1., 3.

2., 4.

clay?   (2.) We'll life we would sing.

tune.   (4.) The   jus - tice and   love.

(3.) The   join   in   your   choir.

5.

(5.) A -

Text: Psalm 98; Thomas Troeger, b.1945, © 1985, Oxford University Press
Tune: COMMON PRAYER, 10 10 11 11; Todd Alan Constable, b.1964, © 1994, GIA Publications, Inc.

669 Joyful, Joyful, We Adore You

1. Joy - ful, joy - ful, we a - dore you, God of glo - ry,
2. All your works with joy sur-round you, Earth and heav'n re -
3. Al - ways giv - ing and for - giv - ing, Ev - er bless-ing,
4. Mor - tals join the might - y cho - rus, Which the morn - ing

Lord of love; Hearts un - fold like flowers be - fore you,
flect your rays, Stars and an - gels sing a - round you,
ev - er blest, Well - spring of the joy of liv - ing,
stars be - gan; God's own love is reign - ing o'er us,

Open - ing to the sun a - bove. Melt the clouds of
Cen - ter of un - bro - ken praise; Field and for - est,
O - cean depth of hap - py rest! Lov - ing Fa - ther,
Join - ing peo - ple hand in hand. Ev - er sing - ing,

sin and sad - ness; Drive the dark of doubt a - way;
vale and moun - tain, Flow - ery mead-ow, flash - ing sea,
Christ our broth - er, Let your light up - on us shine;
march we on - ward, Vic - tors in the midst of strife;

Giv - er of im - mor - tal glad - ness, Fill   us with the   light of day!
Chant - ing bird and flow - ing foun - tain, Prais - ing you   e - ter - nal - ly!
Teach us   how to love each oth - er, Lift   us to   the   joy di - vine.
Joy - ful   mu - sic leads us   sun - ward In   the tri - umph song of life.

Text: Henry van Dyke, 1852-1933, alt., © Charles Scribner's Sons
Tune: HYMN TO JOY, 8 7 8 7 D; arr. from Ludwig van Beethoven, 1770-1827, by Edward Hodges, 1796-1867

670 All Creatures of Our God and King

1. All crea-tures of our God and King, Lift
2. O rush-ing wind and breez-es soft, O
3. O flow-ing wa-ters, pure and clear, Make
4. Dear moth-er earth, who day by day Un -
5. O ev - 'ry one of ten-der heart, For -

up your voice and with us sing: Al-le-lu - ia! Al-le-
clouds that ride the winds a-loft: Al-le-lu - ia! Al-le-
mu - sic for your Lord to hear. Al-le-lu - ia! Al-le-
folds rich bless-ings on our way, Al-le-lu - ia! Al-le-
giv - ing oth-ers, take your part, Al-le-lu - ia! Al-le-

lu - ia! O burn-ing sun with gold-en beam And
lu - ia! O ris-ing morn, in praise re - joice, O
lu - ia! O fire so mas-ter-ful and bright, Pro -
lu - ia! The fruits and flow'rs that ver-dant grow, Let
lu - ia! All you who pain and sor-row bear, Praise

sil - ver moon with soft - er gleam:
lights of eve - ning, find a voice.
vid - ing us with warmth and light, Al - le -
them God's glo - ry al - so show.
God and cast on God your care.

lu - ia! Al-le - lu - ia! Al-le-lu - ia, al-le-

lu - ia, al-le-lu - ia!

6. And you, most kind and gentle death,
   Waiting to hush our final breath,
      Alleluia! Alleluia!
   You lead to heav'n the child of God,
   Where Christ our Lord the way has trod.
      Alleluia! Alleluia!
      Alleluia, alleluia, alleluia!

7. Let all things their Creator bless,
   And worship God in humbleness,
      Alleluia! Alleluia!
   Oh praise the Father, praise the Son,
   And praise the Spirit, Three in One!
      Alleluia! Alleluia!
      Alleluia, alleluia, alleluia!

Text: *Laudato si, mi Signor;* Francis of Assisi, 1182-1226; tr. by William H. Draper, 1855-1933, alt., © J. Curwen and Sons
Tune: LASST UNS ERFREUEN, LM with alleluias; *Geistliche Kirchengesänge*, 1623; harm. by Ralph Vaughan Williams, 1872-1958, © Oxford
   University Press

671 Cantai ao Senhor

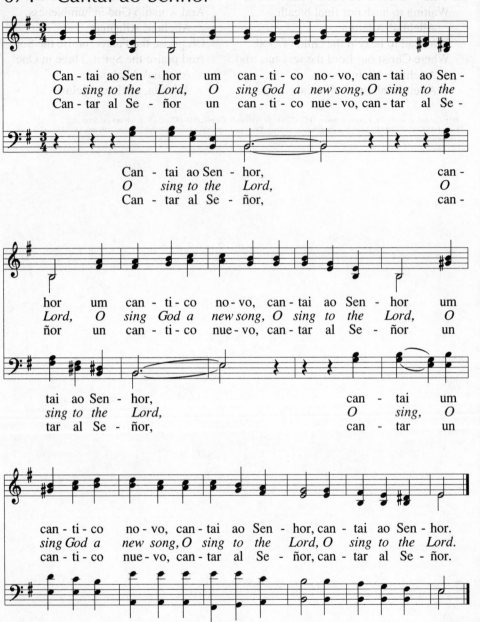

Can - tai ao Sen - hor um can - ti - co no - vo, can - tai ao Sen -
O sing to the Lord, O sing God a new song, O sing to the
Can - tar al Se - ñor un can - ti - co nue - vo, can - tar al Se -

Can - tai ao Sen - hor, can -
O sing to the Lord, O
Can - tar al Se - ñor, can -

hor um can - ti - co no - vo, can - tai ao Sen - hor um
Lord, O sing God a new song, O sing to the Lord, O
ñor un can - ti - co nue - vo, can - tar al Se - ñor un

tai ao Sen - hor, can - tai um
sing to the Lord, O sing, O
tar al Se - ñor, can - tar un

can - ti - co no - vo, can - tai ao Sen - hor, can - tai ao Sen - hor.
sing God a new song, O sing to the Lord, O sing to the Lord.
can - ti - co nue - vo, can - tar al Se - ñor, can - tar al Se - ñor.

Text: Psalm 98; Anonymous
Tune: Traditional Brazilian, © Editora Sinodal, Sao Leopoldo; arr. by John L. Bell, b. 1949, © 1991, Iona Community, GIA Publications, Inc., agent

Santo, Santo, Santo / Holy, Holy, Holy 672

1. San - to, san - to, san - to, san - to, san - to, san - to es nues - tro
2.   san - to, san - to, san - to, san - to, san - to es nues - tro
1. *Ho - ly, ho - ly, ho - ly, ho - ly, ho - ly, ho - ly is our*
2.   *ho - ly, ho - ly, ho - ly, ho - ly, ho - ly is our*

Dios,   Se - ñor de   to - da   la   tie - rra. San - to,
Dios,   Se - ñor de   to - da   la his - to - ria. San - to,
God,   God, the Lord of earth   and heav - en. Ho - ly,
God,   God, the Lord of all   of his - t'ry. Ho - ly,

1.

2. ⌢ *Last time*

san - to es nues - tro Dios. San - to,
san - to es nues - tro   Dios.
ho - ly is our God. Ho - ly,
ho - ly is our   God.

Que a - com - pa - ña a   nues - tro   pue - blo, que
Ben - di - tos los que en su   nom - bre el
Who ac - com - pa - nies our   peo - ple, who
Bless - ed those who in the   Lord's name an -

vi - ve en nues - tras   lu - chas, del   u - ni - ver - so en -
e - van - ge - lio a - nun - cian, la   bue - na y gran no -
lives with - in our strug - gles, of all the earth and
nounce the ho - ly gos - pel, pro - claim - ing the good

1.

2.   **D.C.**

te - ro el ú - ni - co Se - ñor.
ti - cia de la li - be - ra -   ción.
heav - en the one and on - ly Lord.
news that our lib - er - a - tion   comes.

Text: Guillermo Cuellar; trans. by Linda McCrae
Tune: Guillermo Cuellar; acc. by Diana Kodner, b.1957
© 1993, 1994, GIA Publications, Inc.

673 World without End

1. Praise to the Lord for the joys of the earth:
2. Praise to the Lord for the pro - gress of life:
3. Praise to the Lord for his care of our kind:
4. Praise to the Lord for the peo - ple we meet,
5. Praise to the Lord for the car - pen - ter's son,

Cy - cles of sea - son and rea - son and birth,
Cra - dle and grave, bond of hus - band and wife,
Faith for the faith - less and sight for the blind,
Safe in our homes or at risk in the street:
Dove - tail - ing wor - ship and work in - to one:

Con - trasts in out - look and land - scape and need,
Pain of youth grow - ing and wrin - kling of age,
Heal - ing, ac - cep - tance, dis - tur - bance, and change,
Kiss of a lov - er and friend - ship's em - brace,
Trades - man and teach - er and va - grant and friend,

Chal - lenge of fam - ine, pol - lu - tion, and greed.
Ques - tions in step with ex - pe - rience and stage.
All the e - mo - tions through which our lives range.
Smile of a stran - ger and words full of grace.
Source of all life in this world with - out end.

Text: John L. Bell, b.1949, © 1987, The Iona Community, GIA Publications, Inc., agent
Tune: BONNIE GEORGE CAMPBELL, 10 10 10 10; Scottish Folk Song; acc. by John L. Bell, b.1949, © 1993, Iona Community,
GIA Publications, Inc., agent

Christians, Lift Up Your Hearts   674

Refrain

Chris - tians, lift up your hearts, and make this a day of re - joic - ing; God is our strength and song; glo - ry and praise to his name!

Verses 1, 3, 5

1. This is the house of the Lord, where
3. Praise that his love o - ver - flowed in the
5. Come, Ho - ly Spir - it, to us, who

seek - ers and find - ers are wel - come; En - ter its
hearts of all who re - ceived him, Join - ing to -
live by your pres - ence with - in us, Come to di -

gates with your praise, fill all its courts with your song:
geth - er in peace those once di - vid - ed by sin:
rect our course, give us your life and your power:

D.C.

Verses 2, 4, 6

2. Strong and a - lert in his grace, God's peo - ple are
4. Those who are bur - dened with sin find here the
6. Al - might - y God, send us out to live to your

one   in   their   wor - ship: Kept   by   his
joy   of   for - give - ness,   Lay - ing   their
praise   and   your   glo - ry;   Yours   is   the

D.C.

peace they de - part,   read - y for   serv - ing   their   Lord:
sins   be - fore Christ,   par - don and peace   their   re - ward:
pow'r and the might,   ours be the   cour - age   and   faith:

Text: John E. Bowers, b.1923, alt., © Canon John E. Bowers
Tune: SALVE FESTA DIES, Irregular with refrain; Ralph Vaughan Williams, 1872-1958, © Oxford University Press

675   Magnificat

Canon

(A)   (B)

Ma-gni-fi-cat,   ma-gni-fi-cat,   Ma-gni-fi-cat a-ni-ma me-a Do-mi-num.

(C)   (D)

Ma-gni-fi-cat,   ma-gni-fi-cat,   Ma-gni-fi-cat a-ni-ma me-a!

Secondary canon (*or unison choir with trumpet*)

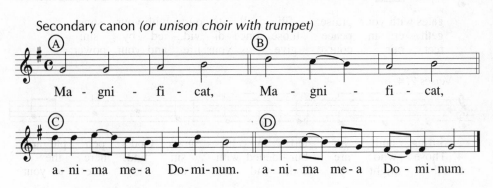

(A)   (B)

Ma - gni - fi - cat,   Ma - gni - fi - cat,

(C)   (D)

a - ni - ma me-a Do-mi-num.   a - ni - ma me-a Do-mi-num.

Text: Luke 1:46, *My soul magnifies the Lord;* Taizé Community, 1978
Tune: Jacques Berthier, 1923-1994
© 1979, Les Presses de Taizé, GIA Publications, Inc., agent

God, We Praise You 676

1. God, we praise you! God, we bless you! God, we
2. True a - pos - tles, faith-ful proph - ets, Saints who
3. Je - sus Christ, the king of glo - ry, Ev - er -
4. Christ, at God's right hand vic - to - rious, You will

name you sov - 'reign Lord! Might - y
set their world a - blaze, Mar - tyrs,
last - ing Son of God, Hum - ble
judge the world you made; Lord, in

King whom an - gels wor - ship, Fa - ther,
once un - known, un - heed - ed, Join one
was your vir - gin moth - er, Hard the
mer - cy help your ser - vants For whose

by your church a - dored: All cre -
grow - ing song of praise, While your
lone - ly path you trod: By your
free - dom you have paid: Raise us

a - tion shows your glo - ry, Heav'n and
church on earth con - fess - es One ma -
cross is sin de - feat - ed, Hell con -
up from dust to glo - ry, Guard us

earth draw near your throne, Sing - ing
jes - tic Trin - i - ty: Fa - ther,
front - ed face to face, Heav - en
from all sin to - day; King en -

"Ho - ly, ho - ly, ho - ly, Lord of
Son, and Ho - ly Spir - it, God, our
o - pened to be - liev - ers, Sin - ners
throned a - bove all prais - es, Save your

hosts, and God a - lone!"
hope e - ter - nal - ly.
jus - ti - fied by grace.
peo - ple, God, we pray.

Text: Based on the *Te Deum*; Christopher Idle, b.1938, © 1982, Hope Publishing Co.
Tune: NETTLETON, 8 7 8 7 D; Wyeth's *Repository of Sacred Music*, Pt. II, 1813

Sing a New Song to the Lord   677

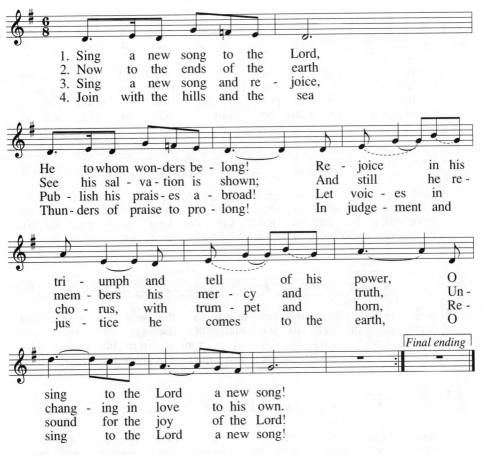

1. Sing a new song to the Lord,
2. Now to the ends of the earth
3. Sing a new song and re - joice,
4. Join with the hills and the sea

He to whom won-ders be - long! Re - joice in his
See his sal - va - tion is shown; And still he re -
Pub - lish his prais - es a - broad! Let voic - es in
Thun - ders of praise to pro - long! In judge - ment and

tri - umph and tell of his power, O
mem - bers his mer - cy and truth, Un -
cho - rus, with trum - pet and horn, Re -
jus - tice he comes to the earth, O

Final ending

sing to the Lord a new song!
chang - ing in love to his own.
sound for the joy of the Lord!
sing to the Lord a new song!

Text: Psalm 98; Timothy Dudley-Smith, b.1926
Tune: CANTATE DOMINO (ONSLOW SQUARE), Irregular; David G. Wilson, b.1940
© 1973, Hope Publishing Co.

678 Canticle of the Turning

Refrain

My heart shall sing of the day you bring. Let the
fires of your jus - tice burn.
fires of your jus - tice burn. Wipe a -
way all tears, for the dawn draws near, and the
world is a - bout to turn!
world is a - bout to turn!

Text: Luke 1:46-58; Rory Cooney, b.1952
Tune: STAR OF THE COUNTY DOWN; Irish traditional; arr. by Rory Cooney, b.1952
© 1990, GIA Publications, Inc.

679 Jesus Christ, Yesterday, Today and for Ever

Ostinato Refrain

Je - sus Christ, Je - sus Christ,

yes- ter - day, to - day and for ev - er.

Verses

Cantor:

1. O ra - diant light, O sun di - vine of our

God's death - less face.

2. You are al - pha and o - me - ga,

you are sav - ior and friend.

3. Im - age of light sub - lime that fills the

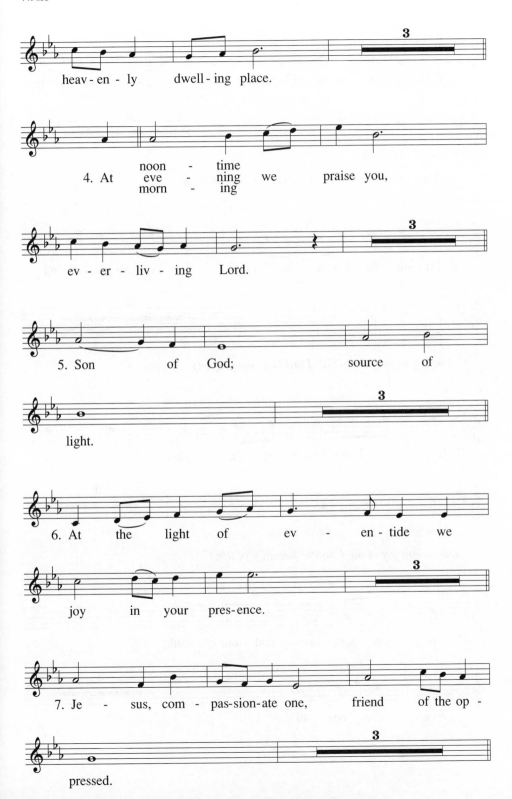

heav - en - ly dwell - ing place.

4. At noon - time
eve - ning we praise you,
morn - ing

ev - er - liv - ing Lord.

5. Son of God; source of

light.

6. At the light of ev - en - tide we

joy in your pres - ence.

7. Je - sus, com - pas - sion-ate one, friend of the op -

pressed.

8. Cris - to nos da la Li - ber-tad; Cris - to nos da la Sal - va - ción.

(Christ gives us freedom; Christ gives us salvation.)

9. Da - me Se - ñor tu pa - la - bra; o - ye Se - ñor mi o - ra - ción.

(Lord, give me your word; Lord hear my prayer.)

10. Joie a - bon - date de l'E - glise, et sour - ce de vie.

(Abundant joy of the Church; fountain of life.)

11. You are our way and our truth; You are our life.

12. Chúa sống Lai tràn dầy sù sống.

(Jesus Christ rose with full life.)

13. Cris - to, pa - ro - la e - ter - na del Di - o vi - ven - te.

(Christ, eternal word of the Living God.)

14. Káy - ud mée - luh fóil - dta r'rho-what ÉE- yo - Sah ah hgrraw.

(A hundred thousand welcomes, Jesus love!)

Text: Suzanne Toolan, SM, b.1927
Tune: Suzanne Toolan, SM, b.1927
© 1988, GIA Publications, Inc.

680 When, in Our Music, God Is Glorified

1. When, in our mu - sic, God is glo - ri -
2. How of - ten, mak - ing mu - sic, we have
3. So has the Church, in lit - ur - gy and
4. And did not Je - sus sing a psalm that
5. Let ev - 'ry in - stru-ment be tuned for

fied, And ad - o - ra - tion leaves no
found A new di - men - sion in the
song, In faith and love, through cen - tu -
night When ut - most e - vil strove a -
praise! Let all re - joice who have a

room for pride, It is as
world of sound, As wor - ship
ries of wrong, Borne wit - ness
gainst the Light? Then let us
voice to raise! And may God

though the whole cre - a - tion cried:
moved us to a more pro - found
to the truth in ev - 'ry tongue: Al - le - lu -
sing, for whom he won the fight:
give us faith to sing al - ways:

ia! Al - le - lu - ia! Al - le - lu - ia!

Text: Fred Pratt Green, b.1903, © 1972, Hope Publishing Co.
Tune: MAYFLOWER, 10 10 10 with alleluias; Marty Haugen, b.1950, © 1989, GIA Publications, Inc.

681 Earth and All Stars

1. Earth and all stars, Loud rush - ing plan - ets
2. En - gines and steel, Loud pound - ing ham - mers
3. Class - rooms and labs, Loud boil - ing test tubes
4. Knowl - edge and truth, Loud sound - ing wis - dom

Sing to the Lord a new song!
Sing to the Lord a new song!
Sing to the Lord a new song!
Sing to the Lord a new song!

Hail, wind, and rain, Loud blow - ing snow - storm
Lime - stone and beams, Loud build - ing work - ers
Ath - lete and band, Loud cheer - ing peo - ple
Daugh - ter and son, Loud pray - ing mem - bers

Sing to the Lord a new song!
Sing to the Lord a new song!
Sing to the Lord a new song!
Sing to the Lord a new song!

God has done mar - vel - ous things.

I too sing prais - es with a new song!

Text: Herbert F. Brokering, b.1926
Tune: EARTH AND ALL STARS, 4 5 7 D with refrain; David N. Johnson
© 1968, Augsburg Publishing House

Joyfully Singing 682

Verses

1. Joy - ful - ly sing - ing to the Lord,
2. God, in your mer - cy, free our hearts to
3. Gath - er the na - tions to you, Lord,

prais - ing God on high, all of the earth in thank-
praise your ho - ly name, help - ing the poor and low -
draw them to your care, com - ing from all the dis -

ful - ness joins in glad re - ply.
ly ones faith - ful - ly pro - claim.
tant lands glad - ly to de - clare.

Refrain

Bless - ed are your days, ho - ly are your nights,

1., 3.

won - drous is your love all of our lives.

2.

Lord, bring us to - geth - er from

east and from the west. Show us your moun - tain, your

D.C.

dwell - ing place, your life of ho - li - ness.

Text: Mike Balhoff, b. 1946, Gary Daigle, b.1957, Darryl Ducote, b.1945
Tune: Mike Balhoff, b. 1946, Gary Daigle, b.1957, Darryl Ducote, b.1945
© 1985, Damean Music. Distributed by GIA Publications, Inc.

683 Sing Praise to God Who Reigns Above

1. Sing praise to God who reigns a-bove, The God of all cre-a-tion, The God of pow'r, the God of love, The God of our sal-va-tion; With
2. What God's al-might-y pow'r has made, His gra-cious mer-cy keep-ing; By morn-ing glow or eve-ning shade His watch-ful eye ne'er sleep-ing; With-
3. Then all my glad-some way a-long, I sing a-loud your prais-es, That all may hear the grate-ful song My voice un-wea-ried rais-es; Be
4. Let all who name Christ's ho-ly name, Give God all praise and glo-ry; All you who own his pow'r, pro-claim A-loud the won-drous sto-ry! Cast

heal - ing balm my soul he fills, And
in the king - dom of his might, Lo!
joy - ful in the Lord, my heart, Both
each false i - dol from its throne, The

ev - 'ry faith - less mur - mur stills: To
all is just and all is right: To
soul and bod - y sing your part: To
Lord is God, and he a - lone: To

God all praise and glo - ry.
God all praise and glo - ry.
God all praise and glo - ry.
God all praise and glo - ry.

Text: *Sei Lob und Ehr' dem höchsten Gut;* Johann J. Schütz, 1640-1690; tr. by Frances E. Cox, 1812-1897
Tune: MIT FREUDEN ZART, 8 7 8 7 88 7; Bohemian Brethren's *Kirchengesänge*, 1566

684 Praise, My Soul, the King of Heaven

1. Praise, my soul, the King of heav - en; To his feet your trib - ute bring; Ran - somed, healed, re - stored, for - giv - en, Ev - er - more his prais - es sing: Al - le - lu - ia! Al - le - lu - ia! Praise the ev - er - last - ing King.

2. Praise him for his grace and fa - vor To his peo - ple in dis - tress; Praise him still the same as ev - er, Slow to chide, and swift to bless: Al - le - lu - ia! Al - le - lu - ia! Glo - rious in his faith - ful - ness.

3. Fa - ther - like he tends and spares us; Well our fee - ble frame he knows; In his hands he gent - ly bears us, Res - cues us from all our foes. Al - le - lu - ia! Al - le - lu - ia! Wide - ly yet his mer - cy flows.

4. Frail as sum - mer's flow'r we flour - ish, Blows the wind and it is gone; But while mor - tals rise and per - ish, God en - dures un - chang - ing on; Al - le - lu - ia! Al - le - lu - ia! Praise the high e - ter - nal one!

5. An - gels, help us to a - dore him; You be - hold him face to face; Sun and moon, bow down be - fore him, Dwell - ers all in time and space: Al - le - lu - ia! Al - le - lu - ia! Praise with us the God of grace.

Text: Psalm (102)103; Henry F. Lyte, 1793-1847, alt.
Tune: LAUDA ANIMA, 8 7 8 7 8 7; John Goss, 1800-1880

The God of Abraham Praise 685

1. The God of A-braham praise, Who reigns en-throned a-bove;
2. The Lord, our God has sworn: I on that oath de-pend;
3. There dwells the Lord, our King, The Lord, our Right-eous-ness,
4. The God who reigns on high The great arch-an-gels sing,

The an-cient of e-ter-nal days, And God of love;
I shall, on ea-gle-wings up-borne, To heav'n as-cend:
Tri-umph-ant o'er the world and sin, The Prince of Peace;
And "Ho-ly, Ho-ly, Ho-ly," cry, "Al-might-y King!

The Lord, the great I AM, By earth and heav'n con-fessed
I shall be-hold God's face, I shall God's pow'r a-dore,
On Zi-on's sa-cred height The king-dom God main-tains,
Who was, and is, the same, For all e-ter-ni-ty,

We bow and bless the sa-cred name For ev-er blest.
And sing the won-ders of God's grace For ev-er-more.
And, glo-rious with the saints in light, For ev-er reigns.
Im-mor-tal God, the great I AM, All glo-ry be."

Text: *Yigdal Elohim Hai;* ascr. to Daniel ben Judah Dayyan, fl.1400; para. by Thomas Olivers, 1725-1799, alt.
Tune: LEONI, 6 6 8 4 D; from the *Yigdal;* transcribed by Meyer Lyon, c.1751-1797

686 Sing a New Song

Refrain

Descant:
Sing a new song; sing

Melody:
Sing a new song un-to the Lord; let your song be

Harmony:

al - le - lu - ia. Sing a

sung from moun-tains high. Sing a new song

new song al - le - lu - ia.

un-to the Lord, sing-ing al - le - lu - ia.

Verses

1. Yah - weh's peo - ple dance for joy. O come be -
2. Rise, O chil - dren, from your sleep; your Sav - ior
3. Glad my soul for I have seen the glo - ry

fore the Lord. And play for him on
now has come. He has turned your
of the Lord. The trum - pet sounds; the

glad tam - bou - rines, and let your trum-pet sound.
sor - row to joy, and filled your soul with song.
dead shall be raised. I know my Sav - ior lives.

D.C.

Text: Psalm 98; Dan Schutte, b. 1947
Tune: Dan Schutte, b. 1947
© 1972, Daniel L. Schutte, administered by New Dawn Music

Sing Praise to the Lord   687

1. Sing praise to the Lord! praise God in the height;
2. Sing praise to the Lord! praise God up - on earth,
3. Sing praise to the Lord, all things that give sound;
4. Sing praise to the Lord! thanks - giv - ing and song

Re - joice in his word, you an - gels of light;
In tune - ful ac - cord, all you of new birth;
Each ju - bi - lant chord re - ech - o a - round;
To him be out - poured all a - ges a - long;

O heav - ens, a - dore him by whom you were made,
Praise him who has brought you his grace from a - bove,
Loud or - gans, his glo - ry tell forth in deep tone,
For love in cre - a - tion, for heav - en re - stored,

And wor - ship be - fore him in bright-ness ar - rayed.
Praise him who has taught you to sing of his love.
And trum-pets, the sto - ry of what God has done.
For grace of sal - va - tion, sing praise to the Lord!

Text: Psalm 150; Henry W. Baker, 1821-1877, alt.
Tune: LAUDATE DOMINUM, 10 10 11 11; Charles H. H. Parry, 1840-1918

688 Praise the Lord, My Soul

Refrain

S., A.:

Al- le - lu- ia! Al- le - lu - ia! Al - le - lu - ia!

Assembly:

Praise the Lord, my soul! Sing al - le -

To verses 1, 3, 5, 7 | To verses 2, 4, 6

Last time

Al - le - lu - ia!

Last time

lu - ia, bless God's name.

Verses 1, 3, 5, 7

1. All prais - es to the Fa - ther of our Lord,
3. How great the sign of God's love for us
5. And now we are God's work of art,
7. We come to you with hearts full of faith,

a God so mer - ci - ful and kind,
in giv - ing us his Son to be our bread:
a new cre - a - tion formed in Christ the Lord.
your voice is call - ing us so deep with - in.

who gives to us a new birth, who
as prom - ised us so long a - go, re -
We know we are his chil - dren now. What
We died with you as grain of wheat, we

brings to us a new hope by rais - ing his
vealed to us in these last days. How hap - py
we shall be in days to come, what tongue can
rise with you to fruit - ful lives, now make us

Son from death to life!
we who put our faith in him!
tell? What ear has heard?
chil - dren of the light!

Verses 2, 4, 6

2. On this moun - tain God will pre - pare a
4. Ev - 'ry tear shall be wiped a - way and
6. Taste and see the good - ness of God! Hap-py

ban - quet for all peo - ples: rich food and fin - est
shame shall be no more for God's own cho - sen
those who take their shel - ter be - neath his watch - ful

wine. On this moun - tain God will re - move the
friends. Then they shall say: "This is the one we
care. Fear the Lord! Proud and rich may

mourn - ing veil that cov - ers all peo - ples
hoped for to bring us sal - va - tion.
find them - selves sent emp - ty a - way;

and will de - stroy death for ev - er.
Now we re - joice that God has freed us."
but those who seek the Lord lack noth - ing.

Text: Tom Parker, b.1947
Tune: Tom Parker, b.1947
© 1981, GIA Publications, Inc.

689 There's a Spirit in the Air

Descant:

Praise the love, Praise the love, Al - le - lu - ia!

1. There's a spir - it in the air, Tell - ing Chris - tians
2. Lose your shy - ness, find your tongue; Tell the world what
3. When be - liev - ers break the bread, When a hun - gry
4. Still the Spir - it gives us light, See - ing wrong and
5. When a stran - ger's not a - lone, Where the home - less

ev - 'ry - where, "Praise the love that Christ re - vealed,
God has done: God in Christ has come to stay,
child is fed: Praise the love that Christ re - vealed,
set - ting right: God in Christ has come to stay,
find a home, Praise the love that Christ re - vealed,

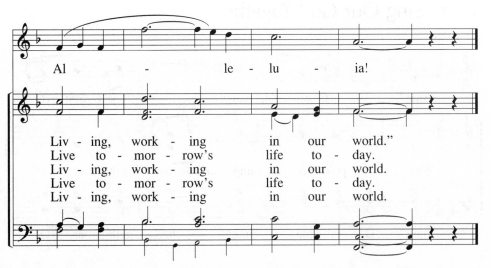

Al - le - lu - ia!

Liv - ing, work - ing	in our	world."
Live to - mor - row's	life to -	day.
Liv - ing, work - ing	in our	world.
Live to - mor - row's	life to -	day.
Liv - ing, work - ing	in our	world.

6. May the Spirit fill our praise,
   Guide our thoughts and change our ways.
   God in Christ has come to stay,
   Live tomorrow's life today.

7. There's a Spirit in the air,
   Calling people ev'rywhere;
   Praise the love that Christ revealed;
   Living, working in our world.

Text: Brian Wren, b.1936
Tune: LAUDS, 77 77; John W. Wilson, b.1905
© 1979, Hope Publishing Co.

690 Sing Our God Together

Refrain

Sing*, O peo - ple, sing* our God to -

Sing*, O peo - ple, sing* our God to - geth - er,

Sing*, O peo - ple, sing* to - geth - er, O

geth - er! O peo-ple, sing *Last time* al - le - lu -

raise your voic - es: sing al - le - lu - ia!

raise your voic - es:

After each verse, repeat key word in the refrain: (Dance/Dance our; Serve/Serve our; Shine/Shine in; Teach/Teach our; Seek/ Seek our; Live/Live our)

Verses

Solo voices:

1. Sing with one an - oth - er:
2. Dance the steps of beau - ty:
3. Serve all those who suf - fer:
4. Shine as bright as day-break!
5. Teach the way of Je - sus:
6. Seek the chil-dren's wis-dom:
7. Live no more un - car - ing:

All:

Sing the love that gave us breath!
Dance the love that gave us breath!
Serve the love that gave us breath!
Shine the love that gave us breath!
Teach the love that gave us breath!
Seek the love that gave us breath!
Live the love that gave us breath!

ia.

Ooh_____ sing* the love that gave us breath!

Solo voices:

Sing, each sis - ter, broth - er:
Dance, de - light and du - ty:
Serve, that love might con - quer:
Shine as true as heart - ache!
Teach the way that frees us:
Seek God's way of free - dom:
Live your love un - spar - ing:

All:

Sing the God be - yond all death!
Dance the God be - yond all death!
Serve the God be - yond all death!
Shine in God be - yond all death!
Teach the God be - yond all death!
Seek the God be - yond all death!
Live the God be - yond all death!

D.C.

Ooh_____ sing* the God be - yond all death!

D.C.

death! O

*as before

Text: David Haas, b. 1957, and Marty Haugen, b. 1950
Tune: David Haas, b. 1957, and Marty Haugen, b. 1950
© 1993, GIA Publications, Inc.

691 Lift Up Your Hearts

Refrain

Descant:
Lift up your hearts, praise God's all-

Melody:
Lift up your hearts to the Lord, praise God's gra-cious

gra-cious mer - cy sing! Sing out to God,

mer - cy! Sing out your joy to the Lord,

To verses | Last time

whose love is en - dur - ing. ing.

whose love is en - dur - ing. ing.

Verses

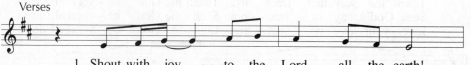

1. Shout with joy to the Lord, all the earth!
2. Let the earth wor-ship, sing - ing your praise.
3. God's right hand made a path through the night,
4. Lis - ten now, all you ser - vants of God,

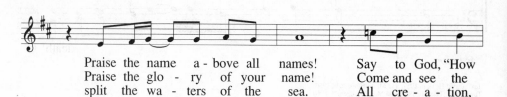

Praise the name a - bove all names! Say to God, "How
Praise the glo - ry of your name! Come and see the
split the wa - ters of the sea. All cre - a - tion,
As I tell of these great works. Bless-ed be the

won-drous your works,   how glo - rious your name!"
deeds of the Lord,   bless God's ho - ly name!
lift up your voice: Our God set us free.
Lord of my life,   whose love shall en - dure!

Text: Psalm 66; Roc O'Connor, SJ, b.1949, © 1981, 1993, and New Dawn Music
Tune: Roc O'Connor, SJ, b.1949, © 1981 and New Dawn Music; acc. by Robert J. Batastini, b.1942, © 1994, GIA Publications, Inc.

692 Halleluya! We Sing Your Praises

Refrain

Hal - le - lu - ya! We sing your prais-es, all our hearts are filled with glad - ness. Hal - le - lu - ya! We sing your prais-es, all our hearts are filled with glad - ness.

Verses

1. Christ the Lord to us said: I am wine, I am bread, I am wine, I am
2. Now he sends us all out, strong in faith, free of doubt, strong in faith, free of

bread, give to all who thirst and hun - ger.
doubt, to pro - claim the joy - ful Gos - pel.

Text: South African
Tune: South African
© 1984, Utryck, Walton Music Corporation, agent

Jubilate Deo 693

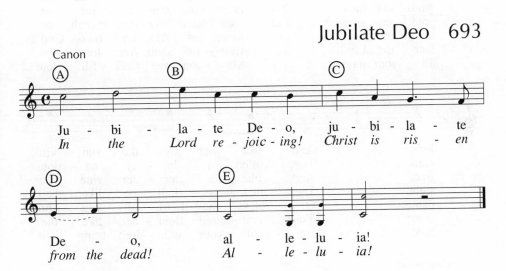

Canon

Ⓐ Ⓑ Ⓒ

Ju - bi - la - te De - o, ju - bi - la - te
In the Lord re - joic - ing! Christ is ris - en

Ⓓ Ⓔ

De - o, al - le - lu - ia!
from the dead! Al - le - lu - ia!

Text: Psalm 100:1; tr. Taizé Community, 1990, © 1978, 1990, Les Presses de Taizé, GIA Publications, Inc., agent
Tune: Michael Praetorius, 1571-1621; acc. by Jacques Berthier, 1923-1994, © 1978, 1990, Les Presses de Taizé, GIA Publications, Inc., agent

694 We Praise You

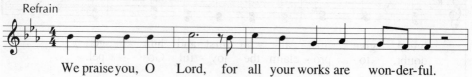

Refrain

We praise you, O Lord, for all your works are won-der-ful.

We praise you, O Lord, for ev - er is your love.

Verses

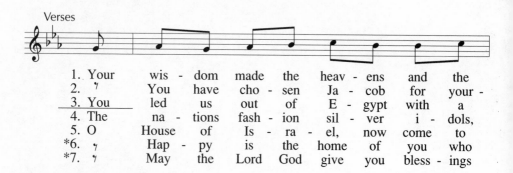

1. Your wis - dom made the heav - ens and the
2. ʼ You have cho - sen Ja - cob for your -
3. You led us out of E - gypt with a
4. The na - tions fash - ion sil - ver i - dols,
5. O House of Is - ra - el, now come to
*6. ʼ Hap - py is the home of you who
*7. ʼ May the Lord God give you bless - ings

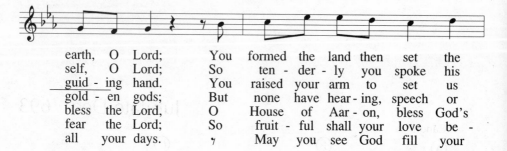

earth, O Lord; You formed the land then set the
self, O Lord; So ten - der - ly you spoke his
guid - ing hand. You raised your arm to set us
gold - en gods; But none have hear - ing, speech or
bless the Lord, O House of Aar - on, bless God's
fear the Lord; So fruit - ful shall your love be -
all your days. ʼ May you see God fill your

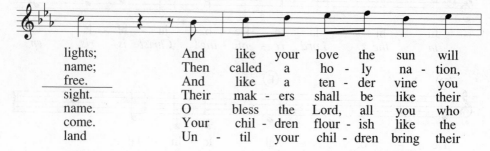

lights; And like your love the sun will
name; Then called a ho - ly na - tion,
free. And like a ten - der vine you
sight. Their mak - ers shall be like their
name. O bless the Lord, all you who
come. Your chil - dren flour - ish like the
land Un - til your chil - dren bring their

wedding verses

rule the day,	And	stars will grace the	night.
Is - ra - el,	To	make them yours, you	came.
plant - ed us	To	grow un - to the	sea.
emp - ty gods,	The	Lord a - lone brings	life.
hon - or God,	And	praise his ho - ly	name.
ol - ive plants,	For	ev - er are you	one.
chil - dren home	To	show God's love a -	gain.

Text: Mike Balhoff, b.1946
Tune: Darryl Ducote, b.1945, Gary Daigle, b.1957
© 1978, Damean Music. Distributed by GIA Publications, Inc.

695 Praise to the Lord, the Almighty

Descant:

4. Praise to the Lord— O let all that is in us a-

1. Praise to the Lord, the Al - might-y, the king of cre-
2. Praise to the Lord, a - bove all things so might - i - ly
3. Praise to the Lord, who shall pros - per our work and de-
4. Praise to the Lord— O let all that is in us a-

dore him! All that has life and breath

a - tion! O my soul, praise him, for
reign - ing; Keep-ing us safe at his
fend us; Sure - ly his good - ness and
dore him! All that has life and breath

come now with prais - es be - fore him!

he is your health and sal - va - tion!
side, and so gent - ly sus - tain - ing.
mer - cy shall dai - ly at - tend us.
come now with prais - es be - fore him!

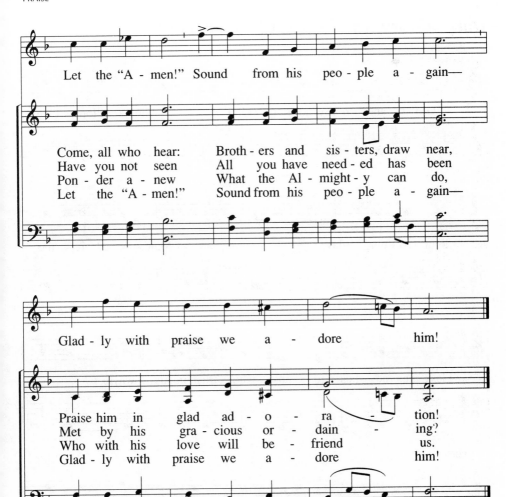

Let the "A - men!" Sound from his peo - ple a - gain—

Come, all who hear: Broth - ers and sis - ters, draw near,
Have you not seen All you have need - ed has been
Pon - der a - new What the Al - might - y can do,
Let the "A - men!" Sound from his peo - ple a - gain—

Glad - ly with praise we a - dore him!

Praise him in glad ad - o - ra - tion!
Met by his gra - cious or - dain - ing?
Who with his love will be - friend us.
Glad - ly with praise we a - dore him!

Text: *Lobe den Herren, den mächtigen König;* Joachim Neander, 1650-1680; tr. by Catherine Winkworth, 1827-1878, alt.
Tune: LOBE DEN HERREN, 14 14 47 8; *Stralsund Gesangbuch,* 1665; descant by C. S. Lang, 1891-1971, © 1953, Novello and Co. Ltd.

696 Glory and Praise to Our God

D.C.

done in   ev - 'ry   heart that   sings.
vails, our   God   is   there to   save.
lost,   to   an - swer   those who   pray.

Verse 4

4. God   has   wa - tered   our   bar - ren   land and   spent his

mer - ci - ful   rain.   Now the   riv - ers of   life   run

D.C.

full for   an - y - one to   drink.

Text: Psalm 65, 66; Dan Schutte, b. 1947
Tune: Dan Schutte, b. 1947; acc. by Sr. Theophane Hytrek, OSF, 1915-1992, alt.
© 1976, Daniel L. Schutte and New Dawn Music

697 For the Beauty of the Earth

1. For the beau - ty of the earth, For the glo - ry
2. For the beau - ty of each hour Of the day and
3. For the joy of ear and eye, For the heart and
4. For the joy of hu - man love, Broth - er, sis - ter,
5. For your church, that ev - er - more Lifts its ho - ly
6. For your - self, best Gift Di - vine! To this world so

of the skies, For the love which from our birth
of the night, Hill and vale, and tree and flow'r,
mind's de - light, For the mys - tic har - mo - ny
par - ent, child, Friends on earth, and friends a - bove;
hands a - bove, Off - 'ring up on ev - 'ry shore
free - ly giv'n; Word In - car - nate, God's de - sign,

O - ver and a - round us lies:
Sun and moon, and stars of light:
Link - ing sense to sound and sight:
For all gen - tle thoughts and mild:
Its pure sac - ri - fice of love:
Peace on earth and joy in heav'n:

Lord of all, to you we raise This our hymn of grate - ful praise.

Text: Folliot S. Pierpont, 1835-1917
Tune: DIX, 7 7 7 7 77; arr. from Conrad Kocher, 1786-1872, by William H. Monk, 1823-1889

Amen Siakudumisa 698

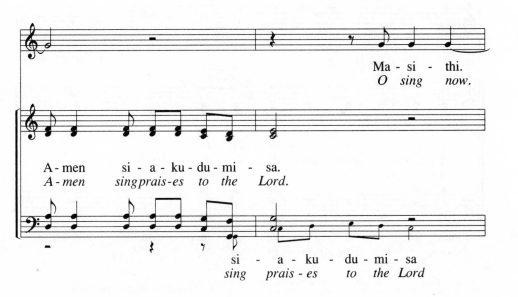

(Omit last time)

A-men ba - wo, A-men ba - wo,
A-men sing praise, A-men sing praise,

ba - wa, ba - wo, ba - wo, ba -
O praise God's name, O praise God's

Ma - si - thi.
O sing now.

A-men si - a - ku - du - mi - sa.
A-men sing prais - es to the Lord.

wo, si - a - ku - du - mi - sa.
name, sing prais - es to the Lord.

Text: *Amen. Praise the name of the Lord.* South African traditional; English text, *Hymnal Version*
Tune: Attr. to S. C. Molefe as taught by George Mxadana; arr. by John L. Bell, b.1949, © 1990, Iona Community, GIA Publications, Inc., agent

Christus Paradox 699

1. You, Lord, are both Lamb and Shep-herd. You, Lord, are both
2. Clothed in light up - on the moun-tain, Stripped of might up -
3. You, who walk each day be - side us, Sit in pow - er
4. Wor - thy is our earth - ly Je - sus! Wor - thy is our

prince and slave. You, peace-mak - er and sword-bring - er
on the cross, Shin - ing in e - ter - nal glo - ry,
at God's side. You, who preach a way that's nar - row,
cos - mic Christ! Wor - thy your de - feat and vic - t'ry.

Of the way you took and gave. You, the ev - er-
Beg - gar'd by a sol - dier's toss, You, the ev - er-
Have a love that reach - es wide. You, the ev - er-
Wor - thy still your peace and strife. You, the ev - er-

last - ing in - stant; You, whom we both scorn and crave.
last - ing in - stant; You, who are our gift and cost.
last - ing in - stant; You, who are our pil - grim guide.
last - ing in - stant; You, who are our death and life.

Text: Sylvia G. Dunstan, 1955-1993, © 1991, GIA Publications, Inc.
Tune: WESTMINSTER ABBEY, 8 7 8 7 8 7; adapt. from an anthem of Henry Purcell, 1659-1695

700 Now Thank We All Our God

1. Now thank we all our God With hearts and hands and
2. O may this gra - cious God Through all our life be
3. All praise and thanks to God The Fa - ther now be

voic - es, Who won - drous things has done, In
near us, With ev - er joy - ful hearts And
giv - en, The Son, and Spir - it blest, Who

whom his world re - joic - es; Who, from our moth-ers'
bless - ed peace to cheer us; Pre - serve us in his
reigns in high - est heav - en, E - ter - nal, Tri - une

arms, Hath blest us on our way With
grace, And guide us in dis - tress, And
God, Whom earth and heav'n a - dore; For

count - less gifts of love, And still is ours to - day.
free us from all sin, Till heav - en we pos - sess.
thus it was, is now, And shall be ev - er - more.

Text: *Nun danket alle Gott;* Martin Rinkart, 1586-1649; tr. by Catherine Winkworth, 1827-1878, alt.
Tune: NUN DANKET, 6 7 6 7 6 6 6 6; Johann Crüger, 1598-1662; harm. by A. Gregory Murray, OSB, 1905-1992

Table Prayer 701

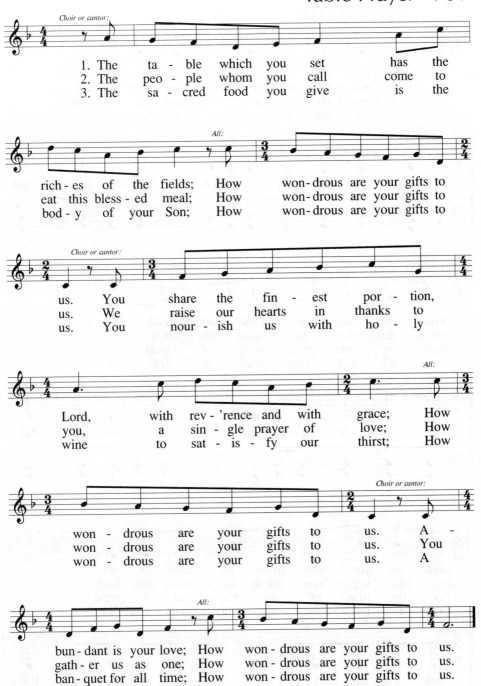

1. The ta - ble which you set has the
2. The peo - ple whom you call come to
3. The sa - cred food you give is the

rich - es of the fields; How won-drous are your gifts to
eat this bless - ed meal; How won-drous are your gifts to
bod - y of your Son; How won-drous are your gifts to

us. You share the fin - est por - tion,
us. We raise our hearts in thanks to
us. You nour - ish us with ho - ly

Lord, with rev - 'rence and with grace; How
you, a sin - gle prayer of love; How
wine to sat - is - fy our thirst; How

won - drous are your gifts to us. A -
won - drous are your gifts to us. You
won - drous are your gifts to us. A

bun - dant is your love; How won - drous are your gifts to us.
gath - er us as one; How won - drous are your gifts to us.
ban - quet for all time; How won - drous are your gifts to us.

Text: Mike Balhoff, b.1946, Gary Daigle, b.1957, Darryl Ducote, b.1945
Tune: Mike Balhoff, b.1946, Gary Daigle, b.1957, Darryl Ducote, b.1945
© 1985, Damean Music. Distributed by GIA Publications, Inc.

702 Blest Are You

Blest be you with ev - 'ry breath,
Gath - er us as one in you,
Spread your love to ev - 'ry land,
In the break - ing of the bread,

uch a - tah A - do - nai El - o - he - nu, Bar -

All:

Blest be you with ev - 'ry breath.
Gath - er us as one in you.
Spread your love to ev - 'ry land.
In the break - ing of the bread.

uch a - tah A - do - nai El - o - he - nu, Bar - uch a - tah

Text: Berakhot and *Didache*; Marty Haugen, b.1950
Tune: Marty Haugen, b.1950
© 1993, GIA Publications, Inc.

703 In the Lord I'll Be Ever Thankful

Ostinato Refrain

In the Lord I'll be ev-er thank-ful, in the Lord I will re-

joice! Look to God, do not be a-fraid; lift up your

voic-es, the Lord is near; lift up your voic-es, the Lord is near.

Verse

Cantor: (In the Lord)

With joy you will draw wa-ter at the foun-tain of sal-va-tion.

Give thanks to the Lord.   Ac-claim God's name.

Text: Taizé Community
Tune: Jacques Berthier, 1923-1994
© 1986, 1991, Les Presses de Taizé, GIA Publications, Inc., agent

For the Fruits of This Creation   704

1. For the fruits of this cre-a-tion, Thanks be to
2. In the just re-ward of la-bor, God's will is
3. For the har-vests of the Spir-it, Thanks be to

God; For these gifts to ev-'ry na-tion,
done; In the help we give our neigh-bor,
God; For the good we all in-her-it,

Thanks be to God; For the plow-ing,
God's will is done; In our world-wide
Thanks be to God; For the won-ders

sow-ing, reap-ing, Si-lent growth while we are sleep-ing,
task of car-ing For the hun-gry and de-spair-ing,
that a-stound us, For the truths that still con-found us,

Fu - ture needs in earth's safe keep-ing, Thanks be to God.
In the har-vests we are shar-ing, God's will is done.
Most of all, that love has found us, Thanks be to God.

Text: Fred Pratt Green, b.1903, © 1970, Hope Publishing Co.
Tune: EAST ACKLAM, 8 4 8 4 888 4; Francis Jackson, b.1917, ©

705 Father, We Thank Thee, Who Hast Planted

1. Fa - ther, we thank thee, who hast plant - ed
2. Watch o'er thy Church, O Lord, in mer - cy,

Thy ho - ly Name with - in our hearts.
Save it from e - vil, guard it still,

Knowl - edge and faith and life im - mor - tal
Per - fect it in thy love, u - nite it,

Je - sus, thy Son, to us im - parts.
Cleansed and con - formed un - to thy will.

Thou, Lord, didst make all for thy plea - sure,
As grain, once scat - ter'd on the hill - sides,

Didst give us food for all our days,
Was in this bro - ken bread made one,

Giv - ing in Christ the Bread e - ter - nal;
So from all lands thy Church be gath - er'd

Thine is the power, be thine the praise.
In - to thy king - dom by thy Son.

Text: From the *Didache*, c.110; tr. by F. Bland Tucker, 1895-1984, alt., © 1940, The Church Pension Fund
Tune: RENDEZ À DIEU, 9 8 9 8 D; *Genevan Psalter*, 1551; attr. to Louis Bourgeois, c.1510-1561

706 Come, Ye Thankful People, Come

1. Come, ye thank-ful peo-ple, come, Raise the song of
2. All the world is God's own field, Fruit un-to God's
3. For the Lord our God shall come, And shall take the
4. E-ven so, Lord, quick-ly come To your fi-nal

har-vest-home: All is safe-ly gath-ered in,
praise to yield; Wheat and tares to-geth-er sown,
har-vest home; From the field shall in that day
har-vest-home; Gath-er all your peo-ple in,

Ere the win-ter storms be-gin; God, our Mak-er,
Un-to joy or sor-row grown; First the blade, and
All of-fens-es purge a-way, Giv-ing an-gels
Free from sor-row, free from sin; There, for ev-er

does pro-vide For our wants to be sup-plied;
then the ear, Then the full corn shall ap-pear:
charge at last In the fire the tares to cast,
pu-ri-fied, In your pres-ence to a-bide:

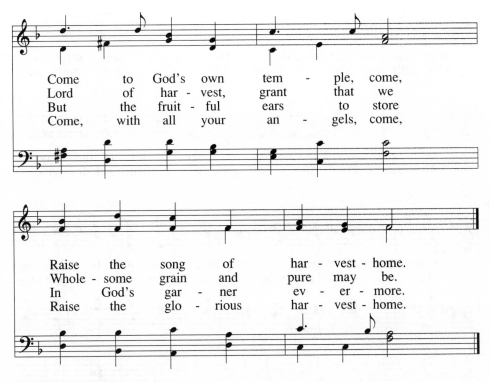

Come to God's own tem - ple, come,
Lord of har - vest, grant that we
But the fruit - ful ears to store
Come, with all your an - gels, come,

Raise the song of har - vest - home.
Whole - some grain and pure may be.
In God's gar - ner ev - er - more.
Raise the glo - rious har - vest - home.

Text: Henry Alford, 1810-1871, alt.
Tune: ST. GEORGE'S WINDSOR, 77 77 D; George J. Elvey, 1816-1893

Let All Things Now Living 707

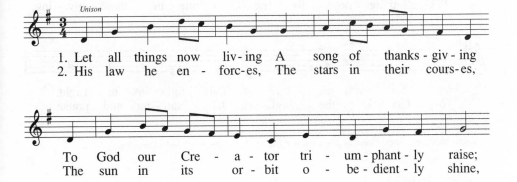

1. Let all things now liv-ing A song of thanks - giv - ing
2. His law he en - forc-es, The stars in their cours-es,

To God our Cre - a - tor tri - um - phant - ly raise;
The sun in its or - bit o - be - dient - ly shine,

Who fash-ioned and made us, Pro - tect - ed and stayed us,
The hills and the moun-tains, The riv - ers and foun-tains,

By guid - ing us on to the end of our days.
The depths of the o - cean pro - claim God di - vine.

Harmony

God's ban - ners are o'er us, Pure light goes be - fore us,
We, too, should be voic - ing Our love and re - joic - ing

A pil - lar of fire shin - ing forth in the night:
With glad ad - o - ra - tion, a song let us raise:

Unison

Till shad - ows have van - ished And dark - ness is ban - ished,
Till all things now liv - ing U - nite in thanks-giv - ing,

As for - ward we trav - el from light in - to Light.
To God in the high - est, ho - san - na and praise.

Text: Katherine K. Davis, 1892-1980, © 1939, E.C. Schirmer Music Co.
Tune: ASH GROVE, 66 11 66 11 D; Welsh; harm. by Gerald H. Knight, 1908-1979, © The Royal School of Church Music

Thanks Be to You   708

1.,3. Praise to you, O God of mer - cy! Thanks be to you for
2. From of old you loved and sought us! Thanks be to you for

ev - er! Rais - ing high the weak and low - ly:
ev - er! Truth and jus - tice you have taught us:

1., 3.   Last time   2.

Thanks be to you for ev - er!
Thanks be to you for ev - er!

Last time

Strong is your faith - ful - ness, strong is your love, re -

D.C.

mem - b'ring your cov - e - nant of life with us.

Text: Marty Haugen, b.1950
Tune: Marty Haugen, b.1950
© 1990, GIA Publications, Inc.

709 We Gather Together

1. We gath-er to-geth-er to ask the Lord's bless-ing;
2. Be-side us to guide us, our God with us join-ing,
3. We all do ex-tol you our lead-er tri-um-phant,

He chas-tens and has-tens his will to make known;
Whose king-dom calls all to the love which en-dures.
And pray that you still our de-fend-er will be.

The wick-ed op-press-ing now cease from dis-tress-ing:
So from the be-gin-ning the fight we were win-ning:
Let your con-gre-ga-tion es-cape trib-u-la-tion:

Sing prais-es to his name; he for-gets not his own.
You, Lord, were at our side; all glo-ry be yours!
Your name be ev-er praised! O Lord, make us free!

Text: *Wilt heden nu treden*, Netherlands folk hymn; tr. by Theodore Baker, 1851-1934, alt.
Tune: KREMSER, 12 11 12 11; *Neder-landtsch Gedenckclanck*, 1626; harm. by Edward Kremser, 1838-1914

Confitemini Domino / Come and Fill   710

Ostinato Refrain

Con - fi - te - mi - ni   Do - mi - no
Come and   fill   our   hearts   with   your   peace.

quo - ni - am   bo-nus.   Con - fi - te - mi - ni
You a-lone, O Lord, are   ho - ly.   Come and   fill our hearts

Do - mi - no,   Al - le - lu - ia!
with   your   peace,   Al - le - lu - ia!

Text: Psalm 137, *Give thanks to the Lord for he is good;* Taizé Community, 1982
Tune: Jacques Berthier, 1923-1994
© 1982, 1991, Les Presses de Taizé, GIA Publications, Inc., agent

711 Creating God

1. Cre - at - ing God, your fin - gers trace The
2. Sus - tain - ing God, your hands up - hold Earth's
3. Re - deem - ing God, your arms em - brace All
4. In - dwell - ing God, your gos - pel claims One

bold de - signs of far - thest space; Let sun and
mys - t'ries known or yet un - told; Let wa - ters
now de - spised for creed or race; Let peace, de -
fam - 'ly with a bil - lion names; Let ev - 'ry

moon and stars and light And what lies hid - den
frag - ile blend with air, En - a - bling life, pro -
scend - ing like a dove, Make known on earth your
life be touched by grace Un - til we praise you

1. - 3.
praise your might.
claim your care.
heal - ing love.

4.
face to face.

Text: Jeffery Rowthorn, b.1934, © 1979, Hymn Society of America, alt.
Tune: PRESENCE, LM; David Haas, b.1957, © 1989, GIA Publications, Inc.

Lead Me, Guide Me 712

Refrain

Lead me, guide me, a - long the way,

For if you lead me, I can - not stray.

Lord, let me walk each day with thee.

Lead me, oh Lord, lead me.

Verses

1. I am weak and I need thy strength and
2. Help me tread in the paths of right - eous -
3. I am lost if you take your hand from

power to help me o - ver my weak - est
ness, Be my aid when Sa - tan and sin op -
me, I am blind with - out thy Light to

hour. Help me through the dark - ness thy face to
press. I am put - ting all my trust in
see, Lord, just al - ways let me thy ser - vant

D.C.

see, Lead me, oh Lord, lead me.
thee. Lead me, oh Lord, lead me.
be. Lead me, oh Lord, lead me.

713 Lord of all Hopefulness

1. Lord of all hope - ful - ness, Lord of all joy,
2. Lord of all ea - ger - ness, Lord of all faith,
3. Lord of all kind - li - ness, Lord of all grace,
4. Lord of all gen - tle - ness, Lord of all calm,

Whose trust, ev - er child - like, no cares can de - stroy,
Whose strong hands were skilled at the plane and the lathe,
Your hands swift to wel - come, your arms to em - brace,
Whose voice is con - tent - ment, whose pres - ence is balm,

Be there at our wak - ing, and give us, we pray,
Be there at our la - bors, and give us, we pray,
Be there at our hom - ing, and give us, we pray,
Be there at our sleep - ing, and give us, we pray,

Your bliss in our hearts, Lord, at the break of the day.
Your strength in our hearts, Lord, at the noon of the day.
Your love in our hearts, Lord, at the eve of the day.
Your peace in our hearts, Lord, at the end of the day.

Text: Jan Struther, 1901-1953, © Oxford University Press
Tune: SLANE, 10 11 11 12; Gaelic; harm. by Erik Routley, 1917-1982, © 1985, Hope Publishing Co.

Jesus, Come! For We Invite You 714

1. Je - sus, come! for we in - vite you,
2. Je - sus, come! trans - form our pleas - ures,
3. Je - sus, come! in new cre - a - tion,
4. Je - sus, come! sur - prise our dull - ness,

Guest and mas - ter, friend and Lord;
Guide us in - to paths un - known;
Heav'n brought near in pow'r di - vine;
Make us will - ing to re - ceive

Now as once at Ca - na's wed - ding,
Bring your gifts, com - mand your ser - vants,
Give your un - ex - pect - ed glo - ry
More than we can yet i - mag - ine,

Speak, and let us hear your word:
Let us trust in you a - lone:
Chang - ing wa - ter in - to wine:
All the best you have to give:

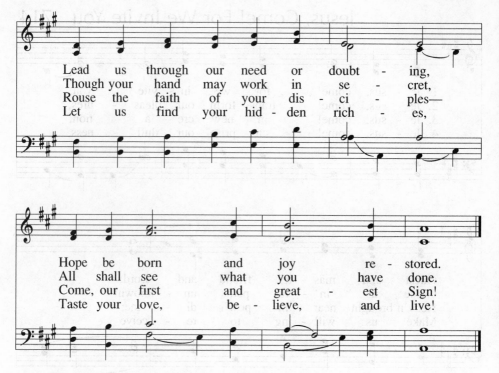

Lead us through our need or doubt - ing,
Though your hand may work in se - cret,
Rouse the faith of your dis - ci - ples—
Let us find your hid - den rich - es,

Hope be born and joy re - stored.
All shall see what you have done.
Come, our first and great - est Sign!
Taste your love, be - lieve, and live!

Text: John 2; Christopher Idle, b.1938, © 1982, Hope Publishing Co.
Tune: BEST GIFT, 8 7 8 7 8 7; Ronald F. Krisman, b.1946, © 1986, GIA Publications, Inc.

Healing River 715

1. O heal - ing riv - er, send down your
2. This land is parch - ing, this land is
3. Let the seed of free - dom, a - wake and

wa - ters, Send down your wa - ters up - on this
burn - ing, No seed is grow - ing in the bar - ren
flour - ish, Let the deep roots nour - ish, let the tall stalks

land. O heal - ing riv - er, send down your
ground. O heal - ing riv - er, send down your
rise. O heal - ing riv - er, send down your

wa - ters, And wash the blood from off the sand.
wa - ters, O heal - ing riv - er, send your wa - ters down.
wa - ters, O heal - ing riv - er, from out of the skies.

The assembly echoes each phrase of the cantor at the interval of one half measure.

Text: Fran Minkoff
Tune: Fred Hellerman; arr. by Michael Joncas, b.1951
© 1964, Appleseed Music, Inc.

716　I Need You to Listen

Refrain

Cantor:　　　　　　　　　　　　　　　　　　　　　　*All:*

I need you to lis-ten. I need you to an-swer. I

need you to lis-ten. I need you to

1.,2.,4.,6.	3.,5.
an - swer.	an - swer.

Last time

an - swer. an - swer.

Verses 1, 2

Cantor or choir:

1. O　God, I need you　to.　I want to see your face. It
2. Do　not a-void my　eyes　or let me an-ger you. Do

D.C.

is this love I have. It makes me search for you.
not toss me a-side. O God, do not drop me.

Verse 3

Cantor or choir:

3. You　are the　on-ly hope I　have;　fa-ther,

moth- er,   they can leave me   or- phaned,   but

Lead me to   you, O God, a -
your love   must nev-er.   Lead   me   a -

D.C.
long   the smooth - est   road.

Verse 4
Cantor or choir:
4. There are those who   hate me.   Do not leave me   to them. They

eat   my   life   a - way   by   ly - ing   un - der

D.C.
oath   or   twist- ing   ev - i - dence.

Verse 5

Cantor or choir:

5. I trust your love. I will see your beau-ty af-ter death in

your land of life. My love will wait for you.

It will be strong wait - ing. O

D.C.

God, my love will wait!

Text: Based on Psalm 27; Francis Patrick Sullivan, © 1987, The Pastoral Press
Tune: Marty Haugen, b.1950, © 1991, GIA Publications, Inc.

Come, My Way, My Truth, My Life   717

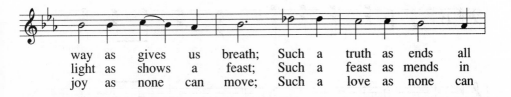

1. Come, my Way, my Truth, my Life: Such a
2. Come, my Light, my Feast, my Strength: Such a
3. Come, my Joy, my Love, my Heart: Such a

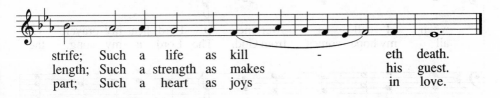

way   as gives   us   breath; Such a truth as ends   all
light as shows a   feast;   Such a feast as mends in
joy   as none   can move; Such a love   as none   can

strife; Such a life as kill - eth death.
length; Such a strength as makes his guest.
part; Such a heart as joys in love.

Text: George Herbert, 1593-1632
Tune: THE CALL, 7 7 7 7; Ralph Vaughan Williams, 1872-1958

718 O Lord, Hear My Prayer

Ostinato Chorale

O Lord, hear my prayer, O Lord, hear my prayer:
*The Lord is my song, the Lord is my praise:

when I call an - swer me. O Lord, hear my prayer, O
all my hope comes from God. The Lord is my song, the

Last time
Lord, hear my prayer. Come and lis - ten to me. O
Lord is my praise: God, the well- spring of life. The

*Alternate text

Text: Psalm 102; Taizé Community, 1982
Tune: Jacques Berthier, 1923-1994
© 1982, Les Presses de Taizé, GIA Publications, Inc., agent

Come to Us, Creative Spirit   719

1. Come to us, cre - a - tive Spir - it,
2. Po - et, paint - er, mu - sic - mak - er,
3. Word from God e - ter - nal spring - ing,
4. In all plac - es and for ev - er

In our Fa - ther's house; Ev - 'ry hu -
All your trea - sures bring; Crafts-man, ac -
Fill our minds, we pray; And in all
Glo - ry be ex - pressed To the Son,

man tal - ent hal - low, Hid - den skills a -
tor, grace - ful danc - er, Make your of - fer -
ar - tis - tic vi - sion Give in - te - gri -
with God the Fa - ther And the Spir - it

rouse, That with - in your earth - ly tem - ple,
ing, Join your hands in cel - e - bra - tion:
ty: May the flame with - in us burn - ing
blessed: In our wor - ship and our liv - ing

Wise and sim - ple, may re - joice.
Let cre - a - tion shout and sing!
Kin - dle yearn - ing day by day.
Keep us striv - ing for the best.

Text: David Mowbray, b.1938, © Stainer and Bell Publications
Tune: CASTLEWOOD, 8 5 8 5 84 3; Richard Proulx, b.1937, © 1986, GIA Publications, Inc.

720 Bwana Awabariki / May God Grant You a Blessing

Bwa - na a - wa - ba - ri - ki, Bwa - na
May God grant you a bless-ing, may God

a - wa - ba - ri - ki, Bwa - na a - wa - ba-ri - ki
grant you a bless-ing, may God grant you a bless-ing

mi - le - le. U - ki - mcha Bwa - na.
ev - er - more. Re - vere the Lord.

Bwa - na a - wa - ba - ri - ki.
May God grant you a bless - ing.

Text: Swahili folk hymn
Tune: Swahili melody

May the Lord, Mighty God   721

Melody:

1.,3. May the Lord, might-y God, bless and
2. Lift your eyes and see God's face full of

Harmony: (verse 2)

keep you for - ev - er, grant you peace,
grace for - ev - er. May the Lord,

per - fect peace, cour - age in ev - 'ry en - deav - or.
might-y God, bless and keep you for - ev - er.

Text: Numbers 6:24-26; unknown
Tune: WEN-TI, Irregular; Chinese, Pao-chen Li; adapted by I-to Loh, © 1983, Abingdon Press; acc. by Diana Kodner, b.1957, © 1993,
   GIA Publications, Inc.

722 I Say "Yes," Lord / Digo "Si," Señor

Verses

Cantor:

1. To the God who can - not die:
   To the God of the op - pressed:
2. I am a ser - vant of the Lord:
   I'm a pris - oner of their wars:
3. For the dream I have to - day:
   To come to love my en - e - mies:
4. Like that of Job, un - ceas - ing - ly:
   Like that of Da - vid in a song:

I say
Di - go

"Yes," my Lord.
"Sí," Se - ñor.

To the
To the
I'm a
Like a pol - i -
To be a
For your
Like that of Ma -
Like Is - ra -

All:

Harmony:

I say "Yes," my Lord.
Di - go "Sí," Se - ñor.

One who hears me cry:
God of all jus - tice:
work - er in the fields:
ti - cian, in - e - vi - ta - bly:
heal - er of all pain:
peace in all the world:
ri - a whole - heart - ed - ly:
el, for you I long:

I say
Di - go

"Yes," my Lord.
"Sí," Se - ñor.

All:

I say "Yes," my Lord. "Yes," my Lord.
Di - go "Sí," Se - ñor. "Sí," Se - ñor.

Harmony:

Refrain

Descant:

I say "Yes," my Lord, in all the good times, through
Di - go "Sí," Se - ñor, en tiem - pos mal - os, en

Melody:

all the bad times, I say "Yes," my Lord to
tiem - pos bue - nos, Di - go "Sí," Se - ñor a

Last time to coda ⊕   D.C.   ⊕ Coda

ev - 'ry word you speak.
to - do lo que ha - blas.

Text: Donna Peña, b.1955
Tune: Donna Peña, b.1955; arr. by Marty Haugen, b.1950
© 1989, GIA Publications, Inc.

723 We Walk By Faith

1., 5. We walk by faith, and not by sight: No
2. We may not touch his hands and side, Nor
3. Help then, O Lord, our un-be-lief, And
4. That when our life of faith is done In

gra-cious words we hear Of him who spoke as
fol-low where he trod; Yet in his prom-ise
may our faith a-bound; To call on you when
realms of clear-er light We may be-hold you

none e'er spoke, But we be-lieve him near.
we re-joice, And cry "My Lord and God!"
you are near, And seek where you are found:
as you are In full and end-less sight.

Text: Henry Alford, 1810-1871, alt.
Tune: SHANTI, CM; Marty Haugen, b.1950, © 1984, GIA Publications, Inc.

We Remember 724

Refrain

us   to your

We re - mem-ber how you loved us   to your   death,

you are with us

and still we cel-e-brate, for   you   are   here;

you   when you come

and we be - lieve that we will see you   when you   come

in your   glo-ry, Lord.   We re - mem - ber,   we

Last time to coda ⊕

cel - e - brate,   we be - lieve.

Verses

1. Here, a mil - lion wound - ed souls are
2. Now we re - cre - ate your love, we
3. Christ, the Fa - ther's great "A - men" to
4. See the face of Christ re - vealed in

yearn - ing just to touch you and be healed.
bring the bread and wine to share a meal.
all the hopes and dreams of ev - 'ry heart,
ev - 'ry per - son stand - ing by your side,

Gath - er all your peo - ple, and
Sign of grace and mer - cy, the
Peace be - yond all tell - ing, and
Gift to one an - oth - er, and

D.C. ⊕ Coda

hold them to your heart.
pres - ence of the Lord.
free - dom from all fear.
tem - ples of your love.

Text: Marty Haugen, b.1950
Tune: Marty Haugen, b.1950
© 1980, GIA Publications, Inc.

Mayenziwe / Your Will Be Done   725

Text: from the Lord's Prayer, South African
Tune: South African traditional, as taught by George Mxadana; transcribed by John L. Bell, b.1949; © 1990, Iona Community,
    GIA Publications, Inc., agent

726 A Living Faith

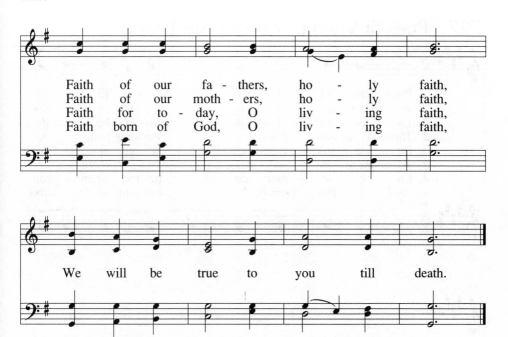

Faith of our fa - thers, ho - ly faith,
Faith of our moth - ers, ho - ly faith,
Faith for to - day, O liv - ing faith,
Faith born of God, O liv - ing faith,

We will be true to you till death.

Text: St. 1, Frederick W. Faber, 1814-1863, alt.; Sts. 2-4, Joseph R. Alfred, © 1981, alt.
Tune: ST. CATHERINE, LM with refrain; Henry F. Hemy, 1818-1888; adapt. by James G. Walton, 1821-1905

727 Pues Si Vivimos / If We Are Living

Descant:

Melody:

1. Pues si vi - vi - mos pa - ra Él vi -
1. *If we are liv - ing we are in the*
2. En es - ta vi - da, fru - tos he - mos de
2. *Through - out our lives we have fruit to*
3. En la tris - te - za y en el do -
3. *When there is sad - ness, when there is*
4. En es - te mun - do, he - mos de en - con -
4. *And in this world we will al - ways*

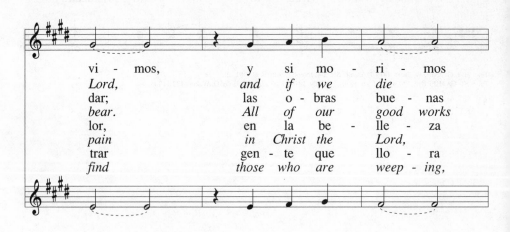

vi - mos, y si mo - ri - mos
Lord, and if we die
dar; las o - bras bue - nas
bear. All of our good works
lor, en la be - lle - za
pain in Christ the Lord,
trar gen - te que llo - ra
find those who are weep - ing,

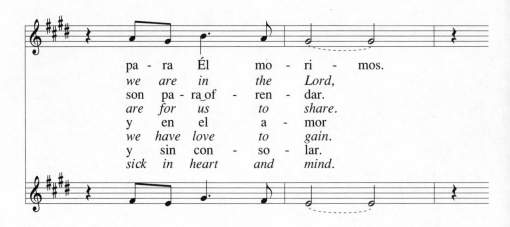

pa - ra Él mo - ri - mos.
we are in the Lord,
son pa - ra_of - ren - dar.
are for us to share.
y en el a - mor
we have love to gain.
y sin con - so - lar.
sick in heart and mind.

Sea que vi - va - mos o que mu -
for if we live or if we
Ya sea que de - mos o que re - ci -
Whe - ther we give, or we re -
Sea que su - fra - mos o que go -
Whe - ther we suf - fer or we re -
Sea que_a - yu - de - mos o que_al - i - men -
They need our help, they need our

ra - mos, so - mos del Señ - or,
die we be - long to God,
ba - mos, so - mos del Señ - or,
ceive we be - long to God,
ce - mos, so - mos del Señ - or,
joice, we be - long to God,
te - mos, so - mos del Señ - or,
care. we be - long to God,

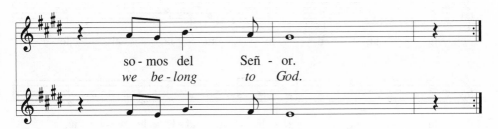

so - mos del Señ - or.
we be - long to God.

Text: Verse 1, Romans 14:8; traditional Spanish; translation by Deborah L. Schmitz, b.1969, © 1994, GIA Publications, Inc.
Tune: Traditional Spanish; arr. by Diana Kodner, b.1957, © 1994, GIA Publications, Inc.

728 Seek Ye First the Kingdom of God

Canon

1. Seek ye first the king - dom of God
2. Ask, and it shall be giv - en un - to you,
3. You do not live by bread a - lone,
4. Where two or three are gath - ered in my name,

and his right - eous - ness,
seek, and ye shall find,
but by ev - 'ry word,
there am I in their midst;

and all these things shall be add - ed un - to you;
knock, and the door shall be o - pened un - to you;
that comes forth from the mouth of God;
and what - so - ev - er you ask I will do;

Al - le - lu, al - le - lu - ia. Al - le -

lu - ia, al - le - lu - ia, al - le -

lu - ia, al - le - lu, al - le - lu - ia.

May be sung as a two-voice canon.

Text: Matthew 6:33, 7:7; St. 1, adapt. by Karen Lafferty, b.1948; St. 2-4, anon.
Tune: SEEK YE FIRST, Irregular; Karen Lafferty, b.1948
© 1972, Maranatha! Music

Awake, O Sleeper, Rise from Death   729

1. A - wake, O sleep - er, rise from death,
2. To us on earth he came to bring
3. There is one Bod - y and one Hope,
4. Then walk in love as Christ has loved
5. For us Christ lived, for us he died

And Christ shall give you light.
From sin and fear re - lease,
One Spir - it and one Call,
Who died that he might save;
And con - quered in the strife.

So learn his love— its length and breadth,
To give the Spir - it's u - ni - ty,
One Lord, one Faith, and one Bap - tism,
With kind and gen - tle hearts for - give
A - wake, a - rise, go forth in faith,

Its full - ness, depth and height.
The ver - y bond of peace.
One Fa - ther of us all.
As God in Christ for - gave.
And Christ shall give you life.

Text: Ephesians 3-5; F. Bland Tucker, 1895-1984, © 1980, Augsburg Publishing House
Tune: AZMON, CM; Carl G. Gläser, 1784-1829; harm. by Lowell Mason, 1792-1872

730 Psalm of Hope

Refrain

A - maz - ing grace! how sweet the sound that saved and set me free. I once was lost, but now am found; was blind, but now I see.

Verses

1. My God, my God, why have you a -
2. But here am I, the scorn of all my
3. The e - vil - do - ers cir - cle in a -
4. I shall pro-claim your name to the full as -
*1. You did not turn your face from all your
*2. And so my soul shall live for you, O

Alternate Easter verses used with v.4 above.

ban - doned me?   Far from my prayers,
peo - ple.   They say, "if God
round me.   I am en - slaved
sem - bly.   Those who fear God,
peo - ple.   You res - cued them
Lord of hope.   My chil - dren shall

far from my cries, all day and night I call.
is now your friend, let God res - cue you."
in chains of death, I can count all my bones.
ex - ult and praise; Glo - ri - fy the Lord.
from chains of death, you raised them from de - spair.
bring forth your deeds and mag - ni - fy your name.

Yet, our an - ces - tors put their trust in
From my moth - er's womb you are my
O my strength, has - ten to my
All gen - er - a - tions, all chil - dren of the
Ev - 'ry na - tion on earth from end to
All my de - scen - dants shall know your ways, O

you.   You res - cued them,
God.   You held me up,
aid.   Come save my life,
earth: Pro - claim for ev - er
end   Shall turn to you
Lord.   May they pro - claim

D.C.

you saved them from all foes.
you placed me in your arms.
come quick - ly to my help.
the won - drous deeds of God.
and bow be - fore your throne.
the jus - tice you have shown.

Text: Refrain, John Newton, 1725-1807; Verses, Psalm 22, adapted by Felix Goebel-Komala, b.1961
Tune: PSALM OF HOPE, irregular with refrain; Felix Goebel-Komala, b.1961
© 1994, GIA Publications, Inc.

731 How Firm a Foundation

1. How firm a foun - da - tion, you saints of the
2. "Fear not, I am with you, O be not dis -
3. "When through the deep wa - ters I call you to
4. "The soul that on Je - sus still leans for re -

Lord, Is laid for your faith in this ex - cel - lent
mayed, For I am your God, and will still give you
go, The riv - ers of woe shall not you o - ver -
pose, I will not, I will not de - sert to its

Word! What more can God say than to you has been
aid; I'll strength - en you, help you, and cause you to
flow; For I will be with you, your trou - bles to
foes; That soul, though all hell should en - deav - or to

said, To you who for ref - uge to Je - sus have fled?
stand, Up - held by my right - eous, om - nip - o - tent hand.
bless, And sanc - ti - fy to you, your deep - est dis - tress.
shake, I'll nev - er, no nev - er, no nev - er for - sake!"

Text: 2 Peter 1:4; "K" in Rippon's *A Selection of Hymns*, 1787
Tune: FOUNDATION, 11 11 11 11; Funk's *Compilation of Genuine Church Music*, 1832; harm. by Richard Proulx, b.1937, © 1975,
  GIA Publications, Inc.

The Lord Is My Light   732

Verses 1, 3

1. The Lord is my light and my sal -
3.   Wait on the Lord and be of good

va - tion, the Lord is my light and my sal -
cour - age, O wait on the Lord and be of good

va - tion, the Lord is my light and my sal -
cour - age,   wait on the Lord and be of good

va - tion; whom shall I fear?
cour - age. He shall strength - en thine heart.

Refrain

Whom shall I fear, whom shall I fear?

The Lord is the strength of my life; whom shall I fear?

Verse 2

2. In the time of trou-ble he shall hide me, O in the time of trou-ble, he shall hide me, in the time of trou-ble,

he shall hide me; whom shall I fear?

D.S.

Text: Lillian Bouknight
Tune: Lillian Bouknight; arr. by Paul Gainer
© 1980, Savgos Music, Inc.

How Can I Keep from Singing 733

1. My life flows on in end-less song A-
2. Through all the tu-mult and the strife, I
3. What, though my joys and com-fort die, The
4. The peace of Christ makes fresh my heart, A

bove earth's lam-en-ta-tion. I hear the real though
hear that mu-sic ring-ing; It sounds and ech-oes
Lord, my sav-ior liv-eth. What though the dark-ness
foun-tain ev-er spring-ing. All things are mine since

far-off hymn That hails a new cre-a-tion.
in my soul; How can I keep from sing-ing?
gath-er 'round? Songs in the night it giv-eth.
I am his; How can I keep from sing-ing?

No storm can shake my in-most calm, While to that rock I'm

cling-ing. Since Christ is Lord of heav-en and earth,

How can I keep from sing-ing?

Text: Robert Lowry, 1826-1899
Tune: HOW CAN I KEEP FROM SINGING, 8 7 8 7 with refrain; Robert Lowry, 1826-1899; harm. by Robert J. Batastini, b.1942, © 1988, GIA
   Publications, Inc.

734 Be Not Afraid

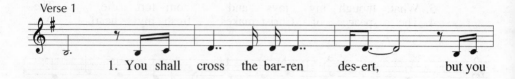

Verse 1

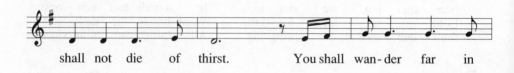

1. You shall cross the bar-ren des-ert, but you

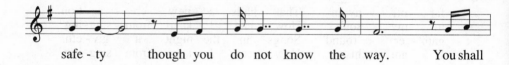

shall not die of thirst. You shall wan-der far in

safe-ty though you do not know the way. You shall

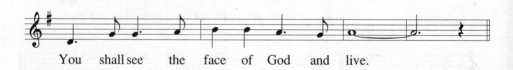

speak your words in for-eign lands and all will un-der-stand.

You shall see the face of God and live.

𝄋 Refrain

Melody:

Be not a - fraid. I go be-

Harmony:

Be not a - fraid. I go be-

Verse 3

Ooh   king-dom shall be theirs.

3. Bless - ed are your poor, for the king-dom shall be theirs.

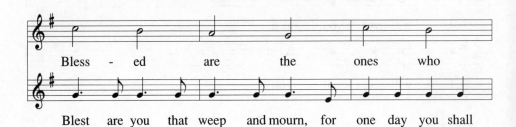

Bless - ed are the ones who

Blest are you that weep and mourn, for one day you shall

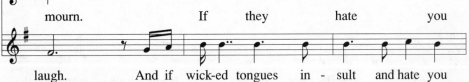

mourn.   If they hate you

laugh.   And if wick-ed tongues in - sult and hate you

D.S.

all be-cause of me, bless-ed, bless-ed are you!

all be-cause of me, bless-ed, bless-ed are you!

Text: Isaiah 43:2-3, Luke 6:20ff; Bob Dufford, SJ, b.1943
Tune: Bob Dufford, SJ, b.1943; acc. by Sr. Theophane Hytrek, OSF, 1915-1992
© 1975, Robert J. Dufford, SJ, and New Dawn Music

O God, Our Help in Ages Past   735

1. O God, our help in ages past,
2. Un - der the shad - ow of your throne
3. Be - fore the hills in or - der stood,
4. A thou - sand a - ges in your sight
5. Time, like an ev - er - roll - ing stream,
6. O God, our help in a - ges past,

Our hope for years to come,
Your saints have dwelt se - cure;
Or earth re - ceived its frame,
Are like an eve - ning gone,
Soon bears us all a - way;
Our hope for years to come,

Our shel - ter from the
Suf - fi - cient is your
From ev - er - last - ing
Short as the watch that
We fly for - got - ten,
Still be our guard while

storm - y blast, And our e - ter - nal home.
arm a - lone, And our de - fense is sure.
you are God, To end - less years the same.
ends the night Be - fore the ris - ing sun.
as a dream Dies at the op - 'ning day.
trou - bles last, And our e - ter - nal home.

Text: Psalm 90; Isaac Watts, 1674-1748
Tune: ST. ANNE, CM; attr. to William Croft, 1678-1727; harm. composite from 18th C. versions

736   Be Still and Know That I Am God

Text: Psalm 46:10; John L. Bell, b.1949
Tune: John L. Bell, b.1949
© 1989, Iona Community, GIA Publications, Inc., agent

Amazing Grace 737

1. A - maz - ing grace! how sweet the sound, That saved a wretch like me! I once was lost, but now am found, Was blind, but now I see.

2. 'Twas grace that taught my heart to fear, And grace my fears re - lieved; How pre - cious did that grace ap - pear The hour I first be - lieved!

3. The Lord has prom - ised good to me, His word my hope se - cures; He will my shield and por - tion be As long as life en - dures.

4. Through man - y dan - gers, toils, and snares, I have al - read - y come; 'Tis grace has brought me safe thus far, And grace will lead me home.

5. When we've been there ten thou - sand years, Bright shin - ing as the sun, We've no less days to sing God's praise Than when we'd first be - gun.

Text: St. 1-4, John Newton, 1725-1807; st. 5, attr. to John Rees, fl.1859
Tune: NEW BRITAIN, CM; *Virginia Harmony*, 1831; harm. by Edwin O. Excell, 1851-1921

738 With a Shepherd's Care

Verses

unis.   *div.*

God
God
God

1. When we are lost, and can-not find the way,
2. When we are weak, and cares press all a-round,
3. When we are scared, and feel so all a-lone,

cares for us and keeps us safe.
strength-ens us to face each day.
loves us and is by our side.

God cares for us. For
God strength - ens us. For
God loves us. For

and
and
and

God is our light and our faith - ful guide,
God is our rock and our sav - ing help,
God is our hope and our con - stant friend,

leads us with a shep - herd's care.
guides us with a fa - ther's strength.
nur - tures with a moth - er's love.

D.C.

with a shep - herd's care.
with a fa - ther's strength.
with a moth - er's love.

Text: James J. Chepponis, b.1956
Tune: James J. Chepponis, b.1956
© 1992, GIA Publications, Inc.

739 Surely It Is God Who Saves Me

1. Sure - ly it is God who saves me; Trust - ing him, I shall not fear. For the Lord de - fends and shields me And his sav - ing help is near. So re - joice as you draw wa - ter From sal - va - tion's liv - ing spring; In the day of your de - liv - 'rance Thank the Lord, his mer - cies sing.

2. Make his deeds known to the peo - ples; Tell out his ex - alt - ed Name. Praise the Lord, who has done great things; All his works his might pro - claim. Zi - on, lift your voice in sing - ing; For with you has come to dwell, In your ver - y midst, the great and Ho - ly One of Is - ra - el.

Text: Isaiah 12:1-6; Carl P. Daw, Jr., b.1944, © 1982
Tune: RAQUEL, 8 7 8 7 D; Skinner Chávez-Melo, 1944-1992, ©

On Eagle's Wings   740

Verse 1

1. You who dwell in the shel-ter of the Lord, who a -
bide in his shad - ow for life, say to the Lord: "My
ref - uge, my rock in whom I trust!"

Refrain

Descant:
And he will raise you up on ea - gle's wings, bear you on the

Melody:

breath of dawn, make you to shine like the sun, and

Last time to coda ⊕

hold you in the palm of his hand.

To verses

2. The

Verse 2

snare of the fowl- er will nev - er cap-ture you, and

3

fam - ine will bring you no fear: un - der his wings your

D.S.

ref - uge, his faith-ful- ness your shield.

Verse 3

3

3. You need not fear the ter - ror of the night, nor the

D.S.

ar - row that flies by day; though thou - sands fall a -

bout you, near you it shall not come.

Verse 4

3

4. For to his an - gels he's giv - en a com - mand to

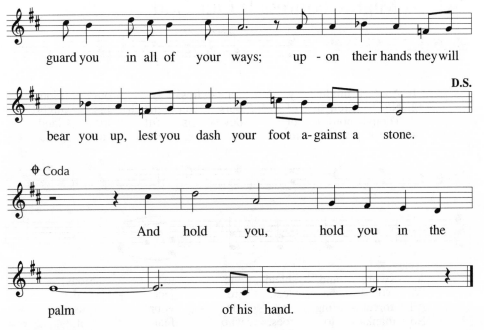

guard you in all of your ways; up - on their hands they will

bear you up, lest you dash your foot a-gainst a stone.

Coda

And hold you, hold you in the

palm of his hand.

Text: Psalm 91; Michael Joncas, b.1951
Tune: Michael Joncas, b.1951
© 1979, New Dawn Music

741 A Mighty Fortress Is Our God

1. A might-y for-tress is our God,
2. No strength of ours can match his might!
3. Though hordes of dev-ils fill the land
4. God's Word for-ev-er shall a-bide,

A sword and shield vic-to-rious,
We would be lost, re-ject-ed.
All threat-n'ing to de-vour us,
No thanks to foes, who fear it;

Who breaks the cruel op-pres-sor's rod
But now a cham-pion comes to fight,
We trem-ble not, un-moved we stand;
For God, our Lord, fights by our side

And wins sal-va-tion glo-rious.
Whom God a-lone e-lect-ed.
They can-not o-ver-pow'r us.
With weap-ons of the Spir-it.

The old sa - tan - ic foe / Has sworn to
You ask who this may be? / The Lord of
Let this world's ty - rant rage; / In bat - tle
Were they to take our house, / Goods, hon - or,

work us woe! / With craft and dread - ful might
hosts is he! / Christ Je - sus, might - y Lord,
we'll en - gage! / His might is doomed to fail;
child, or spouse, / Though life be wrenched a - way,

He arms him - self to fight.
God's on - ly Son, a - dored.
God's judge - ment must pre - vail!
They can - not win the day.

On earth he has no e - qual.
He holds the field vic - to - rious.
One lit - tle word sub - dues him.
The King - dom's ours for - ev - er!

Text: Psalm (45) 46; *Ein' feste Burg ins unser Gott;* Martin Luther, 1483-1546; tr. © 1978, *Lutheran Book of Worship*
Tune: EIN' FESTE BURG, 8 7 8 7 66 66 7; Martin Luther, 1483-1546; harm by J.S. Bach, 1685-1750

742 There's a Wideness in God's Mercy

1. There's a wide-ness in God's mer-cy Like the wide-ness of the sea; There's a kind-ness in God's jus-tice Which is more than lib-er-ty. There is plen-ti-ful re-demp-tion In the blood that has been shed;

2. For the love of God is broad-er Than the meas-ures of our mind, And the heart of the E-ter-nal Is most won-der-ful-ly kind. If our love were but more sim-ple We should take him at his word,

3. Trou-bled souls, why will you scat-ter Like a crowd of fright-ened sheep? Fool-ish hearts, why will you wan-der From a love so true and deep? There is wel-come for the sin-ner And more grac-es for the good;

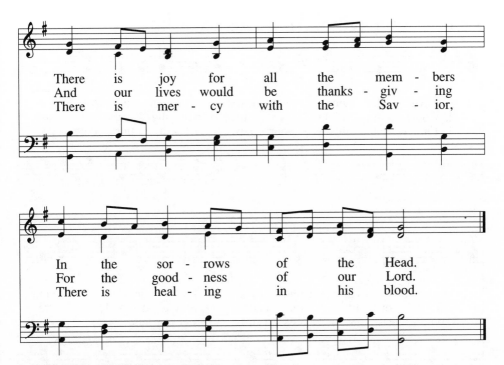

There is joy for all the mem - bers
And our lives would be thanks - giv - ing
There is mer - cy with the Sav - ior,

In the sor - rows of the Head.
For the good - ness of our Lord.
There is heal - ing in his blood.

Text: Frederick W. Faber, 1814-1863, alt.
Tune: IN BABILONE, 8 7 8 7 D; *Oude en Nieuwe Hollanste Boerenlities*, c.1710

743 Love Divine, All Loves Excelling

1. Love di - vine, all loves ex - cel - ling, Joy of
2. Come, al - might - y to de - liv - er, Let us
3. Fin - ish then your new cre - a - tion, Pure and

heav'n to earth come down! Fix in us your
all your life re - ceive; Sud - den - ly re -
spot - less, gra - cious Lord, Let us see your

hum - ble dwell - ing, All your faith - ful mer - cies crown.
turn and nev - er, Nev - er more your tem - ples leave.
great sal - va - tion Per - fect - ly in you re - stored.

Je - sus, source of all com - pas - sion, Love un -
Lord, we would be al - ways bless - ing, Serve you
Changed from glo - ry in - to glo - ry, Till in

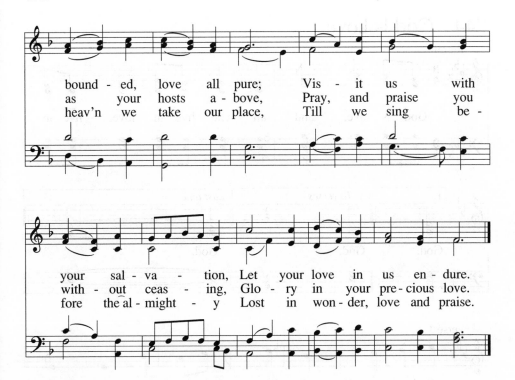

bound - ed, love   all   pure;   Vis - it   us   with
as   your hosts a - bove,   Pray, and praise you
heav'n we   take   our place, Till   we   sing   be -

your   sal - va - tion, Let your love in us en - dure.
with - out ceas - ing, Glo - ry in your pre - cious love.
fore   the al - might - y Lost in won - der, love and praise.

Text: Charles Wesley, 1707-1788, alt.
Tune: HYFRYDOL, 8 7 8 7 D; Rowland H. Prichard, 1811-1887

744 God Is Love

Refrain

God is love, and all who live in love, live in

1. God. 2. *To verses* God. *Last time* God.

Verse 1

1. God is light, in God there is no dark - ness. Come

live in the love of the Lord.

D.C.

Verse 2

2. Come to the Lord, re - ceive the light, and

live in the love of the Lord.

D.C.

Verse 3

3. We are called to be God's own chil - dren, to

live in the love of the Lord.

D.C.

Verse 4

D.C.

4. All of you are one, u - nit - ed in Je - sus, to

live in the love of the Lord.

Text: 1 John 1:5, 3:2, 4:15, Psalm 33:6, Galatians 3:28; David Haas, b.1957
Tune: David Haas, b.1957
© 1987, GIA Publications, Inc.

745 Love One Another

Refrain

Descant:
Love one an - oth - er, love is of God.

Melody:
Love one an - oth - er, for love is of God.

Love one an - oth - er, God is love.

Love one an - oth-er, for God is love.

Verses 1, 5

1. God loved the world so much he
5. God is love, and

sent us his on - ly son, that all who be-lieve in
they who a-bide in love, a - bide in

D.C.

him might have e - ter - nal life.
God, and God in them.

Verse 2

2. Since God has giv-en his love to us,

there - fore let us love one an - oth- er. If we love one an-oth-er,

God will love us, and live in us in per - fect love.

Verse 3

3. Ev - 'ry-one who loves is be -

got - ten of God and knows him as the Fa - ther. But

they who do not love do not know God, for God is love.

Verse 4

4. Let not your hearts be trou - bled, for

love has no room for fear. In love all fear is for -

got - ten, for God is here with us.

Text: 1 John 4; James J. Chepponis, b.1956
Tune: James J. Chepponis, b.1956
© 1983, GIA Publications, Inc.

746 Ubi Caritas

Refrain

U - bi ca - ri - tas   et a - mor,
Live in char - i - ty   and stead - fast   love,

u - bi ca - ri - tas   De - us i - bi est.
live in char - i - ty;   God will   dwell with   you.

Verses

1. Your love, O Je-sus Christ, has gath-ered us to - geth-er.

2. May your   love, O Je-sus Christ,   be fore-most in our   lives.

3. Let us   love one an - oth - er   as   God has   loved   us.

4. Let us be   one   in love to - geth-er   in the one bread of Christ.

* Choose either part.

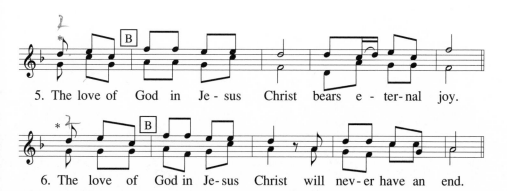

5. The love of God in Je-sus Christ bears e - ter-nal joy.

6. The love of God in Je-sus Christ will nev-er have an end.

Text: I Corinthians 13:2-8; *Where charity and love are found, God is there;* Taizé Community, 1978
Tune: Jacques Berthier, 1923-1994
© 1979, Les Presses de Taizè, GIA Publications, Inc., agent

Where Charity and Love Prevail   747

1. Where char - i - ty and love pre - vail,
2. With grate - ful joy and ho - ly fear
3. For - give we now each oth - er's faults
4. Let strife a - mong us be un - known,
5. Let us re - call that in our midst
6. No race nor creed can love ex - clude,

There God is ev - er found; Brought here to - geth - er
God's char - i - ty we learn; Let us with heart and
As we our faults con - fess; And let us love each
Let all con - ten - tion cease; Be God's the glo - ry
Dwells God's be - got - ten Son; As mem - bers of his
If hon - ored be God's name; Our fam - i - ly em -

by Christ's love, By love are we thus bound.
mind and soul Now love him in re - turn.
oth - er well In Chris - tian ho - li - ness.
that we seek, Be ours God's ho - ly peace.
bod - y joined, We are in him made one.
brac - es all Whose Fa - ther is the same.

Text: *Ubi caritas;* trans. by Omer Westendorf, b.1916
Tune: CHRISTIAN LOVE, CM; Paul Benoit, OSB, 1893-1979
© 1961, 1962, World Library Publications, Inc.

748 May Love Be Ours

Intro-Coda

To verses

Last time

Verses

1. Not for tongues of heav - en's an - gels,
2. Love is hum - ble, love is gen - tle,
3. Nev - er jeal - ous, nev - er self - ish,
4. In the day this world is fad - ing,

Not for wis-dom to dis - cern, Not for faith that mas-ters
Love is ten - der, true, and kind; Love is gra-cious, ev - er
Love will not re - joice in wrong; Nev - er boast-ful nor re -
Faith and hope will play their part; But when Christ is seen in

moun - tains, For this bet - ter gift we yearn:
pa - tient, Gen - er - ous of heart and mind—
sent - ful, Love be - lieves and suf - fers long—
glo - ry, Love shall reign in ev - 'ry heart:

Refrain

May love be ours, Lord; may love be ours.

Last time D.C.

May love be ours, O Lord.

Text: Timothy Dudley-Smith, b.1926, © 1985, Hope Publishing Co.
Tune: COMFORT, 8 7 8 7 with refrain; Michael Joncas, b.1951, © 1988, GIA Publications, Inc.

What Wondrous Love Is This   749

1. What won-drous love is this, O my soul, O my soul?
2. To God and to the Lamb I will sing, I will sing;
3. And when from death I'm free, I'll sing on, I'll sing on;

What won-drous love is this, O my soul?
To God and to the Lamb, I will sing;
And when from death I'm free, I'll sing on;

What won-drous love is this that caused the Lord of bliss
To God and to the Lamb who is the great I Am,
And when from death I'm free, I'll sing and joy-ful be,

To bear the dread-ful curse for my soul, for my soul;
While mil-lions join the theme, I will sing, I will sing;
And through e-ter-ni-ty I'll sing on, I'll sing on!

To bear the dread-ful curse for my soul?
While mil-lions join the theme, I will sing.
And through e-ter-ni-ty I'll sing on.

Text: Alexander Means, 1801-1853
Tune: WONDROUS LOVE, 12 9 12 12 9; *Southern Harmony*, 1835; harm. from *Cantate Domino, 1980*, © 1980, World Council of Churches

750 Love Is His Word

1. Love is his word, love is his way.
2. Love is his way, love is his mark.
3. Love is his mark, love is his sign.
4. Love is his sign, love is his news.
5. Love is his news, love is his name.

Feast - ing with all, fast - ing a - lone,
Shar - ing his last Pass - o - ver feast.
Bread for our strength, wine for our joy.
"Do this," he said, "lest you for - get
We are his own, cho - sen and called,

Liv - ing and dy - ing, Ris - ing a - gain.
Guest at his ta - ble, Host to the Twelve,
"This is my bod - y, This is my blood."
All my deep sor - row, All my dear blood."
Fam - i - ly, breth - ren, Cous - ins and kin.

Love, on - ly love, is his way.
Love, on - ly love, is his mark.
Love, on - ly love, is his sign.
Love, on - ly love, is his news.
Love, on - ly love, is his name.

Rich - er than gold is the love of my Lord,

bet - ter than splen - dor and wealth.

Rich - er than gold is the love of my Lord,

bet - ter than splen - dor and wealth.

6. Love is his name, love is his law.
Hear his command, all who are his:
"Love one another, I have loved you."
Love, only love, is his law.

7. Love is his law, love is his word:
Love of the Lord, Father and Word.
Love of the Spirit, God ev'ry one.
Love, only love, is his word.

Text: Luke Connaughton, 1917-1979, © 1970, Mayhew McCrimmon, Ltd.
Tune: JULINORMA, 4 4 8 5 4 7 with refrain; Robert M. Hutmacher, OFM, b.1948, © 1986, GIA Publications, Inc.

Lord of All Nations, Grant Me Grace   751

1. Lord of all na - tions, grant me grace To love all
2. Break down the wall that would di - vide Your chil - dren,
3. For - give me, Lord, where I have erred By love - less
4. Give me your cour - age, Lord, to speak When - ev - er
5. With your own love may I be filled And by your

peo - ple, ev - 'ry race To see each mor - tal as I
Lord, on ev - 'ry side. My neigh - bor's good let me pur -
act and thought-less word. Make me to see the wrong I
strong op - press the weak. Should I my - self as vic - tim
Ho - ly Spir - it willed, That all whose lives are touched by

ought, My kin - dred, whom your love has bought.
sue, Let Chris - tian love bind warm and true.
do Will cru - ci - fy my Lord a - new.
live, Re - mem - b'ring you, may I for - give.
mine, May know your heal - ing touch di - vine.

Text: Philippians 2:1-18; Olive W. Spannaus, b.1916, © 1969, Concordia Publishing House
Tune: BEATUS VIR, LM; Slovak; harm. by Richard Hillert, b.1923, © 1969, Concordia Publishing House

752 Where True Love and Charity Are Found / Ubi Caritas

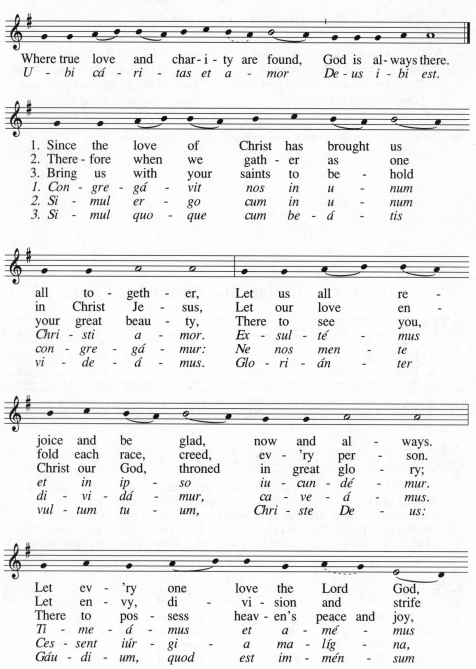

Where true love and char-i-ty are found, God is al-ways there.
U - bi cá - ri - tas et a - mor De - us i - bi est.

1. Since the love of Christ has brought us
2. There-fore when we gath - er as one
3. Bring us with your saints to be - hold
1. *Con - gre - gá - vit nos in u - num*
2. *Si - mul er - go cum in u - num*
3. *Si - mul quo - que cum be - á - tis*

all to - geth - er, Let us all re -
in Christ Je - sus, Let our love en -
your great beau - ty, There to see you,
Chri - sti a - mor. Ex - sul - té - mus
con - gre - gá - mur: Ne nos men - te
vi - de - á - mus. Glo - ri - án - ter

joice and be glad, now and al - ways.
fold each race, creed, ev - 'ry per - son.
Christ our God, throned in great glo - ry;
et in ip - so iu - cun - dé - mur.
di - vi - dá - mur, ca - ve - á - mus.
vul - tum tu - um, Chri - ste De - us:

Let ev - 'ry one love the Lord God,
Let en - vy, di - vi - sion and strife
There to pos - sess heav - en's peace and joy,
Ti - me - á - mus et a - mé - mus
Ces - sent iúr - gi - a ma - líg - na,
Gáu - di - um, quod est im - mén - sum

the   liv - ing   God;   And   with   sin -   cere
cease   a - mong   us;   May   Christ our   Lord
your   truth and   love,   For   end - less   a -
De -   um   vi - vum.   *Et   ex   cor -   de*
ces -   sent   li - tes.   *Et   in   mé -   di -*
at -   que   pro - bum.   *Sáe - cu -   la   per*

D.C.

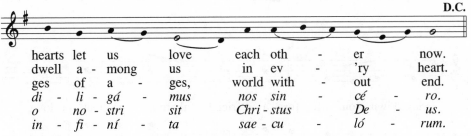

hearts let   us   love   each   oth -   er   now.
dwell   a - mong   us   in   ev -   'ry   heart.
ges   of   a -   ges,   world   with -   out   end.
di -   li - gá -   mus   *nos   sin -   cé -   ro.*
o   no - stri   sit   *Chri - stus   De -   us.*
in -   fi - ní -   ta   *sae - cu -   ló -   rum.*

Text: Latin, 9th C.; tr. by Richard Proulx, b.1937, © 1975, 1986, GIA Publications, Inc.
Tune: UBI CARITAS, 12 12 12 12 with refrain; Mode VI; acc. by Richard Proulx, b.1937, © 1986, GIA Publications, Inc.

753 No Greater Love

Refrain

There is no great - er love, says the Lord, than to

lay down your life for a friend; there is no great - er love,

no great - er love, than to lay down your life for a friend.

Verse 1

1. As the Fa-ther has loved me, so I have loved you.

Live on in my love. You will live in my love if you

keep my com-mands, ev-en as I have kept my Fa - ther's.

rit. **D.C.**

Verse 2
2. All this I tell you that my joy may be yours and your joy may be com-plete. Love one an-oth-er as I have loved you: This is my com-mand. *rit.* **D.C.**

Verse 3
3. You are my friends if you keep my com-mands; no long-er slaves but friends to me. All I heard from my Fa-ther, I have made known to you: Now I call you friends. *rit.* **D.C.**

Verse 4
4. It was not you who chose me, it was I who chose you, chose you to go forth and bear fruit. Your fruit must en-dure, so you will re-ceive all you ask the Fa-ther in my name. *rit.* **D.C.**

Text: John 15: 9-17; Michael Joncas, b.1951
Tune: Michael Joncas, b.1951
© 1988, GIA Publications, Inc.

754 Precious Lord, Take My Hand

1. Pre - cious Lord, take my hand, Lead me on, let me
2. When my way grows drear, Pre - cious Lord, lin - ger
3. When the dark - ness ap-pears And the night draws

stand, I am tired, I am weak, I am
near, When my life is al - most
near, And the day is past and

worn. (I am worn.) Through the storm, through the
gone, (al - most gone,) Hear my cry, hear my
gone, (past and gone,) At the riv - er I

night, Lead me on to the light, Take my
call, Hold my hand lest I fall. Take my
stand, Guide my feet, hold my hand. Take my

hand,   pre - cious Lord,   lead me   home. (Lead me home.)
hand,   pre - cious Lord,   lead me   home. (Lead me home.)
hand,   pre - cious Lord,   lead me   home. (Lead me home.)

Text: Thomas A. Dorsey, 1899-1993, © 1938, Unichappell Music, Inc.
Tune: PRECIOUS LORD 66 9 D; George N. Allen, © 1938, Unichappell Music, Inc.; arr. by Kelly Dobbs Mickus, b. 1966, © 1994,
    GIA Publications, Inc.

755 Jesus, Lead the Way

1. Je - sus, lead the way Through our life's long day,
2. Je - sus be our light, In the midst of night,
3. When in deep - est grief, Strength - en our be - lief.
4. Je - sus, still lead on 'Til our rest be won:

When at times the way is cheer - less,
Let not faith - less fear o'er - take us,
When temp - ta - tions come al - lur - ing,
If you lead us through rough plac - es,

Help us fol - low, calm and fear - less;
Let not faith and hope for - sake us;
Make us pa - tient and en - dur - ing;
Grant us your re - deem-ing grac - es.

Guide us by your hand To the prom - ised land.
May we feel you near As we wor - ship here.
Lord we seek your grace In this ho - ly place.
When our course is o'er, O - pen heav - en's door.

Text: *Jesu, geh voran;* Nicholas L. von Zinzendorf, 1700-1760; tr. by Jane Borthwick, 1813-1897, alt.
Tune: ROCHELLE, 55 88 55; Adam Drese, 1620-1701; harm. alt.

Shepherd Me, O God   756

Refrain

Shep-herd me, O God, be - yond my wants, be-yond my fears, from death in-to life.

Shep-herd me, be - yond my wants, be-yond my fears, from death to life.

To verses 1, 2, 3, 5

To verse 4

Verses 1, 2, 3

1. God is my shep-herd, so noth-ing shall I want, I rest in the mead-ows of faith-ful-ness and love, I walk by the qui - et wa - ters of peace.
2. Gent - ly you raise me and heal my wea-ry soul, you lead me by path-ways of right-eous-ness and truth, my spir - it shall sing the mu - sic of your name.
3. Though I should wan - der the val - ley of death, I fear no e - vil, for you are at my side, your rod and your staff, my com - fort and my hope.

D.C.

Verse 4

4. You have set me a ban-quet of love in the face of ha-tred, crown-ing me with love be-yond my pow'r to hold.

Verse 5

5. Sure - ly your kind-ness and mer-cy fol-low me all the days of my life; I will dwell in the house of my God for ev - er - more.

Final Refrain

Shep-herd me, O God, be - yond my wants, be - yond my fears, from death in - to life.

Text: Psalm 23; Marty Haugen
Music: Marty Haugen
© 1986, GIA Publications, Inc.

Nada Te Turbe / Nothing Can Trouble 757

*Choose either part

Text: St. Teresa of Jesus; Taizé Community, 1986, 1991
Tune: Jacques Berthier, 1923-1994
© 1986, 1991, Les Presses de Taizé, GIA Publications, Inc., agent

758 Eye Has Not Seen

Refrain

Eye has not seen, ear has not heard what God has read-y for those who love him;

Spir-it of love, come, give us the mind of Je-sus,

teach us the wis-dom of God.

Last time

Verses 1-3

1. When pain and sor-row weigh us down, be
2. Our lives are but a sin-gle breath, we
3. To those who see with eyes of faith, the

near to us, O Lord, for - give the weak - ness
flow - er and we fade, yet all our days are
Lord is ev - er near, re - flect - ed in the

of our faith, and bear us up with - in your peace - ful
in your hands, so we re - turn in love what love has
fac - es of all the poor and low - ly of the

word.
made.
world.

Verse 4

4. We sing a mys - t'ry from the past in halls where saints have

trod, yet ev - er new the mu - sic rings to Je - sus, Liv - ing

Song of God.

Text: 1 Corinthians 2:9-10; Marty Haugen, b.1950
Tune: Marty Haugen, b.1950
© 1982, GIA Publications, Inc.

759 O Jesus, Joy of Loving Hearts

1. O Jesus, joy of loving hearts, The fount of life and our true light, We seek the peace your love imparts, And stand rejoicing in your sight.
2. We taste in you our living bread, And long to feast upon you still; We drink of you, the fountainhead, Our thirsting souls to quench and fill.
3. For you our restless spirits yearn Where'er our changing lot is cast; Glad, when your presence we discern, Blest, when our faith can hold you fast.
4. O Jesus, ever with us stay; Make all our moments calm and bright; O chase the night of sin away, Shed o'er the world your holy light.

Descant

4. O Jesus, ever with us stay; Make all our moments calm and bright; O chase the night of sin away, Shed o'er the world your holy light.

Text: *Jesu, dulcedo cordium;* attr. to Bernard of Clairvaux, 1091-1153; para. by Ray Palmer, 1808-1887, alt.
Tune: WAREHAM, LM; William Knapp, 1698-1768

A Touching Place 760

Verses

1. Christ's is the world in which we move,
2. Feel for the peo-ple we most a-void,
3. Feel for the par-ents who've lost their child,
4. Feel for the lives by life con-fused,

Christ's are the folk we're sum-moned to love,
Strange or be-reaved or nev-er em-ployed;
Feel for the wom-en whom men have de-filed,
Rid-dled with doubt, in lov-ing a-bused;

Christ's is the voice which calls us to care, And
Feel for the wom-en, and feel for the men Who
Feel for the ba-by for whom there's no breast, And
Feel for the lone-ly heart, con-scious of sin, Which

Christ is the one who meets us here.
fear that their liv-ing is all in vain.
feel for the wea-ry who find no rest.
longs to be pure but fears to be-gin.

Refrain

To the lost Christ shows his face; To the un-loved he

gives his em-brace; To those who cry in pain or dis-

grace, Christ makes, with his friends, a touch-ing place.

Text: John L. Bell, b.1949, © 1989, Iona Community, GIA Publications, Inc., agent
Tune: DREAM ANGUS, Irregular; Scottish folk song; acc. by John L. Bell, b.1949, © 1993, Iona Community, GIA Publications, Inc., agent

761 My Shepherd Will Supply My Need

1. My Shepherd will supply my need; The God of love supreme; In pastures green you make me feed, Beside the living stream. You bring my wan - d'ring spir - it back, When I for - sake your ways; In paths of truth and grace.

2. When I walk through the shades of death, Your presence is my stay; One word of your sup - port - ing breath Drives all my fears a - way. Your hand, in sight of all my foes, Does still my ta - ble spread; My cup with bless - ings o - ver - flows, Your oil a - noints my head.

3. The sure pro - vi - sions of my God At - tend me all my days; O may your house be my a - bode, And all my work be praise! There would I find a set - tled rest, While oth - ers go and come, No more a stran - ger nor a guest; But like a child at home.

Text: Psalm 23; Isaac Watts, 1674-1748, alt.
Tune: RESIGNATION, CMD; Funk's *Compilation of Genuine Church Music*, 1832; harm. by Richard Proulx, b.1937, © 1975, GIA Publications, Inc.

You Are Mine 762

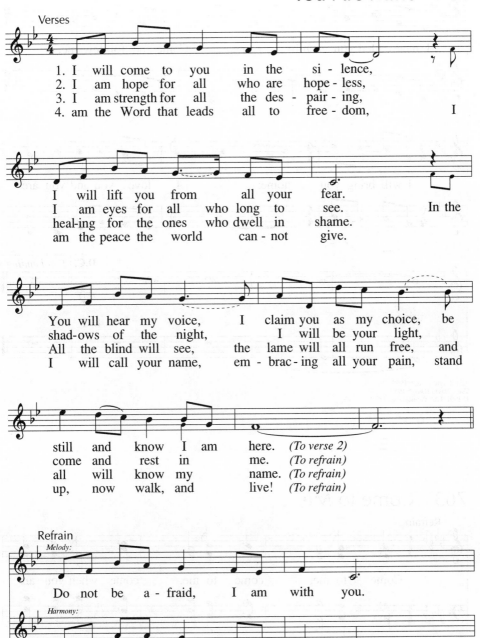

Verses

1. I will come to you in the si - lence,
2. I am hope for all who are hope - less,
3. I am strength for all the des - pair - ing,
4. am the Word that leads all to free - dom,   I

I will lift you from all your fear.
I am eyes for all who long to see.   In the
heal-ing for the ones who dwell in shame.
am the peace the world can - not give.

You will hear my voice, I claim you as my choice, be
shad-ows of the night, I will be your light,
All the blind will see, the lame will all run free, and
I will call your name, em - brac - ing all your pain, stand

still   and   know   I   am   here. *(To verse 2)*
come   and   rest   in   me. *(To refrain)*
all   will   know   my   name. *(To refrain)*
up,   now   walk,   and   live! *(To refrain)*

Refrain

Melody:

Do not be a - fraid,   I   am   with   you.

Harmony:

I have called you each by name. Come and fol-low me,

I will bring you home; I love you and you are

D.C. | Final ending

mine. 4. I

Text: David Haas, b.1957
Tune: David Haas, b.1957
© 1991, GIA Publications, Inc.

763 Come to Me

Refrain

Come to me, come to me, come when you are

wea-ry; come to me, come to me, and

COMFORT

Text: Matthew 11:28-30; Michael Joncas, b.1951
Tune: Michael Joncas, b.1951
© 1989, GIA Publications, Inc.

764 There Is a Balm in Gilead

Refrain

There is a balm in Gil-e-ad To make the wound-ed whole,

There is a balm in Gil-e-ad To heal the sin-sick soul.

Verses

1. Some - times I feel dis - cour - aged   And
2. If you can - not preach like Pe - ter,   If you
3. Don't ev - er feel dis - cour - aged,   For

think my work's in vain, But then the Ho - ly
can - not pray like Paul, You can tell the love of
Je - sus is your friend; And if you lack for

D.C.

Spir - it Re - vives my soul a - gain.
Je - sus, And say, "He died for all!"
knowl - edge He'll ne'er re - fuse to lend.

Text: Jeremiah 8:22, African-American spiritual
Tune: BALM IN GILEAD, Irregular; African-American spiritual; acc. by Robert J. Batastini, b.1942, © 1987, GIA Publications, Inc.

765 Shelter Me, O God

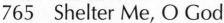

Refrain

Shel - ter me, O God; hide me in the shad-ow of your wings.

To verses | Last time

You a - lone are my hope.

Verses

1. When my foes sur - round me, set me high a - bove their
2. As a moth - er gath - ers her young be - neath her
3. Though I walk in dark - ness, through the nee - dle's eye of

D.C.

reach. Hear me when I call your name.
care, gath - er me in - to your arms.
death, you will nev - er leave my side.

Text: Psalm 16, 61, Luke 13:34; Bob Hurd, b. 1950, © 1984
Tune: Bob Hurd, b. 1950, © 1984; harm. by Dominic MacAller, © 1984, OCP Publications
Published by OCP Publications

The King of Love My Shepherd Is   766

1. The King of love my shep - herd is, Whose good - ness
2. Where streams of liv - ing wa - ter flow My ran - somed
3. Con - fused and fool - ish oft I strayed, But yet in
4. In death's dark vale I fear no ill With you, dear
5. You spread a ta - ble in my sight; Your sav - ing
6. And so through all the length of days Your good - ness

fails me nev - er; I noth - ing lack if
soul he's lead - ing, And where the ver - dant
love he sought me; And on his shoul - der
Lord, be - side me, Your rod and staff my
grace be - stow - ing; And O what trans - port
fails me nev - er; Good Shep - herd, may I

I am his, And he is mine for ev - er.
pas - tures grow With food ce - les - tial feed - ing.
gent - ly laid, And home, re - joic - ing, brought me.
com - fort still, Your cross be - fore to guide me.
of de - light From your pure chal - ice flow - ing!
sing your praise With - in your house for ev - er.

767 Within Our Darkest Night

Text: Taizé Community, 1991
Tune: Jacques Berthier, 1923-1994
© 1991, Les Presses de Taizé, GIA Publications, Inc., agent

I Heard the Voice of Jesus Say 768

1. I heard the voice of Je - sus say, "Come
2. I heard the voice of Je - sus say, "Be -
3. I heard the voice of Je - sus say, "I

un - to me and rest; Lay down, O wea - ry
hold, I free - ly give The liv - ing wa - ter;
am this dark world's light; Look un - to me, your

one, lay down Your head up - on my breast." I
thirst - y one, Stoop down, and drink, and live." I
morn shall rise, And all your day be bright." I

came to Je - sus as I was, So
came to Je - sus, and I drank Of
looked to Je - sus, and I found In

wea - ry, worn, and sad; I found in him a
that life - giv - ing stream; My thirst was quenched, my
him my star, my sun; And in that light of

rest - ing place, And he has made me glad.
soul re - vived, And now I live in him.
life I'll walk Till trav - 'ling days are done.

Text: Horatius Bonar, 1808-1889
Tune: KINGSFOLD, CMD; English; harm. by Ralph Vaughan Williams, 1872-1958, © Oxford University Press

Come to Me, O Weary Traveler 769

1. Come to me, O wea-ry trav-'ler; Come to me with
2. Do not fear, my yoke is eas-y; Do not fear, my
3. Take my yoke and leave your trou-bles; Take my yoke and
4. Rest in me, O wea-ry trav-'ler; Rest in me and

your dis-tress; Come to me, you heav-y bur-dened;
bur-den's light; Do not fear the path be-fore you;
come with me. Take my yoke, I am be-side you;
do not fear. Rest in me, my heart is gen-tle;

Come to me and find your rest.
Do not run from me in fright.
Take and learn hu-mil-i-ty.
Rest and cast a-way your care.

1.-3.   4.

Text: Matthew 11:28-30; Sylvia G. Dunstan, 1955-1993, © 1991, GIA Publications, Inc.
Tune: DUNSTAN, 8 7 8 7; Bob Moore, b.1962, © 1993, GIA Publications, Inc.

770 Jesus, Remember Me

Ostinato Refrain

Je-sus, re-mem-ber me when you come in-to your King-dom.

Je-sus, re-mem-ber me when you come in-to your King-dom.

Text: Luke 23:42; Taizé Community, 1981
Tune: Jacques Berthier, 1923-1994
© 1981, Les Presses de Taizé, GIA Publications, Inc., agent

I Will Not Die   771

Verses

1., 5. I will not die be-fore I've lived to see that land;
2. I will not rest un-til your dawn is in my eyes;
3. And I will breathe in that might-y wind of jus-tice;
4. You will stand up for the poor and the need-y;

firm as the earth, your own prom-ise.
that frag-ile light, new like morn-ing.
I'll know my name and rise up sing-ing.
you'll break the chains that bind your peo-ple.

I'll not let go un-til I've held it in my hand;
I will not sleep be-fore I've wak-ened to that sun-rise;
And I will call un-til my words bring on the thun-der;
For you are home for the lost and the des-p'rate;

Last time

that word of hope, and gen-tle laugh-ter.
and all the world knows your glo-ry.
washed in that rain, then I'll know you.
your strong right hand goes be-fore us.

Refrain

For your right hand has de-liv-ered us from death;

you have re-gard-ed our tears,

D.C.

3

you who are good-ness and grace.

Text: Tom Conry, b.1951
Tune: Tom Conry, b.1951; acc. by Patrick Loomis, 1951-1990

772   Bring Forth the Kingdom

Verses

1. You are salt for the earth, O peo-ple:
2. You are a light on the hill, O peo-ple:
3. You are a seed of the Word, O peo-ple:
4. We are a blest and a pil - grim peo-ple:

Salt for the King-dom of God! Share the fla - vor of
Light for the Cit - y of God! Shine so ho - ly and
Bring forth the King-dom of God! Seeds of mer - cy and
Bound for the King-dom of God! Love our jour - ney and

life, O peo - ple: Life in the King-dom of God!
bright, O peo - ple: Shine for the King-dom of God!
seeds of jus - tice, Grow in the King-dom of God!
love our home - land: Love is the King-dom of God!

Refrain

Bring forth the King-dom of mer - cy, Bring forth the

King-dom of peace; Bring forth the King-dom of jus - tice,

Bring forth the Cit - y of God!

Text: Marty Haugen, b.1950
Tune: Marty Haugen, b.1950
© 1986, GIA Publications, Inc.

When Jesus Came Preaching 773

1. When Je - sus came preach-ing the King-dom of God With the
2. Since Je - sus came preach-ing the King-dom of God, What a
3. Still Je - sus comes preach-ing the King-dom of God In a

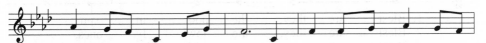

love that has pow'r to per - suade, The sick were made whole, both in
change in our lives he has made! How man - y have shared in the
world that is sick and a - fraid; His gos - pel has spread like the

bod - y and soul, And e - ven the de - mons o -
joy of their Lord, In self - giv - ing have loved and o -
leav - en in bread By the love that has a pow'r to per -

beyed. But he need-ed a few he could trust to be true, To
beyed! But let none of us doubt what re - li-gion's a-bout, Or by
suade. So let none of us swerve from our mis-sion to serve, That has

share in his work from the start: When Je - sus came preach-ing the
what it is shamed and be - trayed: Do just - ly, love mer - cy, walk
made us his Church from the start, May Je - sus, the light of the

King - dom of God, God's gift to the hum-ble of heart.
hum - bly with God, Is the rule of life Je - sus o - beyed.
world, send us out In the strength of the hum-ble of heart.

Text: Fred Pratt Green, b.1903, © 1974, Hope Publishing Co.
Tune: SAMANTHRA, 11 8 11 8 D; *Southern Harmony*, 1835; harm. by Austin C. Lovelace, b.1919, © 1986, GIA Publications, Inc.

774 Blest Are They

Verses 1-3

1. Blest are they, the poor in spir - it,
2. Blest are they, the low - ly ones,
3. Blest are they who show mer - cy,

theirs is the king - dom of God.
they shall in - her - it the earth.
mer - cy shall be theirs.

Blest are they, full of sor - row,
Blest are they who hun - ger and thirst,
Blest are they, the pure of heart,

they shall be con - soled.
they shall have their fill.
they shall see God!

Refrain

Descant:
Re - joice and be glad!

Melody:
Re - joice and be glad!

Men's voices:
Re - joice and be glad!

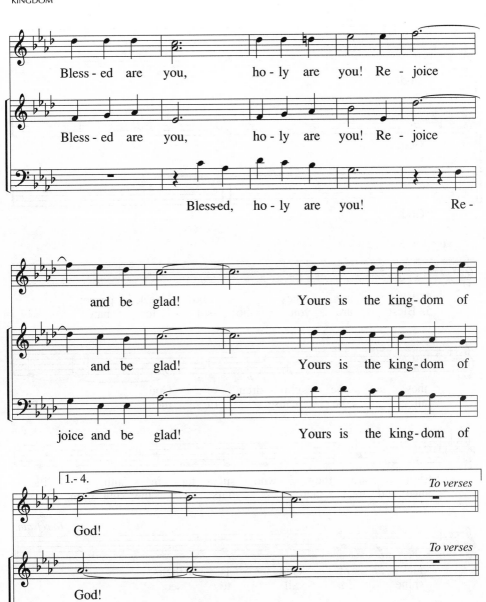

Bless - ed are you, ho - ly are you! Re - joice

Bless - ed are you, ho - ly are you! Re - joice

Bless-ed, ho - ly are you! Re -

and be glad! Yours is the king - dom of

and be glad! Yours is the king - dom of

joice and be glad! Yours is the king - dom of

1.- 4.   *To verses*

God!

                                          To verses

God!

                                          To verses

God!

Last time

God!

God!

God!

Verses 4, 5

4. Blest are they who seek peace;
5. Blest are you who suf - fer hate,

they are the chil - dren of God.
all be - cause of me. Re -

Blest are they who suf - fer in faith, the
joice and be glad, yours is the king - dom;

To refrain

glo - ry of God is theirs.
shine for all to see.

Text: Matthew 5:3-12; David Haas, b.1957
Tune: David Haas, b.1957; vocal arr. by David Haas, b.1957, Michael Joncas, b.1951
© 1985, GIA Publications, Inc.

The Kingdom of God 775

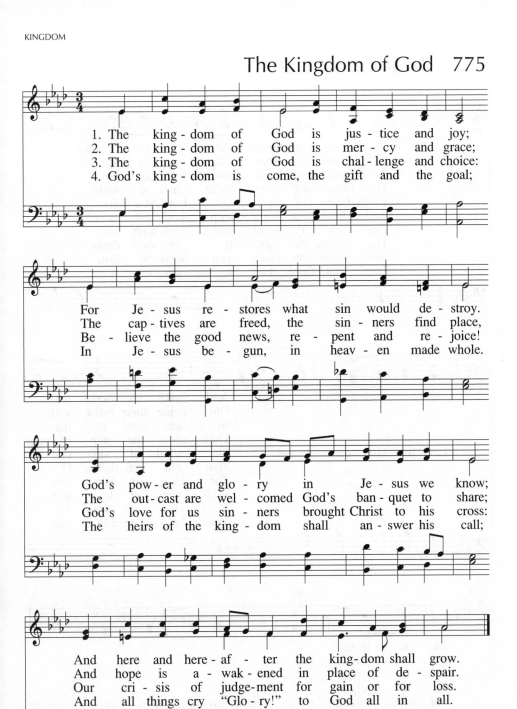

1. The king-dom of God is jus-tice and joy;
2. The king-dom of God is mer-cy and grace;
3. The king-dom of God is chal-lenge and choice:
4. God's king-dom is come, the gift and the goal;

For Je-sus re-stores what sin would de-stroy.
The cap-tives are freed, the sin-ners find place,
Be-lieve the good news, re-pent and re-joice!
In Je-sus be-gun, in heav-en made whole.

God's pow-er and glo-ry in Je-sus we know;
The out-cast are wel-comed God's ban-quet to share;
God's love for us sin-ners brought Christ to his cross:
The heirs of the king-dom shall an-swer his call;

And here and here-af-ter the king-dom shall grow.
And hope is a-wak-ened in place of de-spair.
Our cri-sis of judge-ment for gain or for loss.
And all things cry "Glo-ry!" to God all in all.

Text: Bryn A. Rees, 1911-1983, © Mrs. Olwen Scott
Tune: LAUDATE DOMINUM, 10 10 11 11; Charles H. H. Parry, 1848-1918

776 Thy Kingdom Come

Verses

Cantor:

1. O you who taught the mud to dream,
   Did spin like tops the stars in space,
2. Like seed and rain your word goes out,
   The blooms that grow there shall re - main,
3. From hearts of stone, O Lord, you drew,
   And won your King - ship with that sword,
4. And ev - 'ry heart that's sick with sin,
   The wound - ed spir - it he shall dress,
5. And when the skies you break at last,
   Then shall there be a joy - ful noise:

O

Lord, thy king - dom come.

Cantor:

And make the world with
Did guide their paths with
In gar - dens of the
Their scent the sign of your
The sword of sin that
That cut you down, O
The Heal - er King has
With balms of love and
Your king - dom come to
Your king - dom praise you

All:

life to teem,
age - less grace.
heart to sprout.
ho - ly reign.
ran them through. O Lord, thy king - dom come.
pre - cious Lord.
come to win.
ten - der - ness.
take at last.
with one voice.

777 Christ's Church Shall Glory

1. Christ's church shall glo - ry in his pow'r
2. Christ's peo - ple serve his way - ward world
3. Christ's liv - ing lamp shall bright - ly burn,
4. Christ's bod - y tri - umphs in his name;

And grow to his per - fec - tion;
To whom he seems a stran - ger;
And to our earth - ly cit - y
One Fa - ther sov - 'reign giv - er,

He is our rock, our might - y tow'r
He knows its wel - come from of old,
For - got - ten beau - ty shall re - turn,
One Spir - it, with his love a - flame,

Our life, our res - ur - rec - tion:
He shares our joy, our dan - ger:
And pu - ri - ty and pit - y:
One Lord, the same for ev - er.

So by his skill - ful hand / The church of
So strong, and yet so weak, / The church of
To give the op - pressed their right / The church of
To you, O God, our prize / The church of

Christ shall stand; / The mas - ter - build - er's plan
Christ shall speak; / His cross our great - est need,
Christ shall fight; / And though the years seem long
Christ shall rise / Be - yond all meas - ured height,

He works, as he be - gan,
His word the vi - tal seed
He is our strength and song,
To that e - ter - nal light

And soon will crown with splen - dor.
That brings a fruit - ful har - vest.
And he is our sal - va - tion.
Where Christ shall reign all - ho - ly.

Text: Christopher Idle, b.1938, © 1982, Hope Publishing Co.
Tune: EIN' FESTE BURG, 8 7 8 7 66 66 7; Martin Luther, 1483-1546; harm. by J.S. Bach, 1685-1750

778 Christ Is Made the Sure Foundation

1. Christ is made the sure foun - da - tion,
2. To this tem - ple where we call you,
3. Here vouch - safe to all your ser - vants
4. Laud and hon - or to the Fa - ther,

Christ the head and cor - ner-stone; Cho - sen of the
Come, O Lord of hosts, to - day; With your wont - ed
What they ask of you to gain; What they gain from
Laud and hon - or to the Son, Laud and hon - or

Lord, and pre - cious, Bind - ing all the Church in one;
lov - ing kind - ness Hear your ser - vants as they pray,
you for ev - er With the bless - ed to re - tain,
to the Spir - it, Ev - er three and ev - er One,

Ho - ly Zi - on's help for ev - er,
And your full - est ben - e - dic - tion
And here - af - ter in your glo - ry
One in might and One in glo - ry,

And her con - fi - dence a - lone.
Shed in all its bright ar - ray.
Ev - er - more with you to reign.
While un - end - ing a - ges run.

Text: Latin hymn, c.7th C.; trans. by John M. Neale, 1818-1866, alt.
Tune: EDEN CHURCH, 8 7 8 7 8 7; Dale Wood, b.1934

As a Fire Is Meant for Burning 779

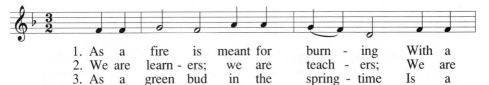

1. As a fire is meant for burn - ing With a
2. We are learn - ers; we are teach - ers; We are
3. As a green bud in the spring - time Is a

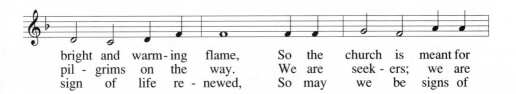

bright and warm - ing flame, So the church is meant for
pil - grims on the way. We are seek - ers; we are
sign of life re - newed, So may we be signs of

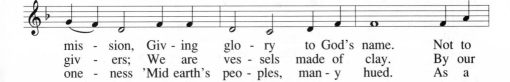

mis - sion, Giv - ing glo - ry to God's name. Not to
giv - ers; We are ves - sels made of clay. By our
one - ness 'Mid earth's peo - ples, man - y hued. As a

preach our creeds or cust - oms, But to build a bridge of
gen - tle, lov - ing ac - tions, We would show that Christ is
rain - bow lights the heav - ens When a storm is past and

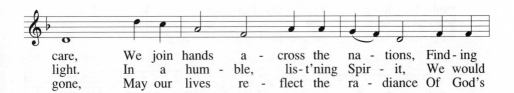

care, We join hands a - cross the na - tions, Find - ing
light. In a hum - ble, lis - t'ning Spir - it, We would
gone, May our lives re - flect the ra - diance Of God's

neigh - bors ev - 'ry - where.
live to God's de - light.
new and glor - ious dawn.

Text: Ruth Duck, b.1947, © 1992, GIA Publications, Inc.
Tune: BEACH SPRING, 8 7 8 7 D; The Sacred Harp, 1844; harm. by Marty Haugen, b.1950, © 1985, GIA Publications, Inc.

780 Singing Songs of Expectation

1. Sing - ing songs of ex - pec - ta - tion,
2. One the light of God's own pres - ence,
3. One the strain the lips of thou - sands

On - ward goes the pil - grim band, Through the night of
O'er his ran - somed peo - ple shed, Chas - ing far the
Lift as from the heart of one; One the con - flict,

doubt and sor - row, March - ing to the prom-ised land.
gloom and ter - ror, Bright - 'ning all the path we tread:
one the per - il, One the march in God be - gun:

Clear be - fore us through the dark - ness Gleams and burns the
One the ob - ject of our jour - ney, One the faith which
One the glad-ness of re - joic - ing On the far e -

guid - ing light: Trust - ing God we march to - geth - er
nev - er tires, One the ear - nest look - ing for - ward,
ter - nal shore, Where the one al - might - y Fa - ther

Step - ping fear - less through the night.
One the hope our God in - spires.
Reigns in love for ev - er - more.

Text: Bernard Severin Ingeman, 1798-1862; tr. by Sabin Baring-Gould, 1834-1924, alt.
Tune: HOLY MANNA, 8 7 8 7 D; William Moore, fl. 1830; acc. by Marty Haugen, b.1950, © 1987, GIA Publications, Inc.

O Christ the Great Foundation 781

1. O Christ the great foun - da - tion On which your peo - ple stand To preach your true sal - va - tion In ev - 'ry age and land: Pour out your Ho - ly Spir - it To make us strong and pure, To keep the faith

2. Bap - tized in one con - fes - sion, One church in all the earth, We bear our Lord's im - pres - sion, The sign of sec - ond birth: One ho - ly peo - ple gath - ered In love be - yond our own, By grace we were

3. Where ty - rants' hold is tight - ened, Where strong de - vour the weak, Where in - no - cents are fright - ened, The right - eous fear to speak, There let your church a - wak - ing At - tack the pow'rs of sin And, all their ram -

4. This is the mo - ment glo - rious When he who once was dead Shall lead his church vic - to - rious, Their cham - pion and their head. The Lord of all cre - a - tion His heav'n - ly king - dom brings The fi - nal con -

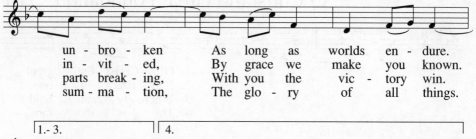

un - bro - ken	As	long	as	worlds	en - dure.
in - vit - ed,	By	grace	we	make	you	known.
parts break - ing,	With you	the	vic -	tory	win.
sum - ma - tion,	The	glo - ry	of	all	things.

A - men.

Text: Timothy T'ingfang Lew, 1891-1947, alt., © Christian Conference of Asia
Tune: ABREU; 76 76 D; Calvin Hampton, 1938-1984, © 1973, Concordia Publishing House

O Christ the Great Foundation 782

1. O Christ the great foun - da - tion On which your peo-ple stand
2. Bap - tized in one con - fes - sion, One church in all the earth,
3. Where ty - rants' hold is tight-ened, Where strong de-vour the weak,
4. This is the mo-ment glo - rious When he who once was dead

To preach your true sal - va - tion In ev - 'ry age and land:
We bear our Lord's im - pres - sion, The sign of sec-ond birth:
Where in - no - cents are fright-ened The right-eous fear to speak,
Shall lead his church vic - to - rious, Their cham-pion and their head.

Pour out your Ho - ly Spir - it To make us strong and pure,
One ho - ly peo - ple gath - ered In love be - yond our own,
There let your church a - wak - ing At - tack the pow'rs of sin
The Lord of all cre - a - tion His heav'n - ly king - dom brings

To keep the faith un - bro - ken As long as worlds en - dure.
By grace we were in - vit - ed, By grace we make you known.
And, all their ram-parts break - ing, With you the vic - tory win.
The fi - nal con - sum - ma - tion, The glo - ry of all things.

Text: Timothy T'ingfang Lew, 1891-1947, alt., © Christian Conference of Asia
Tune: AURELIA, 7 6 7 6 D; Samuel Sebastian Wesley, 1810-1876

783 Church of God

Refrain

Melody:
Church of God, cho - sen peo - ple, sing your praise to

Harmony:
Church of God, cho - sen peo - ple,

God. He has called you out of dark - ness

sing your praise to God. He has called you

1.-7. *To verses* | *Last time*
in - to his mar - vel - ous light. light.

in - to his mar - vel - ous light. light.

Verses

1. Come, peo - ple of God, with joy - ful song, Praise
2. The church is built with liv - ing stones With
3. As heirs of Christ, re - deemed by love We
4. As wa - ter spring - ing from the rock Once
5. We gath - er here to wor - ship God, Our
6. May fra - grant smoke of in - cense rise To
7. The light of Christ has come to us Dis -

God the Fa - ther of all. Bap -
Christ as cor - ner - stone. In
wait for his re - turn; A
brought God's peo - ple life, The
eu - cha - rist to share. We
fill this house of prayer. May
pel - ling all our fears. His

tized	in	Christ,	re -	born	in	him,	Our
him	we	trust	who	makes	us	one,	U -
priest -	ly	peo -	ple	of -	f'ring	praise	To
liv -	ing	wa -	ter	giv'n	by	Christ	Cre -
give	him	thanks	and	cel -	e -	brate	The
we	who	gath -	er	find	true	peace,	God's
light	re -	veals	the	path	of	life.	We

hearts	are	filled	with	joy.	He	cleans -	es	our
nit -	ing	us	in	love.	We	build	on	the
God,	the	source	of	hope.	For	Je -	sus	is
ates	our	lives	a -	new.	So	come	you	who
mys -	t'ry	of	his	love;	The	Word	is	made
pres -	ence	fill - ing	our	lives.	Our	hearts	lift	with
fol -	low	him	with	joy,	The	glo -	ry	of

D.C.

sin,	Re -	new -	ing	our	lives.
rock	Of	faith		in	Christ.
Lord,	Our	Sav -	ior	and	God.
thirst	To	springs	of	new	life.
flesh	And	giv -	en	for	us.
praise,	Our	lips	sing	in	joy.
God,	The	light	of	the	world.

Text: Sr. Pamela Stotter
Tune: Margaret Daly
© 1980, International Commission on English in the Liturgy, Inc.

784 Not Alone Where Silent Woodlands

1. Not a - lone where si - lent wood - lands Shel - ter crea - tures great and small; Not a - lone in peace - ful mead - ows Where the birds in con - cert call; Not a - lone where rays of star - light Pierce the

2. Where the cit - y's cease - less clam - or Nev - er ends by day, by night; Where the heav - ens' star - ry splen - dor Hides be - hind its gar - ish light; Where the lurk - ing threat of vio - lence Dai - ly

3. Not a - lone where vast ca - the - drals Send their arch - es soar - ing high; Not a - lone in hum - bler chap - els Where the still - ness draws you nigh; Not a - lone in qui - et cham - bers Where we

4. Lord of life, a - mid the la - bor Fill - ing all our crowd - ed days, There your love no less sus - tains us; There our work may be your praise. Help us make each shop a tem - ple, Ev - 'ry

vel - vet skies of night, Can your
strikes the heart with fear; There, where
kneel in sol - i - tude Can our
desk a ho - ly place, Farms and

peo - ple seek your pres - ence, God of
life is bruised and bro - ken, You, O
hearts pour out be - fore you Prayers of
fac - t'ries, homes and high - ways Shrines trans-

mer - cy, God of might.
God of grace, are near.
trust and grat - i - tude.
fig - ured by your grace.

Text: Herman Stuempfle, b.1923; © 1993, GIA Publications, Inc.
Tune: NETTLETON, 8 7 8 7 D; Wyeth's *Repository of Sacred Music, Pt. II*, 1813

785 What Does the Lord Require

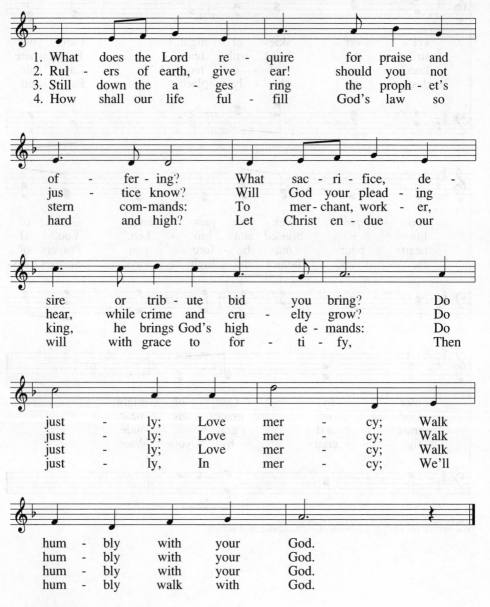

1. What does the Lord re - quire for praise and
2. Rul - ers of earth, give ear! should you not
3. Still down the a - ges ring the proph - et's
4. How shall our life ful - fill God's law so

of - fer - ing? What sac - ri - fice, de -
jus - tice know? Will God your plead - ing
stern com-mands: To mer - chant, work - er,
hard and high? Let Christ en - due our

sire or trib - ute bid you bring? Do
hear, while crime and cru - elty grow? Do
king, he brings God's high de - mands: Do
will with grace to for - ti - fy, Then

just - ly; Love mer - cy; Walk
just - ly; Love mer - cy; Walk
just - ly; Love mer - cy; Walk
just - ly, In mer - cy; We'll

hum - bly with your God.
hum - bly with your God.
hum - bly with your God.
hum - bly walk with God.

Text: Micah 6:6-8; Albert F. Bayly, 1901-1984, alt., © Oxford University Press
Tune: SHARPTHORNE, 6 6 6 6 33 6; Erik Routley, 1917-1982, © 1969, Hope Publishing Co.

Renew Your People 786

1. Lov - ing Fa - ther, gra-cious God,
2. Thank you for your gift of Love:
3. Fa - ther, make us car - ing neigh - bors;

praise and glo - ry to you. Bur-dened
Christ the Lord, Prince of Peace. Je - sus
teach us, Lord, how to give. Help us

by our sin and its dark-ness, we long for
is our friend and our Sav - ior; make us like
strive for true peace and jus - tice, liv - ing as

light, our souls re - new. Mer - ci - ful
him, your pow'r re - lease. Send us your
Christ taught us to live. May all our

Fa - ther, we ask of you, Sal - va - tion and heal-ing, our
Spir - it in all we do, With joy - ful de - vo-tion, our
ef - forts give praise to you, U - nite us in Spir - it, our

hearts re - new.
hearts re - new. Re - new your peo-ple, O
lives re - new.

Lord; re - new our lives with your Word.

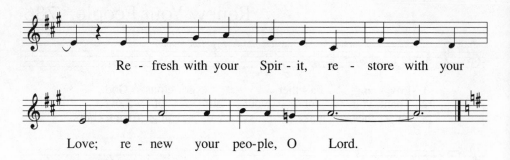

Re - fresh with your Spir - it, re - store with your
Love; re - new your peo-ple, O Lord.

Text: Lucia Welch
Tune: Randolph N. Currie, b.1943
© 1983, GIA Publications, Inc.

787 The Temple Rang with Golden Coins

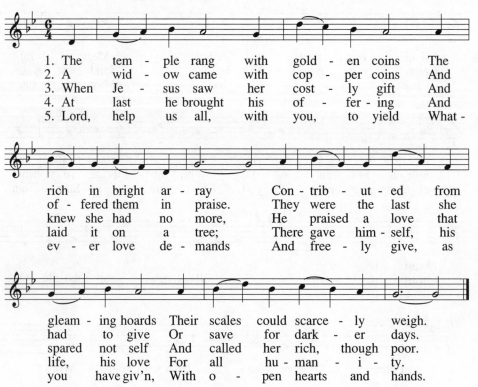

1. The tem - ple rang with gold - en coins The
2. A wid - ow came with cop - per coins And
3. When Je - sus saw her cost - ly gift And
4. At last he brought his of - fer - ing And
5. Lord, help us all, with you, to yield What -

rich in bright ar - ray Con - trib - ut - ed from
of - fered them in praise. They were the last she
knew she had no more, He praised a love that
laid it on a tree; There gave him - self, his
ev - er love de - mands And free - ly give, as

gleam - ing hoards Their scales could scarce - ly weigh.
had to give Or save for dark - er days.
spared not self And called her rich, though poor.
life, his love For all hu - man - i - ty.
you have giv'n, With o - pen hearts and hands.

Text: Mark 12:41-44; Herman Stuempfle, b.1923; © 1993, GIA Publications, Inc.
Tune: LEWIS-TOWN, CM; William Billings, 1746-1800; harm. by Donald A. Busarow, b.1934, © 1978, *Lutheran Book of Worship*

The Servant Song   788

1.,6. Will you let me be your ser - vant,
2. We are pil - grims on a jour - ney,
3. I will hold the Christ - light for you
4. I will weep when you are weep - ing;
5. When we sing to God in heav - en

Let me be as Christ to you; Pray that I may
We are trav - 'lers on the road; We are here to
In the night-time of your fear; I will hold my
When you laugh I'll laugh with you. I will share your
We shall find such har - mo - ny, Born of all we've

have the grace to Let you be my ser - vant, too.
help each oth - er Walk the mile and bear the load.
hand out to you, Speak the peace you long to hear.
joy and sor - row 'Til we've seen this jour - ney through.
known to - geth - er Of Christ's love and ag - o - ny.

Text: Richard Gillard
Tune: Richard Gillard; harm. by Betty Pulkingham, b.1929
© 1977, Scripture in Song

789 We Are Your People

1. We are your peo - ple: Spir - it of grace,
2. Joined in com - mu - ni - ty, Treas - ured and fed;
3. Rich in di - ver - si - ty, Help us to live
4. Glad of tra - di - tion, Help us to see
5. Give, as we ven - ture Jus - tice and care
6. Spir - it, u - nite us, Make us, by grace,

You dare to make us To all our neigh-bors,
May we dis - cov - er Gifts in each oth - er,
Clos - er than neigh-bors, O - pen to stran - gers,
In all life's chang - ing Where you are lead - ing,
(Peace-ful, re - sist - ing, Wait - ing or risk - ing)
Will - ing and read - y, Christ's liv - ing bod - y,

1., 6.
Christ's liv - ing voice, hands and face.

2.- 5.
Will - ing to lead and be led.
A - ble to clash and for - give.
Where our best ef - forts should be.
Wis - dom to know when and where.
Lov - ing the whole hu - man race.

Optional Descant for Stanza 6

Spir - it, Make us, by grace, Will-ing and read - y,

Christ's liv - ing bod - y, Lov - ing the whole hu-man race.

Text: Brian Wren, b.1936, © 1975, Hope Publishing Co.
Tune: WHITFIELD, 5 4 5 5 7; John W. Wilson, b.1905, © 1980, Hope Publishing Co.

I Bind My Heart   790

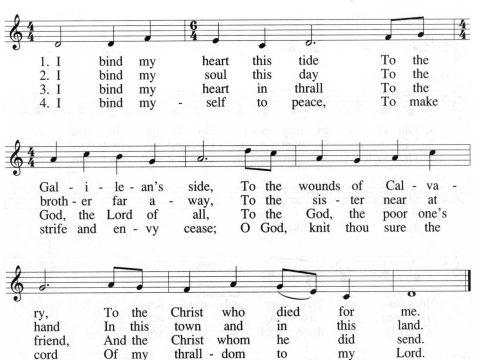

1. I bind my heart this tide
2. I bind my soul this day
3. I bind my heart in thrall
4. I bind my - self to peace,

To the
To the
To the
To make

Gal - i - le - an's side,
broth - er far a - way,
God, the Lord of all,
strife and en - vy cease;

To the wounds of Cal - va -
To the sis - ter near at
To the God, the poor one's
O God, knit thou sure the

ry,
hand
friend,
cord

To the Christ who died for me.
In this town and in this land.
And the Christ whom he did send.
Of my thrall - dom to my Lord.

Text: "Thraldom," *The Tryst,* 1907, Lauchlan McLean Watt, 1853-1931
Tune: Suzanne Toolan, SM, b.1927, © 1979, Resource Publications, Inc.

791 Glorious in Majesty

Introduction and Optional Interlude

Triangle:

Verses

1. Glo-ri-ous in maj-es-ty, Ho-ly in his prais-es,
2. Vic-to-ry he won for us, Free-ing us from dark-ness,
3. One in love, as fam-i-ly, Liv-ing with each oth-er,

(doo)　　　(doo)　　　*simile*

Je-sus, our Sav-ior and our King.
Dy-ing and ris-ing from the dead.
Glad-ly we share each oth-er's pain.

Born a man, yet God of old, Let us all a-dore him:
Liv-ing with the Fa-ther now, Yet he is a-mong us:
Yet he will not leave us so, Soon he is re-turn-ing,

Filled with his Spir-it, let us sing.
We are the bod-y, he the head.
Tak-ing us back with him to reign.

Refrain

Liv - ing is to love him, serv - ing him to know his free-dom.

Come a - long with us to join the praise of Je - sus.

Come to Je - sus now, Go to live his word re - joic - ing.

(doo) *simile*

Text: Jeff Cothran, fl.1972, © 1972, GIA Publications, Inc.
Tune: SHIBBOLET BASADEH, 7 6 8 D with refrain; Jewish melody; harm. by Jeff Cothran, fl.1972, © 1972, GIA Publications, Inc.

792 'Tis the Gift to Be Simple

'Tis the gift to be sim-ple, 'tis the gift to be free, 'tis the

gift to come down where we ought to be, and

when we find our-selves in the place just right, 'twill

be in the val - ley of love and de - light.

When true sim - plic-i - ty is gained to bow and to bend we

shan't be a-shamed, to turn, turn, will be our de-light till by

turn - ing, turn - ing we come round right.

Text: Shaker Song, 18th. C.
Tune: SIMPLE GIFTS; arr. Margaret W. Mealey, © 1984

Lord, Whose Love in Humble Service   793

1. Lord, whose love in hum - ble serv - ice Bore the
2. Still your chil - dren wan - der home - less; Still the
3. As we wor - ship, grant us vi - sion, Till your
4. Called from wor - ship in - to serv - ice Forth in

weight of hu - man need, Who did on the Cross for -
hun - gry cry for bread; Still the cap - tives long for
love's re - veal - ing light, Till the height and depth and
your great name we go, To the child, the youth, the

sak - en, Show us mer - cy's per - fect deed; We, your
free - dom; Still in grief we mourn our dead. As, O
great - ness Dawns up - on our hu - man sight: Mak - ing
a - ged, Love in liv - ing deeds to show; Hope and

ser - vants, bring the wor - ship Not of voice a - lone, but
Lord, your deep com - pas - sion Healed the sick and freed the
known the needs and bur - dens Your com - pas - sion bids us
health, good - will and com - fort, Coun - sel, aid, and peace we

heart: Con - se - crat - ing to your pur - pose Ev - 'ry
soul, Use the love your Spir - it kin - dles Still to
bear, Stir - ring us to faith - ful serv - ice, Your a -
give That your chil - dren, Lord, in free - dom, May your

gift which you im - part.
save and make us whole.
bun - dant life to share.
mer - cy know and live.

Text: Albert F. Bayly, 1901-1984, © Oxford University Press, alt.
Tune: BEACH SPRING, 8 7 8 7 D; *The Sacred Harp*, 1844; harm. by Marty Haugen, b.1950, © 1985, GIA Publications, Inc.

794 God, Whose Giving Knows No Ending

1. God, whose giv-ing knows no end-ing, From your rich and end-less store: Na-ture's won-der, Je-sus' wis-dom, Cost-ly cross, grave's shat-tered door, Gift-ed by you, we turn to you, Of-f'ring

2. Skills and time are ours for press-ing Toward the goals of Christ, your Son: All at peace in health and free-dom, Rac-es joined, the Church made one. Now di-rect our dai-ly la-bor, Lest we

3. Treas-ure, too, you have en-trust-ed, Gain through pow'rs your grace con-ferred; Ours to use for home and kin-dred, And to spread the Gos-pel Word. O-pen wide our hands in shar-ing, As we

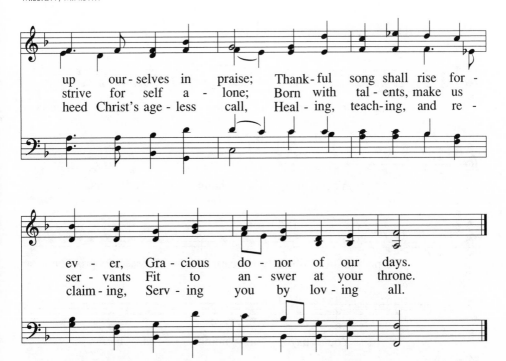

up   our - selves in   praise;   Thank - ful   song shall rise for -
strive   for   self   a -   lone;   Born with   tal - ents, make us
heed Christ's age - less   call,   Heal - ing,   teach - ing, and   re -

ev - er,   Gra - cious   do - nor   of   our   days.
ser - vants Fit   to   an - swer at   your   throne.
claim - ing, Serv - ing   you   by   lov - ing   all.

Text: Robert L. Edwards, b.1915, © 1961, Hymn Society of America
Tune: RUSTINGTON, 8 7 8 7 D; Charles H. H. Parry, 1848-1918

795 You Have Anointed Me

Verse 1

1. To bring glad tid-ings to the low-ly, to heal the bro-ken heart,

You have a - noint - ed me.

To pro-claim lib-er-ty to cap-tives, re-lease to pris-on-ers,

You have a - noint - ed me.

Refrain

Melody:

Your Spir - it, O God, is up-on me,

Harmony:

Your Spir - it, O God, is up-on me,

me, You have a - noint - ed

me.

1. me.

To verse 2

2. me.

Verse 2

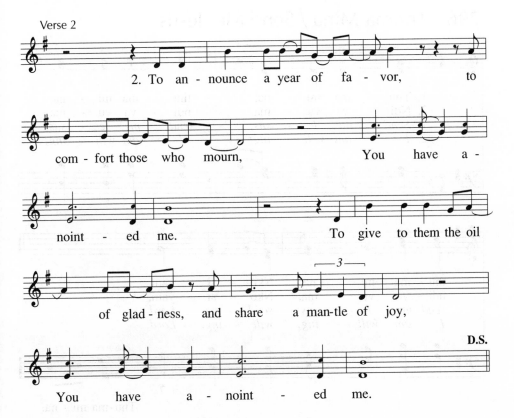

2. To an-nounce a year of fa-vor, to com-fort those who mourn, You have a-noint - ed me. To give to them the oil of glad-ness, and share a man-tle of joy,

D.S.

You have a - noint - ed me.

Text: Mike Balhoff, b.1946, Gary Daigle, b.1957, Darryl Ducote, b.1945
Tune: Mike Balhoff, b.1946, Gary Daigle, b.1957, Darryl Ducote, b.1945; acc. by Gary Daigle
© 1981, Damean Music. Distributed by GIA Publications, Inc.

796 Thuma Mina / Send Me, Jesus

1. Thu - ma mi - na, thu - ma mi - na,
2. Ndi - ya vu - ma, ndi - ya vu - ma,
1. Send me, Je - sus; send me, Je - sus;
2. I am will - ing; I am will - ing;

thu - ma mi - na, Nko - si yam.
ndi - ya vu - ma, Nko - si yam.
send me, Je - sus; send me, Lord.
I am will - ing, will - ing, Lord.

Cantor:

Thu - ma mi - na.

Text: Traditional South African
Tune: Traditional; transcribed from Lulu Dumazweni by John Bell, b.1949, © 1991, Iona Community, GIA Publications, Inc., agent

797 Good News

Verses

1. When Je - sus worked here on earth he preached in
2. The eld - ers of the syn - a - gogue were shocked by
3. The way he lived was proof of it: he qui - et -
4. So pass it on to - day, good friend: the mes - sage

his home - town,
Mar - y's son,
ed our strife.
is the same.

I - sa - iah's hopes now ful-
that he was des - tined to
The cross it - self he would not
De - liv - 'rance Christ a - lone can

filled, those claims of great re - nown.
be the Christ for ev - 'ry - one.
flee e'en though it cost his life.
give, for this to earth he came.

Refrain

To bring good news to the need - y, to make the blind to

see, the bro - ken hearts healed a - gain, to

1.
set the cap - tive free.

2.
cap - tive free.

Text: Howard S. Olson
Tune: Almaz Belihu; Yemissrach Dimts Literature Program, Ethiopia
© 1993, Howard S. Olson

798 Go Make of All Disciples

1. "Go make of all dis-ci-ples:" We hear the call, O
2. "Go make of all dis-ci-ples:" Bap-tiz-ing in the
3. "Go make of all dis-ci-ples:" We at your feet would
4. "Go make of all dis-ci-ples:" We wel-come your com-

1. Lord, That comes from you, our Fa-ther, In
2. name Of Fa-ther, Son, and Spir-it— From
3. stay Un-til each life's vo-ca-tion Ac-
4. mand; "Lo, I am with you al-ways:" We

1. your e-ter-nal Word. In-spire our ways of
2. age to age the same. We call each new dis-
3. cents your ho-ly way. We cul-ti-vate the
4. take your guid-ing hand. The task looms large be-

1. learn-ing Through earn-est, fer-vent prayer, And
2. ci-ple To fol-low you, O Lord, Re-
3. na-ture God plants in ev-'ry heart, Re-
4. fore us— We fol-low with-out fear. In

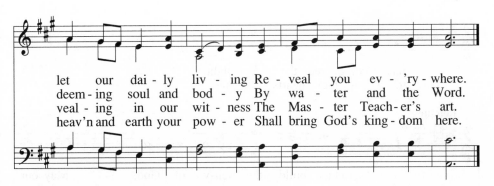

let our dai - ly liv - ing Re - veal you ev - 'ry - where.
deem - ing soul and bod - y By wa - ter and the Word.
veal - ing in our wit - ness The Mas - ter Teach - er's art.
heav'n and earth your pow - er Shall bring God's king - dom here.

Text: Matthew 28:19-20; Leon M. Adkins, b.1896, alt., © 1955,1964, Abingdon Press
Tune: ELLACOMBE, 7 6 7 6 D; *Gesangbuch der Herzogl*, Wirtemberg, 1784

City of God   799

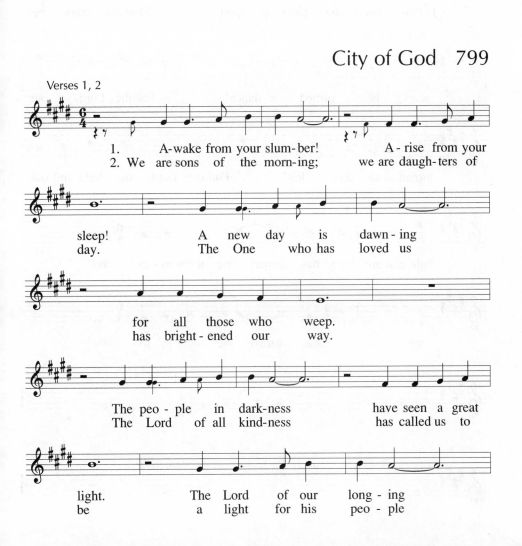

Verses 1, 2

1.   A-wake from your slum-ber!   A - rise from your
2. We are sons of the morn-ing;   we are daugh-ters of

sleep!   A new day is dawn - ing
day.   The One who has loved us

for all those who weep.
has bright - ened our way.

The peo - ple in dark-ness   have seen a great
The Lord of all kind-ness   has called us to

light.   The Lord of our long - ing
be   a light for his peo - ple

has con-quered the night.
to set their hearts free.

Refrain

Descant:

Let us build the cit-y of God. May our

Melody:

Let us build the cit-y of God. May our tears be

tears be turned to dance! For the Lord, our

turned in-to danc - ing! For the Lord, our light and our

light and our love, has turned the night in - to day!

love, has turned the night in - to day!

1.

2. *To next section (v.3)* 3. *D.S. (v.4)* 4.

Verse 3

3. God is light; in him there is no dark-ness. Let us walk in his light, his chil - dren, one and all.

𝄋 (Verse 4)

(3.) O com - fort my peo - ple; make gen-tle your words. Pro-claim to my cit - y the day of her birth.
4. O cit-y of glad-ness, now lift up your voice. Pro-claim the good ti - dings that all may re - joice!

To refrain

800 You Are Called to Tell the Story

1. You are called to tell the sto - ry, pass - ing
2. You are called to teach the rhy - thm of the
3. You are called to set the ta - ble, bless - ing
4. May the One whose love is broad - er than the

words of life a - long, Then to
dance that nev - er ends, Then to
bread as Je - sus blessed, Then to
meas - ure of all space Give us

blend your voice with oth - ers as you
move with - in the cir - cle, hand in
come with thirst and hun - ger, need - ing
words to sing the sto - ry, move a -

sing the sa - cred song. Christ be
hand with stran - gers, friends. Christ be
care like all the rest, Christ be
mong us in this place. Christ be

known in all our sing - ing,
known in all our danc - ing,
known in all our shar - ing,
known in all our liv - ing,

fill - ing all with songs of love.
touch - ing all with hands of love.
feed - ing all with signs of love.
fill - ing all with gifts of love.

Text: Ruth Duck, b.1947, © 1992, GIA Publications, Inc.
Tune: GHENT, 8 7 8 7 8 7; M.D. Ridge, b.1938; acc. by Patrick Loomis, 1951-1990, © 1987, GIA Publications, Inc.

Moved by the Gospel, Let Us Move   801

1. Moved by the Gos-pel, let us move With ev-'ry gift and art. The im-age of cre-a-tive love In-dwells each hu-man heart. The Mak-er calls cre-a-tion good, So

2. Let weav-ers form from bro-ken strands A tap-es-try of prayer. Let art-ists paint with skill-ful hands Their joy, la-ment, and care. Then mime the sto-ry: Christ has come. With

3. O Spir-it, breathe a-mong us here; In-spire the work we do. May hands and voic-es, eye and ear At-test to life made new. In wor-ship and in dai-ly strife Cre-

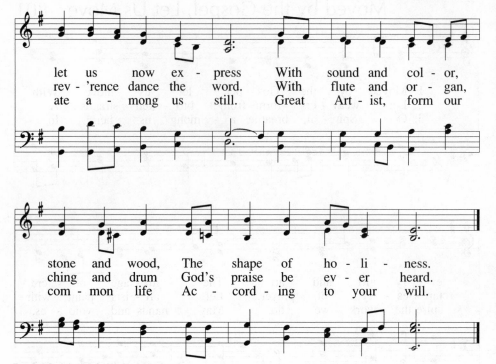

let us now ex - press With sound and col - or,
rev - 'rence dance the word. With flute and or - gan,
ate a - mong us still. Great Art - ist, form our

stone and wood, The shape of ho - li - ness.
ching and drum God's praise be ev - er heard.
com - mon life Ac - cord - ing to your will.

Text: Ruth Duck, b. 1947, © 1992, GIA Publications, Inc.
Tune: KINGSFOLD, CMD; English; harm. by Ralph Vaughan Williams, 1872-1958

Here I Am, Lord   802

sat - is - fied.   I will give my   life to them.

dark - ness bright.   Who will bear   my light to them?
love a - lone.   I will speak   my word to them.
sat - is - fied.   I will give   my life to them.

Whom shall I send?

Whom shall I send?
Whom shall I send?
Whom shall I send?

Refrain

Here I am, Lord.   Is it I, Lord?

I have heard you call-ing in the night.   I will

go, Lord, if you lead me.   I will hold your

1., 2.   **3.**

peo-ple in my heart.   heart.

Text: Isaiah 6; Dan Schutte, b.1947
Tune: Dan Schutte, b.1947; arr. by Michael Pope, SJ, John Weissrock
© 1981, Daniel L. Schutte and New Dawn Music

The Church of Christ in Every Age   803

1. The Church of Christ in ev - 'ry age Be - set by change but Spir - it led, Must claim and test its her - it - age And keep on ris - ing from the dead.
2. A - cross the world, a - cross the street, The vic - tims of in - jus - tice cry For shel - ter and for bread to eat, And nev - er live un - til they die.
3. Then let the ser - vant Church a - rise, A car - ing Church that longs to be A part - ner in Christ's sac - ri - fice, And clothed in Christ's hu - man - i - ty.
4. For he a - lone, whose blood was shed, Can cure the fe - ver in our blood, And teach us how to share our bread And feed the starv - ing mul - ti - tude.
5. We have no mis - sion but to serve In full o - be - dience to our Lord: To care for all, with - out re - serve, And spread his lib - er - at - ing Word.

Text: Fred Pratt Green, b.1903, © 1971, Hope Publishing Co.
Tune: DUNEDIN, LM; Vernon Griffiths, 1894-1985, © 1971, Faber Music Ltd.

804 Unless a Grain of Wheat

Refrain

Un - less a grain of wheat shall fall up - on the ground and die, it re - mains but a sin - gle grain with no life.

1.- 6. *To verses* — *Last time*

2. If

Verses

1. If we have died with him then we shall
2. an - y - one serves me then they must
3. Make your home in me as I make
4. If you re - main in me and my word
5. Those who love me are loved by my
6. Peace I leave with you, my peace I

live with him; if we hold firm we shall
fol - low me; where - ev - er I am my
mine in you; those who re - main in me
lives in you, then you will be my dis -
Fa - ther; we shall be with them and
give to you; peace which the world can - not

D.C.

reign with him.
ser - vants will be.
bear much fruit.
ci - ples.
dwell in them.
give is my gift.

Text: John 12:24; Bernadette Farrell, b.1957
Tune: Bernadette Farrell, b.1957
© 1983, Bernadette Farrell, published by OCP Publications

Those Who Love and Those Who Labor   805

1. Those who love and those who la - bor Fol - low in the
2. Where the man - y work to - geth - er, They with Christ him -
3. Let the seek - er nev - er fal - ter Till the truth is

way of Christ; Thus the first dis - ci - ples found him,
self a - bide, But the lone - ly work - ers al - so
found a - far With the wis - dom of the a - ges

Thus the gift of love suf - ficed. Je - sus says to
Find him ev - er at their side. Lo, the Prince of
Un - der - neath a gi - ant star, With the rich - est

those who seek him, I will nev - er pass you by;
com - mon wel - fare Dwells with - in the mar - ket strife;
and the poor - est, Of the sum of things pos - sessed,

Raise the stone and you shall find me;
Lo, the bread of heav'n is bro - ken
Like a child at first to won - der,

Cleave the wood, and there am I.
In the sac - ra - ment of life.
Like a king at last to rest.

Text: Geoffrey Dearmer, b.1893, © Oxford University Press
Tune: HYMN TO JOY, 8 7 8 7 D; arr. from Ludwig van Beethoven, 1770-1827, by Edward Hodges, 1796-1867

806 Jesu Tawa Pano / Jesus, We Are Here

Je - su ta- wa pa- no; Je - su ta- wa pa- no;
Je - sus, we are here; Je - sus, we are here;

Solo: *Mam - bo Je - su.

Je - su ta- wa pa- no; ta- wa pa- no, mu zi- ta re- nyu.
Je - sus, we are here; we are here for you.

*Omit last time

Text: Zimbabwean; Patrick Matsikenyiri
Tune: Patrick Matsikenyiri
© 1990, Patrick Matsikenyiri

You Walk Along Our Shoreline   807

1. You walk a - long our shore-line Where land meets un-known sea.
2. You call us, Christ, to gath - er The peo - ple of the earth.
3. We cast our net, O Je - sus; We cry the king-dom's name;

We hear your voice of pow - er, "Now come and fol - low me.
We can - not fish for on - ly Those lives we think have worth.
We work for love and jus - tice; We learn to hope through pain.

And if you still will fol - low Through storm and wave and shoal,
We spread your net of gos - pel A - cross the wa - ter's face,
You call us, Lord, to gath - er God's daugh - ters and God's sons,

Then I will make you fish - ers But of the hu - man soul."
Our boat a com - mon shel - ter For all found by your grace.
To let your judg-ment heal us So that all may be one.

Text: Sylvia Dunston, 1955-1993, © 1991, GIA Publications, Inc.
Tune: AURELIA, 7 6 7 6 D; Samuel Sebastian Wesley, 1810-1876

808 Take Up Your Cross

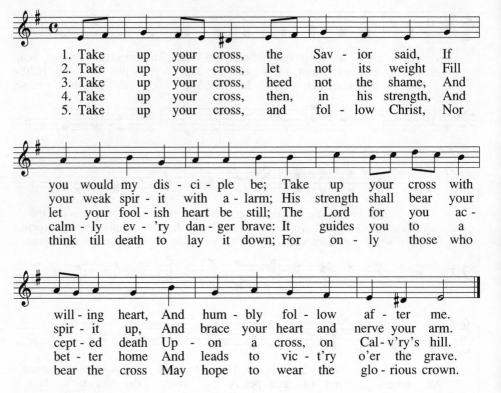

1. Take up your cross, the Sav - ior said, If
2. Take up your cross, let not its weight Fill
3. Take up your cross, heed not the shame, And
4. Take up your cross, then, in his strength, And
5. Take up your cross, and fol - low Christ, Nor

you would my dis - ci - ple be; Take up your cross with
your weak spir - it with a - larm; His strength shall bear your
let your fool - ish heart be still; The Lord for you ac -
calm - ly ev - 'ry dan - ger brave: It guides you to a
think till death to lay it down; For on - ly those who

will - ing heart, And hum - bly fol - low af - ter me.
spir - it up, And brace your heart and nerve your arm.
cept - ed death Up - on a cross, on Cal - v'ry's hill.
bet - ter home And leads to vic - t'ry o'er the grave.
bear the cross May hope to wear the glo - rious crown.

Text: Charles W. Everest, 1814-1877, alt.
Tune: ERHALT UNS HERR, LM; Klug's *Geistliche Lieder*, 1543; harm. by J.S. Bach, 1685-1750

I Danced in the Morning   809

1. I danced in the morn-ing when the
2. I danced for the scribe and the
3. I danced on the Sab-bath and I
4. I danced on a Fri-day when the
5. They cut me down and I

world was be-gun, And I danced in the moon and the
phar - i - see, But they would not dance, and they
cured the lame: The ho - ly peo - ple said it
sky turned black; It's hard to dance with the
leapt up high; I am the life that - 'll

stars and the sun, And I came down from heav - en and I
would-n't fol-low me; I danced for the fish - er-men, for
was a shame. They whipped and they stripped and they
dev - il on your back. They bur - ied my bod - y and they
nev - er, nev - er die; I'll live in you if you'll

danced on the earth; At Beth-le - hem I had my birth.
James and John; They came with me and the dance went on.
hung me high, And left me there on a Cross to die.
thought I'd gone; But I am the dance and I still go on.
live in me: I am the Lord of the Dance, said he.

Dance then wher - ev - er you may be; I am the Lord of the

Dance, said he, And I'll lead you all, wher - ev - er you may be, And I'll

| 1.- 4. | 5. |

lead you all in the Dance, said he.   Dance, said he.

Text: Sydney Carter, b.1915, © Stainer and Bell Ltd., London, England
Tune: LORD OF THE DANCE, Irregular; adapted from a traditional Shaker melody; harm. by Sydney Carter, b.1915, © Stainer and Bell Ltd.,
    London, England

810 Wherever He Leads

1. "Take up thy cross and fol - low Me," I
2. He drew me clos - er to His side, I
3. It may be through the shad - ows dim, Or
4. My heart, my life, my all I bring To

heard my Mas - ter say; "I gave My life to
sought His will to know, And in that will I
o'er the storm - y sea, I take my cross and
Christ who loves me so; He is my Mas - ter,

ran - som thee, Sur - ren-der your all to - day."
now a - bide, Wher - ev - er He leads I'll go.
fol - low Him, Wher - ev - er He lead - eth me.
Lord, and King, Wher - ev - er He leads I'll go.

Wher - ev - er He leads I'll go, Wher -

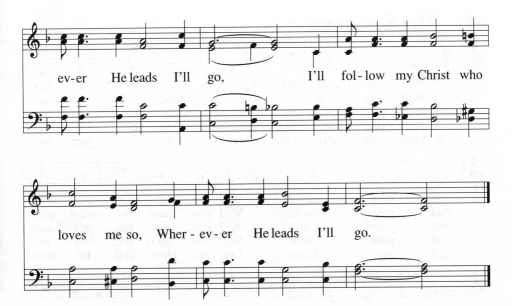

ev-er He leads I'll go, I'll fol-low my Christ who

loves me so, Wher-ev-er He leads I'll go.

Text: B. B. McKinney, 1886-1952
Music: FALLS CREEK; B. B. McKinney, 1886-1952
© 1936, 1964, Broadman Press

811 The Summons

1. Will you come and fol - low me If I but
2. Will you leave your - self be - hind If I but
3. Will you let the blind - ed see If I but
4. Will you love the 'you' you hide If I but
5. Lord, your sum - mons ech - oes true When you but

call your name? Will you go where you don't
call your name? Will you care for cruel and
call your name? Will you set the pris - 'ners
call your name? Will you quell the fear in -
call my name. Let me turn and fol - low

know And nev - er be the same? Will you
kind And nev - er be the same? Will you
free And nev - er be the same? Will you
side And nev - er be the same? Will you
you And nev - er be the same. In your

let my love be shown, Will you let my
risk the hos - tile stare Should your life at -
kiss the lep - er clean, And do such as
use the faith you've found To re - shape the
com - pa - ny I'll go Where your love and

name be known, Will you let my life be
tract or scare? Will you let me an - swer
this un - seen, And ad - mit to what I
world a - round, Through my sight and touch and
foot - steps show. Thus I'll move and live and

grown In you and you in me?
pray'r In you and you in me?
mean In you and you in me?
sound In you and you in me?
grow In you and you in me.

Text: John L. Bell, b.1949, © 1987, Iona Community, GIA Publications, Inc., agent
Tune: KELVINGROVE, 7 6 7 6 777 6; Scottish traditional; arr. by John L. Bell, b.1949, © 1987, Iona Community, GIA Publications, Inc., agent

Two Fishermen   812

1. Two fish-er-men, who lived a-long The Sea of Gal-i-
2. And as he walked a-long the shore 'Twas James and John he'd
3. O Si-mon Pe-ter, An-drew, James And John be-lov-ed
4. And you, good Chris-tians, one and all Who'd fol-low Je-sus'

lee, Stood by the shore to cast their nets In-
find, And these two sons of Zeb-e-dee Would
one, You heard Christ's call to speak good news Re-
way, Come leave be-hind what keeps you bound To

to an age-less sea. Now Je-sus watched them
leave their boats be-hind. Their work and all they
vealed to God's own Son. Su-san-na, Mar-y,
trap-pings of our day, And lis-ten as he

from a-far Then called them each by name; It
held so dear They left be-side their nets. Their
Mag-da-lene Who trav-eled with your Lord, You
calls your name To come and fol-low near, For

changed their lives, these sim-ple men; They'd nev-er be the same.
names they'd heard as Je-sus called; They came with-out re-gret.
min-is-tered to him with joy For he is God a-dored.
still he speaks in var-ied ways To those his call will hear.

Leave all things you have And come and fol-low

me,   And   come   and fol - low   me.

Text: Suzanne Toolan, SM, b.1927, © 1986, GIA Publications, Inc.
Tune: LEAVE ALL THINGS, CMD with refrain; Suzanne Toolan, SM, b.1927, © 1970, GIA Publications, Inc.

813   Now We Remain

Refrain

We hold the   death of the   Lord   deep in our   hearts.

Liv-ing;   now we re - main   with Je - sus the

Liv -   ing;

Christ.

Verses 1, 4

1. Once we   were   peo - ple a - fraid,   lost in the
4. We   are   the   pres - ence of God;   this is our

To Coda, Verse 4

D.C.

night.   Then   by   your   cross   we   were   saved;
call.   Now   to   be - come   bread   and   wine:

Dead   be - came   liv - ing,   life   from   your   giv - ing.
Food   for   the   hun - gry,   life   for   the   wea - ry,

Verse 2

2. Some - thing   which   we   have   known,   some - thing   we've

touched,   what   we   have   seen   with   our

D.C.

eyes: this   we   have   heard;   life   giv - ing   word.

Verse 3

3. He   chose   to   give   of   him - self,   be - came   our

bread.   Bro - ken,   that   we   might

D.C.

live.   Love   be - yond   love,   pain   for   our   pain.

Coda

D.C.

for   to   live   with   the   Lord,   we   must   die   with   the   Lord.

Text: Corinthians, 1 John, 2 Timothy; David Haas, b.1957
Tune: David Haas, b.1957

814 The Love of the Lord

Intro-Coda

To verses

Last time

Verses

1. All that I count - ed as gain
2. Rich - es and hon - ors will fade,
3. Sil - ver and gold have I none,
4. Faith is the wealth I pos - sess

now I con - sid - er as loss,
earth - ly de - light dis - ap - pear,
no land to count as my home, yet
Find - ing its source in my God:

emp - ty and worth - less to me in the
fade like the grass of the field in the
wealth be - yond meas - ure I own in the
faith in the prom - ise of Christ is my

1., 3.

2., 4.

light of the love of the Lord.
light of the love of the Lord.
light of the love of the Lord.
life and my love of the Lord.

Text: Philippians 3:7-11; Michael Joncas, b.1951
Tune: Michael Joncas, b.1951
© 1988, GIA Publications, Inc.

815   We Have Been Told

We have been told, we've seen his face, and heard his voice a - live in our hearts; "Live in my love with all your heart, as the Fa - ther has loved me, so I have loved you."

1.- 3.   *To verses*   4.

Verse 1

1. "I am the vine, you are the branch - es, and
all who live in me will bear great fruit."

Verses 2, 3

2. "You are my friends, if you keep my com - mands,
3. "No great-er love is there than this: to

no long - er slaves, I call you friends."
lay down one's life, for a friend."

Text: David Haas, b.1957
Tune: David Haas, b.1957; vocal arr. by David Haas, b.1957, Marty Haugen, b.1950
© 1983, GIA Publications, Inc.

816 On the Journey to Emmaus

1. On the jour - ney to Em - ma - us with our
2. And our hearts burned with - in us as we
3. And that eve - ning at the ta - ble as he
4. On our jour - ney to Em - ma - us, in our

hearts cold as stone— The One who would
talked on the way, How all that was
blessed and broke bread, We saw it was
sto - ries and feast, With Je - sus we

save us had left us a - lone. Then a
prom - ised was ours on that day. So we
Je - sus a - ris'n from the dead; Though he
claim that the great - est is least: And his

stran - ger walks with us and, to our sur -
begged him, "Stay with us and grant us your
van - ished be - fore us we knew he was
words burn with - in us— let none be ig -

prise,   He   o - pens   our
word."   We   wel - comed   the
near—   The   life   in   our
nored—   Who   wel - comes   the

sto - ries   and he   o - pens   our   eyes.
stran - ger and we   wel - comed the   Lord.
dy - ing   and the hope in   our   fear.
stran - ger shall   wel - come the   Lord.

Text: Luke 24:13-35; Marty Haugen b.1950
Tune: COLUMCILLE, Irregular; Gaelic, arr. by Marty Haugen, b.1950

817 Lord, When You Came / Pescador de Hombres

Verses

1. Lord, when you came to the sea - shore
2. Lord, you knew what my boat car - ried:
3. Lord, have you need of my la - bor,
4. Lord, send me where you would have me,
1. Tú has ve - ni - do_a la_o - ri - lla,
2. Tú sa - bes bien lo que ten - go,
3. Tú ne - ce - si - tas mis ma - nos,
4. Tú pes - ca - dor de_o-tros, ma - res,

You weren't seek - ing the wise or the
Nei - ther mon - ey nor weap - ons for
Hands for serv - ice, a heart made for
To a vil - lage, or heart of the
no_has bus - ca - do ni_a sa - bios, ni_a
en mi bar - ca no_hay o - ro ni_es -
mi can - san - cio que_a o - tros des -
an - sia_e - ter - na, al - mas que es -

wealth - y, But on - ly ask - ing
fight - ing, But nets for fish - ing,
lov - ing, My arms for lift - ing
cit - y; I will re - mem - ber
ri - cos, tan só - lo quie - res
pa - das, tan só - lo re - des
can - se, a - mor que quie - ra
pe - ran. A - mi - go bue - no,

that I might fol - low.
my dai - ly la - bor.
the poor and bro - ken?
that you are with me.
que yo te si - ga.
y mi tra - ba - jo.
se - guir a - man - do.
que_a - sí me lla - mas.

Refrain

O Lord, in my eyes you were gaz - ing,
Se - ñor me has mi - ra - do a los o - jos,

Kind-ly smil - ing, my name you were
son - ri - en - do has di - cho mi

say - ing; All I treas - ured,
nom - bre, *en la a - re - na*

I have left on the sand there; Close to
he de - ja - do mi bar - ca, *jun - to a*

you, I will find oth - er seas.
ti *bus - ca - ré o - tro mar.*

Text: *Pescador de Hombres,* Cesáreo Gabaráin, © 1979, published by OCP Publications; trans. by Willard Francis Jabusch, b.1930, © 1982, administered by OCP Publications
Tune: Cesáreo Gabaráin, © 1979, published by OCP Publications; acc. by Diana Kodner, b.1957, © 1994, GIA Publications, Inc.

818 God It Was

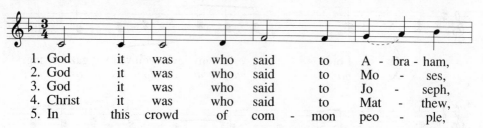

1. God it was who said to A - bra - ham,
2. God it was who said to Mo - ses,
3. God it was who said to Jo - seph,
4. Christ it was who said to Mat - thew,
5. In this crowd of com - mon peo - ple,

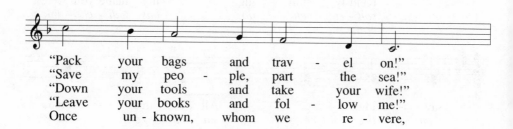

"Pack your bags and trav - el on!"
"Save my peo - ple, part the sea!"
"Down your tools and take your wife!"
"Leave your books and fol - low me!"
Once un - known, whom we re - vere,

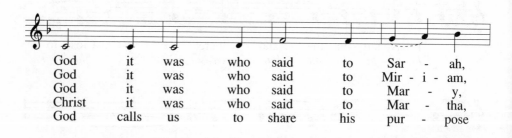

God it was who said to Sar - ah,
God it was who said to Mir - i - am,
God it was who said to Mar - y,
Christ it was who said to Mar - tha,
God calls us to share his pur - pose

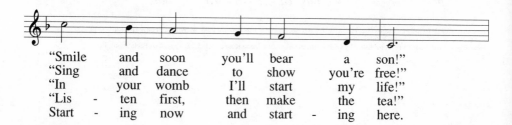

"Smile and soon you'll bear a son!"
"Sing and dance to show you're free!"
"In your womb I'll start my life!"
"Lis - ten first, then make the tea!"
Start - ing now and start - ing here.

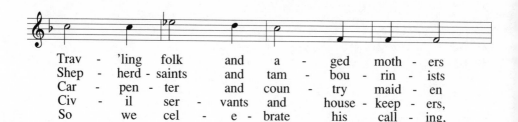

Trav - 'ling folk and a - ged moth - ers
Shep - herd - saints and tam - bou - rin - ists
Car - pen - ter and coun - try maid - en
Civ - il ser - vants and house - keep - ers,
So we cel - e - brate his call - ing,

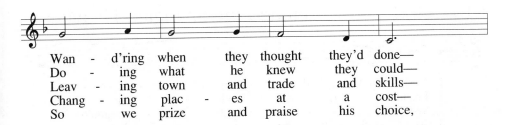

Wan	-	d'ring	when	they	thought	they'd	done—
Do	-	ing	what	he	knew	they	could—
Leav	-	ing	town	and	trade	and	skills—
Chang	-	ing	plac	- es	at	a	cost—
So		we	prize	and	praise	his	choice,

This	is	how	God	calls	his	peo	-	ple,
This	is	how	God	calls	his	peo	-	ple,
This	is	how	God	calls	his	peo	-	ple,
This	is	how	Christ	calls	dis	- ci	-	ples,
As	we	pray	that	through	this	com	- pa	- ny

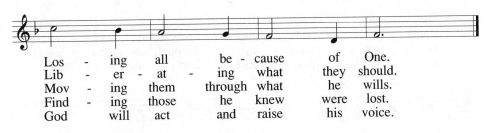

Los	-	ing	all	be - cause	of	One.
Lib	-	er - at	- ing	what	they	should.
Mov	-	ing	them	through what	he	wills.
Find	-	ing	those	he	knew	were	lost.
God		will	act	and	raise	his	voice.

Text: John L. Bell, b.1949
Tune: JESUS CALLS US, Irregular; adapt. from a Gaelic Air by John L. Bell, b.1949
© 1989, Iona Community, GIA Publications, Inc., agent

819 God, Who Stretched the Spangled Heavens

1. God, who stretched the span - gled heav - ens
2. Proud - ly rise our mod - ern cit - ies,
3. We have ven - tured worlds un - dreamed of
4. As each far ho - ri - zon beck - ons,

In - fi - nite in time and place, Flung the suns in
State - ly build - ings, row on row; Yet their win - dows,
Since the child - hood of our race; Known the ec - sta -
May it chal - lenge us a - new, Chil - dren of cre -

burn - ing ra - diance Through the si - lent
blank, un - feel - ing, Stare on can - yoned
sy of wing - ing Through un - trav - eled
a - tive pur - pose, Serv - ing oth - ers,

fields of space; We, your chil - dren, in your like - ness,
streets be - low, Where the lone - ly drift un - no - ticed
realms of space; Probed the se - crets of the at - om,
hon - oring you. May our dreams prove rich with prom - ise,

Share in - ven - tive pow'rs with you; Great Cre - a - tor,
In the cit - y's ebb and flow, Lost to pur - pose
Yield-ing un - i - mag - ined pow'r, Fac - ing us with
Each en - deav - or, well be - gun: Great Cre - a - tor,

still cre - a - ting, Show us what we yet may do.
and to mean - ing, Scarce-ly car - ing where they go.
life's de - struc - tion Or our most tri - um - phant hour.
give us guid - ance Till our goals and yours are one.

Text: Catherine Cameron, b.1927, © 1967, Hope Publishing Co.
Tune: HOLY MANNA, 8 7 8 7 D; William Moore, fl.1830; harm. by Charles Anders, b.1929, © 1969, *Contemporary Worship I: Hymns*

We Are Called   820

1. Come! Live in the light!
2. Come! O - pen your heart!
3. Sing! Sing a new song!

Shine with the joy and the love of the Lord! We are
Show your mer - cy to all those in fear! We are
Sing of that great day when all will be one! God will

called to be light for the king - dom, to
called to be hope for the hope - less so all
reign, and we'll walk with each oth - er as

live in the free - dom of the cit - y of God!
ha - tred and blind-ness will be no more!
sis - ters and broth-ers u - nit - ed in love!

We are called to act with jus - tice,   we are

called to love ten - der - ly,   we are called to

serve one an - oth-er;   to walk hum - bly with

1., 2. | 3.

God!

Text: Micah 6:8; David Haas, b.1957
Tune: David Haas, b.1957
© 1988, GIA Publications, Inc.

821 Freedom Is Coming

Text: South African
Tune: South African, © 1984, Utryck

822 Here Am I

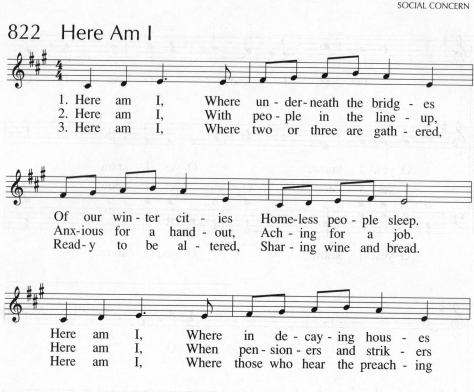

1. Here am I, Where un - der-neath the bridg - es
2. Here am I, With peo - ple in the line - up,
3. Here am I, Where two or three are gath - ered,

Of our win - ter cit - ies Home-less peo - ple sleep.
Anx-ious for a hand - out, Ach - ing for a job.
Read-y to be al - tered, Shar - ing wine and bread.

Here am I, Where in de - cay - ing hous - es
Here am I, When pen - sion - ers and strik - ers
Here am I, Where those who hear the preach - ing

Lit - tle chil - dren shiv - er, Cry - ing at the
Sing and march to - geth - er, Want - ing some-thing
Change their way of liv - ing, Find the way to

cold. Where are you?
new. Where are you?
life. Where are you?

Text: Brian Wren, b.1936
Tune: STANISLAUS, 3 7 6 5 D 3; Dan Damon, b.1955
© Words 1983, music 1995, Hope Publishing Co.

For the Healing of the Nations   823

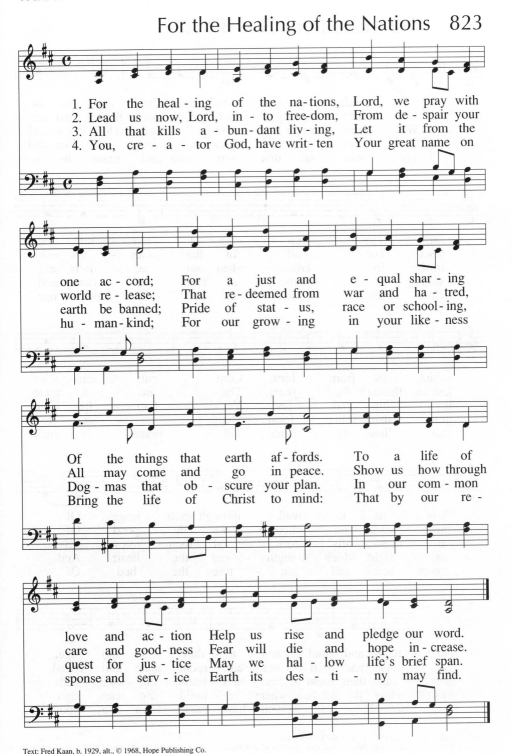

1. For the heal-ing of the na-tions, Lord, we pray with
2. Lead us now, Lord, in-to free-dom, From de-spair your
3. All that kills a-bun-dant liv-ing, Let it from the
4. You, cre-a-tor God, have writ-ten Your great name on

one ac-cord; For a just and e-qual shar-ing
world re-lease; That re-deemed from war and ha-tred,
earth be banned; Pride of stat-us, race or school-ing,
hu-man-kind; For our grow-ing in your like-ness

Of the things that earth af-fords. To a life of
All may come and go in peace. Show us how through
Dog-mas that ob-scure your plan. In our com-mon
Bring the life of Christ to mind: That by our re-

love and ac-tion Help us rise and pledge our word.
care and good-ness Fear will die and hope in-crease.
quest for jus-tice May we hal-low life's brief span.
sponse and serv-ice Earth its des-ti-ny may find.

Text: Fred Kaan, b. 1929, alt., © 1968, Hope Publishing Co.
Tune: ST. THOMAS, 8 7 8 7 8 7; John Wade, 1711-1786

824 God Made from One Blood

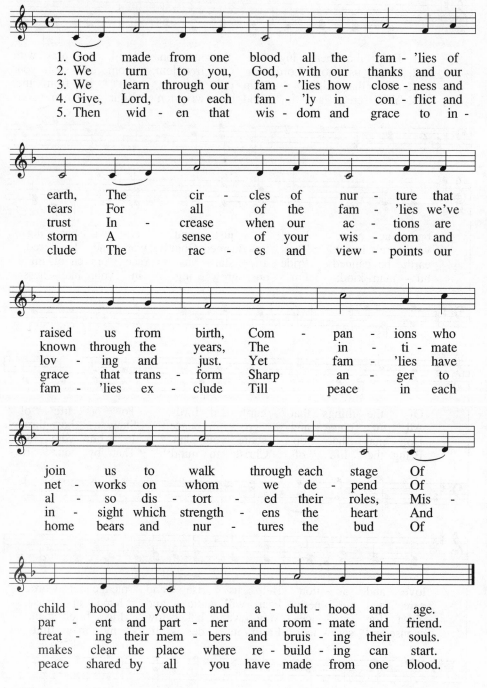

1. God made from one blood all the fam-'lies of earth, The cir-cles of nur-ture that raised us from birth, Com-pan-ions who join us to walk through each stage Of child-hood and youth and a-dult-hood and age.

2. We turn to you, God, with our thanks and our tears For all of the fam-'lies we've known through the years, The in-ti-mate net-works on whom we de-pend Of par-ent and part-ner and room-mate and friend.

3. We learn through our fam-'lies how close-ness and trust In-crease when our ac-tions are lov-ing and just. Yet fam-'lies have al-so dis-tort-ed their roles, Mis-treat-ing their mem-bers and bruis-ing their souls.

4. Give, Lord, to each fam-'ly in con-flict and storm A sense of your wis-dom and grace that trans-form Sharp an-ger to in-sight which strength-ens the heart And makes clear the place where re-build-ing can start.

5. Then wid-en that wis-dom and grace to in-clude The rac-es and view-points our fam-'lies ex-clude Till peace in each home bears and nur-tures the bud Of peace shared by all you have made from one blood.

Text: Thomas H. Troeger, b.1945, © 1991, Oxford University Press
Tune: FOUNDATION, 11 11 11 11; Funk's *Compilation of Genuine Church Music*, 1832; harm. by Richard Proulx, b.1937, © 1975, GIA Publications, Inc.

If You Believe and I Believe   825

Text: Zimbabwean traditional
Tune: Zimbabwean traditional; adapt. of English traditional; as taught by Tarasai; arr. by John L. Bell, b.1949, © 1991, Iona Community,
   GIA Publications, Inc., agent

826 God of Day and God of Darkness

1. God of day and God of dark-ness, Now we stand be-fore the night; As the shad-ows stretch and deep-en, Come and make our dark-ness bright. All cre-a-tion still is groan-ing For the dawn-ing of your might, When the Sun of peace and jus-tice Fills the earth with ra-diant light.

2. Still the na-tions curse the dark-ness, Still the rich op-press the poor; Still the earth is bruised and bro-ken By the ones who still want more. Come and wake us from our sleep-ing, So our hearts can-not ig-nore All your peo-ple lost and bro-ken, All your chil-dren at our door.

3. Show us Christ in one an-oth-er, Make us ser-vants strong and true; Give us all your love of jus-tice So we do what you would do. Let us call all peo-ple ho-ly, Let us pledge our lives a-new, Make us one with all the low-ly, Let us all be one in you.

4. You shall be the path that guides us, You the light that in us burns; Shin-ing deep with-in all peo-ple, Yours the love that we must learn, For our hearts shall wan-der rest-less 'Til they safe to you re-turn; Find-ing you in one an-oth-er, We shall all your face dis-cern.

5. Praise to you in day and dark-ness, You our source and you our end; Praise to you who love and nur-ture us As a fa-ther, moth-er, friend. Grant us all a peace-ful rest-ing, Let each mind and bod-y mend, So we rise re-freshed to-mor-row, Hearts re-newed to King-dom tend.

Text: Marty Haugen, b.1950, © 1985, 1994, GIA Publications, Inc.
Tune: BEACH SPRING, 8 7 8 7 D; *The Sacred Harp,* 1844; harm. by Marty Haugen, b.1950, © 1985, GIA Publications, Inc.

Now Join We to Praise the Creator 827

1. Now   join   we   to   praise   the   cre - a - tor,
2. We   thank   you,   O   God,   for   your   good - ness,
3. But   al - so   of   need   and   star - va - tion
4. We   cry   for   the   plight   of   the   hun - gry
5. The   song   grows   in   depth   and   in   wide - ness:
6. Then   teach   us,   O   Lord   of   the   har - vest,

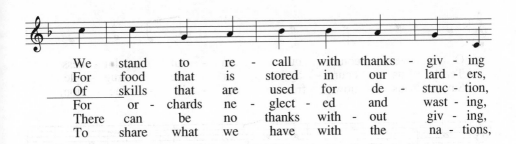

Our   voic - es   in   wor - ship   and   song;
For the   joy   and   a - bun - dance   of   crops,
We   sing   with   con - cern   and   de - spair,
While   har - vests   are   left   on   the   field,
The   earth   and   its   peo - ple   are   one.
To   be   hum - ble   in   all   that   we   claim;

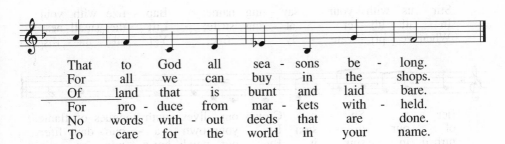

We   stand   to   re - call   with   thanks - giv - ing
For   food   that   is   stored   in   our   lard - ers,
Of   skills   that   are   used   for   de - struc - tion,
For   or - chards   ne - glect - ed   and   wast - ing,
There   can   be   no   thanks   with - out   giv - ing,
To   share   what   we   have   with   the   na - tions,

That   to   God   all   sea - sons   be - long.
For   all   we   can   buy   in   the   shops.
Of   land   that   is   burnt   and   laid   bare.
For   pro - duce   from   mar - kets   with - held.
No   words   with - out   deeds   that   are   done.
To   care   for   the   world   in   your   name.

Text: Fred Kaan, b.1929, © 1968, Hope Publishing Co.
Tune: HARVEST, 9 8 9 8; Geoffrey Laycock, b.1927, © 1971, Faber Music Ltd.

828 God, Whose Purpose Is to Kindle

1. God, whose pur - pose is to kin - dle:
2. God, who in your ho - ly gos - pel
3. God, who still a sword de - liv - ers

Now ig - nite us with your fire; While the earth a -
Wills that all should tru - ly live, Make us sense our
Rath - er than a plac - id peace, With your sharp - ened

waits your burn - ing, With your pas - sion us in - spire.
share of fail - ure, Our tran - quil - li - ty for - give.
word dis - turb us, From com - pla - cen - cy re - lease!

O - ver - come our sin - ful calm - ness,
Teach us cour - age as we strug - gle
Save us now from sat - is - fac - tion,

Stir us with your sav - ing name; Bap - tize with your
In all lib - er - at - ing strife; Lift the small - ness
When we pri - vate - ly are free, Yet are un - dis -

fier - y Spir - it, Crown our lives with tongues of flame.
of our vi - sion By your own a - bun - dant life.
turbed in spir - it By our neigh - bor's mis - er - y.

Text: Luke 12:49; David E. Trueblood, b.1900; © 1967, David Elton Trueblood
Tune: HOLY MANNA, 8 7 8 7 D; William Moore, fl.1830; harm. by Charles Anders, b.1929, © 1969 *Contemporary Worship I:Hymns*

How Long, O Lord, How Long 829

1. "How long, O Lord, how long," The
2. How long, O Lord, how long Must
3. How long, O Lord, how long Will
4. How long, O Lord, how long Will
5. How long, O Lord, how long Must
6. "How long, O Lord, how long?" We
7. How long, O Lord, how long? Grant
8. How long, O Lord, how long Will

starv - ing mil - lions cry, "Shall fam - ine's blight our
home - less peo - ple lie With - out a bed in
jus - tice bow to greed, And wealth and pow - er
walls we build di - vide, And pride of gen - der,
war its car - nage spread And leave be - hind in
cry in our de - spair; Yet, nailed up - on the
strength of heart and nerve To share your work of
e - vil's pow'r pre - vail? We hope in Christ who

lives de - stroy, Our chil - dren waste and die?"
street and camp While oth - ers pass them by?
forge the chains That hold the poor in need?
race or class An - oth - er's worth de - ride?
ru - ined rows The har - vest of the dead?
cross we see The em - blem of your care.
truth and love, To suf - fer and to serve.
con - quered death, Whose pur - pose can - not fail.

Text: Herman Stuempfle, b.1923; © 1993, GIA Publications, Inc.
Tune: SOUTHWELL, 6 6 8 6; Damon's *Psalmes*, 1579

830 Make Me a Channel of Your Peace

Verses 1, 2, 4

1. Make me a chan-nel of your peace. Where
2. Make me a chan-nel of your peace. Where
4. Make me a chan-nel of your peace. It

there is ha-tred, let me bring your love. Where
there's de-spair in life, let me bring hope. Where
is in par-don-ing that we are par-doned, in

there is in-ju-ry, your par-don, Lord, And
there is dark-ness, on-ly light, And
giv-ing of our-selves that we re-ceive, and in

1.
where there's doubt, true faith in you.
where there's sad-ness, ev-er joy.
dy-ing that we're born to e-ter-nal life.

Verse 3

3. Oh, Mas-ter, grant that I may nev-er seek So much to be con-

soled as to con-sole. To be un-der-stood as to un-der-

D.C.

stand. To be loved as to love with all my soul.

Text: *Prayer of St. Francis;* adapt. by Sebastian Temple, b.1928, ©1967, OCP Publications
Tune: Sebastian Temple, b.1928, © 1967, OCP Publications; acc. by Robert J. Batastini, b.1942, © 1996, GIA Publications, Inc.
Dedicated to Mrs. Frances Tracy

Let There Be Peace on Earth 831

Let there be peace on earth, and let it be-gin with me.

Let there be peace on earth, the peace that was meant to be. With

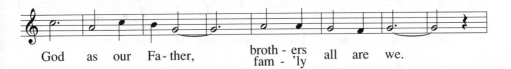

God as our Fa-ther, broth-ers / fam-'ly all are we.

Let me / us walk with my broth-er / each oth-er in per-fect har-mo-ny.

Let peace be-gin with me; let this be the mo-ment now.

With ev-'ry step I take, let this be my sol-emn vow; To

take each mo-ment, and live each mo-ment in peace e-ter-nal-ly!

Let there be peace on earth, and let it be-gin with me.

Text: Sy Miller, 1908-1941, Jill Jackson, © 1955, 1983, Jan-Lee Music
Tune: Sy Miller, 1908-1941, Jill Jackson © 1955, 1983, Jan-Lee Music; acc. by Diana Kodner, b.1957, © 1993, GIA Publications, Inc.
Used with permission

832 Dona Nobis Pacem in Terra

Do - na   no - bis   pa - cem in   ter - ra,

do - na   no - bis   pa - cem, Do - mi - ne.

Music: The Iona Community, © 1987, The Iona Community, GIA Publications, Inc., agent

O God of Love, O King of Peace   833

1. O God of love, O King of peace, Make
2. Whom shall we trust but you, O Lord? Where
3. Where saints and an - gels dwell a - bove, All

wars through - out the world to cease; Our vio - lent ways help
rest but on your faith - ful word? None ev - er called on
hearts are joined in ho - ly love; O bind us in that

us con - tain; Give peace, O God, give peace a - gain!
you in vain; Give peace, O God, give peace a - gain!
heav'n - ly chain; Give peace, O God, give peace a - gain!

*May be sung as a two or four-voice canon.

Text: Henry W. Baker, 1821-1877
Tune: TALLIS' CANON, LM; Thomas Tallis, c.1505-1585

834 O God of Every Nation

1. O God of ev - 'ry na - tion, Of
2. From search for wealth and pow - er And
3. Lord, strength - en all who la - bor That
4. Keep bright in us the vi - sion Of

ev - 'ry race and land, Re -
scorn of truth and right, From
we may find re - lease From
days when wars shall cease, When

deem your whole cre - a - tion With
trust in bombs that show - er De -
fear of rat - tling sa - ber, From
ha - tred and di - vi - sion Give

your al - might - y hand; Where
struc - tion through the night, From
dread of war's in - crease; When
way to love and peace, Till

hate   and   fear   di - vide   us   And
pride   of   race   and   sta - tion   And
hope   and   cour - age   fal - ter,   Your
dawns   the   morn - ing   glo - rious   When

bit - ter   threats   are   hurled,   In
blind - ness   to   your   way,   De -
still   small   voice   be   heard;   With
Christ   a - lone   shall   reign   And

love   and   mer - cy   guide   us   And
liv - er   ev - 'ry   na - tion,   E -
faith   that   none   can   al - ter,   Up -
he   shall   rule   vic - to - rious   O'er

heal   our   strife - torn   world.
ter - nal   God,   we   pray.
hold   us   by   your   word.
all   the   world's   do - main.

Text: William W. Reid, b.1923, alt., © 1958, Hymn Society of America
Tune: PASSION CHORALE, 7 6 7 6 D; Hans Leo Hassler, 1564-1612; harm. by J. S. Bach, 1685-1750

835 There Is One Lord

Ostinato Refrain

There is one Lord, one faith, one bap - tis-m,

There is one God who is Fa - ther of all.

Verses

Cantor:

1. Bear with one an - oth - er in love and char - i - ty, be

hum - ble, be pa - tient, be self - less, be as one.

2. There is one bod - y, there is one Spir - it,

there is one hope to which we are called.

3. We are all to come to u - ni - ty, in our

faith and knowl - edge of the Son of God, un - til

we be-come per - fect-ed in the full-ness of Christ.

Text: Ephesians 4, Taizé Community, 1984
Tune: Jacques Berthier, 1923-1994
© 1984, Les Presses de Taizé, GIA Publications, Inc., agent

In Christ There Is No East or West   836

1. In Christ there is no east or west, In
2. In him shall true hearts ev - 'ry - where Their
3. Join hands, dis - ci - ples in the faith, What -
4. In Christ now meet both east and west, In

him no south or north, But one great fam - 'ly
high com - mun - ion find; His serv - ice is the
e'er your race may be! Who serve each oth - er
him meet south and north, All Christ - ly souls are

bound by love Through - out the whole wide earth.
gold - en cord Close - bind - ing hu - man - kind.
in Christ's love Are sure - ly kin to me.
one in him, Through - out the whole wide earth.

Text: Galatians 3:23; John Oxenham, 1852-1941
Tune: MC KEE, CM; African-American; adapt. by Harry T. Burleigh, 1866-1949

837 Diverse in Culture, Nation, Race

1. Di - verse in cul - ture, na - tion, race, We
2. God, let us be a bridge of care Con -
3. When cha - sms wid - en, storms a - rise, O
4. God, let us be a ta - ble spread With

come to-geth-er by your grace. God, let us be a
nect - ing peo - ple ev - 'ry - where. Help us con - front all
Ho - ly Spir - it, make us wise. Let our re - solve, like
gifts of love and bro - ken bread, Where all find wel - come,

meet - ing ground Where hope and heal - ing love are found.
fear and hate And lust for pow'r that sep - a - rate.
steel, be strong To stand with those who suf - fer wrong.
grace at - tends, And en - e - mies a - rise as friends.

May be sung as a two or four voice canon.

Text: Ruth Duck, b.1947, © 1992, GIA Publications, Inc.
Tune: TALLIS' CANON, LM; Thomas Tallis, c.1510-1583

Help Us Accept Each Other   838

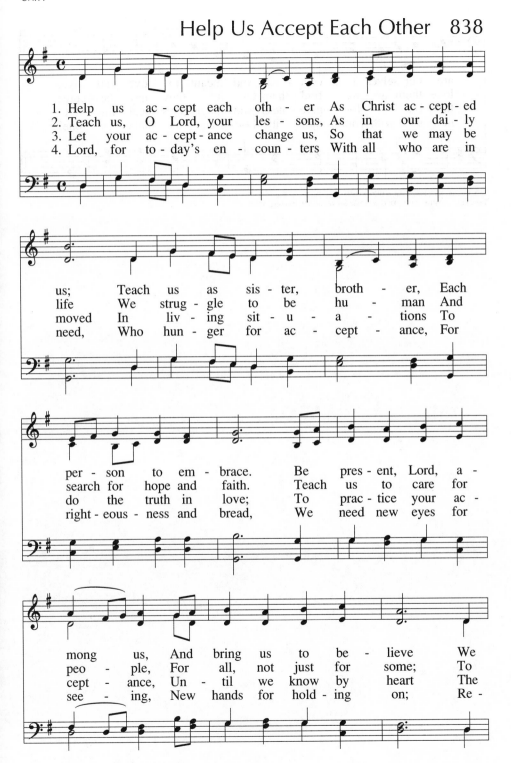

1. Help us ac-cept each oth - er As Christ ac-cept-ed
2. Teach us, O Lord, your les - sons, As in our dai - ly
3. Let your ac-cept-ance change us, So that we may be
4. Lord, for to-day's en - coun - ters With all who are in

us; Teach us as sis - ter, broth - er, Each
life We strug - gle to be hu - man And
moved In liv - ing sit - u - a - tions To
need, Who hun - ger for ac - cept - ance, For

per - son to em - brace. Be pres - ent, Lord, a -
search for hope and faith. Teach us to care for
do the truth in love; To prac - tice your ac -
right - eous - ness and bread, We need new eyes for

mong us, And bring us to be - lieve We
peo - ple, For all, not just for some; To
cept - ance, Un - til we know by heart The
see - ing, New hands for hold - ing on; Re -

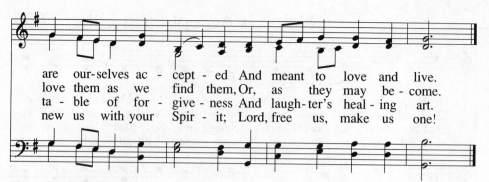

are our-selves ac - cept - ed And meant to love and live.
love them as we find them, Or, as they may be - come.
ta - ble of for - give - ness And laugh-ter's heal - ing art.
new us with your Spir - it; Lord, free us, make us one!

Text: Romans 15:7; Fred Kaan, b.1929, © 1975, Hope Publishing Co.
Tune: ELLACOMBE, 7 6 7 6 D; *Gesangbuch der Herzogl*, Wirtemberg, 1784

Father, Lord of All Creation 839

1. Fa - ther, Lord of all cre - a - tion,
2. Je - sus Christ, the man for oth - ers,
3. Ho - ly Spir - it, rush - ing, burn - ing

Ground of be - ing, life and love; Height and depth be -
We, your peo - ple, make our prayer: Give us grace to
Wind and flame of Pen - te - cost, Fire our hearts a -

yond de - scrip - tion On - ly life in you can prove:
love all oth - ers, Those whose bur - dens we can share.
fresh with yearn - ing To re - gain what we have lost.

You are mor - tal life's de - pen - dence:
Where your name binds us to - geth - er
May your love u - nite our ac - tion,

Thought, speech, sight are ours by grace; Yours is ev - 'ry
You, Lord Christ, will sure - ly be; Where no self - ish -
Nev - er - more to speak a - lone: God, in us a -

hour's ex - ist - ence, Sov - 'reign Lord of time and space.
ness can sev - er, There your love we all may see.
bol - ish fac - tion. God, through us your love make known.

Text: Stewart Cross, b.1928, ©
Tune: GENEVA, 8 7 8 7 D; George H. Day, 1883-1966, © 1942, The Church Pension Fund

one, the cross   that we   bear.

Last time

Verses
unis.

1. God of all,   we   look to   you,
2. So my pain   is   pain for   you,
3. All you seek - ers,   great and   small,

we would be   your ser-vants   true,
in your joy   is   my joy,   too;
seek the great - est   gift of   all;

div.   D.C.

let us be   your love   to   all   the   world.
all is brought   to - geth - er   in   the   Lord.
if you love,   then you   will know the   Lord.

div.

Text: 1 Corinthians 12, 13; Marty Haugen, b.1950
Tune: Marty Haugen, b.1950
© 1980, 1986, GIA Publications, Inc.

841   Many Are the Lightbeams

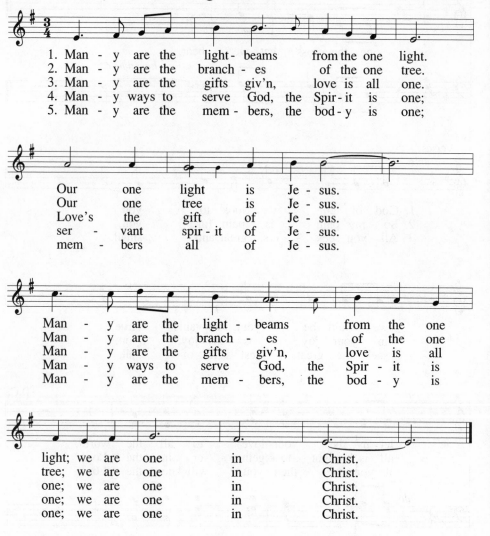

1. Man - y are the light-beams from the one light.
2. Man - y are the branch - es of the one tree.
3. Man - y are the gifts giv'n, love is all one.
4. Man - y ways to serve God, the Spir-it is one;
5. Man - y are the mem - bers, the bod-y is one;

Our one light is Je - sus.
Our one tree is Je - sus.
Love's the gift of Je - sus.
ser - vant spir-it of Je - sus.
mem - bers all of Je - sus.

Man - y are the light - beams from the one
Man - y are the branch - es of the one
Man - y are the gifts giv'n, love is all
Man - y ways to serve God, the Spir - it is
Man - y are the mem - bers, the bod - y is

light; we are one in Christ.
tree; we are one in Christ.
one; we are one in Christ.
one; we are one in Christ.
one; we are one in Christ.

Text: *De unitate ecclesiae,* Cyprian of Carthage, 252 A.D, by Anders Frostenson © A-F Foundation Hymns and Songs
Tune: Olle Widestrand ©; acc. by Marty Haugen, b.1950, © 1987, GIA Publications, Inc.

This Is the Day When Light Was First Created   842

1. This is the day when light was first cre - a - ted,
2. This is the day of our com - plete sur - pris - ing,
3. We join to praise, with ev - 'ry race and na - tion,
4. This is the day of wor - ship and of vi - sion,
5. We pray that this, the day of re - cre - a - tion,

Sym - bol and gift of or - der and de - sign.
Re - peat of Eas - ter: Christ has come to life!
The God who with the world his Spir - it shares;
Great birth - day of the church in ev - 'ry land.
May hal - low all the week that is to come.

In light is God's in - ten - tion clear - ly stat - ed,
Now is the feast of love's re - volt and ris - ing
Strong wind of change and earth's il - lu - mi - na - tion,
Let Chris - tians all con - fess their sad di - vi - sion,
Help us, O Lord, to lay a good foun - da - tion

The break of day re - veals his lov - ing mind.
A - gainst the rule of hell and death and grief.
Dis - pel - ling stat - ic thoughts and dark - est fears.
And seek the strength a - gain as one to stand.
For all we do at work, at school, at home.

Text: Fred Kaan, b.1929, © 1968, Hope Publishing Co.
Tune: NORTHBROOK, 11 10 11 10; Reginald S. Thatcher, 1888-1957, © Oxford University Press

843 On This Day, the First of Days

1. On this day, the first of days,
2. On this day the e - ter - nal Son
3. Word - made - flesh, all prais - es be!
4. Ho - ly Spir - it, you im - part
5. God, the bless - ed Three in One,

God our Mak - er's name we praise;
O - ver death his tri - umph won;
You from sin have set us free;
Gifts of love to ev - 'ry heart;
May your ho - ly will be done;

Who, cre - a - tion's Lord and Spring,
On this day the Spir - it came
And with you we die and rise
Give us light and grace, we pray,
In your word our souls are free,

Did the world from dark - ness bring.
With its gifts of liv - ing flame.
Un - to God in sac - ri - fice.
Fill our hearts this ho - ly day.
As we praise the Trin - i - ty.

Text: *Die parente temporum; Le Mans Breviary,* 1748; tr. by Henry W. Baker, 1821-1877
Tune: LÜBECK, 77 77; Freylinghausen's *Gesangbuch,* 1704

God Is Here! As We His People 844

1. God is here! As we his peo - ple,
2. Here are sym - bols to re - mind us
3. Here our chil - dren find a wel - come
4. Lord of all, of church and king - dom,

Meet to of - fer praise and prayer,
Of our life - long need of grace;
In the Shep - herd's flock and fold;
In an age of change and doubt,

May we find in ful - ler meas - ure
Here are ta - ble, font and pul - pit,
Here, as bread and wine are tak - en,
Keep us faith - ful to the gos - pel,

What it is in Christ we share:
Here the cross has cen - tral place:
Christ sus - tains us as of old:
Help us work your pur - pose out:

Here, as in the world a - round us,
Here in hon - es - ty of preach - ing,
Here the ser - vants of the Ser - vant
Here, in this day's ded - i - ca - tion,

All our var - ied skills and arts
Here in si - lence as in speech,
Seek in wor - ship to ex - plore
All we have to give, re - ceive;

Wait the com - ing of his Spir - it
Here in new - ness and re - new - al
What it means in dai - ly liv - ing
We who can - not live with - out you,

In - to o - pen minds and hearts.
God the Spir - it comes to each.
To be - lieve and to a - dore.
We a - dore you! We be - lieve!

Text: Fred Pratt Green, b.1903, © 1979, Hope Publishing Co.
Tune: ABBOT'S LEIGH, 8 7 8 7 D; Cyril V. Taylor, 1907-1991, © 1942, 1970, Hope Publishing Co.

All Who Hunger, Gather Gladly   845

1. All who hun - ger, gath - er glad - ly;
2. All who hun - ger, nev - er stran - gers,
3. All who hun - ger, sing to - geth - er;

Ho - ly man - na in our bread. Come from wil - der -
Seek - er, be a wel - come guest. Come from rest - less -
Je - sus Christ is liv - ing bread. Come from lone - li -

ness and wan - d'ring. Here, in truth, we will be fed.
ness and roam-ing. Here, in joy, we keep the feast.
ness and long - ing. Here, in peace, we have been led.

You that yearn for days of full - ness,
We that once were lost and scat - tered
Blest are those who from this ta - ble

All a - round us is our food. Taste and see the
In com - mun - ion's love have stood. Taste and see the
Live their days in grat - i - tude. Taste and see the

grace e - ter - nal. Taste and see that God is good.
grace e - ter - nal. Taste and see that God is good.
grace e - ter - nal. Taste and see that God is good.

Text: Sylvia G. Dunstan, 1955-1993, © 1991, GIA Publications, Inc.
Tune: HOLY MANNA, 8 7 8 7 D; William Moore, fl.1830; harm. by Charles Anders, b.1929, © 1969, *Contemporary Worship 1: Hymns*

846 All Are Welcome

Descant (verse 5):

5. Let us build so all are named,

Melody:

1. Let us build a house where love can dwell And
2. Let us build a house where proph - ets speak, And
3. Let us build a house where love is found In
4. Let us build a house where hands will reach Be -
5. Let us build a house where all are named, Their

their songs and vi - sions heard,

all can safe - ly live, A place where saints and
words are strong and true, Where all God's chil - dren
wa - ter, wine and wheat: A ban - quet hall on
yond the wood and stone To heal and strength - en,
songs and vi - sions heard And loved and treas - ured,

taught and claimed As words with - in the

chil - dren tell How hearts learn to for -
dare to seek To dream God's reign a -
ho - ly ground, Where peace and jus - tice
serve and teach, And live the Word they've
taught and claimed As words with - in the

Word. Built of tears and cries and laugh - ter,

give. Built of hopes and dreams and vi - sions, Rock of
new. Here the cross shall stand as wit - ness And as
meet. Here the love of God, through Je - sus, Is re -
known. Here the out - cast and the stran - ger Bear the
Word. Built of tears and cries and laugh - ter, Prayers of

Prayers and songs of grace, Let this

faith and vault of grace; Here the
sym - bol of God's grace; Here as
vealed in time and space; As we
im - age of God's face; Let us
faith and songs of grace, Let this

house pro - claim from floor to raft - er;

love of Christ shall end di - vi - sions:
one we claim the faith of Je - sus:
share in Christ the feast that frees us:
bring an end to fear and dan - ger:
house pro - claim from floor to raft - er:

All are wel - come, all are wel - come, wel - come

All are wel - come, all are wel - come, all are wel - come

Last time

in this place.

Last time

in this place.

Text: Marty Haugen, b.1950
Tune: TWO OAKS, 9 6 8 6 8 7 10 with refrain; Marty Haugen, b.1950
© 1994, GIA Publications, Inc.

847 Come, Rejoice before Your Maker

1. Come, re-joice be-fore your Mak-er
2. Know for cer-tain, our Cre-a-tor
3. Come with grate-ful hearts and voic-es
4. For the Lord our God is gra-cious

All you peo-ples of the earth; Serve the Lord your
Is the true and on-ly God; We the crea-tures
En-ter now God's courts with praise; Show your thank-ful-
Ev-er-last-ing is God's love, And to ev-'ry

God with glad-ness, Come re-joic-ing with a song!
of our Mak-er Sheep with-in the Shep-herd's fold.
ness with glad-ness, Give due hon-or to God's name.
gen-er-a-tion That great faith-ful-ness en-dures.

Text: Psalm 100; Michael Baughen, b.1930, alt.
Tune: JUBILATE DEO, 8 7 8 7; Noel H. Tredinnick, b.1949
© 1973, Hope Publishing Co.

As We Gather at Your Table 848

1. As we gath - er at your Ta - ble, As we lis - ten to your Word, Help us know, O God, your pres - ence: Let our hearts and minds be stirred. Nour - ish us with sa - cred sto - ry Till we

2. Turn our wor - ship in - to wit - ness In the sac - ra - ment of life; Send us forth to love and serve you, Bring - ing peace where there is strife. Give us, Christ, your great com - pas - sion To for -

3. Gra - cious Spir - it, help us sum - mon Oth - er guests to share that feast Where tri - um - phant Love will wel - come Those who had been last and least. There no more will en - vy blind us Nor will

claim it as our own; Teach us
give as you for - gave; May we
pride our peace de - stroy, As we

through this ho - ly ban - quet How to
still be - hold your im - age In the
join with saints and an - gels To re -

make Love's vic - tory known.
world you died to save.
peat the sound - ing joy.

Text: Carl P. Daw, Jr. b.1944; © 1989, Hope Publishing Co.
Tune: NETTLETON, 8 7 8 7 D; Wyeth's *Repository of Sacred Music, Pt. II*, 1813

849   All People That on Earth Do Dwell

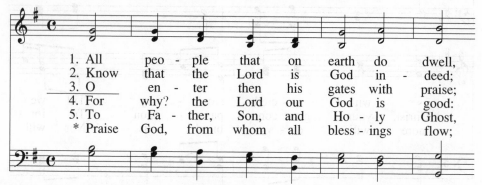

1. All   peo - ple   that   on   earth   do   dwell,
2. Know   that   the   Lord   is   God   in - deed;
3. O   en - ter   then   his   gates   with   praise;
4. For   why?   the   Lord   our   God   is   good:
5. To   Fa - ther,   Son,   and   Ho - ly   Ghost,
* Praise   God,   from   whom   all   bless - ings   flow;

May be sung alone or as an alternate to stanza 5.

Sing to the Lord with cheer - ful voice;
With - out our aid he did us make;
Ap - proach with joy his courts un - to;
His mer - cy is for ev - er sure;
The God whom heaven and earth a - dore,
Praise him, all crea - tures here be - low;

Him serve with mirth, his praise forth tell,
We are his folk, he does us feed,
Praise, laud, and bless his Name al - ways,
His truth at all times firm - ly stood,
From us and from the an - gel host
Praise him a - bove, you heav'n - ly host:

Come we be - fore him, and re - joice.
And for his sheep he does us take.
For it is seem - ly so to do.
And shall from age to age en - dure.
Be praise and glo - ry ev - er - more.
Praise Fa - ther, Son and Ho - ly Ghost.

Text: Psalm (99)100; William Kethe, d. c.1593; Doxology, Thomas Ken, 1637-1711
Tune: OLD HUNDREDTH, LM; Louis Bourgeois, c.1510-1561

850 Gather Us In

1. Here in this place new light is stream-ing,
2. We are the young— our lives are a mys-t'ry,
3. Here we will take the wine and the wa - ter,
4. Not in the dark of build - ings con - fin - ing,

Now is the dark - ness van - ished a - way,
We are the old— who yearn for your face,
Here we will take the bread of new birth,
Not in some heav - en, light - years a - way, But

See in this space our fears and our dream-ings,
We have been sung through - out all of his - t'ry,
Here you shall call your sons and your daugh-ters,
here in this place the new light is shin - ing,

Brought here to you in the light of this
Called to be light to the whole hu - man
Call us a - new to be salt for the
Now is the King - dom, now is the

day. Gath-er us in— the
race. Gath-er us in— the
earth. Give us to drink the
day. Gath-er us in and

lost and for - sak - en, Gath - er us in— the
rich and the haugh - ty, Gath - er us in— the
wine of com - pas - sion, Give us to eat the
hold us for ev - er, Gath - er us in and

blind   and   the   lame;
proud   and   the   strong;
bread   that   is   you;
make   us   your   own;

Call   to   us   now,   and
Give   us   a   heart   so
Nour - ish   us   well,   and
Gath - er   us   in—   all

we   shall   a - wak - en,
meek and   so   low - ly,
teach   us   to   fash - ion
peo - ples   to - geth - er,

We   shall   a - rise   at   the
Give   us   the   cour - age   to
Lives   that   are   ho - ly   and
Fire   of   love   in   our

sound   of   our
en -   ter   the
hearts   that   are
flesh   and   our

name.
song.
true.
bone.

Text: Marty Haugen, b.1950
Tune: GATHER US IN, Irregular; Marty Haugen, b.1950
© 1982, GIA Publications, Inc.

851 I Rejoiced When I Heard Them Say

1. I re - joiced when I heard them
2. Strong - ly built is Je - ru - sa -
3. Pray for peace in Je - ru - sa -
4. For the love of my fam - i - ly and

say: "Let us go to the house of the
lem, There the tribes of the Lord go
lem, May they pros - per who love you
friends And the sake of the house of the

Lord." Our feet are stand - ing with - in your
up, Seek - ing their jus - tice and bring - ing
well; E - ter - nal peace be with - in your
Lord, I ev - er pray for your health and

gates, O Je - ru - sa - lem.
thanks, O Je - ru - sa - lem.
walls, O Je - ru - sa - lem.
peace, O Je - ru - sa - lem.

I re - joiced when I heard them say:

"Let us go to the house of the Lord!"

I re - joiced when I heard them say:

"Let us go to the house of the Lord!"

Text: Psalm 121; Richard Proulx, b.1937
Tune: MA YEDIDUT; Chassidic Melody, arr. by Richard Proulx, b.1937
© 1993, GIA Publications, Inc.

Only-begotten, Word of God Eternal   852

1. On - ly - be - got - ten, Word of God e -
2. Ho - ly this tem - ple where our Lord is
3. Lord, we be - seech you, as we throng your
4. God in Three Per - sons, Fa - ther ev - er -

ter - nal, Lord of cre - a - tion, mer - ci - ful and
dwell - ing, This is none oth - er than the gate of
tem - ple, By your past bless - ings, by your pres - ent
liv - ing, Son co - e - ter - nal, ev - er - bless - ed

might - y, Hear now your ser - vants, when their tune - ful
heav - en; Stran - gers and pil - grims, seek - ing homes e -
boun - ty, Smile on your chil - dren, and with ten - der
Spir - it, Yours be the glo - ry, praise and ad - or -

voic - es Rise to your pres - ence.
ter - nal, Pass through its por - tals.
mer - cy Hear our pe - ti - tions.
a - tion, Now and for ev - er.

Text: *Christe cunctorum dominator alme;* Latin, 9th C.; tr. by Maxwell J. Blacker, 1822-1888
Tune: ISTE CONFESSOR, 11 11 11 5; Rouen Church Melody; harm. by Carl Schalk, b.1929, © 1969, Concordia Publishing House

853   Now the Feast and Celebration

slain, whose blood has freed and u -

nit - ed us to be one great

D.C.

peo - ple of God.

Verse 2

2. Pow - er and rich - es, wis - dom and might, all

hon - or and glo - ry to Christ for -

D.C.

ev - er.

Verse 3

3. For God has come to dwell with us, to

make us peo - ple of God; to make all

D.C.

things new.

Text: Marty Haugen, b.1950
Tune: Marty Haugen, b.1950
© 1990, GIA Publications, Inc.

854 I Come with Joy

1. I come with joy, a child of God, For-
2. I come with Chris - tians far and near To
3. As Christ breaks bread, and bids us share, Each
4. The Spir - it of the ris - en Christ, Un -
5. To - geth - er met, to - geth - er bound By

giv - en, loved, and free, The life of Je - sus
find, as all are fed, The new com - mu - ni -
proud di - vi - sion ends. The love that made us,
seen, but al - ways near, Is in such friend - ship
all that God has done, We'll go with joy, to

to re - call, In love laid down for me.
ty of love In Christ's com - mu - nion bread.
makes us one, And stran - gers now are friends.
bet - ter known, A - live a - mong us here.
give the world The love that makes us one.

Text: Brian Wren, b.1936, © 1971, Hope Publishing Co.
Tune: LAND OF REST, CM; American; harm. by Annabel M. Buchanan, 1888-1983, © 1938, 1966, J. Fisher and Bro.

Song Over the Waters 855

Refrain

God, you have moved up-on the wa-ters, you have

sung in the rush of wind and flame; and in your

love, you have called us sons and daugh-ters, make us

Last time to coda ⊕ | *To verses* | *To repeat refrain or to sprinkling rite*

peo-ple of the wa-ter and your name. name.

Verses

1. Come fill our wait - ing hearts with the
2. Give us a thirst for love, give us a
3. You are the breath of life, you are the
4. Come, o - pen ev - 'ry heart, come now and

spir - it of Je - sus, let us shine with your
hun - ger for jus - tice, make us one with the
hope of the hope - less, come and fill us with
wake us to won - der, make us ves - sels of

D.S.

light and peace.
mind of Christ.
light and peace.
light and peace.

Coda

unis.

name.   Make us peo - ple of the

unis.

rit.

wa - ter and your name.

rit.

Sprinkling Rite

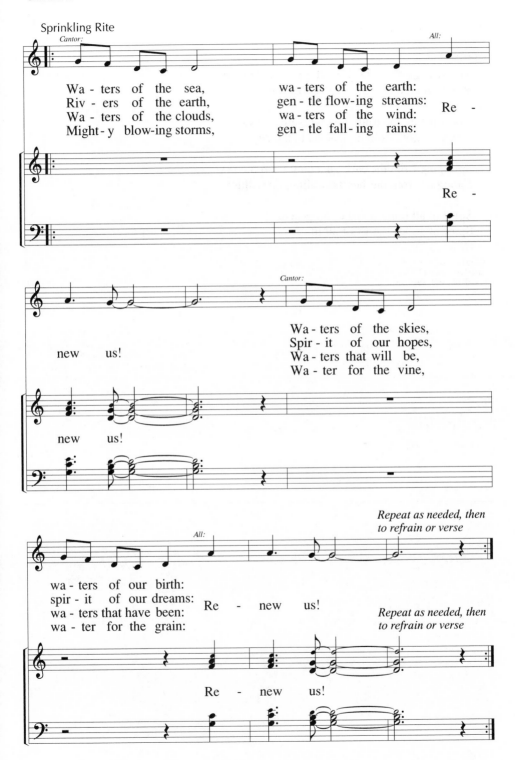

Wa - ters of the sea, wa - ters of the earth:
Riv - ers of the earth, gen - tle flow-ing streams:
Wa - ters of the clouds, wa - ters of the wind:
Might - y blow-ing storms, gen - tle fall - ing rains:

Re - new us!

Wa - ters of the skies,
Spir - it of our hopes,
Wa - ters that will be,
Wa - ter for the vine,

new us!

Repeat as needed, then
to refrain or verse

wa - ters of our birth:
spir - it of our dreams:
wa - ters that have been:
wa - ter for the grain:

Re - new us!

Repeat as needed, then
to refrain or verse

Additional verses for Sprinkling Rite:

Cantor:

You who give us life, you who give us breath:
You beyond our fears, you beyond our death:

You who are the truth, you who are the way:
You who give us light, lead us in the day:

Springing from the earth, dancing from the sky:
Springing from our hearts, welling up within:

Spirit of all hope, spirit of all peace:
Spirit of all joy, spirit of all life:

Text: Marty Haugen, b.1950
Tune: Marty Haugen, b.1950
© 1987, GIA Publications, Inc.

This Day God Gives Me   856

1. This day God gives me Strength of high
2. This day God sends me Strength as my
3. God's way is my way, God's shield is
4. Ris - ing I thank you, Might - y and

heav - en, Sun and moon shin - ing,
guar - dian, Might to up - hold me,
'round me, God's host de - fends me,
strong One, King of cre - a - tion,

Flame in my hearth, Flash - ing of light - ning,
Wis - dom as guide. Your eyes are watch - ful,
Sav - ing from ill. An - gels of heav - en,
Giv - er of rest, Firm - ly con - fess - ing

Wind in its swift - ness, Depths of the
Your ears are lis - t'ning, Your lips are
Drive from me al - ways All that would
God in three Per - sons, One - ness of

Last time

o - cean, Firm - ness of earth.
speak - ing, Friend at my side.
harm me, Stand by me still.
God - head, Trin - i - ty blest.

Text: Ascribed to St. Patrick; James Quinn, S.J., b.1919, © 1969. Used by permission of Selah Publishing Co., Inc., Kingston, N.Y.
Tune: ANDREA, 5 5 5 4 D; David Haas, b.1957, © 1993, GIA Publications, Inc.

857 Today I Awake

1. To - day I a - wake and God is be - fore me. At
2. To - day I a - rise and Christ is be - side me. He
3. To - day I af - firm the Spir - it with - in me At
4. To - day I en - joy the Trin - i - ty round me, A -

night, as I dreamt, he sum-moned the day; For
walked through the dark to scat - ter new light. Yes,
wor - ship and work, in strug - gle and rest. The
bove and be - neath, be - fore and be - hind; The

God nev - er sleeps but pat - terns the morn - ing With
Christ is a - live, and beck - ons his peo - ple To
Spir - it in - spires all life which is chang - ing From
Mak - er, the Son, the Spir - it to - geth - er— They

slith - ers of gold or glo - ry in gray.
hope and to heal, re - sist and in - vite.
fear - ing to faith, from bro - ken to blest.
called me to life and call me their friend.

Text: John L. Bell, b.1949
Tune: SLITHERS OF GOLD, 11 10 11 10; John L. Bell, b.1949
© 1989, Iona Community, GIA Publications, Inc., agent

When Morning Gilds the Skies   858

1. When morn-ing gilds the skies, My heart, a-wak-ing, cries, "May Je-sus Christ be praised!" A-like at work and prayer To Je-sus I re-pair: "May Je-sus Christ be praised!"

2. To God, the Word, on high The hosts of an-gels cry: "May Je-sus Christ be praised!" Let mor-tals, too, up-raise Their voice in hymns of praise: "May Je-sus Christ be praised!"

3. Let earth's wide cir-cle round In joy-ful notes re-sound: "May Je-sus Christ be praised!" Let air, and sea, and sky, From depth to height, re-ply: "May Je-sus Christ be praised!"

4. Be this while life is mine My can-ti-cle di-vine: "May Je-sus Christ be praised!" Be this the e-ter-nal song, Through all the a-ges long: "May Je-sus Christ be praised!"

Text: *Wach ich früh Morgens auf; Katholiches Gesangbuch,* 1828; tr. by Edward Caswall, 1814-1878
Tune: LAUDES DOMINI, 66 6 D; Joseph Barnby, 1838-1896

859 Morning Has Broken

1. Morn-ing has bro-ken Like the first morn-ing, Black-bird has
2. Sweet the rain's new fall Sun-lit from heav-en, Like the first
3. Mine is the sun-light! Mine is the morn-ing Born of the

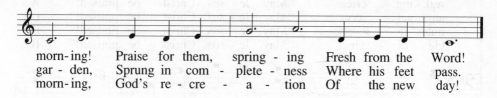

spo-ken Like the first bird. Praise for the sing-ing! Praise for the
dew-fall On the first grass. Praise for the sweet-ness Of the wet
one light E-den saw play! Praise with e - la-tion, Praise ev-'ry

morn-ing! Praise for them, spring-ing Fresh from the Word!
gar-den, Sprung in com - plete - ness Where his feet pass.
morn-ing, God's re-cre - a - tion Of the new day!

Text: Eleanor Farjeon, 1881-1965, *The Children's Bells,* © David Higham Assoc., Ltd.
Tune: BUNESSAN, 5 5 5 4 D; Gaelic; acc. by Marty Haugen, b.1950, © 1987, GIA Publications, Inc.

860 Father, We Praise You

1. Fa - ther, we praise you, now the night is o - ver,
2. Mak - er of all things, fit us for your man-sions;
3. All - ho - ly Fa - ther, Son and e - qual Spir - it,

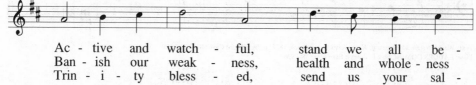

Ac - tive and watch - ful, stand we all be -
Ban - ish our weak - ness, health and whole - ness
Trin - i - ty bless - ed, send us your sal -

fore you; Sing- ing we of - fer pray'r and med- i -
send - ing; Bring us to heav- en, where your saints u -
va - tion; Yours is the glo - ry, gleam- ing and re -

ta - tion: Thus we a - dore you.
nit - ed Joy with- out end - ing.
sound - ing Through all cre - a - tion.

Text: *Nocte Surgentes;* Attr. to St. Gregory the Great, 540-604; tr. by Percy Dearmer, 1867-1936, alt., © Oxford University Press
Tune: CHRISTE SANCTORUM, 11 11 11 5; La Feillees *Methode du plain-chant,* 1782

Kindle a Flame to Lighten the Dark 861

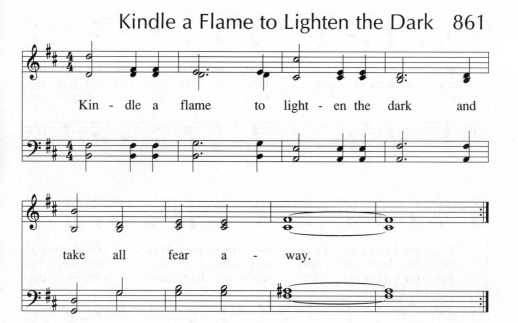

Kin - dle a flame to light - en the dark and

take all fear a - way.

Text: John L. Bell, b.1949
Tune: John L. Bell, b.1949
© 1987, Iona Community, GIA Publications, Inc., agent

862 Day Is Done

1. Day   is   done,   but   love   un-fail-ing Dwells   ev - er
2. Dark   de-scends, but   light un-end-ing Shines   through   our
3. Eyes   will close, but   you   un-sleep-ing Watch   by   our

here;   Shad - ows fall, but   hope,   pre-vail - ing,
night;   You   are with us,   ev - er lend - ing
side;   Death may come, in   love's   safe keep - ing

Calms   ev - 'ry fear.   God,   our Mak - er, none for-sak - ing,
New   strength to sight: One   in   love, your truth con-fess - ing,
Still   we   a - bide.   God   of   love, all   e - vil quell-ing,

Take our hearts, of Love's   own mak - ing, Watch   our sleep-ing
One in hope of   heav - en's bless-ing, May   we see, in
Sin for - giv-ing,   fear   dis - pel - ling, Stay   with us, our

guard   our   wak - ing,   Be   al -   ways   near.
love's   pos - sess - ing,   Love's   end -   less   light!
hearts in - dwell - ing,   This   e -   ven - tide.

Text: James Quinn, SJ, b.1919, © 1969, Used by permission of Selah Publishing, Inc., Kingston, N.Y.
Tune: AR HYD Y NOS, 8 4 8 4 888 4; Welsh

Our Darkness / La Ténèbre 863

Our   dark - ness is nev - er dark-ness in your   sight: the
La té - nè - bre n'est point té - nè - bre de - vant   toi: la

deep - est night is   clear as the   day -   light.
nuit com - me le   jour est lu - miè -   re.

Text: Taizé Community
Tune: Jacques Berthier, 1923-1994
© 1991, Les Presses de Taizé, GIA Publications, Inc., agent

864　At Evening

1. Now it is eve - ning: Lights of the cit - y
2. Now it is eve - ning: Lit - tle ones sleep - ing
3. Now it is eve - ning: Food on the ta - ble
4. Now it is eve - ning: Here in our meet - ing

Bid us re - mem - ber Christ is our Light.
Bid us re - mem - ber Christ is our Peace.
Bids us re - mem - ber Christ is our Life.
May we re - mem - ber Christ is our Friend.

Man - y are lone - ly, Who will be neigh- bor?
Some are ne - glect - ed, Who will be neigh- bor?
Man - y are hun - gry, Who will be neigh- bor?
Some may be stran - gers, Who will be neigh- bor?

Where there is car - ing Christ is our Light.
Where there is car - ing Christ is our Peace.
Where there is shar - ing Christ is our Life.
Where there's a wel - come Christ is our Friend.

Text: Fred Pratt Green, b.1903, © 1974, Hope Publishing Co.
Tune: EVENING HYMN, 5 5 5 4 D; David Haas, b.1957, © 1985, GIA Publications, Inc.

Christ, Mighty Savior 865

1. Christ, might - y Sav - ior, Light of all cre -
2. Now comes the day's end as the sun is
3. There - fore we come now eve - ning rites to
4. Give heed, we pray you, to our sup - pli -
5. Though bod - ies slum - ber, hearts shall keep their

a - tion, You make the day - time
set - ting: Mir - ror of day - break,
of - fer, Joy - ful - ly chant - ing
ca - tion: That you may grant us
vig - il, For ev - er rest - ing

ra - diant with the sun - light And to the
pledge of res - ur - rec - tion; While in the
ho - ly hymns to praise you, With all cre -
par - don for of - fens - es, Strength for our
in the peace of Je - sus, In light or

night give glit - ter - ing a - dorn - ment,
heav - ens choirs of stars ap - pear - ing
a - tion join - ing hearts and voic - es
weak hearts, rest for ach - ing bod - ies,
dark - ness wor - ship - ing our Sav - ior

Stars in the heav - ens.
Hal - low the night - fall.
Sing - ing your glo - ry.
Sooth - ing the wea - ry.
Now and for - ev - er.

Text: *Christe, lux mundi;* Mozarabic Rite, 10th C.; tr. by Alan G. McDougall, 1895-1964, rev. by Anne K. LeCroy, b.1930, and others, ©
Tune: MIGHTY SAVIOR, 11 11 11 5; David Hurd, b.1950, © 1985, GIA Publications, Inc.

866 The Day You Gave Us, Lord, Is Ended

1. The day you gave us, Lord, is end-ed, The
2. We thank you that your Church, un-sleep-ing While
3. A-cross each con-ti-nent and is-land As
4. The sun that bids us rest is wak-ing Your
5. So be it, Lord; your throne shall nev-er, Like

dark-ness falls at your be-hest; To
earth rolls on-ward in-to light, Through
dawn leads on an-oth-er day, The
friends be-neath the west-ern sky, And
earth's proud em-pires, pass a-way: Your

you our morn-ing hymns as-cend-ed, Your
all the world its watch is keep-ing, And
voice of prayer is nev-er si-lent, Nor
hour by hour fresh lips are mak-ing Your
king-dom stands, and grows for ev-er, Till

praise shall sanc-ti-fy our rest.
rests not now by day or night.
dies the strain of praise a-way.
won-drous do-ings heard on high.
all your crea-tures own your sway.

Text: John Ellerton, 1826-1893, alt.
Tune: ST. CLEMENT, 9 8 9 8; Clement C. Scholefield, 1839-1904

Praise and Thanksgiving 867

1. Praise and thanks - giv - ing, Fa - ther, we of - fer,
2. Lord, bless the la - bor We bring to serve you,
3. Fa - ther, pro - vid - ing Food for your chil - dren,
4. Then will your bless - ing Reach ev - 'ry peo - ple,

For all things liv - ing You have made good.
That with our neigh - bor We may be fed.
Your wis - dom guid - ing Teach-es us share
Free - ly con - fess - ing Your gra - cious hand.

Har - vest of sown fields, Fruits of the or - chard,
Sow - ing or till - ing, We would work with you,
One with an - oth - er, So that re - joic - ing
Where you are reign - ing No one will hun - ger,

Hay from the mown fields, Blos - som and wood.
Har - vest - ing, mill - ing, For dai - ly bread.
With us, all oth - ers May know your care.
Your love sus - tain - ing, Fruit - ful the land.

Text: Albert F. Bayly, 1901-1984, © Oxford University Press
Tune: BUNESSAN, 5 5 5 4 D; Gaelic; harm. by A. Gregory Murray, OSB, 1905-1992, © Downside Abbey

868 When the Lord in Glory Comes

1. When the Lord in glo - ry comes not the
   shout the heav - ens raise, not the
2. When the Lord is seen a - gain not the
   pomp and pow'r a - lone, not the
3. When the Lord to hu - man eyes shall be -
   man by all de - nied, not the

trum - pets, not the drums, not the an - them, not the
cho - rus, not the praise, not the si - lenc - es sub-
glo - ries of his reign, not the light - nings through the
splen - dors of his throne, not his robe and di - a-
stride our nar - row skies, not the child of hum - ble
vic - tim cru - ci - fied, but the God who died to

1., 3., 5.

psalm, not the thun - der, not the calm, not the
lime, not the sounds of space and
storm, not the ra - diance of his form, not his
dems, not the gold and not the
birth, not the car - pen - ter of earth, not the
save, but the vic - tor of the

Text: Timothy Dudley-Smith, b.1926, © 1967, Hope Publishing Co.
Tune: ST. JOHN'S, 77 77 77D; Bob Moore, b.1962, © 1993, GIA Publications, Inc.

869 Mine Eyes Have Seen the Glory

1. Mine eyes have seen the glo - ry of the
2. I have seen him in the watch - fires of a
3. He has sound - ed forth the trum - pet that shall
4. In the beau - ty of the lil - ies Christ was

com - ing of the Lord; He is tram - pling out the
hun - dred cir - cling camps; They have build - ed him an
nev - er call re - treat; He is sift - ing out all
born a - cross the sea, With a glo - ry in his

vin - tage where the grapes of wrath are stored; He hath
al - tar in the eve - ning dews and damps; I can
hu - man hearts be - fore his judg - ment seat; O be
bos - om that trans - fig - ures you and me; As he

loosed the fate - ful light - ning of his ter - ri - ble swift
read the right - eous sen - tence by the dim and flar - ing
swift, my soul, to an - swer him; be ju - bi - lant, my
died to make us ho - ly, let us die that all be

sword; His truth is march - ing on.
lamps; His day is march - ing on.
feet! Our God is march - ing on.
free! While God is march - ing on.

Glo - ry! Glo - ry! Hal - le - lu - jah! Glo - ry!

Glo - ry! Hal - le - lu - jah! Glo - ry! Glo - ry!

Hal - le - lu - jah! His truth is march - ing on.

Text: Julia W. Howe, 1819-1910
Tune: BATTLE HYMN OF THE REPUBLIC, 15 15 15 6 with refrain; attr. to William Steffe, d.1911

870 Soon and Very Soon

1. Soon and ver - y soon we are goin' to see the King,
2. No more cry - in' there we are goin' to see the King,
3. No more dy - in' there we are goin' to see the King,
4. Soon and ver - y soon we are goin' to see the King,

Soon and ver - y soon we are
No more cry - in' there we are
No more dy - in' there we are
Soon and ver - y soon we are

goin' to see the King, Soon and ver - y soon
goin' to see the King, No more cry - in' there
goin' to see the King, No more dy - in' there
goin' to see the King, Soon and ver - y soon

we are goin' to see the King, Hal - le -

lu - jah, Hal - le - lu - jah, we're goin' to see the King!

Hal - le - lu - jah, Hal - le - lu - jah, Hal - le - lu - jah, Hal - le - lu - jah.

Text: Andraé Crouch
Tune: Andraé Crouch
© 1976, Bud John Songs, Inc./Crouch Music/ASCAP

871 Jerusalem, My Happy Home

1. Je - ru - sa - lem, my hap - py home, When
2. Your saints are crowned with glo - ry great; They
3. There Da - vid stands with harp in hand As
4. Our La - dy sings Mag - nif - i - cat With
5. There Mag - da - lene has left her tears, And
6. Je - ru - sa - lem, Je - ru - sa - lem, God

shall I with you be? When shall my sor - rows
see God face to face; They tri - umph still, they
mas - ter of the choir: Ten thou - sand times that
tune sur - pass - ing sweet; And all the vir - gins
cheer - ful - ly does sing With bless - ed saints, whose
grant that I may see Your end - less joy, and

have an end? Your joys when shall I see?
still re - joice: In that most ho - ly place.
we were blest That might this mu - sic hear.
join the song While sit - ting at her feet.
har - mo - ny In ev - 'ry street does ring.
of the same Par - tak - er ev - er be!

Text: Joseph Bromehead, 1747-1826, alt.
Tune: LAND OF REST, CM; American; harm. by Richard Proulx, b.1937, © 1975, GIA Publications, Inc.

872 We Shall Rise Again

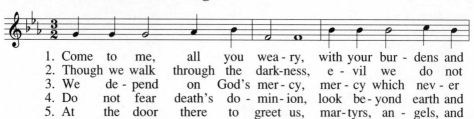

1. Come to me, all you wea - ry, with your bur - dens and
2. Though we walk through the dark-ness, e - vil we do not
3. We de - pend on God's mer - cy, mer - cy which nev - er
4. Do not fear death's do - min - ion, look be - yond earth and
5. At the door there to greet us, mar - tyrs, an - gels, and

pain. Take my yoke on your shoul - ders and
fear. You are walk - ing be - side us with your
fades. We re - mem - ber our cov - e - nant and the
grave. See the bright - ness of Je - sus shin - ing
saints, And our fam - 'ly and loved ones, ev - 'ry -

learn from me: I am gen - tle and hum - ble,
rod and your staff. On - ly good - ness and kind - ness
prom - ise Je - sus made: If we die with Christ Je - sus,
out to light our way. Lov - ing Fa - ther and Spir - it,
one freed from their chains. We shall feel their ac - cep - tance,

and your soul will find rest, For my yoke is
fol - low us all our lives. We shall dwell in the
we shall live with him, And if we are
lov - ing Je - sus the Son, All God's peo - ple to -
and the joy of new life. We shall join in the

eas - y and my bur - den is light.
Lord's house for so man - y years to come!
faith - ful, we shall reign with him! We shall
geth - er, we shall live on as one!
gath - er - ing, re - u - nit - ed in God's love!

rise a - gain on the last day with the faith - ful, rich and poor. Com - ing

to the house of Lord Je - sus, we will find an o - pen

door there, we will find an o - pen door.

1.-4   5.

Text: Matthew 11:29-30, Psalm 23, John 11, 2 Timothy 2; Jeremy Young, b.1948
Tune: RESURRECTION; Irregular with refrain; Jeremy Young, b.1948
©1987, GIA Publications, Inc.

873 Steal Away to Jesus

Refrain

Steal a-way, steal a-way, steal a-way to Je-sus!

Steal a-way, steal a-way home, I ain't got long to stay here.

Verses

1. My Lord, he calls me, He calls me by the thun-der; The
2. Green trees are bend-ing, Poor sin-ners stand a trem-bling; The
3. My Lord, he calls me, He calls me by the light-ning; The

D.C.

trum-pet sounds with-in my soul; I ain't got long to stay here.

Text: African-American spiritual
Tune: African-American spiritual

Lord, Bid Your Servant Go in Peace 874

1. Lord, bid your ser - vant go in peace, Your word is now ful - filled. These eyes have seen sal - va - tion's dawn, This child so long fore - told.

2. This is the Sav - ior of the world, The gen - tiles' prom - ised light, God's glo - ry dwell - ing in our midst, The joy of Is - ra - el.

3. This child shall see the rise, the fall, Of those in Is - ra - el, God's sign raised high for all to see, Whom some shall yet de - ny.

4. His moth - er's soul a sword shall pierce, Of sor - row keen and deep; And se - cret thoughts of man - y hearts Through him shall be re - vealed.

5. Blest be the Fa - ther, who has giv'n His Son to be our Lord, Blest too that Son, and with them both The Spir - it of their love.

875 Come Now, and Praise the Humble Saint

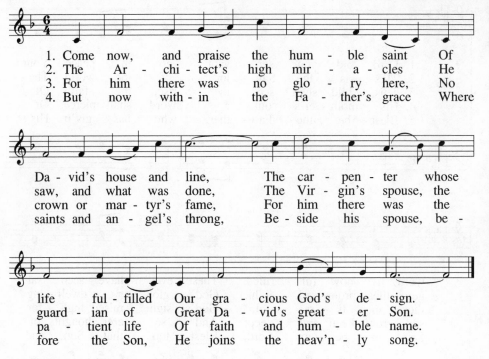

1. Come now, and praise the hum - ble saint Of
2. The Ar - chi - tect's high mir - a - cles He
3. For him there was no glo - ry here, No
4. But now with - in the Fa - ther's grace Where

Da - vid's house and line, The car - pen - ter whose
saw, and what was done, The Vir - gin's spouse, the
crown or mar - tyr's fame, For him there was the
saints and an - gel's throng, Be - side his spouse, be -

life ful - filled Our gra - cious God's de - sign.
guard - ian of Great Da - vid's great - er Son.
pa - tient life Of faith and hum - ble name.
fore the Son, He joins the heav'n - ly song.

Text: G. W. Williams, b.1922, © 1979, Hymn Society of America
Tune: LAND OF REST, CM; American; harm. by Richard Proulx, b.1937, © 1975, GIA Publications, Inc.

876 No Wind at the Window

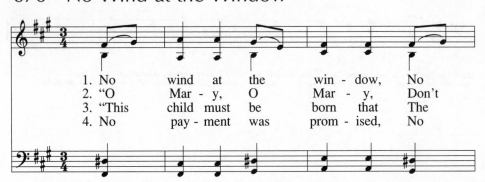

1. No wind at the win - dow, No
2. "O Mar - y, O Mar - y, Don't
3. "This child must be born that The
4. No pay - ment was prom - ised, No

knock on the door; No light from the lamp-stand, No
hide from my face. Be glad that you're fa - vored And
king - dom might come: Sal - va - tion for man - y, De -
prom - is - es made; No wed - ding was dat - ed, No

foot on the floor; No dream born of
filled with God's grace. The time for re -
struc - tion for some; Both end and be -
blue - print dis - played. Yet Mar - y, con -

tired - ness, No ghost raised by fear: Just an
deem - ing The world has be - gun; And
gin - ning, Both mes - sage and sign; Both
sent - ing To what none could guess, Re -

an - gel and a wom - an And a voice in her ear.
you are re - quest - ed To moth - er God's son.
vic - tor and vic - tim, Both yours and di - vine."
plied with con - vic - tion, "Tell God I say yes."

Text: John L. Bell, b.1949
Tune: COLUMCILLE, Irregular; Gaelic, arr. by John L. Bell, b.1949

877 Praise We the Lord This Day

1. Praise we the Lord this day, This day so long fore-told, Whose prom-ise shone with cheer-ing ray On wait-ing saints of old.
2. The Proph-et gave the sign For faith-ful folk to read: A vir-gin, born of Da-vid's line, Shall bear the prom-ised Seed.
3. Ask not how this should be, But wor-ship and a-dore Like her whom God's own maj-es-ty Came down to shad-ow o'er.
4. She meek-ly bowed her head To hear the gra-cious word, Mar-y, the pure and low-ly maid, The fa-vored of the Lord.
5. Bless-ed shall be her name In all the Church on earth, Through whom that won-drous mer-cy came, The in-car-nate Sav-ior's birth.
6. O Christ, the Vir-gin's Son, We praise you and a-dore, You are with God the Fa-ther One And Spir-it ev-er-more.

Text: Matthew 1:23; *Hymns for the Festivals and Saints' Days*, 1846
Tune: SWABIA, SM; Johann M. Speiss, 1715-1772; adapt. by William H. Havergal, 1793-1870

When Jesus Came to Jordan 878

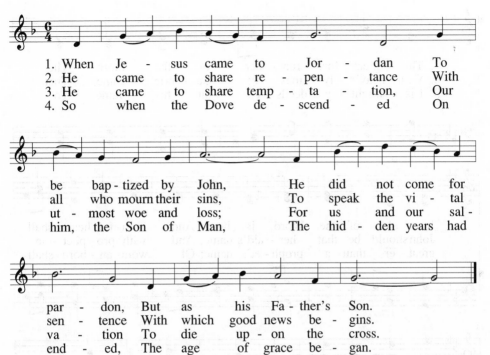

1. When Je - sus came to Jor - dan To
2. He came to share re - pen - tance With
3. He came to share temp - ta - tion, Our
4. So when the Dove de - scend - ed On

be bap - tized by John, He did not come for
all who mourn their sins, To speak the vi - tal
ut - most woe and loss; For us and our sal -
him, the Son of Man, The hid - den years had

par - don, But as his Fa - ther's Son.
sen - tence With which good news be - gins.
va - tion To die up - on the cross.
end - ed, The age of grace be - gan.

Text: Fred Pratt Green, b.1903, © 1980, Hope Publishing Co.
Tune: DE EERSTEN ZIJN DE LAATSTEN, 7 6 7 6; Frits Mehrtens, 1922-1975, © Interkerkelijke Stichting voorhet Kerklied

879 The Great Forerunner of the Morn

1. The great fore-run-ner of the morn, The
2. With heav'n-ly mes-sage Ga-briel came, That
3. His might-y deeds ex-alt his fame To

her-ald of the Word, is born; And faith-ful hearts shall
John should be that her-ald's name, And with pro-phet-ic
great-er than a proph-et's name; Of wom-an-born shall

nev-er fail With thanks and praise his light to hail.
ut-t'rance told His ac-tions great and man-i-fold.
nev-er be A great-er proph-et than was he.

Text: *Praecursor altus luminis;* Venerable Bede, 673-735; tr. by John M. Neale, 1818-1866, alt.
Tune: WINCHESTER NEW, LM; adapt. from *Musikalisches Handbuch,* Hamburg, 1690

880 Two Noble Saints

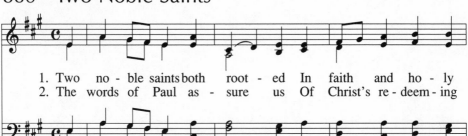

1. Two no-ble saints both root-ed In faith and ho-ly
2. The words of Paul as-sure us Of Christ's re-deem-ing

love,   By hope of God u - nit - ed They
word;   The works of Pe - ter show us How

reach to heaven a - bove. One on a cross is
we may serve the Lord. So praise we the Cre -

mar - tyred, One by the sword is slain; Both tri - umph
a - tor, And praise we Christ the Son, Who with the

in their dy - ing, Both glo - rious saint- hood gain.
Ho - ly Spir - it, Now reign, blest Three in One.

Text: Based on *Decora lux aeternitatis auream*, by Anne K. LeCroy, b.1930, ©
Tune: ELLACOMBE, 7 6 7 6 D; *Gesangbuch der Herzogl*, Wirtemberg, 1784

881 Transform Us

1. Trans - form us as you, trans - fig - ured,
2. Trans - form us as you, trans - fig - ured,
3. Trans - form us as you, trans - fig - ured,

Stood a - part on Ta - bor's height.
Once spoke with those ho - ly ones.
Would not stay with - in a shrine.

Lead us up our sa - cred moun - tains,
We, sur - round - ed by the wit - ness
Keep us from our great temp - ta - tion—

Search us with re - veal - ing light.
Of those saints whose work is done,
Time and truth we quick - ly bind,

Lift us from where we have fall - en,
Live in this world as your Bod - y,
Lead us down those dai - ly path - ways

Full of ques - tions, filled with fright.
Cho - sen daugh - ters cho - sen sons.
Where our love is not con - fined.

Text: Sylvia Dunstan, 1955-1993, © 1993, GIA Publications, Inc.
Tune: PICARDY, 8 7 8 7 8 7; French Carol; harm. by Richard Proulx, b.1937, © 1986, GIA Publications, Inc.

'Tis Good, Lord, to Be Here   882

1. 'Tis good, Lord, to be here! Your
2. 'Tis good, Lord, to be here, Your
3. Ful - fill - er of the past! Prom -
4. Be - fore we taste of death, We
5. 'Tis good, Lord, to be here! Yet

glo - ry fills the night; Your face and gar - ments,
beau - ty to be - hold, Where Mo - ses and E -
ise of things to be! We hail your bod - y
see your king - dom come; We long to hold the
we may not re - main; But since you bid us

like the sun, Shine with un - bor - rowed light.
li - jah stand, Your mes - sen - gers of old.
glo - ri - fied, And our re - demp - tion see.
vi - sion bright, And make this hill our home.
leave the mount, Come with us to the plain.

Text: Luke 9:32-33; Joseph A. Robinson, 1858-1933, alt., © Esme. D. E. Bird
Tune: SWABIA, SM; Johann M. Speiss, 1715-1772; adapt. by William H. Havergal, 1793-1870

883 Hail, Holy Queen Enthroned Above

1. Hail, ho - ly Queen en - throned a - bove, O Ma -
2. The cause of joy to all be - low, O Ma -
3. O gen - tle, lov - ing, ho - ly one, O Ma -

ri - a. Hail, Queen of mer - cy and of love,
ri - a. The spring through which all grac - es flow,
ri - a. The God of light be - came your Son,

O Ma - ri - a. Tri - umph, all ye
O Ma - ri - a. An - gels, all your
O Ma - ri - a. Tri - umph, all ye

Cher - u - bim, Sing with us, ye Ser - a - phim,
prais - es bring, Earth and heav - en, with us sing,
Cher - u - bim, Sing with us, ye Ser - a - phim,

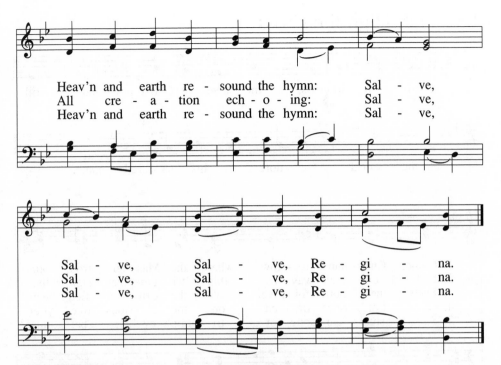

Heav'n and earth re - sound the hymn: Sal - ve,
All cre - a - tion ech - o - ing: Sal - ve,
Heav'n and earth re - sound the hymn: Sal - ve,

Sal - ve, Sal - ve, Re - gi - na.
Sal - ve, Sal - ve, Re - gi - na.
Sal - ve, Sal - ve, Re - gi - na.

Text: *Salve, Regina, mater misericordia;* c.1080; tr. *Roman Hymnal,* 1884; st. 2-3 adapt. by M. Owen Lee, CSB, b.1930
Tune: SALVE REGINA COELITUM, 8 4 8 4 777 4 5; *Choralmelodien zum Heiligen Gesänge,* 1808; harm. by Healey Willan, 1880-1968, © Willis
    Music Co.

884 Lift High the Cross

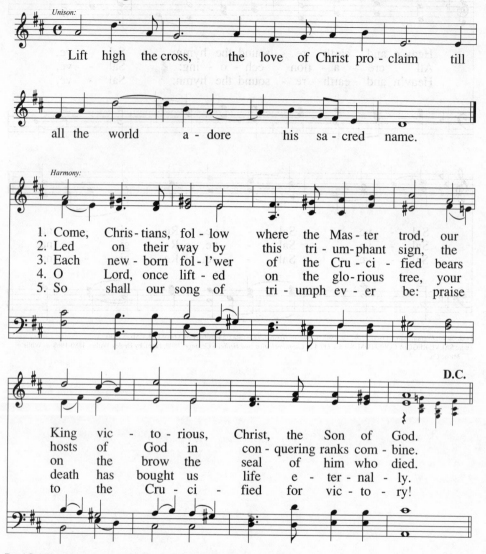

Lift high the cross, the love of Christ pro-claim till
all the world a-dore his sa-cred name.

1. Come, Chris-tians, fol-low where the Mas-ter trod, our
2. Led on their way by this tri-um-phant sign, the
3. Each new-born fol-l'wer of the Cru-ci-fied bears
4. O Lord, once lift-ed on the glo-rious tree, your
5. So shall our song of tri-umph ev-er be: praise

King vic-to-rious, Christ, the Son of God.
hosts of God in con-quering ranks com-bine.
on the brow the seal of him who died.
death has bought us life e-ter-nal-ly.
to the Cru-ci-fied for vic-to-ry!

Text: 1 Corinthians 1:18; George W. Kitchin, 1827-1912, and Michael R. Newbolt, 1874-1956, alt.
Tune: CRUCIFER, 10 10 with refrain; Sydney H. Nicholson, 1875-1947
© 1978, Hope Publishing Co.

For All the Faithful Women 885

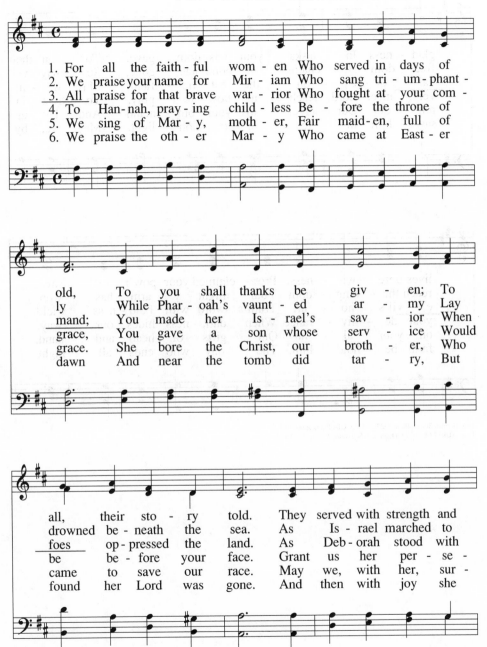

1. For all the faith-ful wom-en Who served in days of old, To you shall thanks be giv - en; To all, their sto - ry told. They served with strength and

2. We praise your name for Mir - iam Who sang tri - um-phant-ly While Phar - oah's vaunt - ed ar - my Lay drowned be - neath the sea. As Is - rael marched to

3. All praise for that brave war - rior Who fought at your com - mand; You made her Is - rael's sav - ior When foes op - pressed the land. As Deb - orah stood with

4. To Han-nah, pray - ing child - less Be - fore the throne of grace, You gave a son whose serv - ice Would be be - fore your face. Grant us her per - se -

5. We sing of Mar - y, moth - er, Fair maid - en, full of grace. She bore the Christ, our broth - er, Who came to save our race. May we, with her, sur -

6. We praise the oth - er Mar - y Who came at East - er dawn And near the tomb did tar - ry, But found her Lord was gone. And then with joy she

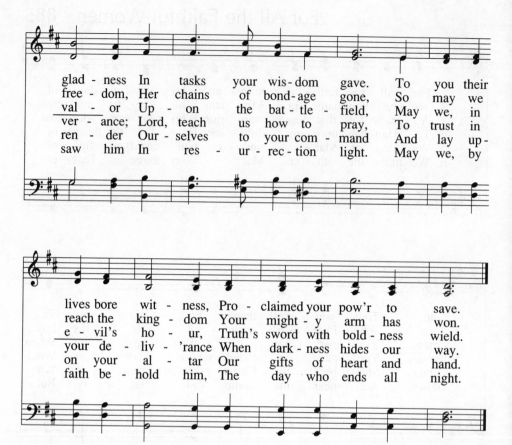

glad - ness In tasks your wis-dom gave. To you their
free - dom, Her chains of bond-age gone, So may we
val - or Up - on the bat - tle - field, May we, in
ver - ance; Lord, teach us how to pray, To trust in
saw him In res - ur - rec-tion light. May we, by

lives bore wit - ness, Pro - claimed your pow'r to save.
reach the king - dom Your might - y arm has won.
e - vil's ho - ur, Truth's sword with bold - ness wield.
your de - liv - 'rance When dark - ness hides our way.
on your al - tar Our gifts of heart and hand.
faith be - hold him, The day who ends all night.

Text: Herman Stuempfle, b.1923, © 1993, GIA Publications, Inc.
Tune: AURELIA, 7 6 7 6 D; Samuel Sebastian Wesley, 1810-1876

Ye Watchers and Ye Holy Ones   886

1. Ye watch - ers and ye ho - ly ones,
2. O high - er than the cher - u - bim,
3. Re - spond, ye souls in end - less rest,
4. O friends, in glad - ness let us sing,

Bright ser - aphs, cher - u - bim, and thrones,
More glo - rious than the ser - a - phim,
Ye pa - tri - archs and proph - ets blest,
Su - per - nal an - thems ech - o - ing,

[⌒]

Raise the glad strain,
Lead their prais - es,
Al - le - lu - ia,   Al - le - lu - ia!
Al - le - lu - ia,

Cry out, do - min - ions, prince - doms, powers,
O bear - er of the e - ter - nal Word,
Ye ho - ly Twelve, ye mar - tyrs strong,
To God the Fa - ther, God the Son,

Vir - tues, arch - an - gels, an - gels' choirs,
Most gra - cious, mag - ni - fy the Lord,
All saints tri - um - phant, raise in song,
And God the Spir - it, Three in One,

Al - le - lu - ia, Al - le - lu - ia, Al - le - lu - ia,

Al - le - lu - ia, Al - le - lu - ia!

Text: Athelstan A. Riley, 1858-1945, © Oxford University Press
Tune: LASST UNS ERFREUEN, LM with alleluias; *Geistliche Kirchengasänge*, Cologne, 1623; harm. by Ralph Vaughan Williams, 1872-1958,
© Oxford University Press

887 By All Your Saints Still Striving

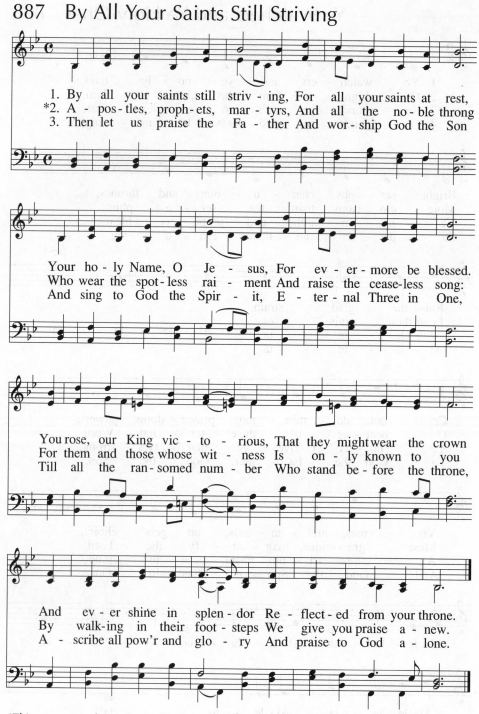

1. By all your saints still striv - ing, For all your saints at rest,
*2. A - pos - tles, proph - ets, mar - tyrs, And all the no - ble throng
3. Then let us praise the Fa - ther And wor - ship God the Son

Your ho - ly Name, O Je - sus, For ev - er - more be blessed.
Who wear the spot - less rai - ment And raise the cease - less song:
And sing to God the Spir - it, E - ter - nal Three in One,

You rose, our King vic - to - rious, That they might wear the crown
For them and those whose wit - ness Is on - ly known to you
Till all the ran - somed num - ber Who stand be - fore the throne,

And ev - er shine in splen - dor Re - flect - ed from your throne.
By walk - ing in their foot - steps We give you praise a - new.
A - scribe all pow'r and glo - ry And praise to God a - lone.

*This stanza may be replaced by an appropriate stanza taken from the following pages.

Text: Based on Horatio Nelson, 1823-1913, by Jerry D. Godwin, b.1944, © 1985, The Church Pension Fund
Tune: ST. THEODULPH, 7 6 7 6 D; Melchior Teschner, 1584-1635

January 25: Conversion of Paul

Praise for the light from heaven
   And for the voice of awe:
Praise for the glorious vision
   The persecutor saw.
O Lord, for Paul's conversion,
   We bless your Name today.
Come shine within our darkness
   And guide us in the Way.

February 22: Chair of Peter

We praise you, Lord, for Peter,
   So eager and so bold:
Thrice falling, yet repentant,
   Thrice charged to feed your fold.
Lord, make your pastors faithful
   To guard your flock from harm
And hold them when they waver
   With your almighty arm.

March 19: Joseph, Husband of Mary

All praise, O God, for Joseph,
   The guardian of your Son,
Who saved him from King Herod,
   When safety there was none.
He taught the trade of builder,
   When they to Naz'reth came,
And Joseph's love made "Father"
   To be, for Christ, God's name.

March 25: Annunciation of Our Lord

We sing with joy of Mary
   Whose heart with awe was stirred
When, youthful and unready,
   She heard the angel's word;
Yet she her voice upraises
   God's glory to proclaim,
As once for our salvation
   Your mother she became.

April 25: Mark

For Mark, O Lord, we praise you,
   The weak by grace made strong:
His witness in his Gospel
   Becomes victorious song.
May we, in all our weakness,
   Receive your power divine,
And all, as faithful branches,
   Grow strong in you, the Vine.

May 3: Philip and James

We praise you, Lord, for Philip,
   Blest guide to Greek and Jew,
And for young James the faithful,
   Who heard and followed you,
O grant us grace to know you,
   The victor in the strife,
That we with all your servants
   May wear the crown of life.

May 14: Matthias

For one in place of Judas,
   The apostles sought God's choice:
The lot fell to Matthias
   For whom we now rejoice.
May we like true apostles
   Your holy Church defend,
And not betray our calling
   But serve you to the end.

June 11: Barnabas

For Barnabas we praise you,
   Who kept your law of love
And, leaving earthly treasures,
   Sought riches from above.
O Christ, our Lord and Savior,
   Let gifts of grace descend,
That your true consolation
   May through the world extend.

June 24: Birth of John the Baptist

All praise for John the Baptist,
   Forerunner of the Word,
Our true Elijah, making
   A highway for the Lord.
The last and greatest prophet,
   He saw the dawning ray
Of light that grows in splendor
   Until the perfect day.

June 29: Peter and Paul

We praise you for Saint Peter;
   We praise you for Saint Paul.
They taught both Jew and Gentile
   that Christ is all in all.
To cross and sword they yielded
   And saw the kingdom come:
O God, your two apostles
   Won life through martyrdom.

July 3: Thomas

All praise, O Lord, for Thomas
　　Whose short-lived doubtings prove
Your perfect twofold nature,
　　The depth of your true love.
To all who live with questions
　　A steadfast faith afford;
And grant us grace to know you,
　　Made flesh, yet God and Lord.

July 22: Mary Magdalene

All praise for Mary Magd'lene,
　　Whose wholeness was restored
By you, her faithful Master,
　　Her Savior and her Lord.
On Easter morning early,
　　A word from you sufficed:
Her faith was first to see you,
　　Her Lord, the risen Christ.

July 25: James

O Lord, for James, we praise you,
　　Who fell to Herod's sword.
He drank the cup of suff'ring
　　And thus fulfilled your word.
Lord, curb our vain impatience
　　For glory and for fame,
Equip us for such suff'rings
　　As glorify your Name.

August 24: Bartholomew

Praised for your blest apostle
　　Surnamed Bartholomew;
We know not his achievements
　　But know that he was true,
For he at the Ascension
　　Was an apostle still.
May we discern your presence
　　And seek, like him, your will.

September 21: Matthew

We praise you, Lord, for Matthew,
　　Whose gospel words declare
That, worldly gain forsaking,
　　Your path of life we share.
From all unrighteous mammon,
　　O raise our eyes anew,
That we, whate'er our station
　　May rise and follow you.

October 18: Luke

For Luke, beloved physician,
　　All praise; whose Gospel shows
The healer of the nations,
　　The one who shares our woes.
Your wine and oil, O Savior,
　　Upon our spirits pour,
And with true balm of Gilead
　　Anoint us evermore.

October 28: Simon and Jude

Praise, Lord, for your apostles,
　　Saint Simon and Saint Jude.
One love, one hope impelled them
　　To tread the way, renewed.
May we with zeal as earnest
　　The faith of Christ maintain,
Be bound in love together,
　　And life eternal gain.

November 30: Andrew

All praise, O Lord, for Andrew,
　　The first to follow you;
He witnessed to his brother,
　　"This is Messiah true."
You called him from his fishing
　　Upon Lake Galilee;
He rose to meet your challenge,
　　"Leave all and follow me."

December 26: Stephen

All praise, O Lord, for Stephen
　　Who, martyred, saw you stand
To help in time of torment,
　　To plead at God's right hand.
Like you, our suff'ring Savior,
　　His enemies he blessed,
With "Lord, receive my spirit,"
　　His faith, in death, confessed.

December 27: John

For John, your loved disciple,
　　Exiled to Patmos' shore,
And for his faithful record,
　　We praise you evermore;
Praise for the mystic vision
　　His words to us unfold.
Instill in us his longing,
　　Your glory to behold.

December 28: Holy Innocents

Praise for your infant martyrs,
   Whom your mysterious love
Called early from life's conflicts
   To share your peace above.
O Rachel, cease your weeping;
   They're free from pain and cares.
Lord, grant us crowns as brilliant
   And lives as pure as theirs.

Give Thanks to God on High   888

1. Give thanks to God on high For saints of
2. Their vi - sion long ful - filled, Our prayer is
3. New tasks to - day are ours Who serve a
4. Give thanks to God on high For all the

oth - er days, Whose hope it was to
still the same; Up - on their work of
world in pain, New calls to chal - lenge
fu - ture sends, In praise of Christ to

live and die In love's con - sum - ing blaze,
faith to build, Their word of truth pro - claim,
all our pow'rs Of heart and hand and brain,
live and die Who calls his ser - vants friends,

For Christ and his king-dom, His glo - ry and his praise.
For Christ and his king-dom, And for his ho - ly name.
For Christ and his king-dom, While life and breath re - main.
For Christ and his king-dom, Whose glo - ry nev - er ends.

Text: Timothy Dudley-Smith, b.1926, © 1985, Hope Publishing Co.
Tune: BALDWIN, 6 6 8 6 6 6; James J. Chepponis, b.1956, © 1987, GIA Publications, Inc.

889 For All the Saints

1. For all the saints who from their la - bors
2. You were their rock, their for - tress and their
3. O may your sol - diers, faith - ful, true and
7. But then there breaks a yet more glo - rious
8. From earth's wide bounds, from o - cean's far - thest

rest, All who by faith be - fore the world con -
might; You, Lord, their Cap - tain in the well - fought
bold, Fight as the saints who no - bly fought of
day: The saints tri - um - phant rise in bright ar -
coast, Through gates of pearl streams in the count - less

fessed, Your name, O Je - sus, be for ev - er blest.
fight; You in the dark - ness drear, their one true light.
old, And win with them, the vic - tor's crown of gold.
ray; The King of glo - ry pass - es on his way.
host, Sing - ing to Fa - ther, Son, and Ho - ly Ghost:

Al - le - lu - ia! Al - le - lu - ia!

Harmony:

4. O blest com - mun - ion, fam - i - ly di - vine!
5. And when the strife is fierce, the war - fare long,
6. The gold - en eve - ning bright - ens in the west;

We feebly struggle, they in glory shine;
Steals on the ear the distant triumph song,
Soon, soon to faithful warriors comes their rest;

Yet all are one within your great design.
And hearts are brave again, and arms are strong.
Sweet is the calm of paradise the blest.

Al - le - lu - ia! Al - le - lu - ia!

Text: William W. How, 1823-1897
Tune: SINE NOMINE, 10 10 10 with alleluias; Ralph Vaughan Williams, 1872-1958, © Oxford University Press

890 Immaculate Mary

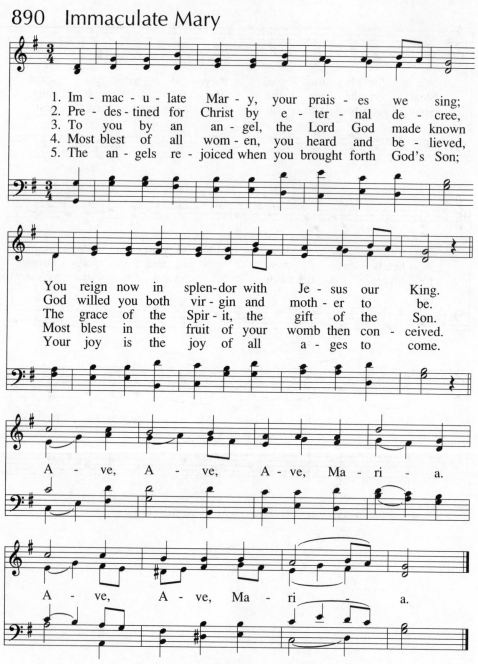

1. Im - mac - u - late Mar - y, your prais - es we sing;
2. Pre - des - tined for Christ by e - ter - nal de - cree,
3. To you by an an - gel, the Lord God made known
4. Most blest of all wom - en, you heard and be - lieved,
5. The an - gels re - joiced when you brought forth God's Son;

You reign now in splen-dor with Je - sus our King.
God willed you both vir - gin and moth - er to be.
The grace of the Spir - it, the gift of the Son.
Most blest in the fruit of your womb then con - ceived.
Your joy is the joy of all a - ges to come.

A - ve, A - ve, A - ve, Ma - ri - a.

A - ve, A - ve, Ma - ri - a.

6. Your child is the Savior, all hope lies in him:
He gives us new life and redeems us from sin.

7. In glory for ever now close to your Son,
All ages will praise you for all God has done.

Text: St. 1 Jeremiah Cummings, 1814-1866, alt.; St. 2-7, Brian Foley, b.1919, © 1971, Faber Music Ltd.
Tune: LOURDES HYMN, 11 11 with refrain; Grenoble, 1882

For Builders Bold 891

1. For build - ers bold whose vi - sion pure Saw
2. As here they raised a soar - ing spire Which
3. Here saints new - born you gen - er - ate Through
4. We come, O Lord, in - her - i - tors From

more than brick or stone, Who laid in hope foun -
thrusts toward worlds a - bove, So may our prayers, like
wa - ter and the Word; Through loaf and cup com -
those whose work is done. Lord, make us now con -

da - tions sure With Christ the cor - ner - stone; For
tongues of fire, Leap kin - dled by your love. And
mu - ni - cate The gift of Christ the Lord. We
trib - u - tors To years be - yond our own. Let

those who hon - ored your com-mands And trust - ed
let your liv - ing Word de - scend As seed on
gath - er, Christ's own fam - i - ly; Christ's meal of
faith's en - kin - dled flame not fail; Let love's best

your strong Word, Who of - fered faith - ful
wait - ing hearts And, fruit - ful there, its
love we share. Come, help us live in
gifts in - crease. Let hope in Christ's sure

hearts and hands, We give you thanks, O Lord.
grace ex - tend To earth's most dis - tant parts.
u - ni - ty, Each oth - er's bur - dens bear.
Word pre - vail Till earth and time shall cease.

Text: Herman Stuempfle, b.1923, © 1993, GIA Publications, Inc.
Tune: FOREST GREEN, CMD; English, Harm. by Ralph Vaughan Williams, 1872-1958, © Oxford University Press, alt.

892 What Is This Place

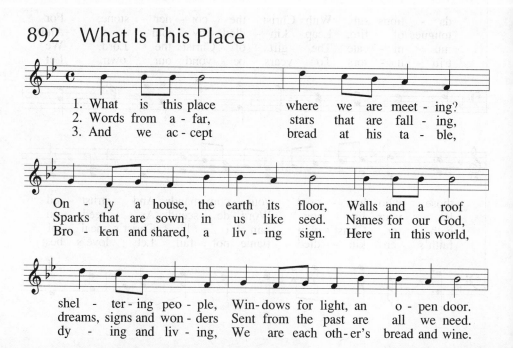

1. What is this place where we are meet - ing?
2. Words from a - far, stars that are fall - ing,
3. And we ac - cept bread at his ta - ble,

On - ly a house, the earth its floor, Walls and a roof
Sparks that are sown in us like seed. Names for our God,
Bro - ken and shared, a liv - ing sign. Here in this world,

shel - ter - ing peo - ple, Win - dows for light, an o - pen door.
dreams, signs and won - ders Sent from the past are all we need.
dy - ing and liv - ing, We are each oth - er's bread and wine.

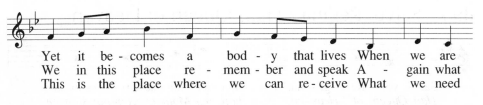

Yet it be - comes a bod - y that lives When we are
We in this place re - mem - ber and speak A - gain what
This is the place where we can re - ceive What we need

gath - ered here, And know our God is near.
we have heard: God's free re - deem - ing word.
to in - crease: Our jus - tice and God's peace.

Text: *Zomaar een dak boven wat hoofen;* Huub Oosterhuis, b.1933; trans. by David Smith, b.1933,
© 1967, Gooi en Sticht, bv., Baarn, The Netherlands. Exclusive English language agent: OCP Publications
Tune: KOMT NU MET ZANG, 9 8 9 8 9 66; Valerius' *Neder-landtsche gedenck-klanck;* acc. by Robert J. Batastini, b.1942,
© 1987, GIA Publications, Inc.

How Blessed Is This Place   893

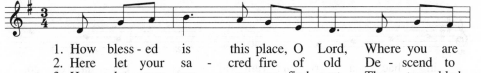

1. How bless - ed is this place, O Lord, Where you are
2. Here let your sa - cred fire of old De - scend to
3. Here let your wea - ry one find rest, The trou - bled
4. Here your an - gel - ic spir - its send Their sol - emn

wor - shiped and a - dored; In faith we here an al - tar
kin - dle spir - its cold; And may our prayers, when here we
heart, your com - fort blest, The guilt - y one, a sure re -
praise with ours to blend, And grant the vi - sion, in - ly

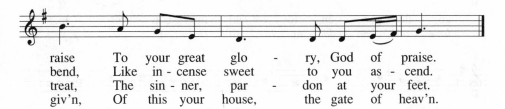

raise To your great glo - ry, God of praise.
bend, Like in - cense sweet to you as - cend.
treat, The sin - ner, par - don at your feet.
giv'n, Of this your house, the gate of heav'n.

Text: Ernest E. Ryden, 1886-1981, alt., © sts. 1-3, Lutheran Church in America, © st. 4, 1958, Service Book and Hymnal
Tune: O WALY WALY, LM; English; harm. by Martin West, b.1929, © 1983, Hope Publishing Co.

894 Salve, Regina / Hail, Queen of Heaven

Sal - ve, Re - gí - na, ma - ter mi - se - ri - cór - di - ae:
Hail, Queen of Heav - en, hail, our Moth - er com - pas - sion - ate,
Vi - ta, dul - cé - do et spes no - stra sal - ve.
True life and com - fort and our hope, we greet you!
Ad te cla - má - mus, éx - su - les fí - li - i He - vae.
To you we ex - iles, chil - dren of Eve, raise our voic - es.
Ad te sus - pi - rá - mus, ge - mén - tes et flen - tes
We send up sighs to you, as mourn - ing and weep - ing,
in hac la - cri - má - rum val - le. E - ia er - go,
we pass through this vale of sor - row. Then turn to us,
ad - vo - cá - ta no - stra, il - los tu - os mi - se - ri -
O most gra - cious Wom - an, those eyes of yours, so full of
cór - des ó - cu - los ad nos con - vér - te.
love and ten - der - ness, so full of pit - y.
Et Je - sum, be - ne - dí - ctum fru - ctum ven - tris tu - i,
And grant us af - ter these, our days of lone - ly ex - ile,

no - bis post hoc ex - sí - li - um o - stén - de.
the sight of your blest Son and Lord, Christ Je - sus.

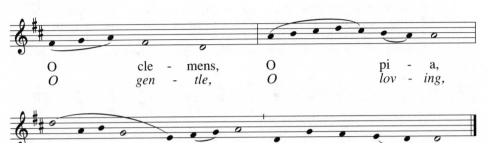

O cle - mens, O pi - a,
O gen - tle, O lov - ing,

O dul - cis Vir - go Ma - rí - a.
O ho - ly, sweet Vir - gin Mar - y.

Text: Latin, c.1080, tr. by John C. Selner, SS, b.1904, © 1954, GIA Publications, Inc.
Tune: SALVE REGINA, Irregular; Mode V; acc. by Gerard Farrell, OSB, b.1919, © 1986, GIA Publications, Inc.

895 Sing We of the Blessed Mother

1. Sing we of the bless-ed Moth-er Who re-ceived the an-gel's word, And o-be-dient to the sum-mons Bore in love the in-fant Lord; Sing we of the

2. Sing we, too, of Mar-y's sor-rows, Of the sword that pierced her through, When be-neath the cross of Je-sus She his weight of suf-f'ring knew, Looked up-on her

3. Sing a-gain the joys of Mar-y When she saw the ris-en Lord, And in prayer with Christ's a-pos-tles, Wait-ed on his prom-ised word: From on high the

4. Sing the great-est joy of Mar-y When on earth her work was done, And the Lord of all cre-a-tion Brought her to his heav'n-ly home: Vir-gin Moth-er,

joys of Mar - y / At whose breast that child was fed
Son and Sav - ior / Reign - ing from the aw - ful tree,
blaz - ing glo - ry / Of the Spir - it's pres - ence came,
Mar - y bless-ed, / Raised on high and crowned with grace,

Who is Son of God e - ter - nal
Saw the price of our re - demp - tion
Heav'n - ly breath of God's own be - ing,
May your Son, the world's re - deem - er,

And the ev - er - last - ing Bread.
Paid to set the sin - ner free.
To - kened in the wind and flame.
Grant us all to see his face.

Text: George B. Timms, b.1910, © 1975, Oxford University Press
Tune: OMNE DIE, 8 7 8 7 D; *Trier Gesängbuch*, 1695

896 Ave Maria

1. Hail Mar - y full of grace, the Lord is with you. Bless - ed are you a - mong all wo - men, Blest is the fruit of your womb.

2. Ho - ly Mar - y moth-er of God, the Lord is with you. Pray for us sin - ners, pray for us sin - ners, Now and at the hour of our death. Je - sus.

A - ve Ma - ri - a, gra - ti - a ple - na, Do - mi - nus te - cum, Be - ne - di - cta in mu - li - e - ri - bus

Text: Hail Mary; additional text by Dan Kantor, b.1960
Tune: Dan Kantor, b.1960; arr. by Rob Glover

897 All Who Claim the Faith of Jesus

1. All who claim the faith of Je - sus Sing the
2. Bless - ed were the cho - sen peo - ple Out of
3. There - fore let all faith - ful peo - ple Sing the
4. "Mag - ni - fy, my soul, God's great - ness; In my

won - ders that were done When the love of God the
whom the Lord did come; Bless - ed was the land of
hon - or of her name; Let the Church, in her fore -
Sav - ior I re - joice; All the a - ges call me

Fa - ther O'er our sins the vic - t'ry
prom - ise Fash - ioned for his earth - ly
shad - owed, Part in her thanks - giv - ing
bless - ed, In his praise I lift my

won, When God made the Vir - gin
home; But more bless - ed far the
claim; What Christ's moth - er sang in
voice; God has cast down all the

Mar - y Moth - er of the on - ly Son.
moth - er, She who bore him in her womb.
glad - ness Let Christ's peo - ple sing the same."
might - y, And the low - ly are his choice."

Text: Vincent Stuckey Stratton Coles, 1845-1929, alt.; St. 4, F. Bland Tucker, 1895-1984
Tune: TILLFLYKT, 87 87 87; *Sionstoner,* 1889; harm. by Marty Haugen, b.1950, © 1987, GIA Publications, Inc.

Ave Maria 898

A - ve Ma - rí - a, grá - ti - a ple - na,

Dó - mi - nus te - cum, be - ne - dí - cta tu in mu - li -

é - ri - bus, et be - ne - dí - ctus fru - ctus ven - tris tu - i,

Je - sus. San - cta Ma - rí - a, Ma - ter De - i,

o - ra pro no - bis pec - ca - tó - ri - bus, nunc et in

ho - ra mor - tis no - strae. A - men.

Text: Luke 1:29; Latin, 13th C.
Tune: AVE MARIA, Irregular; Mode I; acc. by Robert LeBlanc, b.1948, © 1986, GIA Publications, Inc.

899 I Sing a Maid

1. I sing a maid of ten - der years To whom an an - gel came, And knelt, as to a might - y queen, And bowed bright wings of flame: A na - tion's hope in her re - ply, This maid of match - less grace; For God's own son be - came her child, And she his rest - ing place.

2. She watched him grow to man - hood's strength To meet his des - tin - y, And when the dan - ger of his truth Brought him to Cal - va - ry, She stood by him all pow - er - less To ease his dy - ing pain, 'Til in the dark - est hour of all, She held her son a - gain.

3. And if the song had end - ed then, Our eyes would fill with tears, But ah! the song had just be - gun To ech - o down the years! Now lift your voic - es, hearts and souls, To sing with one ac - cord To hon - or Mar - y, Moth - er of The Christ, the Ris - en Lord!

Text: M. D. Ridge, b.1938, © 1987, GIA Publications, Inc.
Tune: THE FLIGHT OF THE EARLS; 14 14 14 14; trad. Celtic melody; harm. by Michael Joncas, b.1951, © 1987, GIA Publications, Inc.

O Sanctissima / O Most Virtuous   900

1. O san - ctís - si - ma, O pi - ís - si - ma,
2. Tu so - lá - ti - um Et re - fú - gi - um,
3. Ec - ce dé - bi - les, Per - quam flé - bi - les,
4. Vir - go ré - spi - ce, Ma - ter, ád - spi - ce,

1. O most vir - tu - ous And most pi - ous,
2. Our pro - tec - tion and Con - so - la - tion,
3. See us pow - er - less In our hope - less-ness:
4. Maid - en, look on us, Moth - er, care for us.

Dul - cis vir - go Ma - rí - a!
Vir - go ma - ter Ma - rí - a!
Sal - va nos, Ma - rí - a!
Au - di nos, Ma - rí - a!

Dear - est maid - en, sweet Mar - y,
Vir - gin moth - er, good Mar - y,
Aid us, save us, Mar - y!
Hear our pleas, O Mar - y!

Ma - ter a - má - ta, In - te - me - rá - ta,
Quid - quid op - tá - mus, Per te spe - rá - mus,
Tol - le lan - guó - res, Sa - na do - ló - res,
Tu me - di - cí - nam, Por - tas di - ví - nam;

Moth - er af - fec - tion-ate, Vir - gin in - vi - o - late,
What - e'er our souls de-sire, May you help us to ac - quire.
Wipe a - way the tears we shed, Heal us of our grief and dread.
Balm and our sur - e - ty, Gate-way to di - vin - i - ty,

O	-	ra,			o	-	ra	pro	no	-	bis.
O	-	ra,			o	-	ra	pro	no	-	bis.
O	-	ra,			o	-	ra	pro	no	-	bis.
O	-	ra,			o	-	ra	pro	no	-	bis.
In	-	ter - cede	and	pray	for	us,	O	Mar	-	y!
In	-	ter - cede	and	pray	for	us,	O	Mar	-	y!
In	-	ter - cede	and	pray	for	us,	O	Mar	-	y!
In	-	ter - cede	and	pray	for	us,	O	Mar	-	y!

Text: St. 1, *Stimmen der Völker in Liedern*, 1807; st. 2, *Arundel Hymnal*, 1902; tr. Neil Borgstrom, b.1953, © 1994, GIA Publications, Inc.
Tune: O DU FRÖLICHE, 55 7 55 7; Tattersall's *Improved Psalmody*, 1794

901 We Are God's Work of Art / Somos la Creación de Dios

Refrain

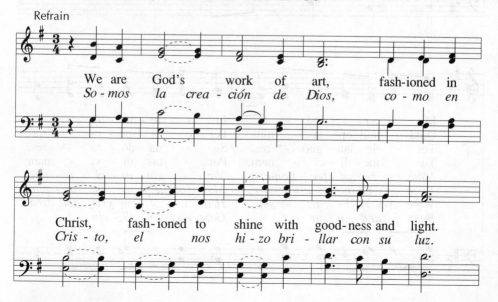

We are God's work of art, fash-ioned in
So - mos la crea - ción de Dios, co - mo en

Christ, fash-ioned to shine with good-ness and light.
Cris - to, el nos hi - zo bri - llar con su luz.

As it was from the start— formed by this great,
A - sí fue al co - men - zar, con gran a - mor,

great love, we are God's great,
el nos for - mó, so-mos gran - des o - bras del

1.- 4., 6.   To verses 1.- 4.   5.   To verse 5
Last time

won-drous work of art.   work of
ar - te del Se - ñor.   del Se -
Last time

Verses 1, 2

1.   When we were dead in sin, you
2.   How rich is the grace of God, how
1. Cuan - do en pe - ca-do mo - ri - mos, nos
2.   Qué ri - ca es la gra-cia de Dios qué

brought us to life in Christ, and raised
strong is the love of God, to send
tra - jo la vi - da en Cris - to y nos
fuer - te es su a - mor, en - vió

D.C.

us up, up to the heav - ens.
us Christ for our sal - va - tion.
lle - vó a las al - tu - ras.
a Cris - to pa - ra nuestra sal - va - cion.

Verse 3

3. We are stran - gers no long - er,
3. No so - mos ex - tran - je - ros,

out - casts no long-er, we are saints in the
no mas des-te - rra-dos, so-mos san - tos en la

D.C.

house of God.
ca - sa del Se - ñor.

Verse 4

4. We are the tem - ple that our God
4. So - mos el tem - plo que el Se - ñor

has fash - ioned,
hi - zo,

has fash - ioned, in Christ we are the
hi - zo, en Cris - to so - mos mo -

D.C.

dwell - ing place of love.
ra - da de su a - mor.

Verse 5

art.   5. From the foun - da - tion   of the world
ñor.   5. Des - de el prin - ci - pio   del mun - do

you have cho - sen   us,   des - tined in
nos es - co - gis - te   el des - ti - no de

love to   be your sons   and   daugh -
ser   tus hi - jos y   tus   hi -

ters.   You have re - vealed to us the
jas.   Nos re - ve - ló el mis - te -

mys - t'ry of grace,   to u - nite
rio de   gra - cia,   pa-ra u - nir

D.C.

all   things   in   Christ.
to - das las   co - sas en   Cris - to.

Text: Ephesians 2:1, 4-7, 10, 19, 21-22; Marty Haugen, b.1950; Spanish trans. by Donna Peña, b.1955
Tune: Marty Haugen, b.1950
© 1991, GIA Publications, Inc.

902 Come and Let Us Drink of That New River

1. Come and let us drink of that new riv - er,
2. Now the world has bright il - lu - mi - na - tion,

Not from bar - ren rock di - vine - ly poured,
Heav - en and all things up - on the earth:

But the fount of life that springs for ev - er
Ris - en is the God of all cre - a - tion,

From the sa - cred bod - y of our Lord.
Christ the Lord who gave cre - a - tion birth.

3. Yes - ter - day with you in bur - ial ly - ing,

Now with you in tri - umph I a - rise,

Yes - ter - day the part - ner of your dy - ing,

Raise me with you far be - yond the skies.

Text: John of Damascus, c.675-746; tr. by John M. Neale, 1818-1866, adapt. by Anthony G. Petti, 1932-1985, © 1971, Faber Music Ltd.
Tune: NEW RIVER, 10 9 10 9; Kenneth D. Smith, b.1928

Baptized in Water   903

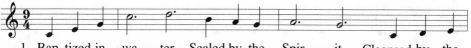

1. Bap-tized in wa - ter, Sealed by the Spir - it, Cleansed by the
2. Bap-tized in wa - ter, Sealed by the Spir - it, Dead in the
3. Bap-tized in wa - ter, Sealed by the Spir - it, Marked with the

blood of Christ our King: Heirs of sal - va - tion, Trust-ing his
tomb with Christ our King: One with his ris - ing, Freed and for -
sign of Christ our King: Born of one Fa - ther, We are his

prom - ise, Faith - ful - ly now God's praise we sing.
giv - en, Thank - ful - ly now God's praise we sing.
chil - dren, Joy - ful - ly now God's praise we sing.

Text: Michael Saward, b.1932, © 1982, Hope Publishing Co.
Tune: BUNESSAN, 5 5 8 D; Gaelic melody; acc. by Marty Haugen, b.1950, © 1987, GIA Publications, Inc.

904 Covenant Hymn

1. Wher - ev - er you go, I will fol - low, Wher -
2. What - ev - er you dream, I am with you, When
3. And though you should fall, you will find me, When
4. Wher - ev - er you die, I will be there To
5. Wher - ev - er you go, I will fol - low, Be -

ev - er you live is my home. Though
stars call your name in the night. Though
no oth - er friend can you claim, When
sing you to sleep with a psalm, To
hold! The ho - ri - zon shines clear. The

days be of bless - ing or sor - row, Though
shad - ows and mist cloud the fu - ture, To -
foes beat you down or be - tray you And
soothe you with tales of our jour - ney, Your
pos - si - ble gleams like a cit - y: To -

house be of can - vas or stone, Though
geth - er we bear there a light. Like
oth - ers de - sert you in shame. When
fears and your doubts I will calm. We'll
geth - er we've noth - ing to fear. So

E - den be lost to the past, Though
A - bram and Sar - ah we stand, With
home and dreams aren't e - nough, And
live when jour - neys are done For -
speak with words bold and true The

moun - tains be - fore us be vast, Wher -
on - ly a prom - ise in hand. But
you run a - way from my love, I'll
ev - er in mem - 'ry as one. And
mes - sage my heart speaks to you. You

905 Blessed Be God, Who Chose You in Christ

Refrain

Bless-ed be God, who chose you in Christ to be
filled with the Spir - it of love.
Bless-ed be God, who chose you in Christ to pro -
claim to all na - tions His deeds.

Verse 1
Cantor:

1. We come to you, Lord Je - sus. You have
filled us with new life, as chil - dren of the
Fa - ther, and one in you.

𝄋 *Bridge to refrain*

Send forth your Ho - ly Spir - it, re -

All:

new the face of the earth. Re -

D.C.

new the face of the earth.

Verse 2

Cantor:

2. From all who have been bap - tized in wa - ter and the Ho - ly Spir-it, you have formed one peo - ple, u - nit - ed in your Son, Je - sus Christ.

D.S.

Verse 3

Cantor:

3. You have set us free, and filled our hearts with the Spir - it of your love, that we may live in your peace.

D.S.

Verse 4

Cantor:

4. You call those who have been bap - tized to an - nounce the Good News of Je - sus Christ to peo - ple ev - 'ry - where.

D.S.

Text: Adapted from the Rite of Baptism, James J. Chepponis, b.1956
Tune: James J. Chepponis, b.1956
© 1982, GIA Publications, Inc.

906 We Know That Christ Is Raised

1. We know that Christ is raised and dies no
2. We share by wa - ter in his sav - ing
3. The Fa - ther's splen - dor clothes the Son with
4. A new cre - a - tion comes to life and

more.   Em - braced by death, he broke its
death.   Re - born, we share with him an
life.   The Spir - it's fis - sion shakes the
grows   As Christ's new bod - y takes on

fear - ful hold,   And our de - spair he turned to
East - er life   As liv - ing mem - bers of our
Church of God.   Bap-tized, we live with God the
flesh and blood.   The u - ni - verse re - stored and

blaz - ing joy.   Al - le - lu - ia!
Sav - ior Christ.   Al - le - lu - ia!
Three in One.   Al - le - lu - ia!
whole will sing: Al - le - lu - ia!

Text: Romans 6:4,9; John B. Geyer, b.1932, ©
Tune: ENGELBERG, 10 10 10 with alleluia; Charles V. Stanford, 1852-1924

O Breathe on Me, O Breath of God   907

1. O breathe on me, O breath of God, Fill
   me with life a - new,
   That I may love the
   things you love, And do what you would do.

2. O breathe on me, O breath of God, Un -
   til my heart is pure;
   Un - til my will is
   one with yours, To do and to en - dure.

3. O breathe on me, O breath of God, My
   will to yours in - cline,
   Un - til this self - ish
   part of me Glows with your fire di - vine.

4. O breathe on me, O breath of God, So
   shall I nev - er die,
   But live with you the
   per - fect life Of your e - ter - ni - ty.

Text: Edwin Hatch, 1835-1889
Tune: ST. COLUMBA, CM; Gaelic; Harm. by A. Gregory Murray, OSB, 1905-1992, © Downside Abbey

908   In Memory of You / Ave Verum

Refrain

Lord, Je - sus! You are here with us.

Lord, Je - sus! You are here with us.

This we do in mem - o - ry of you.

This we do in mem - o - ry of you.

Verse 1

1. A - ve ve - rum Cor - pus na -

D.C.

tum de Ma - rí - a Vír - gi - ne:

Verse 2

2. Ve - re pas - sum im - mo - lá -

D.C.

tum in cru - ce pro hó - mi - ne:

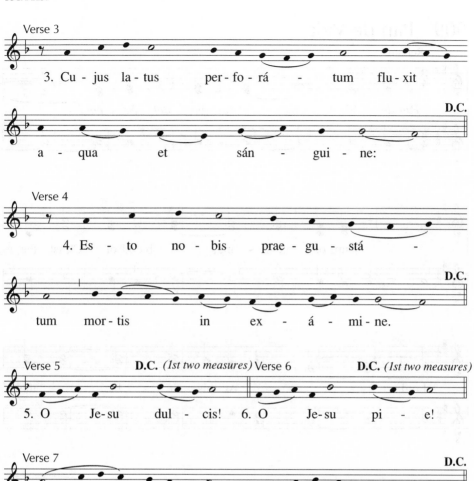

Verse 3
3. Cu - jus la - tus per - fo - rá - tum flu - xit

a - qua et sán - gui - ne:

D.C.

Verse 4
4. Es - to no - bis prae - gu - stá -

tum mor - tis in ex - á - mi - ne.

D.C.

Verse 5
D.C. (1st two measures) Verse 6 D.C. (1st two measures)
5. O Je-su dul - cis! 6. O Je-su pi - e!

Verse 7
D.C.
7. O Je - su fi - li Ma - rí - ae.

Text: Refrain, Alexander Peloquin, b.1918; verses ascr. to Innocent VI, d.1362
Tune: Refrain, Alexander Peloquin, b.1918; verses, Chant mode VI
© 1976, GIA Publications, Inc.

909   Pan de Vida

Refrain

Pan de Vi - da, cuer-po del Se - ñor,

cup of bless - ing, blood of Christ the

Lord. At this ta - ble the

last shall be first, ** po-der es ser - vir,

por-que Dios es a - mor.

1.- 3. | Last time

* Bread of Life, body of the Lord,
** power is for service, because God is love.

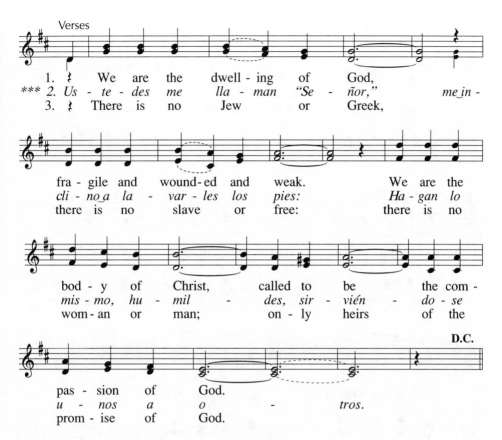

Verses

1. ⁀ We are the dwell - ing of God,
*** 2. Us - te - des me lla - man "Se - ñor," me_in -
3. ⁀ There is no Jew or Greek,

fra - gile and wound-ed and weak. We are the
cli - no_a la - var - les los pies: Ha - gan lo
there is no slave or free: there is no

bod - y of Christ, called to be the com -
mis - mo, hu - mil - des, sir - vién - do - se
wom - an or man; on - ly heirs of the

D.C.

pas - sion of God.
u - nos a o - tros.
prom - ise of God.

*** You call me "Lord", and I bow to wash your feet:
you must do the same, humbly serving each other.

Text: John 13: 1-15, Galatians 3: 28-29; Bob Hurd, b.1950, and Pia Moriarty, © 1988, Bob Hurd
Tune: Bob Hurd, b.1950, © 1988; acc. by Craig Kingsbury, b.1952, © 1988, OCP Publications; arr. © 1988, OCP Publications
Published by OCP Publications

ev - er you go, I am with you, I
lead where you dream: I will fol - low. To
raise you from where you have fall - en.
we will be bur - ied to - geth - er, And
won't be a - lone, I have prom - ised. Wher -

nev - er will leave you a - lone.
dream with you is my de - light.
Faith - ful to you is my name.
wak - en to greet a new dawn.
ev - er you go, I am here.

Text: Ruth 1:16; Rory Cooney, b.1952
Tune: Gary Daigle, b.1957
© 1993, GIA Publications, Inc.

910 Take and Eat

Refrain

Take and eat; take and eat: this is my bod - y giv-en up for you. Take and drink; take and drink: this is my blood giv-en up for you.

Verses

1. I am the Word that spoke and light was made;
2. I am the way that leads the ex - ile home;
3. I am the Lamb that takes a - way your sin;
4. I am the cor - ner-stone that God has laid;
5. I am the light that came in - to the world;
6. I am the first and last, the Liv - ing One;

I am the seed that died to be re - born;
I am the truth that sets the cap - tive free;
I am the gate that guards you night and day;
A cho-sen stone and pre - cious in his eyes;
I am the light that dark - ness can - not hide;
I am the Lord who died that you might live;

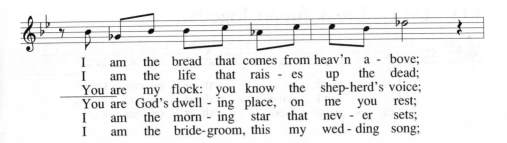

I am the bread that comes from heav'n a - bove;
I am the life that rais - es up the dead;
You are my flock: you know the shep-herd's voice;
You are God's dwell - ing place, on me you rest;
I am the morn - ing star that nev - er sets;
I am the bride-groom, this my wed - ding song;

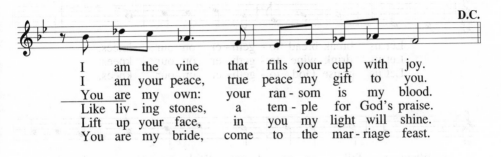

D.C.

I am the vine that fills your cup with joy.
I am your peace, true peace my gift to you.
You are my own: your ran - som is my blood.
Like liv - ing stones, a tem - ple for God's praise.
Lift up your face, in you my light will shine.
You are my bride, come to the mar - riage feast.

Text: Verse text, James Quinn, SJ, b.1919, © 1989. Used by permission of Selah Publishing., Inc., Kingston, N.Y.; refrain text, Michael Joncas,
    b.1951, © 1989, GIA Publications, Inc.
Tune: Michael Joncas, b.1951, © 1989, GIA Publications, Inc.

911   Let Us Break Bread Together

1. Let us break bread to-geth-er on our knees;
2. Let us drink wine to-geth-er on our knees;
3. Let us praise God to-geth-er on our knees;

Let us break bread to-geth-er on our knees;
Let us drink wine to-geth-er on our knees;
Let us praise God to-geth-er on our knees;

When I fall on my knees, With my face to the ris-ing

sun, O Lord, have mer-cy on me.

Text: American folk hymn
Tune: LET US BREAK BREAD, 10 10 6 8 7; American folk hymn; harm. by David Hurd, b.1950, © 1968, GIA Publications, Inc.

912   You Satisfy the Hungry Heart

Refrain

You sat-is-fy the hun-gry heart With

gift of fin-est wheat; Come give to us, O

sav-ing Lord, The bread of life to eat.

Verses

1. As when the shep - herd calls his sheep, They
2. With joy - ful lips we sing to you Our
3. Is not the cup we bless and share The
4. The mys-t'ry of your pres-ence, Lord, No
5. You give your-self to us, O Lord; Then

know and heed his voice; So when you call your
praise and grat - i - tude, That you should count us
blood of Christ out-poured? Do not one cup, one
mor - tal tongue can tell: Whom all the world can -
self - less let us be, To serve each oth - er

fam - 'ly, Lord, We fol - low and re - joice.
wor - thy, Lord, To share this heav'n-ly food.
loaf, de - clare Our one - ness in the Lord?
not con - tain Comes in our hearts to dwell.
in your name In truth and char - i - ty.

D.C.

Text: Omer Westendorf, b.1916
Tune: BICENTENNIAL, CM, with refrain; Robert E. Kreutz, b.1922
© 1977, Archdiocese of Philadelphia

I Received the Living God 913

Refrain

I re-ceived the liv-ing God, and my
heart is full of joy. I re-ceived the liv-ing
God, and my heart is full of joy.

Verses

1. Je-sus said: "I am the Bread Knead-ed
2. Je-sus said: "I am the Way, And my
3. Je-sus said: "I am the Truth; If you
4. Je-sus said: "I am the Life Far from

long to give you life; You who will par-take of
Fa-ther longs for you; So I come to bring you
fol-low close to me, You will know me in your
whom no thing can grow, But re-ceive this liv-ing

D.C.

me Need not ev-er fear to die."
home To be one with him a-new."
heart, And my word shall make you free."
bread, And my Spir-it you shall know."

Text: Anonymous
Tune: LIVING GOD, 7 7 7 7 with refrain; Anonymous; harm. by Richard Proulx, b.1937, © 1986, GIA Publications, Inc.

914 Alleluia! Sing to Jesus

1. Al - le - lu - ia! sing to Je - sus!
2. Al - le - lu - ia! not as or - phans
3. Al - le - lu - ia! Bread of An - gels,
4. Al - le - lu - ia! King e - ter - nal,

His the scep - ter, his the throne;
Are we left in sor - row now;
Here on earth our food, our stay!
You the Lord of lords we own;

Al - le - lu - ia! his the tri - umph,
Al - le - lu - ia! he is near us,
Al - le - lu - ia! here the sin - ful
Al - le - lu - ia! born of Mar - y,

His the vic - to - ry a - lone;
Faith be - lieves, nor ques - tions how:
Flee to you from day to day:
Earth your foot - stool, heav'n your throne:

Hark! the songs of peace - ful Zi - on
Though the cloud from sight re - ceived him,
In - ter - ces - sor, friend of sin - ners,
You, with - in the veil, have en - tered,

Thun - der like a might - y flood;
When the for - ty days were o'er,
Earth's re - deem - er, plead for me,
Robed in flesh, our great high priest;

Je - sus out of ev - 'ry na - tion
Shall our hearts for - get his prom - ise,
Where the songs of all the sin - less
Here on earth both priest and vic - tim

Has re - deemed us by his blood.
"I am with you ev - er - more?"
Sweep a - cross the crys - tal sea.
In the eu - cha - ris - tic feast.

Text: Revelation 5:9; William C. Dix, 1837-1898
Tune: HYFRYDOL, 8 7 8 7 D; Rowland H. Prichard, 1811-1887

915   One Bread, One Body

Verses

1. Gen - tile or Jew, ser - vant or
2. Man - y the gifts, man - y the
3. Grain for the fields, scat - tered and

free, wom - an or man
works, one in the Lord
grown, gath-ered to one

D.C.

no more.
of all.
for all.

Coda

Lord.

Text: 1 Corinthians 10:16; 17, 12:4, Galatians 3:28; the *Didache* 9; John Foley, SJ, b.1939
Tune: John Foley, SJ, b.1939
©1978, John B. Foley, SJ, and New Dawn Music

916 In Christ There Is a Table Set for All

1. Wel-come, all you no - ble saints of old,   As
2. El - ders, mar-tyrs, all are fall - ing down;
3. Beg-gars, lame, and har - lots al - so here;   Re -
4. Who is this who spreads the vic - t'ry feast?
5. Here he gives him - self to us as bread:
6. Wor-ship in the pres-ence of the Lord.   With
7. When at last this earth shall pass a - way.   When

now be - fore your ver - y eyes un - fold.   The
Proph-ets, pa - tri - archs are gath - 'ring 'round.   What
pen - tant pub - li - cans are draw - ing near;
Who is this who makes our war - ring cease?
Here, as wine, we drink the blood he shed.
joy - ful songs and hearts in one ac - cord.   And
Je - sus and his bride are one to stay.   The

won - ders all so long a - go fore - told:
an - gels long to see now we have found.
Way-ward sons come home with - out a fear.
Je - sus, ris - en Sav - ior, Prince of Peace.   In
Born to die, we eat and live in - stead!
let our host at ta - ble be a - dored.
feast of love is just be - gun that day.

Christ there is a ta - ble set for all.   In all.

Text: Robert J. Stamps
Tune: CENÉDIUS, Irregular, Robert J. Stamps
© 1972, Dawn Treader Music

Draw Us in the Spirit's Tether   917

1. Draw us in the Spir - it's teth - er, For when
2. As dis - ci - ples used to gath - er In the
3. All our meals and all our liv - ing Make as

hum - bly in your name, Two or
name of Christ to sup, Then with
sac - ra - ments of you, That by

three are met to - geth - er, You are in the
thanks to God the Fa - ther Break the bread and
car - ing, help-ing, giv - ing, We may be dis -

midst of them; Al - le - lu - ia! Al - le - lu - ia!
bless the cup, Al - le - lu - ia! Al - le - lu - ia!
ci - ples true. Al - le - lu - ia! Al - le - lu - ia!

Touch we now your gar - ment's hem.
So now bind our friend - ship up.
We will serve with faith a - new.

Text: Percy Dearmer, 1867-1936, alt., © Oxford University Press
Tune: UNION SEMINARY, 8 7 8 7 44 7; Harold Friedell, 1905-1958, © 1957, H. W. Gray Co., Inc.; harm. by Jet Turner, 1928-1984, © Chalice Press

918 Seed, Scattered and Sown

Refrain

Seed, scat-tered and sown, wheat, gath-ered and grown, bread, bro-ken and shared as one, the Liv - ing Bread of God. Vine, fruit of the land, wine, work of our hands, one cup that is shared by all; the Liv - ing Cup, the

Liv - ing Bread of God.

Verses

1. Is not the bread we break a
2. The seed which falls on rock will
3. As wheat up - on the hills was

shar - ing in our Lord?   Is not the
with - er and will die.   The seed with-
gath - ered and was grown,   So may the

cup we bless the blood of Christ out - poured?
in good ground will flow - er and have life.
church of God be gath - ered in - to one.

D.C.

Text: *Didache* 9, 1 Corinthians 10:16-17, Mark 4:3-6; Dan Feiten
Tune: Dan Feiten; keyboard arr. by Eric Gunnison, R.J. Miller
© 1987, Ekklesia Music, Inc.

919 Taste and See

Refrain

Taste and see, taste and see the

Lord.

good - ness of the good - ness of the

Taste and see,

Lord. O taste and see the

Last time to coda

good - ness of the Lord.

Verses

1. I will nev - er stop thank - ing my God
2. Join the sing - ing in praise of our God;
3. Look to God and be ra - diant with joy;
4. God of jus - tice, rain down on the poor,

with my words of praise. My
tell the world of the Name. I
you will nev - er know shame. The
giv - ing hope to their days. Come

soul will boast, will boast in the Lord. The
cried to the Lord: "Have mer - cy on me." God
weight of your bur - den is light to the Lord. With
vis - it your peo - ple, each child of the earth; come

D.C.

low - ly will hear me and be lift - ed in praise.
calmed all my fears and then set me free.
ten - der com - pas - sion God will call you by name.
vis - it us now and bring us to a new birth.

Coda

good - ness of the Lord.

Text: Psalm 34:1-3; Francis Patrick O'Brien, b.1958
Tune: Francis Patrick O'Brien, b.1958
© 1992, GIA Publications, Inc.

920 Life-giving Bread, Saving Cup

Refrain

Descant (beginning after verse one or two):

Life - giv-ing bread, sav - ing

Melody:

Life - giv - ing bread, sav - ing cup, we

cup, we of - fer you. Life - giv-ing bread, life -

of - fer in thanks-giv-ing, O God. Life - giv-ing bread

sav - ing cup, as a sign of love.

sav - ing cup, we of-fer as a sign of our love.

Verses

1. For bread that is bro - ken, we give thanks. For
2. We thank you, O Fa - ther, for your name which
3. Cre - a - tor of all, we of - fer thanks. You
4. Re - mem - ber your Church which sings your praise. Per -

wine that is poured, we give praise. For
you give to dwell in our hearts. You
give us a share in your life. You
fect it in truth and in love. And

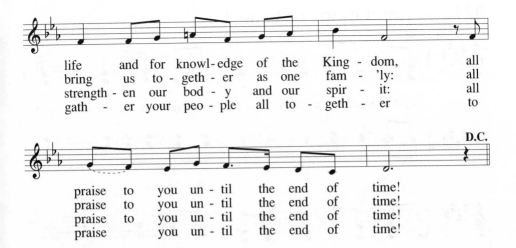

life   and for knowl-edge of the   King - dom,   all
bring   us   to - geth - er   as one   fam - 'ly: all
strength - en   our bod - y   and our   spir - it: all
gath   -   er your peo - ple   all to - geth - er   to

D.C.

praise   to you un - til   the end   of   time!
praise   to you un - til   the end   of   time!
praise   to you un - til   the end   of   time!
praise   you un - til   the end   of   time!

Text: Adapted from the *Didache,* 2nd C.; James J. Chepponis, b.1956
Tune: James J. Chepponis, b.1956
© 1987, GIA Publications, Inc.

921 As the Grains of Wheat

Refrain

As the grains of wheat once scat-tered on the hill were

gath-ered in - to one to be - come our bread;

so may all your peo-ple from all the ends of earth be

Last time
gath - ered in - to one in you.

Verses

1. As this cup of bless-ing is shared with-in our midst,
2. Let this be a fore-taste of all that is to come when

D.C.

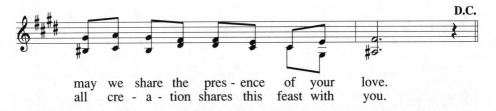

may we share the pres - ence of your love.
all cre - a - tion shares this feast with you.

Text: Marty Haugen, b.1950
Tune: Marty Haugen, b.1950
© 1990, GIA Publications, Inc.

922 At That First Eucharist

1. At that first Eu - cha - rist be - fore you died,
2. For all your church, O Lord, we in - ter - cede;
3. We pray for those who wan - der from the fold;

O Lord, you prayed that all be one in you;
O make our lack of char - i - ty to cease;
O bring them back, Good Shep - herd of the sheep,

At this our Eu - cha - rist a - gain pre - side,
Draw us the near - er each to each we plead,
Back to the faith which saints be - lieved of old,

And in our hearts your law of love re - new.
By draw - ing all to you, O Prince of Peace.
Back to the Church which still that faith does keep.

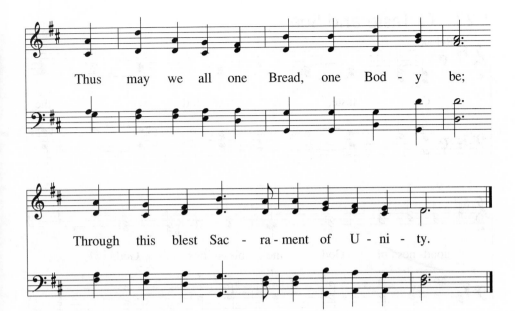

Thus may we all one Bread, one Bod - y be;

Through this blest Sac - ra - ment of U - ni - ty.

Text: William H. Turton, 1859-1938, alt.
Tune: UNDE ET MEMORES, 10 10 10 10 with refrain; William H. Monk, 1823-1889, alt.

923 O Taste and See

Refrain

O taste, taste and see the good-ness of God, the bless-ings of God.

Verse 1

1. I will sing God's prais-es all the days that I shall live. My soul will glo-ry in my God, the low-ly will hear and be glad. O glo-ri-fy God's name with me, to-geth-er let us re - joice.

D.C.

Text: Psalm 34:2-4, 5-6, 7-8, 9, 11, 12-13, 19; Marty Haugen, b.1950
Tune: Marty Haugen, b.1950
© 1993, GIA Publications, Inc.

924 Song of the Body of Christ / Canción del Cuerpo de Cristo

Refrain

We come to share our sto - ry, we
Ve - ni-mos a de - cir del mis - te - rio, *y par -*

come to break the bread, We
tir el pan de vi - da. *Ve -*

come to know our ris - ing from the dead. *Last time*
ni - mos a sa - ber de nues-tra_e - ter - ni - dad. *Last time*

Verses in English

1. We come as your peo - ple, we
2. We are called to heal the bro - ken, to be
3. Bread of life and cup of prom - ise, in this
4. You will lead and we shall fol - low, you will
5. We will live and sing: "A - lo - ha," "Al - le -
   (live and sing your prais - es,)

come   as   your own,   u - nit - ed with each
hope   for   the poor,   we are called   to feed the
meal we   all   are one.   In our dy - ing and our
be   the breath of   life;   liv-ing wa - ter, we are
lu - ia" is our   song.   May we live   in love and

D.C.

oth - er,   love   finds a   home.
hun - gry   at   our   door.
ris - ing,   may your king-dom   come.
thirst - ing   for   your   light.
peace   our   whole life   long.

Verses in Spanish

1. Ve - ni-mos, co - mo   su pueb - lo   en es -
2. Nos   lla -   ma pa - ra cu - rar   y
3. Pan de vi - da y co-pa de pro-me - sa,   so-mos
4. Nos guia-rás   y   te   se-gui-re-mos,   por-que
5. Vi - vi - re - mos can-tan - do "A - lo - ha." "A - le -

pí - ri - tu de ver - dad.   U - ni - dos en   su a -
ser su   es - per-an - za.   So-mos su-yos pa-ra a - li-men-
u - no en es - ta co - mi-da. Ven - drá su   rei-no en
e - res la luz que bus-ca-mos. En el di - a o en la
lu-ya" es nues-tra can - ción. Por   siem-pre vi - vi -

D.C.

mor,   so - mos   un   cor - a - zón.
tar   a   los   po -   bres.
nues - tra   trans - for-ma - ción.
no - che,   bri -   lla -   rás.
re - mos   en   su   paz.

Text: David Haas, b.1957, Spanish translation by Donna Peña, b. 1955
Tune: NO KE ANO' AHI AHI, Irregular, Hawaiian traditional, arr. by David Haas, b.1957
© 1989, GIA Publications, Inc.

925 Take the Bread, Children

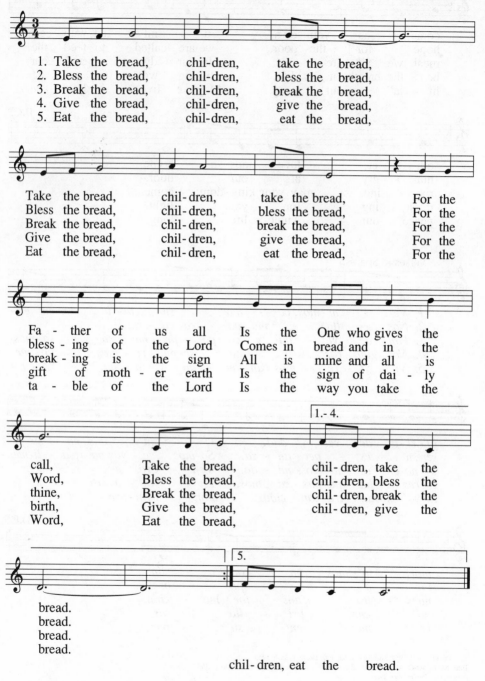

1. Take the bread, chil-dren, take the bread,
2. Bless the bread, chil-dren, bless the bread,
3. Break the bread, chil-dren, break the bread,
4. Give the bread, chil-dren, give the bread,
5. Eat the bread, chil-dren, eat the bread,

Take the bread, chil-dren, take the bread, For the
Bless the bread, chil-dren, bless the bread, For the
Break the bread, chil-dren, break the bread, For the
Give the bread, chil-dren, give the bread, For the
Eat the bread, chil-dren, eat the bread, For the

Fa - ther of us all Is the One who gives the
bless - ing of the Lord Comes in bread and in the
break - ing is the sign All is mine and all is
gift of moth - er earth Is the sign of dai - ly
ta - ble of the Lord Is the way you take the

1.- 4.

call, Take the bread, chil-dren, take the
Word, Bless the bread, chil-dren, bless the
thine, Break the bread, chil-dren, break the
birth, Give the bread, chil-dren, give the
Word, Eat the bread,

5.

bread.
bread.
bread.
bread.

chil-dren, eat the bread.

Text: Herbert Brokering, b.1926, © 1981
Tune: BREAD, 88 77 8; Carl F. Schalk, b.1929, © 1981, GIA Publications, Inc.

All Who Hunger 926

Verses

Cantor(s):

1. All who hun - ger, gath - er glad - ly;
2. All who hun - ger, nev - er stran - gers,
3. All who hun - ger, sing to - geth - er;

ho - ly man - na is our bread.
seek-er, be a wel - come guest.
Je - sus Christ is liv - ing bread.

Come from wil - der - ness and wan - d'ring.
Come from rest - less - ness and roam - ing.
Come from lone - li - ness and long - ing.

Here, in truth, we will be fed. You that
Here, in joy, we keep the feast. We that
Here, in peace, we have been led. Blest are

yearn for days of full - ness, all a -
once were lost and scat - tered in com -
those who from this ta - ble live their

round us is our food.
mun - ion's love have stood.
lives in grat - i - tude.

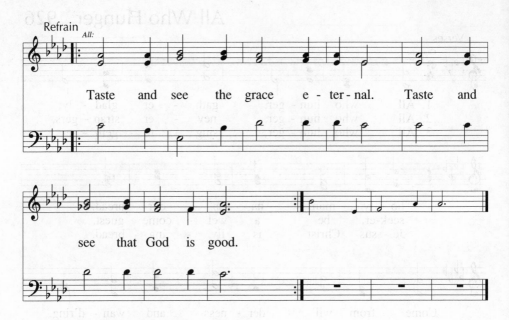

Taste and see the grace e-ter-nal. Taste and see that God is good.

Text: Sylvia G. Dunstan, 1955-1993, © 1991, GIA Publications, Inc.
Tune: Bob Moore, b.1962, © 1993, GIA Publications, Inc.

Bread to Share   927

*Use bread, fish, wine, *or* room *according to the preceeding verse.*

Verses

Cantor:

1. Bread for ev - 'ry hun - ger: the
2. Bread for those who sor - row: and
3. Bread for ev - 'ry sis - ter: and
4. Bread of hope and kind - ness: the
5. Fish for those who hun - ger: and
6. Wine of our re - mem - brance: the
7. Wine of our for - give - ness: the
8. Room for those for - got - ten: and
9. Room for all the chil - dren: and
10. Room for those who suf - fer: and

Choir and assembly:

(Hum)   You have plen - ty to share.

bread of joy and glad - ness: the
bread of life and laugh - ter: the
bread for ev - 'ry broth - er: and
bread of your com - pas - sion: the
joy for all who sor - row: and
wine of dreams and vi - sions: the
wine of our re - demp - tion: the
room for those re - ject - ed: and
room for all the el - ders: and
room for all the dy - ing: a

(Hum)   You have plen - ty to share.

bread of grace   and   mer - cy:
bread of strength and   jus - tice:
bread for   free - dom's jour - ney:
bread of   love   and   wel - come:
faith   for   un - be - liev - ers:
wine   of   cel - e - bra - tion:
wine   of   our   to - mor - rows:
room   for   all   the   out - casts:
room   for   all   the   lone - ly:
room that sings   of   new   life:

(Hum)   You have plen-ty   to share, you have

plen - ty   of bread   to   share.

D.C.

Text: John 6:1-15; Marty Haugen, b.1950
Tune: Marty Haugen, b.1950
© 1995, GIA Publications, Inc.

928 Eat This Bread

Refrain

Eat this bread, drink this cup, come to me and nev-er be hun-gry.

Eat this bread, drink this cup, trust in me and you will not thirst.

Verse 1

1. I am the bread of life, the

true bread sent from the Fa - ther.

D.C.

Verse 2

2. Your an - ces - tors ate man - na in the des - ert, but

this is the bread come down from heav - en.

D.C.

Verse 3

3. Eat my flesh and drink my blood, and

D.C.

I will raise you up on the last day.

Verse 4

4. An - y - one who eats this bread, will

D.C.

live for ev - er.

Verse 5

5. If you be - lieve and eat this bread,

D.C.

you will have e - ter - nal life.

Choose either part

Text: John 6; adapt. by Robert J. Batastini, b.1942, and the Taizé Community
Tune: Jacques Berthier, 1923-1994
© 1984, Les Presses de Taizé, GIA Publications, Inc., agent

929 Let Us Be Bread

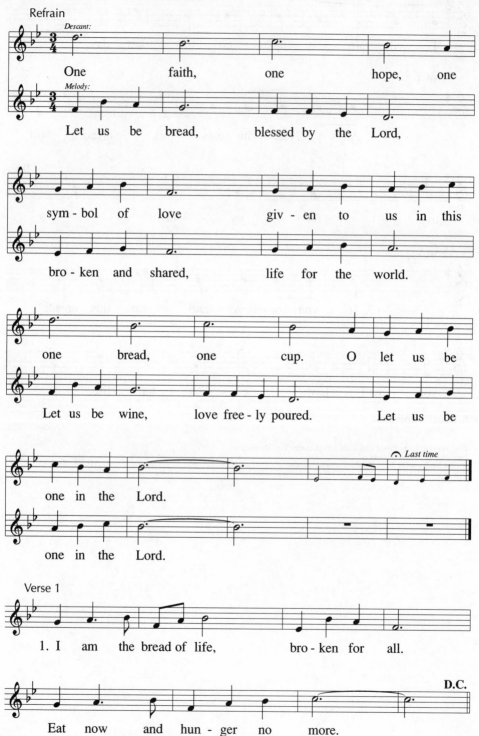

Refrain

Descant:

One faith, one hope, one

Melody:

Let us be bread, blessed by the Lord,

sym - bol of love giv - en to us in this

bro - ken and shared, life for the world.

one bread, one cup. O let us be

Let us be wine, love free - ly poured. Let us be

one in the Lord.

one in the Lord.

Last time

Verse 1

1. I am the bread of life, bro - ken for all.

Eat now and hun - ger no more.

D.C.

Verse 2

2. You are my friends if you keep my com-mands,

no long - er ser - vants but friends.

Verse 3

3. See how my peo - ple have noth-ing to eat.

Give them the bread that is you.

Verse 4

4. As God has loved me so I have loved you.

Go and live on in my love.

Text: Thomas J. Porter, b.1958
Tune: Thomas J. Porter, b.1958
© 1990, GIA Publications, Inc.

930 Jesus Is Here Right Now

Refrain

Je - sus is here right now. Je - sus is here; With this bread and wine his peace you'll find, Christ Je - sus is here right now. (right

To verses

now).

Last time

now).

Verse 1

1. Do not let your old hearts be troub-led. Have faith in God and have faith in me. In my Fa-ther's house there are man - y man - sions; oth - er-wise, how could I have told you so?

D.C.

Text: Leon C. Roberts; verses, John 14:1-4
Tune: Leon C. Roberts
© 1986, GIA Publications, Inc.

I Am the Bread of Life / Yo Soy el Pan de Vida   931

Verses

1.___ I am the Bread of life. You who
2. The bread that___ I will give is my
3. Un - less___ you___ eat of the
4.___ I am the Res - ur - rec - tion,___
5. Yes, Lord,___ I be - lieve that___

1.___ Yo soy el pan de vi - da. El que
2. El pan que___ yo da - ré___ es mi
3.___ Mien - tras no co - mas el___
4.___ Yo soy la re - su - rrec - ción.___
5.___ Sí, Se - ñor, yo cre - o que___

come to me shall not hun - ger; and who be -
flesh for the life of the world,___ and if you
flesh of the Son of Man___ and___
I___ am the life.___ If you be -
you___ are the Christ,___ the___

vie - ne_a mí no ten - drá ham - bre.___ El que
cuer - po___ vi - da del mun - do, y el que
cuer - po del hi - jo del hom - bre,___ y___
Yo___ soy la vi - da.___ El que
tú e - res el Cris - to,___ El___

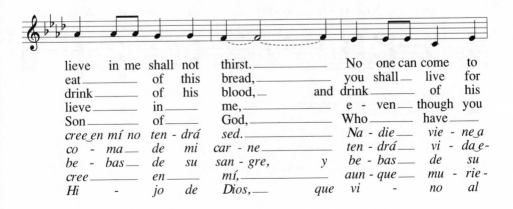

lieve in me shall not thirst.___ No one can come to
eat___ of this bread,___ you shall___ live for
drink___ of his blood,___ and drink___ of his
lieve___ in___ me,___ e - ven___ though you
Son___ of___ God,___ Who___ have___

cree_en mí no ten - drá sed.___ Na - die___ vie - ne_a
co - ma___ de mi car - ne___ ten - drá___ vi - da_e-
be - bas___ de su san - gre, y be - bas___ de su
cree___ en___ mí,___ aun - que___ mu - rie-
Hi - jo de Dios,___ que vi - no al

me	un - less	the___	Fa - ther___	beck-ons.
ev - er,_____	you shall___	live	for___	ev - er.
blood,	you shall	not have life	with -	in you.
die,_____	you shall___	live	for___	ev - er.
come	in - to_____	the_____		world.___
*mí*_____	*mien - tras el*	*Pa - dre nos*	*lla - me.*	
ter - na,_____	*ten - drá___*	*vi - da e - *	*ter - na.*	
san - gre,	*no*	*ten - drá___*	*vi - da___*	*en ti.*
ra,_____		*ten - drá vi - da*	*e - *	*ter - na.*
mun - do_____	*pa - *	*ra sal - *	*var - nos.*	

Refrain

And I will raise you up, and I will raise you
Yo le re - su - ci - ta - ré, *Yo le re - su - ci - ta -*

up, and I will raise you up on the last day.
ré, *Yo le re - su - ci - ta - ré el di - a de El.*

Text: John 6; Suzanne Toolan, SM, b.1927
Tune: BREAD OF LIFE, Irregular with refrain; Suzanne Toolan, SM, b.1927
© 1966, 1970, 1986, 1993, GIA Publications, Inc.

In the Breaking of the Bread / 932
Cuando Partimos el Pan del Señor

Refrain

In the break - ing
Cuan-do par - ti - mos

of the bread We have known
pan del Se - ñor, lo co - no - ce -

him; we have been fed.
mos, nos da de co - mer.

Je - sus the stran - ger,
sús des - co - no - ci - do,

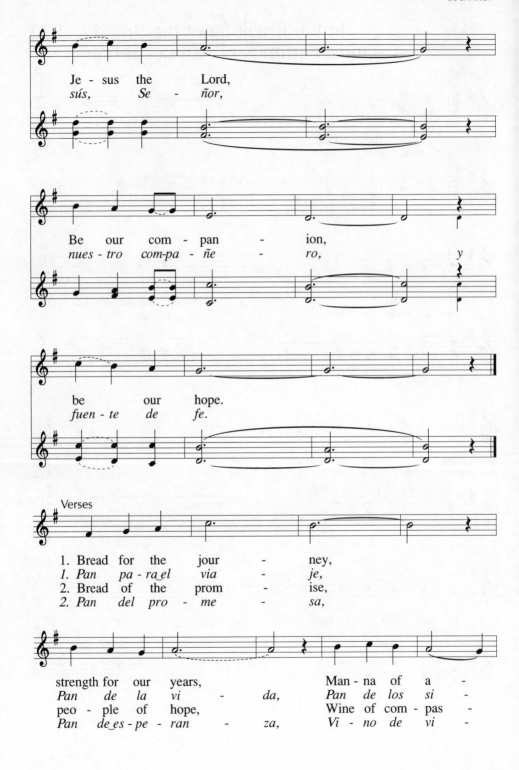

Je - sus the Lord,
sús, *Se* - *ñor,*

Be our com - pan - ion,
nues - tro com-pa - ñe - ro, *y*

be our hope.
fuen - te de fe.

Verses

1. Bread for the jour - ney,
1. Pan pa - ra el via - je,
2. Bread of the prom - ise,
2. Pan del pro - me - sa,

strength for our years,
Pan de la vi - da,
peo - ple of hope,
Pan de es - pe - ran - za,

Man - na of a -
Pan de los si -
Wine of com - pas -
Vi - no de vi -

ges,   of   strug - gle   and   tears.
glos   de   lu - cha y do - lor,
sion,   life   for   the   world
da,   de   su   com - pa - sión,

Cup   of   sal - va   -   tion,
y   es - te   vi   -   no,   fru -
Gath- ered at   ta   -   ble,
En   es - ta   me   -   sa

fruit   of   the   land,
to   de   la   tie   -   rra   ben -
joined as   his   bod   -   y,
un   so - lo   cuer   -   po

Bless   and   re -   ceive   now,   the
dí -   ce - lo,   Pa   -   dre,   es
Sealed in   the   Spir -   it,
en   un   es -   pí -   ri -   tu,   con

D.C.

work   of   our   hands.
tu -   yo,   mi   Dios.
sent   by   the   Word.
u -   na   mi -   sión.

Original Verses:

1. Once I was helpless, sad and confused; darkness surrounded me, courage removed.
   And then I saw him by my side. Carry my burden, open my eyes.

2. There is no sorrow, pain or woe; there is no suffering he did not know.
   He did not waver; he did not bend. He is the victor. He is my friend.

Text: Bob Hurd, b. 1950, and Michael Downey, © 1984, 1987; Spanish text by Stephen Dean and Kathleen Orozco, © 1989, OCP Publications
Tune: Bob Hurd, b. 1950, © 1984; acc. by Dominic MacAller, b. 1959, © 1984, OCP Publications
Published by OCP Publications

933 Now in This Banquet

Refrain

Now in this ban-quet,   Christ is our bread;
Advent: God of our jour-neys,   day-break to night;
Lent: Lord, you can o-pen   hearts that are stone;

Here shall all hun-gers be fed.
Lead us to jus-tice and light.
Live in our flesh and our bone;

Bread that is bro-ken,   wine that is poured,
Grant us com-pas-sion,   strength for the day,
Lead us to won-der,   mys-t'ry and grace,

To verses

Love is the sign of our Lord.
Wis-dom to walk in your way.
One in your lov-ing em-brace.

Last time

Lord.
way.
brace.

May be sung in canon.

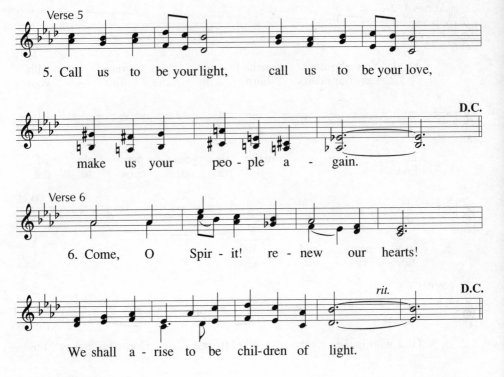

Verse 5
5. Call us to be your light, call us to be your love,

D.C.

make us your peo - ple a - gain.

Verse 6
6. Come, O Spir - it! re - new our hearts!

rit.   D.C.

We shall a - rise to be chil-dren of light.

Text: Marty Haugen, b.1950
Tune: Marty Haugen, b.1950
© 1986, GIA Publications, Inc.

In Paradisum / May Choirs of Angels   934

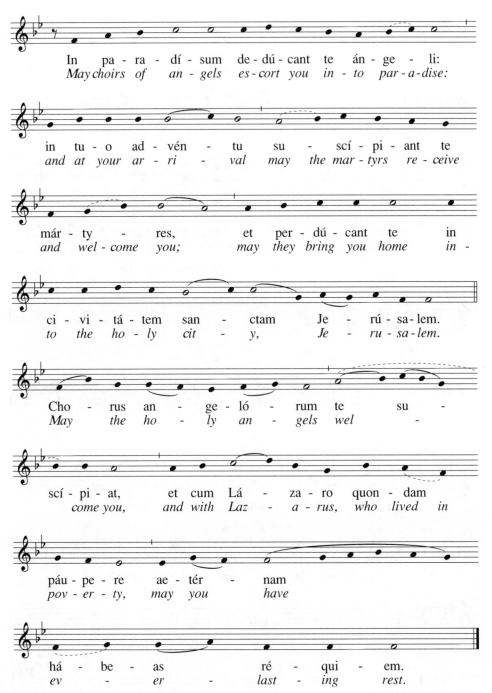

In pa-ra-dí-sum de-dú-cant te án-ge-li:
May choirs of an-gels es-cort you in-to par-a-dise:

in tu-o ad-vén - tu su - scí-pi-ant te
and at your ar-ri - val may the mar-tyrs re-ceive

már-ty - res, et per-dú-cant te in
and wel-come you; may they bring you home in -

ci-vi-tá-tem san - ctam Je-rú-sa-lem.
to the ho-ly cit - y, Je-ru-sa-lem.

Cho-rus an - ge-ló-rum te su -
May the ho - ly an - gels wel -

scí-pi-at, et cum Lá - za-ro quon-dam
come you, and with Laz - a-rus, who lived in

páu-pe-re ae-tér - nam
pov-er-ty, may you have

há-be-as ré-qui - em.
ev - er - last-ing rest.

Text: *In Paradisum*, tr. © 1986, GIA Publications, Inc.
Tune: Mode VII; acc. by Richard Proulx, b.1937, © 1986, GIA Publications, Inc.

935 Song of Farewell

Refrain

Dy - ing you de - stroyed our death! Ris - ing you re-
stored our life! Lord Je - sus, Lord Je - sus,
Lord Je - sus, Lord Je - sus,
come in glo - ry!

Verse 1

1. May Christ who died for you
lead you in - to his king - dom;
may Christ who died for you
lead you this day in - to par - a - dise.

Verse 2

2. May Christ, the Good Shep - herd,

lead you home to - day and give you a

D.C.

place with - in his flock.

Alternate children's verse:

2. May Christ, the Good Shep-herd, take you on his

shoul-ders and bring you home,

D.C.

bring you home to - day.

Verse 3

3. May the an - gels lead you in - to par - a- dise;

may the mar - tyrs come to wel - come you and

take you to the Ho - ly Cit - y, the

D.C.

new and e - ter - nal Je - ru - sa - lem.

Verse 4

4. May the choirs of an-gels come to meet you,

may the choirs of an-gels come to meet you; where

Laz-a-rus is poor no long-er

D.C.

may you have e-ter-nal life in Christ.

Alternate children's verse:

4. May the choirs of an-gels come to meet you,

may the choirs of an-gels come to meet you;

and with all God's chil-dren

D.C.

may you have e-ter-nal life in Christ.

Text: Memorial Acclamation © 1973, ICEL; *In paradisum;* Michael Marchal, © 1988, GIA Publications, Inc.
Tune: Michael Joncas, b.1951, © 1988, GIA Publications, Inc.

I Know That My Redeemer Lives   936

Gently

rall.

Cantor (with simplicity and confidence): **mf**

I know that my Re-deem-er lives,

and on the last day I shall rise a-gain; in my

rall.   *All:*   *a tempo*

bod-y I shall look on God, my Sav-ior, in my bod-y I shall

mf
Cantor:

look on God, my Sav - ior. I my-self shall see him;

more intensely   *rall.*

my own eyes will gaze on him, my own eyes will gaze on him;

a tempo   *rall.*   *a tempo*   *All:*

in my bod-y I shall look on God, my Sav - ior, in my

rall.

bod - y I shall look on God, my Sav - ior.

mf *a tempo*
Cantor: *rall.*

This is the hope I cher-ish, this is the hope I cher-ish in my

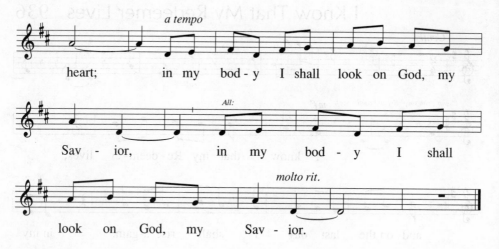

a tempo

heart; in my bod - y I shall look on God, my

All:

Sav - ior, in my bod - y I shall

molto rit.

look on God, my Sav - ior.

Text: *Rite of Funerals,* © 1970, ICEL
Music: *Music for Rite of Funerals and Rite of Baptism for Children,* Howard Hughes, SM, © 1977, ICEL

937 Rest in Peace

Descant:

3. Re -

Melody:

1. Rest in peace, earth's jour - ney end - ed,
2. Hap - py soul, to Christ u - nit - ed,
3. May we meet, dear Lord, in heav - en,

qui - em, Re -

You whom Christ re - deemed, de - fend - ed:
Calm - er now and clear - er - sight - ed:
Each for - giv - ing, each for - giv - en,

qui - em,

To   the   place   where   saints   are   one,
Your   new   jour - ney   now   be   -   gins,
Each   more   gift - ed   to   pur -   sue

Re   -   qui - em,

Safe - ly   brought by   him a - lone—   May   he   grant   us
Freed from earth's be - set - ting   sins: Press-ing   on   to -
All   you   have for   us to   do.   By   your Spir - it's

Do   -   na,   do - na,

like   pro - tec - tion—   Rest   in   peace,   Rest   in   peace,
wards per - fec - tion,   Hap - py soul,   Hap - py soul,
sure   di - rec - tion   May   we meet,   May   we meet,

do - na   e   -   is   re   -   qui - em.

Rest   in   peace,   earth's   jour   -   ney   end - ed.
Hap - py   soul,   to   Christ   u - nit - ed.
May   we   meet,   dear   Lord,   in heav   - en.

Text: Fred Pratt Green, b.1903, © 1982, Hope Publishing Co.
Music: MOEHR, Russell Schulz-Widmar, b.1944, © 1987, GIA Publications, Inc.

938 May the Angels Lead You into Paradise

Gently

Cantor or choir: **p**

May the an-gels lead you in-to par-a-dise;

mf may the mar-tyrs come to wel-come you and take you to the ho-ly cit-y, the new and e-ter-nal Je-ru-sa-lem.

All: May the an-gels lead you in-to par-a-dise; may the mar-tyrs come to wel-come you and take you to the ho-ly cit-y, the new and e-ter-nal Je-ru-sa-lem.

Cantor or choir: May the choir of an-gels wel-come you Where Laz-a-rus is poor no long-er,

p may you have e-ter-nal rest,

rall. may you have e-ter-nal rest.

Text: *In paradisum; Rite of Funerals,* © 1970, ICEL
Tune: *Music for Rite of Funerals and Rite of Baptism for Children,* Howard Hughes, SM, © 1977, ICEL

May Saints and Angels Lead You On   939

1. May saints and an - gels lead you on, Es -
2. Come to the peace of A - bra - ham And

cort - ing you where Christ has gone. Now he has called you,
to the sup - per of the Lamb: Come to the glo - ry

come to him Who sits a - bove the ser - a - phim.
of the blessed, And to per - pet - ual light and rest.

Text: *In Paradisum,* © 1985, ICEL
Tune: TALLIS' CANON, LM; Thomas Tallis, c.1505-1585

940 Keep in Mind

Refrain

Keep in mind that Je-sus Christ has died for us and is ris-en from the dead. He is our sav-ing Lord, he is joy for all a-ges.

Verse 1

D.C.

1. If we die with the Lord, we shall live with the Lord.
If we en-dure with the Lord, we shall reign with the Lord.

Verses 2, 3

D.C.

2. In Christ all our sor-row, in Christ all our joy.
In him hope of glo-ry, in him all our love.
3. In Christ our re-demp-tion, in Christ all our grace.
In him our sal-va-tion, in him all our peace.

Text: 2 Timothy 2:8-12, Lucien Deiss, CSSp, b.1921
Tune: Lucien Deiss, CSSp, b.1921
© 1965, World Library Publications, Inc.

A Nuptial Blessing   941

Refrain

May God bless you, hold and keep you;
may God's mer-cy shine on you,
guide your work and guard your rest-ing,
keep your love for ev-er new.

Verses

1. May God sat - is - fy your long - ing,
2. May God join your hope - ful spir - its,
3. May God make your home a ref - uge

be re - fresh - ment at your ta - ble,
fill your hearts with truth and cour - age,
where you warm - ly wel - come stran - gers

and pro - vide your dai - ly bread,
trust to share both joy and tears,
and the low - ly find a place;

and pro - vide your dai - ly bread,
trust to share both joy and tears,
and the low - ly find a place;

guard your go - ing and your com - ing,
teach love to your chil - dren's chil - dren;
make you car - ing, kind com - pan - ions,

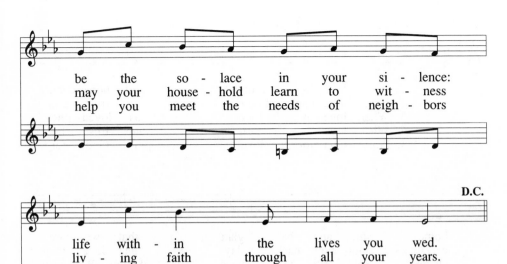

be   the   so -   lace   in   your   si -   lence:
may   your   house - hold   learn   to   wit -   ness
help   you   meet   the   needs   of   neigh - bors

D.C.

life   with - in   the   lives   you   wed.
liv -   ing   faith   through all   your   years.
find - ing   Christ in   ev -   'ry   face.

Text: Vicki Klima; adapt. by Michael Joncas, b.1951, and George Szews
Tune: Michael Joncas, b.1951
© 1989, GIA Publications, Inc.

942 When Love Is Found

1. When love is found and hope comes
2. When love has flow'red in trust and
3. When love is tried as loved-ones
4. When love is torn and trust be -
5. Praise God for love, praise God for

home, Sing and be glad that two are
care, Build both each day that love may
change, Hold still to hope though all seems
trayed, Pray strength to love till tor - ments
life, In age or youth, in calm or

one. When love ex - plodes and fills the
dare To reach be - yond home's warmth and
strange, Till ease re - turns and love grows
fade, Till lov - ers keep no score of
strife. Lift up your hearts let love be

sky, Praise God and share our Mak - er's joy.
light, To serve and strive for truth and right.
wise Through lis - t'ning ears and o - pened eyes.
wrong But hear through pain love's Eas - ter song.
fed Through death and life in bro - ken bread.

Text: Brian Wren, b.1936
Tune: O WALY WALY, LM; English; harm. by Martin West, b.1929
© 1983, Hope Publishing Co.

Wherever You Go   943

Verse 1

1. Wher - ev - er you go   I   shall go.

Wher - ev - er you live   so shall I   live.

Your peo-ple will be   my peo - ple,   and

your God   will be   my God   too.

Verse 2

2. Wher - ev - er you die   I   shall die

and there   shall I   be bur - ied be - side   you.

We will be to - geth-er   for ev - er,   and

our love   will be the gift   of our   life.

Text: Ruth 1:16, 17; Gregory Norbet, b.1940
Tune: Gregory Norbet, b.1940; arr. by Mary David Callahan, b.1923
© 1972, 1980, The Benedictine Foundation of the State of Vermont, Inc.

944 Bridegroom and Bride

1. God, in the plan-ning and pur-pose of life,
2. Je-sus was found, at a sim-i-lar feast,
3. There-fore we pray that his spir-it pre-side
4. Praise then the Mak-er, the Spir-it, the Son,

Hal-lowed the un-ion of hus-band and wife:
Tak-ing the roles of both wait-er and priest,
O-ver the wed-ding of bride-groom and bride,
Source of the love through which two are made one.

This we em-bod-y where love is dis-played,
Turn-ing the world-ly to-wards the di-vine,
Ful-fill-ing all that they've hoped will come true,
God's is the glo-ry, the good-ness, and grace

Rings are pre-sent-ed and prom-is-es made.
Tears in-to laugh-ter and wa-ter to wine.
Light-ing with love all they dream of and do.
Seen in this mar-riage and known in this place.

Text: John L. Bell, b.1949, © 1989, Iona Community, GIA Publication, Inc., agent
Tune: SLANE, 10 10 10 10; Irish traditional; harm. by Erik Routley, 1917-1982, © 1985, Hope Publishing Co.

Blessing the Marriage   945

1. That hu - man life might rich - er be, That
2. As two we love are wed this day And
3. Par - ents and fam - i - lies they leave, Their
4. This is as God meant it to be, That
5. Then, bless the bride - groom, bless the bride, The

chil - dren may be named and known, That love finds its own
we stand wit - ness to their vow, We call on God, the
own new fam - i - ly to make; And, shar - ing what their
man and wom - an should be one And live in love and
dreams they dream, the hopes they share; And thank the Lord whose

sanc - tua - ry, That those in love stay not a - lone.
Trin - i - ty, To sanc - ti - fy their pledg - es now.
pasts have taught, They shape it for the fu - ture's sake.
love through life, As Christ on earth has taught and done.
love in - spires The joy their lips and ours de - clare.

Praise, praise the Mak - er, Spir - it, Son,

bless - ing this mar - riage now be - gun.

Text: John L. Bell, b.1949, © 1989, Iona Community, GIA Publications, Inc., agent
Tune: SUSSEX CAROL, 8 8 8 8 8 88; harm. by Ralph Vaughan Williams, 1872-1958

946 Love Is the Sunlight

1. Love is the sun - light
2. Love is the spa - cious
3. May we in glad - ness

Shaped of your
Qui - et of
Grow in your

splen - dor, Love is the star bright Born of your
shad - ows, Love is the gra - cious Shade of re -
sun - shine, May we in sad - ness Rest in your

hand, Bless-ing of heav - en Gra-cious-ly giv - en,
lease, Mist of the morn - ing, Mid-day a - dorn - ing,
shade, Giv - ing and gain - ing, Ev - er re - main - ing,

Ra - diant with glo - ry From your com - mand.
Cool with the twi - light Breath of your peace.
One in the mar - riage Your love has made.

Text: Borghild Jacobson, © 1981, Concordia Publishing House
Tune: BUNESSAN, 5 5 5 4 D; Gaelic; harm. by A. Gregory Murray, OSB, 1905-1992, © Downside Abbey

Out of the Depths 947

1. Out of the depths, O God, we call to you.
2. Out of the depths of fear, O God, we speak.
3. God of the lov - ing heart, we praise your name.

Wounds of the past re-main, af - fect-ing all we do.
Break - ing the si - len - ces, the sear-ing truth we seek.
Dance through our lives and loves; a - noint with Spir - it flame.

Fac - ing our lives, we need your love so much.
Safe a - mong friends, our grief and rage we share.
Your light il - lu - mines each fa - mil - iar face.

Here in this com - mun - i - ty, heal us by your touch.
Here in this com - mun - i - ty, hold us in your care.
Here in this com - mun - i - ty, meet us with your grace.

Text: Psalm 130:1; Ruth Duck, b.1947, © 1992, GIA Publications, Inc.
Tune: FENNVILLE, 10 12 10 12; Robert J. Batastini, b.1942, © 1994, GIA Publications, Inc.

948 Lord Jesus Christ, Lover of All

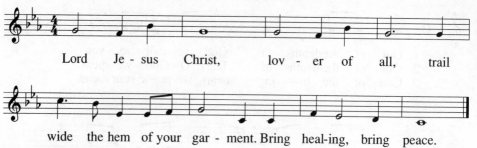

Lord Je-sus Christ, lov-er of all, trail

wide the hem of your gar-ment. Bring heal-ing, bring peace.

Text: John L. Bell, b.1949
Tune: John L. Bell, b.1949
© 1987, Iona Community, GIA Publications, Inc., agent

949 Your Hands, O Lord, in Days of Old

1. Your hands, O Lord, in days of old Were
2. And then your touch brought life and health, Gave
3. O be our might-y heal-er still, O

strong to heal and save; They tri-umphed o-ver
speech, and strength, and sight; And youth re-newed and
Lord of life and death; Re-store and strength-en,

pain and death, Fought dark-ness and the grave. To
health re-stored, Claimed you, the Lord of light: And
soothe and bless, With your al-might-y breath: On

you they went, the blind, the mute, The
so, O Lord, be near to bless, Al -
hands that work and eyes that see, Your

pal - sied, and the lame, The lep - er set a -
might - y now as then, In ev - 'ry street, in
heal - ing wis - dom pour, That whole and sick, and

part and shunned The sick and those in shame.
ev - 'ry home, In ev - 'ry trou - bled friend.
weak and strong, May praise you ev - er - more.

Text: Matthew 14:35-36; Edward H. Plumtre, 1821-1891, alt., © 1986, GIA Publications, Inc.
Tune: MOZART, CMD; adapt. from Wolfgang A. Mozart, 1756-1791

950   O Christ, the Healer

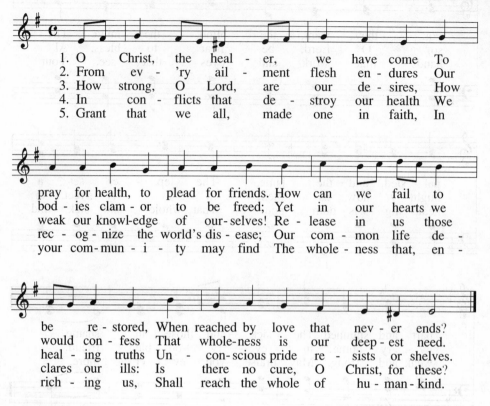

1. O   Christ,   the   heal - er,   we   have   come   To
2. From   ev - 'ry   ail - ment   flesh   en - dures   Our
3. How   strong,   O   Lord,   are   our   de - sires,   How
4. In   con - flicts that   de - stroy   our   health   We
5. Grant   that   we   all,   made   one   in   faith,   In

pray   for health, to   plead   for friends. How   can   we   fail   to
bod - ies clam - or   to   be   freed; Yet   in   our   hearts we
weak   our knowl-edge   of   our-selves! Re - lease   in   us   those
rec - og - nize   the world's dis - ease;   Our   com - mon   life   de -
your com-mun - i - ty   may find   The   whole - ness   that,   en -

be   re - stored, When reached by   love   that   nev - er   ends?
would con - fess   That   whole-ness   is   our   deep - est   need.
heal - ing   truths   Un - con-scious pride   re - sists   or shelves.
clares   our   ills: Is   there   no   cure,   O   Christ, for these?
rich - ing   us,   Shall   reach   the whole   of   hu - man - kind.

Text: Fred Pratt Green, b.1903, © 1969, Hope Publishing Co.
Tune: ERHALT UNS HERR, LM; Klug's *Geistliche Lieder*, 1543; harm. by J.S. Bach, 1685-1750

He Healed the Darkness of My Mind 951

1. He   healed the dark - ness of my mind   The
2. Let   oth - ers call   my faith a   lie,   Or
3. Ask   me not how! But I know who   Has

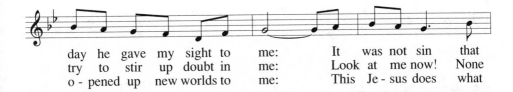

day he gave my sight to   me: It was not sin   that
try to stir up doubt in   me: Look at me now! None
o - pened up new worlds to   me: This Je - sus does what

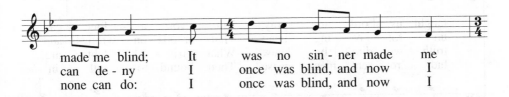

made me blind;   It   was no sin - ner made   me
can de - ny   I   once was blind, and now   I
none can do: I   once was blind, and now   I

1., 2.   3.

see.
see.

                   see.

Text: John 9; Fred Pratt Green, b.1903, © 1982, Hope Publishing Co.
Tune: ARLINGTON, LM; David Haas, b.1957, © 1988, GIA Publications, Inc.

952 Forgive Our Sins

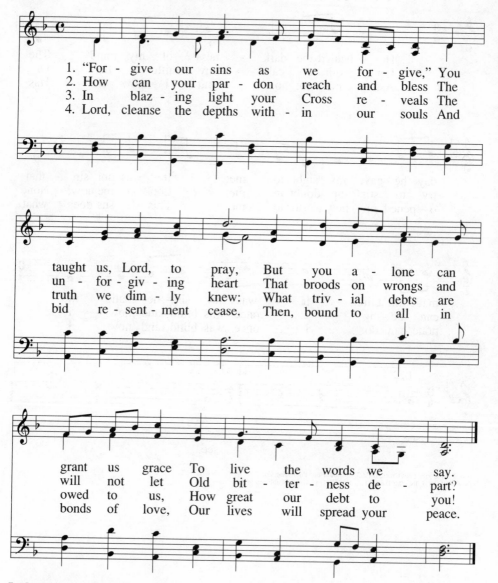

1. "For - give our sins as we for - give," You
2. How can your par - don reach and bless The
3. In blaz - ing light your Cross re - veals The
4. Lord, cleanse the depths with - in our souls And

taught us, Lord, to pray, But you a - lone can
un - for - giv - ing heart That broods on wrongs and
truth we dim - ly knew: What triv - ial debts are
bid re - sent - ment cease. Then, bound to all in

grant us grace To live the words we say.
will not let Old bit - ter - ness de - part?
owed to us, How great our debt to you!
bonds of love, Our lives will spread your peace.

Text: Rosamond Herklots, 1905-1987, © Oxford University Press
Tune: DETROIT, CM; Supplement to *Kentucky Harmony*, 1820; harm. by Gerald H. Knight, 1908-1979, © The Royal School of Church Music

Softly and Tenderly Jesus Is Calling 953

1. Soft - ly and ten - der - ly Je - sus is call - ing,
2. Why should we tar - ry when Je - sus is plead - ing,
3. Time is now fleet - ing, the mo - ments are pass - ing,
4. O for the won - der - ful love He has prom - ised,

Call - ing for you and for me; See, on the
Plead - ing for you and for me? Why should we
Pass - ing from you and from me; Shad - ows are
Prom - ised for you and for me; Though we have

por - tals He's wait - ing and watch - ing,
lin - ger and heed not His mer - cies,
gath - er - ing, death - beds are com - ing,
sinned He has mer - cy and par - don,

Watch - ing for you and for me.
Mer - cies for you and for me?
Com - ing for you and for me.
Par - don for you and for me.

Text: Will L. Thompson, 1847-1909
Music: Will L. Thompson, 1847-1909

Come, You Sinners, Poor and Needy 954

1. Come, you sin - ners, poor and need - y,
2. Come, you thirst - y, come, and wel - come,
3. Come, you wea - ry, heav - y lad - en,

Weak and wound - ed, sick and sore, Je - sus, Son of
God's free boun - ty glo - ri - fy; True be - lief and
Lost and ru - ined by the fall; If you tar - ry

God, will save you, Full of pit - y, love, and pow'r.
true re - pent - ance, Ev - 'ry grace that brings you nigh.
till you're bet - ter, You will nev - er come at all.

I will a - rise and go to Je - sus, He will em - brace me

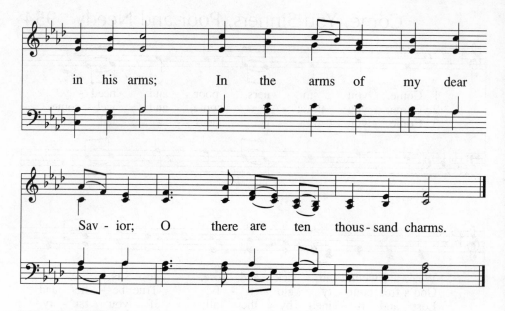

in his arms; In the arms of my dear

Sav - ior; O there are ten thous - and charms.

Text: Joseph Hart, 1712-1768, alt.
Tune: RESTORATION, 8 7 8 7 with refrain; American; harm. by George Mims, b.1938, © 1979, Church of the Redeemer, Houston

955 Our Father, We Have Wandered

1. Our Fa - ther, we have wan - dered And
2. And now at length dis - cern - ing The
3. O Lord of all the liv - ing, Both

hid - den from your face; In fool - ish - ness have
e - vil that we do, Be - hold us, Lord, re -
ban - ished and re - stored, Com - pas - sion - ate, for -

squan - dered Your leg - a - cy of grace. But
turn - ing With hope and trust to you. In
giv - ing And ev - er car - ing Lord, Grant

now, in ex - ile dwell - ing, We
haste you come to meet us And
now that our trans - gress - ing, Our

rise with fear and shame, As dis - tant but com -
home re - joic - ing bring, In glad - ness there to
faith - less - ness may cease. Stretch out your hand in

pell - ing, We hear you call our name.
greet us With calf and robe and ring.
bless - ing, In par - don and in peace.

Text: Kevin Nichols, b.1929, © 1980, ICEL
Tune: PASSION CHORALE, 7 6 7 6 D; Hans Leo Hassler, 1564-1612; harm. by J.S. Bach, 1685-1750

956 The Master Came to Bring Good News

1. The Mas - ter came to bring good news, The
2. The Law's ful - filled through Je - sus Christ, The
3. To seek the sin - ners Je - sus came, To
4. For - give us, Lord, as we for - give And

news of love and free - dom, To heal the sick and
man who lived for oth - ers, The law of Christ is:
live a - mong the friend - less, To show them love that
seek to help each oth - er. For - give us, Lord, and

seek the poor, To build the peace - ful king - dom.
Serve in love Our sis - ters and our broth - ers.
they might share The king - dom that is end - less.
we shall live To pray and work to - geth - er.

Fa - ther, for - give us! Through Je - sus hear us!

As we for-give one an-oth - er!

Text: Ralph Finn b.1941, © 1965, GIA Publications, Inc.
Tune: ICH GLAUB AN GOTT, 8 7 8 7 with refrain; *Mainz Gesangbuch*, 1870; harm. by Richard Proulx, b.1937, © 1986, GIA Publications, Inc.

957 Ashes

1. We rise a - gain from ash - es, from the
2. We of - fer you our fail - ures, we
3. Then rise a - gain from ash - es, let
4. ξ Thanks be to the Fa - ther, who

good we've failed to do. We rise a - gain from
of - fer you at - tempts, The gifts not ful - ly
heal - ing come to pain, Though spring has turned to
made us like him - self. Thanks be to the

ash - es, to cre - ate our - selves a - new. If
giv - en, the dreams not ful - ly dreamt. Give our
win - ter, and sun - shine turned to rain. The
Son, who saved us by his death.

all our world is ash - es, then must our lives be
stum - bl - ings di - rec - tion, give our vi - sions wid - er
rain we'll use for grow - ing, and cre - ate the world a -
Thanks be to the Spir - it, who cre - ates the world a -

true, An of - fer - ing of ash - es, an
view, An of - fer - ing of ash - es, an
new From an of - fer - ing of ash - es, an
new From an of - fer - ing of ash - es, an

1.- 3. *4.*

of - fer - ing to you.
of - fer - ing to you.
of - fer - ing to you.
of - fer - ing to you.

Text: Tom Conry, b.1951
Tune: Tom Conry, b.1951; acc. by Michael Joncas, b.1951
© 1978, New Dawn Music

Healer of Our Every Ill   958

Refrain

Descant:

Melody:

Heal - er of our ev - 'ry ill, light of each to - mor - row, give us peace be - yond our fear, and hope be - yond our sor - row.

Last time

Verses

1. You who know our fears and sad - ness,
2. In the pain and joy be - hold - ing,
3. Give us strength to love each oth - er,
4. You who know each thought and feel - ing,

Grace us with your peace and glad - ness,
How your grace is still un - fold - ing,
Ev - 'ry sis - ter, ev - 'ry broth - er,
Teach us all your way of heal - ing,

D.C.

Spir - it of all com - fort: fill our hearts.
Give us all your vi - sion: God of love.
Spir - it of all kind - ness: be our guide.
Spir - it of com - pas - sion: fill each heart.

Text: Marty Haugen, b.1950
Tune: Marty Haugen, b.1950
© 1987, GIA Publications, Inc.

959 God of Eve and God of Mary

Refrain

Descant:
God of Eve, God of Mar - y,

Melody:
God of Eve and God of Mar - y,

God of moth - er earth,

God of love and moth - er earth,

Thank you for the ones who with us

Thank you for the ones who with us

Shared their life and gave us birth.

Shared their life and gave us birth.

Verses

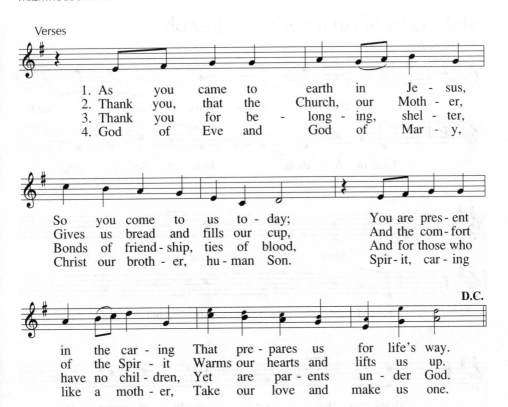

1. As you came to earth in Je - sus,
2. Thank you, that the Church, our Moth - er,
3. Thank you for be - long - ing, shel - ter,
4. God of Eve and God of Mar - y,

So you come to us to - day; You are pres - ent
Gives us bread and fills our cup, And the com - fort
Bonds of friend - ship, ties of blood, And for those who
Christ our broth - er, hu - man Son. Spir - it, car - ing

D.C.

in the car - ing That pre - pares us for life's way.
of the Spir - it Warms our hearts and lifts us up.
have no chil - dren, Yet are par - ents un - der God.
like a moth - er, Take our love and make us one.

Text: Fred Kaan, b.1929, © 1989, Hope Publishing Co.
Tune: FARRELL, 8 7 8 7 with refrain, Thomas J. Porter, b.1958, © 1994, GIA Publications, Inc.

960 God of Adam, God of Joseph

Refrain

God of A - dam, God of Jo - seph,

God of A - dam, God of Jo - seph,

God of sow - ing,

God of sow - ing, soil and seed,

Thank you for your world of prom - ise:

Thank you for your world of prom - ise:

Milk and hon - ey, wine and bread.

Milk and hon - ey, wine and bread.

Verses

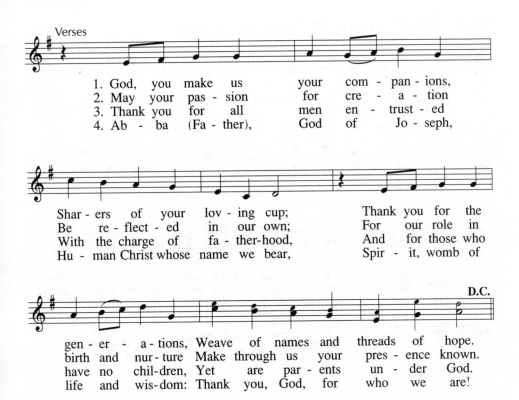

1. God, you make us your com - pan - ions,
2. May your pas - sion for cre - a - tion
3. Thank you for all men en - trust - ed
4. Ab - ba (Fa - ther), God of Jo - seph,

Shar - ers of your lov - ing cup;   Thank you for the
Be re - flect - ed in our own;   For our role in
With the charge of fa - ther-hood,   And for those who
Hu - man Christ whose name we bear,   Spir - it, womb of

D.C.

gen - er - a - tions, Weave of names and threads of hope.
birth and nur - ture Make through us your pres - ence known.
have no chil-dren, Yet are par - ents un - der God.
life and wis-dom: Thank you, God, for who we are!

Text: Fred Kaan, b.1929, © 1989, Hope Publishing Co.
Tune: FARRELL, 8 7 8 7 with refrain, Thomas J. Porter, b.1958, © 1994, GIA Publications, Inc.

961 Our Father, by Whose Name

1. Our Fa-ther, by whose name All par-ent-hood is known,
2. O Christ, thy-self a child With-in an earth-ly home,
3. O Spir-it, who dost bind Our hearts in u-ni-ty,

Who dost in love pro-claim Each fam-i-ly thine own.
With heart still un-de-filed, Thou didst to man-hood come;
And teach-est us to find The love from self set free,

Bless thou all par-ents, guard-ing well, With con-stant love as
Our chil-dren bless, in ev-'ry place, That they may all be-
In all our hearts such love in-crease, That ev-'ry home, by

sen-ti-nel, The homes in which thy peo-ple dwell.
hold thy face, And know-ing thee may grow in grace.
this re-lease, May be the dwell-ing place of peace.

Text: F. Bland Tucker, 1895-1984, alt., © 1941, The Church Pension Fund
Tune: RHOSYMEDRE, 6 6 6 6 888; John Edwards, 1806-1885

O Saving Victim / O Salutaris 962

1. O Sav - ing Vic - tim, o - p'ning wide The
2. To your great name be end - less praise, Im -
1. O sa - lu - tá - ris hó - sti - a, Quae
2. U - ni tri - nó - que Dó - mi - no Sit

gate of heav'n to us be - low! Our foes press on from
mor - tal God - head, One in Three; O grant us end - less
cae - li pan - dis ó - sti - um: Bel - la pre - munt ho -
sem - pi - tér - na gló - ri - a: Qui vi - tam si - ne

ev - 'ry side: Your aid sup - ply, your strength be - stow.
length of days When our true na - tive land we see.
stí - li - a, Da ro - bur fer au - xí - li - um.
tér - mi - no No - bis do - net in pá - tri - a.

Text: Thomas Aquinas, 1227-1275; tr. by Edward Caswall, 1814-1878, alt.
Tune: DUGUET, LM; Dieu donne Duguet, d.1767

963 Come Adore / Tantum Ergo

1. Come a-dore this won-drous pres-ence, Bow to Christ the
2. Glo-ry be to God the Fa-ther, Praise to his co-
1. *Tan-tum er-go Sa-cra-mén-tum Ve-ne-ré-mur*
2. *Ge-ni-tó-ri, Ge-ni-tó-que Laus et ju-bi-*

source of grace. Here is kept the an-cient prom-ise
e-qual Son, Ad-o-ra-tion to the Spir-it,
cér-nu-i: Et an-tí-quum do-cu-mén-tum
lá-ti-o, Sa-lus, ho-nor, vir-tus quo-que

Of God's earth-ly dwell-ing-place. Sight is blind be-
Bond of love, in God-head one. Blest be God by
No-vo ce-dat rí-tu-i: Prae-stet fi-des
Sit et be-ne-dí-cti-o: Pro-ce-dén-ti

fore God's glo-ry, Faith a-lone may see his face.
all cre-a-tion Joy-ous-ly while a-ges run.
sup-ple-mén-tum Sén-su-um de-fé-ctu-i.
ab u-tró-que Com-par sit lau-dá-ti-o.

Text: Thomas Aquinas, 1227-1274; tr. by James Quinn, SJ, b.1919, © 1969. Used by permission of Selah Publishing Co., Inc.
Tune: ST. THOMAS, 8 7 8 7 8 7; John F. Wade, 1711-1786

This Is My Song 964

1. This is my song, O God of all the na - tions,
2. My coun-try's skies are blu - er than the o - cean,
3. This is my prayer, O God of all earth's king - doms,

A song of peace for lands a - far and mine.
And sun-light beams on clo - ver - leaf and pine.
Your king-dom come; on earth your will be done.

This is my home, the coun-try where my heart is;
But oth - er lands have sun-light too, and clo - ver,
Let Christ be lift - ed up till all shall serve him,

Here are my hopes, my dreams, my ho - ly shrine;
And skies are ev - 'ry - where as blue as mine.
And hearts u - nit - ed learn to live as one.

maj - es - ties A - bove the fruit - ed plain! A -
free - dom beat A - cross the wil - der - ness! A -
coun - try loved, And mer - cy more than life! A -
cit - ies gleam, Un - dimmed by hu - man tears! A -

mer - i - ca! A - mer - i - ca! God
mer - i - ca! A - mer - i - ca! God
mer - i - ca! A - mer - i - ca! May
mer - i - ca! A - mer - i - ca! God

shed his grace on thee, And crown thy good with
mend thine ev - 'ry flaw, Con - firm thy soul in
God thy gold re - fine, Till all suc - cess be
shed his grace on thee, And crown thy good with

broth - er - hood From sea to shin - ing sea.
self - con - trol, Thy lib - er - ty in law.
no - ble - ness, And ev - 'ry gain di - vine.
broth - er - hood From sea to shin - ing sea.

Text: Katherine L. Bates, 1859-1929
Tune: MATERNA, CMD; Samuel A. Ward, 1848-1903

966 God of Our Fathers

1. God of our fa - thers, whose al - might - y hand
2. Your love di - vine has led us in the past,
3. From war's a - larms, from dead - ly pes - ti - lence,
4. Re - fresh your peo - ple on their toil - some way,

Leads forth in beau - ty all the star - ry band
In this free land by you our lot is cast;
Your might - y arm our ev - er sure de - fense;
Lead us from night to nev - er - end - ing day;

Of shin - ing worlds in splen - dor through the skies,
Be our strong rul - er, guar - dian, guide, and stay,
Your true re - li - gion in our hearts in - crease,
Fill all our lives with heav'n-born love and grace,

Our grate - ful songs be - fore your throne a - rise.
Your word our law, your paths our cho - sen way.
Your boun - teous good - ness nour - ish us in peace.
Un - til at last, we meet be - fore your face.

Text: Daniel C. Roberts, 1841-1907
Tune: NATIONAL HYMN, 10 10 10 10; George W. Warren, 1828-1902

The God of All Eternity   967

1. The God of all e-ter-ni-ty, Un-bound by
2. What shall we of - fer God to-day— Our dreams of
3. God does not share our doubts and fears, Nor shrinks from
4. Let faith or for - tune rise or fall, Let dreams and
5. God grant that we, in this new year, May show the

space yet al - ways near, Is pres - ent
what we can - not see, Or, with eyes
the un - known or strange: The one who
dread both have their day; Those whom God
world the King - dom's face, And let our

where his peo - ple meet To cel - e -
fas - tened to the past, Our dread of
fash - ioned heav'n and earth Makes all things
loves walk un - a - fraid With Christ their
work and wor - ship thrive As signs of

brate the com - ing year.
what is yet to be?
new and ush - ers change.
guide and Christ their way.
hope and means of grace.

Text: John L. Bell, b.1949, © 1989, Iona Community, GIA Publications, Inc., agent
Tune: O WALY WALY, 8 8 8 8; English traditional; arr. by John L. Bell, b.1949, © 1989, Iona Community, GIA Publications, Inc., agent

968 Greet Now the Swiftly Changing Year

1. Greet now the swift-ly chang-ing year With
2. This Je-sus came to wage sin's war; The
3. His love a-bun-dant far ex-ceeds The
4. With such a Lord to lead our way In
5. "All glo-ry be to God on high And

joy and pen-i-tence sin-cere; Re-joice, re-joice, with
Name of names for us he bore; Re-joice, re-joice, with
vol-ume of a whole year's needs; Re-joice, re-joice, with
want and in pros-per-i-ty, What need we fear in
peace on earth," the an-gels cry; Re-joice, re-joice, with

thanks em-brace An-oth-er year of grace.
thanks em-brace An-oth-er year of grace.
thanks em-brace An-oth-er year of grace.
earth or space In this new year of grace?
thanks em-brace An-oth-er year of grace.

Text: Slovak, 17th C.; tr. Jaroslav J. Vajda, b.1919, alt. © 1969, Concordia Publishing House
Tune: SIXTH NIGHT, 88 86; Alfred V. Fedak, © 1989, Selah Publishing Co.

But oth - er hearts in oth - er lands are beat - ing
So hear my song, O God of all the na - tions,
So hear my prayer, O God of all the na - tions.

With hopes and dreams as true and high as mine.
A song of peace for their land and for mine.
My - self I give you; let your will be done.

Text: St. 1-2, Lloyd Stone, b.1912, © 1934, Lorenz Publishing Co., st. 3, Georgia Harkness, 1891-1974, © 1964, Lorenz Publishing Co.
Tune: FINLANDIA, 11 10 11 10 11 10; Jean Sibelius, 1865-1957

965 America the Beautiful

1. O beau - ti - ful for spa - cious skies, For
2. O beau - ti - ful for pil - grim feet, Whose
3. O beau - ti - ful for he - roes proved In
4. O beau - ti - ful for pa - triot dream That

am - ber waves of grain, For pur - ple moun - tain
stern, im - pas - sioned stress A thor - ough - fare for
lib - er - at - ing strife, Who more than self their
sees be - yond the years Thine al - a - bas - ter

Appendix

Passion or Palm Sunday is the last Sunday in Lent. Its closeness to the end of Lent has given this liturgy two distinct features: the procession with palms and the gospel reading of the Lord's passion. The blessing and carrying of palms celebrates Jesus' entrance into Jerusalem to accomplish his paschal mystery. The reading of the passion comes as a conclusion to all the gospel readings of the Lenten Sundays: these scriptures yearly prepare catechumens and the faithful to approach the celebration of Christ's death and resurrection. That celebration takes place most especially in the sacraments of initiation at the Easter Vigil.

COMMEMORATION OF THE LORD'S ENTRANCE INTO JERUSALEM

This rite may be very simple or may involve the entire assembly in a procession with the blessing of palms and the gospel reading of Jesus' entrance into Jerusalem.

OPENING ANTIPHON
The following or another appropriate acclamation may be sung.

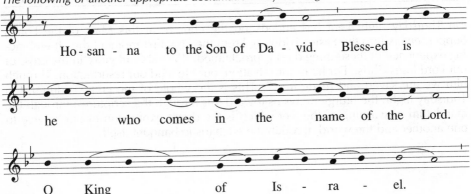

Ho - san - na to the Son of Da - vid. Bless-ed is

he who comes in the name of the Lord.

O King of Is - ra - el.

Ho - san - na   in   the   high - est.

Music: Chant Mode VII; acc. by Richard Proulx, © 1985, GIA Publications, Inc.

BLESSING OF BRANCHES

All hold branches as these are blessed. The branches may be of palm or from a tree that is native to the area. The green or flowering branches signify the victory of life.

PROCESSION

All join in the procession or at least in the song. Such a movement of people expresses the experience of Lent: the church has been called to move on, to go ever further toward the paschal mystery of death and resurrection. The hymn, "All Glory, Laud, and Honor" (no. 563) or another appropriate song is sung during the procession.

The commemoration of the Lord's entrance into Jerusalem, whether this is done in a simple or solemn manner, concludes with the opening prayer of the Mass.

---

970   EASTER TRIDUUM

"The Easter Triduum of the passion and resurrection of Christ is...the culmination of the entire liturgical year. What Sunday is to the week, the solemnity of Easter is to the liturgical year." (General Norms for the Liturgical Year, #18)

Lent ends quietly on Thursday afternoon. The church enters the Triduum ("three days"). On Thursday night the church begins a time of prayer and fasting, a time of keeping watch, that lasts into the great Vigil between Saturday and Sunday. The church emphasizes that the fasting of Good Friday and, if possible, of Holy Saturday are integral to the keeping of these days and the preparation for the sacraments of initiation celebrated at the Vigil. On Thursday night and on Friday afternoon or evening the church gathers to pray and to remember the many facets of the single mystery.

---

971   HOLY THURSDAY: EVENING MASS OF THE LORD'S SUPPER

On Thursday night Lent has ended and the church, at this Mass of the Lord's Supper, enters into the Easter Triduum. From the very first moment the all-embracing experience of these three days is proclaimed: "We should glory in the cross of our Lord Jesus Christ. For he is our salvation, our life, and our resurrection. Through him we are saved and made free." This is the whole of the great Triduum. On Thursday night, the liturgy draws us toward this through the scriptures, through the mandatum or washing of the feet which is the direct expression of our service to one another and the world, through the eucharistic banquet itself.

WASHING OF FEET

The homily is followed by the washing of feet, the mandatum (from the Latin word for "command": "A new commandment I give to you..."). This is a simple gesture of humble service: the priest washes the feet of various members of the assembly. Such a gesture, with the song which accompanies it, speaks directly of the way of life Christians seek.

Appropriate songs are: Ubi Caritas, no. 746 or 752, and Jesus Took a Towel, no. 566.

The Mass continues with the general intercessions.

TRANSFER OF THE HOLY EUCHARIST 972

When the communion rite is concluded, the eucharistic bread that remains is solemnly carried from the altar. The following hymn accompanies the procession.

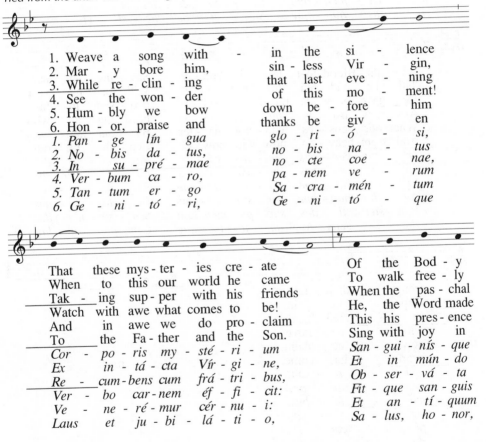

of | the | Sav - ior | Who | was | tor - tured | for | our | sake
through the | fur - rows | Scat - ter - ing | his | Fa - ther's | grain
meal | was | end - ed | With | the | rites | the | Law | de - | mands
flesh, | has | spo - ken | And | the | bread | and | wine | per - | ceived
on | our | al - tar | Glo - | ri - fied | be - yond | all | pain.
their | own | Spir - it | Who | a - lone | can | make | us | one,
pre - | ti - | ó - si, | Quem | in | mún - di | pré - ti - | um
con - | ver - | sá - tus, | Spar - so | vér - bi | sé - mi - ne,
le - | ge | ple - ne | Ci - bis | in | le - gá - li - bus,
Chri - sti | me - rum, | Et | si | sen - sus | dé - fi - cit,
do - | cu - | mén - tum | No - | vo | ce - dat | rí - tu - i;
vir - | tus | quo - que | Sit | et | be - ne - dí - cti - o:

And | the | Blood that | left | his | bod - y | Sav - ing | sin - ners
Till | he | end - ed | his | brief | vis - it | With | a | har - vest
He | gave | them | as | bread | his | bod - y | Bro - ken | in | his
Are | now | tru - ly | his | own | bod - y | Feed - ing | all | who
What our | sens - es | can - not | mas - ter | By | our | faith | we
And from | heav - en | now | with | pow - er | Gen - tly | to | our
Fru - ctus | ven - tris | ge - ne - ró - si | Rex | ef - fú - dit
Su - i | mo - ras | in - co - lá - tus | Mi - ro | clau - sit
Ci - bum | tur - bae | du - o - dé - nae | Se | dat | su - is
Ad | fir - mán - dum | cor | sin - cé - rum | So - la | fi - des
Prae - stet | fi - des | sup - ple - mén - tum | Sén - su - um | de -
Pro - ce - dén - ti | ab | u - tró - que | Com - par | sit | lau -

from | their | fate.
reaped | in | pain.
sa - | cred | hands.
will | be - lieve.
now | ac - claim.
hearts | has | come. | A - men.
gén - | ti - um.
ór - | di - ne.
má - | ni - bus.
súf - | fi - cit.
fé - | ctu - i.
dá - | ti - o. | A - men.

Text: *Pange lingua,* Thomas Aquinas, 1227-1274; tr. by Ralph Wright, OSB, b.1938, © 1989, GIA Publications, Inc.
Tune: PANGE LINGUA, 8 7 8 7 8 7; Mode III; acc. by Eugene Lapierre, © 1964, GIA Publications, Inc.

The liturgy has no concluding rite, no dismissal. Rather, the church continues to watch and pray throughout the Triduum.

GOOD FRIDAY 973

In Good Friday's liturgy of the word and veneration of the cross there is great solemnity: a pondering of the "mystery of our faith," the passion, death and resurrection of our Lord Jesus Christ. Fasting and praying during these days, the catechumens and the baptized assemble on Good Friday in the afternoon or evening for a time of prayer together. This begins a time of silence.

LITURGY OF THE WORD

GENERAL INTERCESSIONS
As at Sunday liturgy, the word service concludes with prayers of intercession. Today these prayers take a more solemn form as the church lifts up to God its own needs and those of the world.

VENERATION OF THE CROSS 974
An ancient liturgical text reads: "See here the true and most revered Tree. Hasten to kiss it and to cry out with faith: You are our help, most revered Cross." For many centuries the church has solemnly venerated the relic or image of the cross on Good Friday. It is not present as a picture of suffering only but as a symbol of Christ's passover, where "dying he destroyed our death and rising restored our life." It is the glorious, the life-giving cross that the faithful venerate with song, prayer, kneeling and a kiss.

As the cross is shown to the assembly, the following is sung.

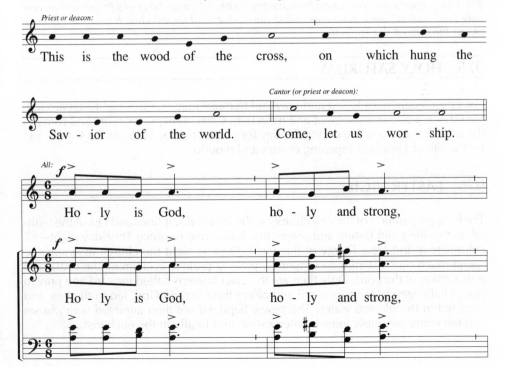

ho - ly and liv - ing for ev - er.

ho - ly and liv - ing for ev - er.

Music: Howard Hughes, SM, © 1979, 1985, GIA Publications, Inc.

As the assembly comes forward to venerate the cross, appropriate hymns and songs may be sung.

HOLY COMMUNION

This liturgy concludes with a simple communion rite. All recite the Lord's Prayer and receive holy communion. There is no concluding rite or dismissal for the church continues to be at prayer throughout the Triduum.

975   HOLY SATURDAY

The church continues to fast and pray and to make ready for this night's great Vigil. Saturday is a day of great quiet and reflection. Catechumens, sponsors and some of the faithful may assemble during the day for prayer, the recitation of the Creed, and for the rite of Ephpheta (opening of ears and mouth).

976   EASTER VIGIL

The long preparation of the catechumens, the lenten disciplines and fast of the faithful, the vigiling and fasting and prayer that have gone on since Thursday night—all culminate in the great liturgy of this night. On this night the church assembles to spend much time listening to scriptures, praying psalms, acclaiming the death and resurrection of the Lord. Only then are the catechumens called forward and prayed over, challenged to renounce evil and affirm their faith in God, led to the font and baptized in the blessed water. The newly baptized are then anointed with chrism and the entire assembly joins in intercession and finally in the eucharist.

INTRODUCTORY RITE

BLESSING OF THE FIRE AND LIGHTING OF THE PASCHAL CANDLE
The night vigil begins with the kindling of new fire and the lighting of the assembly's paschal candle.

PROCESSION
The ministers and assembly go in procession to the place where the scriptures will be read. The following is sung during the procession.

Christ our light.   Thanks be to God.

EASTER PROCLAMATION: THE EXSULTET
In this ancient text the church gives thanks and praise to God for all that is recalled this night: Adam's fall, the deliverance from Egypt, the passover of Christ, the wedding of earth and heaven, our reconciliation.

LITURGY OF THE WORD
At the Vigil, the liturgy of the word is an extended time of readings, silence and the chanting of psalms. On this night when the faithful know the death and resurrection of the Lord in baptism and eucharist, the church needs first to hear these scriptures which are the foundation of our life together: the creation story, Abraham and Isaac, the dividing of the sea, the poetry of Isaiah and Baruch and Ezekiel, the proclamation of Paul to the Romans and the gospel account of Jesus' resurrection.

977 LITURGY OF BAPTISM

After the homily the catechumens are called forward. The assembly chants the litany of the saints, invoking the holy women and men of all centuries. Patron saints of the church and of the catechumens and the faithful may be included in the litany.

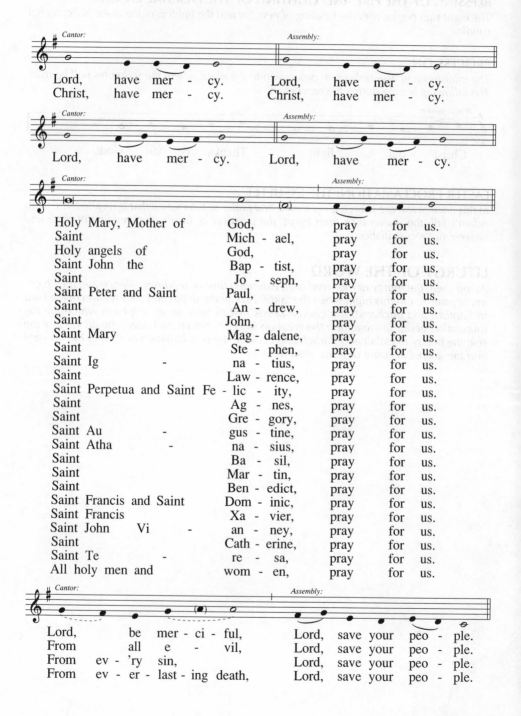

Cantor: Lord, have mer - cy.   Assembly: Lord, have mer - cy.
         Christ, have mer - cy.   Christ, have mer - cy.

Cantor: Lord, have mer - cy.   Assembly: Lord, have mer - cy.

Cantor:		Assembly:		
Holy Mary, Mother of	God,	pray	for	us.
Saint	Mich - ael,	pray	for	us.
Holy angels of	God,	pray	for	us.
Saint John the	Bap - tist,	pray	for	us.
Saint	Jo - seph,	pray	for	us.
Saint Peter and Saint	Paul,	pray	for	us.
Saint	An - drew,	pray	for	us.
Saint	John,	pray	for	us.
Saint Mary	Mag - dalene,	pray	for	us.
Saint	Ste - phen,	pray	for	us.
Saint Ig -	na - tius,	pray	for	us.
Saint	Law - rence,	pray	for	us.
Saint Perpetua and Saint Fe -	lic - ity,	pray	for	us.
Saint	Ag - nes,	pray	for	us.
Saint	Gre - gory,	pray	for	us.
Saint Au -	gus - tine,	pray	for	us.
Saint Atha -	na - sius,	pray	for	us.
Saint	Ba - sil,	pray	for	us.
Saint	Mar - tin,	pray	for	us.
Saint	Ben - edict,	pray	for	us.
Saint Francis and Saint	Dom - inic,	pray	for	us.
Saint Francis	Xa - vier,	pray	for	us.
Saint John Vi -	an - ney,	pray	for	us.
Saint	Cath - erine,	pray	for	us.
Saint Te -	re - sa,	pray	for	us.
All holy men and	wom - en,	pray	for	us.

Cantor:		Assembly:			
Lord,	be mer - ci - ful,	Lord,	save your	peo - ple.
From	all e - vil,	Lord,	save your	peo - ple.
From	ev - 'ry sin,	Lord,	save your	peo - ple.
From	ev - er - last - ing death,	Lord,	save your	peo - ple.

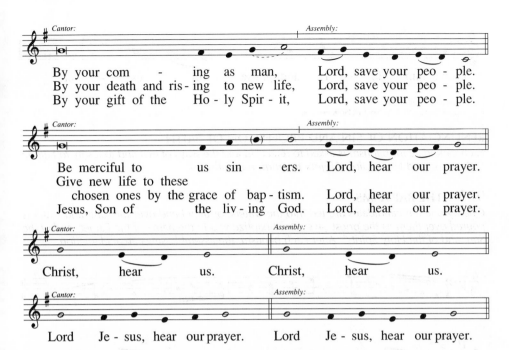

By your com - ing as man, Lord, save your peo - ple.
By your death and ris - ing to new life, Lord, save your peo - ple.
By your gift of the Ho - ly Spir - it, Lord, save your peo - ple.

Be merciful to us sin - ers. Lord, hear our prayer.
Give new life to these
chosen ones by the grace of bap - tism. Lord, hear our prayer.
Jesus, Son of the liv - ing God. Lord, hear our prayer.

Christ, hear us. Christ, hear us.

Lord Je - sus, hear our prayer. Lord Je - sus, hear our prayer.

Text: *Litany of the Saints, Roman Missal*
Music: *Litany of the Saints, Roman Missal*

BLESSING OF WATER 978

The priest gives thanks and praise to God over the waters of baptism. This acclamation is sung by all.

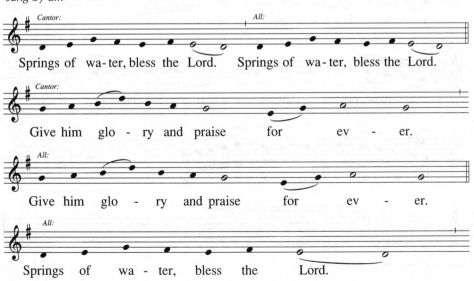

Springs of wa - ter, bless the Lord. Springs of wa - ter, bless the Lord.

Give him glo - ry and praise for ev - er.

Give him glo - ry and praise for ev - er.

Springs of wa - ter, bless the Lord.

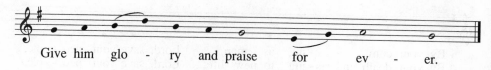

Give him glo - ry and praise for ev - er.

Text: Refrain trans. © 1973, ICEL
Tune: Richard Proulx, b.1937, © 1985, GIA Publications, Inc.

RENUNCIATION OF SIN AND PROFESSION OF FAITH

Each candidate for baptism is asked to reject sin and the ways of evil and to testify to faith in Father, Son and Holy Spirit. All join to affirm this faith.

979   THE BAPTISMS

One by one the candidates are led into the waters, or they bend over the font, and water is poured over them as the priest says: "N., I baptize you in the name of the Father, and of the Son, and of the Holy Spirit." After each baptism, the assembly sings an acclamation.

Cantor:
You have put on Christ, in him you have been bap - tized.

Al - le - lu - ia, al - le - lu - ia.

All:
You have put on Christ, in him you have been bap - tized.

Al - le - lu - ia, al - le - lu - ia.

Music: Howard Hughes, SM, © 1977, ICEL

Each of the newly baptized is then clothed in a baptismal garment.

RECEPTION INTO FULL COMMUNION
Those who have been previously baptized are now called forward to profess their faith and to be received into the full communion of the Roman Catholic Church.

CONFIRMATION
Infants who have been baptized are anointed with chrism. Children and adults are usually confirmed: the priest prays and lays hands on them, then anoints each of the newly baptized with chrism saying: "N., be sealed with the Gift of the Holy Spirit."

RENEWAL OF BAPTISMAL PROMISES
All of the faithful repeat and affirm the rejection of sin made at baptism and profess faith in the Father, Son and Holy Spirit. The assembly is sprinkled with the baptismal water. The newly baptized then take their places in the assembly and, for the first time, join in the prayer of the faithful, the prayers of intercession.

LITURGY OF THE EUCHARIST
The gifts and table are prepared and the eucharist is celebrated in the usual way.

Sequence for Easter 980

1. Chris - tians, praise the pas - chal vic-tim! Of - fer thank- ful sac - ri- fice!
1. Ví - cti - mae Pa-schá - li lau-des im - mó-lent Chri - sti - á - ni.

2. Christ the Lamb has saved the sheep, Christ the just one paid the
3. Death and life fought bit - ter - ly For this won-drous vic - to -
2. A - gnus ré - de - mit ó - ves: Chri - stus ín - no - cens Pá -
3. Mors et vi - ta du - él - lo con - fli - xé - re mi - rán -

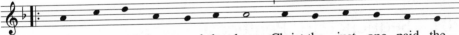

price, Re - con - cil - ing sin - ners to the Fa - ther.
ry; The Lord of life who died reigns glo - ri - fied!
tri re - con - ci - li - á - vit pec - ca - tó - res.
do: dux vi - tae mór - tu - us re - gnat vi - vus.

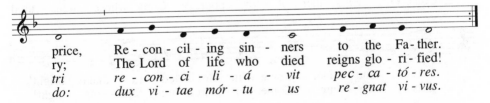

4. O Mar - y, come and say what you saw at break of day.
6. Bright an - gels tes - ti - fied, Shroud and grave clothes side by side!
4. Dic no - bis Ma - rí - a, quid vi - dí - sti in vi - a?
6. An - gé - li - cos te - stes, su - dá - ri - um, et ve-stes.

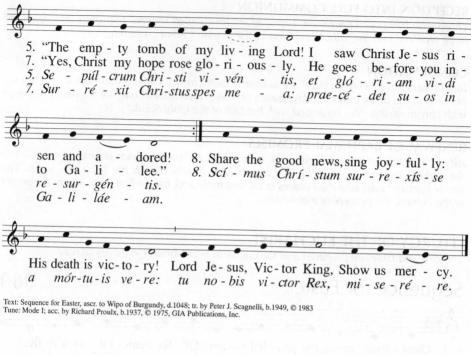

5. "The emp - ty tomb of my liv - ing Lord! I saw Christ Je - sus ri -
7. "Yes, Christ my hope rose glo - ri - ous - ly. He goes be - fore you in -
5. *Se - púl - crum Chri - sti vi - vén - tis, et gló - ri - am vi - di*
7. *Sur - ré - xit Chri - stus spes me - a: prae-cé - det su - os in*

sen and a - dored! 8. Share the good news, sing joy - ful - ly:
to Ga - li - lee." 8. *Scí - mus Chrí - stum sur - re - xís - se*
re - sur - gén - tis.
Ga - li - láe - am.

His death is vic - to - ry! Lord Je - sus, Vic - tor King, Show us mer - cy.
a mór - tu - is ve - re: tu no - bis vi - ctor Rex, mi - se - ré - re.

Text: Sequence for Easter, ascr. to Wipo of Burgundy, d.1048; tr. by Peter J. Scagnelli, b.1949, © 1983
Tune: Mode I; acc. by Richard Proulx, b.1937, © 1975, GIA Publications, Inc.

981 Sequence for Pentecost

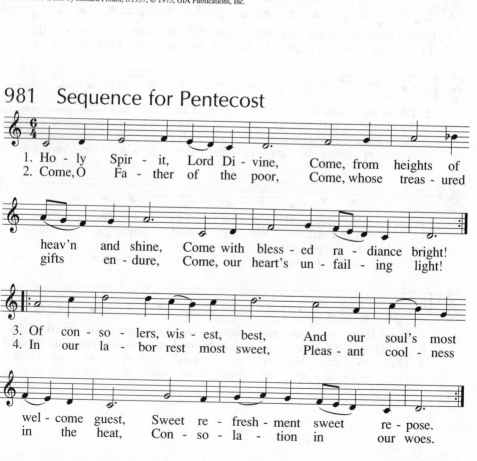

1. Ho - ly Spir - it, Lord Di - vine, Come, from heights of
2. Come, O Fa - ther of the poor, Come, whose treas - ured

heav'n and shine, Come with bless - ed ra - diance bright!
gifts en - dure, Come, our heart's un - fail - ing light!

3. Of con - so - lers, wis - est, best, And our soul's most
4. In our la - bor rest most sweet, Pleas - ant cool - ness

wel - come guest, Sweet re - fresh - ment sweet re - pose.
in the heat, Con - so - la - tion in our woes.

5. Light most bless - ed, shine with grace In our heart's most
6. Left with - out your pres - ence here, Life it - self would

se - cret place, Fill your faith - ful through and through.
dis - ap - pear, Noth - ing thrives a - part from you!

7. Cleanse our soil - ed hearts of sin, Ar - id souls re -
8. Bend the stub - born heart and will, Melt the fro - zen,

fresh with - in, Wound - ed lives to health re - store.
warm the chill, Guide the way - ward home once more!

9. On the faith - ful who are true And pro - fess their
10. Give us vir - tue's sure re - ward, Give us your sal-

faith in you, In your sev'n - fold gift de - scend!
va - tion, Lord, Give us joys that nev - er end!

Text: Sequence for Pentecost, 13th. C.; tr. by Peter J. Scagnelli; b.1949, © 1983
Tune: Mode I; acc. by Adriaan Engels, b.1906, © Interkerkelijke Stichting voor het Kerklied Den Haag

SERVICE MUSIC

2 Text: Antiphons © 1974, ICEL; Verses © 1963, 1993, The Grail, GIA Publications Inc., agent. Music: © 1974, ICEL

4 Text: © 1969, James Quinn, SJ. Used by permission of Selah Publishing Co., Inc., (North American agent, Kingston NY 12401. All rights reserved. Used by permission.) Music: © 1987, GIA Publications, Inc.

6 Text: © 1974, ICEL. Music © 1986, GIA Publications, Inc.

7 Text: © 1992, GIA Publications, Inc. Music harm.: © Oxford University Press

8 © 1979, GIA Publications, Inc.

10 © 1979, GIA Publications, Inc.

13 Text trans.: © WGS (William G. Storey). Music acc.: © 1975, GIA Publications, Inc.

15 Text: © 1963, 1993, The Grail, GIA Publications, Inc., agent. Music: © 1985, GIA Publications, Inc.

16 Text: © 1974, ICEL. Music: © 1986, GIA Publications, Inc.

17 Text: © 1992, GIA Publications, Inc. Music harm.: from *The English Hymnal* © Oxford University Press

19 through 20: © 1979, GIA Publications, Inc.

22 Text: © 1967, Benedictine Nuns of St. Mary's Abbey, West Malling, Kent. Music: © 1982, GIA Publications, Inc.

25 through 26: Text: © 1974, ICEL. Music: © 1986, GIA Publications, Inc.

27 © 1979, GIA Publications, Inc.

28 Antiphon text: © 1969, 1981, ICEL. Antiphon Music: © 1975, GIA Publications. Psalm tone: © 1979, Robert Knox Kennedy. Gelineau tone and psalm text: © 1963,1993, The Grail, GIA Publications, Inc., agent

29 Antiphon I text: © 1974, ICEL. Antiphon II text: © 1969, ICEL. Antiphon Music: © 1986, GIA Publications, Inc. Psalm tone: © L.J. Carey and Co. Ltd. Gelineau tone and psalm text: © 1963, 1993, The Grail, GIA Publications, Inc., agent

30 © 1980, GIA Publications, Inc.

31 Antiphon I: © 1963, The Grail, GIA Publications, Inc., agent. Antiphon II text: © 1969, 1981, ICEL. Antiphon II music: © 1986, GIA Publications, Inc. Psalm tone: © 1975, GIA Publications, Inc. Text and Gelineau tone: © 1963, 1993, The Grail, GIA Publications, Inc., agent

32 © 1990, GIA Publications, Inc.

33 Antiphon text: © 1981, ICEL. Antiphon Music: © 1995, GIA Publications, Inc. Psalm tone: © Gethsemani Abbey. Gelineau tone and psalm text: © 1963, 1993, The Grail, GIA Publications, Inc., agent

34 Antiphon I text: © 1974, ICEL. Antiphons II-IV texts: © 1969, 1981, ICEL. Antiphon music: © 1986, GIA Publications, Inc. Psalm tone: © 1969, Ampleforth Abbey Trust. Gelineau tone and psalm text: © 1963, 1993, The Grail, GIA Publications, Inc., agent.

35 Text: © 1993, GIA Publications, Inc. Refrain trans.: © 1969, ICEL. Music: © 1993, GIA Publications, Inc.

36 Refrain III trans.: © 1969, ICEL. Text and music: © 1988, GIA Publications, Inc.

37 Refrain trans.: © 1969, ICEL. Text and music: © 1993, GIA Publications, Inc.

38 Refrain trans.: © 1969, ICEL. Text: © 1963, 1993, The Grail, GIA Publications, Inc., agent. Music: © 1994, GIA Publications, Inc.

39 Antiphon I-IV texts: © 1969, ICEL. Antiphon I music © 1975, GIA Publications, Inc. Antiphon II-IV music: © 1986, GIA Publications, Inc. Psalm tone: © L.J. Carey and Co. Ltd. Gelineau tone and psalm text: © 1963, 1993, The Grail, GIA Publications, Inc., agent.

40 Refrain trans.: © 1969, ICEL. Text and music: © 1983, GIA Publications, Inc.

41 Refrain trans.: © 1969, ICEL. Text: © 1963, 1993, The Grail, GIA Publications, Inc., agent. Music: © 1994, GIA Publications, Inc.

42 Refrain music: © 1975, GIA Publications, Inc. Refrain text and psalm text: © 1963, 1993 The Grail, GIA Publications, Inc., agent

43 Refrain trans.: © 1969, ICEL. Text and music: © 1983, GIA Publications, Inc.

44 © 1994, GIA Publications, Inc.

45 Antiphon III-IV texts: © 1969, ICEL. Antiphon III-IV music and psalm tone: © 1975, GIA Publications, Inc. Antiphons I-II: © 1963, The Grail, GIA Publications, Inc., agent. Gelineau tone and psalm text: © 1963, 1993, The Grail, GIA Publications, Inc., agent.

46 © 1988, 1993, GIA Publications, Inc.

47 Refrain I trans.: © 1969, ICEL. Text and music © 1993, GIA Publications, Inc.

48 Refrain text: © 1969, ICEL. Text: © 1963, 1993, The Grail, GIA Publications, Inc., agent. Music: © 1975, GIA Publications, Inc.

49 Refrain trans.: © 1969, ICEL. Text: © The Grail, GIA Publications, Inc., agent. Music: © 1995, GIA Publications, Inc.

50 Refrain text: © 1963, The Grail, GIA Publications, Inc., agent. Text: © 1963, 1993, The Grail, GIA Publications, Inc., agent. Music: © 1975, GIA Publications, Inc.

51 Refrain trans.: © 1969, ICEL. Text: © 1963, 1993, The Grail, GIA Publications, Inc., agent. Music: © 1995, GIA Publications, Inc.

52 © 1988, 1993, GIA Publications, Inc.

53 Refrain trans.: © 1969, ICEL. Text and music: © 1982, GIA Publications, Inc.

54 Refrain trans.: © 1969, ICEL. Text and music: © 1985, GIA Publications, Inc.

55 Antiphon I-II texts: © 1969, ICEL. Antiphon music © 1975, GIA Publications, Inc. Text: © 1963, 1993, The Grail, GIA Publications, Inc., agent

56 Text: From *The Jerusalem Bible*, by Alexander Jones, ed. Copyright © 1966, Darton, Longman and Todd, Ltd. and Doubleday, a division of Bantam Doubleday Dell Publishing Group, Inc. Used by permission of Doubleday, a division of Bantam Doubleday Dell Publishing Group, Inc. Music: © 1993, GIA Publications, Inc.

57 © 1983, GIA Publications, Inc.

58 Antiphon text: © 1981, ICEL. Antiphon music: © 1995, GIA Publications, Inc. Text: © 1963, 1993, The Grail, GIA Publications, Inc., agent

59 Refrain trans.: © 1969, ICEL. Text: © 1963, 1993, The Grail, GIA Publications, Inc., agent. Music: © 1995, GIA Publications, Inc.

60 Psalm text: © 1963, 1993, The Grail, GIA Publications, Inc., agent. Refrain text and music: © 1985, Paul Inwood. Published by OCP Publications. All rights reserved.

61 © 1993, GIA Publications, Inc.

62 Text: From *New American Bible* © 1970, Confraternity of Christian Doctrine, Washington DC 20017-1194. Refrain trans: © 1969, ICEL. Music: © 1980, GIA Publications, Inc.

63 Antiphon I-II texts: © 1969, 1981, ICEL. Antiphon III text: © 1974, ICEL. Antiphon I music: © 1975, GIA Publications, Inc. Antiphon II-III music: © 1986, GIA Publications, Inc. Psalm tone: © L.J. Carey and Co. Ltd. Gelineau tone and psalm text: © 1963, 1993, The Grail, GIA Publications, Inc., agent

64 Refrain trans.: © 1969, ICEL. Text and music: © 1993, GIA Publications, Inc.

65 Refrain trans.: © 1969, ICEL. Text: © 1963, 1993, The Grail, GIA Publications, Inc., agent. Music: © 1995, GIA Publications, Inc.

66 Refrain I trans.: © 1969, ICEL. Refrains II, III, verses and music: © 1987, 1994, GIA Publications, Inc.

67 Antiphon texts: © 1969, 1981, ICEL. Antiphon music: © 1975, GIA Publications. Text: © 1963, 1993, The Grail, GIA Publications, Inc., agent.

68 Refrain trans.: © 1969, ICEL. Text: © 1963, 1993, The Grail, GIA Publications, Inc., agent. Music: © 1995, GIA Publications, Inc.

69 © 1978, 1990, John B. Foley SJ and New Dawn Music, P.O. Box 13248, Portland, OR 97213-0248. All rights reserved. Used with permission.

70 Refrain trans.: © 1969, ICEL. Text and music: © 1980, GIA Publications, Inc.

71 Refrain trans.: © 1969, ICEL. Text: © 1963, 1993, The Grail, GIA Publications, Inc., agent. Music: © 1995, GIA Publications, Inc.

72 © 1981, Stephen Dean. Published by OCP Publications. All rights reserved.

73 Antiphon texts: © 1969, 1981, ICEL. Antiphon music © 1975, GIA Publications, Inc. Psalm tone: © 1986, GIA Publications, Inc. Gelineau tone and psalm text: © 1963, 1993, The Grail, GIA Publications, Inc., agent

74 © 1971, 1991, New Dawn Music, PO Box 13248, Portland OR 97213-0248. All rights reserved. Used with permission.

75 Antiphon texts: © 1969, 1981, ICEL. Antiphon I music: © 1986, GIA Publications, Inc. Antiphon II music: © 1975, GIA Publications, Inc. Text: © 1963, 1993, The Grail, GIA Publications, Inc., agent.

76 and 77: Antiphon text: © 1969, 1981, ICEL. Antiphon music: © 1975, GIA Publications, Inc. Text: © 1963, 1993, The Grail, GIA Publications, Inc., agent.

78 Refrain trans.: © 1969, ICEL. Text: © 1963, 1993, The Grail, GIA Publications, Inc. Music: © 1995, GIA Publications, Inc.

79 Antiphon trans.: © 1969, 1981, ICEL. Antiphon music: © 1975, GIA Publications, Inc. Text: © 1963, 1993, The Grail, GIA Publications, Inc., agent

80 Refrain trans.: © 1969, ICEL. Text and music: © 1983, GIA Publications, Inc.

81 Refrain trans.: © 1969, ICEL. Text: © 1963, 1993, The Grail, GIA Publications, Inc., agent. Music: © 1994, GIA Publications, Inc.

82 Antiphons II, IV text: © 1969, 1981, ICEL. Antiphon III text: © 1969, ICEL. Antiphon II, III music: © 1975, GIA Publications, Inc. Antiphon IV music: © 1986, GIA Publications, Inc. Antiphon V: © 1979, 1995, GIA Publications, Inc. Psalm Tone: © Gethsemani Abbey. Antiphon I, psalm text and Gelineau tone: © 1963, 1993, The Grail, GIA Publications, Inc., agent

83 Refrain trans.: © 1969, ICEL. Text and music: © 1983, GIA Publications, Inc.

84 Refrain trans.: © 1969, ICEL. Text: © 1963, 1993, The Grail, GIA Publications, Inc., agent. Music: © 1995, GIA Publications, Inc., agent.

85 © 1987, GIA Publications, Inc.

86 Refrain trans.: © 1969, ICEL. Text: © 1963, 1986, The Grail, GIA Publications, Inc., agent. Music: © 1994, GIA Publications, Inc.

87 Antiphon text: © 1969, 1981, ICEL. Antiphon music: © 1975, GIA Publications, Inc. Text: © 1963, 1993, The Grail, GIA Publications, Inc., agent

88 © 1989, GIA Publications, Inc.

89 Antiphon I text: © 1969, 1981, ICEL. Antiphon I music: © 1975, GIA Publications, Inc. Antiphon II: © 1979, GIA Publications, Inc. Psalm tone: © 1986, GIA Publications, Inc. Gelineau tone and psalm text: © 1963, The Grail, GIA Publications, Inc., agent

90 Verses trans.: © 1970, Confraternity of Christian Doctrine, Washington, DC 20017-1194; refrain text and music: © 1987, GIA Publications, Inc.

91 Refrain trans.: © 1969, ICEL. Text and music: © 1993, GIA Publications, Inc.

92 Refrain trans.: © 1969, ICEL. Text: © 1963, 1993, The Grail, GIA Publications, Inc., agent. Music: © 1994, GIA Publications, Inc.

93 © 1982, GIA Publications, Inc.

94 Refrain trans.: © 1969, ICEL. Text: © 1963, 1993, The Grail, GIA Publications, Inc., agent. Music: © 1994, GIA Publications, Inc.

95 Antiphon texts: © 1969, 1981, ICEL. Antiphon music: © 1975, GIA Publications, Inc. Psalm tone: © 1969, Ampleforth Abbey Trust. Gelineau tone and psalm text: © 1963, 1993 The Grail, GIA Publications, Inc., agent

96 Refrain trans.: © 1969, 1981, ICEL. Text: © 1963, 1993, The Grail, GIA Publications, Inc., agent. Refrain music: © 1991, GIA Publications, Inc.

97 Refrain trans.: © 1969, ICEL. Text: © 1963, 1993, The Grail, GIA Publications, Inc., agent. Refrain music: © 1994, GIA Publications, Inc.

98 Refrain trans.: © 1969, 1981, ICEL. Text: © 1963, 1993, The Grail, GIA Publications, Inc., agent. Refrain music: © 1975, GIA Publications, Inc.

99 Refrain trans.: © 1969, ICEL. Text: © 1963, 1993, The Grail, GIA Publications, Inc., agent. Refrain music: © 1995, World Library Publications, a division of J.S. Paluch Company, Inc. Schiller Park, IL 60176. All rights reserved. Used by permission

100 through 101: Refrain trans.: © 1969, ICEL. Text: © 1963, 1993, The Grail, GIA Publications, Inc., agent. Refrain music: © 1995, GIA Publications, Inc.

102 © 1987, 1994, GIA Publications, Inc.

103 Refrain trans.: © 1969, ICEL. Text: © 1963, 1993, The Grail, GIA Publications, Inc., agent. Refrain music: © 1995, GIA Publications, Inc.

104 Refrain trans.: © 1969, 1981, ICEL. Text: © 1963, 1993, The Grail, GIA Publications, Inc., agent. Refrain music: © 1975, GIA Publications, Inc.

105 Refrain trans.: © 1969, 1981, ICEL. Text: © 1963, 1993, The Grail, GIA Publications, Inc., agent. Refrain music: © 1975, GIA Publications, Inc.

106 Refrain trans.: © 1969, ICEL. Text: © 1963, 1993, The Grail, GIA Publications, Inc., agent. Refrain music: © 1994, GIA Publications, Inc.

107 © 1982, GIA Publications, Inc.

108 Refrain trans.: © 1969, ICEL. Text: © 1963, 1993, The Grail, GIA Publications, Inc., agent. Refrain music: © 1995, GIA Publications, Inc.

109 Refrain trans.: © 1969, 1981, ICEL. Text: © 1963, 1993, The Grail, GIA Publications, Inc., agent. Refrain music: © 1986, GIA Publications, Inc.

110 Psalm tone: © Gethsemani Abbey. Antiphon, psalm text and Gelineau tone: © 1963, 1993, The Grail, GIA Publications, Inc., agent

111© 1987, GIA Publications, Inc.

112 Refrain trans.: © 1969, ICEL. Text and music: © 1983, GIA Publications, Inc.

113 Antiphon texts: © 1969, 1981, ICEL. Text: © 1963, 1993, The Grail, GIA Publications, Inc., agent. Antiphon I music: © 1975, GIA Publications, Inc. Antiphon II music: © 1986, GIA Publications, Inc.

114 Refrain texts: © 1969, ICEL. Verse text and music: © 1978, 1993, Damean Music. Distributed by GIA Publications, Inc.

115 Antiphon I text: © 1974, ICEL. Antiphon II text: © 1969, 1981, ICEL. Antiphon music: © 1986, GIA Publications, Inc. Psalm tone: © 1969, Ampleforth Abbey Trust. Gelineau tone and psalm text: © 1963, 1993, The Grail, GIA Publications, Inc., agent.

116 Antiphon text: © 1974, ICEL. Antiphon music: © 1986, GIA Publications, Inc. Psalm tone: © Gethsemani Abbey. Gelineau tone and psalm text: © 1963, 1993, The Grail, GIA Publications, Inc., agent.

117 Refrain trans.: © 1969, ICEL. Text: © 1963, 1993, The Grail, GIA Publications, Inc., agent. Music: © 1995, GIA Publications, Inc.

118 Refrain trans.: © 1969, ICEL. Text: © 1963, 1993, The Grail, GIA Publications, Inc., agent. Alt. text and music: © 1988, 1994, GIA Publications, Inc.

119 Antiphon texts: © 1969, 1981, ICEL. Antiphon I music: © 1975, GIA Publications, Inc. Antiphon II music: © 1986, GIA Publications, Inc. Verse text: © 1963, 1993, The Grail, GIA Publications, Inc., agent

120 Antiphon texts: © 1969, 1981, ICEL. Antiphon I and III music: © 1986, GIA Publications, Inc. Antiphon II music: © 1975, 1995, GIA Publications, Inc. Psalm tone: © L.J. Carey and Co. Ltd. Gelineau tone and psalm text: © 1963, 1993, The Grail, GIA Publications, Inc., agent

121 Refrain trans.: © 1969, ICEL. Text and music: © 1993, GIA Publications, Inc.

122 Antiphon III text: © 1974, ICEL. Psalm tone and Antiphon III music: © 1986, GIA Publications, Inc. Antiphons I-II, Gelineau tone and psalm text: © 1963, 1993, The Grail, GIA Publications, Inc., agent

123 © 1980, GIA Publications, Inc.

124 Refrain trans.: © 1969, ICEL. Text: © 1963, 1993, The Grail, GIA Publications, Inc., agent. Music: © 1994, GIA Publications, Inc.

125 Refrain trans.: © 1969, 1981, ICEL. Refrain music: © 1975, GIA Publications, Inc. Text: © 1963, 1993, The Grail, GIA Publications, Inc., agent

126 Psalm tone: © 1975, GIA Publications, Inc. Antiphons, Gelineau tone and psalm text: © 1963, 1993, The Grail, GIA Publications, Inc., agent

127 Refrain trans.: © 1969, ICEL. Text: © 1963, 1993, The Grail, GIA Publications, Inc., agent. Music: © 1995, GIA Publications, Inc.

128 Refrain trans.: © 1969, ICEL. Text and music: © 1993, GIA Publications, Inc.

129 © 1983, 1994, GIA Publications, Inc.

130 Refrain trans.: © 1969, ICEL. Verse trans.: © 1970, Confraternity of Christian Doctrine, Washington DC 20017-1194. Music: © 1976, GIA Publications, Inc.

131 Antiphon III-IV texts: © 1969, 1981, ICEL. Antiphon III music: © 1975, GIA Publications, Inc. Antiphon IV music: © 1986, GIA Publications, Inc. Antiphons I-II and psalm text: © 1963, 1993, The Grail, GIA Publications, Inc., agent

132 Refrain trans.: © 1969, ICEL. Text: © 1989, GIA Publications, Inc. Music: © 1989, 1994, GIA Publications, Inc.

133 through 134: Antiphon text: © 1969, 1981, ICEL. Antiphon music: © 1975, GIA Publications, Inc. Text: © 1963, 1993, The Grail, GIA Publications, Inc., agent.

135 © 1983, 1994, GIA Publications, Inc.

136 Refrain trans: © 1969, ICEL. Text: © 1963, 1993, The Grail, GIA Publications, Inc., agent. Music: © 1995, GIA Publications, Inc.

137 Antiphon texts: © 1969, 1981, ICEL. Antiphon I-II music: © 1975, GIA Publications, Inc. Antiphon III music: © 1986, GIA Publications, Inc. Text: © 1963, 1993, The Grail, GIA Publications, Inc., agent

138 © 1983, GIA Publications, Inc.

139 Psalm tone: © 1975, GIA Publications, Inc. Antiphons, Gelineau tone and psalm texts: © 1963, 1993, The Grail, GIA Publications, Inc., agent

140 © 1993, GIA Publications, Inc.

141 Antiphon texts: © 1969, 1981, ICEL. Antiphon I-II music: © 1986, GIA Publications, Inc. Antiphon III music and psalm tone: © 1975, GIA Publications, Inc. Gelineau tone and psalm text: © 1963, 1993, The Grail, GIA Publications, Inc., agent

142 Refrain trans.: © 1969, ICEL. Text: © 1963, 1993, The Grail, GIA Publications, Inc., agent. Music: © 1995, GIA Publications, Inc.

143 Refrain trans.: © 1969, ICEL. Text and music: © 1983, GIA Publications, Inc.

144 Refrain trans.: © 1969, 1981, ICEL. Text: © 1963, 1993, The Grail, GIA Publications, Inc., agent. Music: © 1971, GIA Publications, Inc.

145 Refrain trans.: © 1969, 1981, ICEL. Text: © 1963, 1993, The Grail, GIA Publications, Inc., agent. Music: © 1975, GIA Publications, Inc.

146 Refrain trans.: © 1969, ICEL. Text and music: © 1985, GIA Publications, Inc.

147 through 148: Refrain trans.: © 1969, 1981, ICEL. Text: © 1963, 1993, The Grail, GIA Publications, Inc., agent. Music: © 1975, GIA Publications, Inc.

Acknowledgments/*continued*

Acknowledgments/*continued*

244 © 1977, ICEL.

248 © Refrain trans: © 1969, 1981, ICEL. Refrain music: © 1975, GIA Publications, Inc. Text and Music: © 1963, 1993, The Grail, GIA Publications, Inc., agent.

249 © 1985, GIA Publications, Inc. Lent acc.: © 1970, GIA Publications, Inc.

254 Refrain trans.: © 1974, ICEL. Refrain music: © 1986, GIA Publications, Inc. Text and music: © 1963, The Grail, GIA Publications, Inc., agent.

255 © 1985, GIA Publications, Inc. Lent acc.: © 1970, GIA Publications, Inc.

259 Refrain trans.: © 1969, ICEL. Text: © 1963, 1993, The Grail, GIA Publications, Inc., agent. Music: © 1994, GIA Publications, Inc.

264 Refrain trans.: © 1969, ICEL. Text: © 1963, 1993, The Grail, GIA Publications, Inc., agent. Music: © 1994, GIA Publications, Inc.

265 © 1985, GIA Publications, Inc. Lent acc.: © 1970, GIA Publications, Inc.

272 (A)Refrain trans.: © 1969, ICEL. Refrain music: © 1975, GIA Publications, Inc. Text and Music: © 1963, 1993, The Grail, GIA Publications, Inc., agent. (B) © 1983, GIA Publications, Inc.

273 © 1985, GIA Publications, Inc. Lent acc.: © 1970, GIA Publications, Inc.

277 © 1984, GIA Publications, Inc.

278 (A) © 1984, GIA Publications, Inc. (B) © 1990, GIA Publications, Inc. (C) & (D) © 1993, GIA Publications, Inc.

279 © 1984, GIA Publications, Inc.

280 © 1975, 1993, GIA Publications, Inc.

281 © 1993, GIA Publications, Inc.

284 (A) Text: © 1985, ICEL. Music: © 1990, GIA Publications, Inc. (B) © 1990, GIA Publications, Inc. (C) © 1975, GIA Publications, Inc.

286 Text: © 1985, ICEL. Music: © 1990, GIA Publications, Inc.

377 Refrain trans.: © 1973, ICEL. Text and Music: © 1994, GIA Publications, Inc.

379 Text and music: © 1975, GIA Publications, Inc.

385 through 386: © 1990, Iona Community, GIA Publications, Inc., agent.

388 © 1981, 1982, Peter Jones. Published by OCP Publications. All rights reserved.

395 © 1985, Fintan O'Carroll and Christopher Walker. Published by OCP Publications. All rights reserved

396 Text and music: © 1990, Iona Community, GIA Publications, Inc., agent. Verses and acc.: © 1993, GIA Publications, Inc.

397 © 1984, Les Presses de Taizé, GIA Publications, Inc., agent

398 © 1958, The Grail, GIA Publications, Inc., agent

401 © 1984, Les Presses de Taizé, GIA Publications, Inc., agent

404 © 1980, ICEL.

410 Text and music: © 1984, Bob Hurd. Acc.: © 1989, OCP Publications. Published by OCP Publications. All rights reserved

415 through 416: © 1980, Les Presses de Taizé, GIA Publications, Inc., agent

439 through 441: Text and Music: © 1973, Robert J. Dufford and Daniel L. Schutte. Administered by New Dawn Music, P.O. Box 13248, Portland, OR 97213-0248. All rights reserved. Used with permission. #439 Acc.: © 1993, GIA Publications, Inc.

442 © 1980, The Church Pension Fund. Acc.: © 1986, GIA Publications, Inc.

456 © 1970, World Library Publications, a division of J.S. Paluch Company, Inc. Schiller Park, IL 60176. All rights reserved. Used by permission

457 © 1973, World Library Publications, a division of J.S. Paluch Company, Inc. Schiller Park, IL 60176. All rights reserved. Used by permission

478 Text: sts. 2-4 © 1928, Oxford University Press. Harm.: © David McK. Williams

479 Harm.: © 1958, Basilian Fathers, assigned 1958 to Ralph Jusko Publications

481 Text and music: © 1971, United Church Press. Acc. © 1987, GIA Publications, Inc.

482 Text: © David Higham Assoc. Ltd. Harm.: © Oxford University Press

483 Text: © 1985, The Church Pension Fund. Acc.: © 1986, GIA Publications, Inc.

484 © 1984, Les Presses de Taizé, GIA Publications, Inc., agent

485 © 1981, 1982, Michael Joncas and Cooperative Ministries, Inc., OCP Publications, agent

486 Text: © 1982, Hope Publishing Co., Carol Stream, IL 60188. All rights reserved. Used by permission. Music: from *Enlarged Songs of Praise* © Oxford University Press

487 Text: © 1982, Hope Publishing Co., Carol Stream, IL 60188. All rights reserved. Used by permission

489 Text: © 1982, Hope Publishing Co., Carol Stream, IL 60188. All rights reserved. Used by permission

491 © 1984, Les Presses de Taizé, GIA Publications, Inc., agent

492 © 1993, GIA Publications, Inc.

493 Acc. © 1975, GIA Publications, Inc.

494 © 1983, GIA Publications, Inc.

495 © 1982, GIA Publications, Inc.

496 © 1981, ICEL.

497 © 1994, GIA Publications, Inc.

500 Text: © 1964, GIA Publications, Inc. Acc.: © 1986, GIA Publications, Inc.

501 Text and music: © 1945, Boosey and Co. Ltd. Copyright renewed. Reprinted by permission of Boosey & Hawkes, Inc. Acc. © 1993, GIA Publications, Inc.

506 © 1991, GIA Publications, Inc.

507 © 1979, 1988, Les Presses de Taizé, GIA Publications, Inc., agent

509 Harm.: © Horfield Baptist Housing Assc. Ltd.

510 © 1985, GIA Publications, Inc.

511 Music: © 1990, Pablo Sosa

512 Text: © 1981, Jaroslav Vajda. Music: © 1981, GIA Publications, Inc.

513 Harm.: *The English Hymnal* © from Oxford University Press

514 Text: © Mrs. John W. Work III. Music: © 1995, GIA Publications, Inc.

515 Music: © 1994, GIA Publications, Inc.

516 © 1987, GIA Publications, Inc.

517 Text: © 1986, Jaroslav J. Vajda. Music: © 1986, GIA Publications, Inc.

518 Alternate text: © 1992, GIA Publications, Inc.

519 Text: © 1990, Iona Community, GIA Publications, Inc., agent

521 © 1992, GIA Publications, Inc.

523 © 1984, GIA Publications, Inc.

525 © 1987, Iona Community, GIA Publications, Inc., agent

526 Harm.: © 1957, Novello and Co. Ltd. 8/9 Frith Street, London

528 Harm.: © 1986, GIA Publications, Inc.

532 © 1965, World Library Publications, a division of J.S. Paluch Company, Inc. Schiller Park, IL 60176. All rights reserved. Used by permission

533 Harm.: © 1987, GIA Publications, Inc.

536 © 1978, Damean Music. Distributed by GIA Publications, Inc.

538 Text: © 1984, Hope Publishing Co., Carol Stream, IL 60188. All rights reserved. Used by permission

539 Text: © 1989, Hope Publishing Co., Carol Stream, IL 60188. All rights reserved. Used by permission. Music: © 1991, GIA Publications, Inc.

540 © 1976, Robert F. O'Connor, SJ, and New Dawn Music, P.O. Box 13248, Portland, OR 07213-0248. All rights reserved. Used with permission.

541 © 1984, GIA Publications, Inc.

542 Music: © 1984, GIA Publications, Inc.

543 Music: © 1995, GIA Publications, Inc.

544 Text: © Peter J. Scagnelli. Acc.: © 1975, GIA Publications, Inc.

545 Text: from *The English Hymnal* © Oxford University Press

546 © 1987, GIA Publications, Inc.

547 Harm.: © 1986, GIA Publications, Inc.

548 Text: © 1993, GIA Publications, Inc.

549 Text: © 1963, The Grail, GIA Publications, Inc., agent. Acc.: © 1986, GIA Publications, Inc.

550 Text: © 1978, Damean Music. Distributed by GIA Publications, Inc.

551 Text: © 1971, Faber Music Ltd. London. Reprinted from *New Catholic Hymnal* by permission of the publishers. Harm.: © 1986, GIA Publications, Inc.

552 Text: © 1980, ICEL. Acc.: © 1975, GIA Publications, Inc.

554 Text: © 1982, Thomas H. Cain. Music: © 1988, GIA Publications, Inc.

555 © 1990, 1991, GIA Publications, Inc.

556 © 1994, GIA Publications, Inc.

557 © 1975, GIA Publications, Inc.

558 © 1965, 1966, 1968, 1973, World Library Publications, a division of J.S. Paluch Company, Inc. Schiller Park, IL 60176. All rights reserved. Used by permission

559 Text: © Peter J. Scagnelli

560 Text: © Oxford University Press. Music: © 1995, GIA Publications, Inc.

561 Text: © 1994, World Library Publications, a division of J.S. Paluch Company, Inc. Schiller Park, IL 60176. All rights reserved. Used by permission

562 Verse 3-9 Text: © 1991, GIA Publications, Inc. Harm.: © 1987, GIA Publications, Inc.

Acknowledgments/*continued*

564 Acc.: © 1982, Hope Publishing Co.

565 © 1984, Les Presses de Taizé, GIA Publications, Inc., agent

566 © Gethsemani Abbey

567 © 1984, Les Presses de Taizé, GIA Publications, Inc., agent

570 Harm.: © 1987, GIA Publications, Inc.

571 © 1991, Les Presses de Taizé, GIA Publications, Inc., agent

572 Music: © John Ireland Trust

573 Harm.: © 1986, GIA Publications, Inc.

574 © 1981, Robert F. O'Connor, SJ and New Dawn Music, P.O. Box 13248, Portland, OR 97213-0248. All rights reserved. Used with permission.

576 © 1981, 1982, Cooperative Ministries, Inc. Exclusive agent: OCP Publications. All rights reserved. The English translation of the psalm response from the *Lectionary for Mass* © 1969, ICEL. All rights reserved. Verse text: © Confraternity of Christian Doctrine

577 © 1984, Les Presses de Taizé, GIA Publications, Inc., agent

579 Acc.: © 1975, GIA Publications, Inc.

580 Text and Music: © 1972, Francisco Gómez Argüello and Editiones Musical PAX. All rights reserved. Sole US agent: OCP Publications. English text: © 1988, OCP Publications. All rights reserved. Acc.: © 1993, GIA Publications, Inc.

581 Text and Music: © 1973, Word of God Music. (Administered by THE COPYRIGHT COMPANY NASHVILLE, TN) All rights reserved. International Copyright Secured. Used by permission. Descant harm.: © 1979, CELEBRATION c/o THE COPYRIGHT COMPANY, NASHVILLE, TN) All rights reserved. International Copyright Secured. Used by permission.

583 Text: © 1978, LUTHERAN BOOK OF WORSHIP. Reprinted by permission of Augsburg Fortress. Music and Harm: © 1975, 1988, Richard Hillert. Used by permission.

584 Acc.: © 1986, GIA Publications, Inc.

585 © 1978, Les Presses de Taizé, GIA Publications, Inc., agent

586 Verses 1-4: © 1958, renewal 1986 by Hope Publishing Co., Carol Stream, IL 60188. All rights reserved. Used by permission. Verse 5: © 1971, Walton Music Corporation. Acc.: © 1987, GIA Publications, Inc.

588 *The English Hymnal* © Oxford University Press

589 © 1987, New Dawn Music, PO Box 13248, Portland, OR 97213-0248. All rights reserved. Used with permission.

590 © 1975, Robert J. Dufford, SJ and New Dawn Music, P.O. Box 13248, Portland, OR 97213-0248. All rights reserved. Used with per-mission.

592 © 1986, GIA Publications, Inc.

594 Acc.: © 1980, GIA Publications, Inc.

596 © 1988, Iona Community, GIA Publications, Inc., agent

597 Text: © Peter J. Scagnelli

598 Harm.: © Concordia Publishing House

600 © 1969, Hope Publishing Co., Carol Stream, IL 60188. All rights reserved. Used by permission

601 Text: © 1975, Hope Publishing Co, Carol Stream, IL 60188. All rights reserved. Used by permission

603 © 1983, GIA Publications, Inc.

604 © 1981, 1982, Word Music (a div. of WORD, INC.). All rights reserved. Used by permission

606 Text: © 1978, LUTHERAN BOOK OF WORSHIP. Reprinted by permission of Augsburg Fortress. Harm.: *The English Hymnal* © Oxford University Press

607 Text: © 1978, Jeffrey Rowthorn. Music:© 1942, 1970, Hope Publishing Co., Carol Stream, IL 60188. All rights reserved. Used by permission.

608 Text: © 1991, GIA Publications, Inc. Music: *The English Hymnal* © Oxford University Press.

609 Text: from *English Praise* © Oxford University Press. Music: © 1983, GIA Publications, Inc.

610 Text: © 1968, Hope Publishing Co., Carol Stream, IL 60188. All rights reserved. Used by permission. Music: © 1985, 1988, GIA Publications, Inc.

611 Harm.: © 1986, GIA Publications, Inc.

612 © 1981, 1982, 1987, GIA Publications, Inc.

613 Text: © 1984, Hope Publishing Co., Carol Stream, IL 60188. All rights reserved. Used by permission. Music: © 1974, Harold Flammer Music, a division of Shawnee Press, Inc. (ASCAP). Reprinted by permission

614 Text: © Oxford University Press

615 © 1979, Les Presses de Taizé, GIA Publications, Inc., agent

616 Text: © 1975, John Webster Grant. Music: © 1975, GIA Publications, Inc.

617 Music: from *The English Hymnal* © Oxford University Press

618 Text: © 1989, Hope Publishing Co., Carol Stream, IL 60188. All rights reserved. Used with permission. Music: © 1991, GIA Publications, Inc.

620 Text: © 1962, World Library Publications, a division of J.S. Paluch Company, Inc. Schiller Park, IL 60176. All rights reserved. Used by permission. Harm.: © 1958, Basilian Fathers, assigned 1958 to Ralph Jusko Publications, Inc.

621 Text: © 1991, GIA Publications, Inc. Harm.: from *The English Hymnal* © Oxford University Press

622 Text: © 1986, Hope Publishing Co., Carol Stream, IL 60188. All rights reserved. Used by permission. Music: © 1993, GIA Publications, Inc.

623 Text: © 1983, Hope Publishing Co., Carol Stream, IL 60188. All rights reserved. Used by permission. Music: © 1994, GIA Publications, Inc.

625 © 1988, GIA Publications, Inc.

628 Text: © 1966, 1984, Willard F. Jabusch. Music: © 1986, GIA Publications, Inc.

629 Text: © 1941, Irene C. Mueller. Harm.: © 1986, GIA Publications, Inc.

630 Text: from *Enlarged Songs of Praise* © Oxford University Press

632 Harm.: © 1995, GIA Publications, Inc.

634 © 1990, Bernadette Farrell. Published by OCP Publications. All rights reserved

636 Text: © 1992, GIA Publications, Inc. Music: © 1994, GIA Publications, Inc.

637 Text: © 1916, Walton Music Corp. Music: © 1993, Iona Community, GIA Publications, Inc., agent

638 © 1980, GIA Publications, Inc.

639 © 1973, Hope Publishing Co., Carol Stream, IL 60188. All rights reserved. Used by permission. Music: © 1986, GIA Publications, Inc.

640 © 1985, GIA Publications, Inc.

641 © 1979, New Dawn Music, P.O. Box 13248, Portland, OR 97213-0248. All rights reserved. Used with permission.

642 © 1991, GIA Publications, Inc.

643 © 1992, GIA Publications, Inc.

644 © 1982, 1988, GIA Publications, Inc.

645 Text: © 1982, Hope Publishing Co., Carol Stream, IL 60188. All rights reserved. Used by permission

646 Music: from *Enlarged Songs of Praise* © Oxford University Press

647 © 1987, GIA Publications, Inc.

648 © 1984, Utryck, Walton Music Corporation, agent

649 © 1982, Les Presses de Taizé, GIA Publications, Inc., agent

650 © 1987, GIA Publications, Inc.

651 © 1970, 1975, CELEBRATION (Administered by THE COPYRIGHT COMPANY, NASHVILLE, TN). All rights reserved. International Copyright Secured. Used by permission. Acc.: © 1987, GIA Publications, Inc.

652 © 1986, Bernadette Farrell. Published by OCP Publications. All rights reserved

653 © 1969, James Quinn SJ. Used by permission of Selah Publishing Co., Inc. (North American agent, Kingston NY 12401. All rights reserved. Used by permission.)

654 Text: © 1953, renewal 1981, The Hymn Society. All rights reserved. Used by permission of Hope Publishing Co., Carol Stream, IL 60188

655 © 1993, GIA Publications, Inc.

656 Music: © 1979, 1988, GIA Publications, Inc.

658 © 1986, GIA Publications, Inc.

659 © 1983, 1987, GIA Publications, Inc.

660 © 1980, Les Presses de Taizé, GIA Publications, Inc., agent

661 Text: © 1975, Hope Publishing Co., Carol Stream, IL 60188. All rights reserved. Used by permission. Music: © 1973, Hope Publishing Co., Carol Stream, IL 60188. All rights reserved. Used by permission

662 Text and Music: © 1979, Manuel José Alonso, Jose Pagán and Ediciones Musical PAX. All rights reserved. Sole U.S. agent: OCP Publications. Acc.: © 1994, GIA Publications, Inc.

663 © 1953, renewed 1981, Manna Music, Inc., 35255 Brooten Road, Pacific City, OR 97135. All rights reserved.

664 Text and Music: © 1976, Resource Publications, Inc. 160 E. Virginia Street #290, San Jose, CA 95112. Acc.: © 1993, GIA Publications, Inc.

665 Text: © 1972, Hope Publishing Co., Carol Stream, IL 60188. All rights reserved. Used by permission

666 Text: © 1969, James Quinn SJ. Used by permission of Selah Publishing Co., Inc., (North American agent, Kingston, NY 12401. All rights reserved. Used by permission.) Music: © 1979, GIA Publications, Inc.

667 © 1979, Les Presses de Taizé, GIA Publications, Inc., agent

668 © 1985, Oxford University Press. Music: © 1994, GIA Publications, Inc.

670 Text: © 1923, (renewed) by J. Curwen & Sons Ltd. All rights throughout the U.S. and Canada controlled by G. Schirmer, Inc. International Copyright Secured. All rights reserved. Reprinted by Permission. Music: from *The English Hymnal* © Oxford University Press.

671 Music: © Editora Sinodal, Sao Leopoldo. Arr.: © 1991, Iona Community, GIA Publications, Inc., agent

672 © 1993, 1994, GIA Publications, Inc.

673 Text: © 1987, Iona Community, GIA Publications, Inc., agent. Acc.: © 1993, Iona Community, GIA Publications, Inc., agent

674 Text: © Canon John E. Bowers. Music: from *The English Hymnal* © Oxford University Press

675 © 1979, Les Presses de Taizé, GIA Publications, Inc., agent

676 Text: © 1982, Hope Publishing Co., Carol Stream, IL 60188. All rights reserved. Used by permission

677 © 1973, Hope Publishing Co., Carol Stream, IL 60188. All rights reserved. Used by permission

678 © 1990, GIA Publications, Inc.

679 ©1988, GIA Publications, Inc.

680 Text: © 1972, Hope Publishing Co., Carol Stream, IL 60188. All rights reserved. Used by permission. Music: © 1989, GIA Publications, Inc.

681 © 1968, Augsburg Publishing House. Reprinted permission of Augsburg Fortress

682 © 1985, Damean Music. Distributed by GIA Publications, Inc.

686 © 1972, Daniel L. Schutte. Administered by New Dawn Music, P.O. Box 13248, Portland, OR 97213-0428. All rights reserved. Used with permission.

688 © 1981, GIA Publications, Inc.

689 © 1979, Hope Publishing Co., Carol Stream, IL 60188. All rights reserved. Used by permission

690 © 1993, GIA Publications, Inc.

691 Text and Music: © 1981, Robert F. O'Connor, SJ and New Dawn Music P.O. Box 13248, Portland, OR 97213-0248. All rights reserved. Used with permission. Acc. © 1994, GIA Publications, Inc.

692 © 1984, Utryck, Walton Music Corporation, agent

693 Text and acc.: © 1978, 1990, Les Presses de Taizé, GIA Publications, Inc., agent

694 © 1978, Damean Music. Distributed by GIA Publications, Inc.

695 Descant: © 1953, Novello and Co. Ltd. 8/9 Frith Street, London

696 © 1976, Daniel L. Schutte and New Dawn Music, P.O. Box 13248, Portland, OR 97213-0248. All rights reserved. Used with permission.

698 © 1990, Iona Community, GIA Publications, Inc.

699 Text: © 1991, GIA Publications, Inc.

701 © 1985, Damean Music. Distributed by GIA Publications, Inc.

702 © 1993, GIA Publications, Inc.

703 © 1986, 1991, Les Presses de Taizé, GIA Publications, Inc., agent

704 Text: © 1970, Hope Publishing Co., Carol Stream IL 60188. All rights reserved. Used by permission. Music: © Francis Jackson

705 Text: © 1940, The Church Pension Fund

707 Text: © 1939, E.C. Schirmer Music Co. Renewed 1966. Music: © Royal School of Church Music

708 © 1990, GIA Publications, Inc.

710 © 1982, 1991, Les Presses de Taizé, GIA Publications, Inc., agent

711 Text: © 1979, The Hymn Society. All rights reserved. Used by permission of Hope Publishing Co., Carol Stream, IL 60188.

712 © 1953, Doris Akers. Copyright renewed. All rights administered by Unichappell Music Inc. International Copyright Secured. All rights reserved.

713 Text: from *Enlarged Songs of Praise* © Oxford University Press. Harm.: © 1975, Hope Publishing Co., Carol Stream, IL 60188. All rights reserved. Used by permission

714 Text: © 1982, Hope Publishing Co., Carol Stream, IL 60188. All rights reserved. Used by permission. Music: © 1986, GIA Publications, Inc.

715 © 1964 (renewed), Appleseed Music Inc. All rights reserved

716 Text: © 1987, The Pastoral Press. Music: © 1991, GIA Publications, Inc.

718 © 1982, Les Presses de Taizé, GIA Publications, Inc., agent

719 Text: © 1979 Stainer & Bell Ltd. All rights reserved. Used by permission of Hope Publishing Co., Carol Stream, IL 60188. Music: © 1986, GIA Publications, Inc.

721 Music: © 1983, Abingdon Press. Acc. © 1993, GIA Publications, Inc.

722 © 1989, GIA Publications, Inc.

723 Music: © 1984, GIA Publications, Inc.

724 © 1980, GIA Publications, Inc.

725 Music: © 1990, Iona Community, GIA Publications, Inc., agent

726 Verses 2-4: © 1981, Joseph Alfred, Immanuel U.C.C. 9185 S. Campbell, Evergreen Park, IL 60805

727 Text trans.: © 1994, GIA Publications, Inc. Music: © 1994, GIA Publications, Inc.

728 © 1972, Maranatha! Music. (Administered by THE COPYRIGHT COMPANY NASHVILLE, TN) All rights reserved. International Copyright Secured. Used by permission.

729 Text: © 1980, Augsburg Publishing House. Reprinted by permission of Augsburg Fortress

730 © 1994, GIA Publications, Inc.

731 Harm.: © 1975, GIA Publications, Inc.

732 © 1980, Savgos Music Inc. Administered by Malaco Music Group, P.O. Box 9287, Jackson, MS 39206

733 Acc: © 1988 GIA Publications, Inc.

734 © 1975, Robert J. Dufford SJ and New Dawn Music, P.O. Box 13248, Portland, OR 07213-0248. All rights reserved. Used with permission.

736 © 1989, Iona community, GIA Publications, Inc., agent

738 © 1992, GIA Publications, Inc.

739 Text: © 1982, Hope Publishing Co.,Carol Stream, IL 60188. All rights reserved. Used by permission. Music: © Skinner Chávez-Melo

740 © 1979, New Dawn Music, P.O. Box 13248, Portland, OR 07213-0248. All rights reserved. Used with permission.

741 Text trans.: © 1978, LUTHERAN BOOK OF WORSHIP. Reprinted by permission of Augsburg Fortress

744 © 1987, GIA Publications, Inc.

745 © 1983, GIA Publications, Inc.

746 © 1979, Les Presses de Taizé, GIA Publications, Inc., agent

747 ©1960, 1961, World Library Publications, a division of J.S. Paluch Company, Inc. Schiller Park, OR 60176. All rights reserved. Used by permission

748 Text: © 1985, Hope Publishing Co., Carol Stream, IL 60188. All rights reserved. Used by permission. Music: © 1988, GIA Publications, Inc.

749 Harm.: © 1980, World Council of Churches, Geneva, Switzerland. Used with permission

750 Text: © 1970, McCrimmon Publishing Co., Ltd. Great Wakering, Essex. Music: © 1986, GIA Publications, Inc.

751 Text and harm.: © 1969, Concordia Publishing House

752 Text and acc.: © 1986, GIA Publications, Inc.

753 © 1988, GIA Publications, Inc.

754 Text and music: © 1938, Unichappel Music Inc. Copyright renewed. International Copyright Secured. All rights reserved. Music arr.: © 1994, GIA Publications, Inc.

756 © 1986, GIA Publications, Inc.

757 © 1986, 1991, Les Presses de Taizé, GIA Publications, Inc., agent

758 © 1982, GIA Publications, Inc.

760 Text: © 1989, Iona Community, GIA Publications, Inc., agent. Acc.: © 1993, Iona Community, GIA Publications, Inc., agent

761 Harm.: © 1975, GIA Publications, Inc.

762 © 1991, GIA Publications, Inc.

763 © 1989, GIA Publications, Inc.

764 Acc.: © 1987, GIA Publications, Inc.

765 Text and music: © 1984, Bob Hurd. Harm.: © 1984, OCP Publications, Inc. Published by OCP Publications,Inc. All rights reserved

766 Harm.: © Downside Abbey, Bath, BA3 4RH UK

767 © 1991, Les Presses de Taizé, GIA Publications, Inc., agent

768 Harm.: from *The English Hymnal* © Oxford University Press

769 Text: © 1991, GIA Publications, Inc. Music: © 1993, GIA Publications, Inc.

770 © 1981, Les Presses de Taizé, GIA Publications, Inc., agent

771 © 1984, 1990, TEAM Publications, published by OCP Publications, Inc.

772 © 1986, GIA Publications, Inc.

773 Text: © 1974, Hope Publishing Co., Carol Stream, IL 60188. All rights reserved. Used by permission. Harm.: © 1986, GIA Publications, Inc.

774 © 1985, GIA Publications, Inc.

776 © 1983, North American Liturgy Resources, PO Box 13248, Portland, OR 97213-0248. All rights reserved. Used with permission.

777 Text: © 1982, Hope Publishing Co., Carol Stream, IL 60188. All rights reserved. Used by permission

779 Text: © 1992, GIA Publications, Inc. Harm.: © 1985, GIA Publications, Inc.

780 Acc.: © 1987, GIA Publications, Inc.

Acknowledgments/*continued*

875 Text: © 1979, The Hymn Society. All rights reserved. Used by permission of Hope Publishing Co., Carol Stream, IL 60188. Harm.: © 1975, GIA Publications, Inc.

876 © 1992, Iona Community, GIA Publications, Inc., agent

878 Text: © 1980, Hope Publishing Co., Carol Stream, IL 60188. All rights reserved. Used by permission. Music: © Interkerkelijke Stichting voor het Kerklied

880 Text: © Anne K. LeCroy

881 Text: © 1993, GIA Publications, Inc. Harm.: © 1986, GIA Publications, Inc.

882 Text: © Esme. D.E. Bird

883 Harm.: © 1958, Basilian Fathers. Assigned 1958 to Ralph Jusko Publications

884 ©1978, Hope Publishing Co., Carol Stream, IL 60188. All rights reserved. Used by permission

885 Text: © 1993, GIA Publications, Inc.

886 Text and harm.: from *The English Hymnal* © Oxford University Press

887 Text: © 1985, The Church Pension Fund

888 Text: © 1985, Hope Publishing Co., Carol Stream, IL 60188. All rights reserved. Used by permission. Music: © 1987, GIA Publications, Inc.

889 Music: from *The English Hymnal* © Oxford University Press

890 Text: © 1971, Faber Music Ltd. London. Reprinted from *New Catholic Hymnal* by permission of the publishers

891 Text: © 1993, GIA Publications, Inc. Harm.: © Oxford University Press

892 Text: © 1967, Gooi en Sticht bv. Baarn The Netherlands. Exclusive English language agent: OCP Publications, Inc. All rights reserved. Music: © 1987, GIA Publications, Inc.

893 Verses 1-3: © Board of Publication, Lutheran Church in America. Verse 4: © 1958 SERVICE BOOK AND HYMNAL. Reprinted by permission of Augsburg Fortress. Harm.: © 1983, Hope Publishing Co., Carol Stream, IL 60188. All rights reserved. Used by permission

894 Text: © 1954, GIA Publications, Inc. Acc.: © 1986, GIA Publications, Inc.

895 from *The English Hymnal* © 1975, Oxford University Press

896 © 1993, GIA Publications, Inc.

897 Harm.: © 1987, GIA Publications, Inc.

898 Acc: © 1986, GIA Publications, Inc.

899 Text and harm.: © 1987, GIA Publications, Inc.

900 Text trans.: © 1994, GIA Publications, Inc.

901 © 1991, GIA Publications, Inc.

902 Text: © 1971, Faber Music Ltd. London. Reprinted from *New Catholic Hymnal* by permission of the publishers

903 Text: © 1982, Hope Publishing Co., Carol Stream, IL 60188. All rights reserved. Used by permission. Acc.: © 1987, GIA Publications, Inc.

904 © 1993, GIA Publications, Inc.

905 © 1982, GIA Publications, Inc.

906 Text: © John B. Geyer

907 Harm: © Downside Abbey, Bath, BA3 4RH UK

908 © 1976, GIA Publications, Inc.

909 Text and Music: © 1988, Bob Hurd. Acc and music arr.: © OCP Publications, Inc. Published by OCP Publications, Inc. All rights reserved.

910 Verse text: © 1989, James Quinn SJ. Used by permission of Selah Publishing Co., Inc. (North American agent. Kingston NY 12401. All rights reserved. Used by permission.) Refrain text and music: © 1989, GIA Publications, Inc.

911 Harm.: © 1968, GIA Publications, Inc.

912 © 1977, Archdiocese of Philadelphia

913 Harm.: © 1986, GIA Publications, Inc.

915 © 1978, John B. Foley SJ and New Dawn Music, P.O. Box 13248, Portland, OR 97213-0248. All rights reserved. Used with permission

916 © 1972, Dawn Treader Music. Admin by EMI Christian Music Publishing. All rights reserved. Reprinted by permission.

917 Text: from *Enlarged Songs of Praise* © Oxford University Press. Music: © 1957, H.W. Gray Co., Inc. Harm.: © Chalice Press

918 © 1987, Ekklesia Music, Inc.

919 © 1992, GIA Publications, Inc.

920 © 1987, GIA Publications, Inc.

921 © 1990, GIA Publications, Inc.

923 © 1993, GIA Publications, Inc.

924 © 1989, GIA Publications, Inc.

925 © 1981, GIA Publications, Inc.

926 Text: © 1991, GIA Publications, Inc. Music: © 1993, GIA Publications, Inc.

927 © 1995, GIA Publications, Inc.

928 © 1984, Les Presses de Taizé, GIA Publications, Inc., agent

929 © 1990, GIA Publications, Inc.

930 © 1986, GIA Publications, Inc.

931 © 1966, 1970, 1986, 1993, GIA Publications, Inc.

932 Text: © 1984, 1987, Bob Hurd and Michael Downey. Spanish text: © 1989, OCP Publications, Inc. Music: © 1984, Bob Hurd. Acc.: © OCP Publications, Inc. Published by OCP Publications.

933 © 1986, GIA Publications, Inc.

934 Text trans. and acc.: © 1986, GIA Publications, Inc.

935 Refrain text: © 1973, ICEL. Verse text and music: © 1988, GIA Publications, Inc.

936 Text: *Rite of Funerals* © 1970, ICEL. Music: *Music for Rite of Funerals and Rite of Baptism for Children* © 1977, ICEL.

937 Text: © 1982, Hope Publishing Co., Carol Stream, IL 60188. All rights reserved. Used by permission. Music © 1987, GIA Publications, Inc.

938 Text: © 1970, ICEL. Music: © 1977, ICEL

939 Text: © 1985, ICEL

940 © 1965, World Library Publications, a division of J.S. Paluch Company, Inc. Schiller Park, IL 60176. All rights reserved. Used by permission

941 © 1989, GIA Publications, Inc.

942 Text and harm.: © 1983, Hope Publishing Co., Carol Stream IL 60188. All rights reserved. Used by permission

943 © 1972, 1980, The Benedictine Foundation of the State of Vermont, Weston Priory, Weston, VT

944 © 1989, Iona Community, GIA Publications, Inc., agent. Harm.: © 1975, Hope Publishing Co., Carol Stream, IL 60188. All rights reserved. Used by permission

945 Text: © 1989, Iona Community, GIA Publications, Inc., agent

946 Text: © 1981, Concordia Publishing House. Harm.: © Downside Abbey, Bath, BA3 4RH UK

947 Text: © 1992, GIA Publications, Inc. Music: © 1994, GIA Publications, Inc.

948 © 1987, Iona Community, GIA Publications, Inc., agent

949 Text: © 1986, GIA Publications, Inc.

950 Text: © 1969, Hope Publishing Co., Carol Stream, IL 60188. All rights reserved. Used by permission

951 Text: © 1982, Hope Publishing Co., Carol Stream, IL 60188. All rights reserved. Used by permission. Music: © 1988, GIA Publications, Inc.

952 Text: © Oxford University Press. Music: © The Royal School of Church Music

954 Harm.: © 1979, Church of the Redeemer, Houston

955 Text: © 1980, ICEL

956 Text: © 1965, GIA Publications, Inc. Harm.: © 1986, GIA Publications, Inc.

957 © 1978, New Dawn Music, P.O. Box 13248, Portland, OR 97213-0248. All rights reserved. Used with permission

958 © 1987, GIA Publications, Inc.

959 Text: © 1989, Hope Publishing Co., Carol Stream, IL 60188. All rights reserved. Used with permission. Music: © 1994, GIA Publications, Inc.

960 Text: © 1989, Hope Publishing Co., Carol Stream, IL 60188. All rights reserved. Used with permission. Music: © 1994, GIA Publications, Inc.

961 Text: © 1941, The Church Pension Fund

963 Text: © 1969, James Quinn SJ. Used by permission of Selah Publishing Co., Inc., (North American agent. Kingston NY 12401. All rights reserved. Used by permission)

964 Text: Verses 1-2 © 1934, 1962, Lorenz Publishing Co., Verse 3 © 1964, Lorenz Publishing Co., reprint license #303926

967 Text and Music arr.: © 1989, Iona Community, GIA Publications, Inc., agent

968 Text: © 1969, Concordia Publishing House. Music: © 1989, Selah Publishing Co., (Kingston NY 12401. All rights reserved. Used by permission.)

969 Acc.: © 1985, GIA Publications, Inc.

972 Text trans.: © 1969, James Quinn, SJ. Used by permission of Selah Publishing Co., Inc., (North American agent, Kingston NY 12401. All rights reserved. Used by permission.) Acc.: © 1964, GIA Publications, Inc.

974 Music: © 1979, 1985, GIA Publications, Inc.

978 Refrain trans.: © 1973, ICEL. Music: © 1985, GIA Publications, Inc.

979 Music: © 1977, ICEL

980 Text trans.: © 1983, Peter J. Scagnelli. Acc.: © 1975, GIA Publications, Inc.

981 Text trans.: © 1983, Peter J. Scagnelli. Acc.: © Interkerkelijke Stichting voor het Kerklied Den Haag.

Scripture Passages Related to Hymns/*continued*

Scripture Passages Related to Hymns/*continued*

55:6-9	Seek the Lord 540
55:10-10	Thy Kingdom Come 776
55:10-11	Word of God, Come Down on Earth 653
58:9-14	Return to God 555
60:1-5	Sion, Sing 532
60:15-15	Sion, Sing 532
60:19-20	Sion, Sing 532
61:1-1	Advent Gathering 492
61:1-1	Song of the Body of Christ / Canción del Cuerpo 924
61:1-2	You Have Anointed Me 795
61:1-4	Good News 797
62:3-3	All Hail the Power of Jesus' Name 632
63:3-3	Mine Eyes Have Seen the Glory 869
66:1-1	Mine Eyes Have Seen the Glory 869
67:7-7	Easter Alleluia 592

JEREMIAH

8:22-22	There Is a Balm in Gilead 764
31:3-3	I Have Loved You 641
31:31-34	Grant to Us, O Lord 558
31:33-33	Deep Within 546
36:26-26	Grant to Us, O Lord 558
51:8-8	Sing Praise to God Who Reigns Above 683

LAMENTATIONS

1:12-12	All You Who Pass This Way 567

BARUCH

4:	City of God, Jerusalem 486
5:	City of God, Jerusalem 486

EZEKIEL

11:19-19	Here I Am, Lord 802
21:14-15	Mine Eyes Have Seen the Glory 869
36:26-28	Deep Within 546
37:23-23	I Will Be with You 603
47:1-12	Healing River 715

DANIEL

3:	Surrexit Christus 577
3:52-57	Daniel 3:52-57/Song of the Three Children 206
3:52-90	Sing Out, Earth and Skies 640
3:57-87	Daniel 3: Benedicite 208
3:57-88	Daniel 3:57-88/Song of the Three Children 207

HOSEA

6:3-3	Mine Eyes Have Seen the Glory 869
14:2-2	Deep Within 546

JOEL

2:12-12	Deep Within 546
2:12-12	Return to God 555
2:12-18	Again We Keep This Solemn Fast 559
2:17-17	Parce Domine 549
3:1-1	Song Over the Waters 855
3:1-5	Praise the Spirit in Creation 609

AMOS

6:1-7	O Christ, the Healer 950

MICAH

6:6-8	What Does the Lord Require 785
6:6-8	When Jesus Came Preaching 773
6:8-8	Lord, Today 536
6:8-8	We Are Called 820

HABAKKUK

2:14-14	God Is Working His Purpose Out 646
2:20-20	Let All Mortal Flesh Keep Silence 658

ZEPHANIAH

3:14-17	Sion, Sing 532

HAGGAI

2:7-7	Angels, from the Realms of Glory 508
2:7-7	Come, O Long Expected Jesus 496

MALACHI

3:1-1	On Jordan's Bank 490
4:2-2	Hark! The Herald Angels Sing 502

MATTHEW

1:4-11	Jesus, Tempted in the Desert 548
1:18-24	God of Adam, God of Joseph 960
1:20-21	God It Was 818
1:23-23	Praise We the Lord This Day 877
2:	Brightest and Best 533
2:	Night of Silence 523
2:1-11	Good Christian Friends, Rejoice 518
2:1-11	The Virgin Mary Had a Baby Boy 501
2:1-12	A Child Is Born in Bethlehem 500
2:1-12	Angels, from the Realms of Glory 508
2:1-12	As with Gladness Men of Old 534
2:1-12	Songs of Thankfulness and Praise 529
2:1-12	The First Nowell 537
2:1-12	We Three Kings of Orient Are 535
2:2-10	What Star Is This 531
2:10-11	O Come, All Ye Faithful / Adeste Fideles 499
2:11-11	What Child Is This 530
2:13-23	God of Adam, God of Joseph 960
2:16-18	By All Your Saints Still Striving 887
3:	When John Baptized by Jordan's River 538
3:13-17	Songs of Thankfulness and Praise 529
4:	When Jesus Came Preaching 773
4:1-11	Lord, Who throughout These Forty Days 553
4:1-11	Tree of Life 541
4:16-16	Child of Mercy 506
4:16-16	Comfort, Comfort, O My People 488
4:18-20	Those Who Love and Those Who Labor 805
4:18-22	Lord, When You Came / Pescador de Hombres 817
4:24-24	The King of Glory 628
5:3-12	Blest Are They 774
5:13-13	Gather Us In 850
5:13-16	Bring Forth the Kingdom 772
5:21-24	Forgive Our Sins 952
5:38-48	Lord of All Nations, Grant Me Grace 751
6:1-6	Again We Keep This Solemn Fast 559
6:9-10	Thy Kingdom Come 776
6:9-13	Lord's Prayer 9
6:9-13	This Is My Song 964
6:9-15	Forgive Our Sins 952
6:10-10	Mayenziwe / Your Will Be Done 725
6:16-18	Again We Keep This Solemn Fast 559
6:25-34	Lord of All Hopefulness 713
6:25-34	Praise and Thanksgiving 867
6:25-34	Today I Awake 857
6:33-33	Seek Ye First the Kingdom of God 728
7:7-7	Seek Ye First the Kingdom of God 728
8:23-27	Psalm 107: Give Thanks to the Lord 147
9:9-13	Come, You Sinners, Poor and Needy 954
9:11-13	The Master Came to Bring Good News 956
10:42-42	There's a Spirit in the Air 689
11:25-30	How Blessed Is This Place 893
11:25-30	I Heard the Voice of Jesus Say 768
11:25-30	O Jesus, Joy of Loving Hearts 759
11:28-30	Come to Me 763
11:28-30	Come to Me, O Weary Traveler 769
11:29-30	We Shall Rise Again 872
13:	Christ's Church Shall Glory in His Power 777
13:1-23	Word of God, Come Down on Earth 653
13:4-23	Bring Forth the Kingdom 772
13:21-43	Come, Ye Thankful People, Come 706
13:44-52	When Jesus Came Preaching 773
14:13-21	Bread to Share 927
14:14-14	Love Divine, All Loves Excelling 743
14:22-33	How Firm a Foundation 731
14:35-36	Your Hands, O Lord, in Days of Old 949
17:1-8	Transform Us 881
17:1-9	'Tis Good, Lord, to Be Here 882
17:2-2	From Ashes to the Living Font 561
18:10-14	My Shepherd Will Supply My Need 761
18:10-14	The King of Love My Shepherd Is 766
18:19-20	Help Us Accept Each Other 838
18:20-20	Draw Us in the Spirit's Tether 917
18:20-20	Here Am I 822
18:20-20	The God of All Eternity 967
19:5-6	Blessing the Marriage 945
20:1-16	For the Fruits of This Creation 704
20:25-28	Lord, Whose Love in Humble Service 793
21:1-17	All Glory, Laud, and Honor 563
21:33-43	O Christ the Great Foundation 781
22:1-10	The Kingdom of God 775

Scripture Passages Related to Hymns/*continued*

19:16-37	Sing, My Tongue, the Song of Triumph 573
19:25-25	At the Cross Her Station Keeping 551
19:25-25	Calvary 568
19:25-25	Immaculate Mary 890
19:25-25	Sing We of the Blessed Mother 895
19:25-27	O Sanctissima 900
19:28-28	All You Who Pass This Way 567
19:34-34	Come and Let Us Drink of That New River 902
19:34-34	Were You There 570
19:36-42	I Danced in the Morning 809
20:	O Sons and Daughters 579
20:	That Easter Day with Joy Was Bright 599
20:1-9	This Is the Day When Light Was First Created 842
20:1-18	For All the Faithful Women 885
20:11-18	Christ the Lord Is Risen Today 594
20:11-18	Christ the Lord Is Risen Today 602
20:24-29	By All Your Saints Still Striving 887
20:27-29	We Walk by Faith 723
21:15-17	Go 604
21:18-19	Two Noble Saints 880

ACTS

1:1-11	A Hymn of Glory Let Us Sing 606
1:8-8	Come Down, O Love Divine 617
1:8-8	Come, Holy Ghost 611
1:8-8	O Holy Spirit, by Whose Breath 616
1:8-8	When God the Spirit Came 613
1:9-11	Hail the Day That Sees Him Rise 605
2:	Christians, Lift Up Your Hearts 674
2:	When God the Spirit Came 613
2:1-2	Song Over the Waters 855
2:1-4	On This Day, the First of Days 843
2:1-11	Diverse in Culture, Nation, Race 837
2:1-11	Spirit of God within Me 610
2:1-11	This Is the Day When Light Was First Created 842
2:1-11	Veni Sancte Spiritus 615
2:43-49	Praise the Spirit in Creation 609
3:6-6	The Love of the Lord 814
3:14-15	My Song Is Love Unknown 572
4:11-11	O Christ the Great Foundation 781 782
7:54-60	By All Your Saints Still Striving 887
10:37-37	On Jordan's Bank 490

ROMANS

1:28-32	O Christ, the Healer 950
6:1-4	Baptized in Water 903
6:3-11	I Know That My Redeemer Lives 582
6:4-5	Christians, Lift Up Your Hearts 674
6:4-9	We Know That Christ Is Raised 906
6:5-11	Christ Is Alive 601
8:14-17	In Christ There Is No East or West 836
8:18-39	There's a Wideness in God's Mercy 742
11:33-35	There's a Wideness in God's Mercy 742
12:15-15	The Servant Song 788
14:8-8	Pues Sí Vivimos / If We Are Living 727
14:17-17	The Kingdom of God 775

1 CORINTHIANS

1:15-20	We Know That Christ Is Raised 906
1:18-18	Lift High the Cross 884
1:18-18	Sing, My Tongue, the Song of Triumph 573
1:25-25	Darkness Is Gone 596
2:9-9	May the Angels Lead You into Paradise 938
2:9-10	Eye Has Not Seen 758
3:13-15	Come, Ye Thankful People, Come 706
5:6-8	Steal Away to Jesus 873
5:18-20	God Is Working His Purpose Out 646
10:16-17	One Bread, One Body 915
10:16-17	Seed, Scattered and Sown 918
10:16-17	You Satisfy the Hungry Heart 912
11:23-26	I Come with Joy to Meet My Lord 854
11:23-26	Life-giving Bread, Saving Cup 920
11:23-26	Now We Remain 813
11:23-27	Take the Bread, Children 925
11:23-27	This Holy Covenant Was Made 621
11:23-29	Draw Us in the Spirit's Tether 917
11:23-29	Let Us Break Bread Together 915
12:	In Christ There Is No East or West 836
12:	There Is One Lord 835
12:	We Are Many Parts 840
12:	When Love Is Found 942

12:4-4	One Bread, One Body 915
12:4-5	Sing Praise to Our Creator 620
12:4-6	Many Are the Lightbeams 841
12:4-11	Come, Holy Ghost 611
12:4-11	Fire of God, Undying Flame 614
12:12-13	Many Are the Lightbeams 841
12:12-13	Sing Praise to Our Creator 620
12:27-33	God Is Here! As We His People 844
13:	We Are Many Parts 840
13:1-13	May Love Be Ours 748
13:2-8	Ubi Caritas 746
13:2-8	Where True Love and Charity Are Found / Ubi Caritas 752
15:10-10	Amazing Grace 737
15:14-19	This Joyful Eastertide 598
15:20-20	Sing with All the Saints in Glory 595
15:20-28	Come, Ye Faithful, Raise the Strain 575
15:22-23	Spirit of God within Me 610
15:51-54	The Strife Is O'er 587
15:54-57	Resucitó 580
15:55-55	Christ the Lord Is Risen Today 594
15:55-55	Christ the Lord Is Risen Today 602

2 CORINTHIANS

4:5-5	God Is Here! As We His People 844
4:11-11	Good Christians All 586
5:7-7	We Walk by Faith 723
5:17-17	Good Christians All 586
5:17-17	Love Divine, All Loves Excelling 743
5:17-17	O Christ the Great Foundation 781
6:2-2	O Sun of Justice 544
6:2-2	Return to God 555
9:10-14	Come, Ye Thankful People, Come 706
9:10-14	Now Join We to Praise the Creator 827

GALATIANS

2:19-19	Alleluia, Alleluia, Give Thanks 581
2:20-20	I Heard the Voice of Jesus Say 768
3:28-28	God Is Love 744
3:28-28	In Christ There Is No East or West 836
3:28-28	One Bread, One Body 915
3:28-29	Pan de Vida 909
4:4-4	Hark! The Herald Angels Sing 502
5:22-22	For the Fruits of This Creation 704
5:22-22	When God the Spirit Came 613
6:14-14	In the Cross of Christ 221
6:14-14	Crucem Tuam / O Lord, Your Cross 571
7:	All Who Claim the Faith of Jesus 897

EPHESIANS

1:9-11	God Is Working His Purpose Out 646
1:18-19	The Church of Christ in Every Age 803
1:19-23	Holy God, We Praise Thy Name 657
2:1-1	We Are God's Work of Art / Somos la Creación de Dios 901
2:4-7	We Are God's Work of Art / Somos la Creación de Dios 901
2:8-8	Amazing Grace 737
2:10-10	We Are God's Work of Art / Somos la Creación de Dios 901
2:12-22	We Are God's Work of Art / Somos la Creación de Dios 901
2:19-19	We Are God's Work of Art / Somos la Creación de Dios 901
2:19-22	What Is This Place 892
3:5-5	Awake, O Sleeper, Rise from Death 729
3:14-14	You Are Called to Tell the Story 800
4:	O Christ, the Healer 950
4:	There Is One Lord 835
4:1-6	In Christ There Is No East or West 836
4:4-6	Let Us Be Bread 929
4:5-7	O Christ the Great Foundation 781
4:6-6	There Is One God 237
5:8-8	We Are Marching 648
5:8-10	I Want to Walk as a Child of the Light 651
5:14-14	Awake, O Sleeper 650
5:14-14	Awake, O Sleeper, Rise from Death 729
5:14-14	Light of Christ / Exsultet 647
5:14-14	Wake, O Wake, and Sleep No Longer 489
5:25-27	O Christ the Great Foundation 781
5:27-27	Love Divine, All Loves Excelling 743

Scripture Passages Related to Hymns/*continued*

PHILIPPIANS

2:1-18	Lord of All Nations, Grant Me Grace 751
2:5-7	Stand Up, Friends 622
2:5-8	Psalm 8: How Great Is Your Name 31
2:8-8	Hark! The Herald Angels Sing 502
2:9-10	All Hail the Power of Jesus' Name 632
2:10-11	Creator of the Stars of Night 483
3:7-11	The Love of the Lord 814
4:4-5	Rejoice, the Lord Is King 627

COLOSSIANS

1:16-16	Ye Watchers and Ye Holy Ones 886
1:17-17	Psalm 8: How Great Is Your Name 31
1:18-18	Christ the Lord Is Risen Today 594
1:18-18	Christ the Lord Is Risen Today 602
2:13-13	Good Christians All 586
3:12-21	Our Father, by Whose Name 961
3:13-14	Forgive Our Sins 952
3:16-16	Come, Rejoice before Your Maker 847

1 THESSALONIANS

13:18-18	When the Lord in Glory Comes 868

2 THESSALONIANS

2:15-15	God Is Here! As We His People 844

1 TIMOTHY

6:12-12	Faith of Our Fathers 726

2 TIMOTHY

2:	Now We Remain 813
2:	We Shall Rise Again 872
2:8-12	Keep in Mind 940
2:12-12	The Head That Once Was Crowned with Thorns 591
4:3-7	Faith of Our Fathers 726
4:6-8	Two Noble Saints 880

TITUS

2:14-14	God Is Here! As We His People 844

HEBREWS

1:3-3	Rejoice, the Lord Is King 627
2:9-10	The Head That Once Was Crowned with Thorns 591
9:	The King of Glory 628
9:11-14	Alleluia, Sing to Jesus 914
10:	The King of Glory 628
10:7-7	Psalm 40: Here I Am 74
11:	Faith of Our Fathers 726
12:1-1	For All the Saints 889
12:1-1	I Want to Walk as a Child of the Light 651
12:1-3	Holy God, We Praise Thy Name 657
12:18-19	How Blessed Is This Place 893
13:6-6	My Shepherd Will Supply My Need 761
13:8-8	I Know That My Redeemer Lives 582

JAMES

1:17-17	America the Beautiful 965
1:17-17	For the Beauty of the Earth 697
1:17-17	I Sing the Mighty Power of God 633
5:13-16	Your Hands, O Lord, in Days of Old 949

1 PETER

1:3-5	Praise the Lord, My Soul 688
2:4-6	Christ's Church Shall Glory in His Power 777
2:4-6	O Christ the Great Foundation 781
2:4-7	For Builders Bold 891
2:4-7	Christ Is Made the Sure Foundation 778
2:4-8	O Christ the Great Foundation 781 782
2:5-5	Take and Eat 910
2:9-9	Light of Christ / Exsultet 647
2:9-10	God Is Here! As We His People 844

2 PETER

1:16-18	Transform Us 881
1:19-19	Take and Eat 910
1:19-19	Up from the Earth 589

1 JOHN

1:	Now We Remain 813
1:	City of God 799
1:5-5	God Is Love 744
1:5-5	I Want to Walk as a Child of the Light 651
1:5-5	Our Darkness / La Ténèbre 863
2:27-27	Come, Holy Ghost 611
3:2-2	God Is Love 744
3:18-18	Faith of Our Fathers 726
4:	God Is Love 744
4:	Where Charity and Love Prevail 747
4:7-7	Love One Another 745
4:7-17	Love Divine, All Loves Excelling 743
4:9-10	What Wondrous Love Is This 749
4:10-16	Where True Love and Charity Are Found / Ubi Caritas 752
4:12-12	Love One Another 745
4:12-12	Ubi Caritas 746
4:16-16	Many Are the Lightbeams 841
4:16-16	Ubi Caritas 746
4:20-21	Now Join We to Praise the Creator 827
5:4-4	How Long, O Lord, How Long 829
5:6-8	Come and Let Us Drink of That New River 902
5:13-13	Good Christians All 586
9:12-16	Easter Alleluia 592

REVELATION

1:8-8	Of the Father's Love Begotten 510
1:18-18	Rejoice, the Lord Is King 627
1:18-18	The Strife Is O'er 587
2:10-10	For All the Saints 889
3:20-20	Somebody's Knockin' at Your Door 547
4:	God, We Praise You 676
4:	Heavenly Hosts in Ceaseless Worship 661
4:	Holy God, We Praise Thy Name 657
4:	Holy, Holy, Holy! Lord God Almighty 624
4:8-8	Of the Father's Love Begotten 510
5:	Heavenly Hosts in Ceaseless Worship 661
5:	Holy God, We Praise Thy Name 657
5:	This Is the Feast of Victory 583
5:9-9	Alleluia, Sing to Jesus 914
5:9-9	At the Lamb's High Feast We Sing 578
5:9-9	Crown Him with Many Crowns 626
5:9-9	To Jesus Christ, Our Sovereign King 629
5:11-12	Alabaré 662
5:11-13	Now the Feast and Celebration 853
5:11-14	All Hail the Power of Jesus' Name 632
5:13-13	All Glory, Laud, and Honor 563
6:2-2	Ride On, Jesus, Ride 562
7:2-4	For All the Saints 889
7:9-14	For All the Saints 889
8:3-4	How Blessed Is This Place 893
14:17-20	Mine Eyes Have Seen the Glory 869
15:4-4	Holy, Holy, Holy! Lord God Almighty 624
19:1-7	Revelation 19:1-7 213
19:6-9	Wake, O Wake, and Sleep No Longer 489
19:11-16	Let All Mortal Flesh Keep Silence 658
19:11-16	The King Shall Come When Morning Dawns 497
19:12-12	Crown Him with Many Crowns 626
19:16-16	Christ the Lord Is Risen 600
21:1-4	Jerusalem, My Happy Home 871
21:1-5	What Is This Place 892
21:9-13	Wake, O Wake, and Sleep No Longer 489
21:23-23	I Want to Walk as a Child of the Light 651
22:	Jerusalem, My Happy Home 871
22:1-1	Come and Let Us Drink of That New River 902
22:5-5	Light of Christ / Exsultet 647
22:5-5	Our Darkness / La Ténèbre 863
22:17-17	In Christ There Is a Table Set for All 916
22:17-17	We Know That Christ Is Raised 906
22:20-20	Each Winter As the Year Grows Older 481
22:20-20	Soon and Very Soon 870

Hymns and Psalms for the Church Year 984

The following hymns and psalms are suggested for the Sundays of the three-year lectionary cycle. Those with an asterisk (*) are directly related to the scriptures of the day, while the others are suggested because of their relationship to the predominant focus of the day's readings.

ADVENT I
- A - Wake, O Wake and Sleep No Longer 489
  - Psalm 122: I Rejoiced When I Heard 165
- B - Wake, O Wake and Sleep No Longer 489
  - Psalm 80: Lord, Make Us Turn to You 108
- C - When the Lord in Glory Comes 868
  - Psalm 25: To You, O Lord 50 51 53
  - Psalm 25: Levanto Mi Alma 52

ADVENT II
- A - On Jordan's Bank* 490
  - A Voice Cries Out* 485
  - Psalm 72: Justice Shall Flourish 101
  - Psalm 72: In His Days Justice Will Flourish 102
- B - Comfort, Comfort, O My People* 488
  - On Jordan's Bank* 490
  - A Voice Cries Out* 485
  - Psalm 85: Lord, Let Us See Your Kindness 112 113 114
- C - City of God, Jerusalem* 486
  - On Jordan's Bank* 490
  - A Voice Cries Out* 485
  - Psalm 126: The Lord Has Done Great Things 169 170 171

ADVENT III
- A - When the King Shall Come Again* 487
  - Psalm 146: O Lord, Come and Save Us 195
- B - On Jordan's Bank* 490
  - A Voice Cries Out* 485
  - Luke 1:46-55/Magnificat 209 211
  - Luke 1:46-55/Magnificat/Holy Is Your Name 210
- C - On Jordan's Bank* 490
  - A Voice Cries Out* 485
  - Isaiah 12: Cry Out with Joy and Gladness 205

ADVENT IV
- A - Savior of the Nations, Come 480
  - Psalm 24: Let the Lord Enter 48
- B - No Wind at the Window* 876
  - A Message Came to a Maiden Young* 478
  - Psalm 89: For Ever I Will Sing 117 118 119
- C - Savior of the Nations, Come 480
  - Psalm 80: Lord, Make Us Turn to You 108

CHRISTMAS
see nos. 498-524
- Vigil - Psalm 89: For Ever I Will Sing 117 118 119
- Midnight - Psalm 96: Today Is Born Our Savior 130 131
- Dawn - Psalm 97: A Light Will Shine 134
- Day - Psalm 98: All the Ends of the Earth 135 136 137

HOLY FAMILY
see nos. 525-526
- Psalm 128: O Happy Are Those 172

MARY, MOTHER OF GOD
see nos. 527-528
- Psalm 67: May God Bless Us in His Mercy 94 95

EPIPHANY
see nos. 529-537
- Psalm 72: Every Nation on Earth 102
- Psalm 72: Lord, Every Nation on Earth 103

BAPTISM OF THE LORD
- When John Baptized by Jordan's River* 538
- Psalm 29: The Lord Will Bless His People 58

ASH WEDNESDAY
- Dust and Ashes 539
- Psalm 51: Be Merciful, O Lord 82 83

LENT I
- A - Jesus, Tempted in the Desert* 548
  - Psalm 51: Be Merciful, O Lord 82 83
- B - Lord, Who throughout These Forty Days* 553
  - This Is the Time* 556
  - Psalm 25: Your Ways, O Lord 53
- C - Jesus, Tempted in the Desert* 548
  - Psalm 91: Be with Me 123

LENT II
- A - 'Tis Good, Lord, to Be Here* 882
  - Transform Us* 881
  - Psalm 33: Let Your Mercy Be on Us 66
  - Psalm 33: Lord, Let Your Mercy 68
- B - 'Tis Good, Lord, to Be Here* 882
  - Transform Us* 881
  - Psalm 116: I Will Walk in the Presence 153 154
- C - 'Tis Good, Lord, to Be Here* 882
  - Transform Us* 881
  - Psalm 27: The Lord Is My Light 55 57 238

LENT III
- A - I Heard the Voice of Jesus Say* 768
  - Psalm 95: If Today You Hear His Voice 127 128
  - Psalm 95: If Today You Hear God's Voice 129
- B - Christ Is Made the Sure Foundation 778
  - Psalm 19: Lord, You Have the Words 39 40
- C - Eternal Lord of Love 554
  - Psalm 103: The Lord Is Kind and Merciful 140 141 143

LENT IV
- A - He Healed the Darkness of My Mind* 951
  - Psalm 23: The Lord Is My Shepherd 44 45
  - Psalm 23: My Shepherd Is the Lord 45
  - Psalm 23: Nada Me Falta 46
  - Psalm 23: Shepherd Me, O God 756
- B - What Wondrous Love Is This 749
  - Psalm 137: Let My Tongue Be Silent 182 183
- C - Our Father, We Have Wandered* 955
  - Psalm 34: Taste and See 70 71 72 73

LENT V
- A - I Am the Bread of Life/Yo Soy el Pan de Vida* 931
  - Psalm 130: With the Lord There Is Mercy 174 175 176
- B - Unless a Grain of Wheat* 804
  - Psalm 51: Create a Clean Heart 82
  - Psalm 51: Create in Me a Clean Heart 84, 85
- C - Forgive Our Sins* 952
  - Psalm 126: The Lord Has Done Great Things 169 170 171

PASSION SUNDAY
see nos. 562-563
- Psalm 22: My God, My God 42 43

HOLY THURSDAY
see nos. 564-566
   Psalm 116: Our Blessing Cup   152 153 155

GOOD FRIDAY
see nos. 567-574
   Psalm 31: I Put My Life in Your Hands/Pongo Mi Vida
   61
   Psalm 31: Father, I Put My Life in Your Hands   62 63

EASTER VIGIL
see nos. 575-602
   I.   Psalm 104: Lord, Send Out Your Spirit   144 145
        146
        or Psalm 33: The Earth Is Full of the Goodness   66
        67
   II. Psalm 16: Keep Me Safe, O God   34 35 36
   III. Exodus 15: Let Us Sing to the Lord   201
        Exodus 15: Song at the Sea   202
   IV. Psalm 30: I Will Praise You, Lord   59 60
   V.   Isaiah 12: You Will Draw Water   204
   VI. Psalm 19: Lord, You Have the Words   39 40
   VII. Psalm 42/43: Like a Deer That Longs   77
        or Psalm 51: Create a Clean Heart   82
        Psalm 51: Create in Me a Clean Heart   84 85

EASTER
see nos. 575-602
   Psalm 118: This Is the Day   158 160

EASTER II
   A - O Sons and Daughters*   579
       We Walk by Faith*   723
       Psalm 118: Give Thanks to the Lord   159
   B - O Sons and Daughters*   579
       We Walk by Faith*   723
       Psalm 118: Give Thanks to the Lord   159
   C - O Sons and Daughters*   579
       We Walk by Faith*   723
       Psalm 118: Give Thanks to the Lord   159

EASTER III
   A - On the Journey to Emmaus*   816
       Psalm 16: Lord, You Will Show   34
       Psalm 16: You Will Show Me the Path of Life   36
   B - On the Journey to Emmaus*   816
       Psalm 4: Lord, Let Your Face Shine on Us   29
       Psalm 4: Lord, Let Your Face Shine upon Us   30
   C - You Walk along Our Shoreline   807
       Psalm 30: I Will Praise You, Lord   59 60

EASTER IV
   A - Christus Paradox   699
       Psalm 23: The Lord Is My Shepherd   44 45
       Psalm 23: My Shepherd Is the Lord   45
       Psalm 23: Nada Me Falta   46
       Psalm 23: Shepherd Me, O God   756
   B - Christus Paradox   699
       Psalm 118: The Stone Rejected   161
   C - Christus Paradox   699
       Psalm 100: We Are God's People   138

EASTER V
   A - Come, My Way, My Truth, My Life*   717
       I Know That My Redeemer Lives*   582
       Psalm 33: Let Your Mercy Be on Us   66
       Psalm 33: Lord, Let Your Mercy   68
   B - We Have Been Told*   815
       Psalm 22: I Will Praise You, Lord   41
   C - Lord of All Nations, Grant Me Grace   751

Love Is His Word*   750
Psalm 145: I Will Praise Your Name   192 193 194

EASTER VI
   A - Come Down, O Love Divine*   617
       If You Believe and I Believe   825
       Psalm 66: Let All the Earth   93
   B - No Greater Love*   753
       Psalm 98: The Lord Has Revealed   137
   C - Come Down, O Love Divine   617
       Unless a Grain of Wheat   804
       Psalm 67: O God, Let All the Nations Praise You
       94 95

ASCENSION
see nos. 603-608
   Psalm 47: God Mounts His Throne   79 80

EASTER VII
   A - Alleluia! Sing to Jesus   914
       Psalm 27: I Believe That I Shall See   55
       Psalm 27: In the Land of the Living   56
   B - Alleluia! Sing to Jesus   914
       Psalm 103: The Lord Has Set His Throne   141 142
   C - Alleluia! Sing to Jesus   914
       Psalm 97: The Lord Is King   133

PENTECOST
see nos. 609-617
   Vigil - Psalm 104: Lord, Send Out Your Spirit   144 145
           146
   Day - Psalm 104: Lord, Send Out Your Spirit   144 145
         146

TRINITY SUNDAY
see nos. 618-625
   A - What Wondrous Love Is This   749
       Daniel 3:52-57/Song of the Three Children   206
   B - Go*   604
       Go to the World*   608
       Psalm 33: Happy Are the People   66
       Psalm 33: Happy the People   67
   C - Alleluia, Sing!   625
       Psalm 8: O Lord, Our God   31
       Psalm 8: How Glorious Is Your Name   32

BODY AND BLOOD
   A - I Am the Bread of Life/Yo Soy el Pan de Vida*   931
       Psalm 147: Praise the Lord   198 199
   B - Take and Eat*   910
       Psalm 116: The Name of God   152
       Psalm 116: I Will Take the Cup of Salvation   153
   C - Plenty of Bread   927
       Psalm 110: You Are a Priest for Ever   148

ORDINARY TIME

SECOND SUNDAY
   A - When Jesus Came to Jordan*   878
       Psalm 40: Here I Am   74
       Psalm 40: Here Am I   75
   B - Those Who Love and Those Who Labor*   805
       Psalm 40: Here I Am   74
       Psalm 40: Here Am I   75
   C - Jesus, Come! For We Invite You*   714
       Psalm 96: Proclaim to All the Nations   132

THIRD SUNDAY
   A - Two Fishermen*   812
       The Summons   811
       You Walk along Our Shoreline   807

Hymns and Psalms for the Church Year/*continued*

Psalm 27: The Lord Is My Light 55 57
B - Two Fishermen* 812
The Summons 811
You Walk along Our Shoreline 807
Psalm 25: Teach Me Your Ways 54
C - You Have Anointed Me* 795
Good News* 797
Psalm 19: Your Words, Lord, Are Spirit and Life
40

FOURTH SUNDAY
A - Blest Are They* 774
Psalm 146: Happy the Poor 196
B - When Jesus Came Preaching 773
Psalm 95: If Today You Hear His Voice 127 128
Psalm 95: If Today You Hear God's Voice 129
C - God Has Spoken by His Prophets 654
May Love Be Ours* 748
Psalm 71: I Will Sing 99

FIFTH SUNDAY
A - Bring Forth the Kingdom* 772
Psalm 112: A Light Rises in the Darkness 149
B - Your Hands, O Lord, in Days of Old* 949
Psalm 147: Praise the Lord 198
C - You Walk along Our Shoreline* 807
Lord, When You Came/Pescador de Hombres* 817
Psalm 138: In the Sight of the Angels 184 185

SIXTH SUNDAY
A - What Does the Lord Require 785
Deep Within 546
Eye Has Not Seen* 758
Psalm 119: Happy Are They 162
B - Your Hands, O Lord, in Days of Old* 949
Psalm 32: I Turn to You 64
C - Blest Are They* 774
Psalm 1: Happy Are They 28

SEVENTH SUNDAY
A - Lord of All Nations, Grant Me Grace* 751
Psalm 103: The Lord Is Kind and Merciful 140 141
143
B - Your Hands, O Lord, in Days of Old 949
Psalm 41: Lord, Heal My Soul 76
C - Lord of All Nations, Grant Me Grace* 751
Psalm 103: The Lord Is Kind and Merciful 140 141
143

EIGHTH SUNDAY
A - Seek Ye First the Kingdom of God* 728
Psalm 62: Rest in God 87
Psalm 62: In God Alone 88
B - Christ Is the King 630
Psalm 103: The Lord Is Kind and Merciful 140 141
143
C - Help Us Accept Each Other 838
Psalm 92: Lord, It Is Good 124 125

NINTH SUNDAY
A - Christ Is Made the Sure Foundation 778
Psalm 31: Lord, Be My Rock of Safety 63
B - I Danced in the Morning 809
Psalm 81: Sing with Joy to God 109
C - Surely It Is God Who Saves Me 739
Psalm 117: Go Out to All the World 157

TENTH SUNDAY
A - Come, You Sinners, Poor and Needy* 954
God It Was 818
Psalm 50: To the Upright 81

B - The Master Came to Bring Good News 956
Psalm 130: With the Lord There Is Mercy 174 175
176
C - Your Hands, O Lord, in Days of Old* 949
Psalm 30: I Will Praise You, Lord 59, 60

ELEVENTH SUNDAY
A - When Jesus Came Preaching 773
Psalm 100: We Are God's People 138
B - The Kingdom of God* 775
Psalm 92: Lord, It Is Good 124 125
C - There's a Wideness in God's Mercy 742
Psalm 32: Lord, Forgive the Wrong 65

TWELFTH SUNDAY
A - Be Not Afraid 734
Psalm 69: Lord, in Your Great Love 98
B - How Firm a Foundation* 731
Psalm 107: Give Thanks to the Lord 147
C - Take Up Your Cross* 808
Wherever He Leads* 810
Psalm 63: My Soul Is Thirsting 89 90 91

THIRTEENTH SUNDAY
A - Take Up Your Cross* 808
Wherever He Leads* 810
Psalm 89: For Ever I Will Sing 117 118 119
B - Draw Us in the Spirit's Tether* 917
Psalm 30: I Will Praise You, Lord 59, 60
C - Jesus, Lead the Way 755
Psalm 16: You Are My Inheritance 34 36

FOURTEENTH SUNDAY
A - Come to Me, O Weary Traveler* 769
Come to Me* 763
I Heard the Voice of Jesus Say* 768
Psalm 145: I Will Praise Your Name for Ever 192
Psalm 145: I Will Praise Your Name 193 194
B - God Has Spoken by His Prophets* 654
Psalm 123: Our Eyes Are Fixed on the Lord 168
264
C - Lord, You Give the Great Commission 607
Psalm 66: Let All the Earth 93

FIFTEENTH SUNDAY
A - Word of God, Come Down on Earth* 653
Psalm 65: The Seed That Falls on Good Ground 92
B - Go to the World 608
Psalm 85: Lord, Let Us See Your Kindness 112 113
114
C - Lord of All Nations, Grant Me Grace* 751
We Are Your People 789
Psalm 69: Turn to the Lord in Your Need 97

SIXTEENTH SUNDAY
A - Come, Ye Thankful People, Come* 706
Psalm 86: Lord, You Are Good and Forgiving 115
B - There's a Wideness in God's Mercy* 742
Psalm 23: My Shepherd Is the Lord 45
Psalm 23: The Lord Is My Shepherd 44 45
Psalm 23: Shepherd Me, O God 756
C - God It Was 818
Psalm 15: The Just Will Live 33

SEVENTEENTH SUNDAY
A - The Kingdom of God 775
Psalm 119: Lord, I Love Your Commands 163
B - Bread to Share 927
Psalm 145: The Hand of the Lord Feeds Us 191
C - Seek Ye First the Kingdom of God* 728
Psalm 138: Lord, on the Day I Called for Help 184

Hymns and Psalms for the Church Year/*continued*

EIGHTEENTH SUNDAY
A - Bread to Share* 927
    Psalm 145: The Hand of the Lord Feeds Us 191
B - All Who Hunger 926 845
    Psalm 78: The Lord Gave Them Bread 105
C - The Love of the Lord 814
    Psalm 95: If Today You Hear His Voice 127 128
    Psalm 95: It Today You Hear God's Voice 129

NINTEENTH SUNDAY
A - How Firm a Foundation* 731
    Psalm 85: Lord, Let Us See Your Kindness 112 113
    114
B - I Am the Bread of Life/Yo Soy el Pan de Vida* 931
    Psalm 34: Taste and See 70 71 72 73 248
C - What Does the Lord Require 785
    God Whose Giving Knows No Ending 794
    Psalm 33: Happy Are the People 66
    Psalm 33: Happy the People 67

TWENTIETH SUNDAY
A - Your Hands, O Lord, in Days of Old 949
    Psalm 67: O God, Let All the Nations Praise You
    94 95
B - I Am the Bread of Life/Yo Soy el Pan de Vida* 931
    Psalm 34: Taste and See 70 71 72 73 248
C - God, Whose Purpose Is to Kindle* 828
    Psalm 40: Lord, Come to My Aid 75

TWENTY-FIRST SUNDAY
A - O Christ the Great Foundation 781 782
    Psalm 138: Lord, Your Love Is Eternal 184
B - I Am the Bread of Life/Yo Soy el Pan de Vida* 931
    Psalm 34: Taste and See 70 71 72 73 248
C - In Christ There Is a Table Set for All 916
    Psalm 117: Go Out to All the World 157

TWENTY-SECOND SUNDAY
A - Take Up Your Cross* 808
    Wherever He Leads* 810
    Psalm 63: My Soul Is Thirsting 89 90 91
B - Deep Within 546
    Psalm 15: The Just Will Live 33
C - Gather Us In 850
    Psalm 68: You Have Made a Home for the Poor 96

TWENTY-THIRD SUNDAY
A - Draw Us in the Spirit's Tether* 917
    Seek Ye First* 728
    Forgive Our Sins 952
    Psalm 95: If Today You Hear His Voice 127 128
    Psalm 95: If Today You Hear God's Voice 129
B - When the King Shall Come Again* 487
    Psalm 146: Praise the Lord, My Soul 195
C - Take Up Your Cross* 808
    Wherever He Leads* 810
    Psalm 90: In Every Age 120

TWENTY-FOURTH SUNDAY
A - Forgive Our Sins* 952
    Psalm 103: The Lord Is Kind and Merciful 140 141
    143
B - Take Up Your Cross* 808
    Wherever He Leads* 810
    Psalm 115: I Will Walk in the Presence 153 154
C - Our Father, We Have Wandered* 955
    Psalm 51: I Will Rise and Go to My Father 82
    Psalm 51: I Will Arise and Go to My God 85

TWENTY-FIFTH SUNDAY
A - For the Fruits of This Creation 704
    Psalm 145: The Lord Is Near 191
B - The Church of Christ in Every Age* 803
    Psalm 54: The Lord Upholds My Life 86
C - God, Whose Giving Knows No Ending 794
    The Love of the Lord 814
    Psalm 113: Praise the Lord 151

TWENTY-SIXTH SUNDAY
A - In Christ There Is a Table Set for All 916
    Psalm 25: Remember Your Mercies 54
B - The Love of the Lord 814
    Psalm 19: The Precepts of the Lord 39
C - God, Whose Purpose Is to Kindle 828
    Come, You Sinners, Poor and Needy 954
    Psalm 146: Praise the Lord, My Soul 195

TWENTY-SEVENTH SUNDAY
A - O Christ the Great Foundation* 781 782
    Psalm 80: The Vineyard of the Lord 106
B - Our Father, by Whose Name 961
    When Love Is Found 942
    Psalm 128: May the Lord Bless and Protect 172
    Psalm 128: May the Lord Bless Us 173
C - The Church of Christ in Every Age 803
    Psalm 95: If Today You Hear His Voice 127 128
    Psalm 95: If Today You Hear God's Voice 129

TWENTY-EIGHTH SUNDAY
A - City of God, Jerusalem* 486
    Gather Us In* 850
    Psalm 23: I Shall Live in the House of the Lord 45
B - The Summons 811
    The Love of the Lord 814
    Psalm 90: Fill Us with Your Love, O Lord 120 121
C - Your Hands, O Lord, in Days of Old 949
    Psalm 98: The Lord Has Revealed to the Nations
    137

TWENTY-NINTH SUNDAY
A - Sing Praise to God Who Reigns Above 683
    Psalm 96: Give the Lord Glory and Honor 131 132
B - Lord, Whose Love in Humble Service 793
    'Tis the Gift to Be Simple 792
    Psalm 33: Let Your Mercy Be on Us 66
    Psalm 33: Lord, Let Your Mercy Be on Us 68
C - Sing Praise to God Who Reigns Above 683
    Psalm 121: Our Help Comes from the Lord 164

THIRTIETH SUNDAY
A - Lord of All Nations, Grant Me Grace* 751
    Psalm 18: I Love You, Lord, My Strength 38
B - Your Hands, O Lord, in Days of Old 949
    Amazing Grace 737
    Psalm 126: The Lord Has Done Great Things 169
    170 171
C - What Does the Lord Require 785
    'Tis the Gift to Be Simple 792
    Psalm 34: The Lord Hears the Cry of the Poor 71

THIRTY-FIRST SUNDAY
A - What Does the Lord Require 785
    'Tis the Gift to Be Simple 792
    Psalm 131: My Soul Is Still 178
    Psalm 131: In You, Lord 179
B - Lord of All Nations, Grant Me Grace 751
    Psalm 18: I Love You, Lord, My Strength 38
C - Come, You Sinners, Poor and Needy 954
    Psalm 145: I Will Praise Your Name 192 193 194

Hymns and Psalms for the Church Year/*continued*

THIRTY-SECOND SUNDAY
- A - Wake, O Wake, and Sleep No Longer* 489
  - Who Can Measure Heaven and Earth 645
  - Psalm 63: My Soul Is Thirsting 89 90 91
- B - The Temple Rang with Golden Coins* 787
  - Psalm 146: Praise the Lord, My Soul 195
- C - Jesus, Lead the Way 755
  - Soon and Very Soon 870
  - Psalm 17: Lord, When Your Glory Appears 37

THIRTY-THIRD SUNDAY
- A - God, Whose Giving Knows No Ending* 794
  - Psalm 128: O Happy Are Those Who Fear the Lord 172
- B - The King Shall Come When Morning Dawns 497
  - When the Lord in Glory Comes 868
  - Psalm 16: Keep Me Safe, O God 34 35 36
- C - Be Not Afraid 734
  - How Can I Keep from Singing 733
  - Psalm 98: The Lord Comes to Rule the Earth 135

CHRIST THE KING
see nos. 626-632
- A- Lord, Whose Love in Humble Service 793
  - A Touching Place 760
  - Psalm 23: The Lord Is My Shepherd 44 45
  - Psalm 23: My Shepherd Is the Lord 45
  - Psalm 23: Nada Me Falta 46
  - Psalm 23: Shepherd Me, O God 756
- B- To Jesus Christ, Our Sovereign King 629
  - Psalm 93: The Lord Is King for Evermore 126
- C- Jesus, Remember Me* 770
  - Psalm 122: I Rejoiced When I Heard 165
  - Psalm 122: I Was Glad 166
  - Psalm 122: Let Us Go Rejoicing 167

FEB. 2: PRESENTATION OF THE LORD
- Lord, Bid Your Servant Go in Peace* 874
- Psalm 24: Who Is This King 49

MARCH 19: JOSEPH, HUSBAND OF MARY
- Come Now, and Praise the Humble Saint 875
- Psalm 89: The Son of David 119

MARCH 25: ANNUNCIATION OF OUR LORD
see nos. 875-876
- Psalm 40: Here I Am 74
- Psalm 40: Here Am I 75

JUNE 24: BIRTH OF JOHN THE BAPTIST
see nos. 878-879
- Vigil - Psalm 71: Since My Mother's Womb 100
- Day - Psalm 139: I Praise You 187

JUNE 29: PETER AND PAUL
- Two Noble Saints 880
- Vigil - Psalm 19: Their Message Goes Out 39
- Day - Psalm 34: The Angel of the Lord 73

JULY 4: INDEPENDENCE DAY
see nos. 964-966
- Psalm 85: The Lord Speaks of Peace 113

AUGUST 6: TRANSFIGURATION
see nos. 881-882
- Psalm 97: The Lord Is King 133

AUGUST 15: ASSUMPTION
- Hail, Holy Queen Enthroned Above 883
- Vigil - Psalm 132: Lord, Go Up 180
- Day - Psalm 45: The Queen Stands 78

LABOR DAY
- Those Who Love and Those Who Labor 805
- Psalm 90: Lord, Give Success 120

SEPTEMBER 14: TRIUMPH OF THE CROSS
- Lift High the Cross 884
- Psalm 78: Do Not Forget 104

NOVEMBER 1: ALL SAINTS
see nos. 885-889
- Psalm 24: O God, This Is the People 47

NOVEMBER 9: DEDICATION OF ST. JOHN LATERAN
see nos. 891-893
- 1Chr 29: We Praise Your Glorious Name 203

THANKSGIVING DAY
see nos. 700-709
- Psalm 67: The Earth Has Yielded 95
- 1Chr 29: We Praise Your Glorious Name 203
- Psalm 145: I Will Praise Your Name 192 193 194

DECEMBER 8: IMMACULATE CONCEPTION
- Immaculate Mary 890
- Psalm 98: Sing to the Lord a New Song 135 136 137

Please refer to the pew or keyboard accompaniment
editions of *RitualSong* for indexes 985 through 989.

991 Index of Service Music

Index of First Lines and Common Titles 992

Index of First Lines and Common Titles/*continued*

Index of First Lines and Common Titles/*continued*

Index of First Lines and Common Titles/*continued*